# Environmental Justice

D1198920

# Environmental Justice
## Law, Policy & Regulation

THIRD EDITION

### Clifford Villa
KELEHER & McLEOD PROFESSOR OF LAW
UNIVERSITY OF NEW MEXICO SCHOOL OF LAW

### Nadia Ahmad
ASSOCIATE PROFESSOR OF LAW
BARRY UNIVERSITY DWAYNE O. ANDREAS SCHOOL OF LAW

### Rebecca Bratspies
PROFESSOR OF LAW, CITY UNIVERSITY OF NEW YORK SCHOOL OF LAW

### Roger Lin
CLINICAL SUPERVISING ATTORNEY, ENVIRONMENTAL LAW CLINIC
UNIVERSITY OF CALIFORNIA BERKELEY SCHOOL OF LAW

### Clifford Rechtschaffen
FORMER PROFESSOR AND CO-FOUNDER, ENVIRONMENTAL LAW &
JUSTICE CLINIC, GOLDEN GATE UNIVERSITY SCHOOL OF LAW

### Eileen Gauna
EMERITUS PROFESSOR OF LAW, UNIVERSITY OF NEW MEXICO SCHOOL OF LAW

### Catherine O'Neill
FORMER PROFESSOR OF LAW, SEATTLE UNIVERSITY SCHOOL OF LAW

CAROLINA ACADEMIC PRESS
Durham, North Carolina

Copyright © 2020
Carolina Academic Press, LLC
All Rights Reserved.

Library of Congress Cataloging-in-Publication Data

Names: Villa, Clifford, author. | Ahmad, Nadia Batool, author. | Bratspies,
    Rebecca M., 1965– author. | Lin, Roger, author. | Rechtschaffen,
    Clifford, 1957– author. | Gauna, Eileen P., 1953– author. | O'Neill,
    Catherine A., author.
Title: Environmental justice : law, policy, and regulation / by Clifford
    Villa, Nadia Ahmad, Rebecca Bratspies, Roger Lin, Clifford
    Rechtschaffen, Eileen Gauna, Catherine A. O'Neill.
Description: Third edition. | Durham, North Carolina : Carolina Academic
    Press, LLC, [2020] | Includes bibliographical references and index.
Identifiers: LCCN 2020006023 | ISBN 9781531012380 (paperback) | ISBN
    9781531012397 (ebook)
Subjects: LCSH: Environmental law—United States. | LCGFT: Casebooks (Law)
Classification: LCC KF3775 .R385 2020 | DDC 344.7304/6—dc23
LC record available at https://lccn.loc.gov/2020006023

Carolina Academic Press
700 Kent Street
Durham, North Carolina 27701
Telephone (919) 489-7486
Fax (919) 493-5668
www.cap-press.com

Printed in the United States of America.

*For Olivia and all graduates of 2020: You will continue to inspire as you take the lead.*
C.V.

*For the young people in New York City (and everywhere) who are speaking out and stepping up for a just transition.*
R.B.

*In memory of Derrick Bell and Federico Cheever.*
N.A.

*For the residents of Allensworth, Arvin, East and West Oakland, and Richmond who continue to further the movement.*
R.L.

# Summary of Contents

# Contents

# Preface

Environmental justice is one of the most significant and dynamic developments in environmental law since modern environmental legislation emerged in the 1970s. Drawing upon principles from environmental law, civil rights statutes, and broader movements for social and economic justice, the environmental justice movement has focused attention on the disparate environmental harms experienced by low-income communities and communities of color. At the same time, the critical methodologies of environmental justice have drawn attention to other groups who may similarly experience disparate impacts from environmental degradation, including women, children, seniors, immigrants, LGBTQ individuals, and persons requiring special accommodations. While the scope of environmental justice may thus have broadened over time, original concerns remain no less relevant today, particularly as stark examples of racism continue to rise and our national commitment to social welfare continues to erode. Consider the drinking water contamination in Flint, Michigan, for example, or construction of the Dakota Access Pipeline over the massive opposition and protest of indigenous peoples.

This book will provide readers with a comprehensive introduction to environmental justice. Oriented towards legal issues and law students, the book also draws from other disciplines including sociology, geography, and economics. As such, beyond law school, the book may be used in undergraduate or graduate courses. The sixteen chapters of this book provide readings for a single semester of study in environmental justice, or supplemental materials for studies in environmental law, civil rights, and related subjects. To improve readability for a broader audience, we have generally omitted footnotes and legal citations from excerpted materials.

At the same time, this book is intended as a reference guide for practitioners, government officials, and community activists. For lawyers, as promised in the subtitle of the book, we provide an enhanced selection of laws and regulations that may help address specific problems in a given context. For government officials, we provide selections of law and policy to assist their important work in protecting the public health and welfare. For community activists and advocates, we provide examples of how environmental justice concerns have been addressed in circumstances that may be different or perhaps similar to their own.

Community activists remind us that, "We speak for ourselves." To promote the habit of listening, we have included materials and narratives collected from communities and community advocates from the Yukon Territory to Puerto Rico; from the Yakama Nation to the Navajo Nation; from Los Angeles to Chicago to New York City.

Many of these landscapes and leaders also appear directly in the photographs included, for the first time, in this third edition of the book—reinforcing the understanding that environmental justice is about real people and places.

This book is about understanding the real challenges of environmental justice across the country, but also about how to begin addressing these challenges. Thus, Chapter 3 introduces the concepts of risk assessment and risk management to encourage and empower community advocates to participate in these vital processes for characterizing threats to public health. Chapter 5 provides background on how regulatory agencies set standards for protecting public health. Chapter 6 explains how these standards may be incorporated into permits for industrial facilities and how these permits may be influenced or challenged by community advocates.

Where proper standards and permits fail to prevent disparate environmental impacts, this edition of the book provides an expanded examination of legal tools available to address cases of environmental injustice. Thus, Chapter 4 provides a broader review of constitutional law, civil rights legislation, and implementing regulations, with applications illustrated through cases including the drinking water contamination in Flint, Michigan. Chapter 7 provides a new overview of enforcement authorities available to government agencies under such federal laws as the Clean Air Act, Clean Water Act, and Toxic Substances Control Act. Chapter 8 provides a deep examination of legal authorities for cleaning up contaminated sites, with an extensive review of opportunities for community engagement in cleanup processes. Chapter 10 considers specific governmental initiatives to promote environmental justice; these include Executive Order No. 12898, directing the engagement of federal agencies, plus more recent initiatives from states including California and New York. Chapter 11 considers land-use planning as a tool for pursuing environmental justice. Chapter 12 examines mechanisms for obtaining environmental information, including new GIS tools such as EJSCREEN, as well as legal authorities for compelling environmental information and analysis, such as the National Environmental Policy Act and the Emergency Planning and Community Right-to-Know Act. Chapter 13 focuses on citizen enforcement, to include citizen suits under the various environmental statutes plus remedies that advocates may seek through the common law.

The last three chapters of the book consider the special challenges for environmental justice in emerging contexts including climate change, disaster response, and food systems. As we will see, each of these contexts may affect all people on the planet, but the disparate effects on certain groups of people are important to comprehend and address. A substantially updated chapter on climate justice (Chapter 14), plus new chapters on disaster justice (Chapter 15) and food justice (Chapter 16), will provide substantive starting points for study and practice in these areas. Readers interested in deeper explorations of these and many other related subjects will benefit from pathfinders included throughout the book.

Finally, the authors of this third edition would like to express their gratitude to the many people who contributed to this book in different ways. First and foremost, we would like to thank the original authors of this book, Clifford Rechtschaffen, Eileen

Gauna, and Catherine O'Neill, whose original work truly advanced the study and practice of environmental justice, and who entrusted us with carrying forward this endeavor as environmental justice approaches forty years as a distinct discipline. We would also like to thank all those who reviewed draft chapters of this edition or otherwise inspired our thinking in this book, including Tony Arnold, Michelle Bryan, Robert Bullard, Robin Craig, Dan Farber, Davida Finger, Lisa Grow Sun, Jacquie Hand, Marianne Engelman Lado, Alice Kaswan, Gregg Macey, J.B. Ruhl, Rob Verchick, Elizabeth Kronk Warner, Jeanette Wolfley, and dedicated EPA regional staff in Seattle, Chicago, and Philadelphia. We are particularly grateful for all those who gave of their time for interviews and community tours, including Richard Moore and Sofia Martinez of Los Jardines Institute; Dennis Chestnut of Groundwork Anacostia River D.C.; Naeema Muhammad of the North Carolina Environmental Justice Network; Vernice Miller-Travis; Ryke Longest of the Duke University School of Law; Jessica Grannis and the Georgetown Climate Center; Paulina López, James Rasmussen, BJ Cummings, Daniela Cortez, and the Duwamish River Cleanup Coalition; Lupe Martinez and staff at the Center on Race, Poverty & the Environment; Stefanie Tsosie and indefatigable colleagues at the Earthjustice Seattle office; the Picardi-Perez family of San Juan, Puerto Rico; Charles Lee, Suzi Ruhl, and all at the EPA Office of Environmental Justice; and all dedicated staff at the New Mexico Environment Department.

For superlative writing spaces, Cliff Villa thanks Chris and Lorrie Malins, and Mark and Teru Lundsten. For financial support, Cliff thanks Dean Sergio Pareja of the University of New Mexico School of Law and the law firm of Keleher & McLeod, P.A. For research assistance, thanks go to Melanie McNett (UNMSOL '20) and Ernesto Longa, UNM law librarian. For her keen eye and valued input throughout the book, Cliff thanks the incomparable Mara Yarbrough. For support and inspiration, Cliff thanks his wonderful faculty colleagues, including Reed Benson, Gabe Pacyniak, Josh Kastenberg, and Maryam Ahranjani; amazing UNM School of Law students and graduates including participants in the Environmental Justice writing seminars of 2018 and 2020; accounting support from Anna Martinez; and family including his lovely wife Angie, his dear mom, and the ever-fabulous Olivia and Julian.

Rebecca Bratspies thanks the many community activists whose work is documented in these pages. In particular, gratitude goes to Peggy Shepard and Cecil Corbin-Mark at WEACT, Barbara Brown at the Eastern Queens Alliance, and Evie Hantzopoulos of Global Kids for inspiring an entire generation of young New Yorkers to speak up and step forward for environmental justice, and to New York City Councilmember Costa Constantinides for his unwavering dedication to realizing environmental justice in New York City. Rebecca thanks her husband Allen and daughter Naomi for their support and encouragement, her colleagues Andrea McArdle and Sarah Lamdan for forever being willing to share their insights and expertise, and the entire CUNY Law School for every day spent living our motto "Law in the Service of Human Needs."

For institutional support, Nadia Ahmad thanks Dean Leticia Diaz of Barry University School of Law and Terri Day, Judy Koons, Seema Mohapatra, Cathren Page, Nancy Cantalupo, Rachel Deming, and Margaret Stewart. Thanks to her wonderful mentors Berta Hernandez-Truyol, Alyson Flournoy, Sharon Rush, Don Smith, Catherine Smith, Ved Nanda, Annecoos Wiersema, K.K. DuVivier, Jason Czarnezki, Nicholas Robinson, Richard Ottinger, Ann Powers, Bridget Crawford, Ann Bartow, Hari Osofsky, and Hannah Wiseman. Thanks to the ABA Environmental Justice Committee of Paula Shapiro, Alli Kielsgard, Kristen Galles, Scott Badenoch, Emily Bergeron, Stephanie Trager, and Jeremy Orr. Special thanks to David Kennedy at the Harvard Institute for Global Law and Policy and Michael Gerrard at the Sabin Center for Climate Change Law for their support. To the students in her environmental justice capstone course for their feedback and comments. Appreciation extended to Barry Law librarians Whitney Curtis, Diana Botluk, and Jason Murray and to the research assistance of Melissa Bryan. Special appreciation to Katherine Lenart, Sammy Zeno, and Owen Gregory. Cheers to her partner and co-pilot, Akmal, for his affirmation and boundless love, and to her children, Senan, Hanan, and Jihan for their unyielding energy through hurricanes, high tides, sick days, and tardy slips. Gratitude to her parents, Shazia, Osman, and Rubina as well as her extended family.

Roger Lin thanks the residents of Allensworth, Arvin, East and West Oakland, Richmond, and other communities who continue to inspire many in their pursuit of environmental justice. For their guidance and significant efforts in the field, Roger thanks Luke Cole, Helen Kang, Alan Ramo, Cliff Rechtschaffen, Greg Karras, Andrés Soto, Richard Drury, Caroline Farrell, Juan Flores, Refugio Valencia, the Pilot Team, and all of the staff, past, present, and future at Communities for a Better Environment, the Center on Race, Poverty & the Environment, and the UC Berkeley Environmental Law Clinic. For their support and patience, Roger thanks his parents, Marcus, Diana, and Camila (born during the drafting of this edition).

All authors of this edition extend our gratitude to the good folks at Carolina Academic Press, who supported this project from the start and made this book possible. We also, of course, thank all readers of this book. Your support and feedback are always welcome as we continue the pursuit of environmental justice together.

# Foreword

I remember as a young boy my grandmother sharing with me the words of Ms. Ida B. Wells, who said, "The way to right wrongs, is to turn the light of truth upon them." The "truth" is, for hundreds of years, vulnerable communities (lower-income, communities of color, and indigenous peoples) have been fighting for justice and equality in voting, housing, transportation, healthcare, and the economy. The "truth" is, for the past 40 years, environmental justice has encompassed all of these areas of inequity.

Unfortunately, fairness for environmental justice communities has often been fleeting at best and replaced with legacy pollution and sacrifice zones. Throughout history, our country's laws, politicians and decisionmakers have seen Black and Brown communities as the dumping grounds for everything wealthier communities would never accept. In these forgotten areas, we find coal-fired power plants bellowing out mercury and arsenic at alarming rates. Antiquated incinerators releasing dioxins and hazardous ash. Petrochemical facilities in places like Cancer Alley filling the lungs of local residents with nitrogen oxides, sulfur dioxide, and carbon monoxide. In 2020, we still hear the echoes of the Flint water crisis, as millions of children are living in unhealthy housing and attending underfunded schools filled with toxic lead across our country. These impacts will follow our children for a lifetime, with generational effects on the mind, body, and spirits of those who have been exposed.

In our country, over 100,000 people die prematurely annually from air pollution, which is more than those dying from gun violence or automobile accidents. We have 25 million adults and 7 million children living with asthma in the United States. African-American and Latinx children are disproportionately rushed to emergency rooms and the ones most likely to lose their lives due to asthma complications. Recently, the Clean Air Act has been under attack, putting many more lives of color in the crosshairs of pollution. We have an additional 94 environmental rules being rolled back, dismantled and deconstructed, further weakening the environmental and public-health safety net that so many in our country depend on for a basic level of protection.

Even with these increasing challenges facing frontline communities, I continue to see new possibilities and promise. Communities and their partners are working diligently to address past problems and place a spotlight on the impacts happening in their immediate areas. They are gathering information and utilizing community-based participatory research and traditional environmental knowledge to document the impacts they have been experiencing in their neighborhoods, barrios, and reservations. Vulnerable communities are continuing to build authentic collaborative partnerships with scientific organizations and universities to anchor their experiences and findings in irrefutable science. Frontline organizations are utilizing the power of the law to hold polluters accountable and push agencies like the EPA to fully enforce the statutes on the books. In 2020, frontline communities, scientists, lawyers, and politicians have a unique opportunity to continue building together and ensure that communities of color will never be toxic dumping grounds again, but places filled with culture, opportunity and promise.

This important book and the study of law is so incredibly critical at this time in the history of our country. At a time when science is under attack and policy is being manipulated, the law has become our greatest defense against the erosion of our civil, human and environmental rights. The law is also our greatest weapon to ensure that our most vulnerable are truly protected. We need men and women of good conscience to stand up, but they must be prepared with the tools to fight injustice of both the past and the present. I'm confident that one day—the not so distant future—we will have a society where all communities will be able to breathe clean air and drink clean water, and our children will have clean soil free from toxics to play on. In the words of Ms. Harriet Tubman, "Every great dream begins with a dreamer. Always remember, you have within you the strength, the patience, and the passion to reach for the stars to change the world." Let the law be the North Star that guides our most vulnerable communities from surviving to thriving.

Mustafa Santiago Ali
March 2020

# Acknowledgments

The authors gratefully acknowledge the permissions granted to reproduce in this book images and excerpts of the following works:

AP, Figure 1-1: Warren County, North Carolina (Sept. 16, 1982).

Randall S. Abate & Elizabeth Kronk Warner, *Commonality Among Unique Indigenous Communities: An Introduction to Climate Change and Its Impact on Indigenous Peoples*, 26 Tulane Envtl. L.J. 179 (2013).

M.R. Allen, et al.: *Framing and Context.* In: *Global Warming of 1.5°C. An IPCC Special Report on the impacts of global warming of 1.5°C above pre-industrial levels and related global greenhouse gas emission pathways, in the context of strengthening the global response to the threat of climate change, sustainable development, and efforts to eradicate poverty* (2018).

Isela Anchondo, Figure 1-2: Farmworker Ruben Ochoa, Jan. 18, 2020.

Tony Anderson, Figure 6-1, Chukchi Sea and Beaufort Sea.

Deborah N. Archer & Tamara C. Belinfanti, *We Built It and They Did Not Come: Using New Governance Theory in the Fight for Food Justice in Low-Income Communities of Color*, 15 Seattle J. Soc. Justice 307 (2016).

Craig Anthony Arnold, *Planning Milagros: Environmental Justice and Land Use Regulation*, 76 Denver U. L. Rev. 1 (1998).

Josephine M. Balzac, *Public Engagement "Reach In, Reach Out": Pursuing Environmental Justice by Empowering Communities to Meaningfully Participate in the Decision-Making Processes of Brownfields Redevelopment and Superfund Cleanup*, 9 Florida A&M L. Rev. 347 (2014).

Subhankar Banerjee, Figure 1-4 and Figure 14-1, from Arctic Voices: Resistance at the Tipping Point (Seven Stories Press, pbk, 2013), by permission.

Vicki Been, *Locally Undesirable Land Uses in Minority Neighborhoods: Disproportionate Siting or Market Dynamics?*, 103 Yale L.J. 1383 (1994).

Emily Bergeron, *Local Justice: How Cities Can Protect and Promote Environmental Justice in a Hostile Environment*, 32 Nat. Resources & Env't. 8 (2018).

Rebecca M. Bratspies, *Hunger and Equity in an Era of Genetic Engineering*, 7 UC Irvine L. Rev. 195 (2017).

Rebecca Bratspies, *Our Climate Moment Is Now! (or How to Change the Story to Save Our World)*, Environmental Law Disrupted (ELI 2020).

Rebecca Bratspies, *Protecting the Environment in an Era of Federal Retreat: The View from New York City*, 13 Florida Int'l U. L. Rev. 5 (2018).

Garrett M. Broad, *After the White House Garden: Food Justice in the Age of Trump*, 13 J. Food L. & Pol'y 33 (2017).

Robert D. Bullard & Beverly Wright, The Wrong Complexion for Protection (NYU Press, 2012). © New York University, by permission.

Maxine Burkett, *Rehabilitation: A Proposal for a Climate Compensation Mechanism for Small Island States*, 13 Santa Clara J. Int'l L. 81 (2015).

Francis Calpotura, *Why the Law?*, Third Force (May/June 1994).

Carnegie Commission on Science, Technology, and Government, Risk and the Environment: Improving Regulatory Decision Making (1993).

Anna Clark, *The Poisoned City: Flint's Water and an Urban American Tragedy* (Metropolitan Books, 2018). Excerpts from the "Prologue" with permission from Henry Holt and Company. All rights reserved.

Cary Coglianese & Gary E. Marchant, *Shifting Sands: The Limits of Science in Setting Risk Standards*, 152 U. Pa. L. Rev. 1255 (2004).

Luke W. Cole, *Empowerment as the Key to Environmental Protection: The Need for Environmental Poverty Law*, 19 Ecology L.Q. 619 (1992).

Luke Cole & Sheila Foster, From the Ground Up: Environmental Racism and the Rise of the Environmental Justice Movement (2000).

Congressional Black Caucus Foundation, African Americans and Climate Change: An Unequal Burden (2004).

Lara Cushing, Dan Blaustein-Rejito, Madeline Wander, Manuel Pastor, James Sadd, Allen Zhu & Rachel Morello-Frosch, *Carbon Trading, Co-pollutants, and Environmental Equity: Evidence from California's Cap-and-Trade Program (2001–2015)*, PLoS Med. 15(7) (2018).

Richard T. Drury, *Moving a Mountain: The Struggle for Environmental Justice in Southeast Los Angeles*, 38 Envtl. L. Rep. News & Analysis 10,338 (2008).

Richard Toshiyuki Drury, Michael E. Belliveau, J. Scott Kuhn & Shipra Bansal, *Pollution Trading and Environmental Injustice: Los Angeles' Failed Experiment in Air Quality Policy*, 9 Duke Envtl. L. & Pol'y Forum 231 (1999).

Daniel A. Farber, *Climate Adaptation and Federalism: Mapping the Issues*, 1 San Diego J. Climate & Energy 259 (2009).

Davida Finger, et al., *Engaging the Legal Academy in Disaster Response*, 10 Seattle J. Soc. Justice 211 (2011).

Christopher H. Foreman, Jr., The Promise and Peril of Environmental Justice (Brookings Institution Press, 1998).

Andrea Freeman, *The Unbearable Whiteness of Milk: Food Oppression and the USDA*, 3 UC Irvine L. Rev. 1251 (2013).

Georgetown Climate Center, Opportunities for Equitable Adaptation in Cities (2017).

Rebecca L. Goldberg, *No Such Thing as a Free Lunch: Paternalism, Poverty, and Food Justice*, 24 Stanford L. & Pol'y Rev. 35 (2013).

Carmen G. Gonzalez, *An Environmental Justice Critique of Comparative Advantage: Indigenous Peoples, Trade Policy, and the Mexican Neoliberal Economic Reforms*, 32 U. Pa. J. Int'l L. 723 (2011).

Jacqueline Hand, Figure 16-2: Detroit hoophouse, March 2014.

Daniel Hernandez, Figure 2-1: Mariachi Plaza, Los Angeles.

Stephen M. Johnson, *Economics v. Equity: Do Market-Based Environmental Reforms Exacerbate Environmental Injustice?*, 56 WASH. & LEE L. REV. 111 (1999).

Helen H. Kang, *Respect for Community Narratives of Environmental Injustice: The Dignity Right to Be Heard and Believed*, 25 WIDENER L. REV. 219 (2019).

Robert R. Kuehn, *A Taxonomy of Environmental Justice*, 30 ENVTL. L. REP. 10,681 (2000).

Robert R. Kuehn, *The Environmental Justice Implications of Quantitative Risk Assessment*, 1996 U. ILLINOIS L. REV. 103 (1996).

Marianne Engelman Lado, *No More Excuses: Building a New Vision of Civil Rights Enforcement in the Context of Environmental Justice*, 22 U. PA. J.L. & SOC. CHANGE 281 (2019).

Sarah Lamdan & Rebecca Bratspies, *Taking a Page from the FDA's Prescription Medicine Information Rules: Reimagining Environmental Information for Climate Change*, 40 U. ARK. LITTLE ROCK L. REV. 573 (2018).

Philip J. Landrigan, Virginia A. Rauh & Maida P. Galvez, *Environmental Justice and the Health of Children*, 77 MOUNT SINAI J. MED. 178 (2010).

Charles R. Lawrence III, *The Id, the Ego, and Equal Protection: Reckoning with Unconscious Racism*, 39 STANFORD L. REV. 317 (1987).

Richard J. Lazarus, *Pursuing "Environmental Justice": The Distributional Effects of Environmental Protection*, 87 NORTHWESTERN U. L. REV. 787 (1993).

Richard J. Lazarus & Stephanie Tai, *Integrating Environmental Justice into EPA Permitting Authority*, 26 ECOLOGY L.Q. 617 (1999).

Charles Lee, Submission to the National Environmental Policy Commission (May 2001).

Roselynn Loaiza, Figures 13-4(a) and 13-4(b): Raul R. Perez Memorial Park. Huntington, Park, CA. Jan. 17, 2020.

mark! Lopez, *The Truth Fairy Project and the Exide Fights to Come* (May 2019).

Julia Mizutani, *In the Backyard of Segregated Neighborhoods: An Environmental Justice Case Study of Louisiana*, 31 GEORGETOWN ENVTL. L. REV. 363 (2019).

Catherine A. O'Neill, *Variable Justice: Environmental Standards, Contaminated Fish, and "Acceptable" Risk to Native Peoples*, 19 STANFORD ENVTL. L.J. 3 (2000).

Solmari Perez Oliveras, Figure 14-3. Flooding in Ocean Park neighborhood of San Juan, Puerto Rico. Sept. 20, 2017.

Jeanne Marie Zokovitch Paben, *Green Power & Environmental Justice—Does Green Discriminate?*, 46 TEXAS TECH L. REV. 1067 (2014).

Manuel Pastor, Jr., Jim Sadd & John Hipp, *Which Came First? Toxic Facilities, Minority Move-In, and Environmental Justice*, 23 J. URBAN AFF. 1 (2001).

Jedediah Purdy, *The Long Environmental Justice Movement*, 44 ECOLOGY L.Q. 809 (2018).

Danielle M. Purifoy, *Food Policy Councils: Integrating Food Justice and Environmental Justice*, 24 DUKE ENVTL. L. & POL'Y FORUM 375 (2014).

Yale Rabin, *Expulsive Zoning: The Inequitable Legacy of* Euclid, *in* ZONING AND THE AMERICAN DREAM 101 (Charles M. Haar & Jerold S. Kayden eds., 1989).

Alan Ramo, *Environmental Justice as an Essential Tool in Environmental Review Statutes: A New Look at Federal Policies and Civil Rights Protections and California's Recent Initiatives*, 19 HASTINGS W.-N.W. J. ENVTL. L. & POL'Y 41 (2013).

Roselynn Loaiza, Figure 13-4: Raul R. Perez Memorial Park. Huntington Park, CA. Jan. 17, 2020.

Robin Saha & Paul Mohai, *Explaining Racial and Socioeconomic Disparities in the Location of Locally Unwanted Land Uses: A Conceptual Framework*, presented at the 1997 Annual Meeting of the Rural Sociological Society (Toronto, Aug. 1997).

Rachael Salcido, *Reviving the Environmental Justice Agenda*, 91 CHICAGO-KENT L. REV. 115 (2016).

Riccardo Savi, Figure 3-1: "Little Miss Flint," Washington, D.C. April 22, 2017.

Sarah Schindler, *Architectural Exclusion: Discrimination and Segregation through Physical Design of the Built Environment*, 124 YALE L.J. 1934 (2015).

Mattathias Schwartz, *Maria's Bodies*, NY MAGAZINE (Dec. 22, 2017).

SEATTLE TIMES, Figure 15-1: front page, Dec. 20, 2006.

Sidney Shapiro, *Preface: An Ounce of Prevention*, in *From Surviving to Thriving: Equity in Disaster Planning and Recovery* (Center for Progressive Reform, 2018).

Brie D. Sherwin, *The Upside Down: A New Reality for Science at the EPA and Its Impacts on Environmental Justice*, 27 NYU ENVTL. L.J. 57 (2019).

Patrice L. Simms, *Leveraging Supplemental Environmental Projects: Toward an Integrated Strategy for Empowering Environmental Justice Communities*, 47 ENVTL. L. REP. NEWS & ANALYSIS 10,511 (2017).

Rena I. Steinzor, *Mother Earth and Uncle Sam: How Pollution and Hollow Government Hurt Our Kids* (U. Texas Press, 2008).

Shirley Trout, Figure 2-3: Walton, Nebraska. Nov. 12, 2019.

Shirley Trout, Figure 16-3: Cornfield, Walton, Nebraska. Nov. 12, 2019.

Vien Truong, *Addressing Poverty and Pollution: California's SB 535 Greenhouse Gas Reduction Fund*, 49 HARVARD CIVIL RIGHTS-CIVIL LIBERTIES L. REV. 493 (2014).

Rebecca Tsosie, *Tribal Environmental Policy in an Era of Self-Determination: The Role of Ethics, Economics and Traditional Ecological Knowledge*, 21 VERMONT L. REV. 225 (1996).

Robert R.M. Verchick, *Disaster Justice: The Geography of Human Capability*, 23 DUKE ENVTL. L. & POL'Y FORUM 23 (2012).

Olivia Villa, Figure 8-4: North Railroad Avenue Plume Superfund Site, Española, NM, July 10, 2019; and Figure 8-7: Daniela Cortez, Seattle, WA, March 30, 2019.

Shirley Trout, Figure 2-3: Walton, Nebraska. Nov. 12, 2019.

Elizabeth Kronk Warner, *Environmental Justice: A Necessary Lens to Effectively View Environmental Threats to Indigenous Survival*, 26 TRANSNAT'L L. & CONTEMP. PROBS. 343 (2017).

Jeanette Wolfley, *Tribal Environmental Programs: Providing Meaningful Involvement and Fair Treatment*, 29 J. ENVTL. L. & LITIG. 389 (2014).

# Environmental Justice

# Chapter 1

# An Introduction to Environmental Justice

**Figure 1-1:** Rev. Benjamin Chavis raises his fist, joining fellow protesters at the Warren County PCB landfill near Afton, North Carolina. Sept. 16, 1982. Photo: AP/Greg Gibson. Used by permission.

## A. History of the Movement

On September 15, 1982, 6,000 truckloads of soil contaminated with polychlorinated biphenyls (PCBs) began rolling into a landfill in the town of Afton, North Carolina. Residents of Afton, located in Warren County, 50 miles north of Raleigh-Durham, objected to the disposal of this highly toxic material in their community. Organizing themselves into the Warren County Citizens Concerned about PCBs, the concerned citizens took to the streets to make their voices heard, many lying down in front of trucks to stop the dumping of toxic waste. Within a couple of weeks, more than 414 protesters had been arrested. The protest attracted the attention and support of a broad coalition of national civil rights leaders, elected officials, environmental activists, and labor leaders. Among national leaders converging on Warren County was the Reverend Benjamin Chavis of the United Church of Christ Commission for Racial Justice, arrested on the third day of the protests. Richard Hart, *39 Arrested in Third Day of PCB Landfill Protest*, NEWS AND OBSERVER 1, Sept. 18, 1982. Reverend Chavis, who had worked alongside Dr. Martin Luther King, Jr., in the 1960s, and would later lead the NAACP, could see what was happening in Warren County. The town of Afton was 84% African American. Warren County had the highest percentage of blacks in the state and was one of the poorest counties in the state. Robert Bullard, DUMPING IN DIXIE: RACE, CLASS, AND ENVIRONMENTAL QUALITY 30–31 (1990). Toxic waste spread out across 14 counties in North Carolina was being hauled and dumped in Afton for reasons that Reverend Chavis termed "environmental racism." The Warren County protests would not stop the dumping at Afton but did give rise to an enduring movement we know today as environmental justice.

After Warren County, communities of color alarmed conventional environmental organizations, regulators, and industry leaders with further allegations of environmental racism. These charges reflected long-standing frustration on the part of such communities, and their view that people of color systematically receive disproportionately greater environmental risk while white communities systematically receive better environmental protection. Across the country, communities of color began to challenge the siting of hazardous waste facilities, landfills, industrial activities, and other risk-producing land practices within their community. The roots of the environmental justice movement lie in diverse political projects: the civil rights movement, the grassroots anti-toxics movement of the 1980s, organizing efforts of Native Americans and labor, and, to a lesser extent, the traditional environmental movement. *See generally* Luke Cole & Sheila Foster, FROM THE GROUND UP: ENVIRONMENTAL RACISM AND THE RISE OF THE ENVIRONMENTAL JUSTICE MOVEMENT (2001).

"Environmental justice" soon came to mean more than skewed distributional consequences of environmental burdens to communities of color. Becoming multi-issue and multi-racial in scope, the movement began to address disparities borne by the poor as well as by people of color, acknowledging the substantial overlap between the two demographic categories. Concerns about regulatory processes surfaced as well. Often, the communities most impacted by environmentally risky activities had been excluded from important decision-making proceedings, sometimes intentionally so and sometimes because of a lack of resources, specialized knowledge, and other structural impediments. Initially, environmental justice activists used direct action such as demonstrations as the primary means to raise public awareness of the issue.

Largely in response to this early activism, several investigations and studies were undertaken which lent support to charges of environmental injustice. For example, a 1983 report by the U.S. General Accounting Office found that, in the Environmental Protection Agency (EPA) Region IV, three of four major offsite hazardous waste facilities in the Southeast were located in predominantly African-American communities.

In 1987, a national study by the United Church of Christ found a positive correlation between racial minorities and proximity to commercial hazardous waste facilities and uncontrolled waste sites. United Church of Christ, COMMISSION FOR RACIAL JUSTICE, TOXIC WASTES AND RACE IN THE UNITED STATES (1987). Significantly, the study found that race was a more statistically significant variable than income. This early activism also culminated in an extraordinary gathering of grassroots activists at the First National People of Color Environmental Leadership Summit in Washington, D.C., on October 24–27, 1991, where the Principles of Environmental Justice, which are reprinted below, were adopted.

In 1992, a National Law Journal investigation indicated that EPA enforcement under various federal statutes and cleanup under the Superfund law was inequitable by race and, to a less pronounced degree, income. The findings of the National Law Journal investigation with respect to enforcement were subsequently called into question by later studies. *See* Chapter 7 ("Public Enforcement"). Nevertheless, the environmental justice (EJ) movement was further galvanized as other national and regional studies began to confirm the patterns of disproportionate location of industrial facilities and waste sites, exposure to contaminants, and adverse health effects in poor areas and in communities of color.

In response to these studies and to continuing pressure from communities of color, President Clinton in 1994 signed an Executive Order on Environmental Justice (No. 12898) requiring all federal agencies to make environmental justice part of their mission and establishing an interagency work group. (Executive Order No. 12898 is reproduced in part in Chapter 10 ("Governmental Initiatives to Promote Environmental Justice").) In 1992, the EPA established what ultimately came to be called the Office of Environmental Justice. The EPA also convened the National Environmental Justice Advisory Council (NEJAC), a diverse federal advisory group charged with making recommendations to the EPA concerning a broad range of environmental justice matters. The EPA further began to take steps to include environmental justice organizations and community residents in a variety of agency projects, such as the EPA-sponsored "Brownfield" initiatives, which involve the reuse of idle industrial sites that are contaminated or perceived to be contaminated. (*See* Chapter 8 ("Environmental Justice and Contaminated Sites"). These actions in the name of environmental justice marked a new course for environmental regulation, as environmental regulators did not traditionally consider demographics and social context in the course of their regulatory activities.

After some progress on environmental justice under the Clinton administration, the Bush administration took a different approach, redefining "environmental justice" to mean environmental protection for *everyone* and de-emphasizing the need to focus special attention on minority and low-income populations. As a result, and because of the perception that the Bush administration generally was hostile to environmental justice claims, advocates largely shifted their attention to state and local governments to remedy environmental disparities. Reinvigorated efforts to address environmental justice returned to the federal government with the Obama administration—and went underground again with the Trump administration, which attempted to eliminate the EPA Office of Environmental Justice through slashed budgets. *See* Uma Outka & Elizabeth Kronk Warner, *Reversing Course on Environmental Justice Under the Trump Administration*, 54 Wake Forest L. Rev. 393 (2019).

Meanwhile, environmental disparities continue to be found in the siting, compliance, and cleanup contexts. In 2007, for example, researchers using increasingly sophisticated statistical methods identified racial disparities in the siting of hazardous waste facilities considerably greater than indicated in the 1987 Toxic Wastes and Race report. Bullard, et al., Toxic Wastes and Race at Twenty: 1987–2007 (Mar. 2007) at 43–44 & fig. 3.3. Environmental inequities also continue to arise because of the failure to consider environmental justice when regulatory standards are set and programs are designed early in an environmental program. Accordingly, it is clear that environmental justice issues must be considered at the earliest stages of regulatory activity, not only at the permitting and enforcement stages, but particularly during the formation of policy, including the design of new programs—for example, programs tackling climate change.

Unfortunately, integrating environmental justice into environmental regulation in a manner that responds meaningfully to both the distributional and process issues has proven to be exceptionally complex. Environmental regulators are often concerned with the scope of their authority to consider environmental justice under environmental statutes, with the extent of any legal duty to do so under the civil rights laws, as well as with the uncertainty and complexity such an undertaking might add to their regulatory programs. The regulated community is concerned about the potential for increased delay to their projects and about compliance costs. Environmental justice advocates continue to attempt to address concerns and participate in various proceedings under severe resource constraints, and in some areas still confront considerable hostility and resistance by government officials. In addition, participation by environmental justice advocates may be hampered by the tendency among other stakeholders and governmental agencies to view environmental justice as a "special interest." Environmental justice advocates emphasize that the relevant issues are not demands for special treatment, but are founded upon precepts of basic fairness and equal environmental protection: that there should be a level playing field for all stakeholders and that environmental burdens and benefits should not fall in disproportionate patterns by race and income.

To address the range of environmental inequities experienced in many communities, advocates for environmental justice continued to organize and began to seek redress under a variety of legal theories. As we begin to explore in Chapter 4, legal challenges have met with mixed success. Claims alleging violations of the Equal Protection Clause of the U.S. Constitution have largely failed because of the difficulty of proving intentional discrimination under standards set by the U.S. Supreme Court. As an alternative to constitutional claims, community advocates have also filed numerous administrative complaints with the EPA alleging violations of the Civil Rights Act of 1964. Civil Rights Act Title VI, which prohibits discrimination in programs or activities that receive federal financial assistance, had historically been applied in the education and employment context but not in the environmental context. The EPA Office of Civil Rights (OCR) proved egregiously slow in investigating and deciding the Title VI cases, but some progress has been made recently. Further progress may be made using § 1983 of the Civil Rights Act, as the case study in Chapter 4 will discuss. Chapters 5, 6, and 7 focus on the federal regulatory process, identifying how government regulators and community activists may work cooperatively in order to address environmental justice concerns. Chapter 9 considers some of the unique concerns raised by environmental injustice in Indian country. Other claims, some using traditional common law theories and others using citizen suit provisions of environmental laws, are evaluated in later chapters, including Chapter 13 ("Citizen Enforcement and Common Law Remedies"). Finally, the last three chapters (Chapters 14, 15, and 16) explore emerging dimensions of environmental justice, including climate justice, disaster justice, and food justice.

The thrust of this book is twofold: first, to examine the complexities presented by environmental inequity, and second, to explore the potential that exists within the current legal system to move environmental regulation forward in a responsible manner toward a more just society and ecologically sustainable environment. Solutions to many cases of environmental injustice are out there: our project in this book is to help readers find those solutions through the best tools of law and policy.

*Pathfinder on Environmental Justice Generally*

Scholarship on environmental justice is particularly rich and varied. Among the numerous books addressing themes on environmental justice are Katrina Smith Korfmacher, Bridging Silos: Collaborating for Environmental Health and Justice in Urban Communities (2019); Harriet A. Washington, A Terrible Thing to Waste: Environmental Racism and Its Assault on the American Mind (2019); The Routledge Handbook of Environmental Justice (Ryan Holifeld, Jayajit Chakraborty & Gordon Walker eds. 2018); Carmen G. Gonzalez, et al., Energy Justice: US and International Perspectives (2018); Barry E. Hill, Environmental Justice: Legal Theory and Practice (4th ed. 2018); Benjamin K. Sovacool & Michael Dworkin, Global Energy Justice (2014); Dorceta Taylor, Toxic Communities: Environmental Racism, Industrial Pollution, and Residential Mobility (2014); Robert Bullard & Beverly Wright, The Wrong Complexion for Protection (2012); The Law of Environmental Justice: Theories and Procedures to Address Disproportionate Risks (Michael B. Gerrard & Sheila R. Foster eds., 2d ed. 2008); Eileen McGurty, Transforming Environmentalism: Warren County, PCBs, and the Origins of Environmental Justice (2007); Craig Anthony Arnold, Fair and Healthy Land Use: Environmental Justice and Planning (2007); Luke Cole & Sheila Foster, From the Ground Up: Environmental Racism and the Rise of the Environmental Justice Movement (2001); Christopher Foreman, The Promise and Peril of Environmental Justice (1998); Bunyan

Bryant, Environmental Justice: Issues, Policies and Solutions (1995); Confronting Environmental Racism: Voices from the Grassroots (Robert D. Bullard ed., 1993); Unequal Protection: Environmental Justice and Communities of Color (Robert D. Bullard ed., 1994); Race and the Incidence of Environmental Hazards: A Time for Discourse (Paul Mohai & Bunyan Bryant eds., 1992); and the classic work by the "Father of Environmental Justice," Robert D. Bullard, Dumping in Dixie: Race, Class, and Environmental Quality (1990).

Among the wealth of scholarly articles on environmental justice are Sarah Krakoff, *Environmental Justice and the Possibilities for Environmental Law*, 49 Envtl. L. 229 (2019); Oliver A. Houck, *Shintech: Environmental Justice at Ground Zero*, 31 Geo. Intl. Envtl. L. Rev. 455 (2019); Nadia Ahmad, *"Mask Off"—The Coloniality of Environmental Justice*, 25 Widener L. Rev. 173 (2019); Logan Glasenapp, *Judicially Sanctioned Environmental Injustice: Making the Case for Medical Monitoring*, 49 NM L. Rev. 59 (2019); Spencer Banzhaf, Lala Ma & Christopher Timmins, *Environmental Justice: The Economics of Race, Place, and Pollution*, 33 J. Econ. Perspectives 185 (2019); Brigham Daniels, Michalyn Steele & Lisa Grow Sun, *Just Environmentalism*, 37 Yale L. & Pol'y Rev. 1 (2018); Jedediah Purdy, *The Long Environmental Justice Movement*, 44 Ecology L.Q. 809 (2018); Benjamin F. Wilson, *It's Not "Just" Zoning: Environmental Justice and Land Use*, 49 Urb. Law. 717 (2017); Rachael E. Salcido, *Reviving the Environmental Justice Agenda*, 91 Chi.-Kent L. Rev. 115 (2016); Carmen G. Gonzalez, *Environmental Justice, Human Rights, and the Global South*, 13 Santa Clara J. Intl. L. 151 (2015); Gregg Macey, *Boundary Work in Environmental Law*, 53 Houston L. Rev. 103, 114–130 (2015); Paul Mohai & Robin Saha, *Which Came First, People or Pollution? Assessing the Disparate Siting and Post-Siting Demographic Change Hypotheses of Environmental Injustice*, 10 Envtl. Res. Letters, no. 11 (Nov. 18, 2015); Tonya Lewis & Jessica Owley, *Symbolic Politics for Disempowered Communities: State Environmental Justice Policies*, 29 BYU J. Pub. L. 183 (2014); Alice Kaswan, *Environmental Justice and Environmental Law*, 24 Fordham Envtl. L. Rev. 149 (2013); Uma Outka, *Environmental Justice Issues in Sustainable Development: Environmental Justice in the Renewable Energy Transition*, 19 J. Envtl. & Sustainability L. 60 (2012); Jonathan C. Augustine, *Environmental Justice and Eschatology in Revelation*, 58 Loy. L. Rev. 325 (2012); Jeanne Marie Zokovitch Paben, *Approaches to Environmental Justice: A Case Study of One Community's Victory*, 20 S. Cal. Rev. L. & Soc. Just. 325 (2011); Clifford Rechtschaffen, *Advancing Environmental Justice Norms*, 37 U.C. Davis L. Rev. 95 (2003); Robert D. Bullard et al., *Toxic Wastes and Race at Twenty: Why Race Still Matters After All of These Years*, 38 Envtl. L. 371 (2008); Catherine O'Neill, *Mercury, Risk, and Justice*, 34 Envtl. L. Rep. 11070 (2004); Tseming Yang, *Melding Civil Rights and Environmentalism: Finding Environmental Justice's Place in Environmental Regulation*, 26 Harv. Envtl. L. Rev. 1 (2002); Carita Shanklin, *Pathfinder: Environmental Justice*, 24 Ecology L.Q. 333 (1997); Denis Binder, *Index of Environmental Justice Cases*, 27 Urb. Law. 163 (1995), *Environmental Justice Index II*, 3 Chapman L. Rev. 309 (2000), and *Environmental Justice Index III*, 35 Envtl. L. Rep. 10,606 (2005); Eileen Gauna, *An Essay on Environmental Justice: The Past, the Present, and Back to the Future*, 42 Nat. Resources J. 701 (2002) and *Farmworkers as an Envi-*

*ronmental Justice Issue: Similarities and Differences*, 25 ENVIRONS ENVTL. L. & POL'Y J. 67 (2002); Craig Anthony Arnold, *Planning Milagros: Environmental Justice and Land Use Regulation*, 76 DENVER U. L. REV. 1 (1998); Robert R. M. Verchick, *In a Greener Voice: Feminist Theory and Environmental Justice*, 19 HARV. WOMEN'S L.J. 23, 73–74 (1996); Richard J. Lazarus, *"Environmental Racism! That's What It Is."*, 2000 U. ILL. L. REV. 255; *Pursuing "Environmental Justice": The Distributional Effects of Environmental Protection*, 87 Nw. U. L. REV. 787 (1993); Robert W. Collin, *Environmental Equity: A Law and Planning Approach to Environmental Racism*, 11 VA. ENVTL. L.J. 495 (1992); Gerald Torres, *Race, Class, and Environmental Regulation, Introduction: Understanding Environmental Racism*, 63 U. COLO. L. REV. 839 (1992); and Luke W. Cole, *Empowerment as the Key to Environmental Protection: The Need for Environmental Poverty Law*, 19 ECOLOGY L.Q. 619 (1992).

In addition to these and many other important works of legal scholarship, environmental justice advocates may find useful materials through myriad other sources, including multidisciplinary journals such as the bimonthly, peer-reviewed ENVIRONMENTAL JUSTICE, and websites maintained by academic institutions, nonprofit organizations, and government agencies. Among useful websites for environmental justice materials, see those for the Deep South Center for Environmental Justice (www.dscej.org); the NAACP Environmental & Climate Justice Program (www.naacp.org/issues/environmental-justice); and the U.S. EPA Office of Environmental Justice (www.epa.gov/environmentaljustice). For readers of all levels interested in environmental justice concerns, see also the series of EJ comic books by Professor Rebecca Bratspies, available through the website of the City University of New York (CUNY) Center for Urban Environmental Reform (CUER) (cuer.law.cuny.edu).

# B. The Meaning of "Environmental Justice"

A fundamental question for this book and for related study and practice is the meaning of "environmental justice." In the excerpt that follows, Professor Robert Kuehn attempts to elucidate the meaning of environmental justice through proposed definitions as well as four concepts of justice: distributive, procedural, corrective, and social justice.

## Robert R. Kuehn,
### *A Taxonomy of Environmental Justice*
30 ENVIRONMENTAL LAW REPORTER 10,681 (2000)

Efforts to understand environmental justice are [] complicated by the term's international, national, and local scope; by its broad definition of the environment— where one lives, works, plays, and goes to school; and by its broad range of concerns—such as public health, natural resource conservation, and worker safety in both urban and rural environs. Disputes at the international level include allegations that governments and multinational corporations are exploiting indigenous peoples and the impoverished conditions of developing nations. At the national level, although an overwhelming number of studies show differences by race and income in exposures to environmental hazards, debate continues about the strength of that evidence and the appropriate political and legal response to such disparities. At the local level, many people of color and lower income communities believe that they have not been treated fairly regarding the distribution of the environmental benefits and burdens....

*Shifting Perspectives and Uses of Terms*

The U.S. Environmental Protection Agency (EPA) initially used the term "environmental equity," defined as the equitable distribution of environmental risks across population groups, to refer to the environmental justice phenomenon. Because this term implies the redistribution of risk across racial and economic groups rather than risk reduction and avoidance, it is no longer used by EPA, though it is still used by some states.

In some instances, the phrase "environmental racism," defined as "any policy, practice or directive that differentially affects or disadvantages (whether intended or unintended) individuals, groups, or communities based on race or color," is used to explain the differential treatment of populations on environmental issues. Commentators disagree over the proper usage of this term, particularly over whether an action having an unequal distributive outcome across racial groups would in itself be a sufficient basis to label an action environmental racism or whether the action must be the result of intentional racial animus. Today, many environmental justice advocates and scholars avoid the term "environmental racism," though the phrase continues to be employed and is useful in identifying the institutional causes of some environmental injustices. This shift is attributable to a desire to focus on solutions rather than mere identification of problems, as well as a desire to encompass class concerns and not to be limited by issues of intentional conduct....

In 1994, President Clinton issued Executive Order No. 12898 ... and adopted the phrase "environmental justice" to refer to "disproportionately high and adverse human health or environmental effects ... on minority populations and low-income populations." The Executive Order's use of the term "environmental justice" is significant in at least three respects. First, the Executive Order focuses not only on the disproportionate burdens addressed by the term environmental equity, but also on issues of enforcement of environmental laws and opportunities for public participation. Second, the Executive Order identifies not just minorities but also low-income populations as the groups who have been subject to, and entitled to relief from, unfair or unequal treatment. Finally, the Executive Order, and in particular the accompanying memorandum, refers to environmental justice as a goal or aspiration to be achieved, rather than as a problem or cause.

In 1998, EPA's Office of Environmental Justice set forth the Agency's "standard definition" of environmental justice:

The fair treatment of people of all races, cultures, incomes, and educational levels with respect to the development and enforcement of environmental laws, regulations, and policies. Fair treatment implies that no population should be forced to shoulder a disproportionate share of exposure to the negative effects of pollution due to lack of political or economic strength.

Going beyond the issues of disproportionate exposures and participation in the development and enforcement of laws and policies, EPA further elaborated that environmental justice:

is based on the premise that: 1) it is a basic right of all Americans to live and work in "safe, healthful, productive, and aesthetically and culturally pleasing surroundings;" 2) it is not only an environmental issue but a public health issue; 3) it is forward-looking and goal-oriented; and 4) it is also inclusive since it is based on the concept of fundamental fairness, which includes the concept of economic prejudices as well as racial prejudices.

Professor Bunyan Bryant defines environmental justice as referring "to those cultural norms and values, rules, regulations, behaviors, policies, and decisions to support sustainable communities, where people can interact with confidence that their environment is safe, nurturing, and protective." Some critics of environmental justice contend that these definitions of environmental justice by government agencies and environmental justice advocates are so broad and aspirational as not to state clearly the ends of environmental justice.

An alternative approach to defining environmental justice that does state its desired ends, albeit very ambitious ones, was developed by environmental justice leaders during the 1991 First People of Color Environmental Leadership Summit. Its "Principles of Environmental Justice" sets forth a 17-point paradigm [excerpted below]....

Dr. Robert Bullard has distilled the principles of environmental justice into a framework of five basic characteristics: (1) protect all persons from environmental degradation; (2) adopt a public health prevention of harm approach; (3) place the burden of proof on those who seek to pollute; (4) obviate the requirement to prove intent to discriminate; and (5) redress existing inequities by targeting action and resources. In his view, environmental justice seeks to make environmental protection more democratic and asks the fundamental ethical and political questions of "who gets what, why and how much." ...

Students and lawyers are often left without an understanding of unifying themes or common political, legal, or economic approaches to addressing allegations of injustice. The classification method set forth in this [a]rticle seeks to overcome this shortcoming and to advance the understanding of environmental justice by disassembling the term into the four traditional notions of "justice" that are implicated by allegations of environmental injustice....

*Environmental Justice as Distributive Justice*

... Distributive justice has been defined as "the right to equal treatment, that is, to the same distribution of goods and opportunities as anyone else has or is given." Aristotle is often credited with the first articulation of the concept and explained it as involving "the distribution of honour, wealth, and the other divisible assets of the community, which may be allotted among its members." The focus of this aspect of justice is on fairly distributed outcomes, rather than on the process for arriving at such outcomes.

In an environmental context, distributive justice involves the equitable distribution of the burdens resulting from environmentally threatening activities or of the environmental benefits of government and private-sector programs. More specifically, in an environmental justice context, distributive justice most commonly involves addressing the disproportionate public health and environmental risks borne by people of color and lower incomes....

Distributive justice in an environmental justice context does not mean redistributing pollution or risk. Instead, environmental justice advocates argue that it means equal protection for all and the elimination of environmental hazards and the need to place hazardous activities in any community. In other words, distributive justice is achieved through a lowering of risks, not a shifting or equalizing of existing risks.

With such a strong focus on the inequitable distribution by race and income of environmental hazards, an often overlooked aspect of distributive justice is that it also involves the distribution of the benefits of environmental programs and policies, such as parks and beaches, public transportation, safe drinking water, and sewerage and drainage....

Some of the best known local environmental justice disputes have involved dramatic evidence of distributive inequities.

In *Chester Residents Concerned for Quality Living v. Seif* [132 F.2d 925 (3rd Cir. 1997), *vacated*, 524 U.S. 974 (1998)], residents of Chester, Pennsylvania, alleged that the state's issuance of a permit for a new waste facility would create an unlawful disparate impact on African-American residents. As evidence, they noted that Chester, with a population of 42,000, 65% of which are African-American, had become the designated dumping grounds for the rest of Delaware County, with a population of 502,000, 91% of which are white. Though one-twelfth the size of the county, Chester already has five permitted waste facilities, while the rest of Delaware County has only two. All of Delaware County's municipal waste and sewage is processed in Chester, although only 7.5% of the county's population resides in the town. Most dramatically, the permitted capacity for the waste facilities in the much smaller city of Chester [is] 1,500 times greater than the permitted capacity for the remaining facilities in Delaware County (2.1 million tons vs. 1,400 tons), and the capacity per person for the waste facilities in the 65% African-American Chester area is almost 18,000 times greater than the capacity per person for the facilities in 91% white Delaware County.

The dispute over a proposal by Shintech to build a new polyvinyl chloride (PVC) plant in the lower income, 84% African-American community of Convent, Louisiana, also raised substantial distributive justice concerns. An analysis of toxic air emissions from the 10 existing petrochemical plants in the Convent area revealed that residents were already exposed to 251,179 pounds of toxic air pollution per square mile per year, and Shintech proposed to emit an additional three million pounds of air pollution per year, over 600,000 pounds of which would be toxic. This existing cumulative impact on the 84% African-American Convent-area residents is 67 times greater than the toxic air pollution burden for the rest of St. James Parish (the third most polluted parish in the state and 43.5% African American), 93 times greater than the average toxic air pollution exposure per square mile for the heavily polluted Louisiana Mississippi River industrial corridor (36.8% African American), 129 times greater than Louisiana's average exposure per square mile (the second most polluted state in the nation and 30.8% African American), and 658 times higher than the average toxic air pollution exposure per square mile in the United States (12% African American). EPA's disparate impact analysis, using its "relative emissions burden ratio" method, found that, were Shintech permitted to operate, African Americans in St. James Parish would experience a 71% to 242% greater toxic air pollution burden than non-African Americans in the parish....

### Environmental Justice as Procedural Justice

Claims of procedural injustice also are common in environmental justice disputes, and it is not [unusual] for people of color and low-income communities to complain about both the distributive and procedural aspects of an environmental policy or decision. Indeed, in many situations, a community's judgment about whether or not an outcome was distributively just will be significantly determined by the perceived fairness of the procedures leading to the outcome.

Procedural justice has been defined as "the right to treatment as an equal. That is the right, not to an equal distribution of some good or opportunity, but to equal concern and respect in the political decision about how these goods and opportunities are to be distributed." Aristotle referred to this as a status in which individuals have an "equal share in ruling and being ruled." It involves justice as a function of the manner in which a decision is made, and it requires a focus on the fairness of the decision-making process, rather than on its outcome....

The Executive Order on environmental justice has a strong focus on procedural justice, directing agencies to ensure greater public participation and access to information for minority and low-income populations. The Principles of Environmental Justice demand that public policy be based on mutual respect and justice for all peoples and free from bias or discrimination, affirm the fundamental right to self-determination, and insist on the right to participate as equal partners at every level of decision-making.

Environmental justice complaints raise both *ex ante* and *ex post* considerations of procedural fairness. Looking at the process in advance of its use (*ex ante*), they question whether the decision-making and public participation procedures are fair to all concerned or whether they favor one side over the other. Also, looking back (*ex post*), the complaints question whether the completed decision-making process did, in fact, treat all with equal concern and respect.

One way to judge procedural justice *ex ante* is to determine if those to be affected by the decision agree in advance on the process for making the decision. Thus, procedural justice requires looking not just to participation in a process but to whether the process is designed in a way to lead to a fair outcome. In this respect, environmental decision-making processes have been roundly criticized by commentators who have examined issues of environmental justice and public participation. One common observation is that the predominant expertise-oriented, interest-group model of environmental decision-making favors those with resources and political power over people of color and low-income communities. Even the [civic] republican process, which outwardly seeks to advance community interests over private interests, may obscure the true private interests at issue and the continuing disparities in resources, power, and influence. In general, to achieve procedural justice, observers advocate developing more deliberative models of decision-making, providing disadvantaged groups with greater legal and technical resources, and ensuring equal access to decision-makers and the decision-making process....

A common procedural justice complaint at the national level is that people of color and lower income communities [have] little influence on the decision-making processes of legislatures and environmental agencies.... Even where citizens are able to participate, environmental decision-makers are skeptical of the validity of citizen information and are biased in favor of the scientific data submitted by regulated industries.

Underrepresentation on the technical or scientific boards and commissions that make environmental decisions and recommendations is also a problem, particularly since the actions of these boards often reflect politics and personal values....

Another procedural justice aspect is the manner in which the government collects and analyzes data on environmental exposures and public health. In one case, EPA and the National Institutes of Health announced a $15 mil-

**Figure 1-2:** Farmworker Ruben Ochoa on pecan farm in Doña Ana County in southern New Mexico. Sharing an airshed with El Paso, Texas, and Ciudad Juárez, Mexico, Doña Ana County has historically struggled with poor air quality, particularly with dust and ozone pollution. The health of farmworkers and farmworker families is also threatened by exposure to pesticides routinely applied to local agricultural areas. Jan. 18, 2020. Photo: Isela Anchondo.

lion, 10-year epidemiological study on the health of farmers and farmworkers that would omit Hispanics from the study, even though farmworkers are largely Hispanic. The justification for the omission? The difficulty of tracking the highly mobile Hispanic population....

In addition to the procedural justice issues arising from the manner in which the state handled the permitting process, the Shintech case illustrates the *ex ante* obstacles that people of color and lower income communities confront. Under the state permitting process, the permit applicant has an automatic right, if requested, to an adjudicatory hearing, yet local residents have no such right....

The county's handling of a permit to build a hazardous waste incinerator near the Hispanic community of Kettleman City, California, illustrates the procedural barriers often encountered by ethnic communities. Despite the repeated, strong interest expressed by [Spanish]-speaking residents to participate in the permitting process, environmental impact documents, meeting notices, and public hearing testimony were never provided in Spanish. The court in *El Pueblo Para el Aire y Agua Limpio v. County of Kings* [22 Envtl. L. Reptr. 20, 357 (Cal. Super. Ct. 1991)] held that the meaningful involvement of local residents was effectively precluded by the failure to provide Spanish translations and set aside the local permit. When similar translation concerns were raised by Vietnamese-speaking residents regarding efforts to reopen the Marine Shale hazardous waste incinerator in Amelia, Louisiana, the state responded that it would take care of the inability of the Vietnamese community to participate in the public hearing process *after* the permit was issued....

An unresolved aspect of procedural justice is whether a fair process can negate a claim that a disproportionate outcome is unjust. Some argue that if the decisionmaker has given impartial attention to and consideration of competing claims to different benefits, an outcome would not be unjust even if the result were to subordinate one group to another....

While environmental justice requires, at a minimum, a procedurally just process, the emphasis on disparate effects, rather than discriminatory intent, in the Executive Order, Principles of Environmental Justice, and Title VI's implementing regulations indicates that a fair process alone will not negate claims of distributive injustice....

### Environmental Justice as Corrective Justice

The third aspect of justice encompassed by the term environmental justice is "corrective justice," a notion of justice that is sometimes referred to by other names and may be subsumed within claims for distributive or procedural justice....

"Corrective justice" involves fairness in the way punishments for lawbreaking are assigned and damages inflicted on individuals and communities are addressed.... Corrective justice involves not only the just administration of punishment to those who break the law, but also a duty to repair the losses for which one is responsible....

Therefore, as reflected in claims made in the environmental justice context, corrective justice encompasses many aspects of wrongdoing and injury and includes the concepts of "retributive justice," "compensatory justice," "restorative justice," and "commutative justice." I adopt the term corrective justice here because environmental justice seeks more than just retribution or punishment of those who violate legal rules of conduct. Corrective justice is also preferred over the phrase compensatory justice because the latter term may imply that, provided compensation is paid, an otherwise unjust action is acceptable. It is also important to note that although some concepts of corrective justice view fault or wrongful gain as a necessary condition for liability, environmental justice principles impose responsibility for damages regardless of fault (e.g., the polluter-pays principle). Corrective justice, therefore, is not used in the narrow Aristotelian rectificatory sense but instead in a broader, applied sense that violators be caught and punished and not reap benefits for disregarding legal standards and that injuries caused by the acts of another, whether a violation of law or not, be remedied....

The theme of corrective justice ... figures prominently in the efforts of indigenous people to achieve environmental justice. Native Americans have long complained that the federal government and mining and oil companies have failed to take responsibility for and address contamination caused by their nuclear testing and resource development activities on Indian lands. In addition, hundreds of open dumps, many originally operated by the Indian Health Service, currently exist in Indian country and are in need of cleanup. The recent, expanded ability of tribes to obtain authority to implement federal environmental laws presents tribal governments with the opportunity to promote corrective justice by directly enforcing compliance with environmental statutes on tribal lands, rather than having to rely on federal agencies, yet finding the financial and technical resources to carry out that authority remains a problem.

Local efforts to achieve corrective justice are illustrated by community efforts to address contamination from lead smelters in West Dallas—"the classic example of government inaction and callous disregard for the law." [quoting Robert Bullard. Eds.] As early as 1972, Dallas officials were aware of significantly elevated lead levels in the blood of children living in a minority neighborhood near a lead smelter that had repeatedly violated the law. EPA's own study in 1981 confirmed the high lead concentrations in children living near the smelters. In spite of repeated complaints by local residents, government officials took no action; EPA even rejected a voluntary cleanup plan, preferring still further tests of local children and suggesting that spreading dirt and planting grass would be sufficient.... Finally, after 50 years of operation without necessary local permits and 20 years after government officials became aware of the public health problems caused by the illegally operated smelter, authorities closed the facility and started a comprehensive cleanup program....

### Environmental Justice as Social Justice

The fourth and final aspect of justice implicated by the term environmental justice is "social justice," a far-reaching, and some say nebulous, goal of the environmental justice movement....

Social justice is "that branch of the virtue of justice that moves us to use our best efforts to bring about a more just ordering of society—one in which people's needs are more fully met." "The demands of social justice are ... first, that the members of every class have enough resources and enough power to live as befits human beings, and second, that the privileged classes, whoever they are, be accountable to the wider society for the way they use their advantages."

Environmental justice has been described as a "marriage of the movement for social justice with environmentalism" integrating environmental concerns into a broader agenda that emphasizes social, racial, and economic justice. Dr. Bullard refers to this aspect of environmental justice as "social equity: ... an assessment of the role of sociological factors (race, ethnicity, class, culture, lifestyles, political power, and so forth) in environmental decision-making."

Professor Sheila Foster has argued that a narrow focus on issues of distributive justice neglects the search for social structures and agents that are causing the environmental problems. A social justice perspective presents environmental justice as part of larger problems of racial, social, and economic justice and helps illustrate the influence of politics, race, and class on an area's quality of life. This broader social perspective contrasts with traditional environmentalism and its narrower focus on wilderness preservation and the technological aspects of environmental regulation.

Environmental justice's focus on social justice reflects reality. As one community organizer explained, oppressed people do not have compartmentalized problems—they do not separate the hazardous waste incinerator from the fact that their schools are underfunded, that they have no daycare, no sidewalks or streetlights, or no jobs. The reason disadvantaged communities do not separate these problems is that their quality of life as a whole is suffering and the political, economic, and racial causes are likely interrelated....

Social justice influences can work in two ways. The same underlying racial, economic, and political factors that are responsible for the environmental threats to the community also likely play a significant role in why the area may suffer from other problems like inadequate housing, a lack of employment opportunities, poor schools, etc. In turn, the presence of undesirable land uses that threaten the health and well-being of local residents and provide few direct economic benefits negatively influences the quality of life, development potential, and attitudes of the community and may lead to further social and economic degradation.

Government officials are often hesitant to embrace the social justice aspects of environmental justice, reflecting a reluctance to take on the broader systemic causes of environmental injustice or to consider issues outside the narrow technical focus of the agency. Nonetheless, the President's Executive Order acknowledges the significance of social justice by directing each federal agency to consider the economic and social implications of an agency's environmental justice activities, and the memorandum accompanying the Executive Order requires analysis of the economic and social, not just environmental, effects of federal actions on minority and low-income communities....

[C]riticism of environmental justice as too myopic and a diversion of scarce resources away from other more important social and public health problems is not well-founded. Most often, environmental justice efforts do not wastefully divert a community's attention but instead bring residents together to focus on a broad array of social justice problems.... [G]overnment officials and firms seeking community acceptance for environmentally risky projects must as a practical, if not also moral, matter consider whether social justice is served by their projects. For if the environmental and other social burdens of a proposed project are imposed on the local community while the economic and other benefits flow elsewhere, "community opposition will be fierce and the chances for success lessened."

\* \* \*

## Notes and Questions

**1. The "standard definition" of environmental justice.** Examine the EPA's 1998 definition of "environmental justice." How does this definition compare to the dimensions of justice articulated by Professor Kuehn? If it does not meet all four dimensions, which dimensions appear missing?

The EPA subsequently amended the 1998 definition. Today, the EPA defines "environmental justice" as follows:

> **Environmental Justice (EJ)** is the **fair treatment** and **meaningful involvement** of all people regardless of race, color, national origin, or income with respect to the development, implementation, and enforcement of environmental law, regulations, and policies.

How does this current definition compare to the 1998 definition? What words do you see added? How do these added words reflect evolving understandings of environmental justice?

As Kuehn notes, notwithstanding the original focus on communities of color and low-income people, the EPA since the Bush administration has defined "environmental justice" as an objective for "all people." What advantages do you see for this broadened scope? Should environmental justice, for example, apply to children? women? the elderly? the undocumented? LGBTQ communities? wealthy political donors? What disadvantages do you see with this boundless scope?

While the utility and wisdom of the EPA's definition of "environmental justice" may be debated, the EPA's definition remains the one most commonly used in the United States, and thus the one to which we will generally refer in this book. It is important to recognize, however, that individual states, tribes, local governments, or community organizations may adopt different definitions of "environmental justice" for their own purposes, and advocates should be sure to check for alternate definitions in their local area.

**2. Alternate definitions of "environmental justice."** In addition to the EPA definition, Kuehn also notes other definitions proposed by EJ experts including Professor Bunyan Bryant. Bryant defined "environmental justice" to mean "those cultural norms and values, rules, regulations, behaviors, policies, and decisions to support sustainable communities, where people can interact with confidence that their environment is safe, nurturing, and protective." How does this definition compare to the EPA definition? What is the function of interacting with "confidence" in this definition? Is confidence always a good thing?

In the excerpt, Kuehn also notes the "alternative approach" to defining "environmental justice" exemplified by the 17-point "Principles of Environmental Justice." Distilled by Dr. Robert Bullard, the principles include such elements as "protect all persons from environmental degradation" and "obviate the requirement to prove intent to discriminate." How helpful do you find this "alternative approach" based upon such ambitious goals? If we really could "protect all persons from environmental degradation," would we really need any other "principles" for environmental justice? And how exactly should we "obviate the requirement to prove intent to discriminate"? Is this requirement, deriving from the Supreme Court's interpretation of the Equal Protection Clause of the U.S. Constitution, subject to protest in the streets or reversal by popular vote? If these goals seem overly ambitious, why do you imagine that EJ advocates made such efforts to develop them?

**3. Fair treatment.** Returning to the EPA's "standard definition" of environmental justice, what is the meaning of "fair treatment"? The EPA itself supplies a definition:

> **Fair treatment** means no group of people should bear a disproportionate share of the negative environmental consequences resulting from industrial, governmental and commercial operations or policies.

Consider the implications of this definition. How does it compare, for example, with the EJ principle that we should "protect all persons from environmental degradation"? Under the EPA's definition of fair treatment, may some people still be harmed by environmental degradation? If so, must all people be harmed equally?

Should fair treatment apply only to "negative environmental consequences"? What about positive environmental amenities? Should all people also have fair access to city parks, wilderness areas, swimming holes, and fishing ponds? Without amending its standard definition posted on the EPA website, the EPA in fact has recently "expanded the concept of fair treatment to include not only consideration of how burdens are distributed across all populations, but the distribution of benefits as well." U.S. EPA, EJ 2020 ACTION AGENDA at 55. Given this recent extension of "fair treatment" to environmental benefits, how should government ensure the fair distribution of such amenities?

Definitions aside, anyone who had siblings growing up already knows (or thinks they know) what is *fair* and (especially) what is *not* fair. To paraphrase Supreme Court Justice Potter Stewart from a different context, with unfair treatment, "we know it when we see it." *Cf., Jacobellis v. Ohio*, 378 U.S. 184 (1964), Stewart, J., concurring. Consider then what fairness demands in the following scenarios:

- Homes in a diverse neighborhood range in property values from $40,000 to $1 million. Asbestos contamination from an old Navy base makes the entire neighborhood uninhabitable, dropping all property values to zero. Notwithstanding the zero value of each property, the Navy offers each property owner a buy-out of $50,000.

- A home in a poor, largely Latino neighborhood becomes severely contaminated with mercury brought into the home by two teenage boys who live there. The home is worth $50,000 and the EPA estimates the cleanup will cost $500,000.

- Sediments contaminated with polychlorinated biphenyls (PCBs) in an urban waterway make resident fish unsafe to eat. Cleanup of the waterway is estimated to cost $300 million and take 20 years. Instead of undertaking this massive cleanup, the government simply issues an order banning consumption of fish from the waterway. After the order goes into effect, the only groups who continue to eat fish from the waterway are homeless people and Asian-Pacific Islander families.

- High levels of asthma and other respiratory ailments are attributed to the cumulative emission of toxic air pollutants from six industrial facilities that surround a residential neighborhood. Each facility remains in compliance individually with its permit requirements under the Clean Air Act.

- Emissions of sulfur dioxide from an old coal-fired power plant owned and operated by a public utility violate federal standards under the Clean Air Act. To bring the old plant into compliance, the public utility would have to spend $50 million. The public utility cannot afford this upgrade and instead shuts down the plant, putting 220 plant employees out of work on an Indian reservation struggling to emerge from poverty.

Does "fairness" then not always seem intuitive? As used in the EPA definition of environmental justice, does fairness include protection of equity in million-dollar homes? Does fairness allow (or require?) spending ten times more to clean up a home than the home is worth on the market? Does fairness allow a blanket ban on fishing, regardless of the disproportionate impacts of the ban on certain groups? Does fairness include fairness to facility operators who comply with their permits individually yet contribute collectively to harm in neighboring communities? Does fairness require each facility operator to meet national standards, regardless of impacts on the local economy?

In the early years of attention to environmental justice, much of the concern involved the siting of industrial facilities in low-income and minority communities, as with the PCBs landfill in Warren County. Much early scholarship on environmental justice thus addressed fairness in the context of siting such **Locally Undesirable Land Uses (LULUs)**. In one such article, Professor Vicki Been proposed several different models of fairness that could be summarized as follows: (1) even apportionment of LULUs among all neighborhoods; (2) compensation of communities hosting LULUs by other communities; (3) progressive siting — wealthier neighborhoods receive more LULUs; (4) cost internalization — those who benefit from LULUs bear the cost; (5) the siting process involves no intentional discrimination; (6) the siting process shows "equal concern and respect" for all neighborhoods; and (7) all communities receive an equal number of vetoes that can be used to exclude a LULU. Vicki Been, *What's Fairness Got to Do with It? Environmental Justice and the Siting of Locally Undesirable Land Uses*, 78 Cornell L. Rev. 1001 (1993).

What model of "fairness" would you favor for the siting of LULUs? Can you see any challenges for administering one or more of these models? For example, if we agreed to adopt "even apportionment" of LULUs among all neighborhoods, who would do this apportioning? The city? The state? What if different neighborhoods had different concerns based on local demographics, such as high populations of children or elderly residents? Moreover, how do we even know what a "LULU" is? Is an old coal-fired power plant necessarily "locally undesirable" if it is also a major employer in the area? As we will see in Chapter 9 ("Environmental Justice in Indian Country"), even waste disposal sites — a classic LULU from many perspectives — may not be a LULU for some communities eager for economic development.

Fairness in the definition of environmental justice clearly remains subject to some level of subjectivity and differing perspectives. Nonetheless, it remains an important substantive dimension of environmental justice, placing some boundaries on the outcome of process to be explored in the following note.

**4. Meaningful involvement.** The second pillar of environmental justice according to the EPA's definition is **meaningful involvement** in the development, implementation, and enforcement of environmental law and policy. As with fair treatment, the EPA also provides a definition of "meaningful involvement" in this context:

---

**Meaningful involvement** means:
- People have an opportunity to participate in decisions about activities that may affect their environment and/or health;
- The public's contribution can influence the regulatory agency's decision;
- Community concerns will be considered in the decision making process; and
- Decision makers will seek out and facilitate the involvement of those potentially affected.

---

Meaningful involvement in this context may be usefully juxtaposed with the older government notion of "community relations" or the more recent popularity of "public involvement." While public involvement may allow opportunities for public comment on proposed actions, meaningful involvement seeks to ensure that such comments may "influence" the final agency decision. Meaningful involvement also suggests that agencies should make affirmative efforts to "seek out" and assist community input, rather than rely exclusively on traditional channels for public communications, such as published notices in newspapers or the *Federal Register*. For a showcase of ideas for meaningful involvement in the site cleanup context, *see* Chapter 8 ("Environmental Justice and Contaminated Sites") (case study on the Lower Duwamish Waterway Superfund Site). Before flipping to Chapter 8, however, imagine that you are an attorney for the Texas Commission on Environmental Quality drafting a new standard for water quality. The new standard will apply to a river valley with a large population of senior citizens who arrived from Vietnam in the early 1970s plus young families who recently arrived from Central America. For public comment on your draft regulation, how might you "seek out" meaningful input from these particular communities?

Note that meaningful involvement is intended to apply to all phases of the regulatory process, explicitly including the "development, implementation, and enforcement" of environmental laws, regulations, and policies. Meaningful involvement in "development" may include public engagement on draft regulations, such as in the example above. Meaningful involvement in "implementation" may include public engagement on draft permits, such as the permits under the Clean Air Act for the six industrial facilities surrounding the neighborhood in the hypothetical above. But what does meaningful involvement in "enforcement" include? Isn't government enforcement inherently confidential? Doesn't the U.S. Department of Justice often tell us that they don't comment on active cases? For ideas on what meaningful involvement may include in the enforcement context, *see* Chapter 7 ("Public Enforcement").

**5. Corrective justice.** Recall the four dimensions of environmental justice articulated by Professor Kuehn: distributive justice, procedural justice, corrective justice, and social justice. As Kuehn describes the scope of corrective justice, to what extent does it appear to be encompassed within the EPA definition of environmental justice? Environmental justice, as defined by the EPA, can obviously reach corrective actions for current problems, such as permit violations or contaminated sites. But can it also reach elements of compensatory justice, such as compensation for the fish that cannot be eaten safely from a contaminated waterway? For exploration of this question, *see* Chapter 8 ("Contaminated Sites").

**6. Social justice.** What is the relationship of environmental justice to social justice? As defined by the EPA? As envisioned by Kuehn? How would you draw the Venn diagram to explain this relationship? How does social justice figure into the conception of environmental justice expressed by grassroots environmental justice activists in the 17 Principles of Environmental Justice discussed in the next section?

Regardless of taxonomy and how one defines "environmental justice," environmental inequities certainly derive from many sources. These sources of inequitable protection surely include racism and other forms of invidious discrimination, but may also include deficiencies in the apparatus of environmental policymaking. For an investigation of these structural defects, see the following excerpt from the classic article by Harvard Law Professor Richard Lazarus:

## Richard J. Lazarus,
### *Pursuing "Environmental Justice":*
### *The Distributional Effects of Environmental Protection*

87 NORTHWESTERN UNIVERSITY L. REV. 787 (1993)

*Exacerbating Causes: The Structure of Environmental Policymaking*

There exist ... factors more endemic to environmental law itself that may exacerbate distributional inequities likely present in the context of any public welfare law. These factors suggest more than the disturbing, yet somewhat irresistible thesis, that the distributional dimension of environmental protection policy likely suffers from the same inequities that persist generally in society. They suggest the far more troubling, and even less appealing, proposition that the problems of distributional inequity may in fact be more pervasive in the environmental protection arena than they are in other areas of traditional concern to civil rights organizations, such as education, employment, and housing.

Indeed, it is the absence of that minority involvement so prevalent in the more classic areas of civil rights concern that may render the distributional problem worse for environmental protection. Minority interests have traditionally had little voice in the various points of influence that strike the distributional balances necessary to get environmental protection laws enacted, regulations promulgated, and enforcement actions initiated. The interest groups historically active in the environmental protection area include a variety of mainstream environmental organizations representing a spectrum of interests (conservation, recreation, hunting, wildlife protection, resource protection, human health), as well as a variety of commercial and industrial concerns. Until very recently, if at all, the implications for racial minorities of environmental protection laws have not been a focal point of concern for any of these organizations.

Much of environmental protection lawmaking has also been highly centralized, with the geographic focus in Washington, D.C. The enactment of environmental statutes within that geo-political setting has required the expenditure of considerable political resources. As evidenced by the thirteen years required to amend the Clean Air Act, it is no easy task to obtain the attention of the numerous congressional committees, and to form the coalitions between competing interest groups, so necessary to secure a bill's passage.

Environmental legislation has ultimately been produced through intense and lengthy horse-trading among interest groups, a process necessary to secure a particular environmental law's passage. This process has often depended upon the forging of alliances between diverse interests both within the environmental public interest community and within government bureaucracy. Often, these unions have included so-called "unholy alliances" between environmentalists and commercial and industrial interests, where the latter have perceived an economic advantage to be gained (or disadvantage to be minimized) by their supporting an environmental protection law that allocates the benefits and burdens of environmental protection in a particular fashion....

It is not surprising, therefore, that those environmental laws enacted by Congress typically address some, but hardly all, environmental pollution problems. And, even with regard to those problems that are explicitly addressed, there are usually discrepancies and gaps within the statutory scheme. Which problems are confronted, and where the discrepancies and gaps occur, is quite naturally an expression of the priorities of those participants who wield the greatest influence and resources in the political process.

For this reason, much environmental legislation may not have focused on those pollution problems that are of greatest concern to many minority communities. For instance, air pollution control efforts typically have focused on general ambient air quality concerns for an entire metropolitan region rather than on toxic hot spots in any one particular area. Accordingly, while there has been much progress made in improving air quality as measured by a handful of national ambient air quality standards, there has been relatively less progress achieved over the last twenty years in the reduction of those toxic air emissions which tend to be of greater concern to persons, disproportionately minorities, who live in the immediate geographic vicinity of the toxic polluting source.... Likewise, and at the behest of mainstream environmental groups, substantial resources have also been directed to improving air and water quality in nonurban areas. Programs for the prevention of significant deteriorations in air quality, the reduction of "acid rain," and the protection of visibility in national parks and wilderness areas, all require significant financial expenditures. Substantial resources have similarly been expended on improving the quality of water resources that are not as readily accessible to many minorities because of their historical exclusion. Without meaning to suggest that these programs lack merit on their own terms (for the simple reason that they possess great merit), their return in terms of overall public health may be less than pollution control programs directed at improving the environmental quality of urban America's poorer neighborhoods, including many minority communities....

[R]acial minorities have had little influence on either the lawmaking or priority-setting processes at any of the legislative, regulatory, or local enforcement levels. They have not been well represented among the interest groups lobbying and litigating before governmental authorities on environmental protection issues. Nor have they been well represented, especially at the national level, within those governmental organizations actively involved in the relevant environmental processes. Their voices have not been heard in the mainstream environmental public interest organizations that participate in the policymaking debates and that, in the absence of governmental enforcement, are behind citizen suits filling the void. Traditional civil rights organizations have historically had little interest in, and have infrequently become involved with, environmental issues. At the same time, mainstream environmental organizations have historically included few minorities in policymaking positions. In 1990, this fact prompted several members of various civil rights organizations and minority groups to send a widely publicized letter to the national environmental public interest organizations charging them with being isolated from minority communities....

\* \* \*

## *Notes and Questions*

**1. Progress?** In the quarter century-plus since publication of this article, the structural defects identified by Professor Lazarus remain mostly in place. As Congress largely quit legislating on environmental matters in 1990 with passage of the Clean Air Act Amendments, the United States still has no federal environmental statute dedicated to addressing concerns for environmental justice. Federal rulemaking to implement the aging collection of federal environmental laws (e.g., the Clean Air Act, Clean Water Act) remains mostly a matter of top-down administrative process. And today, almost every federal rule that is proposed to address real environmental concerns becomes the immediate subject of nationwide litigation. *See, e.g., National Ass'n of Manufacturers v. Dept. of Defense*, 138 S.Ct. 617 (2018) (allowing challenges to rule defining Clean Water Act jurisdiction to be brought in U.S. district courts across the country).

**2. Hope?** Notwithstanding the lack of progress on defects within policymaking structures in the United States, some advancements must be noted. For example, through formation of the National Environmental Justice Advisory Council (NEJAC) in 1993 and the NEJAC's diligent work to investigate matters of environmental injustice across the country, grassroots activists have developed direct channels for communications with EPA officials in Washington, D.C. EJ activists have also established working relations not just with mainstream environmental organizations but also with supportive civil rights organizations. The American Civil Liberties Union (ACLU), for example, was an early advocate for safe drinking water when the lead contamination in Flint, Michigan, came to light. The ACLU has also taken the lead in litigation challenging construction of the proposed border wall along the U.S.-Mexico border, in support of interests from both environmental and immigrant rights groups. At the same time, the NAACP has become a recognized leader in developing tools and advocacy materials to address concerns for environmental and climate justice. *See* Chapter 14 ("Climate Justice").

# C. "We Speak for Ourselves"

Environmental justice advocates have long observed that environmental laws have not prevented disproportionate environmental harms from occurring. The reasons for this are many and examined throughout this book. One fundamental concern, as noted by Professor Lazarus, is that environmental regulation focuses on improving overall ambient environmental conditions, and does not consider the distributional consequences of where pollution is occurring. Therefore, the relationship between environmental justice activists, on the one hand, and conventional environmental organizations, industry, and government agencies, on the other, has been marked by suspicion and hobbled to some degree by a framework that did not envision the considerations that environmental justice advocates bring to the table. Yet individuals in each of these groups understand the pragmatic need to work collaboratively to address serious problems. The wariness felt by environmental justice leaders toward environmental regulators, environmental laws, and mainstream environmental organizations was reflected in a 1990 letter sent by environmental justice activists to leaders of the ten largest environmental organizations (the "Group of Ten" letter). In addition, many activists were concerned that business interests, academics, and others were misinterpreting their positions. Thus, in 1991, environmental justice activists gathered in an historic summit and proposed a set of principles to guide their efforts and clearly state their positions. A decade later, a group of activists again sent a letter, this time to then-President George W. Bush. These writings reflect the view strongly held by many activists, a view that people living in heavily impacted communities can and do "speak for themselves."

## Letter, Circa Earth Day 1990

March 16, 1990

Addressed individually to Jay Hair, National Wildlife Federation; Michael Fisher and others from the Sierra Club; Frederick Sutherland, Sierra Club Legal Defense Fund; Peter Berle and others from the National Audubon Society; Frederick Krupp, Environmental Defense Fund; Mike Clark, Environmental Policy Institute/Friends of the Earth; Jack Lorenz and others, Izaak Walton League; George Frampton and others from the Wilderness Society; Paul Pritchard, National Parks and Conservation Association; John Adams, Natural Resources Defense Council

Dear [Representative]:

We are writing this letter in the belief that through dialogue and mutual strategizing we can create a global environmental movement that protects us all.

We are artists, writers, academics, students, activists, representatives of churches, unions, and community organizations writing you to express our concerns about the role of your organization and other national environmental groups in communities of people of color in the Southwest.

For centuries, people of color in our region have been subjected to racist and genocidal practices including the theft of lands and water, the murder of innocent people, and degradation of our environment. Mining companies extract minerals leaving economically depressed communities and poisoned soil and water. The U.S. military takes lands for weapons production, testing and storage, contaminating surrounding communities and placing minority workers in the most highly radioactive and toxic worksites. Industrial and municipal dumps are intentionally placed in communities of color, disrupting our cultural lifestyle and threatening our communities' futures. Workers in the fields are dying and babies are born disfigured as a result of pesticide spraying.

Although environmental organizations calling themselves the "Group of Ten" often claim to represent our interests, in observing your activities it has become clear to us that your organizations play an equal role in the disruption of our communities. There is a clear lack of accountability by the Group of Ten environmental organizations towards Third World communities in the Southwest, in the United States as a whole, and internationally.

**Figure 1-3:** Environmental justice pioneers Dr. Sofia Martinez and Richard Moore. Among other things, Moore signed the 1990 "Group of Ten" letter and served as past and present chair of the National Environmental Justice Advisory Council. Albuquerque, NM, Jan. 29, 2019. Photo: Cliff Villa.

Your organizations continue to support and promote policies which emphasize the clean-up and preservation of the environment on the backs of working people in general and people of color in particular. In the name of eliminating environmental hazards at any cost, across the country industrial and other economic activities which employ us are being shut down, curtailed or prevented while our survival needs and cultures are ignored. We suffer from the end results of these actions, but are never full participants in the decision-making which leads to them.

[Selected examples from the letter follow. Eds.]:

Organizations such as the National Wildlife Federation have been involved in exchanges where Third World countries will sign over lands (debt-for-nature swaps) to conservation groups in exchange for creditors agreeing to erase a portion of that country's debt. In other cases the debt is purchased at reduced rates; the creditors can then write it off. This not only raises the specter of conservation groups now being "creditors" to Third World countries, but legitimizes the debt itself through the further expropriation of Third World resources. The question arises whether such deals are in the long term economic interests of both the countries involved and of the people living on the land.

The lack of people of color in decision-making positions in your organizations such as executive staff and board positions is also reflective of your histories of racist and exclusionary practices. Racism is a root cause of your inaction around addressing environmental problems in our communities.

Group of Ten organizations are being supported by corporations such as ARCO, British Petroleum, Chemical Bank, GTE, General Electric, Dupont, Dow Chemical, Exxon, IBM, Coca Cola, and Waste Management, Incorporated. Several of these companies are known polluters whose disregard for the safety and well-being of workers has resulted in the deaths of many people of color. It is impossible for you to represent us in issues of our own survival when you are accountable to these interests. Such accountability leads you to pursue a corporate strategy towards the resolution of the environmental crisis, when what is needed is a *people's strategy* which fully involves those who have historically been without power in this society.

Comments have been made by representatives of major national environmental organizations to the effect that only in the recent past have people of color begun to realize the impacts of environmental contamination. We have been involved in environmental struggles for many years and we have not needed the Group of Ten environmental organizations to tell us that these problems have existed.

We again call upon you to cease operations in communities of color within 60 days, until you have hired leaders from those communities to the extent that they make up between 35–40 percent of your entire staff. We are asking that Third World leaders be hired at all levels of your operations....

Sincerely,

/S/ 117 signatures of organizations and individuals.

* * *

## Principles of Environmental Justice, Proceedings, The First National People of Color Environmental Leadership Summit
### xiii (October 24–27, 1991)

WE THE PEOPLE OF COLOR, gathered together at this multinational *People of Color Environmental Leadership Summit*, to begin to build a national and international movement of all peoples of color to fight the destruction and taking of our lands and communities, do hereby re-establish our spiritual interdependence to the sacredness of our Mother Earth; to respect and celebrate each of our cultures, languages and beliefs about the natural world and our roles in healing ourselves; to ensure environmental justice; to promote economic alternatives which would contribute to the development of environmentally safe livelihoods; and, to secure our political, economic and cultural liberation that has been denied for over 500 years of colonization and oppression, resulting in the poisoning of our communities and land and the genocide of our peoples, do affirm and adopt these Principles of Environmental Justice:

1. Environmental justice affirms the sacredness of Mother Earth, ecological unity and the interdependence of all species, and the right to be free from ecological destruction.

2. Environmental justice demands that public policy be based on mutual respect and justice for all peoples, free from any form of discrimination or bias.

3. Environmental justice mandates the right to ethical, balanced and responsible uses of land and renewable resources in the interest of a sustainable planet for humans and other living things.

4. Environmental justice calls for universal protection from nuclear testing, extraction, production and disposal of toxic/hazardous wastes and poisons and nuclear testing that threaten the fundamental right to clean air, land, water, and food.

5. Environmental justice affirms the fundamental right to political, economic, cultural and environmental self-determination of all peoples.

6. Environmental justice demands the cessation of the production of all toxins, hazardous wastes, and radioactive materials, and that all past and current producers be held strictly accountable to the people for detoxification and the containment at the point of production.

7. Environmental justice demands the right to participate as equal partners at every level of decision-making including needs assessment, planning, implementation, enforcement and evaluation.

8. Environmental justice affirms the right of all workers to a safe and healthy work environment, without being forced to choose between an unsafe livelihood and unemployment. It also affirms the right of those who work at home to be free from environmental hazards.

9. Environmental justice protects the right of victims of environmental injustice to receive full compensation and reparations for damages as well as quality health care.

10. Environmental justice considers governmental acts of environmental injustice a violation of international law, the Universal Declaration of Human Rights, and the United Nations Convention on Genocide.

11. Environmental justice must recognize a special legal and natural relationship of Native Peoples to the U.S. government through treaties, agreements, compacts, and covenants affirming sovereignty and self-determination.

12. Environmental justice affirms the need for urban and rural ecological policies to clean up and rebuild our cities and rural areas in balance with nature, honoring the cultural integrity of all our communities, and providing fair access for all to the full range of resources.

13. Environmental justice calls for the strict enforcement of principles of informed consent, and a halt to the testing of experimental reproductive and medical procedures and vaccinations on people of color.

14. Environmental justice opposes the destructive operations of multinational corporations.

15. Environmental justice opposes military occupation, repression and exploitation of lands, peoples and cultures, and other life forms.

16. Environmental justice calls for the education of present and future generations which emphasizes social and environmental issues, based on our experience and an appreciation of our diverse cultural perspectives.

17. Environmental justice requires that we, as individuals, make personal and consumer choices to consume as little of Mother Earth's resources and to produce as little waste as possible; and make the conscious decision to challenge and reprioritize our lifestyles to insure the health of the natural world for present and future generations.

Adopted today, October 24, 1991, in Washington, D.C.

* * *

Ten years later, many prominent grassroots environmental justice activists prepared the following letter to the President of the United States, this time reflecting growing concern with the impact of climate change on low-income and minority communities.

## Letter, Circa Earth Day 2001

April 19, 2001

George W. Bush
President of the United States of America
The White House
1600 Pennsylvania Avenue NW
Washington, DC 20500
USA

Dear Mr. President,

We are writing you today to express our profound concern with your new climate change policies with respect to their impacts on poor people and people of color in the United States and around the world.

It is our firmly held belief that climate change is not only an ecological, economic or political question, but it is a moral issue with profound ramifications for all of the inhabitants of this planet Earth. It is a question of environmental justice and human rights. It is also an issue of equity between nations.

Particularly hard hit will be low-lying countries like Bangladesh and small island states whose very existence is threatened. The poor here in the United States—especially poor people of color—will also bear the brunt of climate change. Your policies will only intensify those impacts.

Given its potentially profound ramifications, climate change must be tackled with serious and vigorous leadership and international cooperation rather than a misguided isolationist approach that protects a handful of powerful fossil fuel corporations.

The United States, whose four percent of the world's population generates one-quarter of all man made carbon dioxide—the leading global warming gas—must take the lead in reversing its role as the main contributor to this looming global crisis.

Certainly, your predecessor's climate change policies came up well short of the measures we believe are necessary to address the problem. But your administration's response so far—your failure to follow through on campaign promises to reduce carbon dioxide emissions ... borders on nothing short of gross global negligence.

Your negation of the increasingly irrefutable scientific evidence on climate change is distressing. It is no longer a question of whether sea levels will rise, but rather of how many coastlines, people, communities, and entire island nations will be submerged.

Global warming is starting to make itself felt. The 1990s was the warmest decade and 1998 was the warmest year on record. The icecap atop Mount Kilimanjaro in Africa is melting away and will completely disappear in less than 15 years. It is an abuse of power to turn your back on this, the most serious environmental issue ever to confront humanity.

If it is not halted, climate change will probably result in increased frequency and severity of storms, floods and drought. And it will cause the spread of diseases, such as malaria. It will increase hunger and bring about displacement and mass migrations of people with ensuing social conflict.

Mr. President, you claim that you don't want to harm the American consumer, yet you're setting us all up to pay a huge price in the future. This is especially true for the poor. Earlier this year, the United Nations Intergovernmental Panel on Climate Change (IPCC) concluded that the impacts of global warming "are expected to fall disproportionately on the poor."

People who are highly dependent on farming, fishing or forestry, especially indigenous people, are most likely to see their livelihoods destroyed by climate change. Meanwhile, the urban poor—mostly people of color in the U.S.—will be most vulnerable to climate change-related heat waves, diseases and respiratory ailments.

Many of us come from or work with communities that are already directly affected by the oil industry. These are communities and workers that are suffering the social and environmental effects of oil exploration, production, transportation, refining, distribution and combustion. These communities are also some of those who will be hardest hit by climate change—whether they are in Nigeria's Niger Delta, in Arctic Village, Alaska, or in Louisiana's "cancer alley." These communities face a "double whammy" suffering oil's acute toxic impacts first and then its long-term effects in the form of the harsh hand of global warming.

Rather than cater to the socially and ecologically destructive oil industry, Mr. President, you should severely curb U.S. carbon emissions and support the Kyoto Protocol. At home you should also support a just transition for fossil fuel industry workers and fenceline communities while investing the United States' resources in energy efficiency and renewable energy resources, such as solar, wind and biomass.

Mr. President, we urge you to reconsider your position on climate change before the United States becomes universally known as an environmental rogue state, and you go down in history as G.W. Bush, the Global Warming President.

Sincerely,

/S/ Nnimmo Bassey, Oilwatch Africa; Ricardo Carrere, World Rainforest Movement, Uruguay; Chee Yoke Ling, Third World Network, Malaysia; Oronto Douglas, Environmental Rights Action/Friends of the Earth, Nigeria; Tom Goldtooth, Indigenous Environmental Network, U.S.; Sarah James, Gwich'in Steering Committee, U.S.; Esperanza Martinez, Oilwatch International, Ecuador; Richard Moore, Southwest Network for Environmental and Economic Justice, U.S.; Ricardo Navarro, CESTA/Friends of the Earth, El Salvador; S. Bobby Peek, GroundWork, South Africa; Amit Srivastava/Joshua Karliner, CorpWatch, U.S.; Connie Tucker, Southern Organizing Committee for Economic and Social Justice, U.S.; Dr. Owens Wiwa, African Environmental and Human Development Agency, Nigeria

* * *

## Notes and Questions

1. **"Bottom-up" or "top-down"?** What are the implications of a "bottom-up" perspective for addressing environmental problems in fora dominated by formal professionalization? As you consider the various strategies—legal and technical—available to reduce environmental disparities, consider which of them are better equipped to work with and utilize a grassroots perspective. Many environmental justice advocates resist top-down government approaches, noting that the decisions of scientists, bureaucrats, lawyers, and judges are often paternalistic and disempower them. Is there an inherent tension between the movement's participatory goals of having greater voice and power, and the movement's substantive goals of eliminating risk of environmental harm altogether? In other words, is it possible greater participation would not lead to the policies environmental justice activists desire, and the adoption of regulatory policies that environmental justice advocates desire would not lead to improved empowerment of these communities?

2. **Values.** How do the 17 Principles of Environmental Justice presented above compare to the two pillars of "fair treatment" and "meaningful involvement" in the EPA definition of environmental justice? How do these principles compare to Professor Kuehn's four dimensions of environmental justice? In your Venn diagram of environmental justice in relation to social justice, where do you place the principle of freedom from "military occupation"? Are these "Principles of Environmental Justice" really about protecting public health and the environment? Or do they embrace a broader set of values? Consider the following observation:

> [T]he established environmental justice framework tends to treat racial minorities as interchangeable and to assume for all communities of color that health and distribution of environmental burdens are main concerns. For some racialized communities, however, environmental justice is not only,

or even primarily, about immediate health concerns or burden distribution. Rather, for them, and particularly for some indigenous peoples, environmental justice is mainly about cultural and economic self-determination and belief systems that connect their history, spirituality, and livelihood to the natural environment....

Eric K. Yamamoto & Jen-L W. Lyman, *Racializing Environmental Justice*, 72 U. COLO. L. REV. 311 (2001). In Chapter 9 ("Environmental Justice in Indian Country"), we will explore values including cultural preservation and self-determination in the context of indigenous communities. However, it is important to recognize that such values may also be cherished in different ways by other communities and may even be placed above more conventional environmental values such as a reduced risk of asthma attacks.

**3. Expectations.** What do you imagine the drafters of the 17 Principles hoped to accomplish? Are the principles directed at one government agency or one level of government? Are the principles framed more as objectives to be achieved or aspirations to be pursued? Are the demands all realistic? If it seems unrealistic to demand the "cessation of the production of all toxins," which might include the production of components for every penny, car battery, and electronic device, then what do you imagine the drafters of these principles did expect? Similarly, when the principles demand "the right to participate as equal partners at every level of decision-making including ... enforcement," what could the drafters expect here? Can these demands be reconciled with existing societal and legal norms, or do they call for radical social and legal reform? Are there middle grounds where progress toward environmental justice may be realized?

**4. The "Group of Ten" letter.** The writing of environmental justice activists is often aspirational and hard-hitting. EJ activists have challenged dominant paradigms in all sectors including government, academia, and the broader environmental movement that began with events such as passage of the Wilderness Act in 1964 and the first Earth Day in 1970. While the letter to the "Group of Ten" in 1990 must have come as some shock to leaders of those mainstream environmental organizations, the letter also succeeded in drawing attention to failure of the broader environmental movement to address concerns such as worker protection, tribal sovereignty, economic development, and leadership within the organizations themselves. Since that time, many of these organizations have made important strides toward addressing these concerns. In 2015, for example, the Natural Resources Defense Council (NRDC) hired Rhea Suh — a daughter of Korean immigrants — to serve as president of the organization. Under Ms. Suh, in 2016, the NRDC joined other organizations in filing a lawsuit to address the drinking water contamination in Flint, Michigan. Similarly, the Sierra Club Legal Defense Fund (now Earthjustice) currently pursues a wide range of environmental justice matters, to include ongoing challenges to the Dakota Access Pipeline. The National Audubon Society and its local chapters now offer a variety of programs to support diverse communities, including programs to provide naturalist training for at-risk youth. *See* https://www.audubon.org/magazine/november-december-2015/birds-offer-way-outside-troubled-kids. Newer environmental organizations, such as the Center for Biological Diversity—formerly dedicated to the preservation of animal species—now include portfolios with significant work to improve environmental health for people, including through campaigns to address toxic exposures to lead, mercury, uranium, and pesticides. *See* https://www.biologicaldiversity.org/programs/environmental_health/. While mainstream environmental organizations must continue to seek ways to support the concerns of diverse communities, 30 years after the Group of Ten letter, it is clear that much progress has been made toward that end.

5. **Animal justice?** Is environmental justice just about protecting people? Or could it also concern protection of fish, wildlife, and other members of the natural world? What does the EPA definition suggest? What do you find in the 17 Principles of Environmental Justice? If environmental justice includes protection of the animal world, can it be distinguished in any meaningful way from environmental law generally? On the other hand, isn't the fate of at least some diverse human communities tied to protection of certain animal communities? *See, e.g.*, Michael L. Chiropolos, *Inupiat Subsistence and the Bowhead Whale: Can Indigenous Hunting Cultures Coexist with Endangered Animal Species?*, 5 COLO. J. INT'L ENVTL. L. & POL'Y 213 (1994). If so, can we say that at least in some circumstances, any definition of environmental justice could encompass protections for the animal world? Toward that end, consider the argument that while "environmental justice research is predominantly an anthropocentric endeavor," it may be "important to expand our frameworks for understanding injustice to include more than human species...." Aelita Neimanis, Heather Castleden & Daniel Rainham, *Examining the Place of Ecological Integrity in Environmental Justice: A Systematic Review*, 17 INT'L J. JUST. & SUSTAINABILITY 349–350 (2012).

**Figure 1-4:** Iñupiat prayer after bowhead whale hunt. Elder Isaac Akootchook and whaling captain James Lampe thank the creator and the whale for providing food to the community. Kaktovik, Alaska. Sept. 2001. Photo: Subhankar Banerjee, from ARCTIC VOICES: RESISTANCE AT THE TIPPING POINT (Seven Stories Press, pbk, 2013).

# D. Critiquing the Environmental Justice Movement

In the following excerpt, Professor Chris Foreman offers a critical review of the environmental justice movement as it had been defined by early leaders of the movement including Dr. Robert Bullard. As you read this critique, consider your own responses to his observations and conclusions. Which if any of these observations would you consider helpful for shaping future endeavors toward achieving the aims of environmental justice? Which of these critiques appear to warrant their own critique?

## Christopher H. Foreman, Jr., *The Promise and Peril of Environmental Justice*
### (1998)

Reducing and avoiding threats to health is a major, but often unproductive, theme of environmental justice advocacy. When activists call attention to alleged unfair environmental burdens, surreptitious mass poisoning is a primary (if sometimes implicit) fear. After all, why care about an inequity unless it makes a difference? And isn't the difference between life and death the biggest difference of all? Given the vehemently articulated community health anxieties evident in countless public forums, including the National Environmental Justice Advisory Council (NEJAC), one might mistakenly conclude that health is the main, or even sole, focus of environmental justice activism.

[P]olicymakers and activists alike have tended to concentrate on questions and mechanisms of community involvement, not community health. This is not surprising. One reason for this focus is that activists and policymakers alike possess a far better understanding of procedural inclusion, and of the tools that seem useful for producing it, than they do of ways to reduce risk and enhance health.... For activists, involvement offers outlets for advocacy, opportunities for dialogue and the casting of blame, and the promise of institutional accountability. Resourceful and well-timed advocacy may even lead to significant material benefits for a community. On the other hand, involvement mechanisms allow policymakers to exhibit responsiveness and deflect criticism. By comparison, channeling health anxieties effectively toward risk reductions and improved health prospects among low-income and minority persons is far more difficult....

The [environmental justice] movement's obsession with disproportionate adverse impact may obscure more important questions relating to the absolute size, scope and source of such impacts. Second, environmental justice proponents generally eschew personal behavior (and necessary changes in it) as a primary variable in the health of low-income and minority communities. Third, from among the vast array of issues raised to date under the environmental justice rubric, adherents have been incapable of fashioning a coherent agenda of substantive public health priorities. Instead the movement is drawn to an overall procedural priority of citizen involvement, an orientation that unrealistically envisions every issue as a substantive priority.

These limitations exist largely because environmental justice is not mainly a public health movement. It is instead a loose coalition of citizens and groups advocating greater grassroots democracy, usually with an eye fixed on broader social justice goals. Because its primary political aims are to bind residents together, to raise their collective profile in policy debates and decision-making, and to reallocate society's resources, environmental justice activism can ill afford an agenda driven solely by health impacts....

Hazards perceived to be imposed on residents by firms—especially by ones viewed as community intruders—or governmental actors suspected of being distant, unaccountable, or racist are more suitable for this purpose. Under such circumstances, anger and suspicion easily overwhelm risk and health as driving forces. Hazards linked strongly to individual behavior (such as smoking and excessive alcohol consumption) generally have far larger implications for personal and collective health but do not easily resonate politically.... [R]eminding residents that they consume too many calories, or the wrong kinds of food, is likely to appear intrusive, insensitive, or simply beside the point.

Once their underlying democratizing aims are clearly understood it is not hard to make sense of the insistent emphasis by environmental justice activists and by grassroots environmentalists generally on relatively unlikely or weakly documented—but nevertheless profoundly fear-inducing—hazards, such as dioxin and Superfund sites. This democratizing imperative accounts for the deference regularly accorded intuitive (as opposed to scientific) perceptions of risk, as illustrated by the enduring folk myth of a so-called cancer alley in Louisiana.... Anemic mobilizing capacity (that is, low usefulness for generating collective outrage) helps explain why many well-established health hazards, including tobacco use, find no place in the litany of environmental justice concerns.

The political imperatives of the movement also explain why environmental justice lacks substantive health priorities. Real priorities would mean downgrading the concerns of at least some movement constituents, creating the great likelihood of conflict.... [Thus, environmental justice advocates] primarily advance general concepts of equality, not wishing to endanger their coalition by specifying the precise methods of achieving "justice," "fairness," or "equity." The egalitarian position that everyone should be heard and that no one should suffer maintains movement harmony, but at the cost of focus....

[M]ovement rhetoric argues that no community should be harmed and that all community concerns and grievances deserve redress. Scholar-activist Robert Bullard proposes that "the solution to unequal protection lies in the realm of environmental justice for all Americans. No community, rich or poor, black or white, should be allowed to become a 'sacrifice zone.'" When pressed about the need for environmental risk priorities, and about how to incorporate environmental justice into priority setting, Bullard's answer is a vague plea for nondiscrimination, along with a barely more specific call for a "federal 'fair environmental protection act'" that would transform "protection from a privilege to a right."

Bullard's position is fanciful and self-contradictory, but extremely telling. He argues essentially that the way to establish environmental priorities is precisely by guaranteeing that such priorities are impossible to implement. This is symptomatic of a movement for which untrammeled citizen voice and overall social equity are cardinal values. Bullard's position also epitomizes the desire of movement intellectuals to avoid speaking difficult truths (at least in public) to their allies and constituents.

Ironically, in matters of health and risk, environmental justice poses a potentially serious, if generally unrecognized, danger to the minority and low-income communities it aspires to help. By discouraging citizens from thinking in terms of health and risk priorities ... environmental justice can deflect attention from serious hazards to less serious or perhaps trivial ones....

From a health perspective, the [environmental justice] model's most serious drawback may be subtle opportunity costs. If one accepts that citizens inherently have limited time and energy to devote to their health, attention to distant or relatively minor health risks—however politically compelling—very likely means less attention for some more substantive health problems. And if one accepts that low-income citizens, in particular, have even fewer resources, and greater vulnerabilities, than more affluent citizens, then a focus on relatively low or unlikely risks could have a particularly insidious effect.

* * *

## Notes and Questions

1. As Professor Kuehn noted, a prominent criticism of the environmental justice movement is that the terms "justice" and "fairness" are too vague to translate into coherent environmental policy. Do you agree? Can you think of other instances in environmental regulation where broad, aspirational concepts generate regulatory and legislative initiatives? In your view, what would be the best way to incorporate environmental justice goals into environmental policy and implementation?

2. The criticisms made by Foreman depend upon three main assertions: (a) environmental justice advocates focus too much on involuntary (public) risks and not enough on voluntary (behavioral) risks; (b) environmental justice advocates refuse to prioritize risks; and (c) environmental justice advocates focus too much on participatory values. How would you evaluate the criticisms made by Foreman? Are his criticisms premised upon a lack of theoretical consistency or political viability? If premised upon political viability—and assuming Foreman's empirical observations are correct—might there be good strategic reasons why advocates focus on public risks and participation while refusing to engage in a debate about priorities and trade-offs? How would you evaluate the "opportunity costs" borne by adopting environmental justice strategies as described by Foreman? In other words, if environmental justice advocates were to change their focus in response to Foreman's criticisms, how would you predict their chances of success?

3. Just as Foreman criticized the work of various scholars and researchers, Foreman has been subsequently criticized for his failure to acknowledge studies with better methodology that supported the (criticized) seminal studies of environmental inequities, his failure to acknowledge the work of environmental justice scholars who advocate

reform (rather than abolition) of risk assessment, and his "indulging in a superficial psychological deconstruction of the movement." Alan Ramo, *Book Review, The Promise and Peril of Environmental Justice*, 40 Santa Clara L. Rev. 941, 942 (2000). *See also* David Lewis Feldman, 9 L. & Pol. Book Rev. 66 (Feb. 1999) (acknowledging Foreman's contribution but questioning his reliance on risk-based studies that are inconclusive).

# E. Conclusion

The readings in this chapter sketch the history of the environmental justice movement, in the process providing a sense of the efforts of multiple and diverse groups to articulate a common critique of mainstream environmental approaches. The readings also suggest that this movement and its claims are not static. Instead, with the passage of time, the movement has identified newly pressing issues, enlisted alternative legal and other tools, and, at times, refined earlier approaches and theories.

Over time, environmental justice advocates have crafted inclusive, multi-racial, and multicultural coalitions, and scholars have attempted to articulate coherent theoretical frameworks for the common claims of this movement. But it is nonetheless important to recognize that each environmental justice campaign is rooted in its locale and unique combination of culture and history. And, while community-based groups have sought to learn from efforts of sister organizations, often forging effective coalitions and regional networks, it is important to consider how each group is different and how the context — historical, social, cultural, political — in which each group's effort takes place inevitably affects the relevant issues and claims. We may use the term "environmental justice communities" or "environmental justice groups" in this book as a shorthand to refer to all of the various groups and subgroups that are affected by any particular issue. In doing so, we mean to embrace the inclusive posture of the environmental justice movement itself and to recognize common institutional and structural forces that generate environmental inequities. But, at the same time, we also mean to recognize that each group's circumstances are, in fact, unique and that each group's claims for justice can only properly be understood in context.

Finally, for analytical coherence, we will generally apply throughout the book the EPA's modern definition of environmental justice, to require the "fair treatment" and "meaningful involvement" of all people in the administration of environmental programs. We do so, of course, recognizing the many diverse conceptions of environmental justice and the continuing responsibility of environmental justice advocates to listen and respect the distinct concerns of the communities and people they serve.

# Chapter 2

# Theories of Causation

**Figure 2-1:** Mariachi Plaza, Boyle Heights Station, Los Angeles County Metro Rail system. Photo: Daniel Hernandez.

## A. Introduction

This chapter considers the who and how behind systemic environmental injustice issues. Explanatory theories offered are numerous and varied, drawing from economics, political science, urban planning, history, sociology, critical race studies, and other disciplines. A multiplicity of factors is at play with what led to the rise of environmental injustice incidents. This chapter outlines some of the major theories that have been advanced to explain the prevalence of environmental inequities. Many current disparities grew from past land-use practices, derived from centuries of land grabbing and exploitation of poor and vulnerable communities of color. More neutral market forces may have led to undesired outcomes both during the initial siting of polluting and risk-generating facilities and as the result of post-siting market dynamics. Alternative theories center on sociopolitical factors, such as a community's social capital, and how those factors interact within the structure of our environmental laws. Yet another explanation examines the forms of racial discrimination currently at play.

The origins of environmental injustice emerged long before the poor, rural, and predominantly African-American community of Warren County, North Carolina, protested the siting of a hazardous waste facility in 1982.

> The concept of environmental justice has been present ever since low-income people, communities of color, and indigenous groups have been marginalized — from ancient times to the height of the transatlantic slave trade to the transmodern era of the current global regimes. There is an ongoing colonial enterprise to subdue and denigrate populations to advance commercial endeavors at the expense of the beleaguered and marginalized classes and groups within societies.... Prior to the colonization of America, the concept of race as it is known now did not exist, but race would become the modality to grant "legitimacy to the relations to domination imposed by the conquest." The conquest of America was the point when race emerged as a position to set forward "ranks, places, and roles in the new society's structure of power." Only once race is recognized as a means of subordination can the next phase begin: environmental subordination. The races considered inferior to the Anglo-Americans were not allowed access to the same level of environmental protection, as they faced greater environmental threats because of displacement, disease, slavery, and migration. The control of labor and production would create new hierarchies in society based on race.... Seeing the origins of race rooted in the origins of the history of the American colonial enterprise shows the lineage of environmental justice. If the discussion of environmental justice begins in Warren County, it overlooks centuries of environmental denigration, pollution, and toxicity in communities who carried the burden of the capital enterprise through the loss of their lands, livelihoods, and lives, while the elite benefited from their toils.

Nadia Ahmad, *"Mask Off" — The Coloniality of Environmental Justice*, 24 Widener L. Rev. 195 (2019).

# B. Land-Use Practices

In part, the current distribution of environmental hazards is the result of land-use and zoning practices that started centuries ago. Restrictive racial covenants, exclusionary zoning practices like density and use restrictions, urban renewal policies that displaced thousands of residents, and other land-use mechanisms all contributed to residential segregation and the prevalence of unwanted land uses in low-income communities and communities of color. In the following excerpt, Professor Yale Rabin describes one such long-standing zoning practice.

# Yale Rabin, *Expulsive Zoning: The Inequitable Legacy of* Euclid

ZONING AND THE AMERICAN DREAM 101
(Charles M. Haar & Jerold S. Kayden eds., 1989)

... What follows sets forth the hypothesis that zoning, in addition to its well-recognized use as an exclusionary mechanism, also has been frequently employed in ways that have undermined the character, quality, and stability of black residential areas; that zoning not only has been used to erect barriers to escape from the concentrated confinement of the inner city, it has been used to permit—even promote—the intrusion into black neighborhoods of disruptive incompatible uses that have diminished the quality and undermined the stability of those neighborhoods. For reasons explained later, I refer to this practice as *expulsive zoning....*

[T]here is evidence to suggest that expulsive zoning practices have been relatively commonplace in black residential areas. The record, while admittedly fragmentary, indicates that in the years following the [Supreme] Court's rejection of racial zoning in 1917 and continuing through the thirties, and perhaps much later, a number of cities—mainly, but not exclusively, in the South—zoned some low-income residential areas occupied mainly, but not exclusively, by blacks for industrial or commercial use. These practices were sometimes carried out even in neighborhoods of single-family detached houses, thus undermining the quality of the very types of neighborhood housing which zoning ostensibly was intended to protect. To the extent that these practices were effective—that is, to the extent that residential uses were replaced by industrial or commercial uses, residents were displaced. Therefore, the term *expulsive zoning*. Because it appears that such areas were mainly black, and because whites who may have been similarly displaced were not subject to racially determined limitations in seeking alternative housing, the adverse impacts of expulsive zoning on blacks were far more severe and included, in addition to accelerated blight, increases in overcrowding and racial segregation....

[T]hese expulsive zoning practices are entirely consistent with the more general findings of my studies: that the land-use-related policies and practices of government at all levels, but particularly the decisions and initiatives of local government, have been and continue to be instrumental influences on both the creation and perpetuation of racial segregation. Expulsive zoning, as one of these practices, does not occur as an isolated or independent action, but as one element in a web-like pattern of interacting public practices that serve to reproduce and reinforce the disadvantages of blacks. Urban renewal, public housing site selection, school segregation, highway route selection, and code enforcement are a few of the other frequently encountered cords in the web....

*Jackson, Tennessee*

The most extensive and blighting effects of expulsive zoning that I have encountered have been in Jackson, Tennessee. Here expulsive zoning has been and continues to be a fundamental influence on other land-use-related policies and actions of the city which adversely affect the welfare of black residents....

South Jackson, a section of the city which until the mid-1960s housed approximately half of the city's black population, had been zoned industrial since the city first adopted zoning in 1928. The other half of the city's black population lived in northeast Jackson, in an area surrounding all-black Lane College. That area had been and continues to be zoned residential. Housing in the Lane College area, while modest, is, with the exception of a few scattered pockets of slum housing, sound and well maintained.

Although South Jackson is bounded along its southern edge by a number of labor-intensive, forestry- and agriculture-related industries, the area itself always has been overwhelming residential. The area's residents have been the city's lowest income blacks; the housing they occupied was of poor quality and what remains has become severely blighted as a direct consequence of city policies and actions.

Since the early 1960s the city has repeatedly and publicly made clear its intentions to redevelop much of south Jackson for industrial and commercial use and since that time has halted all code enforcement and municipal improvement in the area. At the time of my first visit in 1978, two urban renewal projects were underway. One, at the southwestern edge of the city, was to provide land for industrial development, and in the other, in the center of south Jackson and adjacent to the central business district, a civic center was already under construction. By the city's own estimates, these two projects involved the displacement of approximately 940 black families including more than 2,600 people — about one-fifth of the city's black population. Between the two projects there remained an all-black-occupied public housing project and nearly 20 city blocks of black-occupied slum housing and unpaved streets....

By failing to require even minimal maintenance of housing and withholding maintenance of infrastructure, the city accelerated the deterioration of the housing in south Jackson and reduced the costs to the city of subsequent property acquisition. By failing to provide relocation resources they caused an increase in the level of racial segregation and overcrowding in the city, and prolonged the time during which south Jackson residents were subject to that area's deplorable living conditions....

*Summary and Conclusions*

The adverse impacts evident in these ... cases of expulsive zoning vary widely. They include environmentally blighting nuisances, displacement, and life threatening hazards.... [T]he evidence to date does appear to support three significant generalizations. First, illustrated most vividly by the case of Detroit, the magnitude and severity of adverse impacts are not necessarily proportional to the scale of intrusion or the extent of displacement. A single intrusive use can sometimes have disastrous effects. Second, the blighting and disruptive effects of expulsive zoning grow, rather than diminish, with the passage of time. Finally, expulsive zoning is not merely an historical remnant of a racially unenlightened past, but a current practice that continues to threaten, degrade, and destabilize black and other minority neighbor-hoods....

* * *

Picking up on the last point, Julia Mizutani considers the intentional and unin-tentional disproportionate siting and effects of environmental hazards on communities of color.

### Julia Mizutani, *In the Backyard of Segregated Neighborhoods: An Environmental Justice Case Study of Louisiana*
31 Georgetown Envtl. L. Rev. 363, 364–72 (2019)

Segregation has both a historical and present-day relationship to the placement of environmental hazards — such as landfills, incinerators, petro-chemical plants, and coal-fired power plants — in predominately black and poor communities.

Exclusionary zoning and land-use laws often lead these hazards to be placed in seg-regated black communities because of the fear that such hazards will diminish property values in white communities. Environmental assessments and siting boards also cause environmental hazards to be placed in vulnerable communities because placing hazards in these areas is often less costly and more politically preferable given that underserved communities have less political power. In fact, government funded studies have at times justified the targeting of poor communities of color for polluting sites. California was once advised by a consulting firm that "ideally ... officials and companies should look for lower socioeconomic neighborhoods that are also in a heavy industrial area with little, if any, commercial activity." [The Cerrell Report, discussed *infra* in the excerpt from Cole & Foster. Eds.] Local planning boards and zoning laws have both contributed to the environmental injustices that black communities face due to segregation....

Today, zoning and land-use laws are important for environmental justice because they affect siting decisions concerning locally undesirable land uses such as toxic waste sites, incinerators, and power plants. State zoning acts are often modeled on the Stan-dard State Zoning Enabling Act of 1922, which grants states the power to regulate land use for the "health, safety, morals, or the general welfare of the community," and includes regulating and restricting "density of population and the location and use of buildings, structures and land of trade, industry, residence or other purposes." Un-fortunately, state and local zoning laws modeled after this language often lead to re-strictions on industrial use in residential neighborhoods in order to protect the health of wealthier, whiter communities, to the detriment of poorer, black communities. In many cases, decisions placing industrial and other hazardous land [uses] in low-income and black communities are made in compliance with local zoning ordinances.

The issue of local officials exercising zoning power to the detriment of black res-idents was highlighted in a 2003 panel report by the National Academy of Public Ad-ministrators ("NAPA") titled, "Addressing Community Concerns: How Environmental

Justice Relates to Land Use Planning and Zoning." The report stated that significant evidence showed that people of color and low-income residents were likely to live close to polluting industries because of unequal distribution of environmental exposures in areas zoned for lower-income and historically segregated communities. Further, local zoning decisions regularly "created these disparities and ... local decision-makers were often fully aware of the likely outcomes." Thus, the report found that federal and state policies created and reinforced local decisions that limited housing for black residents to areas where hazardous and polluting industries were located, and then continued to place more such industries in those areas.…

Local police powers for zoning were affirmed in what is now known as the landmark case, *Village of Euclid v. Ambler Realty Corp.*, in 1926. The repercussions of *Euclid* were broad, as the general principle of exercising police power to separate "incompatible uses" to protect residential environments from industrialization was upheld. Justice Sutherland noted that a "nuisance may be merely a right thing in the wrong place, like a pig in the parlor instead of the barnyard." The implications of the decision were significant because many municipalities figuratively deemed black neighborhoods to be barnyards, polluting industries to be pigs, and white residential neighborhoods to be parlors. *Euclid* thus provided a legal basis for local municipalities to disproportionately place polluting facilities in black neighborhoods, while keeping such facilities out of white neighborhoods.

Professor Yale Rabin, of the Massachusetts Institute of Technology, has called this phenomenon "expulsive zoning." Black residents who were not automatically displaced by racially restrictive covenants and zoning laws eventually found their neighborhoods filled with landfills, incinerators, factories, and power plants. Meanwhile, "white neighborhoods were consistently protected from intrusive traffic, noise, and pollution generated by such nonresidential uses." Even in jurisdictions without codified zoning variances, such as Houston, local government authorities placed eight of ten solid waste facilities in black communities from 1920 to 1970, even though the black population of Houston was only a quarter of the city's population. A national report published by the United Church of Christ's Commission for Racial Justice showed that race was the most significant factor nationwide in determining where a hazardous waste facility would be sited. The report also found that black residents were heavily over-represented in areas with the largest number of uncontrolled hazardous waste sites.…

Local officials have used zoning laws supposedly meant to protect the health, safety, morals, or general welfare of the community to the detriment of black neighborhoods by restricting industries from existing in white neighborhoods and thus relegating toxic industries to segregated communities. These communities have limited modes of redress under existing civil rights laws because the evidentiary bar for proving discriminatory intent is too high.

The site selection process in many localities often fails to prevent discriminatory siting. Most site selection processes go to a board that may be comprised of local experts, of those who have been elected by the locality, or sometimes of board members chosen by the governor. These boards are restrained by land-use laws that may already confine industrial sites to predominately black neighborhoods, and even if states pre-empt local land-use statutes to allow sites to be placed in a wealthier neighborhood, boards can be prone to fall to NIMBYism. NIMBY stands for "Not In My Back Yard," and it is a phenomenon where communities with economic and political power will use their advantages to block a toxic site selection planned for their neighborhood, thus relegating the site to a less wealthy and well-connected neighborhood. Robert Bullard ... asserts that politicians and industrialists respond to the NIMBY phenom-enon using the "PIBBY" principle: "Place in Black's Back Yard." Because of the power of NIMBYism, noxious sites are often designated for communities of color so that industry can avoid any siting delays and expenses that might occur if the site was slated for a predominately white, middle class, residential neighborhood.

It should be noted that all states that use siting boards have preemption clauses in their documents that allow them to override opposition to a siting decision by res-idents of a whiter, wealthier neighborhood. However, in the end, private developers often still choose the sites regardless of the board's final decision because they have a cost incentive to choose sites with lower land values, which are typically the neigh-borhoods of economically disadvantaged communities of color because of the history of segregation. Thus, even when a local planning board may be willing to allow a toxic site to be placed in a wealthier neighborhood, developers of the site often choose to build in communities of color due to economic incentives created by the legacy of discrimination....

\* \* \*

Professor Sarah Schindler considers the impact of the built environment and how what she describes as "architectural exclusion" also leads to segregation and carries broader environmental justice impacts.

## Sarah Schindler, *Architectural Exclusion: Discrimination and Segregation through Physical Design of the Built Environment*
### 124 Yale L.J. 1934, 1944–53 (2015)

The idea that architecture regulates is found at the core of much urban planning and geography scholarship, though that body of literature does not always describe architecture as "regulation." At the most general level, it is not controversial among planning and geography scholars to assert that the built environment often is con-structed in a way that furthers political goals. Moreover, these scholars generally agree that architectural decisions will favor some groups and disfavor others. Many would also agree that architecture can be, and is, used to exclude. As one planning scholar acknowledged, "[r]ace is a ubiquitous reality that must be acknowledged ... if [planners] do not want simply to be the facilitators of social exclusion and eco-nomic isolation."

Despite this deep theoretical understanding of the powerful role that architecture plays in crafting experience, practicing planners sometimes fail to afford sufficient weight to the concept of exclusion by design....

The metaphorical use of architecture implies an underlying recognition—foundational to planners and architects—that physical design regulates and that the built environment controls human behavior. Legal scholars use architecture as an analogue in their work with the understanding that "small and apparently insignificant [architectural] details can have major impacts on people's behavior...."

Although legal scholars do not often write directly about architecture as regulation, some—especially law and geography scholars and critical race theorists—have confronted concepts like architecture, the built environment, municipal infrastructure, space, and place in the context of class and race. As one commentator has noted:

> It is hard to understate the central significance of geographical themes—space, place, and mobility—to the social and political history of race relations and antiblack racism in the United States.... [S]egregation, integration, and separation are spatial processes; ... ghettos and exclusionary suburbs are spatial entities; ... access, exclusion, confinement ... are spatial experiences.

For example, Lior Jacob Strahilevitz examines "exclusionary amenities," which are features of residential developments that are generally expensive and that only appeal to certain demographic groups. By including these features in a common interest community, a developer can deter unwanted potential residents—generally poor people and people of color—from buying homes in that development. Strahilevitz therefore recognizes that architecture and design can be employed to steer human behavior and to promote desired ends....

We often expect certain biases in our residential neighborhoods, both due to Fischel's Homevoter Hypothesis—suggesting that homeowners are more likely than renters to vote and more likely to vote in ways that will protect their property investment—and our country's long history of intentional discrimination and exclusion. However, people tend to believe that the plan and structures of cities are created for purposes of efficiency or with the goal of furthering the general public interest, and they overlook the ways that design can exclude.

Legal academics have also proposed the idea that spaces themselves have racial meanings. For example, Elise C. Boddie argues that places have racial identities based on their history of or reputation for exclusion, and that courts should consider this racial meaning for purposes of racial discrimination claims. She further suggests that the racial meaning of a place can allow those in charge, such as police officers, to determine who belongs in that place and who does not. Similarly, Stephen Clowney has addressed the way in which landscapes, parks, and statues create a narrative that often marginalizes African Americans. Despite this recognition from scholars, Boddie points out that "law overlooks the racial identifiability of spaces," and Clowney notes that "landscape is one of the most overlooked instruments of modern race-making...."

However, architectural exclusion is different in that it is concerned with the place-ment and location of infrastructure that physically separates and inhibits access, not just disparities in treatment based on geographic location.

Although regulation through architecture is just as powerful as law, it is less iden-tifiable and less visible to courts, legislators, and potential plaintiffs. While this ob-servation suggests that decision makers should be even more diligent in analyzing the impact of architecture, research demonstrates that they often fail to take it seriously. To be clear, officials may understand that an architectural decision could have an exclusionary effect — they might even intend that result — but they generally do not see their decisions as a form of regulation that should be analyzed and patrolled in the same way that a law with the same effect would be. Exclusion through archi-tecture should be subject to scrutiny that is equal to that afforded to other methods of exclusion by law.

* * *

## Notes and Questions

1. **Expulsive zoning.** Julia Mizutani discusses the exclusionary impacts of local land-use and zoning regulations. Does her article suggest that greater or lesser local control of the siting process is desirable? Practices such as expulsive zoning and ex-clusionary zoning can have profound impacts on the character of communities and the land uses that are sited in and near them.

2. Professor Schindler draws attention to exclusionary practices embedded within architecture to show their adverse impacts on communities and local residents. How do controls and expectations of the built environment heighten disparities that lead to environmental injustice?

3. Another potential threat to neighborhood stability in many urban areas is **gen-trification**, a phenomenon that grew substantially throughout the 1990s. In response to skyrocketing housing costs, the high market demand for land, the growth in in-formation technology-based companies, and other factors, urban neighborhoods, including low-income communities or communities of color that had long received little development attention, became much more attractive to investors. While increased economic development can bring important benefits to these areas, it also can make neighborhoods unaffordable and displace longtime residents. San Francisco's Mission District, for example, long an enclave for working class and recent immigrant Latino families, was targeted for development by many investors. This had the result of "squeezing out longtime tenants, small mom-and-pop stores, non-profits, artists and working class people of all colors." As noted by one environmental justice organization, such displacement is particularly devastating in San Francisco, where rental vacancies are scarce and 40% of renters pay more than a third of their incomes for housing. An-tonio Diaz, People Organizing to Demand Environmental & Economic Rights (PODER), Race & Space: Dot-Colonization, Dislocation and Resistance en la Misíon de San Francisco (2001).

**4.** The legacy of urban renewal policies can persist for decades, as evidenced in this description of Boston's Chinatown, which engaged in a heated battle to preserve open space in the 1990s:

> Chinatowns are some of the most vibrant ethnic neighborhoods in America's landscape. Home to recent immigrants and old-timers alike, a city's Chinatown is the heart of many urban Asian American communities. But Chinatowns are often found in city centers and in crowded and polluted environments. Boston's Chinatown, the fourth largest in the United States, is no exception.

> What explains a Chinatown's location and circumstance? Is it pure chance? Unfortunately, no. At least not with Boston's Chinatown. Since the 1950s, urban planning has given Boston's Chinatown two massive highways, land-hungry medical institutions, and a red light district. Half a century of such policy came to a head in 1993, when the city of Boston tried to sell open land in the heart of Chinatown to build a mammoth garage. The proposed sale of this land, known as "Parcel C," sparked protest and organized resistance....

> Boston's Chinatown is a small but densely populated community.... For many, Chinatown is a purely commercial district of "exotic" shops, markets, and restaurants, which are toured on weekend excursions. However, Chinatown is also a residential community and home to more than 5,000 people.

> The Chinese community was well settled and growing during the early and mid-twentieth century.... Starting in the 1950s, Chinatown became a victim of "urban renewal." Cities such as Boston adopted urban renewal strategies specifically to attract businesses and industries back into downtown, to refurbish its tax base, and to entice urban residents to remain in the area. Unfortunately, all communities did not equally share in the burdens and benefits of urban renewal. Certainly, Boston's Chinatown did not....

> Chinatown has only 2.9 acres of open space. That means a mere 0.6-acre of open space per 1,000 residents — the least amount of open space per resident in the city. Although approximately twelve open spaces exist in and around Chinatown, three of them (city-owned) are unsafe.... [O]nly three are of the appropriate size to be actively used by the residents. The only open space with recreational facilities, such as volleyball and basketball courts, is adjacent to the Central Artery ramps, where thousands of cars enter and exit the highway daily....

Zenobia Lai, Andrew Leong & Chi Chi Wu, *The Lessons of the Parcel C Struggle: Reflections on Community Lawyering*, 6 ASIAN PACIFIC AMERICAN L.J. 1 (2000).

**5.** Some land-use practices that may give rise to disparities go even further back than zoning, and this history has significant consequences to this day. Consider the following:

Control over land and water remains the primary bone of contention in the relations among Indian, Hispano, and Anglo populations in northern New Mexico. This multifaceted set of issues has evolved out of a historical context of successive conquest, land expropriation, and sociopolitical domination by one ethnic group over another.... The most fundamental contrasts between Pueblo Indian and Hispano cases of enclavement derive from the differences in their respective political and legal positions vis-à-vis the state. Trust status has meant, among other things, that Indians cannot alienate their land and do not pay taxes on it, and that legal defense of their land, water, and other tribal claims is the responsibility of the federal government.... Today the land tenure situation of Taos Pueblo appears, at least superficially, far more favorable in comparison to that of rural and semi-rural Hispanos in the area, whose farmland is being expropriated at an escalating rate by the luxury tourism real estate boom....

Today these settlements are each struggling to protect their traditionally differentiated spheres of local land and water control, as always in competition or cooperation with one another, but also against the town's urban spread, and a corresponding escalation of Anglo in-migration and ubiquitous real estate development....

[C]ore elements in the Hispano niche have been occupation of contiguous village farmland and associated water rights ownership and management.... Both Indian and Hispano attachments to a land base are rooted in their traditional subsistence economies. Attachment to a land base remains intrinsic to the ethnic self-identities of both groups, even though neither subsists any longer by agriculture, pastoralism, or hunting....

Sylvia Rodríguez, *Land, Water, and Ethnic Identity in Taos*, in LAND, WATER, AND CULTURE: NEW PERSPECTIVES ON HISPANIC LAND GRANTS 313, 313–60 (Charles L. Briggs & John R. Van Ness eds., 1987). To what extent do you believe that the roots of current inequities may lie in very old land-use practices? Tribal sovereignty issues and the trust obligation of the federal government to American Indians are discussed in greater detail in Chapter 9 ("Environmental Justice in Indian Country").

6. Given the long history of some land-use practices, the intensely local nature of zoning, and, more currently, gentrification, and given the absence of a demonstrated national pattern of zoning practices, would federal or state preemption of local zoning matters be justified? If not, how should these causes of environmental injustice be remedied?

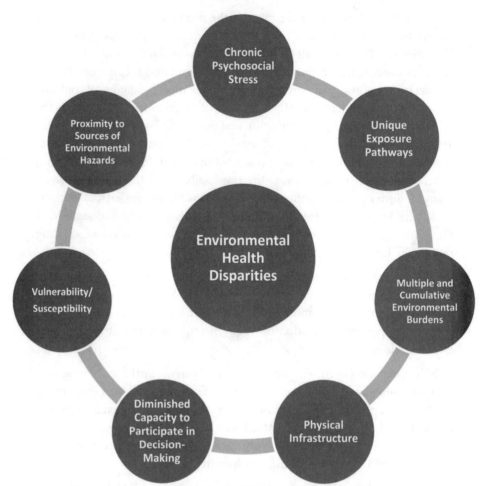

**Figure 2-2:** In 2010, EPA collaborated with government and nongovernmental organizations for a symposium, "Strengthening Environmental Justice Research and Decision Making: A Symposium on the Science of Disproportionate Environmental Health Impacts." The program gave "a forum for discourse on the state of scientific knowledge about factors identified by EPA that may contribute to higher burdens of environmental exposure or risk in racial/ethnic minorities and low-income populations." Figure by Devon C. Payne-Sturges, *Symposium on Integrating the Science of Environmental Justice into Decision-Making at the Environmental Protection Agency: An Overview* in American Journal of Public Health 101 Suppl 1(S1): S19–26, December 2011.

## C. The Market

Many critics who challenge the salience of race and/or ethnicity in explaining environmental disparities argue that market forces best account for these differences. This section considers the debates surrounding two types of "market force" explanations—the first focusing on market forces in the site-selection process, the second examining market-driven changes that occur after siting decisions are made.

# 1. Market Forces in Site Selection

## Robin Saha & Paul Mohai, *Explaining Racial and Socioeconomic Disparities in the Location of Locally Unwanted Land Uses: A Conceptual Framework*

(Conference paper presented at the Annual Meeting of the Rural Sociological Society, Toronto, Canada, August 1997)

The economic explanation of disproportionate siting relies on classic economic theory and focuses on industry's site selection rationale, reducing it down to strictly economic criteria.... In calculating the feasibility of a particular location, a company evaluates the transaction costs associated with the siting process and anticipated operating costs which affect the competitiveness and profitability of the service that can be offered at a particular location.... The transaction costs are associated with site selection, design, permitting, and construction. These costs can be quite high, especially if public opposition results in long delays, court costs, large financial compensation packages, or other exactions....

It has been argued that disproportionate conditions arise coincidentally out of private site selection decisions concerning the transaction costs of acquiring land for proposed facilities. The sole purported basis of these decisions is to minimize property value costs. Disproportionate siting is said to occur because cost-efficient industrial areas with low property values are also likely to be near areas with low residential property values. These areas, in turn, typically suffer from depressed economic conditions relative to other areas. Thus, the reasonable presumption that areas with low property values coincide with areas with high proportions of persons of low socioeconomic status (SES) is used to explain disproportionate siting with respect to SES. In addition, the interaction between low SES and race has been used to explain racial siting disparities.

Another aspect of the economic explanation holds that the calculation of transaction costs stemming from potential public opposition may result in disproportionate siting. According to [Professor James] Hamilton:

> A firm's anticipation of the price of public opposition from a given area can thus be thought of as an aggregation of the costs imposed on the firm by residents: the costs of participating in extensive regulatory proceedings and court battles ... and direct payments to the community in terms of corporate donations and taxes....

A rejected proposal is a costly matter for a sponsoring firm. Numerous activities are involved with putting forward a siting proposal such as securing finances and guarantees, conducting site assessments (e.g., geotechnical testing), developing business plans, negotiating and letting design contracts, and filing permit applications. These efforts represent "sunk costs" and are largely unrecoverable, since these investments of time, personnel, and money do not simply transfer to another proposal but must be carried out anew if a different location must be selected....

[I]t has been suggested that industry considers the potential costs of public opposition and selects a location where the probability of incurring such costs is minimized.... One way of avoiding the high costs of siting delays or defeats is to select communities where the likelihood of public opposition is reduced.... Evidence exists to support the claim that middle-income, affluent, and better educated communities are better equipped to wage effective opposition campaigns....

[A]s part of their transaction and operating costs firms are likely to consider the compensation costs that might be demanded in order for a community to accept a proposal.... Studies on class differences in the value placed on environmental quality suggest that communities with relatively well-educated and affluent residents are willing to pay more to preserve environmental amenities than communities with less educated and low-income residents. Even though these findings may reflect differences in ability to pay, they suggest that communities of lower SES would accept relatively smaller compensation packages in order to accept new facilities (disamenities).... More importantly, it appears that anticipated class differences in levels of acceptable compensation could be a factor firms consider, which, in turn, may contribute to disproportionate siting....

* * *

Attorney Luke Cole and Professor Sheila Foster question the assumption that race-neutral "market" forces are what drive siting decisions.

## Luke Cole & Sheila Foster, *From the Ground Up: Environmental Racism and the Rise of the Environmental Justice Movement*
### 70–74 (2000)

*Social Structure and the Siting Process*

... Conventional industry wisdom counsels private companies to target sites that are in neighborhoods "least likely to express opposition"—those with poorly educated residents of low socioeconomic status. Not surprisingly, many communities that host toxic waste sites possess these characteristics. State permitting laws remain neutral, or blind, toward these inequalities; they therefore perpetuate, and indeed exacerbate, distributional inequalities.

In most states, the hazardous wastes siting process begins when the private sector chooses a site for the location of a proposed facility. Because the proposed location of a hazardous waste facility near, particularly, a neighborhood of white people of high socioeconomic status often faces strong public opposition, there is a limited supply of land on which to site such facilities. Inevitably, the siting process focuses on industrial, or rural, communities, many of which are populated predominantly by people of color. Because land values are lower in heavily industrial and rural communities than in white suburbs, these areas are attractive to industries that are seeking to reduce the cost of doing business. Furthermore, these communities are presumed to pose little threat of political resistance because of their subordinate socioeconomic, and often racial, status.

Rarely does a "smoking gun" — explicit racial criteria or motivation — exist behind the decision to locate a toxic waste facility in a community of color. The reasons frequently given by companies for siting facilities are that such communities have low-cost land, sparse populations, and desirable geological attributes. Notably, however, there is evidence that portions of the waste industry target neighborhoods that possess the attributes of many poor communities of color, using "race-neutral criteria." In 1984, the California Waste Management Board commissioned a study on how to site waste incinerators. The report, written by the political consulting firm Cerrell Associates of Los Angeles and entitled *Political Difficulties Facing Waste-to-Energy Conversion Plant Siting* (popularly known as the Cerrell Report), set out "to assist in selecting a site that offers the least potential of generating public opposition." The report acknowledged that "since the 1970s, political criteria have become every bit as important in determining the outcome of a project as engineering factors." The Cerrell Report suggests that companies target small, rural communities whose residents are low income, older people, or people with a high school education or less; communities with a high proportion of Catholic residents; and communities whose residents are engaged in resource extractive industries such as agriculture, mining, and forestry. Ideally, the report states, "officials and companies should look for lower socioeconomic neighborhoods that are also in a heavy industrial area with little, if any, commercial activity." ...

Likewise, even the "race-neutral" criteria used by government and industry for siting waste facilities — such as the presence of cheap land values, appropriate zoning, low population densities, proximity to transportation routes, and the absence of proximity to institutions such as hospitals and schools — turn out not to be "race neutral" after all, when seen in their social and historical context. Race potentially plays a factor in almost every "neutral" siting criterion used. "Cheap land values" is, understandably, a key siting criteria for the waste industry and other developers. However, because of historical segregation and racism, land values in the United States are integrally tied to race. In urban areas across the United States, this is starkly clear: an acre of land in the San Fernando Valley of Los Angeles has roughly the same physical characteristics as an acre of land in South Central Los Angeles, but people are willing to pay a premium to live in all-white neighborhoods. In rural areas, the pattern is similar: low land values tend to be found in poor areas, and people of color are overrepresented among the rural poverty population.

The land value cycle is vicious, too: once a neighborhood becomes host to industry, land values typically fall or do not increase as quickly as those in purely residential neighborhoods. Thus, a community that initially has low land values because it is home to people of color becomes a community that has low land values because it has a preponderance of industry, which in turn attracts more industry, creating a cumulative effect on land values.... [C]alling these changes "market driven" naturalizes the underlying racism in the valuation of the land....

Zoning is inextricably linked with race, as well.... Yale Rabin's studies of historical zoning decisions have documented numerous instances where stable African American residential communities were "down-zoned" to industrial status by biased decision makers.... Such "expulsive zoning" permanently alters the character of a neighborhood, often depressing property values and causing community blight. The lower property values and the zoning status are then easily invoked as "neutral" criteria upon which siting decisions are made....

Proximity to major transportation routes may also skew the siting process toward communities of color, as freeways appear to be disproportionately sited in such communities. Similarly, locational criteria — prohibitions against the siting of waste facilities near neighborhood amenities like hospitals and schools — skews the process toward underdeveloped communities of color, since such communities are less likely to have hospitals and schools. Hence, siting criteria that prohibit the siting of waste facilities close to such facilities perpetuate the historical lack of such amenities in these communities.

The sociologist Robert Bullard documented this underlying racial discrimination in an otherwise "neutral" siting process. Bullard's documentation was recognized in a 1997 decision by the Nuclear Regulatory Commission's Atomic Safety and Licensing Board, which overturned a facility's permit.... The race-neutral siting criteria — including the criteria of low population and the need to site the facility five miles from institutions such as schools, hospitals, and nursing homes — operated in conjunction with the current racial segregation and the resulting inferior infrastructure (e.g., lack of adequate schools, road paving, water supply) to ensure that the location selected would be a poor community of color....

* * *

Professor Carmen Gonzalez further explores how historical segregation and racism have impacted international investment and neoliberal trade formulations through U.S.-Mexico relations.

## Carmen G. Gonzalez, *An Environmental Justice Critique of Comparative Advantage: Indigenous Peoples, Trade Policy, and the Mexican Neoliberal Economic Reforms*

32 U. Pennsylvania J. Int'l. L. 723, 736–58 (2011)

The theory of comparative advantage plays a central role in legitimating both the ideology of free trade and the economic policy recommendations of the World Trade Organization ("WTO"), the World Bank, and the International Monetary Fund ("IMF"). Developed by David Ricardo, the theory of comparative advantage posits that each country should specialize in the goods that it produces relatively more efficiently and should import the goods that it produces relatively less efficiently. For example, countries with abundant natural resources and scarce capital should specialize in agricultural exports and should import manufactured goods. Furthermore, subsidies and tariffs are inefficient because they distort comparative advantage and encourage countries to produce goods in which they do not have a comparative advantage and which might be produced more cheaply elsewhere. In order to elucidate the relevance of the theory of comparative advantage to contemporary debates over trade policy, it is useful to summarize the ongoing controversy over international trade in agricultural products. Global agricultural trade is currently distorted by high levels of protectionism in industrialized countries. The lavish agricultural subsidies provided by the United States and the European Union to domestic farmers encourage overproduction and depress world market prices for agricultural commodities. Many agricultural commodities are being sold in world markets at below the cost of production, thereby undermining the livelihoods of poor farmers in Asia, Africa, and Latin America....

The poverty and desperation produced by the collapse of Mexican corn prices caused many subsistence farmers to migrate to northern Mexico or to the United States in order to earn the cash necessary to support their families. Indeed, from 1990 to 2000, the highest levels of out-migration in Mexico occurred in the regions with the highest levels of cultural diversity and corn agro-biodiversity. This exodus of able-bodied male workers is fracturing families, leaving fields unplanted, and forcing women and children to work the land and to seek off-farm employment in order to supplement the family's income. Unfortunately, many of these rural migrants have been unable to find employment in Mexico's urban areas because trade liberalization under NAFTA failed to create sufficient manufacturing jobs to keep pace with the rural exodus. At least 500,000 Mexican workers migrate to the United States every year, many of them from Mexico's impoverished rural areas. Indeed, approximately two-thirds of the estimated twelve million undocumented workers in the United States came after 1995 and many are regarded as casualties of NAFTA. Recognizing the relationship between U.S. agricultural trade policy and immigration, a *New York Times* editorial acknowledged that "ending subsidies for agribusiness would be far more effective than beefing up the border patrol"....

Migration also has important cultural, environmental, and economic consequences in Mexico and poses risks to global food security. Mexico's impoverished, indigenous peasants are the custodians of Mexico's genetically diverse varieties of corn. This genetic diversity protects farmers from catastrophic crop loss in the event of environmental disturbances and is also vital to global food security. The out-migration of farmers with traditional knowledge or experience may disrupt the transfer of this knowledge to future generations, leading to the replacement of traditional corn varieties with other crops or with commercial high-yield corn varieties, or, alternatively, to the abandonment of farming altogether. In short, the migration of Mexican farmers threatens Mexico's genetic diversity as well as the survival of Mexico's indigenous population.

### Notes and Questions

1. Professor Sheila Foster and attorney Luke Cole explained the complicated ways in which race interacts with facially neutral criteria and decisions. In light of the ways that race might conceivably, if indirectly, constrain choices in this context, by what metric should voluntariness be measured? More broadly, to what extent are the pref-

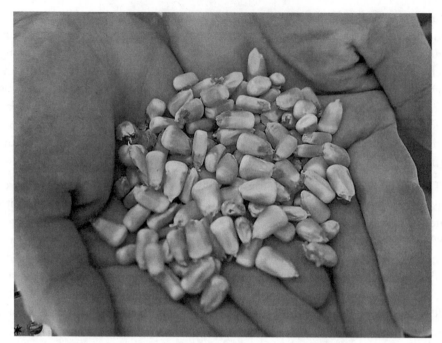

**Figure 2-3:** Nobel Prize winner and famed Mexican poet Octavio Paz once observed, "the invention of corn by Mexicans is only comparable to the invention of fire by man." Photo: Shirley Trout. Walton, Nebraska, Nov. 12, 2019.

erences of individuals as revealed in the market or political process themselves shaped by non-market forces and social institutions, such as racial discrimination in housing and employment?

2. **Smoking guns?** As Cole and Foster point out, rarely does a "smoking gun" document exist in which companies explicitly target low-income communities or communities of color for siting unwanted land-use facilities. The few documents that candidly express such sentiments appeared relatively early, before environmental justice became a high-profile issue. In addition to the 1984 Cerrell Report, another example of such a document is a 1991 internal memo authored by Lawrence Summers (then chief economist of the World Bank, later U.S. Treasury Secretary, president of Harvard University, and director of President Obama's National Economic Council). This memo advocated siting toxic waste facilities in the world's poorest countries because workers there had lower earnings. Summers queried: "Shouldn't the World Bank be encouraging more migration of the dirty industries to LDCs [Less Developed Countries]?" In his view, such targeting was appropriate because:

> [t]he measurement of the costs of health impairing pollution depends upon the foregone earnings from increased morbidity and mortality. From this point of view a given amount of health impairing pollution should be done in the country with the lowest cost, which will be the country with the lowest

wages. I think the economic logic behind dumping a load of toxic waste in the lowest wage country is impeccable and we should face up to that.

Memorandum from Lawrence Summers, Chief Economist, World Bank (Dec. 12, 1991), *quoted in* Robert Bullard, *Anatomy of Environmental Racism and the Environmental Justice Movement, in* CONFRONTING ENVIRONMENTAL RACISM: VOICES FROM THE GRASSROOTS 15, 19–20 (Robert Bullard ed., 1993). Summers also noted that there was likely to be less demand in developing countries for a clean and healthy environment. *Id.* When the memorandum was publicized, Summers issued a statement claiming that his remarks were intended as a "sardonic counter-point, an effort to sharpen the analysis." *World Bank Dumps on Third World Again,* RACE, POVERTY & THE ENV'T. Fall 1991/Winter 1992, at 12. His response is strikingly similar to the response of decision-makers in the wake of the Cerrell Report. In both instances, the suggestion is that the expressed preference for siting polluting or risk-generating facilities in relatively more impoverished areas was in fact not acted upon. Implicit in these subsequent positions is that the "economic logic" was in fact ignored, presumably because of overriding ethical considerations. Should additional safeguards be put into place to guard against these economic impulses? If so, what safeguards might be appropriate?

3. The material above illustrates how difficult it can be to distinguish and categorize different but interrelated factors underlying siting decisions. How would you classify, for instance, a decision by a company to favor siting in areas with less-educated and lower-income residents because of a perception that these residents will accept smaller compensation packages in order to accept a new LULU? Are ethnically neutral criteria really employed when firms are counseled to look for communities with a high percentage of Catholic residents within a particular locale?

4. If market forces are in fact primarily responsible for the current distribution of LULUs, or environmental "disamenities" (a term empirical researchers in this area often use), does this make the distribution less unfair and more acceptable?

5. Businesses were quick to disavow use of the 1984 Cerrell Report, referenced above. What role do you think factors like those discussed in the report actually play in siting decisions? How should firms establish the factors upon which to base their siting decisions? Should they develop written policies, or other mechanisms to reduce the risk that siting decisions are founded upon impermissible factors?

* * *

Professor Brie D. Sherwin considers how data management and the interpretation of scientific results have strong guiding principles. She examines the rubric for environmental justice through the use of scientific studies and how this rubric can be manipulated through attacks on science.

### Brie D. Sherwin, *The Upside Down: A New Reality for Science at the EPA and Its Impact on Environmental Justice*

27 N.Y.U. Envtl. L.J. 57, 62–70 (2019)

The concept of environmental justice can best be measured by scientific studies of the effects of pollution on vulnerable populations. Science sheds light on disproportionate environmental risks in a way that is measurable and that provides public assurance that the process is honest, truthful, and reliable. Politicians, however, are increasingly questioning the integrity of the scientists who are involved in assessing risk; working to sow doubt in the minds of political constituents and the public.

But, there is a fundamental difference in how scientists and politicians work. Scientists aim to discover the truth. Indeed, many believe that science "is the pinnacle of human achievement not because of its actual successes but in virtue of the fact that its practice, both in attaining truth and in lapsing into error, is thoroughly informed by reason." These virtuous thoughts are the very ideals that scientists should, and for the most part do, ascribe to without fault. However, when scientists become involved in the administrative rulemaking process, science becomes politicized to a certain extent.

With the Trump Administration's efforts to remove objective oversight of the scientific process, it is likely that the public's trust in science will continue to erode. The slow demise of public's trust in science has occurred over the past fifteen years, most notably with the Bush Administration's intervention in the scientific processes underlying environmental policy and rulemaking and its subsequent distortion or suppression of scientific findings. This included withholding comments from scientists at the U.S. Fish and Wildlife Service on the destructive impacts of proposed regulatory changes, stacking scientific advisory committees with unqualified members who had industry ties, altering websites, and suppressing agency reports. Most notably, in 2003, the White House infamously edited a discussion of climate change in EPA's *Draft Report on the Environment*. At that time, EPA's scientists complained that the altered draft "no longer accurately represented scientific consensus on climate change," which ultimately led the Agency to eliminate the discussion in its entirety from the report.

The distortion of scientific findings extends beyond policy to legislation also meant to protect environmental and human health. In 2005, Congress exempted hydraulic fracturing (fracking) from EPA oversight under the 1974 Safe Drinking Water Act based on a controversial 2002 draft EPA study which found that fracking posed a low risk to drinking water supplies. Many of these fracking sites are located in rural areas, where much of the population lives below the poverty level, triggering environmental justice concerns.

We have also seen profound impacts on environmental justice, particularly as it relates to safe drinking water, with industry insiders replacing scientists on scientific advisory boards. In the early 1990s, while high levels of lead in drinking water was a rising concern, the George H.W. Bush Administration replaced three national experts in lead poisoning on the Advisory Committee on Childhood Lead Poisoning Prevention with several individuals who had ties to the lead industry. In fact, one of the appointees was a leading industry consultant, who had previously testified that a lead level that was seven times higher than the current Center for Disease Control (CDC) recommendations was safe for children's brains. Over the following decade, little changed in the regulations that were meant to protect children from lead in drinking water. Arguably, it was that lack of urgency in revising the Lead and Copper Rule to better reflect the most recent scientific evidence of risk, along with the economic crisis and agency apathy, that culminated in the environmental justice crisis in Flint, Michigan, in 2015.

Recently, however, under Acting Administrator Wheeler's watch, the apathy has been replaced with an outward rejection of EPA scientists who are meant to advocate for children. Dr. Ruth Etzel, a leading pediatrician and epidemiologist in the field of children's health for over thirty years, was put on administrative leave on September 25, 2018. John Konkis, an EPA spokesman, refused to provide a reason for her leave. Her office, the Department of Children's Health Protection, is, by design, meant to inform the Agency "on the specific health and environmental-protection needs of children," who often require more protective standards than adults. In addition to placing Dr. Etzel on leave, EPA also stalled a year-long project, headed by Etzel's former office, to develop an interagency effort to reduce children's lead exposure.

And, it was not long after President Trump took office that scientific data and reports quietly disappeared within EPA. Mere moments after President Trump's inauguration, the official website of the White House deleted almost all mention of climate change, save one: the new President's vow to eliminate climate change policies created by the Obama Administration. But, although the policy changes were alarming, scientists were even more concerned about the disappearance of climate change data gathered and stored by administrative agencies for years, which is considered some of the most complete and solid data in the world. Since his election, a minimum of fifty academic scientists have taken to preserving and monitoring data stored on government websites like those of EPA, NASA, and National Oceanic and Atmospheric Administration (NOAA).

The disregard for scientific methods is not limited to policy changes on government websites. In May 2017, under Administrator Pruitt, EPA dismissed at least five of the eighteen members of the Agency's Scientific Advisory Board, whose key purpose is to provide objective oversight of the highly technical research collected and reviewed by EPA scientists and draft regulations based on that research that cover issues from $CO_2$ emissions to pollution discharges into waterways. The firings happened, as a spokesman for Mr. Pruitt stated, because he planned to replace the academic research scientists with people "who understand the impact of regulations on the regulated community" — in other words, industry representatives from the exact entities that EPA is meant to regulate.

Although industry representation on advisory panels is not unusual, there is a push to replace even more scientists with industry representatives. Representative

Lamar Smith (R) of Texas, who is Chair of the House Committee on Science, Space and Technology, recently authored a bill which would replace academic scientists with business representatives. At a hearing in February 2017, Representative Smith accused EPA of using *biased* scientists, stating, "The EPA routinely stacks this board with friendly scientists who receive millions of dollars in grants from the federal government. The conflict of interest here is clear." Scientists were shocked by this policy, because it sharply contrasted the policies of major grant-funding agencies, like the National Institutes of Health, and more importantly, because industry-funded scientists did not receive a similar mandate. As a result, as of 2017, eighteen of the forty-four members of the Scientific Advisory Board are now Pruitt appointees.

Two weeks after the members of the EPA's Scientific Advisory Board were dismissed, Dr. Deborah Swackhamer, an environmental chemist and head of the Advisory Board, was called to testify before Congress about the dismissals. Before she testified, Ryan Jackson, EPA's Chief of Staff, pulled her aside and advised her to "stick to 'the agency's talking points'" on the Board dismissals that had just occurred. "The Board of Scientific Counselors had 68 members two months ago. It will have 11, come Sept. 1," Dr. Swackhamer said. "They've essentially suspended scientific activities by ending these terms. We have no meetings scheduled, no bodies to do the work."

Do these actions by the executive branch reach beyond what has happened in the past? James Thurber, the founder of the Center for Congressional American Studies at American University, seems to think so. He recently told *The New York Times* that "he had never heard of an administration pressuring a witness, particularly a scientist, to alter testimony already submitted for the official record."

There is no question that altering scientific testimony fundamentally affects scientific integrity. Despite an admirable effort by the Obama Administration to require agencies to enact policies promoting scientific integrity, agencies are still ill-equipped to protect themselves from political interference. President Obama issued a Presidential Memorandum in 2009 directing federal agencies, including the EPA, CDC, and NOAA, to adopt internal scientific integrity policies to ensure that administrators could not censor inconvenient facts. In response, at least twenty-six of the agencies adopted policies to protect scientific integrity by encouraging the open dissemination of scientific information, allowing employees to speak with the media, and authorizing employees to use social media and blogs.

In 2017, the Trump Administration allegedly told agencies, including EPA and the United States Department of Agriculture (USDA), to curtail all messages to the press and the public. While it is common for incoming administrations to make agency-level policy changes, how the directives are perceived by agency scientists matters. Professor Cary Coglianese, who directs the University of Pennsylvania Law School's Program on Regulation, commented that while the exact wording of the directives may vary with the Administration, "what we're hearing about seems to go against the grain of the broader spirit of scientific integrity."

If the executive branch has the power to undermine scientific integrity to suit its ideological agenda, then agencies arguably become nothing more than political arms of an administration, incapable of carrying out their missions and purposes. And, undermining the scientific process makes it even more difficult for EPA to consider environmental justice issues in rule implementation and agency actions because they will lack information on the quantitative and qualitative impacts of environmental deregulation on poorer communities.

\* \* \*

## Notes and Questions

1. Professor Sherwin argues that politicians are questioning the findings of the scientists who are involved in assessing environmental risks. How does creating doubt in the mind of political constituents and the public impact environmental compliance and enforcement?

2. Environmental justice activists often dispute the claim that LULUs bring significant economic benefits to local residents in their communities. Professor Robert Kuehn gives the following examples:

> In the Shintech case [a proposed polyvinyl chloride plant in Convent, Louisiana], Louisiana offered Shintech, which was already realizing an annual $750,000 per-employee after-tax profit at its comparable PVC plant in Texas, a taxpayer-financed subsidy of almost $800,000 for each permanent job created.... [B]ecause of Shintech's need for employees with computer knowledge and the low educational level of most Convent residents, the staff director of the state agency promoting the plant admitted that "very few" of the permanent jobs created by the company would go to local residents.... Similarly, residents of West Harlem complain that although they are saddled with a disproportionate number of New York's sewage treatment plants, no minority contractors were hired to construct the most recent $1.1 billion plant; the few local minorities that were hired as plant workers were all gone within a year. In the Genesee Power Station case [discussed in Chapter 4 ("Constitutional and Civil Rights Claims")], no minorities from the majority African-American area were hired to construct or were working at the $80 million plant, and the owners all resided outside the community. The judge found these facts "to be appalling" and opined that, in permitting industrial facilities, society ought to take into consideration that the people living in the polluted surrounding communities get no job benefits from the plants. Robbins, Illinois, stands as an example of a town that thought its support of a new waste incinerator would bring jobs and economic development but finds itself "arguably worse off than before" as the economic benefits never materialized and the town is now "saddled with a soaring, smoke-belching trash burner that shoos away commercial investment like a scarecrow guarding a cornfield."

Robert R. Kuehn, *A Taxonomy of Environmental Justice*, 30 ENVTL. L. REP. 10,681, 10,701 (2000). To what extent should demonstrated, tangible benefits to a host community be required to justify a siting?

## 2. Post-Siting Changes

One of the earlier arguments in environmental justice scholarship was that the prevalence of LULUs in low-income communities and communities of color resulted from market-driven changes that occurred in neighborhoods after an unwanted land use was located there. This thesis, called the "market dynamics" or "minority move-in" theory, was prominently developed by Professor Vicki Been, who also discusses why it is important to know which came first, the community or the unwanted land use.

### Vicki Been, *Locally Undesirable Land Uses in Minority Neighborhoods: Disproportionate Siting or Market Dynamics?*
103 YALE L.J. 1383, 1384–1395 (1994)

The environmental justice movement contends that people of color and the poor are exposed to greater environmental risks than are whites and wealthier individuals.... [R]esearch does not, however, establish that [communities hosting LULUs] were disproportionately minority or poor at the time the sites were selected. Most of the studies compare the *current* socioeconomic characteristics of communities that host various LULUs to those of communities that do not host such LULUs. This approach leaves open the possibility that the sites for LULUs were chosen fairly, but that subsequent events produced the current disproportion in the distribution of LULUs. In other words, the research fails to prove environmental justice advocates' claim that the disproportionate burden poor and minority communities now bear in hosting LULUs is the result of racism and classism in the *siting process* itself.

In addition, the research fails to explore an alternative or additional explanation for the proven correlation between the current demographics of communities and the likelihood that they host LULUs. Regardless of whether the LULUs originally were sited fairly, it could well be that neighborhoods surrounding LULUs became poorer and became home to a greater percentage of people of color over the years following the sitings. Such factors as poverty, housing discrimination, and the location of jobs, transportation, and other public services may have led the poor and racial minorities to "come to the nuisance"—to move to neighborhoods that host LULUs—because those neighborhoods offered the cheapest available housing....

*Market Dynamics and the Distribution of LULUs*

The residential housing market in the United States is extremely dynamic. Every year, approximately 17% to 20% of U.S. households move to a new home. Some of those people stay within the same neighborhood, but many move to different neighborhoods in the same city, or to different cities. Some people decide to move, at least in part, because they are dissatisfied with the quality of their current neighborhoods. Once a household decides to move, its choice of a new neighborhood usually depends somewhat on the cost of housing and the characteristics of the neighborhood. Those two factors are interrelated because the quality of the neighborhood affects the price of housing.

The siting of a LULU can influence the characteristics of the surrounding neighborhood in two ways. First, an undesirable land use may cause those who can afford to move to become dissatisfied and leave the neighborhood. Second, by making the neighborhood less desirable, the LULU may decrease the value of the neighborhood's property, making the housing more available to lower income households and less attractive to higher income households. The end result of both influences is likely to be that the neighborhood becomes poorer than it was before the siting of the LULU.

The neighborhood also is likely to become home to more people of color. Racial discrimination in the sale and rental of housing relegates people of color (especially African-Americans) to the least desirable neighborhoods, regardless of their income level. Moreover, once a neighborhood becomes a community of color, racial discrimination in the promulgation and enforcement of zoning and environmental protection laws, the provision of municipal services, and the lending practices of banks may cause neighborhood quality to decline further. That additional decline, in turn, will induce those who can leave the neighborhood—the least poor and those least subject to discrimination—to do so.

The dynamics of the housing market therefore are likely to cause the poor and people of color to move to or remain in the neighborhoods in which LULUs are located, regardless of the demographics of the communities when the LULUs were first sited....

If the siting process is primarily responsible for the correlation between the location of LULUs and the demographics of host neighborhoods, the process may be unjust under current constitutional doctrine, at least as to people of color....

On the other hand, if the disproportionate distribution of LULUs results from market forces which drive the poor, regardless of their race, to live in neighborhoods that offer cheaper housing because they host LULUs, then the fairness of the distribution becomes a question about the fairness of our market economy. Some might argue that the disproportionate burden is part and parcel of a free market economy that is, overall, fairer than alternative schemes, and that the costs of regulating the market to reduce the disproportionate burden outweigh the benefits of doing so. Others might argue that those moving to a host neighborhood are compensated through the market for the disproportionate burden they bear by lower housing costs, and therefore that the situation is just. Similarly, some might contend that while the poor suffer lower quality neighborhoods, they also suffer lower quality food, housing, and medical care, and that the systemic problem of poverty is better addressed through income redistribution programs than through changes in siting processes.

Even if decisionmakers were to agree that it is unfair to allow post-siting market dynamics to create disproportionate environmental risk for the poor or minorities, the remedy for that injustice would have to be much more fundamental than the remedy for unjust siting *decisions*. Indeed, if market forces are the primary cause of the correlation between the presence of LULUs and the current socioeconomic characteristics of a neighborhood, even a siting process radically revised to ensure that LULUs are distributed equally among all neighborhoods may have only a short-term effect. The areas surrounding LULUs distributed equitably will become less desirable neighborhoods, and thus may soon be left to people of color or the poor, recreating the pattern of inequitable siting....

### The Evidence of Disproportionate Siting

Several recent studies have attempted to assess whether locally undesirable land uses are disproportionately located in neighborhoods that are populated by more people of color or are more poor than is normal.... [One frequently cited study,] which is often credited for first giving the issue of environmental justice visibility, was conducted by the United States General Accounting Office (GAO).... [The GAO found that in three of the four communities where hazardous waste landfills were sited in eight southeastern states, the population was disproportionately African American and poor. Eds.] Another frequently cited local study was conducted by sociologist Robert Bullard and formed important parts of his books, *Invisible Houston* and *Dumping in Dixie*. Professor Bullard found that although African-Americans made up only 28% of the Houston population in 1980, six of Houston's eight incinerators and mini-incinerators and fifteen of seventeen landfills were located in predominantly African-American neighborhoods.

[Professor Been then re-analyzed the GAO study and the Bullard study, looking at demographic characteristics of the host communities at the time of siting decisions and tracing subsequent changes in the demographics of these communities. She found mixed support for her thesis: of the four communities reviewed by the GAO, all were disproportionately African American at the siting, and in each case the percentage of African Americans decreased after siting decisions were made. For ten communities studied by Professor Bullard, she found 50% were sited in predominantly African-American communities, and that the percentage of African Americans in all neighborhoods surrounding the landfills subsequently increased (as did the percentage of the population with incomes below the poverty level in all but two host neighborhoods). Eds.]

* * *

## *Notes and Questions*

1. **Chicken or the egg?** The which-came-first question continued to be discussed and debated in subsequent environmental justice literature. In 2006, a group of researchers summarized the state of the empirical evidence:

> Research on the temporal dimension—which came first, the minority communities or the hazards—has been the subject of a more limited range of quantitative research, primarily because of the methodological challenges of such time-series analysis. The results have been mixed. In keeping with the work of Douglas Anderton and various colleagues (Anderton, Anderson, Rossi et al. 1994; Anderton, Anderson, Oakes, and Fraser 1994), John Oakes, Douglas Anderton, and Andy Anderson (1996) found little evidence of either contemporary disparity or historical patterns. Using an improved database, Vicki Been and Francis Gupta (1997) [in the previous excerpt] found no evidence for the move-in view but did find that some Latino communities were the subject of disproportionate siting. Sabina Shaikh and John Loomis (1999) found in a study of Denver that minority populations rose faster in areas without hazards, countering the market dynamics view. James Mitchell, Deborah Thomas, and Susan Cutter (1999) find evidence of minority move-in for South Carolina. A study of the Los Angeles area by Manuel Pastor, James Sadd, and John Hipp (2001) [excerpted below] found that siting was significantly disproportionate, and that the movement of minorities into affected neighborhoods was no faster than in the rest of the region.

Manuel Pastor et al., In the Wake of the Storm: Environment, Disaster, and Race After Katrina 14 (2006).

2. Some scholars have criticized the fact that while Professor Been identifies racial discrimination in housing as a factor in post-siting demographic change, she nonetheless includes this under the rubric of market forces.

> Housing choices among whites may be determined by the market, what is available and affordable, individual preferences (of which the neighborhood racial mix may be one), and utility functions. In contrast, choices among minorities may be severely limited by various forms of institutionalized discrimination altogether separate from ability and willingness to pay. Been recognizes that market processes may result in a gradual downgrading in the economic status of residents of a host neighborhood and that housing discrimination may have a separate effect of concentrating minorities. Yet in combining both factors under the label of market dynamics, Been seems to negate the fact that demographic change due to housing discrimination is a fundamentally different process.

Saha & Mohai, *supra*, at 19.

**3.** How does Professor Been's market dynamics theory square with Professor Rabin's findings documenting expulsive zoning practices in communities of color? Is expulsive zoning an indication of a well-functioning market allocating risks and amenities efficiently, i.e., to those willing to pay the most for the resource in question (either an environmental good or the absence of an environmental risk)? Or, alternatively, is expulsive zoning evidence of a poorly functioning market?

**4.** While public opinion polls and research on risk perception and environmental attitudes support the notion that LULUs render host areas less desirable places to live, Professors Saha and Mohai caution that a mix of factors influences the decision of residents to leave a neighborhood. They argue, for example, that a neighborhood's pre-existing level of stability or change may be equally or more important than the impact of the LULU itself. Saha & Mohai, *supra*, at 21.

**5.** Some scholars seeking to explain disproportionate siting point to a complicated set of sociopolitical and legal factors. Their theories are examined in the following section.

# D. Politics, Social Capital, and the Structure of Environmental Laws

As described above, companies may choose to site noxious facilities in low-income communities or communities of color because this represents the path of least political resistance. Minority and poor residents often have less political power than wealthier communities for a variety of reasons: lack of access to elected officials, lack of awareness of the appropriate officials to contact in order to express concerns about environmental conditions, and under-representation in local government. They are "likely to lack the know-how, the administrative, legal, and scientific expertise to participate effectively in administrative process of siting decisions." Saha & Mohai, *supra*, at 9, 11–13. Explanations that center upon these sociopolitical factors essentially posit that environmental burdens are shifted to groups that lack social capital.

> Social capital can be defined as resources embedded in a social structure that are accessed and/or mobilized in purposive actions. By this definition, the notion of social capital contains three ingredients: resources embedded in a social structure; accessibility to these social resources by individuals; and use or mobilization of them by individuals engaged in purposive action. Thus conceived, social capital contains both structural (accessibility) and action-oriented (mobilization or use) elements.... [S]ocial capital captures the extent to which individuals have differential accessibility to collective resources....
>
> [I]t is incumbent on a theory of social capital to delineate the patterns and determinants of the two ingredients of social capital or *the inequality of social capital* as accessible social resources and mobilized social resources....

Nan Lin et al., *The Position Generator: Measurement Techniques for Investigations of Social Capital, in* SOCIAL CAPITAL: THEORY AND RESEARCH 57, 58–59 (Nan Lin, Karen Cook & Ronald S. Burt eds., 2001).

With this in mind, consider that researchers found that ethnic demographic shifts, a previously overlooked variable in the empirical data on disparities, significantly correlated with the siting of commercial hazardous waste facilities (called treatment, storage, and disposal facilities, or "TSDFs", under federal hazardous waste law). The excerpt below, describing this study, attempts to identify and measure the lack of social capital that explains some environmental disparities.

## Manuel Pastor, Jr., Jim Sadd & John Hipp, *Which Came First? Toxic Facilities, Minority Move-In, and Environmental Justice*
### 23 J. URBAN AFFAIRS 1, 3–19 (2001)

... Many have assumed that contemporary inequity is the result of discriminatory siting practices. The general argument is that low levels of political power in minority communities may induce polluters to locate hazards in these areas. Such a political argument is often implicitly based on notions of social capital and community efficacy: Where residents have more ability to organize and affect policy, perhaps because of their income or racial status in a stratified society, they will be more able to resist the placement of a hazardous facility. Of course, social capital may in fact be affected by other factors, such as the level of education of residents or the ability to bridge differences between minority groups, a topic we explore below....

[W]e focus on the effects of a new dimension of ethnic change. Previous work has stressed the percentage of minorities. But while a 40% increase in Latinos that is matched by a corresponding 40% decrease in African Americans may leave the percentage of minorities unchanged, the neighborhood will in fact be transformed. Such ethnic transitions may weaken the usual social bonds constituted by race and make an area more susceptible to siting. We investigate this "social capital" effect [] finding that it does indeed have an effect on the likelihood of receiving a TSDF....

Black to Brown shifts have been especially prevalent in South Los Angeles, an area laden with hazardous or toxic facilities and air pollution.... Such shifting neighborhood patterns can cause tensions between minority groups, weakening neighborhood social capital and increasing the area's vulnerability to siting locally undesirable land uses.... We label this measure of dynamics within a census tract "ethnic churning." ...

To see whether a change in the ethnic composition of an area—even if it remains minority—weakens social capital and makes areas more vulnerable to disproportionate siting, we re-estimated the model by using ethnic churning during the 1970s and 1980s and TSDF siting over the same period.... [The researchers then found that the churning variable is highly significant at predicting TSDF siting at the one-mile level; they also found that, controlling for other factors, minorities attract TSDFs, but TSDFs do not generally attract minorities. Eds.]

This study offers a lesson consistent with the experience of many environmental justice advocates: Demographics reflecting political weakness—including a higher presence of minorities, a lower presence of home owners, or a significant degree of ethnic churning—seem to be the real attractors of TSDFs. A special challenge is posed by the fact that areas undergoing transition and unable to lay claim to pre-existing racially based social capital may be especially vulnerable. If this is so, then the current strategy of most of the environmental justice movement—building social capital across ethnic lines by an explicit commitment to a people of color movement—may be an effective way to combat the environmental degradation often found in urban minority communities.

\* \* \*

## Notes and Questions

1. Two early campaigns illustrate the points made by Professors Pastor, Sadd, and Hipp, and underscore the potential of the environmental justice movement to promote social capital:

> Los Angeles, the nation's second largest city ... is one of the most culturally and ethnically diverse cities in the United States. People of color—Latino Americans, Asian Americans, Pacific Islanders, African Americans, and Native Americans—now constitute 63 percent of the city's population....
>
> The South Central Los Angeles neighborhoods suffer from a double whammy of poverty and pollution. [An] article in the *San Francisco Examiner* described the ZIP code in which South Central Los Angeles lies (90058) as the "dirtiest" in the state. The 1990 population in the ZIP code is 59 percent African American and 38 percent Latino American. Abandoned toxic-waste sites, freeways, smokestacks, and waste water pipes from polluting industries saturate the one-square-mile area....
>
> Why has South Central Los Angeles become the dumping ground of the city? Local government decisions are in part responsible. Trying to solve them, the city (under a contract with the EPA) developed a plan to build three waste-to-energy incinerators....
>
> After learning about the incinerator project ... residents organized themselves in a group called Concerned Citizens of South Central Los Angeles, most of whom were African American women. Local activists from Concerned Citizens were able to form alliances with several national and grassroots environmental groups, as well as with public interest law groups to block the construction of the city-initiated municipal solid-waste incinerator....
>
> Just as Los Angeles's largest African American community was selected for the city's first state-of-the-art municipal solid waste incinerator, the state's

first state-of-the-art hazardous-waste incinerator was slated to be built near East Los Angeles, the city's largest Latino community....

Several East Los Angeles neighborhoods, made up mostly of Latino Americans, are located only a mile downwind from the proposed hazardous-waste incinerator site.... Residents of East Los Angeles questioned the selection of their community as host for the state's first hazardous-waste incinerator. Opponents of the incinerator saw the project as just another case of industry dumping on the Latino American community....

Mothers of East Los Angeles (MELA) led the opposition to the ... incinerator. MELA consisted of Latino American women who had originally organized against the state's plan to locate a prison in East Los Angeles....

Robert D. Bullard, *Anatomy of Environmental Racism*, in TOXIC STRUGGLES: THE THEORY AND PRACTICE OF ENVIRONMENTAL JUSTICE 25, 30–32 (Richard Hofrichter ed., 1993).

2. Attorney Nicholas Targ, former general counsel to the U.S. EPA Office of Environmental Justice, describes ways in which social capital indicators correlate with environmental regulatory indicators:

Using indicators, such as voter turn-out, as a measure of social capital, the following indicators strongly suggest the importance of community social capital in achieving the environmental policy and civil rights aspects of environmental justice:

• Communities that have high rates of voter turn-out in general elections (normalized for race, income, and education factors) have a higher rate of Toxic Release Inventory (TRI) chemical reduction than communities with lower voter turn-out;

• The level of clean-up and funds expended, on a risk of cancer basis, is greater in communities with higher voter turn-out. Researchers have found that the correlation between voter turn-out and level of clean-up was most significant at the least cost-effective site clean-ups and the lowest risk sites;

• A survey of 200 corporate counsels found that the overwhelming majority of attorneys said that they were more likely to recommend reducing their facilities' emissions if a community group could make a credible threat to take political or legal action against the facility;

• The best predictor for the location of new TRI facilities in Los Angeles is not race or income, but the rate of a community's ethnic change (ethnic churning), an indicator of social capital; and

• The occurrence of urban restoration projects (community gardens, reclamation of vacant lots, etc.) in New Haven, Connecticut, correlates with a sense of "being part of a solid community."

Community social capital is, therefore, a critical asset both for community-led efforts to halt unwanted projects and those community-led efforts that seek to work collaboratively with other stakeholders (e.g., government at all levels, industry, environmentalists, etc.) to achieve mutually consistent goals.

Nicholas Targ, *A Third Policy Avenue to Address Environmental Justice: Civil Rights and Environmental Quality and the Relevance of Social Capital Policy*, 16 TUL. ENVTL. L.J. 167, 169–70 (2002). Mr. Targ recommends ways for governmental officials to enhance the social capital of communities by designing initiatives that will increase the capacity of environmental justice communities to identify and address community needs and goals. *Id.* at 171–72. (Governmental initiatives are examined in Chapter 10.)

3. Rather than stopping a facility, a group of residents may choose instead to negotiate with a facility sponsor to mitigate impacts from a new facility, or alternatively to provide community benefits. Scholars have implicitly examined a relationship between a community's social capital and the community's ability to form and maintain the coalitions necessary to undertake a successful negotiation, ultimately memorialized in what is often termed a "Good Neighbor Agreement." *See, e.g.,* Douglas S. Kenney, et al., *Evaluating the Use of Good Neighbor Agreements for Environmental and Community Protection*, Nat. Resources L. Center, U. Colo. School of Law (Aug. 2004). The potential uses of Good Neighbor Agreements (also known as "Community Benefits Agreements") will be examined in Chapter 13 ("Citizen Enforcement and Common Law Remedies"). For now, consider the following analysis of the social capital that may be required for successful negotiation of a Community Benefits Agreement, or CBA:

> Usually framed as private agreements (with or without municipal involvement), CBAs may require a developer to mitigate potential impacts of the development. But often they go even farther, asking the developer to work with the community to improve housing, employment options, and recreational and cultural facilities. As a result, CBAs can empower communities to become active participants in the planning process.
>
> ... CBAs ... function best when the community base is large and where the developer needs community support in order to obtain subsidies, approvals, or regulatory variances (as is often the case in dense urban neighborhoods). As urban areas become more popular locations for large developments, residents are becoming increasingly empowered to demand that such developments "give back" to the community with benefits that improve urban quality of life....
>
> When developers do choose to engage in talks with community groups, they may persist in attempts to weaken the coalition's bargaining power. The "divide and conquer" techniques used by developers to balkanize coalitions require community groups to be united and to have coherent goals. Otherwise, a developer may attempt to appease some community groups without meeting others' needs — to "buy off" the minimum number of stakeholders to be able to spin the project as being community-supported....
>
> While developers may try to damage coalitions' reputations or seek to win over constituent groups, CBA coalitions have developed some tactics of their

own to boost their bargaining power. From the start, coalitions must develop a language to frame the issues in their favor. This often involves emphasizing positive visions of the community's future, win-win solutions, inclusiveness, the grassroots character of the campaign and the nature of the CBA as fostering equitable development rather than preventing development altogether. These positions reflect strong social values, and they may draw more community members to the coalition and attract positive media attention....

The costs of negotiating a CBA can be high. Organizing a coalition, holding meetings, conducting community research and preparing reports will all require funding. Coalitions that have no experience with CBAs, moreover, will likely need technical and legal assistance throughout the negotiation process. The funding required for all of this may inhibit the process....

Patricia E. Salkin & Amy Lavine, *Understanding Community Benefits Agreements: Equitable Development, Social Justice and Other Considerations for Developers, Municipalities and Community Organizations*, 26 UCLA J. ENVTL. L. & POL'Y 291, 292–323 (2008). The excerpt above reveals a cyclical relationship. While community benefits agreements can promote social capital, to what extent must there be preexisting social capital to prompt formation of the coalition and to avoid its disintegration? For example, would a community undergoing significant ethnic churning have enough social capital to form a coalition to either resist the siting or negotiate a favorable community benefits agreement?

4. In addition to a community's lack of social capital, some political explanations of disparities focus on the structure of environmental law and environmental policymaking (this also includes land-use practices, discussed above). The following two excerpts on green power and the long road to environmental justice explore these issues in greater detail.

\* \* \*

## Jeanne Marie Zokovitch Paben, *Green Power & Environmental Justice — Does Green Discriminate?*

46 TEXAS TECH L. REV. 1067, 1092–100 (2014)

Overall, it is clear that a shift towards green energy is occurring in the United States. Perhaps the shift is not happening as quickly as some envisioned, but nonetheless, the increased proportion of energy coming from renewable sources is undeniable. Not all of these renewable energy sources are created equal in terms of their contribution to environmental problems, which pose environmental justice consequences and risks. Further, no renewable source of energy is devoid of environmental justice risks. And although the green energy movement is thriving, it is a long way from displacing historical energy sources and their history of environmental justice impacts.

As indicated, some of the emerging green power technologies that are getting more attention today are wind, solar, biomass, and biofuels (for comparison purposes, it is these four green power sources that are predominately evaluated in this Article).

The next question is: Are these emerging green power technologies free from environmental justice impacts? And the simple answer is "No." With respect to environmental justice impacts, the green power industry sometimes remains the same, but in other instances it presents new challenges.

## A. Wind

Wind has the lowest pollution emission risks…although there have been complaints of health effects associated with flicker or low-level frequency, sub-audible sounds (infrasounds). Although scientific evidence does not support a direct link between infrasounds generated by wind turbines and health effects, there are psychological complaints associated with infrasounds and wind turbines that are likely attributable to scare tactics of the anti-wind propagandists. Research has indicated that only a very small portion of people living near wind turbines actually complain about health symptoms, and when they do, the complaints coincide with campaigning from anti-wind groups. It is interesting to note that one of the largest proponents of helping the public understand the health risks of wind energy are anti-wind advocates, including the nuclear power industry. Despite the lack of scientifically documented health effects of wind turbines, some of the most prolific battles fought against the siting of green power facilities have been against wind farms. The most famous of these has been the Cape Wind project in the water of Nantucket Sound. One of the groups opposing the Cape Wind project presented a potential environmental justice issue. The Wampanoag Tribe opposed the project because the placement of the turbines would affect tribal religious ceremonies—the turbines were to be placed on burial grounds, which would have obstructed the view for these ceremonies. Even though this is not a traditional environmental justice argument, it does pose the question central to the core of environmental justice: Would these turbines still be placed if the proposed location were a Catholic church or a Christian cemetery, rather than a tribe's burial ground?

## B. Solar

While solar power is generally perceived to be clean, it raises the same environmental justice considerations associated with other types of energy sources with respect to transportation and disposal of waste. The disposal of photovoltaic cells and, in particular, those containing cadmium sulfide and gallium arsenide is problematic because these are very persistent chemicals, increasing the duration of exposure risks. The time required to break down photovoltaic cells is extremely long. As with the disposal of other energy sources, the disposal of solar energy waste from production facilities in the United States presents the risk of the same negative effects on environmental justice communities. These effects include the possibility of disposing of solar energy waste at a hazardous facility. Additionally, some solar battery production is occurring in the United States; these facilities are creating real environmental risks for those living near them.

What is also interesting in the solar context is that just as with electronics, we are seeing export of our waste to third world countries; consequently, the environmental justice impact is not just within the United States. In China, where the polysilicon component of the solar panels is created, there have been reports regarding toxins being improperly discarded. Silicon tetrachloride, a byproduct of solar panel production, has been reported to cause various problems in Gaolong, an impoverished farming community. Residents of the village reported problems with crop growth, soil left in a state not proper for humans or plants, and air quality problems resulting in wilting plants and cases of fainting.

## C. Biomass

Unlike potential health problems of solar energy, the impacts of biomass energy production are more direct. In the context of biomass, during the 2009 energy bill discussions, the American Lung Association urged the Legislature not to promote the combustion of biomass; it stated that burning biomass can lead to significant increases and emissions of nitrous oxide, particulate matter, and sulfur dioxide, which has a severe impact on the health of our children, older adults, and people with lung disease. In Florida, rural residents have fought several battles against the construction of new biomass energy facilities, at least two of which successfully prevented biomass plants in Gadsden, the only county in Florida with a majority African-American population, and in Tallahassee, which does not have a majority African-American population, but sought to place the facility in a predominately African-American minority section of the city. The American Lung Association has indicated that there was a nationwide pattern of biomass plants being proposed for rural areas away from cities, where less protective pollution control restrictions and weaker permitting requirements apply. This is due to the fact that urban areas are more likely to qualify as nonattainment areas under the Clean Air Act for one or more of the criteria pollutants. Under the Clean Air Act, these nonattainment areas have much greater restrictions on new sources. Some might contend that this propels an argument for a more proportionate share because if you put them further away from urban centers, you can pollute more and you are not competing with the polluting rights of other industries. But others argue that this is just going to ship the trend into rural, low-income communities.

## D. Biofuels

Biofuels, though related to biomass as the result of biomass processing, have been used in at least some form for energy production for a long time. They are primarily used as a source of mobile power. The thinking that biofuels have no environmental justice impact overlooks the energy and land costs as well as the pollution associated with refining biofuels....

Recognizing that green power is also potentially fraught with both environmental justice impacts and future risks, solutions need to be offered to address environmental justice issues in the context of green energy so that they actually earn the "green" name and are indeed sustainable over the long term. These themes—the siting of facilities that pollute; air and water pollution that results from these polluting facilities, superfund, and other contaminated sites; the disposal of hazardous waste; raw material development; and transportation of hazardous material—are still the primary issues that give rise to the environmental justice movement. If we hope to start improving the lives of those most affected by the environmental burdens, then solutions that are offered today must become more than lip service and must be put into motion. Because the environmental justice problems posed by green energy sources are in many ways the same problems posed by traditional energy sources and other industrial processes, many of the solutions proffered over the years to address these issues also remain the same....

* * *

# Jedediah Purdy,
## *The Long Environmental Justice Movement*
### 44 Ecology L.Q. 809, 831–35 (2018)

Both the environmental statutes and the environmental movement that took form in the 1970s and early 1980s bore the stamp of a conception of law's role in legal and social reform that was regnant among elite reformers in the 1960s and 1970s. Steven Teles has termed this view "legal liberalism" and linked it with a more general view of the law's role in a democratic society. Legal liberalism was defined by its emphasis on the use of litigation and adjudication-like procedures to protect individuals against arbitrary discrimination with respect to their basic interests — that is, to ensure the formal preconditions of their full participation in political, economic, and social institutions. It implied a central but also quite specifically delimited role for legal advocacy, focused on securing formal rights and procedural attention for those who lacked organized voice backed by money or institutional heft, such as the disorganized poor and consumers.

Legal liberalism took plausibility from the distributional optimism of the mid-twentieth century: its procedural emphases made sense on the view that formally equal and open economic participation overcame rather than reinforced embedded inequality. But legal liberalism was by no means determined by economic optimism alone. Rather, it formed a key part of what is often termed the "consensus liberalism" of the Cold War period in U.S. history. Procedural guarantees promised to bring neglected interests into decision making within a pluralist democracy that discarded ambitious visions of collective self-rule and also recast class conflict as interest-group politics. In light of its picture of politics as the rotation of groups in and out of transient majorities, pluralist-democratic thought adopted a version of the concern with overcoming exclusion that also preoccupied the thinking of the time on economic policy. John Hart Ely's conception of constitutional review as filling persistent structural gaps in political decision makers' consideration of the interests of disadvantaged or disorganized groups represents the elevation of legal liberalism to constitutional theory, explicitly portraying judges' remit as the procedural defense of those disadvantaged by an otherwise legitimate democratic pluralism.

The institutional trajectory of "mainstream environmentalism" in the early and mid-1970s took much of its shape from the legal-liberal conception of advocacy. These years shaped environmental politics for decades thereafter in the litigation and elite advocacy that the environmental justice movement critiqued. The key events in this history of influence were pivotal institutional investments in nascent environmental groups by the Ford Foundation, which had already been at the center of building up clinical programs in law schools and developing pro bono expectations for the bar, two key sites of implementation for the legal-liberal ideal of representation as advocacy. In the early and mid-1970s, the Ford Foundation made major grants to EDF and NRDC. Ford guidance helped to build up EDF from a grassroots coalition of scientists, lawyers, and citizens on Long Island. It also effectively founded NRDC by brokering the merger of a band of young, liberal, well-connected Yale Law School graduates with a Republican director of old-line conservationist impulses, the Simpson Thacher lawyer, John Adams. Ford made some of its largest cumulative Resources and Environment grants of the 1970s to these groups: $3,635,000 to NRDC, $1,079,500 to EDF, $1,509,000 to the Southern California Center for Law in the Public Interest, and $760,000 to the Sierra Club Legal Defense Fund, which later became Earthjustice. Ford's account of the reasons for these investments exemplifies the legal-liberal conception of advocacy: "The Foundation has been assisting the environmental law movement since 1970 in the belief that in a pluralistic society the views and interests of all segments of opinion should have their *day in court.*" The ideal was to bring all "views and interests" before an impartial decision maker, not to engage in political contests to form views and challenge or reshape interests.

The deliberately bipartisan NRDC answered, like EDF, to a litigation review board carefully stocked with law-firm partners and sympathetic figures from the business world. Although this has been interpreted as evidence of elite control of these organizations, that view hardly comports with the controversial and radical cases that the young lawyers brought, particularly in their first decade. It is more convincing to see NRDC and EDF as instances of a general pattern in the institutions of legal liberalism: collaboration between senior professionals whose politics were often cast in a New Deal/Great Society mold and young activists, frequently with moderate New Left sympathies, who saw in the law an institutional path to very basic changes, including welfare rights, death-penalty and criminal-justice reform, and revolutions in sex and gender. Legal liberalism did not necessarily narrow or moderate the substantive scope of environmental politics. It did, however, imply a persistent tilt toward professionalized and elite advocacy that was less likely to engage ordinary people as active constituents than as donors or clients. The legal-liberal model of reform also meant that legally oriented activism followed the ideological peregrinations of the federal courts, not because the advocates became personally more moderate in their goals (whether or not they in fact did so), but because their strategy entailed that what was possible was a function of the arguments that judges would embrace. An advocate who started out with visions of enforcing a progressive conception of the public interest through public-trust or substantive National Environmental Policy Act suits in a green 1970s soon modified her expectations, much as reproductive-rights and poverty lawyers did as the Burger Court and its successors took hold of legal interpretation.

The shaping influence of legal liberalism on environmental law also tilted the definition of environmental problems toward professionals and established groups. The Ford Foundation expressed confidence that its grantees' carefully calibrated litigation, in which clients were often well-established groups, ensured responsiveness to what the foundation seems to have regarded as an uncontroversial "public interest." A 1976 internal report on the foundation's involvement in public-interest law posed the question, "Are there substantial interests in the community that do not get represented adequately because of the way in which public interest law firms tend to choose their clientele?" and responded, "[M]ost of the time public interest law firms represent established and well-informed groups or organizations. The environmental ... cases are the best examples of this." This answer seems to have satisfied the report's authors that their model of advocacy was adequately representing relevant environmental interests. Those who did not identify with well-established advocacy organizations might not have agreed.

The architects of "mainstream environmentalism's" flagship organizations knew, or so they believed, which problems were "environmental issues" and what interest the public had in those issues. This self-confidence was partly owing to a view about the empirical character of the natural world. The influential "climax" theory of ecology described ecosystems as tending toward stable equilibriums with high levels of biological energy and diversity. This in turn seemed to imply natural baselines of health and flourishing—the climax condition—that policy makers could aim to respect. This self-confidence also expressed the unchallenged dominance of a network of elite reformers who shared a substantially overlapping set of ideas about "the environment" and the public interest in it. Homogeneity among decision makers allowed their view of the scope and valence of "environmental issues" to feel, so to speak, natural. This invisible uniformity was a key support for the melding of traditional environmentalism with legal liberalism, an institutional strategy that then proceeded to reinforce the same uniformity.

* * *

## Notes and Questions

**1.** As of 2020, there still is no federal environmental legislation explicitly addressing environmental justice. Although a few states have enacted such laws, these laws typically provide little more than enhanced procedures (governmental initiatives, including state laws addressing environmental justice concerns, are discussed in Chapter 10).

**2.** Does the current pattern of environmental inequities represent a failure of our environmental protection laws, or the *success* of these laws, as Luke Cole argues?

**3.** Given the decentralized nature of the environmental justice movement, and the limited resources available, what would be the most potentially useful points of intervention? Direct action (e.g., demonstrations), litigation, collaborative projects, legislative lobbying, or pressure upon agencies? Can you think of other means? In which venues would lawyers likely be the most helpful?

# E. Racial Discrimination

Another set of explanations for disproportionate environmental burdens and benefits involves racial discrimination. In part this refers to intentional racism, i.e., targeting communities of color based on pure racial bigotry. In today's society, such conduct is far less frequent than in the past, and given the prevailing societal opprobrium toward overt racial discrimination, far less likely to occur in the open. A softer, but related view of intentional discrimination posits that communities of color are targeted for unwanted land uses by those who believe they will be less likely to organize effective opposition than white communities, or by those who believe these communities to be more willing to trade off environmental risks for possible economic benefits.

A broader view of discrimination encompasses actions that are not grounded in intentional, conscious prejudice, but that, because of the structure or workings of social and political institutions, have discriminatory effects. For example, an all-white zoning board may render decisions with discriminatory effects because of unconscious racial prejudices, or because minority citizens, who do not live in the same neighborhoods and are not part of the same social networks as the board members, have less access to them, or because the white board members do not live in the area impacted by a proposed LULU, or because the decision-makers are less interested in the fate of minority residents for political reasons. In some respects, all of the above authors' insights point to specific mechanisms by which this form of "structural" or "institutional" racism works. For example, attorney Luke Cole and Professor Sheila Foster discuss instances where public officials employ seemingly technical criteria — such as that a facility should not be sited in proximity to schools, hospitals, or other sensitive institutions — that can discriminate against minority residents who because of past and present housing discrimination disproportionately live in areas without such facilities. In the following article, Professor Charles Lawrence adds to the general theory of structural racism. By using the insights of psychology, he articulates a theory of why racial discrimination may be far more prevalent than appears on the surface and, accordingly, more persistent throughout our society.

## Charles R. Lawrence III, *The Id, the Ego, and Equal Protection: Reckoning with Unconscious Racism*

### 39 STANFORD L. REV. 317, 322–341 (1987)

… Americans share a common historical and cultural heritage in which racism has played and still plays a dominant role. Because of this shared experience, we also inevitably share many ideas, attitudes, and beliefs that attach significance to an individual's race and induce negative feelings and opinions about nonwhites. To the extent that this cultural belief system has influenced all of us, we are all racists. At the same time, most of us are unaware of our racism. We do not recognize the ways in which our cultural experience has influenced our beliefs about race or the occasions on which those beliefs affect our actions. In other words, a large part of the behavior that produces racial discrimination is influenced by unconscious racial motivation….

*Racism: A Public Health Problem*

Not every student of the human mind has agreed with Sigmund Freud's description of the unconscious, but few today would quarrel with the assertion that there is an unconscious—that there are mental processes of which we have no awareness that affect our actions and the ideas of which we are aware. There is a considerable, and by now well respected, body of knowledge and empirical research concerning the workings of the human psyche and the unconscious. Common sense tells us that we all act unwittingly on occasion. We have experienced slips of the tongue and said things we fully intended not to say, and we have had dreams in which we experienced such feelings as fear, desire, and anger that we did not know we had.

… Racism is in large part a product of the unconscious. It is a set of beliefs whereby we irrationally attach significance to something called race. I do not mean to imply that racism does not have its origins in the rational and premeditated acts of those who sought and seek property and power. But racism in America is much more complex than either the conscious conspiracy of a power elite or the simple delusion of a few ignorant bigots. It is a part of our common historical experience and, therefore, a part of our culture. It arises from the assumptions we have learned to make about the world, ourselves, and others as well as from the patterns of our fundamental social activities.

… [H]ow is the unconscious involved when racial prejudice is less apparent—when racial bias is hidden from the prejudiced individual as well as from others? Increasingly, as our culture has rejected racism as immoral and unproductive, this hidden prejudice has become the more prevalent form of racism. The individual's Ego must adapt to a cultural order that views overly racist attitudes and behavior as unsophisticated, uninformed, and immoral. It must repress or disguise racist ideas when they seek expression.

Joel Kovel refers to the resulting personality type as the "aversive racist" and contrasts this type with the "dominative racist," the true bigot who openly seeks to keep blacks in a subordinate position and will resort to force to do so. The aversive racist believes in white superiority, but her conscience seeks to repudiate this belief, or, at least, to prevent her from acting on it. She often resolves this inner conflict by not acting at all. She tries to avoid the issue by ignoring the existence of blacks, avoiding contact with them, or at most being polite, correct, and cold whenever she must deal with them. Aversive racists range from individuals who lapse into demonstrative racism when threatened—as when blacks get "too close"—to those who consider themselves liberals and, despite their sense of aversion to blacks (of which they are often unaware), do their best within the confines of the existing societal structure to ameliorate blacks' condition....

*A Cognitive Approach to Unconscious Racism*

Cognitive psychologists offer a contrasting model for understanding the origin and unconscious nature of racial prejudice.... [T]hey view human behavior, including racial prejudice, as growing out of the individual's attempt to understand his relationship with the world (in this case, relations between groups) while at the same time preserving his personal integrity. But while the ultimate goal of the cognitive process is understanding or rationality, many of the critical elements of the process occur outside of the individual's awareness....

Cognitivists see the process of "categorization" as one common source of racial and other stereotypes. All humans tend to categorize in order to make sense of experience. Too many events occur daily for us to deal successfully with each one on an individual basis; we must categorize in order to cope. When a category—for example, the category of black person or white person—correlates with a continuous dimension—for example, the range of human intelligence or the propensity to violence—there is a tendency to exaggerate the differences between categories on that dimension and to minimize the differences within each category....

The content of the social categories to which people are assigned is generated over a long period of time within a culture and transmitted to individual members of society by a process cognitivists call "assimilation." Assimilation entails learning and internalizing preferences and evaluations. Individuals learn cultural attitudes and beliefs about race very early in life, at a time when it is difficult to separate the perceptions of one's teacher (usually a parent) from one's own. In other words, one learns about race at a time when one is highly sensitive to the social contexts in which one lives....

Furthermore, because children learn lessons about race at this early stage, most of the lessons are tacit rather than explicit. Children learn not so much through an intellectual understanding of what their parents tell them about race as through an emotional identification with who their parents are and what they see and feel their parents do. Small children will adopt their parents' beliefs because they experience them as their own. If we do learn lessons about race in this way, we are not likely to be aware that the lessons have even taken place. If we are unaware that we have been taught to be afraid of blacks or to think of them as lazy or stupid, then we may not be conscious of our internalization of those feelings and beliefs....

Case studies have demonstrated that an individual who holds stereotyped beliefs about a "target" will remember and interpret past events in the target's life history in ways that bolster and support his stereotyped beliefs and will perceive the target's actual behavior as reconfirming and validating the stereotyped beliefs. While the individual may be aware of the selectively perceived facts that support his categorization or simplified understanding, he will not be aware of the process that has caused him to deselect the facts that do not conform with his rationalization. Thus, racially prejudiced behavior that is actually the product of learned cultural preferences is experienced as a reflection of rational deduction from objective observation, which is nonprejudicial behavior. The decisionmaker who is unaware of the selective perception that has produced her stereotype will not view it as a stereotype. She will believe that her actions are motivated not by racial prejudice but by her attraction or aversion to the attributes she has "observed" in the groups she has favored or disfavored.

*Unconscious Racism in Everyday Life*

Whatever our preferred theoretical analysis, there is considerable commonsense evidence from our everyday experience to confirm that we all harbor prejudiced attitudes that are kept from our consciousness.

When, for example, a well-known sports broadcaster is carried away by the excitement of a brilliant play by an Afro-American professional football player and refers to the player as a "little monkey" during a nationally televised broadcast, we have witnessed the prototypical parapraxes, or unintentional slip of the tongue. This sportscaster views himself as progressive on issues of race. Many of his most important professional associates are black, and he would no doubt profess that more than a few are close friends. After the incident, he initially claimed no memory of it and then, when confronted with videotaped evidence, apologized and said that no racial slur was *intended*. There is no reason to doubt the sincerity of his assertion. Why would he intentionally risk antagonizing his audience and damaging his reputation and career? But his inadvertent slip of the tongue was not random. It is evidence of the continuing presence of a derogatory racial stereotype that he has repressed from consciousness and that has momentarily slipped past his Ego's censors. Likewise, when Nancy Reagan appeared before a public gathering of then-presidential-candidate Ronald Reagan's political supporters and said that she wished he could be there to "see all these beautiful white people," one can hardly imagine that it was her self-conscious intent to proclaim publicly her preference for the company of Caucasians.

Incidents of this kind are not uncommon, even if only the miscues of the powerful and famous are likely to come to the attention of the press. But because the unconscious also influences selective perceptions, whites are unlikely to hear many of the inadvertent racial slights that are made daily in their presence. . . .

\* \* \*

## *Notes and Questions*

1. Under current jurisprudence, only acts of intentional discrimination are unconstitutional. Professor Lawrence argues that this view is unduly narrow and that "the law should be equally concerned when the mind's censor successfully disguises a socially repugnant wish like racism if that motive produces behavior that has a discriminatory result as injurious as if it flowed from a consciously held motive." *Id.* at 344. These issues are discussed further in Chapter 4. *See also*, Charles R. Lawrence III, *Racism Revisited: Reflections on the Impact and Origins of the Id, the Ego, and Equal Protection*, 40 Conn. L. Rev. 931 (2008).

2. How might unconscious racism play a role in a decision to site a hazardous waste facility or other unwanted land use? In *Bean v. Southwestern Waste Management Corp.*, 482 F. Supp. 673 (S.D. Tex. 1979), *aff'd without op.*, 782 F.2d 1038 (5th Cir. 1986), a case discussed in more detail in Chapter 4, plaintiffs alleged that the siting of a solid waste facility in a minority community in Houston was part of a pattern

of racially discriminatory sitings by the Texas Department of Health (TDH). In rejecting plaintiffs' request for an injunction, the trial court noted:

> It simply does not make sense to put a solid waste site so close to a high school, particularly one with no air conditioning. Nor does it make sense to put the land site so close to a residential neighborhood. But I am not TDH and for all I know, TDH may regularly approve of solid waste sites located near schools and residential areas, as illogical as that may seem.... At this juncture, the decision of TDH seems to have been insensitive and illogical. Sitting as the hearing examiner for TDH, based upon the evidence adduced, this Court would have denied the permit. But this Court has a different role to play, and that is to determine whether the plaintiffs have established a substantial likelihood of proving that TDH's decision to issue the permit was motivated by purposeful discrimination.... [The Court found plaintiffs had not made this showing.]

*Id.* at 679–681.

Do you think that TDH's decision, described by the judge as "insensitive and illogical," might have resulted from unconscious racism? Would it be appropriate for a judge to somehow take into consideration the phenomenon of unconscious racism?

**3.** One of the more highly charged issues surrounding the environmental justice movement is the claim that environmental racism underlies disproportionate environmental outcomes. The term "environmental racism" reportedly was coined by Rev. Dr. Benjamin Chavis in 1987, as he was preparing to publicly present the findings of the United Church of Christ study on toxic waste sites and race. Should the term be used to describe practices that unintentionally disadvantage groups based on race? Professor Richard Lazarus notes that Chavis' statement deliberately eschews the more neutral rhetoric of equity in favor of the far more volatile claim of racism, and that as a result "has had a transforming effect on environmental law. If environmental justice had not been so cast in terms of race, it is quite doubtful that the movement would have enjoyed such a strong political half-life." Richard J. Lazarus, *"Environmental Racism! That's What It Is."*, 2000 U. ILL. L. REV. 255, 259 (2000). Do you agree?

**4.** All of the theories of causation described in this chapter are discussed and debated as competing—but also complementary—theories for the disparities among groups of individuals. For example, the empirical studies that control for both race and class have often found that race, not class, is the more significant predictor of location near a polluting or risk-producing activity. Given the above material, what do you think is the relative role in explaining disparities of the following: our discriminatory history of land use, the current structure of land-use and environmental laws, market forces, economics, sociopolitical factors, and race?

# Chapter 3

# Risk and Health

**Figure 3-1:** Mari Copeny, "Little Miss Flint," with Megan Smith, former U.S. Chief Technology Officer, at the National Mall in Washington, D.C. April 22, 2017. Photo: Riccardo Savi.

## A. Introduction

Health risks are a fact of life in our world. Every time you go outside, cross a street, or drive a car, you are placing your health at risk for some adverse consequence. Risks may be life-threatening, such as the risk of a car crash, or perhaps threatening only to the quality of life, such as a child living with asthma. Health risks may occur naturally. In the United States, for example, current estimates are that one in five Americans will develop skin cancer in their lifetime. Of course, risks may also be associated with exposures to environmental toxins. Additionally, the reduction of the stratospheric ozone layer, which protects against ultraviolet radiation, could increase the prevalence of skin cancer. In this context, we may speak of "acute" risks—where exposure over a weekend, for example, may have an adverse impact—or "chronic" risks—where adverse impacts might develop only after exposure for a period of years.

Recognizing that we all face risks to our lives and health every day, environmental justice concerns the extraordinary health risks that certain groups may experience because of who they are or where they live. Health disparities cut across various ethnicities, races, and socioeconomic statuses. These harms include adverse impacts to physical, psychological, social, cultural, and spiritual health. In many instances, these harms represent an affront not only to an individual, but also to the group.

These harms, as environmental justice advocates have pointed out, result from multiple contributing "stressors." For example, in order to understand fully the adverse human health impacts of an individual's exposure to a chemical stressor such as mercury (which is now present in fish that live in contaminated aquatic environments), one needs to account for her circumstances of susceptibility and exposure (e.g., was she exposed *in utero*? to how much mercury?); appreciate the potential for the chemical stressor's interaction with other chemical stressors, such as PCBs, that may also be present in the fish; and consider the impact of social and economic stressors, such as a lack of access to adequate health care, a deficient diet, or a community fabric frayed by poverty and other pressures. The Flint water crisis emerged as a flashpoint for environmental justice and public health in 2014. The excerpt below shows the decades-long human failures that led to that ongoing environmental health tragedy.

## Anna Clark, *The Poisoned City: Flint's Water and the Urban American Tragedy*

(2018)

I.

On a hot day in the summer of 2014, in the Civic Park neighborhood where Pastor R. Sherman McCathern preached in Flint, Michigan, water rushed out of a couple of fire hydrants. Puddles formed on the dry grass and splashed the skin of the delighted kids who ran through it. But the spray looked strange. "The water was coming out, dark as coffee, for hours," McCathern remembered. The shock of it caught in his throat. "Something is wrong here."

Something had been wrong for months. That spring, Flint, under direction from state officials, turned off the drinking water that it had relied upon for nearly fifty years. The city planned to join a new regional system called the Karegnondi Water Authority, and while it waited for the KWA to be built, it began bringing in its water from the Flint River. McCathern didn't pay much attention to the politicking around all this; he had enough to worry about at his busy parish. But after the switch, many of his neighbors grew alarmed at the water that flowed from their kitchen faucets and shower heads. They packed public meetings, wrote questioning letters, and protested at city hall. They filled clear plastic bottles from their taps to show how the water looked brown, or orange, and sometimes had particulates floating in it. Showering seemed to be connected with skin rashes and hair loss. The water smelled foul. A sip of it put the taste of a cold metal coin on your tongue.

But the authorities "said everything was all right and you could drink it, so people did," McCathern said later. Residents were advised to run their faucets for a few minutes before using the water to get a clean flow. As the months went by, the city plant tinkered with treatment and issued a few boil-water advisories. State environmental officials said again and again that there was nothing to worry about. The water was fine.

Whatever their senses told them, whatever the whispers around town, whatever Flint's troubled history with powerful institutions telling them what was best for them, this wasn't actually hard for people like McCathern to believe. Public water systems are one of this country's most heroic accomplishments, a feat so successful that it is almost invisible. By making it a commonplace for clean water to be delivered to homes, businesses, and schools, we have saved untold lives from what today sound like antiquated diseases in a Charles Dickens novel: cholera, dysentery, typhoid fever. Here in Flint, it was instrumental in turning General Motors—founded in 1908 in Vehicle City, as the town was known—into a global economic giant. The advancing underground network of pipes defined the growing city and its metropolitan region, which boasted of being home to one of the strongest middle classes in the country....

## II.

... This is the story of how the City of Flint was poisoned by its own water. It was not because of a natural disaster, or simple negligence, or even because some corner-cutting company was blinded by profit. Instead, a disastrous choice to break a crucial environmental law, followed by eighteen months of delay and cover-up by the city, state, and federal governments, put a staggering number of citizens in peril.

Their drinking water, it turned out, was full of lead and other toxins. No amount of lead exposure is safe. There is no known cure for lead poisoning. The threat invaded the most intimate spaces of people's lives: their bodies, their homes, their meals, the baths they gave their children, the formula they fed their babies. Yet it will be years before we can fully assess the effect of lead exposure on a whole generation of children. We must wait for them to grow up and see.

The tainted water also triggered an outbreak of deadly Legionnaires' disease, a severe form of pneumonia caused by waterborne bacteria that can be contracted by inhaling tiny droplets. And, according to one research team, the water switch correlated with a serious drop in fertility for women in Flint and a 58 percent increase in fetal deaths. In an echo of how women once ingested lead to control their reproduction, an estimated 275 fewer children were born than expected during the emergency.

When residents noticed that there was something odd about their water, they asked for help. But they were routinely dismissed. Among the many ravages attributed to the water crisis—the rashes, the hair loss, the ruined plumbing and pipes, the devalued homes, the diminished businesses, the homeowners who left the city once and for all, the children poisoned by lead, the people sickened or killed by Legionnaires' disease—the lost faith in those who were supposed to be working for the common good was among the most devastating. That this happened in the Great Lakes State, which is surrounded by one fifth of all the freshwater on the face of the Earth, makes it all the more haunting.

Fifty years ago, civil unrest tore through American cities—Flint included—and re-vealed how inequality was built into their very foundations. It cued a national reflection from which the Kerner Report emerged, a six-volume investigation into the riots of the 1960s by a bipartisan presidential commission. With passion, the Kerner Report urged the country to recommit to its cities and to rebuild them as places of opportunity. "These programs will require unprecedented levels of funding and performance," the authoring commission wrote, "but they neither probe deeper nor demand more than the problems which called them forth. There can be no higher priority for national action and no higher claim on the Nation's conscience." Avoiding the issue, it warned, was itself a choice. And it was one that would send cities on a downward spiral.

That's exactly what happened. After decades of negligence by both public and pri-vate actors, the well-being of residents in twenty-first-century Flint sat atop a teetering tower of debt, dysfunctional urban policy, disappearing investment, disintegrating infrastructure, and a compromised democratic process. It didn't take much to tip the city into catastrophe.

Flint was not alone. Thousands of communities across the country are in a similarly precarious situation. From Akron to Albany, South Bend to St. Louis, Baltimore to Buffalo, Flint is just one of a large class of shrinking cities. Once among America's finest communities, they have been hollowed out by generations of public policy that incentivized suburban living. The subsidized freeways, shopping malls, and segregated real estate all contributed to an outmigration of mostly middle- and upper-class peo-ple—white folks first, and then, more recently, African Americans and other commu-nities of color. The cities they left are pressured to cut spending at all costs while at the same time maintaining the services and infrastructure designed for a much larger pop-ulation. It is impossible. There isn't enough money to fix a broken window at city hall, and there certainly isn't enough to upgrade the aging lead-laced water infrastructure.

The Flint water crisis illustrates how the challenges in America's shrinking cities are not a crisis of local leadership—or, at least, not solely that—but a crisis of systems. Paternalism, even if it is well meaning, cannot transcend the political, eco-nomic, and social obstacles that relegate places such as Flint to the bottom. The chronic underfunding of American cities imperils the health of citizens. It also stunts their ability to become full participants in a democratic society, and it shatters their trust in the public realm. Communities that are poor and communities of color—and especially those that are both—are hurt worst of all.

If "Watts" came to represent the twentieth-century urban crisis, then "Flint" rep-resents that of the twenty-first. Systemic inequality and disenfranchisement are at the heart of both tragedies. But what happened in Flint reveals a new hydra of dangers in civic life: environmental injustice, the limits of austerity, and urban disinvestment. Neglect, it turns out, is not a passive force in American cities, but an aggressive one.

While there is moral cowardice in the story of Flint, there is also heroism. It's found most especially in the lionhearted residents who chose, again and again, to act rather than be acted upon. They turned themselves into top-notch community organizers and citizen scientists, and they built relationships with a diverse ensemble of professionals—including journalists in Detroit and Ann Arbor, a regulations manager at the Environmental Protection Agency in Chicago, an engineer who was working from her suburban home, a pediatrician at a local hospital, and a team of scientists and civil engineers all the way down in rural Virginia—to make themselves visible.

This city did not deserve what happened to it. Neither does any other shrinking city. Half a century after the Kerner Report tried to inspire a new approach to urban life, we are at another crossroads between how things were once done and how we can choose to do them in the future. In a way, public drinking water systems are the perfect embodiment of the ideal that we might reach toward. The sprawling pipelines articulate the shape of a community. House by house, they are a tangible affirmation that each person belongs. They tie the city together, and often the metropolitan region as well. If only some have good, clean water and others do not, the system breaks down. It isn't safe. The community gets sick. But when we are all connected to the water, and to each other, it is life-giving—holy, even.

*  *  *

When health and environmental agencies evaluate and respond to the harms of environmental contamination, they frequently consider the problem in terms of risk to human health—understood in the narrow, individual, physiological sense of the term. Agencies for the most part proceed chemical by chemical and consider whether human contact with that chemical is expected to result in an increased likelihood of various human health "endpoints" such as neurological damage or cancer. Agencies make this determination by means of risk assessment, an analytical tool that produces a quantitative prediction of this increase for given levels of environmental contamination. In the example of Flint, Michigan, the federal and state environmental agencies have to set particular drinking water standards in consideration of lead's toxic "endpoints," and then address how these factors impact risk assessment as part of the equation.

Quantitative risk assessment enjoyed a striking ascendancy during the 1980s, when it was increasingly employed by health, environmental, and safety agencies to set human health-based standards. Although the use of risk assessment in this regulatory context has been criticized from numerous quarters, the method appears to be here to stay. In view of risk assessment's prominent role in environmental decision-making, it is important to understand the particulars of the method as well as the paradigm within which it operates. *See* Chapter 5 ("Standard Setting").

Section B of this chapter begins by outlining the four steps of the risk assessment method and highlighting some of the limitations of the method. This section next canvasses the criticisms of risk assessment that have been raised from an environmental justice perspective, as well as from other perspectives. Finally, this section considers issues with risk assessment that are particular to children and, then, to other identifiable groups, including tribal populations. Section C discusses one of the major criticisms leveled by environmental justice advocates in greater depth, elaborating the issues involved in cumulative risk assessment. Section D takes a brief look at the concept of risk management. Generally, risk regulation is thought to involve a separation between risk assessment, which is the measurement of risk according to objective, scientific principles, and risk management, which involves subjective, value-laden policy judgments on how to address risks deemed "unacceptable." As will become apparent, however, a strict separation of these two components of agencies' responses to risk may not be possible (or advisable) in practice.

The seminal discussion of the risk assessment process in the regulatory context is the National Research Council, Risk Assessment in the Federal Government: Managing the Process (1983) (known as the "Red Book"). Three later reports of similar national significance are National Research Council, Issues in Risk Assessment (1993); National Research Council, Science and Judgment in Risk Assessment (1994); and National Research Council, Science and Decisions: Advancing Risk Assessment (2008).

In addition to the materials discussed in this chapter, other pieces that examine risk assessment and environmental justice include Brie D. Sherwin, *Pride and Prejudice and Administrative Zombies: How Economic Woes, Outdated Environmental Regulations, and State Exceptionalism Failed Flint, Michigan*, 88 U. Colo. L. Rev. 653 (2017); Catherine O'Neill, *Exposed: Asking the Wrong Question in Risk Regulation*, 48 Ariz. St. L.J. 704 (2016); Vincent R. Johnson, *Nanotechnology, Environmental Risks, and Regulatory Options*, 121 Penn St. L. Rev. 471 (2016); Mike Ewall, Esq., *Legal Tools for Environmental Equity vs. Environmental Justice*, 13 Sustainable Dev. L. & Pol'y 4 (2013); Arden Rowell, *Allocating Pollution*, 79 U. Chi. L. Rev. 985 (2012); Catherine A. O'Neill, *Environmental Justice in the Tribal Context: A Madness to EPA's Method*, 38 Envtl. L. 495 (2008); Carl F. Cranor, *Risk Assessment, Susceptible Subpopulations, and Environmental Justice, in* The Law of Environmental Justice: Theories and Procedures to Address Disproportionate Risks 341 (Michael B. Gerrard & Sheila R. Foster eds., 2d ed. 2008); Ashley C. Schannauer, *Science and Policy in Risk Assessments: The Need for Effective Public Participation*, 24 Vt. L. Rev. 31 (1999); and Brian Israel, *An Environmental Justice Critique of Risk Assessment*, 3 N.Y.U. Envtl. L. J. 469 (1995).

# B. Quantitative Risk Assessment

## 1. An Introductory Note on Quantitative Risk Assessment

Although "risk" is not inherently or necessarily a quantitative concept, environmental agencies' formalized assessments of the harm that can be expected to result from exposure to toxic contamination start from the assumption that risk can be estimated and expressed in numerical terms. Today, the dominant paradigm for considering risk from environmental hazards entails a quantitative description of the likelihood and severity of adverse effects. Of course, contamination may adversely affect both human and non-human components of ecosystems, and agencies may need to consider both sorts of effects. However, the assessment methods that have evolved for each are somewhat different, with assessments of the impacts on humans termed "human health risk assessments" and assessments of the broader environmental impacts termed "ecological risk assessments." Throughout this chapter, we will be concerned primarily with efforts in the former category.

The quantitative risk assessment method is explained in the following excerpt.

## The Carnegie Commission on Science, Technology, and Government, *Risk and the Environment: Improving Regulatory Decision Making*
### 76–78 (1993)

Risk assessment is a composite of established disciplines, including toxicology, biostatistics, epidemiology, economics, and demography. The goals of risk assessment are to characterize the nature of the adverse effects and to produce quantitative estimates of one or both of the following fundamental quantities: (1) the *probability* that an individual (a hypothetical or identified person) will suffer disease or death as a result of a specified exposure to a pollutant or pollutants; and (2) the *consequences* of such an exposure to an entire population (i.e., the number of cases of disease or death).

Risk assessment can either be generic (e.g., an estimate of the number of excess annual cancers caused by all 189 hazardous air pollutants identified in the 1990 Clean Air Act Amendments) or site- and/or chemical-specific (e.g., the probability that a specified child will suffer neurological impairment as a result of exposure to lead in his household drinking water).

The regulatory process is generally thought to encompass two elements, risk assessment and risk management. The distinction between the two components is important, though controversial. Risk assessment is usually conceived as the "objective" part of the process, and risk management the subjective part. In risk assessment the analyst decides how big the problem is, while in risk management political decision makers decide what to do about the problem. The "conventional wisdom" (which some believe needs rethinking) stresses that risk management must not influence the processes and assumptions made in risk assessment, so the two functions must be kept conceptually and administratively separate.

Numerical estimates derived from risk assessment serve as inputs to several very different kinds of decisions, including (1) "acceptable risk" determinations (wherein action is taken if the risk exceeds some "bright line," which can be zero); (2) "cost-benefit" determinations, where the risks reduced by a proposed action are translated into benefits (e.g., lives saved, life-years extended), expressed in dollar amounts, and compared to the estimated costs of implementing the action and some rule of thumb regarding how much cost it is wise to incur to achieve a given level of benefit (e.g., $10 million to save one additional life); and (3) "cost-effectiveness" determinations, where the action that maximizes the amount of risk reduction (not necessarily expressed in dollar terms) per unit cost is favored.

Since at least 1983 (with the publication of the National Research Council's "Red Book"), the dominant paradigm for risk assessment has been a sequential, four-step process:

• *Hazard Identification*: in which a qualitative determination is made of what kinds of adverse health or ecological effects a substance can cause. Typically, agencies have focused on cancer as the effect that drives further analysis and regulation. So, for example, a typical hazard identification for vinyl chloride released from industrial facilities would involve the collection and critical analysis of short-term test-tube assays (for mutagenicity, etc.), of long-term animal assays (typically, two-year rodent carcinogenicity tests), and of human epidemiologic data — either cohort studies (in which populations exposed to vinyl chloride are followed to assess whether their rates of any disease were significantly greater than those of unexposed or less-exposed populations) or case-control studies (which focus on victims of a particular disease to see whether they were significantly more likely to have been exposed to vinyl chloride than similar but disease-free individuals).

• *Exposure assessment*: in which a determination is made of the amounts of a substance to which a hypothetical person (usually the "maximally exposed individual") and/or the total population are exposed. To return to the vinyl chloride example, this part of risk assessment would bring to bear techniques of emissions characterization (how much vinyl chloride leaves the plant in a given time?), fate-and-transport analysis (how is the chemical dispersed in the atmosphere and transformed into other compounds?), uptake analysis (how much air do people breathe, both outdoors and indoors?), and demographic analysis (how many hours per day do people spend in various locations near the plant, and how long do they reside in one locale before moving away?).

• *Dose-response assessment*: in which an estimate is made of the probability or extent of injury at the exposure levels determined above, by quantifying the "potency" of the chemical in question. For vinyl chloride again, scientists would determine its carcinogenic potency by fitting the bioassay data (number of tumors produced at different exposure levels) to a mathematical model (usually one that is linear at low doses), and then transforming the resultant potency estimate for rodents into a human potency estimate through the use of a "scaling factor" (usually, a ratio of the body surface areas of the two species). Additionally, human epidemiologic data could be used to validate or supplant the animal-based potency estimate.

• *Risk characterization*: in which the results of the above steps are integrated to describe the nature of the adverse effects and the strength of the evidence and to present one or more "risk numbers." For example, EPA might say, "This vinyl chloride plant is estimated to produce up to 3 excess cases of liver cancer every 70 years among the 100,000 people living within 1 mile of the facility" or "the maximally exposed individual faces an excess lifetime liver cancer risk of $5.4 \times 10^{-4}$."

Risk assessment is essentially a tool for extrapolating from scientific data to a risk number. The tool is made up of a host of assumptions, which are an admixture of science and policy. Sometimes either science or policy predominates, but it is often difficult to get a broad consensus that this is so....

* * *

## Notes and Questions

1. "Excess" cancers. In the preceding excerpt, note the references to "excess" cancers, a measure of the number of cancer cases that may be attributed directly to some exposure to an environmental toxin. Estimations of excess cancers recognize that people get cancer whether or not they are exposed to environmental toxins. Based on recent estimates, more than one third of all Americans will be diagnosed with cancer at some point in their lives. *See* National Cancer Institute, Cancer Statistics, available at www.cancer.gov. Given that more than three thousand in ten thousand people would be expected to be diagnosed with cancer anyway, should we still care that one additional person in that same group of ten thousand might get cancer from environmental exposure? What is your best argument for why we should still care about this one person?

2. Non-cancer risks. Often lost in the debate about risk calculations and "excess cancers" is the fact that many devastating health impacts from pollution have nothing to do with cancer. Poor air quality from smog and particulate matter may trigger asthma attacks in children and adults, a leading cause of emergency room visits and lost days of school and work. Acute exposure to polychlorinated biphenyls (PCBs) may produce persistent skin lesions known as chloracne. Acute exposure to mercury may cause behavioral changes and loss of muscle control. Exposure to lead, as through the drinking water in Flint but also through indoor dusts from lead paint in older housing stock and through contaminated soils in old mining districts, can permanently impair cognitive functioning. Accordingly, advocates for environmental justice should always consider the complete range of contaminants of concern in a particular community and the potential effects of each contaminant. For a comprehensive listing of toxic substances and associated health effects, *see* the website of the federal Agency for Toxic Substances and Disease Registry (ATSDR): www.atsdr.cdc.gov.

3. Dawn of the "dread." Fear of cancer, like fear of shark attacks and terrorist strikes, occupies a substantial share of public and private concerns, regardless of the likelihood — or *unlikelihood* — of each threat. Psychologists and other researchers have long observed that the risks perceived by the public often vary dramatically from the risks calculated by experts. As recounted by Professor Cass Sunstein:

> In the late 1980s, the Environmental Protection Agency (EPA) embarked on an ambitious project, designed to compare the views of the public and EPA experts on the seriousness of environmental problems. The project revealed some striking anomalies, for the two groups sharply diverged on some crucial issues.
>
> With respect to health risks, the public's top ten concerns included radioactive waste, radiation from nuclear accidents, industrial pollution of wa-

terways, and hazardous waste sites. But in the view of EPA experts, not one of these problems deserved a high level of concern. Two of the public's top concerns (nuclear accident radiation and radioactive waste) were not even ranked by EPA experts. Of health risks considered by the public, among the lowest ranked were indoor air pollution and indoor radon — even though both were ranked among the worst environmental problems by experts. The EPA concluded that there was a remarkable disparity between the views of the public and the views of its own experts. It also noted, with evident concern, that EPA policies and appropriations seemed to reflect the public's preoccupations, not its own. If regulatory law and policy reflect what has been called a combination of "paranoia and neglect," the public's own concerns may be largely responsible.

Cass Sunstein, *Book Review: The Perception of Risk, by Paul Slovic* (2000), 115 Harv. L. Rev. 1119, 1120 (2002).

Explanations for the disparity between public and expert perceptions of risk often center around the concept of "dread risks." Drawing on the influential research of psychologist Paul Slovic, dread risks may be explained in large part using two variables:

> The first variable represents the extent to which a risk is dreaded — that is, "catastrophic, hard to prevent, fatal, inequitable, threatening to future generations, not easily reduced, increasing, involuntary, and [personally] threatening." The second variable relates to the familiarity of a risk — that is, its "observability, knowledge, immediacy of consequences, and familiarity." Examples of the high-dread, low-familiarity risks are nuclear power, nuclear waste disposal, uranium mining, liquefied natural gas, pollution associated with burning coal, DNA technology, and satellite crashes. Examples of low-dread, high-familiarity risks are bicycles, shock from electric appliances, recreational boating, chainsaws, and trampolines. As one might expect, the higher a risk is on the dread and unfamiliarity scales, the more people tend to want strict regulation in hopes of reducing the risk.

> Certainly not everyone perceives even high-dread risks in the same way. Cultural cognition theory (CCT) hypothesizes that individuals perceive risks in ways that reflect and reinforce their cultural worldviews — whether they are individualists, egalitarians, hierarchs, or fatalists. Take geographic variations in risk perception. France, for example, is far more accepting of nuclear power than the United States. French people, however, are more likely to hold hierarchical worldviews than individualistic Americans. Thus, they are both more accepting of the risks associated with nuclear power, and more comfortable with the ability of elite experts to manage those risks.

Emily Hammond, *Public Participation in Risk Regulation: The Flaws of Formality*, 2016 Utah L. Rev. 169, 174–175 (2016).

One conclusion flowing from these observations is that "merely educating the public will not lead to enlightened public opinions about risk. Instead, people are more likely to further entrench their views when confronted with new information that is inconsistent with their cultural predispositions." *Id.* at 175.

If education of the public will simply "further entrench" people in their own established views, how then should regulators seek meaningful public involvement in risk regulation? Should regulators such as the EPA still seek to address serious health risks such as indoor radon even if these risks are not widely recognized by the public? Is it wrong for the EPA to continue investing substantial resources on cleaning up hazardous waste sites even if these sites are not the highest health risks according to risk experts? What are the arguments on either side of this question?

In considering the disparity between the public and expert perceptions of risk, it must be observed that risk assessment is never perfect and always continues to develop. The EPA provides a history of the use of risk assessments as they gained recognition within the agency:

## History of Risk at EPA
### EPA Staff Paper on Risk Assessment
### Principles & Practices, 2004

Shortly after the publication of the Red Book, EPA began issuing a series of guidelines for conducting risk assessments (e.g., in 1986 for cancer, mutagenicity, chemical mixtures, developmental toxicology, and in 1992 for estimating exposures). Although EPA efforts focused initially on human health risk assessment, the basic model was adapted to ecological risk assessment in the 1990s to deal with risks to plants, animals and whole ecosystems.

Over time, the [National Academy of Sciences (NAS)] expanded on its risk assessment principles in a series of subsequent reports, including Pesticides in the Diets of Infants and Children, Science and Judgment in Risk Assessment (also known as the "Blue Book"), and Understanding Risk: Informing Decisions in a Democratic Society (1996). For example, the NAS places equal emphasis on fully characterizing the scope, uncertainties, limitations, and strengths of the assessment and on the social dimensions of interacting with decision makers and other users of the assessment in an iterative, analytic-deliberative process. The purpose of this process is to ensure that the assessments meet the intended objectives and are understandable. EPA risk assessment practices have evolved over time along with this progression of thought, and in many cases helped drive the evolution of thinking on risk assessment.

In 1995, EPA updated and issued the current Agency-wide Risk Characterization Policy (USEPA, 1995). The Policy calls for all risk assessments performed at EPA to include a risk characterization to ensure that the risk assessment process is transparent; it also emphasizes that risk assessments be clear, reasonable, and consistent with other risk assessments of similar scope prepared by programs across the Agency.

Effective risk characterization is achieved through transparency in the risk assessment process and clarity, consistency, and reasonableness of the risk assessment product-TCCR. EPA's Risk Characterization Handbook (USEPA, 2000) was developed to implement the Risk Characterization Policy.

The Congressional/Presidential Commission on Risk Assessment and Risk Management (CRARM) was created by the Clean Air Act Amendments of 1990 and formed in 1994. Its mandate was to make a full investigation of the policy implications and appropriate uses of risk assessment and risk management in regulatory programs, under various federal laws, designed to prevent cancer and other chronic health effects that may result from exposure to hazardous substances. More specifically, its mandate was to provide guidance on how to deal with residual emissions from Section 112 hazardous air pollutants (HAPs) after technology-based controls have been placed on stationary sources of air pollutants. In 1997, the Commission published its report in two volumes (CRARM, 1997; CRARM, 1997). These discussed the importance of better understanding and quantification of risks, as well as the importance of evaluating strategies to reduce human and ecological risks....

* * *

## Notes and Questions

1. **Objectivity vs. subjectivity.** In your view, does this description of the risk assessment method convey a sense of scientific precision? If so, consider that, in practice, the process entails numerous subjective judgment calls. The National Research Council (NRC) of the National Academy of Sciences has emphasized that "completion of the four steps rests on many judgments for which a scientific consensus has not been established. Risk assessors might be faced with several scientifically plausible approaches (e.g., choosing the most reliable dose-response model for extrapolation beyond the range of observable effects) with no definitive basis for distinguishing among them." National Research Council, SCIENCE & JUDGMENT, *supra*, at 27. The selection of any one approach under these circumstances involves what the NRC terms a "science-policy" choice—to be distinguished from determinations that are more purely a matter of science. For a critique of the notion that quantitative risk assessment is an objective, precise scientific enterprise, *see* Wendy E. Wagner, *The Science Charade in Toxic Risk Regulation*, 95 COLUM. L. REV. 1613 (1995); *see also* Annise Katherine Maguire, *Permitting Under the Clean Air Act: How Current Standards Impose Obstacles to Achieving Environmental Justice*, 14 MICH. J. RACE & L. 255 (2009); Raina Wagner, *Adapting Environmental Justice: In the Age of Climate Change, Environmental Justice Demands a Combined Adaptation-Mitigation Response*, 2 ARIZ. J. ENVTL. L. & POL'Y 153, 153 (2011); Laura A. W. Pratt, *Decreasing Dirty Dumping? A Reevaluation of Toxic Waste Colonialism and the Global Management of Transboundary Hazardous Waste*, 41 TEX. ENVTL. L.J. 147, 150 (2011); Hannah Reed, *Indiana's Public Health Is in Jeopardy: Lessons to Learn from Toxic Chemical Contamination in East Chicago*, 15 IND. HEALTH L. REV. 109 (2018).

## The 4 Step Risk Assessment Process

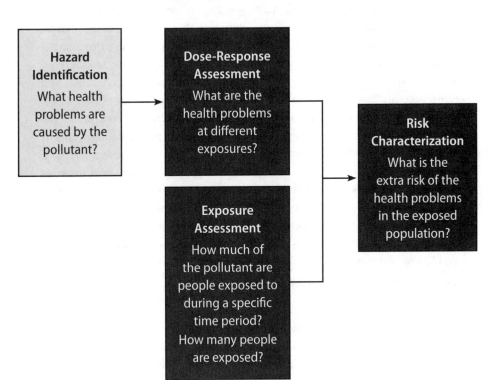

Figure 3-2: The Four-Step Risk Assessment Process. Adapted from U.S. Environmental Protection Agency.

**2. Science or policy?** The fact that risk assessors must make so many judgment calls can have an extraordinary impact on the outcome of a particular risk assessment. The National Research Council has identified 50 quantitative risk assessment "components," each with "inference options," requiring the risk assessor to select between different plausible scientific judgments about uncertain data or theoretical connections. At each point, the consequences of selecting one assumption over another may be substantial. National Research Council, RISK ASSESSMENT IN THE FEDERAL GOVERN- MENT, *supra*, at 28–33. In fact, a risk assessment's "bottom line"—its numerical es- timate of risk—can differ by several orders of magnitude, depending on whether the risk assessor has chosen a more or a less conservative response in the face of un- certainty and on whether she has chosen a more or less protective response to the presence of interindividual variability. Risk assessment scholar Catherine O'Neill considers how compounded conservatism impacts risk assessment:

Meanwhile the claims of "compounded conservatism" that had started being lodged in the 1980s began to encompass the exposure portion of a risk assessment. Commentators sounding this theme generally took aim at the risk assessment process as a whole, citing a litany of instances in which conservative or protective judgments were being made in the process and arguing that the net effect of these judgments was to produce estimates of risk that were unduly conservative. However, some of these commentators began training their arguments on the methods and assumptions used to characterize exposure. Critics took issue, for example, with exposure assessments' focus on the "maximally exposed individual"—sometimes characterized more potently as a "worst-case" exposure scenario. Whether implicitly or explicitly, these criticisms tended to rest on the assertion that no one's actual circumstances of exposure were described by a composite of high-end or maximum values for the relevant parameters. No one, it was assumed, in fact lived their entire life at the fenceline of a factory that emitted toxic air pollutants. No one's children, it was suggested, actually played in and ingested dirt at a site in their neighborhood that had become contaminated with PCBs, benzene and other chemicals. Indeed, critics sometimes caricatured EPA's exposure assumptions as extreme—meant to protect "porch potatoes" and "naked farmers."

Catherine A. O'Neill, *Exposed: Asking the Wrong Question in Risk Regulation*, 48 ARIZ. ST. L.J. 703, 727–29 (2016).

In your view, is the choice to use a conservative input (where the true value is not known, i.e., in the face of uncertainty) or to choose a protective input (where the true value is known to vary, i.e., in the presence of variability) a matter of science, or a matter of policy? Can the two be completely separated in the applied context of risk regulation?

**3. From "Red Book" to "Silver Book."** As risk science has developed, so has the color of the governing guidance documents.

In 2009, a National Research Council committee issued an influential report, *Science and Decisions: Advancing Risk Assessment* (the "Silver Book"), which was developed in response to a request from EPA. The report offers substantial guidance on improving the *scientific status* of risk assessments and on increasing their *utility for decision-making*. A number of EPA efforts to implement the recommendations found in the Silver Book are under way (EPA 2014)....

The Silver Book reaffirms most of the risk-assessment principles and concepts first elucidated in the National Research Council's 1983 report *Risk Assessment in the Federal Government: Managing the Process* (the "Red Book"): the framework within which risk assessments are to be conducted, the need for inference assumptions (defaults) when data and basic knowledge are lacking, the importance of guidelines that specify the types of scientific evidence and default assumptions that will be used in the conduct of risk assessments, and the important distinctions between risk assessment and risk management. The Silver Book builds on those principles and concepts to offer detailed guidance on scientific improvements in risk assessments, some of which can be implemented in the near term and some of which will require substantial study before they can be implemented. The Silver Book also focuses on improving the usefulness of risk assessments.

Board on Environmental Studies and Toxicology; Division on Earth and Life Studies; National Research Council, NATIONAL REVIEW OF CALIFORNIA'S RISK-ASSESSMENT PROCESS FOR PESTICIDES 15–16 (2015).

Although quantitative risk assessment has become a staple of environmental decision-making, it remains controversial. The next section considers criticisms leveled by environmental justice advocates, who tend to be skeptical of both the method and its premises, as well as by others, who see the need to refine what is otherwise a useful analytic tool.

## 2. Criticisms of Quantitative Risk Assessment

Many of the criticisms of quantitative risk assessment are related to environmental justice. In some instances, the criticisms have been raised by environmental justice advocates and may be unique to environmental justice communities. In other instances, the criticisms are more general in origin, but may apply with particular force to environmental justice communities, given their greater "vulnerability" to the harms of environmental contamination — a comprehensive term that has emerged to describe an affected individual's susceptibility or sensitivity to the contaminant(s) in question; her circumstances of exposure to the contaminant(s); and her ability to prepare for and recover from the effects of contact with the contaminant(s), given the various other chemical and non-chemical stressors (for example, physical, social, cultural) that affect that individual. The risk assessment process also has been criticized for instating a highly technical process reserved to a cadre of "experts," one that ignores the expertise of those most affected and tends to diminish opportunities for public participation. Professor Robert Kuehn discusses some of these points in one of the first critiques of risk assessment from the perspective of environmental justice.

### Robert R. Kuehn, *The Environmental Justice Implications of Quantitative Risk Assessment*
1996 UNIVERSITY OF ILLINOIS L. REV. 103, 116–125 (1996)

*Methodological Limitations of Quantitative Risk Assessment and Their Impact on Environmental Justice*

Quantitative risk assessment is frequently described as merely a tool to aid decision makers, not a process that dictates certain risk management results. The methodology, however, raises serious environmental justice concerns, because the results of risk assessments often are not representative of the risks borne by all segments of the population, and the aspects of risk that risk assessment seeks to measure do not capture the concerns of all members of the public.

*1 + 1 Does Not Always Equal 2*

On a daily basis, people are exposed to numerous pollutants from a variety of different sources. The National Academy of Sciences estimated in 1984 that there were more than 64,000 different chemicals currently produced, with over 12,000 manufactured in substantial amounts. In 1989 alone, almost six trillion pounds of chemicals were produced in the United States.... The effects of such multiple exposures and mixing, however, are a matter of dispute and a problem for risk assessment.

Quantitative risk assessment has problems addressing the aggregation of risks, which include multiple exposure, cumulative exposures, and existing exposures. Multiple exposures occur when a person is exposed to a combination of two or more different chemicals or pollutants, while cumulative exposures result when an individual is exposed to one or more chemicals or pollutants from different media or over time. Existing or "background" exposures or risks are those exposures that a person presently experiences, before the addition of any new exposures or risks. Risk assessments generally address the risks posed by one chemical or one source, and a regulatory decision of what is an "acceptable" risk customarily focuses on the risk posed by that single chemical or source. The total risk that a person faces, however, is an aggregate of these many, many risks, each of which individually may be deemed acceptable but in the aggregate may be quite substantial. If a person already has a significant level of existing or background exposure or risk, then the addition of even a small exposure or risk may have a greater effect on that person than on another person who is not already above or near some threshold of safety.... Because minorities and low-income communities face greater exposures to environmental contaminants, it is reasonable to conclude that the failure of risk assessment to account for multiple and cumulative exposures impacts these subpopulations more adversely than other population groups....

Synergistic effects among pollutants that mix also pose a methodological problem for quantitative risk assessment. Possible effects when pollutants mix include "additivity," "synergism," and "antagonism." "Additivity," the simplest effect, occurs when chemicals or pollutants mix and result in an exact combination of all the individual effects. "Synergists" are chemicals or pollutants that, when combined, result in a greater than additive effect. "Antagonism" occurs when the mixture results in diminished toxicity....

The phenomenon of synergism may be widespread among pollutants. Approximately 5% of chemicals exhibit effects that are more or less than additive. Although this percentage may seem relatively small, because there are so many chemicals, synergistic possibilities are huge. For example, if there were 12,000 chemicals in commerce today, and 2.5% reacted synergistically, almost 1.8 million pairs of chemicals would act synergistically.

Despite the propensity for chemicals to react synergistically and increase in toxicity, risk assessments rarely take synergism into account....

*A 70 kg, White Male Complex*

... There is a high degree of variability in the response of humans to different levels of pollution. Age, lifestyle, genetic background, sex, ethnicity, and race may all play an important role in enhancing the susceptibility of persons to environmentally related disease. Studies have shown human variability of more than 1,000-fold in drug metabolism and between 3 and 150-fold in the carcinogenic metabolism of various chemicals.

Variability in susceptibility may not only be large, but also widespread. Five percent of humans may be as much as twenty-five times less or more susceptible to cancer than the average person; one percent may be more than 100 times more susceptible....

The National Academy of Sciences found that interindividual variability is not generally considered in the EPA's cancer risk assessment.... The default assumption usually employed in a risk assessment is that humans on average have the same susceptibility as persons in epidemiologic studies or as the most sensitive of the few animal species tested. Most epidemiology studies used in risk assessments are based on studies of healthy white male workers.... [C]ertain genetic traits that increase susceptibility to environmental pollutants are more prevalent in racial minorities. In addition, biological differences may make certain diseases such as hypertension, chronic liver disease, chronic respiratory disease, and sickle-cell anemia more prevalent among minority populations and increase their risk of adverse outcomes to environmental exposures.

Lifestyle and socio-demographic factors also place minority populations at higher risk. Alcohol, tobacco, and drug use are more frequent in minority populations and result in impaired respiratory, cardiovascular, and metabolic processes, and in reduced ability to metabolize or eliminate toxic substances. Most minority populations also have a higher proportion of young persons and women of childbearing age. Because fetuses, neonates, infants, children, and pregnant women are more susceptible to the adverse effects of pollution, minority groups are more severely impacted by pollution because a higher proportion of these susceptible individuals are found in minority populations. Inadequate diets due to poverty and high-risk diets due to cultural or historical reasons also may be more prevalent in minority communities and increase susceptibility; lack of access to health care or poorer quality care may increase the adverse effects of environmental exposures on poorer minority and ethnic communities....

[R]isk assessment most accurately portrays the risks of a particular subgroup— the healthy, seventy-kilogram, white male. Risk assessments use a seventy-kilogram male with the general biology of a Caucasian, as a so-called reference man, in developing dose-response predictions and assume that this reference man is an appropriate surrogate for minorities, as well as women and children. In addition, the dose-response models used to extrapolate from high-dose animal studies to lower-dose human exposures are based on the assumption that the exposed population is of uniform susceptibility. The result of relying on this reference man is a risk assessment characterization that fits far less than half the nation's population, because the majority are women, children, the elderly, sick, or people of color....

* * *

Law professors Cary Coglianese and Gary Marchant theorize "four basic approaches" that agencies such as the EPA may adopt for greater consistency in risk management decisions. As you read the following article, consider the apparent virtues as well as the political and physical limitations to each theoretical approach.

## Cary Coglianese & Gary E. Marchant, *Shifting Sands: The Limits of Science in Setting Risk Standards*

152 University of Pennsylvania L. Rev.<br>1255, 1325–40 (2004)

Regulatory decisions, such as the selection of air quality standards, involve enormous stakes in terms of both health consequences and economic burdens. How can EPA provide a more coherent justification for these significant decisions than it offered in its most recent NAAQS revisions? A regulatory agency such as EPA has four basic approaches available that it can use to provide a consistent justification for making risk management decisions such as setting ambient standards: (1) eliminate all risks (or all nonnaturally occurring risks); (2) avoid unacceptable risks; (3) avoid unacceptable costs (sometimes described as the feasibility approach); and (4) balance costs and benefits. Although these approaches are not all equally sound strategies—nor are they all currently permissible under the Supreme Court's interpretation of the Clean Air Act—they do illustrate the range of possible ways to provide a consistent explanation for risk management decision making.

### Eliminate All Risks

The first approach is conceptually straightforward: eliminate all risks. This principle could be consistently applied if EPA set its standards at levels at which it believed there would be absolutely no health risks. The Agency also could take a consistent risk management approach if it chose to minimize risk by setting standards at background levels, thereby opting to eliminate all risks except those that are naturally occurring (a zero additive risk approach).

More generally, the EPA could decide to follow an approach aimed at minimizing all risk. A minimize risk approach could in some cases lead to a nonzero risk level if a pollutant provides some beneficial health effects that countervail its adverse health effects. For example, commentators in the ozone rulemaking alleged that, despite the adverse pulmonary effects of ground level ozone, concentrations of the pollutant also screen out harmful ultraviolet radiation. If a reduction of the pollutant would create offsetting risks, such as an increase in skin cancer, then a standard that minimizes health risks would be set above zero. In cases with such so-called risk-risk tradeoffs, EPA could opt for a standard set at a level that achieves the lowest possible adverse health effects, namely the level at which the marginal adverse health effects equal the marginal beneficial health effects....

*Avoid Unacceptable Risks*

A second approach would be for the Agency to establish a level of acceptable risk for its air quality standards. Rather than minimizing all risks, the Agency would only reduce risks to a consistent and tolerable level. As with the minimize risk principle, the acceptable risk approach focuses exclusively on the benefits to be reaped from a risk standard. It does not try to maximize those benefits, but simply to deliver a desirable level of health benefits.

The acceptable risk approach has been used in other regulatory contexts. For example, in setting standards for hazardous air pollutants, EPA has presumptively defined "acceptable risk" to mean a maximum individual mortality risk of no greater than one in ten thousand. The Agency has similarly set acceptable risk targets in other contexts, including the regulation of water quality, hazardous wastes, and pesticides. The Occupational Safety and Health Administration (OSHA) follows a similar approach, using a benchmark mortality risk of one in one thousand as the level of "significant risk" on which it bases its occupational health standards....

The problem with relying only on levels of risk to individuals, of course, is that it overlooks the number of people exposed to the risk, something that clearly affects overall health benefits.

If EPA were to measure and compare the overall benefits of different regulatory alternatives, it would need to use consistent methods to quantify all the benefits that it predicted from each proposed standard and its alternatives. Such a careful "benefits analysis," as Professor Cass Sunstein has called it, would enable the Agency to determine whether any given regulatory option can be expected to achieve an acceptable level of risk. A benefits analysis would detail all the health effects associated with different levels of exposure as well as report the predicted incidence of these effects on all exposed individuals, including those in any sensitive subgroups within the overall population. Such a benefits analysis would contain EPA's best range (or point) of estimates for the number of people likely to be exposed to the pollutant under an alternative standard, the probabilities that they will suffer various health effects, and the severity of those effects. These benefits could be monetized using willingness-to-pay (WTP) measures, a standard way of aggregating different kinds of environmental health effects across an entire population.

...

*Avoid Unacceptable Costs*

A third approach to consistent risk management is the mirror image of the acceptable risk approach. Instead of focusing exclusively on benefits, the cost of a regulation should be the key factor. In other words, EPA could set its standards as low as possible while keeping the costs of compliance below an acceptable level.

This approach typically has been couched in terms of feasibility—what can be achieved without high costs or severe economic disruptions. Saying that a standard is feasible implies that its costs are acceptable. For example, OSHA is charged by statute with developing regulations to protect workers from exposure to toxic substances "to the extent feasible." Of course, just stating that a regulatory standard is "feasible" or "infeasible" is rather imprecise. However, just as agencies have defined the concept of acceptable risk by setting specific risk targets, they could similarly develop precise standards establishing acceptable levels of costs and then reduce risk to the point at which compliance costs reached the specified level.

Such an approach, it should be noted, would disregard the benefits of risk standards. If a standard with exceedingly high costs (or that would cause severe economic disruption) would also save thousands of lives, then society almost certainly would be better off even if the costs might seem unacceptably high. For example, government regulations eliminating lead from gasoline resulted in hundreds of millions of dollars in annual costs and appeared to threaten not only layoffs in the industrial firms that produced lead additives but also gasoline shortages during the transition to unleaded fuels. Nevertheless, these regulations also resulted in dramatic health benefits that substantially dwarfed the costs. If regulatory agencies had adhered to an approach that avoided all regulations that imposed costs exceeding a specified level or threatened economic dislocation, without any concern for the level of corresponding benefits, they may well have delayed or avoided phasing out lead additives in gasoline.

When regulatory agencies justify their risk management decisions based only on either costs or benefits, they can achieve consistent, principled decision making simply by using the same level of acceptable costs or risks across different rulemakings. Nevertheless, all the approaches we have discussed so far truncate the range of risk management criteria and may therefore lead regulatory agencies, in some cases, to make decisions that make little sense, even though they are consistent. Under the acceptable risk approach, however, agencies can affirm standards that impose significant costs without proportional health protection gains. Under the acceptable cost approach, agencies can reject opportunities to achieve significant net social benefits simply because costs are high.

*Balance Costs and Benefits*

With precisely these kinds of perverse outcomes in mind, a fourth approach for risk management would take both benefits and costs into consideration and seek to achieve a consistent balance of the two. By considering both costs and benefits, regulators could set risk management standards to maximize net benefits. Several environmental statutes other than the Clean Air Act actually require agencies to balance benefits and costs when they are setting risk standards. Indeed, absent statutory prohibitions to the contrary (such as now in the Clean Air Act), regulatory agencies are directed by Executive Order No. 12,866 to assess both costs and benefits of significant proposed regulations and to "propose or adopt a [new] regulation only upon a reasoned determination that the benefits of the intended regulation justify its costs."

Of course, in practice, there will be important issues regarding measurement, valuation, and discount rates that must be treated consistently. But this is true for any other approach to risk management decision making, and regulators have developed guidelines for approaching these operational issues in consistent ways. When conducted responsibly, cost-benefit analysis can prove quite valuable in explaining regulatory agencies' decision making. It offers a consistent and systematic approach to risk management.

What is most striking is that EPA has not only rejected a cost-benefit approach but also all of the other general policy principles for risk management. It has explicitly ruled out zero-risk and acceptable-risk approaches, and it has successfully argued that the Clean Air Act precludes it from adopting a feasibility or cost-benefit balancing approach. Instead, EPA has taken an explicitly ad hoc approach.

Given this predicament, it is by no means surprising that the EPA's account of its recent NAAQS decisions has been so inconsistent. At the core of EPA's position lies a fundamental inconsistency: The Agency rejects any need to achieve a level of zero risk, but the reason to reject a zero-risk approach is its complete infeasibility. Thus, an important step toward achieving a more principled and consistent account of EPA's air quality standard would be to free the Agency from its conceptual straitjacket.

\* \* \*

## Notes and Questions

1. **Transparency.** Professor Kuehn, noting that "some form of risk assessment is not just here to stay, but … is likely to increase in use," advances numerous suggestions for reforming the risk assessment process. For example, he proposes that distributional information (the demographic characteristics of the populations at risk) and information on multiple and cumulative exposures be included in all risk assessments. Another suggestion is to provide for meaningful public participation at all stages of the risk assessment process, including its design, data collection, and analysis. He also recommends that risk assessors should inform the public about the pervasive uncertainties underlying the risk assessment process, suggesting that "[w]hen these unknown factors and assumptions are revealed, the public may see the lack of confidence in the estimates and may well question the reliability and relevance of risk assessment in resolving questions about environmental exposures." *Id.* at 150–153, 158–166. The latter suggestion is essentially a call for greater transparency in the risk assessment enterprise.

2. **Susceptibility.** Among the issues that Professor Kuehn raises are those stemming from variability in *susceptibility*. As he explains, two people may be exposed to the same amount of a contaminant in the environment, for the same period of time, yet have markedly different responses. These differences in susceptibility may stem from a variety of factors, including gender, lifestage, and genetic predisposition.

For example, because lead is a neurodevelopmental toxin, humans are more susceptible to this adverse effect during periods of neurological development, i.e., from prenatal through childhood lifestages. As such, the infants and children exposed to lead contamination in the drinking water in Flint may be at much greater risk of injury than adults whose brains and neurological systems are fully formed.

**3. Exposure.** Variability in *exposure* has also emerged as a basis for criticism of risk assessment from the perspective of environmental justice. A group or subpopulation may be more vulnerable to a given level of environmental contamination because its members' circumstances and lifeways leave them more exposed to the contaminants than members of the general population. These people might live nearer to the fenceline of industrial facilities that emit multiple toxic air pollutants; they might live in older, deteriorated housing that harbors lead dust; they might depend to a greater extent on fish that has become contaminated with PCBs and other pollutants. The National Environmental Justice Advisory Council (NEJAC), an advisory body to the EPA representing multiple stakeholders and convened under the auspices of the Federal Advisory Committee Act, discusses the issue of urgent water infrastructure needs in the following excerpt. *See* Chapter 6 ("Environmental Permits").

* * *

## National Environmental Justice Advisory Council, *EPA's Role in Addressing the Urgent Water Infrastructure Needs of Environmental Justice*
17–20 (2018)

Goal 2: REQUEST CONGRESS TO ALLOCATE MORE FUNDING TO HELP COMMUNITIES WITH INFRASTRUCTURE BUILDING AND PUBLIC HEALTH PROTECTION.

**Across the United States, communities are struggling to keep clean, safe water flowing to the tap and to safely dispose of wastewater.** These struggles are directly tied to the fact that we, as a nation, have not made significant investments in our water infrastructure since the 1970s when Congress passed the Clean Water Act and the Safe Drinking Water Act. Over the last few decades, Congress has slashed federal funding that helps states pay for water infrastructure maintenance and upgrades. Faced with a myriad of other pressing issues, water utilities and states are failing to set aside enough money for drinking water infrastructure, sewer repairs, and upgrades. The lack of available federal funds for infrastructure means municipalities have deferred upgrades, which in turn has increased the risk of water line breaks and sewage overflows. Deferring critical maintenance increases the risk of catastrophic failure of water infrastructure for millions of Americans.

When deferring maintenance results in infrastructure failures, the utility will have to raise water rates to pay for required maintenance, repairs, and replacement. But those increased water rates are making basic water and wastewater service unaffordable for low-income communities across the country. Small, unincorporated com-

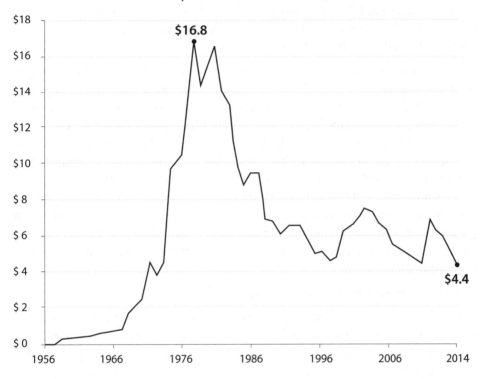

**Federal spending on water and wastewater utility infrastructure decreased in the 1980s and after 2000**

Reported in billions of dollars

**Figure 3-3:** Public Spending on Transportation and Water Infrastructure, 1956 to 2014. Source: Congressional Budget Office (March 2015).

munities, orphaned systems, and those serving vulnerable, impoverished populations require urgent attention. These communities do not have adequate resources to repair and replace infrastructure, or to build new systems. Some rural communities have not had working septic systems despite decades of pleas for help. Nearly every community across the U.S. needs sufficient funding, along with well-trained staff, to provide safe drinking water and manage sewage. Doing so helps protect public health and the environment. Yet, EPA has documented enormous national needs for investment in water infrastructure. National reports have documented long-time problems with lead service lines in communities such as Washington, D.C. and in New Jersey that have had significant consequences. The agency's most recent nationwide surveys of local governments and utilities conservatively estimated approximately $473 billion needs to be invested within the next twenty years to bring our nation's infrastructure up to environmental and public health standards. Strangely, this number is down from the estimated $660 billion 20-year investment need estimated in 2012, despite new concerns about lead in drinking water and other drinking water threats.

The American Water Works Association estimates it will cost over $1 trillion over the next 25 years to upgrade existing drinking water systems and expand them to meet our growing population. In 2010, EPA estimated the cost of capital investments required to maintain and upgrade nation-wide drinking-water and wastewater treatment systems at $91 billion but only $36 billion was funded, leaving a capital funding gap of nearly $55 billion. For 2017, EPA allotted just over $2 billion in loans for the Clean Water and Drinking Water State Revolving Funds.

These federal loans can be leveraged through the sale of tax-exempt bonds to generate additional funds that can be loaned to municipalities for eligible drinking water systems. While the state revolving loan funds are an asset to communities, some water utilities do not receive funding because they have poor credit or are considered a bond risk and/or they do not rank high on the Integrated Priority Ranking System compared to others who are applying. For example, a water utility that requires pipe replacement will rank much lower on the list than one who is in violation of a health-based standard. The Federal Rural Development Authority strongly suggests that states award parties that are able to repay the money back to the Fund. This pressure puts states in a bind to award funding to a party when most likely they will fold on their bond and/or funding, even though those communities might have the greatest need for financial support.

### Lack of expertise compounds the problem.

Small communities typically do not have well-paid, well-trained staff to run their wastewater systems. Competition can be strong for water and wastewater professionals, especially those with considerable experience and higher-level certifications. Small and economically disadvantaged communities are most in need of expert operators and managers, but frequently are least able to pay a full-time salary. These systems often rely too heavily on unpaid volunteers or part-time operators with limited technical knowledge, obscuring the system's true operating costs. Programs like the Rural Water Utilities' Circuit Rider program provides technical support for rural water operations experiencing day-to-day financial, operational, or management challenges. Rural water system officials may request assistance from the Rural Utilities Service, or Rural Utilities Service staff may request assistance on behalf of the system.

Additionally, many medium and large system operators are anticipating a significant loss of skilled, senior operators with many in transition for retirement and too few trainees in position to serve as a next generation of water and wastewater professionals. A lack of expertise and infrastructure management at all levels can lead to a costly and devastating public health crisis. For example, one cause of the Flint Water Crisis was Michigan Department of Environmental Quality (MDEQ) budget cuts and staffing changes. In Puerto Rico, Hurricane Maria decimated the island's drinking water infrastructure for more than nine months, leaving over 3.5 million residents without adequate potable water and sanitation. This U.S. territory resembles many rural regions on the mainland with small water systems that serve fewer than 10,000 people that oftentimes are locally owned and operated. Puerto Rico has approximately

300 of these small water utilities, and the residents who operate them also lost their homes, adding to the difficulty of rebuilding operations.

**Water-related public health problems require attention.**

Our nation's leading public health organizations, including the Centers for Disease Control and Prevention and the American Public Health Association, recognize lack of access to safe and clean water—either due to a non-existent or inadequate system or because water service has been shut off—as a serious public health concern.

Water shutoffs have become a common practice among water system operators to induce payment from delinquent customers. But this collections strategy fails to recognize or address the household and public health problems that are created when residents cannot properly hydrate, prepare meals or manage their personal hygiene for work or school. In Michigan, public health officials and the Department of Health and Human Services (DHHS) have issued daily alerts about Hepatitis A since its outbreak in August 2016. This highly contagious virus is fecal to oral transmitted and can be transferred by eating contaminated food or water. Vaccination and frequent hand washing are recommended to prevent the spread of Hepatitis A, yet there continues to be an elevated number of cases. Fears about its multi-county and long-standing occurrence have led to travel advisories by several U.S. state and Canadian travel bureaus.

Another cause for public health concern among older water systems is the anticipated end of life expectancy among many lead service lines and galvanized pipes across the country. Thousands of miles of water lines have reached their expiration for safety and strength as public officials and system operators grapple with how and when to remove and pay for much needed replacements. New and emerging Superfund clean-up sites overseen by the EPA add further imperative to protect surface and ground water supplies.

\* \* \*

## Notes and Questions

1. **Variable exposures.** How should variability in exposure be taken into account in assessing risk? What if agencies were simply to assess the risk to the maximally exposed individual and then establish regulatory protections accordingly? Are there drawbacks to this protective response to variability in exposure?

2. **Exaggerated risks?** While environmental justice advocates often fear that quantitative risk assessment will underestimate health risks in certain communities, risk assessment has also come under substantial criticism from those who believe that, as currently practiced by environmental agencies, risk assessment leads to overestimates of risk and, consequently, an overinvestment by society in regulations requiring risk reduction. Those who offer this perspective tend to be proponents of risk assessment and other quantitative methods of analysis (e.g., cost-benefit analysis). While supportive of risk assessment as a theoretical matter, they contend nonetheless that agencies' methods ought to be refined in several ways. Two influential sources espousing

this view are Cass R. Sunstein, RISK AND REASON: SAFETY, LAW, AND THE ENVIRON-MENT (2002); and Stephen Breyer, BREAKING THE VICIOUS CIRCLE: TOWARD EFFECTIVE RISK REGULATION (1993).

Among the arguments by those who fear overestimates of risk are two with particular import for environmental justice: arguments favoring the use of "central estimates" of risk and arguments favoring a focus on "population risk" in lieu of individual risk. First, critics have argued that environmental agencies inappropriately respond to both uncertainty and variability when they undertake a risk assessment, producing high-end estimates of risk. They cite the fact that EPA currently uses conservative responses to each instance of uncertainty, choosing, for example, an assumption about the mechanism of carcinogenesis that yields a much higher estimate of a chemical's potency than would competing assumptions. Additionally, they claim that EPA selects protective responses to each instance of variability, focusing on the highly exposed individuals represented by the 90th or 95th percentile of the distribution for the total population. While each of these assumptions might be plausible in isolation, they argue, taken together, they produce an effect of "cascading conservatism" such that the resulting estimate of risk is likely to be unrealistically high and to reflect no one's actual circumstances of exposure.

Justice Breyer, prior to his appointment to the U.S. Supreme Court, presented the following argument:

> EPA sometimes makes a strictly mechanical assumption that the individual is exposed to emissions at a point 200 meters from the factory, all day, every day, for 70 years. OSHA assumes a factory worker exposed 8 hours per day, 5 days a week, 50 weeks per year, for 45 years. Other agencies use such "conservative" assumptions as that householders spend 70 years in the same house (they spend 9, on average); that adults drink 2 liters of water per day (they drink 1.4 liters of all liquids); that half of all houses near toxic waste dumps contain children … and so forth.
>
> If an agency uses these assumptions when calculating the risks run by individuals who are *maximally* exposed, they may be realistic; if it uses them to estimate effects on typical workers or citizens across the nation, they may be unrealistically conservative; if it uses them as "presumptions"— asking industry to come forward with proof of the contrary—they may, in practice, come to resemble the latter use. OMB argues that the agencies apply these assumptions too conservatively; it concludes that, taken together, they "often" overstate risks by factors of a thousand or even a million or more.

Stephen Breyer, BREAKING THE VICIOUS CIRCLE: TOWARD EFFECTIVE RISK REGULATION (1993).

One solution, from the perspective of those who raise the argument advanced here by Justice Breyer, is for agencies to conduct risk assessments that focus on a central estimate of risk. This would counsel agencies to choose a "best" or "plausible" assumption in the face of uncertainty — as opposed to a conservative assumption — and to select a mean or average value from the distribution of values where there is variability.

**3. "Individual risk" vs. "population risk."** Critics have also argued that environmental agencies' focus on "individual risk" is misplaced, again leading to the over-regulation of risks and to a misallocation of resources toward risks to which very few people are actually exposed:

> EPA's rule for cleanups under the Superfund statute is ... risk-based: toxic waste dumps are to be remedied so that the lifetime fatality risk to the "maximally exposed individual" from carcinogens in the dump is within the range of 1 in 10,000 to 1 in 1 million.... What accounts for this regulatory focus on "individual risk"? One answer is tempting, but wrong. The temptation is to say that regulatory agencies inevitably take the maximal level of "individual risk" as the test of safety, at least for substances and activities that cannot be removed from our lives without massive cost.... How else to determine which toxic exposures merit a regulatory response except by setting an "individual risk" threshold which seems very low — say, 1 in 1 million to the maximally exposed individual — and taking that as the trigger for regulatory intervention? But this response overlooks a crucial deficit in "individual risk" tests of this kind: their insensitivity to population size. Compare an isolated toxic waste dump that (under worst-case modeling) leaches contaminants to a radius of ten miles, affecting a population of 10,000; a workplace toxin employed in certain industries, to which one million workers are exposed; and a chemical in drinking water that is consumed by 100 million. For simplicity, assume that in each case every person in the exposed population incurs a 1 in 1 million risk of dying from the hazard. Then in the waste-dump case it is overwhelmingly likely that the hazard will cause no fatalities; in the workplace case it is reasonably likely that the hazard will cause one or more fatalities, with one incremental death the expected outcome; and in the drinking water case it is overwhelmingly likely that the hazard will cause one or more fatalities, with 100 incremental deaths the expected outcome.

> Risk assessors typically distinguish between "individual risk" — the risk of death borne by a particular individual, either a named person or someone identified by her exposure characteristics — and "population risk." "Population risk" (also sometimes called "societal risk") is the total number of fatalities resulting from a toxin, a hazardous activity, or some other threat to human life....

> Whether regulators should intervene to abate some hazard depends, morally, on the number of persons at risk from the hazard.

Matthew D. Adler, *Against "Individual Risk": A Sympathetic Critique of Risk Assessment,* 153 U. PENN. L. REV. 1121, 1122–1132 (2005).

According to commentators such as Professor Adler, if regulatory agencies were to reform risk assessment as urged above, agency estimates of the risks that attend environmental contamination could decrease, and the case for regulating the sources of risk might, correspondingly, be weakened. Professors Jim Hamilton and Kip Viscusi conclude that their survey of EPA's assessment of the risks associated with 150 Superfund sites bears out this point. They argue that, due to "conservative biases" in EPA's method, "[e]ven though actual risk exposures are usually low, individual lifetime cancer rates estimated to arise at sites under EPA's risk assessment methodology are extremely high.... Many of these risk estimates drop to levels deemed acceptable in EPA's remediation guidelines, however, if one uses more realistic parameter values [i.e., central estimates] in the risk assessment process.... Our analysis reveals that once individual risk levels are combined with data on exposed populations, the magnitude of apparent cancer risks diminishes...." James T. Hamilton & W. Kip Viscusi, CALCULATING RISKS? THE SPATIAL AND POLITICAL DIMENSIONS OF HAZARDOUS WASTE POLICY 108 (1999).

What do Professors Hamilton and Viscusi mean by their statement that, if agencies combine individual risk levels with data on exposed populations, "the magnitude of *apparent* cancer risks diminishes"? Is the risk faced by an individual who in fact lives at the fenceline of a polluting factory for his entire life lessened by the fact that few others also live in the vicinity? Similarly, would a case where 10,000 residents of a city were poisoned by lead in their drinking water be diminished by 100,000 people in the same city who were not similarly poisoned? How should regulatory agencies frame the relevant questions?

## 3. Risks to Children

Risk assessment practices are beginning to take into account the disproportionate risks faced by children. Children are especially vulnerable to environmental hazards because their systems are still developing, because they eat proportionately more food, drink more fluids, and breathe more air than adults, and because their behavior patterns, such as playing close to the ground and hand-to-mouth activity, increase their exposure to hazards. In 1995, EPA adopted a policy requiring that the environmental health risks of children be evaluated in risk assessments. EPA also pledged that it would set new regulatory standards at levels protective enough to address the potentially heightened risks faced by children and that it would re-evaluate a number of existing regulations to see if they met this standard. In 1997, President Clinton issued an executive order requiring that each agency make it a high priority to identify and assess environmental health and safety risks that may disproportionately affect children, and ensure that its actions address these disproportionate risks. Protection of Children from Environmental Health Risks and Safety Risks, Exec. Order No. 13,045, 62 Fed. Reg. 19,885 (April 23, 1997). The 1996 Food Quality Protection Act also explicitly requires EPA to address the special risks to infants and children when setting pesticide tolerances, the levels of chemical pesticide residues permissible on foods. If EPA does not have complete or reliable data to assess risks to children or infants, it can require an additional tenfold safety factor. 21 U.S.C. § 346a(b)(2)(C). In 2008, EPA published a handbook setting forth the different factors that describe children's circumstances of exposure. U.S. Envtl. Prot. Agency, CHILD-SPECIFIC EXPOSURE FACTORS HANDBOOK (2008). While EPA had previously provided some guidance as to how risk assessors ought to account for children's unique circumstances, this was the first time in which EPA issued comprehensive guidance exclusively devoted to children. The following excerpt from a medical journal shows the risk of environmental injustice to children and the link to toxic environmental exposures.

## Philip J. Landrigan, Virginia A. Rauh & Maida P. Galvez, *Environmental Justice and the Health of Children*

MOUNT SINAI JOURNAL OF MEDICINE, 77:178–187 (2010)

Evidence has been building for 100 years that toxic exposures in the environment can cause and aggravate disease in children. This body of evidence has become especially compelling in the past 2 decades:

- Rates of asthma are increased in children exposed to second-hand cigarette smoke.
- Rates of asthma are increased in children exposed to particulate air pollution.
- Risk of sudden infant death syndrome is increased in babies exposed to particulate air pollution.
- Neurodevelopmental impairment with a reduced intelligence quotient (IQ), shortening of attention span, and disruption of behavior is increased in children exposed to lead.
- Neurodevelopmental impairment with a reduction of IQ is increased in children exposed to polychlorinated biphenyls.
- Neurodevelopmental impairment with a reduction of IQ and shortening of attention span is increased in children exposed prenatally to methyl mercury.
- Lower birth weight, smaller head circumference at birth, and subsequent developmental delays are increased in children exposed prenatally to the organophosphate pesticide chlorpyrifos.
- Neurodevelopmental impairment with a reduction of IQ and disruption of behavior is increased in children exposed prenatally to ethyl alcohol; this is called fetal alcohol syndrome.
- There is an increased risk of preterm birth associated with prenatal exposure to tobacco smoke and dichlorodiphenyltrichloroethane....

Disease of environmental origin is preventable. Disease caused by environmental degradation and environmental injustice is the result of human activity and is therefore preventable through modification or cessation of the activity that damages or pollutes the environment. To begin to address environmental injustice and its consequences for human health, we need solid evidence-based research on the long-term human health effects of exposure to a range of physical, chemical, and social exposures beginning before conception and continuing throughout childhood into adulthood....

In addition, we need to recognize that inequalities in exposures arise at both the community and individual levels, so efforts to redress these disparities cannot be limited to behavioral interventions. Broad societal efforts and a reordering of priorities are needed to redress social and structural conditions that result in unacceptably high levels of toxic exposure for whole populations. Protection of the vulnerable must become a moral and ethical beacon that guides decision making at all levels of government and business. An example of such enlightened decision making is to be found in the Food Quality Protection Act of 1996. This is [a] major federal pesticide law in the United States, and it is the only federal environmental statute that makes explicit provision for the protection of children's health in the setting of pesticide standards. As a result of environmental injustice, too many American children live their lives burdened by biological and social conditions that severely limit their potential for success. The effects on children are the cruelest consequences of environmental injustice.

Beyond childhood, the disproportionate exposure in early life of children in poor communities to environmental hazards sets the stage for a lifetime of suboptimal health and diminished achievement and thus helps to perpetuate the intergenerational cycle of disenfranchisement and poverty.

* * *

## Notes and Questions

1. "Cycle of disenfranchisement." In the excerpt above, the authors posit that early childhood exposures to toxic substances may help "perpetuate the intergenerational cycle of disenfranchisement and poverty." How would you understand this "cycle" to work? Using childhood exposure to lead as an example, how do the neurological impacts on children perpetuate poverty in poor, urban communities?

2. Moving targets. Dr. Philip Landrigan is one of the leading advocates for children's health, following landmark studies he conducted in the early 1970s demonstrating the effects of lead smelter emissions on children's health. The standard test for children exposed to lead involves drawing a blood sample and analyzing it for lead, with results reported in micrograms (one millionth of a gram) per deciliter (µg/dL) of blood. In 1971, the threshold for childhood lead poisoning in the United States was defined as 40 µg/dL. By 1991, due in part to the work of Dr. Landrigan, the U.S. threshold had fallen to 10 µg/dL. Today, we know there is no safe level of lead in children, with amounts even between 0 and 5 µg/dL showing significant impacts in cognitive development as measured by decrements in IQ. Bruce P. Lanphear, et al., *Low-Level Environmental Lead Exposure and Children's Intellectual Function: An International Pooled Analysis*, 113 ENVTL. HEALTH PERSP. 894 (2005). Given that the early defini-

tions of childhood lead poisoning proved very wrong, how should environmental justice advocates today approach supposed "safe" levels of exposure for any toxic substances? What should be the respective roles of science and policy so that a community will feel confident that their health is being protected?

# C. Cumulative Risk Assessment

Environmental justice advocates have long argued that risk assessment, as currently practiced, grossly understates the risks actually faced by those in tribes, communities of color, and low-income communities. This is so because agencies typically focus on a single chemical or source in isolation (for example, "a risk assessment for dioxin," or "an assessment of risk from TCE in the groundwater at a particular contaminated site"). But, as affected communities have pointed out, people are not exposed to only one chemical contaminant; rather, they are often exposed to multiple chemicals present in their environment. To the extent that agencies account for the cumulative effects of these multiple exposures, as noted above, they tend to treat the consequences as merely additive. However, as noted by Professor Kuehn, there are often synergistic interactions among the various chemicals to which humans are exposed, such that the actual consequences are multiplicative—as Professor Kuehn puts it: "1 + 1 does not always equal 2." While this failure to account for cumulative exposures and synergistic effects is a shortcoming of risk assessment that affects all those at risk, its import is amplified for environmental justice communities, who are often among the most exposed to the mixtures of chemical contaminants present in their environments—the urban toxic soup or the rural pesticide slurry.

Moreover, environmental justice advocates have pointed out, agencies' narrow focus on chemical stressors fails to account for the fact that the actual health consequences for those exposed can only be understood if one accounts for the complete roster of contributing stressors that affect human health. Thus, the same amount of a contaminant present in the environment can result in widely differing health consequences for members of two different communities or subpopulations, depending on the extent to which these other non-chemical (e.g., physical, social, cultural) stressors are also present. Environmental justice communities are often historically overburdened with contamination, disadvantaged in terms of services that would permit members to withstand or recover from environmental insults, and isolated or lacking in political influence. Agencies' failure to account for multiple stressors in their assessments of risk, therefore, is likely again to lead to especially large understatements of risk to these communities.

Wilma Subra, a chemist and environmental justice activist with the Louisiana Environmental Action Network, developed a matrix of the myriad factors that are relevant to a complete understanding of the risk faced by those in the Mississippi River Industrial Corridor—also known as "Cancer Alley"—the 2,000 square-mile area between Baton Rouge and New Orleans, Louisiana.

Environmental agencies, for their part, have long been aware of the limitations of risk assessment's chemical-by-chemical approach. EPA nonetheless continues to employ the "additivity assumption" to address cumulative risks because, in most cases, EPA simply does not have the scientific data on which to base more accurate assessments of the risk from simultaneous or sequential exposure to multiple chemical or other agents. Still, prompted by a variety of sources (e.g., criticism from scientific advisory boards and the public; statutory requirements, such as the Food Quality Protection Act of 1996) and enabled by developments in research, the EPA has made strides in accounting for cumulative risk. In 2003, the EPA published its *Framework for Cumulative Risk Assessment*, which sets forth the principles and features of cumulative risk assessment. The *Framework* remains somewhat aspirational, however, given that it sets forth a process that relies on methods and data that may not currently exist. Michael A. Callahan & Ken Sexton, *If Cumulative Risk Assessment Is the Answer, What Is the Question?*, 115 ENVTL. HEALTH PERSP. 799 (2007).

The National Environmental Justice Advisory Council applauded the EPA's *Framework* as an important advance in addressing environmental justice advocates' concerns. The NEJAC cited with approval the *Framework*'s adoption of the term "vulnerability," which usefully clarified the terms of the discussion (concerns in this regard had sometimes been discussed by reference to "co-risk" factors or other terms). As well, the *Framework*'s process envisioned a different orientation to the problem — one that situates risk assessment in context and envisions a more prominent role for the affected community.

## National Environmental Justice Advisory Council, *Ensuring Risk Reduction in Communities with Multiple Stressors: Environmental Justice and Cumulative Risks/Impacts*

(2004)

*Vulnerability*

The concept of vulnerability goes to the heart of the meaning of environmental justice. Vulnerability recognizes that disadvantaged, underserved, and overburdened communities come to the table with pre-existing deficits of both a physical and social nature that make the effects of environmental pollution more, and in some cases unacceptably, burdensome. As such, the concept of vulnerability fundamentally differentiates disadvantaged, underserved, and overburdened communities from healthy and sustainable communities. Moreover, it provides the added dimension of considering the nature of the receptor population when defining disproportionate risks or impacts.

The *Framework* includes a definition of vulnerability that can serve as a starting point for discussing this concept. According to the *Framework*, a subpopulation is vulnerable if it is more likely to be adversely affected by a stressor than the general population. There are four basic ways in which a population can be vulnerable: susceptibility/sensitivity, differential exposure, differential preparedness, and differential ability to recover. Each of these types of vulnerabilities is discussed below.

*Susceptibility/Sensitivity:* A subpopulation may be susceptible or sensitive to a stressor if it faces an increased likelihood of sustaining an adverse effect due to a life state (e.g., pregnant, young, old), an impaired immune system, or a pre-existing condition, such as asthma. A subpopulation could have been previously sensitized to a compound, or have prior disease or damage. In some cases, susceptibility also could arise because of genetic polymorphisms, which are genetic differences in a portion of a population. For example, a community with a large subpopulation of young children could be more susceptible to the effects of lead poisoning. A community with many elderly residents could be more vulnerable to a stressor such as a heat wave. And a community with a high number of asthmatics will be more susceptible to air pollution. The environmental justice implications of this phenomenon are significant. For example, given the fact that children are considered to be a highly susceptible subpopulation, then children in low-income and people of color communities must be considered an even more susceptible group within that subpopulation.

*Differential Exposure:* A subpopulation can be more vulnerable because it is living or working near a source of pollution and is therefore exposed to a higher level of the pollutant than the general population. Children living in older, deteriorated housing are more likely to receive greater exposure to lead paint dust, and their breathing zone is closer to the ground where such dust is more likely to be found. Communities situated close to the fence line of a facility that is emitting air pollutants, or living near a major roadway, will most likely experience higher levels of air pollution. Due to contaminated fish or wildlife, subpopulations, such as Native Americans, that are dependent on subsistence consumption represent another example of differential exposure.

In reviewing differential exposure, it is important to take into consideration what is sometimes referred to as background exposure or historical exposure. It is particularly important to recognize historical exposures in communities and tribes suffering environmental injustice. In some cases, community members were exposed to pollutants for many years in the past from facilities that are no longer functioning or in business. These past exposures could act to increase the body burden of a subpopulation so that vulnerable individuals start off at a higher dose....

*Differential Preparedness:* Differential preparedness refers to subpopulations which are less able to withstand an environmental insult. This is linked to what kind of coping systems an individual, population, or community has: the more prepared, the less vulnerable. Examples of lessened ability to withstand insult include lack of actions to prepare for a stressor (vaccination, for example, to ward off disease) or poor access to preventive health care (which has the potential to improve community response to stressors). Poverty, poor nutrition, or psycho-social stress may affect the strength of one's coping system. Preparedness against many stressors also can depend on the general state of social and cultural health of a subpopulation.... [P]reparedness in [American Indian] communities often will be linked directly to the balance between emotional, physical, spiritual, and mental health.

*Differential Ability to Recover:* Differential preparedness and differential ability to recover are closely related categories of vulnerability. Some subpopulations are more able to recover from an insult or stressor because they have more information about environmental risks, health, and disease; ready access to better medical and health care; early diagnosis of disease; or better nutrition.

Clearly, social factors, including but not limited to income, employment status, access to insurance, discrimination in the health care system, language ability, and the existence of social capital, can play an important role in determining the ability to prevent, withstand, or recover from environmental insults. Last, isolation, whether economic, racial, linguistic, or otherwise, leads to fewer connections, less access to information or influence, and, thus, less ability to prevent, withstand, or recover from environmental stressors. Indices which measure such isolation, such as dissimilarity indexes, may be useful in this area. Once again, this may point to the relationship of health disparities to all four categories of vulnerability....

[More generally, the EPA's *Framework*] is key to ensuring the goal of environmental justice for all communities because of the following features:

 • *It takes a broad view of risk.* The *Framework* explicitly states that the formulation of risk can include areas outside EPA's regulatory authority, and poses questions for which a quantitative method or answer does not yet exist.

 • *It utilizes a population-based and place-based analysis.* Conventional human health risk assessments usually focus on the source or stressor ("a risk assessment for benzene, an industrial plant, etc.") and follow the stressor to various populations affected. Cumulative risk assessment, like many ecological assessments, will be done with the focus on a population or place, and consideration of various stressors affecting them ("a cumulative risk assessment for a community, etc.").

 • *It promotes a comprehensive and integrated assessment of risk.* Although combining human health and ecological concerns has been a challenge for risk assessors for decades, the possible interaction between ecological and health risks makes this even more important in cumulative assessments than it has been in conventional risk assessment.

 • *It involves multiple stressors (chemical and non-chemical).* While past risk assessments have often addressed a number of chemical stressors individually, the *Framework for Cumulative Risk Assessment* requires the consideration of how these multiple stressors act together. It also discusses broadly considering not only chemical stressors, but also other stressors such as biological, physical, or even cultural, and how they affect the cumulative risk.

 • *It posits an expanded definition of vulnerability to include biological and social factors.* Using the definition of vulnerability from the *Framework*, "vulnerability" is broader than just another word for biological susceptibility or sensitivity. The *Framework* adopts a social science view of vulnerability which allows consideration of any number of types of stressors that result in a widely different effect for two populations who suffer the same intensity of insult.

• *It places a premium on community involvements and partnerships.* Cumulative risk assessment will largely play out geographically or in population-based settings. Because of this, the *Framework* puts heavy emphasis on making use of local expertise of various sorts available within the areas studied.

• *It emphasizes the importance of planning, scoping, and problem-formulation.* Cumulative risk assessment has the potential to be much more complex than conventional risk assessment. It is essential that the questions to be answered be clearly identified and articulated, and that the participants have clear agreement on what is to be done and the limitations of the potential results of the assessments.

• *It links risk assessment to risk management within the context of community health goals.* Because of its potentially broad scope, including many different types of stressors, cumulative risk assessment has a high potential for bringing attention to a variety of sources of risk. Managing these risks may require a wide variety of approaches (not all regulatory) discussed jointly among the participants.

*  *  *

## *Notes and Questions*

1. Although the NEJAC was generally supportive of the EPA's *Framework*, it nonetheless flagged some concerns:

> As important an advance as the Agency's Cumulative Risk Framework is, the NEJAC Work Group fears that … it can be used to slow down progress if it causes analysis of risk to be more complicated and time consuming in order to reach the answers needed for action to take place. In fact, the increased complexity can easily become an excuse for never taking action.

*Id.* at 16. In light of this concern—and given the considerable gaps in the data needed to conduct a cumulative risk assessment in most cases—how would you advise a community seeking cleanup of a nearby contaminated site (say a stretch of river contaminated with mercury and PCBs, or an aquifer contaminated with TCE) to proceed? Should they seek a full-blown cumulative risk assessment or should they advocate a more traditional quantitative risk assessment? Are there other approaches beyond this "either/or" formulation?

2. Does the NEJAC understand the terms "population-based analysis" to have the same meaning as the "population-based assessment" of risk advocated by Professors Adler, Hamilton, and Viscusi, above?

3. According to those familiar with the process, one of the major ways in which EPA's *Framework* differs from the traditional human health risk assessment is that "cumulative risk assessment does not necessarily have to be quantitative; a qualitative

analysis may be appropriate depending on the circumstances." Callahan & Sexton, *supra*, at 801. What challenges do you anticipate in those instances in which a cumulative risk assessment produces a qualitative description of the risk posed, when the outcome of a traditional risk assessment is ordinarily a quantitative assessment? Keep this question in mind when you consider the materials in Chapter 5 ("Standard Setting"), which discusses how agencies use the results of a risk assessment as an input into the equation that determines the numerical standards for, e.g., quantities of pollutants emitted to the air or released to the water or allowed to remain in the soil.

# Chapter 4

# Constitutional and Civil Rights Claims

## A. Introduction

With roots in the civil rights movement, it seems natural that the environmental justice movement would seek remedies from legal authorities such as the U.S. Constitution and the Civil Rights Act of 1964. Such authorities, however, have rarely succeeded in delivering judicial victories to plaintiffs seeking environmental justice (EJ). So far, there is nothing like a *Brown v. Board of Education* for environmental justice plaintiffs. To this day, the EPA has never made a formal finding of discrimination under Civil Rights Act Title VI that led to denying or withdrawing financial assistance to a funding recipient. The reasons why the EPA has been so "spectacularly unsuccessful" with enforcing Title VI are varied and examined thoroughly in Marianne Engelman Lado, *No More Excuses: Building a New Vision of Civil Rights Enforcement in the Context of Environmental Justice*, 22 U. PENN. J. L. & SOC. CHANGE 281 (2019) (attributing failures, in part, to EPA theories of exceptionalism and lack of political will). Nevertheless, the U.S. Constitution, including the Equal Protection Clause of the Fourteenth Amendment, and civil rights legislation, including § 1983 and Title VI of the Civil Rights Act, remain important authorities for seeking to advance the cause of environmental justice, providing bases for legal action as well as leverage for negotiation.

This chapter reviews efforts by impacted communities to use constitutional and civil rights remedies to address environmental harms. Part B addresses why EJ advocates should consider constitutional or civil rights claims at all, given many other alternatives, including citizen suits under the various environmental statutes (*see* Chapter 13). Part C examines claims under the Equal Protection Clause of the U.S. Constitution. Part D focuses on enforcement of the Civil Rights Act Title VI. Finally, Part E will take a quick look at § 1983, through the lens of a case responding directly to the drinking water contamination in Flint, Michigan.

*Pathfinder on Constitutional and Civil Rights Claims for Environmental Justice*

In addition to the articles discussed in this chapter, the following is a selected group of materials that discuss constitutional rights or civil rights legislation in the environmental justice context: Mehmet K. Konar-Steenburg, *Root and Branch: The*

*Thirteenth Amendment and Environmental Justice*, 19 Nevada L.J. 509 (2018); David A. Dana & Deborah Tuerkheimer, *After Flint: Environmental Justice as Equal Protection*, 111 Nw. U. L. Rev. 879 (2017); Claire Glenn, *Upholding Civil Rights in Environmental Law: The Case for Ex Ante Title VI Regulation and Enforcement*, 41 N.Y.U. Rev. L. & Soc. Change 5 (2017); Daria E. Neal, *Recent Developments in Federal Implementation of Executive Order 12898 and Title VI of the Civil Rights Act of 1964*, 57 Howard L.J. 941 (2014); Tony LoPresti, *Realizing the Promise of Environmental Civil Rights: The Renewed Effort to Enforce Title VI of the Civil Rights Act of 1964*, 65 Admin. L. Rev. 757 (2013); Elizabeth Ann Kronk, *Application of Title VI in Indian Country: The Key Is Tribal Sovereignty*, 6 Fla. A & M U. L. Rev. 215 (2011); Carlton Waterhouse, *Abandon All Hope Ye That Enter? Equal Protection, Title VI, and the Divine Comedy of Environmental Justice*, 20 Fordham Envtl. L. Rev. 51 (2009); Philip Weinberg, *Equal Protection*, and Bradford C. Mank, *Title VI, in* The Law of Environmental Justice: Theories and Procedures to Address Disproportionate Risks (Michael B. Gerrard & Sheila R. Foster eds., 2d ed. 2008); Robert J. Klee, *What's Good for School Finance Should Be Good for Environmental Justice: Addressing Disparate Environmental Impacts Using State Courts and Constitutions*, 30 Columbia J. Envtl. L. 135 (2005); Kyle W. La Londe, *Who Wants to Be an Environmental Justice Advocate?: Options for Bringing an Environmental Justice Complaint in the Wake of* Alexander v. Sandoval, 31 B.C. Envtl. Aff. L. Rev. 27 (2004); Scott Michael Edson, *Title VI or Bust? A Practical Evaluation of Title VI of the 1964 Civil Rights Act as an Environmental Justice Remedy*, 16 Fordham Envtl. L. Rev. 141 (2004); Sten-Erik Hoidal, *Returning to the Roots of Environmental Justice: Lessons from the Inequitable Distribution of Municipal Services*, 88 Minn. L. Rev. 193 (2003); Tseming Yang, *The Form and Substance of Environmental Justice: The Challenge of Title VI of the Civil Rights Act of 1964 for Environmental Regulation*, 29 B.C. Envtl. Aff. L. Rev. 143 (2002); Bradford C. Mank, South Camden Citizens in Action v. New Jersey Department of Environmental Protection: *Will Section 1983 Save Title VI Disparate Impact Suits?*, 32 Envtl. L. Rep. 10,454 (2002); Alice M. Shanahan, *Permitting Justice: EPA's Revised Guidance for Investigating Title VI Administrative Complaints*, 7 Envtl. Law. 403 (2001); Jill E. Evans, *Challenging the Racism in Environmental Racism: Redefining the Concept of Intent*, 40 Ariz. L. Rev. 1219 (1998); Rodolfo Mata, Comment, *Inequitable Siting of Undesirable Facilities and the Myth of Equal Protection*, 13 B.C. Third World L.J. 233 (1993); Richard J. Lazarus, *Pursuing "Environmental Justice": The Distributional Effects of Environmental Protection*, 87 Nw. U. L. Rev. 787, 834–842 (1993); and Robert W. Collin, *Environmental Equity: A Law and Planning Approach to Environmental Racism*, 11 Va. Envtl. L. J. 495 (1992). *See also* U.S. Comm. on Civil Rights, Environmental Justice: Examining the Environmental Protection Agency's Compliance and Enforcement of Title VI and Executive Order 12898 (Sept. 2016); U.S. Comm. on Civil Rights, Not in My Backyard: Executive Order 12898 and Title VI as Tools for Achieving Environmental Justice (Oct. 2003); Nat'l Advisory Council for Envtl. Pol'y & Tech., Report of the Title VI Implementation Advisory Committee: Next Steps for EPA, State, and Local Environmental Justice Programs (1999).

# B. Constitutional and Civil Rights Claims for Environmental Injustice

Students and practitioners of environmental law understand that the United States (like most countries now) has a robust set of environmental statutes protecting the air we breathe, the water we drink, and the land where we live, learn, work, play, and pray. With all of these laws, and implementing regulations that fill linear feet of shelf space, one might naturally wonder why environmental justice advocates would consider bringing claims under constitutional provisions or civil rights litigation, given the extraordinary hurdles some of these alternatives may present. For one compelling response to this question, consider the following excerpt:

## Marianne Engelman Lado, *No More Excuses: Building a New Vision of Civil Rights Enforcement in the Context of Environmental Justice*

22 U. Pennsylvania J. Law & Social Change
281, 291–294 (2019)

... Over time, EPA has struggled with the question whether environmental health standards under the Clean Air Act or other environmental laws are sufficiently protective of human health as to serve as a defense to a claim that a permit for a polluting facility has an adverse impact on the basis of race or ethnicity. If a recipient is not violating an environmental health standard set by EPA, how can EPA find that its action has an adverse impact? Isn't stronger environmental enforcement across the board sufficient? Don't environmental laws guarantee clean water, clean air? Does civil rights enforcement just distract from the goal of EPA, "to protect human health and the environment"?

The argument that civil rights enforcement is not necessary or, worse, is a distraction of needed resources, relies on a belief that if fully implemented and enforced, environmental laws are sufficiently protective. Most broadly, though, environmental laws have failed to eliminate the adverse and disparate impacts on communities of color that Title VI and its implementing regulations seek to forbid. To use an analogy, many states have a constitutional obligation to provide all children with a thorough and effective or sound basic education. Yet in reality, state and local educational programs may reinforce rather than ameliorate, or perhaps just insufficiently mitigate inequality in education. We recognize that despite across-the-board responsibilities, inequalities on the basis of race and ethnicity in educational opportunities continue. Given the power of the argument that enforcement of environmental laws precludes the need for attention to civil rights in this context, this section will address the inadequacy of reliance on environmental laws as a means of ensuring racial equality and, particularly, achieving procedural and distributional justice in the environmental context....

[A]s in the educational context, significant gaps in environmental protection create the space for exacerbating racial inequalities in the distribution of environmental benefits and burdens, especially when layered on top of geographic patterns of racial segregation created by racially explicit federal, state, and local government policies. Significantly, environmental statutes, regulations, and standards are the outcome of political and administrative processes, which take into account statutory goals and an array of competing interests and criteria. The EPA has acknowledged that there is no safe exposure level for lead, for example: even small, discrete doses can cause adverse health impacts, particularly for children. Indeed, the EPA has identified a "broad range of adverse health effects" from lead emissions, including "damage to the central nervous system, cardiovascular function, kidneys, immune system, and red blood cells." Yet the National Ambient Air Quality Standard (NAAQS) for lead is not zero, and lack of evidence that emissions from a facility will violate the NAAQS standard does not mean that such emissions are safe, nor should it preclude a finding that a facility will have an adverse impact.

To examine the adequacy of environmental statutes in addressing racial disparities in exposure to sources of environmental pollution, it is worth returning to the complaint filed by groups in North Carolina against [the North Carolina Department of Environmental Quality (DEQ)] claiming that its decision to allow more than 2,100 hog facilities to operate on North Carolina's coastal plain has an unjustified disparate impact on the basis of race. Surely the alphabet soup of federal environmental laws, including the Clean Water Act (CWA), Resource Conservation and Recovery Act (RCRA), the National Environmental Policy Act (NEPA), the Endangered Species Act (ESA), the Clean Air Act (CAA), the Comprehensive Environmental Response, Compensation and Liability Act (CERCLA, otherwise known as the Superfund law), or the Emergency Planning and Community Right to Know Act (EPCRA), should provide ample protection, particularly when combined with state nuisance laws. Without delving into the inadequacies of each of these laws as applied to the disproportionate impact of the inordinate amount of swine waste on communities of color in eastern North Carolina, a few observations are in order. For years before filing their complaint, residents of the region complained to DEQ that the high concentration of swine facilities generated staggering quantities of feces and urine, which are stored in open-air cesspools, called lagoons, and sprayed on fields with high volume spreaders. Residents can live within three miles of upwards of ten facilities and, thus, ten such cesspools for facilities with 2,000 pigs or more.

Residents attest that the stench can be unbearable, and numerous studies over time have documented the adverse impacts of the industry on air and water. The Clean Water Act prohibits discharge of a pollutant from a point source—explicitly including confined animal feeding operations such as the swine facilities in eastern North Carolina—into waters of the United States, and residents and clean water advocates have, in fact, investigated and brought litigation to enforce the law. Yet enforcement actions face significant hurdles. Initially, although neighbors may be impacted by odors and the flow of waste from sprayfields to ditches and waterways, they lack access onto the property of nearby facilities to identify potential discharges. Even when advocates monitor pollutants such as fecal coliform and find high levels downstream from facilities, they must overcome a number of legal barriers to bringing

**Figure 4-1:** Hog farm and waste lagoon, eastern North Carolina. March 8, 2019. Photo: Cliff Villa.

claims under the Clean Water Act. To prove a discharge, for example, they must show that pollutants are entering jurisdictional "waters of the United States" and that the discharge will not be considered "agricultural stormwater" and, thus allowed under the Clean Water Act.

These barriers to Clean Water Act enforcement fail to capture the full scale of the gap between the promise of environmental protection and the reality. In theory, [CERCLA] and EPCRA would require facility owners and operators to report releases from swine operations over certain threshold levels. However, a 2008 rule finalized in the closing hours of the Bush Administration largely exempted confined animal feeding operations from the rule. Moreover, animal operations are all but exempted from coverage under the Clean Air Act. Advocacy groups have filed a number of petitions with EPA to address issues of air pollution from animal operations under the CAA. One, for example, filed in 2009, asked EPA to list emissions from CAFOs— including hydrogen sulfide, ammonia, particulates, volatile organic compounds, methane, and nitrogen oxide—as air pollutants that endanger public health and welfare. The listing would, in turn, require EPA to issue new regulatory standards for CAFOs. The point here is not to debate the merits of additional regulation but, rather, to suggest that the current regime of environmental laws leaves significant gaps in protection and does not negate the potential for disparate impacts on the basis of race.

\* \* \*

## Notes and Questions

1. **Environmental compliance vs. environmental protection.** In the above excerpt, the author (a long-time legal advocate for environmental justice communities) notes many of the means by which environmental law may fail to protect human health.

Failures may stem from a lack of political will on the part of enforcement agencies, but may also follow from problems of proving environmental violations or from the design of environmental laws and regulations themselves. The design of the National Ambient Air Quality Standards (NAAQS) under the Clean Air Act is one classic example. Under the NAAQS, compliance with air quality standards is measured broadly by Air Quality Control Regions or subregions, which may have a broad geographic scope encompassing multiple municipalities within the same county, or even multiple counties. The Air Quality Control Region of the "South Coast Air Basin," encompassing the Los Angeles metro area, says nothing about the air quality that children breathe on a school playground in East L.A. Similarly, the NAAQS attainment status of eastern North Carolina may tell you nothing about the air quality in Warsaw, North Carolina, and a family home surrounded by 20,000 pigs on ten "industrial hog operations," with acrid odor and particulate matter wafting in the wind. Conflating environmental compliance with environmental protection is, unfortunately, a common mistake — one made by the EPA itself in the *Select Steel* decision (1998), discussed later in this chapter.

**2. Filling the regulatory gaps.** Students and scholars familiar with legislative or administrative processes may see many obvious needs for new laws or regulations to provide genuine protection for human health. Efforts to fill gaps in existing regulatory schemes have proven increasingly difficult, however, at least on a federal level. Even where there is widespread agreement on the need for regulation, such as the need to clarify the meaning of "waters of the United States" under the Clean Water Act, there is now likely to be years of litigation challenging any new federal rule, complemented by continuing proposals to withdraw or amend the rule as new administrations come and go. On a state, tribal, or municipal level, efforts to fill regulatory gaps may fare better, and will be explored later in this book. *See* Chapter 5 ("Standard Setting") and Chapter 10 ("Governmental Initiatives"). What is it about federal legislation and rulemaking now that makes progress toward protecting human health so unlikely? What advantages do older authorities such as the U.S. Constitution or the Civil Rights Act of 1964 bring to the problem of gaps in environmental regulation?

# C. Equal Protection Claims

To address concerns for the disparate treatment of racial minorities and the inequitable distribution of environmental burdens, perhaps the most obvious authority for EJ advocates to consider is the Equal Protection Clause of the Fourteenth Amendment to the U.S. Constitution. The Equal Protection Clause provides that "[n]o State shall ... deny to any person within its jurisdiction the equal protection of the laws." By its plain terms, without limitation, the Equal Protection Clause should guarantee the equal protection of the environmental laws. Under this authority, some of the earliest legal challenges to the siting of undesirable land uses in communities of color alleged violations of the Equal Protection Clause. The challenges largely failed, however, for lack of evidence of discriminatory intent. Of course, there is no textual requirement to prove discriminatory intent under the Equal Protection Clause; for better or worse, the intent standard was established by a majority of justices on the U.S. Supreme Court. As Professor Alice Kaswan explains below:

> The current understanding of [the Equal Protection standard] was established in 1975 in *Washington v. Davis* [426 U.S. 229 (1976)]. Stating that the "central purpose of the Equal Protection Clause ... is the prevention of official conduct discriminating on the basis of race," the Court held that a plaintiff must prove that the defendant acted with discriminatory intent.
>
> ... The Court observed that a "racially disproportionate impact," standing alone, is generally insufficient to demonstrate a violation.... The Supreme Court did, however, recognize that since government actors rarely announce their intent to discriminate, discriminatory intent may not be explicit. The justifications presented by government actors may, in some instances, be pretexts for discriminatory conduct.... The Supreme Court addressed the question of what types of facts are relevant to inferring discriminatory intent in the 1976 case of *Village of Arlington Heights v. Metropolitan Housing Development Corp.* [429 U.S. 252 (1977)].... [T]he Court identified the following five factors as potentially probative of intentional discrimination: (1) disparate impact; (2) historical background to the decision; (3) history of the decision-making process; (4) departures from normal substantive factors or procedures; and (5) legislative or administrative history. The Court made clear that its five-factor test was not "exhaustive." Nevertheless, courts have continued to use the five-factor test to determine whether direct and circumstantial evidence reveal that a facially neutral decision is discriminatory.

Alice Kaswan, *Environmental Laws: Grist for the Equal Protection Mill*, 70 U. COLO. L. REV. 387, 408–412 (1999).

In several early cases in the mid-1980s, courts inferred discriminatory intent and found violations of the Equal Protection Clause based on the disparate provision of municipal services such as water hookups, street paving, and storm-sewer capacity to minority residents. One example is the case below:

## Dowdell v. City of Apopka

698 F.2d 1181 (11th Cir. 1983)

*Vance, Senior Circuit Judge:*

The situs of this case is the small city of Apopka, Florida, located in the fern and foliage growing region north of Orlando. More specifically, it is the poor, geographically separate, black community of that city. The plaintiffs (appellees and cross-appellants here) are a Fed. R. Civ. P. 23(b)(2) class comprising the black residents of Apopka "who are, or have been, subjected to the discriminatory provision of municipal services." ... Plaintiffs charged the City of Apopka, its mayor, and four council members with discrimination in the provision of seven municipal services: street paving and maintenance, storm water drainage, street lighting, fire protection, water distribution, sewerage facilities, and park and recreation facilities....

The district court found intentional discrimination in the provision of street paving, the water distribution system, and storm drainage facilities in violation of the fourteenth amendment; Title VI of the Civil Rights Act of 1964, 42 U.S.C. § 2000d, and the State and Local Fiscal Assistance Act of 1972, 31 U.S.C. § 1242 (Revenue Sharing Act)....

To trigger strict scrutiny analysis under the fourteenth amendment, preliminary findings of both disparate impact and discriminatory intent are required. Appellants contend that the facts adduced in evidence do not support a finding of discriminatory intent....

We can reach no such conclusion. Substantial evidence, including video tapes, photographs, charts, and the testimony of community residents and of qualified experts who made on-site surveys revealed a disparity in the provision of street paving, water distribution, and storm water drainage.[3] Appellants do not question the accuracy of these statistical findings. Rather, they assert an absence of responsibility for them, claiming them, variously, to be beyond municipal jurisdiction or the result of historical and environmental forces. Their arguments are insubstantial and were properly rejected by the trial court.

Refutation of Apopka's attempt to deny municipal responsibility for these services one by one does not conclude our inquiry into discriminatory intent. The gravamen of plaintiffs' claim is that Apopka has intentionally maintained a racially and geographically segregated system of municipal services as a result of which the disparities in the provision of street paving, water distribution, and storm drainage facilities have reached constitutional proportions. Discriminatory intent is not synonymous with a racially discriminatory motive. Neither does it require proof that racial discrimination is the sole purpose behind each failure to equalize these services. It is, rather, the cumulative evidence of action and inaction which objectively manifests discriminatory intent.

Although the fluid concept of discriminatory intent is sometimes subtle and difficult to apply, there is ample evidence in this case of the correlation between municipal service disparities and racially tainted purposiveness to mandate a finding of discriminatory intent. Nearly every factor which has been held to be highly probative of discriminatory intent is present.

---

3. The district court found that 42% of the street footage in the black community was unpaved as compared to 9% in the white community and that 33% of the black community residences fronted on such unpaved streets while only 7% of the residences in the white community did so. As regards storm drainage, the court found that while 60% of the residential streets in the white community had curbs and gutters, no streets in the black community had curbs and gutters. Additionally, it found that water service in many homes in the black community was so inadequate that at many times of the day there was insufficient water for such normal purposes as bathing.

**Figure 4-2:** Apopka, Florida. Aug. 31, 2019. Photo: Nadia Ahmad.

First, the magnitude of the disparity, evidencing a systematic pattern of municipal expenditures in all areas of town except the black community, is explicable only on racial grounds. Second, the legislative and administrative pattern of decision-making, extending from nearly half a century in the past to Apopka's plans for future development, indicates a deliberate deprivation of services to the black community. A municipal ordinance restricting blacks to living only on the south side of the railroad tracks remained in force in Apopka until 1968. The ordinance contributed to the ghetto-like qualities of the black residential area. Blacks continue to be significantly under-represented in administrative and elective positions, and their requests for improved municipal services continue to be ignored while substantial funds are expended to annex and develop the new predominantly white sections of town. Third, the continued and systematic relative deprivation of the black community was the obviously foreseeable outcome of spending nearly all revenue sharing monies received on the white community in preference to the visibly underserviced black community. While voluntary acts and "awareness of consequences" alone do not necessitate a finding of discriminatory intent, "actions having foreseeable and anticipated disparate impact are relevant evidence to prove the ultimate fact, forbidden purpose."

Although none of these factors is necessarily independently conclusive, "the totality of the relevant facts," *Washington v. Davis*, amply supports the finding that the City of Apopka has engaged in a systematic pattern of cognitive acts and omissions, selecting and reaffirming a particular course of municipal services expenditures that inescapably evidences discriminatory intent....

\* \* \*

Plaintiffs have had far less success using the Equal Protection Clause in the facility siting context. The following decision involves one of the most famous cases in environmental justice, where field research led by Dr. Robert Bullard indicated the disparate siting of waste facilities in minority neighborhoods of Houston, Texas. Plaintiffs filed suit seeking to invalidate a decision by the Texas Department of Health (TDH) to grant a permit to Southwestern Waste Management to operate a Type I solid waste facility in the East Houston-Dyersdale Road area in Harris County, Texas. They sought a preliminary injunction to restrain the project from going forward. The court ruled as indicated below.

## Bean v. Southwestern Waste Management Corporation
### 482 F. Supp. 673 (S.D. Texas 1979), *affirmed* 780 F.2d 1038 (5th Cir. 1986)

*McDonald, District Judge*:

Before getting to the merits, the Court must address one other procedural matter. The plaintiffs did not name the Texas Department of Water Resources (TDWR) as a defendant in this case. That, of course, is not particularly surprising. That agency did not participate in the decision to grant Permit No. 1193 and nothing it did with respect to the issuance of that permit is being challenged here. The plaintiffs have, however, submitted a large quantity of data related to solid waste sites in Houston operating under the auspices of TDWR and a dispute has arisen as to the relevance of this data. The Court is of the opinion that the evidence as to TDWR's actions is entirely irrelevant to the question of whether it was an historical policy or practice of TDH to discriminate, since TDH should not be held responsible for the commission of acts, e.g., issuance of permits by TDWR, over which it had no control. Evidence as to TDWR's action is relevant, however, to the question of whether TDH, being aware of the placement of solid waste sites throughout the city of Houston, if it was so aware, discriminated by approving the permit for the East Houston-Dyersdale Road site, since a state agency must not put its stamp of approval on a discriminatory practice or policy even if it did not initiate the practice or policy....

The burden on [plaintiffs] is to prove discriminatory purpose. That is, the plaintiffs must show not just that the decision to grant the permit is objectionable or even wrong, but that it is attributable to an intent to discriminate on the basis of race. Statistical proof can rise to the level that it, alone, proves discriminatory intent, as in *Yick Wo v. Hopkins*, 118 U.S. 356 (1886), and *Gomillion v. Lightfoot*, 364 U.S. 339 (1960), or, this Court would conclude, even in situations less extreme than in those two cases, but the data shown here does not rise to that level. Similarly, statistical proof can be sufficiently supplemented by the types of proof outlined in *Arlington*

*Heights* to establish purposeful discrimination, but the supplemental proof offered here is not sufficient to do that.

Two different theories of liability have been advanced in this case. The first is that TDH's approval of the permit was part of a pattern or practice by it of discriminating in the placement of solid waste sites. In order to test that theory, one must focus on the sites which TDH has approved and determine the minority population of the areas in which the sites were located on the day that the sites opened. The available statistical data, both city-wide and in the target area, fails to establish a pattern or practice of discrimination by TDH. City-wide, data was produced for the seventeen (17) sites operating with TDH permits as of July 1, 1978. That data shows that 58.8% of the sites granted permits by TDH were located in census tracts with 25% or less minority population at the time of their opening and that 82.4% of the sites granted permits by TDH were located in census tracts with 50% or less minority population at the time of their opening. In the target area, an area which roughly conforms to the North Forest Independent School District and the newly created City Council District B and is 70% minority in population, two (2) sites were approved by TDH. One, the McCarty Road site, was in a census tract with less than 10% minority population at the time of its opening. The other, the site being challenged here, is in a census tract with close to 60% minority population. Even if we also consider the sites approved by TDWR in the target area, which, as discussed earlier, are not really relevant to TDH's intent to discriminate, no pattern or practice of discrimination is revealed. Of all the solid waste sites opened in the target area, 46.2 to 50% were located in census tracts with less than 25% minority population at the time they opened. It may be that more particularized data would show that even those sites approved in predominantly Anglo census tracts were actually located in minority neighborhoods, but the data available here does not show that. In addition, there was no supplemental evidence, such as that suggested by *Arlington Heights, supra*, which established a pattern or practice of discrimination on the part of TDH.

The plaintiffs' second theory of liability is that TDH's approval of the permit, in the context of the historical placement of solid waste sites and the events surrounding the application, constituted discrimination. Three sets of data were offered to support this theory. Each set, at first blush, looks compelling. On further analysis, however, each set breaks down. Each fails to approach the standard established by *Yick Wo, supra*, and *Gomillion, supra*, and, even when considered with supplementary proof, *Arlington Heights, supra*, fails to establish a likelihood of success in proving discriminatory intent.

The first set of data focuses on the two (2) solid waste sites to be used by the City of Houston. Both of these sites are located in the target area. This proves discrimination, the plaintiffs argue, because "the target area has the dubious distinction of containing 100% of the type I municipal landfills that Houston utilizes or will utilize, although it contains only 6.9% of the entire population of Houston." There are two problems with this argument. First, there are only two sites involved here. That is not a statistically significant number. Second, an examination of the census tracts in the target area in which the sites are located reveals that the East Houston-Dyersdale Road proposed site is in a tract with a 58.4% minority population, but that the McCarty Road site is in a tract with only an 18.4% minority population. Thus, the evidence shows that, of the two sites to be used by the City of Houston, one is in a primarily Anglo census tract and one is in a primarily minority census tract. No inference of discrimination can be made from this data.

The second set of data focuses on the total number of solid waste sites located in the target area. The statistical disparity which the plaintiffs point to is that the target area contains 15% of Houston's solid waste sites, but only 6.9% of its population. Since the target area has a 70% minority population, the plaintiffs argue, this statistical disparity must be attributable to race discrimination. To begin with, in the absence of the data on population by race, the statistical disparity is not all that shocking. One would expect solid waste sites to be placed near each other and away from concentrated population areas. Even considering the 70% minority population of the target area, when one looks at where in the target area these particular sites are located, the inference of racial discrimination dissolves. Half of the solid waste sites in the target area are in census tracts with more than 70% Anglo population. Without some proof that the sites affect an area much larger than the census tract in which they are in, it is very hard to conclude that the placing of a site in the target area evidences purposeful racial discrimination.

The third set of data offered by the plaintiffs focuses on the city as a whole. This data is the most compelling on its surface. It shows that only 17.1% of the city's solid waste sites are located in the southwest quadrant, where 53.3% of the Anglos live. Only 15.3% of the sites are located in the northwest quadrant, where 20.1% of the Anglos live. Thus, only 32.4% of the sites are located in the western half of the city, where 73.4% of the Anglos live. Furthermore, the plaintiffs argue, 67.6% of the sites are located in the eastern half of the city, where 61.6% of the minority population lives. This, according to the plaintiffs, shows racial discrimination.

The problem is that, once again, these statistics break down under closer scrutiny. To begin with, the inclusion of TDWR's sites skew[s] the data. A large number of TDWR sites are located around Houston's ship channel, which is in the eastern half of the city. But those sites, the Assistant Attorney General argues persuasively, are located in the eastern half of the city because that is where Houston's industry is, not because that is where Houston's minority population is. Furthermore, closer examination of the data shows that the city's solid waste sites are not so disparately located as they first appear. If we focus on census tracts, rather than on halves or quadrants of the city, we can see with more particularity where the solid waste sites are located. Houston's population is 39.3% minority and 60.7% Anglo. The plaintiffs argue, and this Court finds persuasive, a definition of "minority census tracts" as those with more than 39.3% minority population and Anglo census tracts as those with more than 60.7% Anglo population.

Using those definitions, Houston consists of 42.5% minority tracts and 57.5% Anglo tracts. Again using those definitions, 42.3% of the solid waste sites in the City of Houston are located in minority tracts and 57.7% are located in Anglo tracts. In addition, if we look at tracts with one or more sites per tract, to account for the fact that some tracts contain more than one solid waste site, 42.2% are minority tracts and 57.8% are Anglo tracts. The difference between the racial composition of census tracts in general and the racial composition of census tracts with solid waste sites is, according to the statistics available to the Court, at best, only 0.3%. That is simply not a statistically significant difference. More surprisingly, from the plaintiffs' point of view, to the extent that it is viewed as significant, it tends to indicate that minority census tracts have a tiny bit smaller percentage of solid waste sites than one would proportionately expect....

*Arlington Heights, supra*, suggested various types of non-statistical proof which can be used to establish purposeful discrimination. The supplementary non-statistical evidence provided by the plaintiffs in the present case raises a number of questions as to why this permit was granted. To begin with, a site proposed for the almost identical location was denied a permit in 1971 by the County Commissioners, who were then responsible for the issuance of such permits. One wonders what happened since that time. The plaintiffs argue that Smiley High School has changed from an Anglo school to one whose student body is predominantly minority. Furthermore, the site is being placed within 1,700 feet of Smiley High School, a predominantly black school with no air conditioning, and only somewhat farther from a residential neighborhood. Land-use considerations alone would seem to militate against granting this permit. Such evidence seemingly did not dissuade TDH.

If this Court were TDH, it might very well have denied this permit. It simply does not make sense to put a solid waste site so close to a high school, particularly one with no air conditioning. Nor does it make sense to put the land site so close to a residential neighborhood. But I am not TDH and for all I know, TDH may regularly approve of solid waste sites located near schools and residential areas, as illogical as that may seem.

It is not my responsibility to decide whether to grant this site a permit. It is my responsibility to decide whether to grant the plaintiffs a preliminary injunction. From the evidence before me, I can say that the plaintiffs have established that the decision to grant the permit was both unfortunate and insensitive. I cannot say that the plaintiffs have established a substantial likelihood of proving that the decision to grant the permit was motivated by purposeful racial discrimination in violation of 42 U.S.C. § 1983....

*Permanent Relief*

The failure of the plaintiffs to obtain a preliminary injunction does not, of course, mean that they are foreclosed from obtaining permanent relief. Because of the time pressures involved, extensive pre-trial discovery was impossible in this case. Assuming the case goes forward, discovery could lead to much more solid and persuasive evidence for either side. Ideally, it would resolve a number of the questions which the Court considers unanswered.

Where, for instance, are the solid waste sites located in each census tract? The plaintiffs produced evidence that in census tract 434, a predominantly Anglo tract, the site was located next to a black community named Riceville. If that was true of most sites in predominantly Anglo census tracts, the outcome of this case would be quite different.

How large an area does a solid waste site affect? If it affects an area a great deal smaller than that of a census tract, it becomes particularly important to know where in each census tract the site is located. If it affects an area larger than that of a census tract, then a target area analysis becomes much more persuasive.

How are solid waste site locations selected? It may be that private contractors consider a number of alternative locations and then select one in consultation with city or county officials. If that is so, it has tremendous implications for the search for discriminatory intent. It may be that a relatively limited number of areas can adequately serve as a Type I solid waste site. If that is so, the placement of sites in those areas becomes a lot less suspicious, even if large numbers of minorities live there. Either way, this is information which should be adduced. At this point, the Court still does not know how, why, and by whom the East Houston-Dyersdale Road location was selected.

What factors entered into TDH's decision to grant the permit? The proximity of the site to Smiley High School and a residential neighborhood and the lack of air conditioning facilities at the former were emphasized to the Court. It is still unknown how much, if any, consideration TDH gave to these factors. The racial composition of the neighborhood and the racial distribution of solid waste sites in Houston were primary concerns of the plaintiffs. It remains unclear to what degree TDH was informed of these concerns....

[P]laintiffs' Motion for a Preliminary Injunction ... [is] DENIED.

\* \* \*

## Notes and Questions

1. *Arlington Heights* **factors.** Consider the evidence analyzed by the *Bean* court in denying the preliminary injunction. Which of the *Arlington Heights* factors does this evidence relate to? Consider also the additional evidence that the court suggests might have been persuasive to it, including where the solid waste sites were located within each census tract, how large an area a solid waste site affects, how solid waste sites are selected, and what factors entered into the Texas Department of Health's decision to grant the permit. How do each of the requested pieces of evidence relate to the *Arlington Heights* factors? Should the prior actions of the Texas Department of Water Resources be considered in applying the *Arlington Heights* factors to the Texas Department of Health?

2. The *McDonnell Douglas* **framework.** In addition to the *Arlington Heights* factors for proving intentional discrimination, federal courts and the U.S. DOJ Civil Rights Division embrace an alternate methodology known as the **McDonnell Douglas framework**, developed through case law under Title VII of the Civil Rights Act (employment discrimination). *See McDonnell Douglas Corp. v. Green*, 411 U.S. 792 (1973).

The Supreme Court in [*McDonnell Douglas*] laid out a tripartite framework for the order and allocation of proof in Title VII individual disparate treatment cases based on circumstantial evidence. Under the *McDonnell Douglas* framework, the plaintiff must first establish a prima facie case of discrimination. Once the prima facie case is established, in order to avoid a verdict for the plaintiff, the employer must articulate "some legitimate, nondiscriminatory reason" for its decision. Finally, at the third stage, the plaintiff must, in the words of the *McDonnell Douglas* Court, "be afforded a fair opportunity to show that [defendant's] stated reason for [plaintiff's] rejection was in fact pretext."

Tristen K. Green, *Making Sense of the McDonnell Douglas Framework: Circumstantial Evidence and Proof of Disparate Treatment under Title VII*, 87 CAL. L. REV. 983, 986 (1999).

In *McDonnell Douglas*, the Court found that the plaintiff, Mr. Green, had established the prima facie case. The Court found that Mr. Green has established the case by showing "(i) that he belongs to a racial minority; (ii) that he applied and was qualified for a job for which the employer was seeking applicants; (iii) that, despite his qualifications, he was rejected; and (iv) that, after his rejection, the position remained open and the employer continued to seek applicants from persons of [plaintiff's] qualifications." *McDonnell Douglas* at 802.

How does the *McDonnell Douglas* framework compare with the *Arlington Heights* factors? Are there cases where the *McDonnell Douglas* framework might support a finding of intentional discrimination when the *Arlington Heights* factors do not? Imagine if your community that is 65% African American was denied state grants for wastewater treatment improvements when the next community, 65% white and with identical qualifications, received these grants. Would intentional discrimination in this case be easier to prove through the *Arlington Heights* factors or the *McDonnell Douglas* framework?

3. **Measuring discriminatory impact.** How should discriminatory impact be measured? This threshold question, which arises in many legal contexts including claims brought under the Fair Housing Act and Title VI of the Civil Rights Act, raises a host of difficult methodological questions. What is the definition of a "minority" community? Is it a community that is more than 50% racial or ethnic minorities? A community that has a higher percentage of racial or ethnic minority residents than in the permitting jurisdiction generally? Than in the relevant city or state? Likewise, for purposes of determining whether a community has suffered a disparate burden, what should be the geographic scope of the impacted community? Should it be defined by city blocks, neighborhoods, zip codes, census tracts, city quadrants, county lines? Or by a geographic radius extending from the unwanted land use? Should it vary depending on type of facility? As *Bean* demonstrates, the units chosen can have a huge impact on the outcome of a given case. For useful guidance and methodology

for establishing disparate impacts, *see* the U.S. DOJ Title VI Legal Manual, available online at https://www.justice.gov/crt/fcs/T6Manual6.

**4. Sympathies and statistics.** Owing perhaps to the large amount of data collected and presented by plaintiffs, the hearing on the motion for preliminary injunction in this case took an extraordinary eleven days. In the decision, Judge McDonald clearly expresses sympathy with the plaintiffs' concerns, yet he seems persuaded by statistics that appear to negate a clear finding of discriminatory intent in this case. What kind of statistics would Judge McDonald find convincing? In his opinion, McDonald points to two cases where discriminatory intent was found: *Yick Wo v. Hopkins* (1886) and *Gomillion v. Lightfoot* (1960). In *Yick Wo v. Hopkins*, as some students may recall, the City of San Francisco established an ordinance requiring a permit to operate a laundry in a wooden building. Of 310 laundries in wooden buildings, 240 had Chinese operators—all of whom were denied city permits. At the same time, all but one non-Chinese laundry received city permits. In *Gomillion v. Lightfoot*, the city of Tuskegee, Alabama, redrew its city boundaries from a square to "an uncouth 28-sided figure" in order to disenfranchise "all save four or five of [the city's] 400 Negro voters." Writing for the Court, Justice Frankfurter observed that if the allegations were proven true, this would be "tantamount ... to a mathematical demonstration" of discriminatory intent. Is this the level of proof that Judge McDonald would have required in *Bean*? If you had eleven days to present the same case today, what statistical evidence would you like the court to consider?

**5. *Bean* and the Bullards.** Like Warren County, the *Bean* case was another epic moment in the development of environmental justice as a field of study and practice. Vigorously litigated by Linda McKeever Bullard, *Bean* plaintiffs included Margaret Bean and other residents of Houston's Northwood Manor neighborhood in one of the first cases to reach a courtroom in a challenge alleging racial discrimination in environmental siting. To support their allegations, plaintiffs relied on data collection and statistical analysis by Mrs. Bullard's husband, sociologist Dr. Robert Bullard, who served as an expert witness on the case. Although the litigation was obviously not decided as plaintiffs hoped, it did signal a new era where advocates for environmental justice would be prepared to turn from protests in the streets to challenges in the courtroom, drawing resources from statistical methods and litigation tactics. For further background on the *Bean* case and its place in EJ history, *see* Robert D. Bullard, Dumping in Dixie: Race, Class, and Environmental Quality 40–45 (1990).

**6. Smiley High School.** So, whatever happened to Smiley High School, where the lack of air conditioning required open windows in classrooms 1,700 feet away from the waste disposal site? As might be expected over the course of nearly 40 years, the school has seen changes resulting from social shifts as well as major incidents including Hurricane Ike in 2008. The school is known today as the North Forest High School. In 2018, North Forest students moved next door to a new, $59.5 million campus funded by the state. The student population remains highly diverse, with approximately 64% of students African American and 35% Hispanic. 82% of students are "economically disadvantaged" and, in 2016, only 17% were classified as "college ready" at graduation, three times below the district-wide level. Texas Education Agency, 2017–18 School Report Card, North Forest High School. As in so many neighborhoods across the country, the struggle for social justice in the community of the former Smiley High School clearly continues.

Some ten years after the decision in *Bean*, another legal challenge to a waste facility went to court and resulted in a decision cited often in the environmental justice literature. This case involved a regional landfill proposed in a predominantly black community of King and Queen County, Virginia. As indicated in the excerpt below, there were three existing landfills in the county. Based upon soil studies, a property identified as the "Piedmont Tract" was determined to be suitable for construction of a new landfill. The county purchased the Piedmont Tract and decided to develop it for a new landfill. The Piedmont Tract is located close to the Second Mt. Olive Baptist Church, founded in 1860 by recently freed slaves. Development of the Piedmont Tract into a landfill would require rezoning from an agricultural to industrial area. The population of the county was approximately 50% black and 50% white. Plaintiffs sued under the Equal Protection Clause in order to stop the county's construction of the landfill.

## R.I.S.E. v. Kay

### 768 F. Supp. 1144 (E.D. Va. 1991)

*Richard L. Williams, District Judge:*

*Demographic Analysis of County Landfill Sites*

… 2. Thirty-nine blacks (64% of total) and twenty-two whites (36% of total) live within a half-mile radius of the proposed regional landfill site.…

3. The Mascot landfill was sited in 1969. None of the present Board members were serving on the Board at that time. At the time the landfill was developed, the estimated racial composition of the population living within a one mile radius of the site was 100% black. The Escobrook Baptist Church, a black church, was located within two miles of the landfill.

4. The Dahlgren landfill was sited in 1971. None of the current Board members were on the Board at that time. An estimated 95% of the population living in the immediate area at the time the landfill was built [was] black. Presently, an estimated 90–95% of the residents living within a two-mile radius are black.

5. The Owenton landfill was sited in 1977. Supervisors Kay and Bourne were serving on the Board when the landfill was developed. In 1977, an estimated 100% of the residents living within a half-mile radius of the landfill were black. The area population is still predominantly black. The First Mount Olive Baptist Church, a black church, is located one mile from the landfill.

[The Court then discussed a controversy surrounding a private landfill opened in 1986 by King Land Corporation. Since the county did not have a zoning ordinance in 1986, the landfill did not require county approval. In response, the county implemented a zoning ordinance and successfully sued to bar the landfill from operating.

The County subsequently denied King Land's application for a variance to use the property as a landfill, finding that the operation would result in a significant decline in property values of the adjacent properties, and that King Land had ignored environmental, health, safety, and welfare concerns. The racial composition of the residential area surrounding the King Land landfill is predominantly white.]

*Conclusions of Law*

... 2. The placement of landfills in King and Queen County from 1969 to the present has had a disproportionate impact on black residents.

3. However, official action will not be held unconstitutional solely because it results in a racially disproportionate impact....

4. The impact of an official action — in this case, the historical placement of landfills in predominantly black communities — provides "an important starting point" for the determination of whether official action was motivated by discriminatory intent.

5. However, the plaintiffs have not provided any evidence that satisfies the remainder of the discriminatory purpose equation set forth in *Arlington Heights*. Careful examination of the administrative steps taken by the Board of Supervisors to negotiate the purchase of the Piedmont Tract and authorize its use as a landfill site reveals nothing unusual or suspicious. To the contrary, the Board appears to have balanced the economic, environmental, and cultural needs of the County in a responsible and conscientious manner....

7. ... [T]he Board was understandably drawn to the Piedmont Tract because the site had already been tested and found environmentally suitable for the purpose of landfill development.

8. The Board responded to the concerns and suggestions of citizens opposed to the proposed regional landfill by establishing a citizens' advisory group, evaluating the suitability of the alternative site recommended by the Concerned Citizens' Steering Committee, and discussing with landfill contractor BFI such means of minimizing the impact of the landfill on the Second Mt. Olive Church as vegetative buffers and improving access roads.

9. Both the King Land landfill and the proposed landfill spawned "Not In My Backyard" movements. The Board's opposition to the King Land landfill and its approval of the proposed landfill was based not on the racial composition of the respective neighborhoods in which the landfills are located but on the relative environmental suitability of the sites.

10. At worst, the Supervisors appear to have been more concerned about the economic and legal plight of the County as a whole than the sentiments of residents who opposed the placement of the landfill in their neighborhood. However, the Equal Protection Clause does not impose an affirmative duty to equalize the impact of official decisions on different racial groups. Rather, it merely prohibits government officials from intentionally discriminating on the basis of race. The plaintiffs have not provided sufficient evidence to meet this legal standard. Judgment is therefore entered for the defendants.

* * *

## Notes and Questions

**1. Getting it wrong?** Professor Alice Kaswan contends that the court's conclusion in *R.I.S.E.* that there were no procedural irregularities in the siting process is "somewhat glib" since the court failed to discuss the need to rezone the property from agricultural to industrial use, a factor considered relevant under *Arlington Heights. See* Kaswan, *supra,* at 444–45. Professor Robert Collin also points to other evidence in the record suggesting that the rezoning was legally suspect. *See* Robert Collin, *Environmental Equity: A Law and Planning Approach to Environmental Racism,* 11 Va. Envtl. L. J. 495, 533 (1992). The *R.I.S.E.* court also did not discuss the project's legislative history, the fifth *Arlington Heights* factor, despite apparent evidence in the record suggesting some decision-makers' discriminatory views. According to plaintiffs' appellate brief, for example, the County Administrator, after hearing the concerns about the landfill expressed by two African-American ministers, told another party that the ministers "should be given a one-way ticket back to Africa." Another white member of the supervisors referred to the "'niggers'" opposition to the landfill. *Id.* at 532.

**2. Discrimination contexts.** Are courts (such as in *City of Apopka,* excerpted at the start of this section) more willing to infer discriminatory intent on the part of government actors and find an equal protection violation when the issue is the inequitable provision of services, rather than when it is the inequitable siting of locally undesirable land uses? For example, in a case alleging racial discrimination in providing municipal services to single-family homeowners and residents of an area of town that was 98.5% minority and 46% low-income, the court applied the *Arlington Heights* factors and denied summary judgment to the city, finding that a genuine issue of material fact of discrimination existed despite an absence of direct evidence of discriminatory intent. *See Miller v. City of Dallas,* 2002 WL 230834 (N.D. Tex.). Consider the consequences that might follow from a successful equal protection claim under, respectively, the municipal services and the siting dispute cases.

**3. Equal Protection: Dead end — or alive and kicking?** Are equal protection challenges a dead end for environmental justice plaintiffs? In her 1999 article, Professor Kaswan argued that "a wholesale abandonment of the equal protection approach is premature," Kaswan, *supra,* at 456, a view that history has largely confirmed. While equal protection victories remain elusive in the environmental justice context, cases in other contexts have proven that the Equal Protection Clause and the *Arlington Heights* factors retain vitality as a check against invidious discrimination in the modern era. *See, e.g., Washington v. Trump,* 847 F.3d 1151 (9th Cir. 2017) (considering *Arlington Heights* factors in denying government's motion to lift TRO against presidential order restricting foreign travel where evidence indicated president intended to establish a "Muslim ban"); *Veasey v. Abbott,* 830 F.3d 216 (5th Cir. 2016) (considering *Arlington Heights* factors in finding evidence "that the cloak of ballot integrity could be hiding a more invidious purpose" behind 2011 Texas voter ID requirement); *Arce v. Douglas,* 793 F.3d 968 (9th Cir. 2015) (applying *Arlington Heights* factors to reverse a finding of summary judgment against students who challenged elimination of the Mexican American Studies program in Tucson public schools).

**4. Substantive Due Process?** While arguments for environmental justice under the U.S. Constitution are most often framed under the Equal Protection Clause, could arguments also be framed effectively as requirements of Due Process? Under the Fifth Amendment (applicable to the federal government) and the Fourteenth Amendment (applicable to the states), no person shall be deprived "of life, liberty, or property, without due process of law...." As interpreted by the U.S. Supreme Court in a long line of cases, the Due Process Clause guarantees substantive as well as procedural rights. *See, e.g., Meyer v. Nebraska*, 262 U.S. 390 (1923) (right of language teacher to engage in "the calling of modern language teachers"); *Pierce v. Society of Sisters*, 268 U.S. 510 (1925) (right of parents to send children to parochial schools); *Griswold v. Connecticut*, 381 US. 479 (1965) (right of married couples to use contraceptives); *Roe v. Wade*, 410 U.S. 113 (1973) (right of women to choose abortion). In *Planned Parenthood v. Casey*, 505 U.S. 833 (1992), affirming the basic right to abortion, the Court observed that the doctrine of Substantive Due Process could be supported by a "rule of personal autonomy and bodily integrity...." *Id.* at 835. Under this rule, could one argue that "personal autonomy" supports a right for parents and children to choose safe places to live, work, and play? Could "bodily integrity" imply a right to protect your lungs against particulate matter from hog farms or lead smelters? At least one federal court so far has indeed found a substantive due process right in the environmental context. *Juliana v. United States*, 217 F.Supp.3d 1224, 1250 (D. Or. 2016) ("Just as marriage is the 'foundation of the family,' a stable climate system is quite literally the foundation" of society and civilization). For a thorough analysis supporting the use of Substantive Due Process to protect public health and welfare, *see* Michael C. Blumm & Mary Christina Wood, *"No Ordinary Lawsuit": Climate Change, Due Process, and the Public Trust Doctrine*, 68 Am. U. L. Rev. 1 (2017).

**5. State constitutions.** Where arguments under the U.S. Constitution appear unlikely to succeed, environmental justice advocates may also consider pursuing similar claims under state constitutions. As Supreme Court Justice William Brennan once observed, "State constitutions, too, are a font of individual liberties, their protections often extending beyond those required by the Supreme Court's interpretation of federal law." William J. Brennan, Jr., *State Constitutions and the Protection of Individual Rights*, 90 Harv. L. Rev. 489, 491 (1977). State courts have found fundamental rights under state constitutions where the U.S. Supreme Court under the U.S. Constitution has not. *Compare Serrano v. Priest*, 557 P.2d 929, 952 (Cal. 1976) (fundamental right to public education under California constitution), with *San Antonio Independent School District v. Rodriguez*, 411 U.S. 1 (1973) (no fundamental right to public education under U.S. Constitution). Moreover, even for rights recognized by both the U.S. and state constitutions, many state courts have established more protective standards for those rights. For example, equal protection clauses in some state constitutions have been interpreted to prohibit disparate impacts, not only actions that are intentionally discriminatory. For one excellent comparative analysis, *see* Robert J. Klee, *What's Good for School Finance Should Be Good for Environmental Justice: Addressing Disparate Environmental Impacts Using State Courts and Constitutions*, 30 COLUM. J. ENVTL. L. 135 (2005). For useful related discussions, *see also* Chasid M. Sapolu, *Dumping on the Wai'anae Coast: Achieving Environmental Justice Through the Hawai'i State Constitution*, 11 ASIAN-PAC. L. & POL'Y J. 204 (2010); Peter Reich, *Greening the Ghetto: A Theory of Environmental Race Discrimination*, 41 U. KAN. L. REV. 271, 301–304 (1992).

**6. Environmental law vs. civil rights?** In a 2002 article, Professor Tseming Yang argued that the law and policy in civil rights and environmental protection are based on fundamentally different paradigms:

> Environmental protection relies in large part on a conception of environmental degradation identified by Garrett Hardin in his seminal article *Tragedy of the Commons*, as well as by Rachel Carson in her book *Silent Spring*. In contrast, civil rights laws and cases have in large part responded to issues of discrimination which are implicit in the Supreme Court's opinion in *Brown v. Board of Education*.... Under ... "the tragedy of the commons," the quintessential focus of environmental regulation is on actions by individuals that, while advantageous and beneficial to that particular individual, are harmful for the community overall. The result is that environmental regulation, like many other forms of government regulations, is primarily directed at protecting the collective from the irresponsible or selfish actions of individuals or small groups.

> That perspective is entirely reversed in anti-discrimination law. The underlying premise of *Brown v. Board of Education* is that prejudice and minority oppression requires the law to focus its protections on minority groups against the majority. Because it was necessary to protect African Americans against continuing discrimination and oppression by whites following the Civil War, the Fourteenth Amendment's Equal Protection Clause was specifically designed to be counter-majoritarian in character.

Tseming Yang, *Melding Civil Rights and Environmentalism: Finding Environmental Justice's Place in Environmental Regulation*, 26 HARV. ENVTL. L. REV. 1 (2002).

What does this suggest about relying on civil rights arguments to remedy environmental disparities at the judicial or regulatory levels? Consider this inherent tension as you read the following materials on the use of civil rights authorities to pursue environmental justice.

# D. Enforcement of the Civil Rights Act, Title VI

## 1. Introduction

Because of lack of success of equal protection claims and the apparent reticence of environmental agencies—at local, state, and federal levels—to condition or deny permits on environmental justice grounds, in the 1990s activists and community residents turned to Title VI of the Civil Rights Act of 1964, a non-environmental statute, as a potential redress for environmental disparities. Title VI has two major provisions:

> **Sec. 601 (42 U.S.C. § 2000d).** No person in the United States shall, on the ground of race, color, or national origin, be excluded from participation in, be denied the benefits of, or be subjected to discrimination under any program or activity receiving Federal financial assistance.

> **Sec. 602 (42 U.S.C. § 2000d-1).** Each Federal department and agency which is empowered to extend Federal financial assistance to any program or activity, by way of a grant, loan, or contract … is authorized and directed to effectuate the provisions of [§ 601] … by issuing rules, regulations, or orders of general applicability which shall be consistent with achievement of the objectives of the [Civil Rights Act of 1964]….

Like the equal protection cases discussed above, section 601 has been interpreted by the Supreme Court to require proof of discriminatory intent to be actionable. The challenge for impacted communities, then, is that the bar is very high to go to court because of the extraordinary difficulty in proving that a state environmental agency specifically intended to discriminate on the basis of race in issuing a permit or taking other actions while administering federal environmental programs (for which it receives funding).

However, pursuant to section 602, federal agencies issued regulations precluding recipients of federal funds from engaging in activities that have a discriminatory "effect," i.e., regulations that prohibit disparate impacts in addition to prohibiting intentional discrimination. Following the practice of many federal agencies, in 1973 EPA promulgated regulations aimed at discriminatory effects. The most recent iteration specifically provides that "[a] recipient shall not use criteria or methods of administering its program or activity which have the effect of subjecting individuals to discrimination because of their race, color, national origin, or sex…." 40 C.F.R. § 7.35(b). Moreover, "A recipient shall not choose a site or location of a facility that has the purpose or effect of excluding individuals from, denying them the benefits of, or subjecting them to discrimination…." *Id.* § 7.35(c).

In many cases, this standard will be easier to satisfy than the intentional discrimination standard applicable to claims brought under the Equal Protection Clause or to section 601 of Title VI. Theoretically, the remedy for a Title VI violation is for the federal agency to withdraw federal funds to the recipient in violation, or alternatively, the federal agency may refer the matter to the Department of Justice, which has the option to file suit to enjoin the discriminatory activity. Agencies must first attempt to negotiate voluntary compliance with recipients of federal funds before withdrawing funding, but historically, agencies that have a record of civil rights enforcement are able to use their clout to address violations of civil rights. EPA, however, has never withdrawn funding nor referred a case to DOJ.

In 1992, community groups began submitting Title VI administrative complaints to the EPA's Office of Civil Rights alleging that the actions of state and local environmental agencies receiving federal funds from the EPA to administer environmental programs were resulting in disparate impacts on the basis of race or national origin. Most of the complaints received by EPA involved the permitting process. The gravamen of these complaints was that state agencies, by continuing to issue permits in heavily impacted minority communities, were using criteria or methods that had the effect of causing or exacerbating existing racial disparities despite any lack of specific intent to discriminate. Initially, EPA had neither the resources nor the analytical framework to begin the task of investigating and administratively adjudicating these claims. In 1998, the Agency issued an 11-page document titled "Interim Guidance for Investigating Title VI Administrative Complaints Challenging Permits" (*Interim Guidance*). The *Interim Guidance* sparked a firestorm of criticism from the industry/ business sector and state/local regulatory agencies, who argued that key terms were left undefined and that the framework was so burdensome that it would discourage economic development.

Partly in response to the strong criticism, the EPA soon established a multi-stakeholder "Title VI Implementation Advisory Committee," which in 1999 submitted its report to the EPA. The Title VI FACA (so named because it was convened under the authority of the Federal Advisory Committee Act) identified eight crucial substantive issues that the EPA needed to address in adjudicating a disparate impact administrative claim, as well as several important procedural issues. In 2000, the EPA replaced the controversial *Interim Guidance* with two lengthy draft guidances; one of these guidances covered the EPA's process for investigating Title VI complaints (*Draft Investigation Guidance*), 65 Fed. Reg. 39,650 (2000). Twenty years later, the EPA still has not issued a "final" guidance for Title VI investigations. However, in 2017, the EPA did issue a "Case Resolution Manual," which is "intended to provide procedural guidance to [EPA civil rights] case managers to ensure EPA's prompt, effective, and efficient resolution of civil rights cases...."

As an alternative to filing a Title VI administrative complaint, community advocates in different contexts tried to bring civil lawsuits to enforce the "disparate impact" regulations promulgated under Title VI, Sec. 602. With a civil complaint in U.S. District Court, the community advocate could potentially bypass an agency's administrative process and directly ask a federal judge for the appropriate relief. However, the Supreme Court in *Alexander v. Sandoval*, 532 U.S. 275 (2001), ruled that there was no private right of action to enforce the Title VI regulations. According to the 5–4 majority opinion of Justice Scalia, plaintiffs could only bring civil claims under Sec. 601 of Title VI, which—like equal protection claims under the Fourteenth Amendment—required findings of intentional discrimination. One consequence of this ruling was renewed focus on administrative proceedings to enforce Title VI regulations.

In this section we first discuss the Title VI administrative process generally and then through contexts involving two Title VI complaints filed on behalf of residents in Flint, Michigan. We then will turn to reforms and modern practice in Title VI enforcement, recognizing the continuing potential of this legal avenue for pursuing environmental justice.

## 2. Administrative Complaints under Title VI Regulations

Administrative complaints alleging violations of the EPA's Title VI regulations must be filed with a designated office of EPA Headquarters in Washington, D.C. Historically, the designated office was the EPA Office of Civil Rights (OCR), but as of 2017, it has been the EPA External Civil Rights Compliance Office (ECRCO). EPA regulations at 40 C.F.R. § 7.120, together with the EPA's *Case Resolution Manual* (2017), set forth the general process for Title VI complaints filed now with the EPA External Civil Rights Compliance Office:

- Concerned citizens may send a complaint letter with supporting information to the EPA. 40 C.F.R. § 7.120(b).

- EPA acknowledges receipt of the complaint within five calendar days, 40 C.F.R. § 7.120(c), assigns a case number, and establishes a file.

- Within 20 calendar days of acknowledging the complaint, EPA "will review the complaint for acceptance, rejection, or referral to the appropriate Federal agency." 40 C.F.R. § 7.120(d)(1)(i).

- EPA reviews the complaint to determine whether it meets four jurisdictional elements: (1) the complaint is in writing; (2) EPA has jurisdiction over the subject matter of the complaint—that is, the complaint sets forth facts that allege a violation of the law or regulations implemented by EPA; (3) the alleged discriminatory actor is an applicant for or recipient of EPA funds; and (4) the allegations are filed timely, within 180 days of the last act of alleged discrimination (unless a waiver is granted).

- EPA issues a letter accepting the complaint and opening an investigation if the complaint satisfies the four jurisdictional elements and no "prudential" factors counsel for rejection.

- EPA proceeds to conduct the investigation while also affording the recipient of EPA funds the opportunity to voluntarily comply with the law. In addition, EPA offers alternative dispute resolution (ADR) to complainants and recipients to resolve matters informally. 40 C.F.R. § 7.120(d)(2).

- "Within 180 calendar days from the start of a … complaint investigation," EPA will notify the recipient of "(i) Preliminary findings; (ii) Recommendations, if any, for achieving voluntary compliance; and (iii) [Recipient's] right to engage in voluntary compliance negotiations where appropriate." 40 C.F.R. §7.115(c)(1).

- If EPA determines that the recipient is not in compliance with Title VI regulations, and if compliance cannot be achieved voluntarily, then EPA "shall make a finding of noncompliance." 40 C.F.R. §7.130(b)(1).
- In the event of a finding of noncompliance, if compliance "cannot be assured by informal means, EPA may terminate or refuse to award or to continue [financial] assistance" to the recipient. 40 C.F.R. §7.130(a).
- Within 30 days of receipt of a notice of noncompliance, the recipient may request a hearing before an administrative law judge, 40 C.F.R. §7.130(b)(2), triggering a new set of adjudicative procedures.

Very few Title VI complaints in EPA's history have ever reached a formal administrative decision. The first one that did arose from concerns for air pollution from a proposed steel mill on the northern edge of Flint, Michigan. Flint residents filed a Title VI complaint to challenge an air permit for the Select Steel facility issued by the Michigan Department of Environmental Quality (MDEQ). As the excerpt below suggests, resolution of this complaint provided no relief or encouragement to advocates for environmental justice.

## The *Select Steel* Administrative Decision

(1998)
*As discussed in* Letter from Ann E. Goode, Director, EPA
Office of Civil Rights, to Father Phil Schmitter and Sister Joanne Chiaverini,
Co-Directors, St. Francis Prayer Center, and Russell Harding, Director,
Michigan Department of Environmental Quality

*Alleged Discriminatory Effect Resulting from Air Quality Impacts*

As outlined in EPA's *Interim Guidance*, EPA follows five basic steps in its analysis of allegations of discriminatory effects from a permit decision. "The first step is to identify the population affected by the permit that triggered the complaint." ... If there is no adverse effect from the permitted activity, there can be no finding of a discriminatory effect which would violate Title VI and EPA's implementing regulations. In order to address the allegation that MDEQ's issuance of a PSD [Prevention of Significant Deterioration] permit for the proposed Select Steel facility would result in a discriminatory effect, EPA first considered the potential adverse effect from the permitted facility using a number of analytical tools consistent with EPA's *Interim Guidance*....

*VOCs [Volatile Organic Compounds]*

To evaluate the impact of VOCs, EPA examined the permit application submitted by Select Steel and a variety of analyses conducted by MDEQ.... In examining VOCs as ozone precursors, EPA studied the additional contribution of VOCs from the proposed Select Steel facility and has determined those emissions will not affect the area's compliance with the national ambient air quality standards (NAAQS) [under the Clean Air Act] for ozone.

The NAAQS for ozone is a health-based standard which has been set at a level that is presumptively sufficient to protect public health and allows for an adequate margin of safety for the population within the area; therefore, there is no affected population which suffers "adverse" impacts within the meaning of Title VI resulting from the incremental VOC emissions from the proposed Select Steel facility....

The Complainants also have alleged that failure to require immediate VOC monitoring for the proposed Select Steel facility will result in a discriminatory effect. Select Steel's permit condition regarding VOC monitoring allows Select Steel one year from plant start-up to implement a continuous emissions monitoring system ("CEMS") for VOCs.... As discussed above, there would be no affected population that suffers "adverse" impacts within the meaning of Title VI resulting from the incremental VOC emissions from the proposed Select Steel facility. For this reason, EPA finds that, with regard to VOC monitoring, MDEQ did not violate Title VI or EPA's implementing regulations.

*Lead*

Similarly, to evaluate potential lead emissions from the facility, EPA studied the additional contribution of airborne lead emissions from the proposed Select Steel facility and has determined those emissions will not affect the area's compliance with the NAAQS for lead. As with ozone, there is a NAAQS for lead that has been set at a level presumptively sufficient to protect public health and allows for an adequate margin of safety for the population within the attainment area. Therefore, there would be no affected population which suffers "adverse" impacts within the meaning of Title VI resulting from the incremental lead emissions from the proposed Select Steel facility....

In this case, MDEQ also appropriately considered information concerning the effect of the proposed facility's lead emissions on blood lead levels in children in response to community concerns. EPA reviewed this information along with other available data on the incidence and likelihood of elevated blood lead levels in Genesee County, particularly in the vicinity of the site of the proposed facility. EPA considered this additional information in response to the Complainants' concerns that the existing incidence of elevated blood lead levels in children in the vicinity of the proposed facility were already high. Overall, EPA found no clear evidence of a prevalence of pre-existing lead levels of concern in the area most likely to be affected by emissions from the proposed facility....

*Air Toxics*

For airborne toxics, EPA conducted its review based on information presented in the permit application, existing TRI [Toxic Release Inventory] data, and MDEQ documents. EPA reviewed MDEQ's analysis of Select Steel's potential air toxic emissions for evidence of adverse impacts based on whether resulting airborne concentrations exceeded thresholds of concern under State air toxics regulations. EPA also considered the potential Select Steel air toxic emissions together with air toxic emissions from [TRI] facilities, the Genesee Power Station, and other major sources in the surrounding area. EPA's review of air toxic emissions from both the proposed site alone, as well as in combination with other sources, found no "adverse" impact in the immediate vicinity of the proposed facility....

### Dioxin

The information gathered from the investigation concerning the monitoring of dioxin emissions is consistent with EAB's [EPA's Environmental Appeals Board's] analysis of the issue. No performance specifications for continuous emissions monitoring systems have been promulgated by EPA to monitor dioxins. Without a proven monitor, MDEQ was unable to impose a monitoring requirement on the source....

### Alleged Discriminatory Public Participation Process

To assess the allegations of discrimination concerning public process, EPA evaluated the information from interviews with Complainants and MDEQ, and from documents gathered from the parties. The first allegation was that the permit was "hastily sped through" by MDEQ to avoid permitting requirements (*i.e.*, conduct a risk assessment; provide opportunity for public comment on risk assessment; provide meaningful opportunity for all affected parties to participate in the permit process) imposed by a State trial court that are under appeal. The five months between receipt of the complete permit application and permit approval is actually slower than the average time of one and a half months for the past twenty-six PSD permits approved by MDEQ. EPA's review found that the public participation process for the permit was not compromised by the pace of the permitting process. MDEQ satisfied EPA's regulatory requirements concerning the issuance of PSD permits....

The Complainants alleged that the manner of publication of the notice of the permit hearing also contributed to the alleged discriminatory process. The Complainants allege that publication in newspapers was insufficient to inform the predominantly minority community because few community members have access to newspapers—something the Complainants allege was brought to MDEQ's attention during the permitting process for another facility in Genesee Township. EPA's regulations for PSD permitting require that notice of a public hearing must be published in a weekly or daily newspaper within the affected area. In this case, MDEQ went beyond the requirements of the regulation and published notices about the hearing in three local newspapers.

Complainants also state that MDEQ's failure to provide individual notice of the hearing to more members of the community also contributed to the alleged discriminatory process. In addition to newspaper notice, EPA's regulations require that notice be mailed to certain interested community members. MDEQ mailed hearing notification letters a month in advance to Fr. Schmitter, Sr. Chiaverini, and nine other individuals in the community who had expressed interest in the Select Steel permit—an action which is consistent with the requirements of EPA's regulations. The mailing list that MDEQ developed was adequate to inform the community about the public hearing, in part, because the Complainants took it upon themselves to contact other members of the community.

The Complainants also alleged that the location of the public hearing (Mount Morris High School) made it difficult for minority members of the community to attend. Complainants felt that the hearing should have been held at Carpenter Road Elementary School. Both schools are approximately two miles from the proposed Select Steel site; however, the elementary school is located in a predominantly minority area, while the high school is in a predominantly white area. MDEQ explored other possible locations and chose the high school, among other reasons, because of its ability to accommodate the expected number of citizens and its close proximity to the proposed site. The high school also is accessible by the general public via Genesee County public transportation.

For all of these reasons, EPA finds that the public participation process for the Select Steel facility was not discriminatory or in violation of Title VI or EPA's implementing regulations....

\* \* \*

## Notes and Questions

1. **Wrongly decided.** The EPA's decision in *Select Steel* is widely recognized as badly reasoned and wrongly decided on many levels. As just one clear example of error, while the *Select Steel* opinion assumed that the affected area met national air quality standards for ozone, in fact, it did not. EPA's Office of Civil Rights noted that the county hosting the facility had been formally designated nonattainment for ozone in 1978, but that it had demonstrated compliance with the one-hour standard based upon three years of air quality data prior to 1998. Thus, reasoned the EPA's Office of Civil Rights, "[i]n practical terms, this means that the old classification of 'nonattainment' has been superseded by a determination that Genesee County was meeting the old ozone standard." *See* Investigative Report, at 14 (a report that accompanied the decision). In other words, OCR did not feel bound by the legal designation of the area. This error was critical because the crux of the EPA's decision was that since the area in question was not violating a health-based standard, then by definition the impact (even assuming a disparity exists) could not be "adverse." The late environmental attorney Luke Cole criticized this approach and argued that, despite the EPA's contentions, as a legal *and* a factual matter Genesee County was not in attainment in 1998, the time of the permit proceeding in the *Select Steel* Title VI investigation:

> When the MDEQ made the decision to grant the permit to Select Steel on May 27, 1998, the area was not in attainment for the "old" one-hour ozone standard. In fact, less than two weeks earlier, on May 15, 1998, Flint hit a one-hour ozone level of 130 parts per billion (ppb)—a full 60 percent above EPA's health-based NAAQS of 80 ppb. On July 22, 1998—after Michigan issued the permit and after the Title VI complaint had been filed—EPA revoked the one-hour NAAQS for the Flint area, and the area was then cov-

ered by the eight-hour ozone NAAQS. On both of these dates—May 27, 1998, for the permit decision and June 9, 1998, for the filing of the complaint—Flint was not in attainment with either the one-hour ozone standard or the eight-hour ozone standard.... Thus, the central underpinning of EPA's decision and theory of no adverse impact—that Flint was in attainment for ozone—is demonstrably false.

Luke W. Cole, *"Wrong on the Facts, Wrong on the Law": Civil Rights Advocates Excoriate EPA's Most Recent Title VI Misstep*, 29 ENVTL. L. REP. 10,775, 10,777–78 (1999).

2. **Wrong—and *wronger*.** Imagine that the Flint region had, in fact, been in compliance with all air standards for ozone when the Select Steel permit had been issued. Would that then have ensured the protection of the community's health? As noted earlier in this chapter, "attainment" of the National Ambient Air Quality Standards (NAAQS) under the Clean Air Act is measured in broad geographies designated as Air Quality Control Regions. Thus, the air quality of Genesee County, at issue in *Select Steel*, may have no relation to the air quality actually experienced by people living in the Flint neighborhood across the street or downwind of the Select Steel facility. Air quality in this neighborhood could potentially exceed the NAAQS by orders of magnitude, while the county as a whole remained in attainment. Moreover, even if the local air quality in this neighborhood remained in compliance with the NAAQS, there is no assurance that EPA set the NAAQS itself at a safe level. Notice the summary assertion in the decision that NAAQS standards are "presumptively sufficient to protect public health." How much should we rely on that? In fact, in the years since the *Select Steel* decision, the EPA has repeatedly recognized that the standards for ozone in place in 1998 were *not* protective of human health. EPA tightened standards for ozone in 2008 and again in 2015, which public health experts believe may still not be protective. *See, Murray Energy v. EPA*, 2019 WL 3977557 (D.C. Cir. 2019) (generally upholding 2015 NAAQS for ozone against challenges by both industry and environmentalists).

Compounding all the EPA's errors concerning ozone was the fact that there were many other air pollutants of concern in this case, which should have alerted the agency to the potential for cumulative impacts on the local community. As noted in the excerpt, in addition to ozone and dioxin, air emissions from the Select Steel facility were anticipated to include lead, which by 1998 was already a problem in Flint soils due to sources including lead-based paint. Lead air emissions from the Select Steel facility would only add to the problem of lead-contaminated soils in the community. While the EPA appeared to consider existing data on elevated blood-lead levels in the community, the EPA appeared to dismiss the concern that more lead contamination in the already-burdened community would lead to greater numbers of lead-poisoned children.

3. **Procedural justice.** While the *Select Steel* decision may serve as an exemplar of distributional injustice, it may also teach hard lessons on procedural injustice. Consider the community complaints about notice by publication in local newspapers. If poor people in the Flint community were unable to afford newspapers, would publication in *more newspapers* do anything to relieve concerns about lack of notice? Direct mail-

ings may help address this concern, but notice how many people actually received the direct mailing in this case. How are the mailing lists compiled and maintained? Are there people that direct mailings might never reach? May the EPA rely legally on the voluntary efforts of a Catholic priest and nun in order to provide actual notice to community members? What more might you have suggested in this case to genuinely serve the interests of procedural justice?

**4. Epilogue.** Perhaps due to the community protest against the Select Steel air permit, the proposed steel mill was never built in Flint. Fr. Phil Schmitter, for his part, remained a staunch advocate for the local community. The Title VI complaint for Select Steel was not, in fact, the first that Fr. Schmitter filed. In 1992, six years before his Select Steel complaint, Fr. Schmitter filed another Title VI complaint with the EPA, this one alleging that the Michigan Department of Natural Resources engaged in disparate treatment in its decision to approve a proposed facility to burn wood waste for energy, a facility to become known as the Genesee Power Station. The EPA, typically, failed to respond to this complaint in a timely manner. However, a quarter of a century later, on the very last day of the Obama administration, the EPA issued the following written decision in this matter.

## EPA letter to Father Phil Schmitter

### Jan. 19, 2017

### UNITED STATES ENVIRONMENTAL PROTECTION AGENCY

#### WASHINGTON, D.C. 20460

EXTERNAL CIVIL RIGHT [sic] COMPLIANCE OFFICE
OFFICE OF GENERAL COUNSEL

January 19, 2017

EPA File No. 01R-R5

Father Phil Schmitter
Flint, Michigan 48503

Dear Father Schmitter:

This letter is to advise you that the US Environmental Protection Agency's (EPA) External Civil Rights Compliance Office (ECRCO) has completed its investigation of the above-referenced Complaint (Genesee Complaint) and is resolving and closing this case as of the date of this letter. The Genesee Complaint was dated December 15, 1992, and filed by you on behalf of the St. Francis Prayer Center (Complainants). The Genesee Complaint was filed under Title VI of the Civil Rights Act of 1964, as amended, 42 U.S.C. §§ 2000d et seq., (Title VI) and EPA's nondiscrimination regulations found at 40 C.F.R. Part 7.

EPA's investigation focused on allegations of discrimination by the Michigan Department of Natural Resources (MDNR) (later becoming the Michigan Department of Environmental Quality (MDEQ)) and the Michigan Air Pollution Control Commission (MAPCC) based on race related to granting of a permit to the Genesee Power

Station (GPS) in Flint, Michigan, under the Clean Air Act (CAA). The MAPCC and MDNR were recipients of EPA financial assistance at the time of the alleged discriminatory acts. The MDEQ has received, and continues to receive, federal grants from EPA to run the Michigan Air Pollution Control Program, which carries out the functions formerly delegated to the MAPCC and the MDNR. The CAA permit function currently resides in the Air Quality Division of the MDEQ.

With this letter, EPA makes findings with respect to the original issues raised in this complaint and closes EPA File No. O1R-94-RS. However, EPA also has additional and current serious concerns, set forth below, that are being examined in the context of another ongoing EPA investigation involving MDEQ. That investigation is focused on alleged discrimination by MDEQ based on race, national origin, and disability in its administration of the Safe Drinking Water Act of 1974 during the Flint drinking water crisis (EPA File No. 17RD-16-R5) (Flint Complaint).

**Summary of Findings**

Title VI provides that "'[n]o person in the United States shall, on the ground of race, color, or national origin, be excluded from participation in, be denied the benefits of, or be subjected to discrimination under any program or activity receiving Federal financial assistance." 42 U.S.C. § 2000d. As implemented by EPA's regulation, these prohibitions include intentional discrimination as well as practices that have a discriminatory effect on the bases of race, color, or national origin. *See* 40 C.F.R. §§ 7.35(a), 7.35(b).

As will be discussed in more detail below, EPA finds that the preponderance of evidence supports a finding of discriminatory treatment of African Americans by MDEQ in the public participation process for the GPS permit considered and issued from 1992 to 1994. In addition, EPA has concerns that MDEQ's current policies are insufficient to address the potential for discrimination given the deficiencies in MDEQ's public participation program and procedures.

With respect to the allegations of adverse disparate health effects raised in the original complaint, EPA conducted four analyses to assess risk of health effects and did not find sufficient evidence to establish adversity/harm with respect to health effects. Therefore, there is insufficient evidence to support a prima facie case of adverse disparate impact.…

*Requests to speak either in advance of or out of order at hearings*

According to MAPCC Commissioners, the MAPCC regularly accommodated elected representatives at MAPCC meetings based upon their schedules. Commissioners stated that they would allow elected representatives to offer their comments on a particular permit before the scheduled hearing if their schedules dictated that they be elsewhere when that permit hearing was to take place. The MAPCC also accommodated other attendees with scheduling conflicts. One MAPCC Commissioner stated that the MAPCC was "in the business of listening to the public," and that it "typically went out of [its] way to try to listen to people who had taken the time to appear before the Commission."

During the December 1, 1992, meeting in Lansing, the MAPCC considered three permits in addition to other five agenda items. In addition to GPS, there were permit hearings scheduled related to two proposed facilities in Marquette County: one in Sands Township and one in Skandia. The GPS permit hearing was the 7th item on the agenda. The MAPCC began its meeting around 9:00 am. At 9:30 a.m. the MAPCC started the first scheduled public hearing for the Marquette County Solid Waste Management Authority. By 11:45 a.m. only 3 people had commented on this permit application. The Chairman of the MAPCC indicated that the MAPCC would break for lunch, but that before it did so, Dr. Robert Soderstrom would speak on the GPS permit application because he had a scheduling conflict and had to leave. Dr. Robert Soderstrom, from the Genesee Medical Society, who is White, then spoke.

State Representative Floyd Clack and Ms. Janice O'Neal, both of whom are African American, each asked to address the MAPCC in advance of the GPS hearing because of scheduling conflicts created by the delay of the hearing. Neither request was granted. Ms. O'Neal provided her oral comments at the GPS hearing later that evening after traveling 120 miles to Flint and back. Ms. Bogardus, who is White, interrupted the MAPCC as they deliberated about whether to postpone the GPS hearing. She did not ask permission to speak in advance of the GPS hearing. She interrupted the Commissioners and was allowed to proceed with her remarks.

The MAPCC deviated from what was described as its standard operating procedures for handling requests to speak in advance of the public comment period resulting in African Americans' requests being denied while requests by Whites to speak in advance were granted....

The GPS hearing began at about 6:40 p.m. with public comment commencing at about 8:40 p.m. Community members interested in providing comments to the MAPCC were given their opportunity more than 11 hours after they had arrived from Flint and the MAPCC meeting had begun. The length of time before the GPS hearing began was irregular for the MAPCC, as most MAPCC meetings had concluded or were wrapping up in the early evening. At no other hearing held in 1992 were community members required to wait 9 hours before their hearing started and 11 hours before they were allowed to provide comment. The GPS public hearing lasted almost 6 hours....

The MAPCC had the discretion to postpone the December 1992 hearing and/or extend the comment period. The decision to continue the hearing into the night and to issue the permit without allowing time for those at the hearing to review and prepare comments on new permit conditions, new analyses, and other information resulted in the commenters from the predominantly African American community being treated less favorably than people at other permit hearings for facilities in predominantly non-African American communities....

*Armed and uniformed officers at hearing*

October 20, 1994, MDEQ held a hearing at the Carpenter Road School, in a predominantly African American neighborhood bordering the GPS facility in Flint, to receive public comment on the proposed Wood Waste Plan. This was the last hearing before GPS would begin normal operation. This was the second GPS public hearing held outside of Lansing and the first to take place in the predominantly African American neighborhood. Two uniformed and armed MDEQ Conservation Officers attended the hearing at the request of the MDEQ. The first two GPS public hearings had been held in Lansing without armed uniformed officers present at the doors of the hearing.

The Law Enforcement Division, for whom the conservation officers work, did not have any written policy on the use of armed and uniformed officers at hearings. In response to the question of why the armed and uniformed officers were present at the Carpenter Road hearing, Michigan state agencies gave a variety of answers. The Law Enforcement Division stated that upon request, conservation officers were typically assigned to state government real estate sales (strong box security) and other public meetings where it was anticipated that personnel safety may be a concern due to the controversial nature of an issue.

Both of the officers at the Carpenter Road hearing stated they had been assigned to guard hearings before, but according to both the officers and other MDEQ staff, having guards at MDEQ meetings was not a frequent occurrence and only occurred when the MDEQ anticipated popular disapproval of MDEQ actions.

There was no strong box to guard at the GPS hearing. There is no persuasive evidence in the record that personnel safety may have been a concern due to the controversial nature of an issue. The state office for whom the conservation officers worked had no record of a request for the presence of armed uniformed officers that might contain an explanation for their presence. Neither of the two Conservation Officers who were present at that GPS hearing recalled being briefed regarding the reason that their presence was required.

In 1999, MDEQ stated that no complaints had been filed regarding the presence of conservation officers at public hearings or meetings since 1994. MDEQ stated that it has held public hearings and meetings in the local affected communities without incident, and that many of these meetings were conducted in inner-city communities. MDEQ's recent response describes a number of reasons, including some not mentioned in 1999, why armed and uniformed officers might be present at hearings and indicates that depending on the circumstances, there are several different types of officers that might be present.

At the time, the use of armed and uniformed officers was uncommon and appears to have only happened at the hearing held in the African American community. In evaluating the use of armed and uniformed officers in this situation, EPA considered the intimidation factor through threat of police force as historically used against African Americans when attempting to exercise their rights.

Without any credible explanation, MDEQ deviated from its stated policy at the time by placing the armed and uniformed guards at the GPS hearing in Flint. MDEQ has not provided a copy of any current policies that apply to the use of armed and uniformed officers at hearings or the criteria used to evaluate whether and when certain types of officers should be used (e.g., plain clothes, armed and uniformed police, conservation officers).

*Close of hearing during testimony*

MDEQ adjourned the October 20, 1994, hearing during the testimony of an African American speaker and before everyone had been given a chance to testify.

The decision to adjourn the hearing surprised MDEQ staff. MDEQ staff stated that, before its adjournment, the October 20, 1994, hearing was not atypically controversial or heated, nor was the audience disorderly. MDEQ staff members stated that the audience at Carpenter Road Elementary was no more emotional than audiences at other hearings that had not been adjourned. One MDEQ employee stated that she had never seen any hearing adjourned before all of the commenters were allowed to speak.

In addition, another witness who attended most of the air permit hearings held in Michigan from 1990 to 1996 stated that he had never seen the MDEQ adjourn a hearing as it did at the October 20, 1994, GPS hearing. The witness stated that commenters at other hearings had made comments similar to Ms. O'Neal's, but the MDEQ had never adjourned a hearing because of it.

The evidence shows that Ms. O'Neal, an African American, was treated less favorably than all other commenters at any MDEQ hearing in anyone's memory. In addition, the witnesses say that to their knowledge the first time, and for some who attended many hearings afterward, the only time a hearing was closed before all commenters could speak was when it was held in the African American community in Flint.

MDEQ did not provide any current information or decision criteria to address whether and when a current hearing might be closed before all those wishing to speak were able to provide comments....

The totality of the circumstances described above supported by a preponderance of the evidence in EPA's record would lead a reasonable person to conclude that race discrimination was more likely than not the reason why African Americans were treated less favorably than non-African Americans during the 1992–1994 public participation for the GPS permit.

[After finding likely race discrimination in the MDEQ permit procedures, the EPA letter proceeds to evaluate the likely health impacts from GPS air emissions. Finding no direct or indirect health effects above EPA's action levels (one in ten thousand excess chance of cancer), the EPA letter concluded that there was insufficient evidence of health impacts (thus insufficient evidence to support a finding of health impacts) on the African-American community of Flint. The EPA accordingly closed this Title VI complaint against MDEQ. Eds.]

\* \* \*

## Notes and Questions

1. **Race discrimination.** As recounted in the above excerpt, what exactly did the state do to support the EPA's finding that "African Americans were treated less favorably than non-African Americans" in the GPS permit process? If you were legal counsel for the state in 1992–1994, how might you have advised your agency clients to avoid any appearance of discrimination in each of the three contexts discussed in the excerpt?

2. **Finally getting it right?** What is the effect of an agency responding to a Title VI complaint 25 years after it has been filed? Is this a mockery of the administrative

process? Or is the letter from the EPA in 2017 vindication of Fr. Schmitter and the African-American community that the EPA found had been so mistreated by MDEQ in the GPS permit process? Could any good come from this?

Consider the effect of the passage of time. If the EPA Office of Civil Rights had responded to the GPS complaint in 1992 as it responded to the Select Steel complaint in 1998, would it similarly have dismissed any allegation of race discrimination? Did OCR (now the External Civil Rights Compliance Office) need time to mature and refine its understanding of distributional and procedural justice?

While failing to find actual health impacts from the GPS facility, the EPA letter found convincing evidence of procedural injustice in the GPS permit process and across MDEQ operations more broadly. After reviewing "30 years of [MDEQ] history," the letter stated that "EPA is deeply concerned that MDEQ will not fulfill its responsibility to implement a fully functioning and meaningful non-discrimination program as required under EPA regulations." EPA letter at 28. To address these "deep[] concerns," the EPA letter provided MDEQ with a number of specific recommendations for improving its public procedures, to include (1) updating and prominently displaying MDEQ's notice of non-discrimination; (2) updating MDEQ's grievance procedures; (3) providing explicit assurances against retaliation for invoking grievance procedures; (4) ensuring appropriate training for MDEQ personnel; (5) developing and updating appropriate public participation plans; (6) taking greater measures to involve Limited English Proficiency communities; and (7) ensuring MDEQ facilities are physically accessible for persons with disabilities.

While closing the Title VI complaint for the Genesee Power Station permit, the EPA letter further noted the existence of another Title VI complaint continuing against MDEQ where the EPA has "additional and serious concerns." This ongoing complaint arises from MDEQ's "administration of the Safe Drinking Water Act ... during the Flint drinking water crisis...." Time will tell whether the EPA will make further findings of race discrimination by MDEQ and whether MDEQ will take actions to ensure future compliance with Title VI of the Civil Rights Act.

## 3. Reform and Modern Practice in Title VI Enforcement

The 25-year saga of the Genesee Power Station Title VI complaint is an extraordinary case on many levels. However, it represents just one of the hundreds of Title VI complaints that have been filed with the U.S. EPA over the same period of time. Like the complaint for the GPS permit, nearly all of the Title VI complaints filed with the EPA have received delayed responses, if they received any response at all. This record of poor performance has not gone unnoticed, including by federal courts and the EPA itself, both of which have contributed to reforms of the Title VI program. Due in part to these reforms, the Title VI enforcement program now appears as vibrant and vital as ever for pursuing cases of environmental injustice across the United States.

After President Obama was elected in 2008, his first EPA Administrator, Lisa Jackson, made environmental justice a renewed emphasis for the Agency. Recognizing the infamous inertia of the EPA Office of Civil Rights, Jackson retained Deloitte Consulting to perform a review of OCR's operations. According to Deloitte's 2011 report, of 247 Title VI complaints filed with OCR between 1993 and 2010, OCR failed to provide timely responses in 94% of the cases. In fact, half of the complaints received no response at all within one year or more. Deloitte Consulting LLP, FINAL REPORT: EVALUATION OF THE EPA OFFICE OF CIVIL RIGHTS 25 (2011). The reasons for OCR's languor were many and complex, but included lack of leadership and vision, as well as difficulty in building and retaining knowledgeable staff. After Deloitte's report, progress came slowly (of course), but did seem to come. In December 2016, the functions of receiving and responding to Title VI complaints were removed from the Office of Civil Rights and assigned to the newly created External Civil Rights Compliance Office, within the EPA Office of General Counsel. The EPA also issued a new *Case Resolution Manual* in 2017 to clarify guidance for Title VI investigators. To provide guidance to the public on filing future Title VI complaints, the agency also issued a new brochure, available on the website of the EPA External Civil Rights Compliance Office.

Since it was established, the EPA External Civil Rights Compliance Office has markedly improved Agency responses to Title VI complaints, although this may not necessarily reflect voluntary action on the part of the Agency. In fact, the Agency's egregious record of delay and inaction on Title VI complaints has attracted the attention and direction of federal courts. In one case arising in Vancouver, Washington, residents of the Rosemere neighborhood, populated by low-income and minority residents, filed a Title VI complaint in 2003 alleging that the City of Vancouver had discriminated in its provision of municipal services such as storm water and septic system management (similar to the claims twenty years earlier against the City of Apopka). In December 2003, the Rosemere residents filed a second Title VI complaint alleging retaliation after the city revoked Rosemere's status as a neighborhood association. Despite the Title VI regulations requiring some response within 20 days, the EPA provided no response to the retaliation complaint within 18 months. The Agency only responded after Rosemere filed suit in federal district court in June 2005 to compel some response to its retaliation complaint. Six weeks later, the EPA accepted the retaliation complaint and moved to dismiss as moot the complaint in district court, which the district court granted. *Rosemere Neighborhood Ass'n v. U.S. EPA*, 2007 WL 9728563 (W.D. Wash. 2007). On appeal, however, the Ninth Circuit reversed, recognizing that after accepting the retaliation complaint, the EPA was immediately in violation of other regulatory deadlines, including the duty to provide some preliminary finding within 180 days. 581 F.3d 1169 (9th Cir. 2009). Citing data from an amicus brief submitted by the Center on Race, Poverty & the Environment, the Ninth Circuit observed that "Rosemere's experience before the EPA appears, sadly and unfortunately, typical of those who appeal to OCR to remedy civil rights violations.... [D]iscovery has shown that the EPA failed to process a single complaint from 2006 or 2007 in accordance with its regulatory deadlines." *Id.* at 1175.

Other courts have demonstrated similar concern for the EPA's historic failure to comply with Title VI regulatory deadlines. *See, e.g., Padres Hacia Una Vida Mejor v. McCarthy*, 614 F.App'x 895, 897 (9th Cir. 2015) (describing as "simply deplorable" the EPA's 17-year delay in responding to a Title VI complaint filed in 1994 alleging discrimination against Latinos in the siting and operation of toxic waste disposal sites in Kettleman City). In a more recent case, community advocates sued in federal court to compel Agency response to Title VI complaints each languishing for more than a decade in California, Michigan, Texas, New Mexico, and Alabama. *Californians for Renewable Energy, et al. v. U.S. EPA*, 2018 WL 1586211 (N.D. Cal. 2018). Rejecting EPA motions to dismiss, and granting summary judgment for the plaintiffs, the court issued the following judgment:

4. The EPA shall timely process any pending and future Title VI complaints submitted by Plaintiffs and accepted for investigation by EPA as follows: for any pending investigation into a Title VI complaint submitted by any Plaintiff, EPA must issue preliminary findings and any recommendations for voluntary compliance, or otherwise resolve the complaint, within 180 days of the date of entry of this judgment; for any Title VI complaint submitted by any Plaintiff and accepted by EPA after the date of entry of this judgment, EPA must issue preliminary findings and any recommendations for voluntary compliance, or otherwise resolve the complaint, within 180 days of acceptance. The requirements of this paragraph shall continue for a period of five years from the date judgment is entered.

5. The Court shall retain jurisdiction to enforce this judgment only as to those complaints subject to Paragraph 4 above.

IT IS SO ORDERED.

DATED at Oakland, California this 13th day of June, 2018.

## Notes and Questions

1. **Message delivered?** Does the outcome of cases like *Californians for Renewable Energy v. EPA* mean that the EPA must always be sued in order to compel compliance with Title VI regulations? Or may it create a deterrent effect, encouraging the EPA to comply with Title VI requirements before it gets sued again? As an agency charged with enforcement of environmental laws (e.g., Clean Air Act, Clean Water Act), the EPA is well aware of the deterrent effect, and one may hope the Agency has learned lessons from its losses in Title VI litigation. If not, precedent appears to be growing in federal court so that more cases may be won by community advocates on summary judgment. For more on Title VI litigation and *Californians for Renewable Energy v. EPA* (by the attorney who served as counsel for the plaintiffs), *see* Marianne Engelman Lado, *No More Excuses, supra*, at 296.

2. **Progress on the ground?** Of course, victory in court does not necessarily mean progress on the ground. Did the lawsuit in *Californians for Renewable Energy* achieve any real benefit for community members concerned with environmental justice? For

at least some of the individual plaintiffs, it does appear to have made a difference. As the court acknowledged in its opinion, the very filing of the lawsuit seemed to encourage the EPA to snap to attention and provide some resolution to each of the five Title VI cases that had languished over a decade. The Michigan case was the one involving the Genesee Power Station, filed by Fr. Schmitter in 1992 and resolved by EPA letter of January 19, 2017 (reprinted in part above). On the same day, the EPA also resolved the New Mexico case, filed on behalf of the Citizens for Alternatives to Radioactive Dumping (CARD), by entering an Informal Resolution Agreement with the New Mexico Environment Department. Previously, the EPA had already closed the California case for "insufficient evidence of current non-compliance with Title VI" or the Title VI regulations. Within three months of resolving the Michigan and New Mexico cases, the EPA closed the Alabama case for "insufficient evidence" and closed the Texas case by entering into an Informal Resolution Agreement with Texas DEQ. *Californians for Renewable Energy* at 4.

While the California and Alabama Title VI complaints were dismissed, the continuing jurisdiction of the court for five years means that the plaintiffs in these cases may now wield significant leverage in negotiations with local regulators, given the plaintiffs' continuing ability to file future Title VI complaints and seek enforcement of regulatory deadlines. The Genesee Power Station case in Flint, Michigan, resulted in a finding that the state likely engaged in race discrimination—a finding any state would seek mightily to avoid—plus specific recommendations from the EPA for improving the state's public involvement processes. For the New Mexico and Texas cases, through the Informal Resolution Agreements, the plaintiffs received specific commitments from state regulators to improve their environmental and community involvement practices. The New Mexico Environment Department, for example, developed a new public involvement policy and took affirmative measures to ensure that key regulatory documents would be translated for Spanish-speaking communities. (One of the book authors served as co-counsel to ensure compliance with the New Mexico agreement.)

Another success through Title VI includes resolution of a complaint against the State of North Carolina alleging failure to address disproportionate impacts from hog farms that had proliferated in the eastern part of the state, including Duplin County. *See* Figure 4-1. The complaint, filed in 2014 on behalf of the North Carolina Environmental Justice Network, community-based Rural Empowerment Association for Community Help (REACH), and Waterkeeper Alliance resulted four years later in a Settlement Agreement with the North Carolina Department of Environmental Quality. Under the Settlement Agreement, the DEQ agreed to specific concessions that will include the following:

- Submission of the Swine Waste Management System General Permit to a public stakeholder process, including use of an independent facilitator;

- Conduct of local air monitoring and water monitoring, carried out in partnership with the complainant community organizations; and

**Figure 4-3:** Naeema Muhammad, North Carolina Environmental Justice Network. March 8, 2019. Photo: Cliff Villa.

- Development and implementation of policies to enhance public involvement and language access.

Whether or not these enhanced public engagement procedures will ultimately relieve the substantial burdens that industrial hog farms pose to people of color and low-income community members around Duplin County and nearby counties, it is clear now that Title VI of the Civil Rights Act of 1964 can be used to draw attention to environmental justice concerns and to compel government response. How Title VI may be used in the future to pursue environmental justice remains to be seen in the dedication and creativity of individual advocates.

# E. Seeking Environmental Justice through § 1983

With origins reaching back to the Civil Rights Act of 1871, the federal law known today as § 1983 provides as follows:

> Every person who, under color of any statute, ordinance, regulation, custom, or usage, of any State or Territory or the District of Columbia, subjects ... any citizen of the United States ... to the deprivation of any rights, privileges, or immunities secured by the Constitution and laws, shall be liable to the party injured in an action at law....

42 U.S.C. § 1983 (2019). As indicated, § 1983 establishes a private right of action for deprivation of rights established under the U.S. Constitution and other federal law. § 1983 is today a major authority for pursuing civil rights claims in every public arena, including education, voting rights, and criminal justice. While a thorough review of § 1983 theory and practice remains beyond the scope of this book, this concluding section of the chapter demonstrates that civil rights claims under § 1983 may also address concerns for environmental justice in certain contexts. Returning to the serious (and in some cases, fatal) poisoning of the drinking water in Flint, Michigan [*see* Part A of Chapter 3 ("Risk and Health")], consider the following decision in a case brought under § 1983 by injured residents of Flint.

## Boler v. Earley

### 865 F.3d 391 (6th Cir. 2017), *cert. denied,*
### 138 S.Ct. 1294 (2018)

JANE B. STRANCH, Circuit Judge

These [] cases arise from the water contamination crisis in Flint, Michigan. Plaintiffs, residents of Flint affected by the contaminated city water, bring suit against various state and local officials and entities, alleging violation of their constitutional rights, pursuant to 42 U.S.C. § 1983, along with other claims. In *Boler*, the district court determined that the § 1983 claims were preempted by the Safe Drinking Water Act (SDWA) and dismissed the case for lack of subject matter jurisdiction. Relying on its preemption analysis in *Boler*, the court dismissed the *Mays* case. The cases have been consolidated on appeal. For the reasons explained below, we REVERSE the judgment of the district court and REMAND for further proceedings.

### I. BACKGROUND

#### A. Factual Background

In March 2011, the Michigan state Legislature passed the Local Government and School District Fiscal Accountability Act ("Act 4"), which authorized the governor to appoint an emergency manager for certain local governments. Act 4 replaced an earlier Michigan law, the Local Government Fiscal Responsibility Act ("Act 72"), which had been in effect since 1990. Act 72 gave the State power to appoint an emergency financial manager to municipalities facing financial crises. Act 4 expanded the scope of the powers granted to these emergency financial managers and changed their title to simply "emergency managers." New emergency managers were subsequently appointed in several areas; in August 2012, Governor Rick Snyder appointed Edward Kurtz in Flint.

On November 5, 2012, Michigan voters rejected Act 4 by referendum. This revived Act 72. In December, the Michigan Legislature responded by enacting the Local Financial Stability and Choice Act ("Act 436"), effective March 28, 2013. Under Michigan law, a public act with an appropriations provision is not subject to referendum. Unlike Act 4, Act 436 added appropriations provisions that prevented voters from subjecting it to a referendum. Act 436, like Act 4, authorized the State to appoint emergency managers with authority to exercise the power of local governments.

Following the passage of Act 436, Kurtz resumed his status as named Emergency Manager for the City of Flint, and remained in that post until July 2013. In November 2013, Governor Snyder appointed Darnell Earley as Emergency Manager for the City of Flint. In January 2015, Earley was replaced by Gerald Ambrose.

Between 1967 and 2014, the City of Flint sourced its water from Lake Huron via the Detroit Water and Sewerage Department (DWSD). On March 29, 2013, one day after Act 436 went into effect, the City of Flint decided to join a water supplier, the Karegnondi Water Authority (KWA), that was to be established. Sourcing water for Flint had been under review. In 2011, Flint had commissioned a study ("2011 Report" or "Report") to evaluate the cost of treating water from the Flint River for municipal use as an alternative to either purchasing from the future KWA or continuing its existing contract with DWSD. The Report determined that water from the Flint River would need to be treated to meet current water safety regulations. It also concluded that the cost of treating water from the Flint River to provide safe municipal use would be greater than the proposed KWA contract, but less than continuing the contract with DWSD. The officials thus decided to go with the cheapest long-term option—the KWA.

Shortly after the decision to switch to the KWA was made, DWSD notified Flint that its current contract would terminate in approximately one year, in April 2014. Because the KWA would take several years to construct, officials were tasked with choosing an interim water source: the Flint River or DWSD. Officials chose the Flint River. Genesee County, which includes Flint but is, according to the Defendants, "[j]urisdictionally separate and distinct from the City of Flint," had also decided to switch its future water supply to the KWA. Unlike the City of Flint, Genesee County officials opted to continue to purchase DWSD water during the KWA's construction. The Defendants state that this was because Genesee County, unlike Flint, does not have its own water treatment plant.

In April 2014, Flint's emergency manager changed the source of the city's water from DWSD to the Flint River. The plaintiffs assert that at this time, the City knew "that the Flint River could not be a source of safe municipal water unless it underwent significant treatment, including the addition of anti-corrosive agents and treatment for microbial contaminants," as explained by the 2011 Report. The Report itself states that its comparison to other alternatives "assumed that the Flint [water treatment plant] w[ould] treat water from the river to provide a finished water of similar quality to other alternatives being considered." There is no evidence that the City upgraded the treatment plants or provided for additional safety measures prior to switching water supply sources on April 25, 2014. The Defendants contend that they operated in accordance with the SDWA's Lead and Copper Rule, which requires a two-step process that begins with "initial monitoring" over two separate six-month periods to determine if treatment is required. The first six-month period did not begin until June 2014.

Following the switch to the Flint River, residents immediately began to complain that the drinking water "smelled rotten, looked foul, and tasted terrible." Larger problems with the water supply soon became apparent. Testing conducted in August and September 2014 detected coliform and *E. coli* bacteria in the water supply. In October 2014, the water was linked to Legionnaire's disease. General Motors discontinued its water service because the Flint River water was corroding its parts.

In January 2015, the City issued a notice that the drinking water violated standards, but that it was safe to drink. In February 2015, further water testing indicated high levels of contaminants such as lead and total trihalomethane. The Defendants state that the City conducted its two required rounds of sampling to determine lead levels, from July to December 2014 and January to June 2015, but the results did not exceed the SDWA Lead and Copper Rule's "action level." The results did indicate that corrosion control treatment measures were needed to counteract lead levels, which "had risen since switching to the Flint River." In March 2015, the Flint City Council voted to reconnect with DWSD rather than continuing to use the Flint River water supply, but the City government's vote was overruled by the Emergency Manager.

Over the next few months, the City issued instructions to residents on their use of water, including advising them to "pre-flush" taps prior to use or to stop drinking the water altogether. In June 2015, the EPA warned of high lead levels in the water. In response, officials provided consumers with water filters, which the Plaintiffs state did not substantially improve the water quality and were incapable of filtering out known contaminants.

In October 2015, Genesee County declared a public health emergency in Flint, advising residents not to drink the water. That same month, the Emergency Manager ordered that Flint reconnect to DWSD. By that point, however, the protective coating in the water supply pipes had been damaged by water from the Flint River, and until the coating could "buil[d] up to appropriate levels," the water would continue to have elevated lead levels. The EPA issued an advisory to Flint residents in February 2016, warning them that unfiltered water was not safe and advising the use of bottled water, especially for young children and pregnant women. Many of these advisories are currently still in place, and Flint remains in a state of emergency.

Flint residents have been billed continuously for their water services since April 2014. The City of Flint has engaged in collection efforts when payments have not been made, including disconnecting water service altogether and issuing liens against real property. The Defendants state that Michigan is providing funds for the reimbursement of water bills, as well as making other efforts to ameliorate the effects of the water crisis.

On January 25, 2016, the Michigan Civil Rights Commission passed a resolution to hold a series of hearings to determine the impact of the Flint water contamination crisis on the civil rights of Michigan's citizens. The Commission, appointed by the Governor, held three hearings that included "expert testimony focusing on the history of Flint's economy and housing, environmental justice, and the application of the ... emergency manager law." Michigan Civil Rights Commission, *The Flint Water Crisis: Systemic*

*Racism Through the Lens of Flint* iii (Feb. 17, 2017). The Commission's 130-page report determined that the response to the Flint water crisis was "the result of systemic racism," *Id.* at 2, and that its finding was "based on a plethora of events and policies that so racialized the structure of public policy that it systemically produced racially disparate outcomes adversely affecting a community that is primarily made up of people of color."

B. Procedural History of *Boler v. Earley*

Plaintiffs Beatrice Boler, Pastor Edwin Anderson and Mrs. Alline Anderson, and EPC Sales, LLC, a Flint business, brought a class action on behalf of purchasers of Flint water. They brought suit against Darnell Earley and Gerald Ambrose, both former emergency managers of Flint; Dayne Walling, the former mayor of Flint; the City of Flint; Governor Rick Snyder; the State of Michigan; the Michigan Department of Environmental Quality (MDEQ); and the Michigan Department of Health and Human Services (MDHHS).

The Plaintiffs filed suit in the Eastern District of Michigan on January 31, 2016, alleging twelve causes of action, five of them pursuant to 42 U.S.C. § 1983: (1) impairment of the constitutional right to contract; (2) deprivation of substantive and procedural due process; (3) breach of the duty to protect against state-created danger; (4) breach of the Equal Protection Clause; and (5) deprivation of property interest without due process or just compensation....

The Plaintiffs filed a motion for a preliminary injunction, seeking to enjoin the defendants from billing and collecting money from Flint residents for water. At a status conference following briefing on the preliminary injunction, the district court asked the parties to provide supplemental briefing on whether the court had jurisdiction over the case. The court subsequently dismissed the case for lack of subject matter jurisdiction, finding that the Plaintiffs' § 1983 claims were precluded by the SDWA, leaving only state law claims over which the court did not have jurisdiction.... This appeal followed....

II. ANALYSIS

A. Preclusion of § 1983 Claims by the Safe Drinking Water Act

The district court's SDWA preemption analysis drew from *Middlesex County Sewerage Authority v. National Sea Clammers Association*, 453 U.S. 1 (1981), in which the Supreme Court found that the § 1983 claims presented were preempted by the statutes alleged. The court primarily relied on the First Circuit's determination that the SDWA foreclosed other federal remedies for an alleged right to "safe and potable water." The Plaintiffs argue that this is not the proper focus of their claims, and more importantly, that the district court misapplied the standard enunciated by the Supreme Court in its line of cases that began with *Sea Clammers* and concluded with *Fitzgerald v. Barnstable School Committee*, 555 U.S. 246 (2009).

The provisions of 42 U.S.C. § 1983 may serve as a vehicle for a plaintiff to obtain damages for violations of the Constitution or a federal statute. Section 1983 provides in part:

> Every person who, under color of any statute, ordinance, regulation, custom, or usage, of any State or Territory or the District of Columbia, subjects, or causes to be subjected, any citizen of the United States … to the deprivation of any rights, privileges, or immunities secured by the Constitution and laws, shall be liable to the party injured in an action at law, suit in equity, or other proper proceeding for redress. …

In *Sea Clammers*, the Court examined claims — brought under the [Clean Water Act], 33 U.S.C. §1251, and the Marine Protection, Research, and Sanctuaries Act (MPRSA), 33 U.S.C. §1401, as well as under §1983 — alleging violations of those statutes as a result of damage to fishing grounds from pollution. Focusing on Congress's intent in enacting [CWA] and MPRSA and finding that they provide "unusually elaborate enforcement mechanisms," the Court held that the plaintiffs could not use §1983 to enforce their rights under those pollution statutes. The Court compared §1983 to [CWA] and MPRSA, primarily examining the extensiveness of the remedial scheme and its relationship to congressional intent: "[w]hen the remedial devices provided in the particular Act are sufficiently comprehensive, they may suffice to demonstrate congressional intent to preclude the remedy of suits under §1983." Based on these statutory provisions, the Court found it "hard to believe that Congress intended to preserve the §1983 right of action" for violations of the statute.

The Court reaffirmed this intent-based analysis in subsequent cases. In *Smith v. Robinson*, 468 U.S. 992, 104 (1984), the plaintiffs brought suit against their child's school district for relief under both the Education of the Handicapped Act (EHA) and, pursuant to §1983, the Due Process and Equal Protection Clauses of the Fourteenth Amendment. The Court first looked to the text of the statute and its legislative history and found Congress's express statements that it had designed the EHA to help the States "comply[] with their constitutional obligations to provide public education for" children with disabilities. It next reviewed the statute's procedural mechanisms, focusing on the "comprehensive nature of the procedures and guarantees" in the EHA. The Court concluded that the language of the statute, its legislative history, and the comprehensive nature of its procedures and remedies reveal Congress's intent that the statute be the "exclusive avenue" for plaintiffs to bring all their claims and, thus, §1983 claims were precluded. …

In the most recent Supreme Court authority on these issues, *Fitzgerald*, the Court explained the distinction between §1983 claims premised on constitutional violations and those based on statutory violations in determining whether a §1983 claim is precluded. "In those cases in which the §1983 claim is based on a statutory right, evidence of such congressional intent may be found directly in the statute creating the right, or inferred from the statute's creation of a comprehensive enforcement scheme that is incompatible with individual enforcement under §1983." The Court then explained:

> In cases in which the §1983 claim alleges a constitutional violation, lack of congressional intent may be inferred from a comparison of the rights and protections of the statute and those existing under the Constitution. Where

the contours of such rights and protections diverge in significant ways, it is not likely that Congress intended to displace § 1983 suits enforcing constitutional rights. Our conclusions regarding congressional intent can be confirmed by a statute's context.

*Id.* at 252–53 (quotation marks and citations omitted). The Court examined Title IX under this framework and found that it contained only an implied private right of action rather than an express private remedy, lacked a comprehensive remedial scheme, and its substantive protections diverged from those provided by the Equal Protection Clause. The Court determined that Title IX did not foreclose the plaintiff's equal protection claim brought under § 1983. In doing so, it acknowledged that it was mindful of *Smith's* admonition to "not lightly conclude that Congress intended to preclude § 1983 as a remedy for a substantial equal protection claim."

*Fitzgerald* was preceded and followed by our own cases that articulate standards in line with the test it set out. We found a § 1983 claim under the First Amendment not precluded by the whistleblower provisions of the SDWA. *Charvat v. E. Ohio Reg'l Wastewater Auth.*, 246 F.3d 607, 615 (6th Cir. 2001). *Communities for Equity*, in which we denied preclusion by Title IX and authorized an equal protection claim under § 1983, was part of the circuit split that preceded and ultimately led to the Supreme Court's decision in *Fitzgerald*. Setting out the governing test, *Fitzgerald* resolved this circuit split by determining, as we did, that Congress did not intend for Title IX to preclude a § 1983 remedy for a plaintiff's equal protection claim.

Based on the case authority set out above, the Plaintiffs in *Boler* and *Mays* aver that they do not "invoke[] § 1983 … as a vehicle to enforce the substantive federal law found in [the SDWA], but as a vehicle to recover for alleged violations" of various constitutional provisions, including the Contract Clause, Equal Protection Clause, and Due Process Clause—allegations that they state would be actionable even if Congress had never enacted the SDWA. Plaintiffs argue that the fact that Congress "created a set of substantive statutory requirements, and adopted a set of procedures for enforcing *those* requirements, does not … suggest that Congress intend[ed] to foreclose a Section 1983 remedy for the violations of independent rights that find their source, not in laws passed by Congress, but in the Constitution itself."

The focus of our inquiry on this question is congressional intent. *See Communities for Equity*, 459 F.3d at 684 ("The question of what Congress intended … concerns not only which remedies Congress sought to provide for [statutory] violations, but whether Congress intended to abandon the rights and remedies set forth in [constitutional jurisprudence] when it enacted [the statute].") "The burden … lies with the defendant in a § 1983 action to prove preclusion."

## 1. Statutory Text and Legislative History

The beginning point for examining congressional intent is the language of the statute. We addressed this very issue in *Charvat*, and determined that the whistleblower provisions of the SDWA and Clean Water Act (CWA) did not preclude the First

Amendment claims brought by that plaintiff pursuant to § 1983. Our analysis focused solely on the SDWA's whistleblower provisions; we found that they provide for an administrative remedy only and determined the remedies provided to be insufficiently comprehensive to foreclose relief under § 1983. The Plaintiffs argue that *Charvat* was an application of the principle that a federal statutory scheme will not preempt independently existing constitutional rights when those rights have contours distinct from the statutory claim.

*Charvat* does not control our decision here, but we find instructive its analysis that emphasizes a focus on the wording of the statute. That focus accords with *Fitzgerald's* analysis, which clarifies that review differs depending on whether "the § 1983 claim is based on a statutory right" or "alleges a constitutional violation." *Fitzgerald* concludes its explanation of that distinction by noting that "[c]ontext, not just literal text, will often lead a court to Congress' intent in respect to a particular statute."

In *Sea Clammers* and *Rancho Palos Verdes*, the Court determined that the statutory remedies at issue were sufficiently comprehensive to evince congressional intent to preclude § 1983 claims for *violations of the statute*. In *Smith*, the Court addressed whether the EHA precludes a § 1983 claim based on *a constitutional violation* and began with a focus on what the legislature said in the Act and its legislative history. The Court found that specific provisions of the EHA evidenced that it was enacted for the very purpose of allowing children with disabilities to pursue their constitutional claims. Explaining its context, the Act noted that "Congress also recognized that in a series of 'landmark court cases,' the right to an equal education opportunity for handicapped children had been established." In addition to protecting that right, the legislative history stated the purpose of Congress in passing the Act: "to provide assistance to the States in carrying out their responsibilities under State law and the *Constitution of the United States* to provide equal protection of the laws." As a result, the Court found that the EHA contained the expression of Congress's intention to preclude a § 1983 claim based on a constitutional violation.

We examine the Safe Drinking Water Act in light of the analysis employed by these precedent cases. The language of the SDWA centers on instructions to the EPA to establish the requirements for national drinking water standards. *See* 42 U.S.C. § 300g-1. Its provisions set out standards identifying particular contaminants selected for regulation and establishing maximum levels that limit the amount of those specified contaminants permitted in public drinking water systems. *See id.* § 300g-1(b). The statutory language also specifies the time frame for the EPA's promulgation of regulations, the use of science in the EPA's decisionmaking, and the technology by which public systems should achieve compliance with the standards. *See id.*

The Defendants have not pointed to any indications of preclusive intent in the text or legislative history of the SDWA in their briefing, nor were they able to do so at argument. The Plaintiffs point to portions of the text and legislative history of the SDWA that they suggest show the statute was *not* intended to foreclose § 1983 claims for constitutional rights. For example, the SDWA was adopted pursuant to Congress's power under the Commerce Clause, U.S. Const. Art. I, § 8, rather than its power under Section 5 of the Fourteenth Amendment to enforce constitutional rights. Accordingly, the Plaintiffs note that the findings enunciated in the SDWA emphasize Congress's focus on the interstate economic impacts of polluted drinking water, not on any constitutional violations that may accompany the pollution.

Unlike the EHA examined in *Smith*, the SDWA does not use language related to constitutional rights, or codify legal standards that appeared in prior cases to enforce rights guaranteed by the Constitution. We find no clear inference from either the text of the statute or its legislative history that Congress intended for the SDWA's remedial scheme to displace § 1983 suits enforcing constitutional rights. This, in turn, informs our next step—evaluating the comprehensiveness of the remedial scheme provided by the statute.

## 2. Remedial Scheme

Lacking textual support from the statute or its legislative history, the Defendants contend that the SDWA's remedial scheme is so comprehensive that it demonstrates congressional intent to preclude remedies under § 1983. They argue that the remedial provisions of the SDWA are similar to those examined in *Sea Clammers* which, along with the First Circuit's holding in *Mattoon*, should direct our inquiry and conclusion, as they did that of the district court.

The SDWA's remedial scheme authorizes the EPA Administrator to compel compliance with the standards promulgated by the statute, 42 U.S.C. § 300g-3(b), and to assess civil penalties against violators of SDWA regulations. *Id.* § 300g-3(g)(3). The statute also provides for judicial review of the Administrator's actions, including the establishment of drinking water regulations, *id.* § 300j-7(a), and contains a citizen-suit provision allowing a private action against any person in violation of the statute for injunctive relief. *Id.* § 300j-8. Plaintiffs bringing claims under the SDWA must also comply with certain procedural requirements, including providing a notice of intent to potential defendants 60 days prior to filing suit. *Id.* § 300j-8(b)(1)(A). This remedial scheme contains a number of similarities to the schemes in the pollution statutes in *Sea Clammers*.

The Plaintiffs respond that the SDWA's savings clause, *id.* § 300j-8(e), demonstrates that Congress intended to preserve independent remedies for conduct also violating the statute. The savings clause states that "[n]othing in this section [establishing the SDWA's private right of action] shall restrict any right which any person (or class of persons) may have under any statute or common law to seek enforcement of any requirement prescribed by or under this subchapter or to seek any other relief." *Id.* § 300j-8(e). *Sea Clammers* rejected a similar argument about the [CWA] and MPRSA's savings clauses, which were similarly worded. The Court found that it was "doubtful that the phrase 'any statute' include[d] the very statute in which [that] statement was contained." But that determination was premised on violations of the statute itself. The Court also recognized that the savings clause was intended to "allow further enforcement of antipollution standards arising under other statutes or state common law." The language of the SDWA's savings clause lends support to a conclusion that

Congress contemplated leaving open § 1983 as an avenue of relief for claims arising under the Constitution....

*Communities for Equity* teaches that where constitutional claims such as those here are at issue, the question of congressional intent "concerns not only what remedies Congress sought to provide" for SDWA violations, "but whether Congress intended to abandon the rights and remedies set forth in Fourteenth Amendment equal protection jurisprudence" when it enacted the SDWA.

The SDWA's remedies are more limited than those generally available under § 1983, as the statute provides for injunctive relief only, not for recovery of damages or other monetary relief available to Plaintiffs with successful § 1983 claims. Though the statute contains a private right of action, it also includes a savings clause establishing that its private action does not restrict rights a person may exercise outside the SDWA. The availability of a private judicial remedy in the SDWA, moreover, does not conclusively establish congressional intent to preclude relief under § 1983. Rather, we examine whether there are statutory indications "express or implicit" that the remedy is meant to "complement, rather than supplant, § 1983." And we do so in accordance with *Fitzgerald*'s admonition that we should be "mindful" to "not lightly conclude that Congress intended to preclude reliance on § 1983 as a remedy for a substantial [constitutional] claim."

In the context of the SDWA and its text and legislative history, we find that the remedial schemes in the SDWA are not so comprehensive as to demonstrate congressional intent to preclude remedies under § 1983 for constitutional violations. This leaves us with the last consideration set out in *Fitzgerald*'s framework—a comparison of the substantive rights and protections of the SDWA to the protections provided by the relevant constitutional provisions. It is Defendants' burden to show that this comparison reveals a congressional intention for the SDWA to preclude remedies provided for under § 1983.

### 3. Contours of the Rights and Protections

*Fitzgerald* teaches that in examining the SDWA, we ask whether "the contours of the rights and protections" provided by the SDWA and those existing under the Constitution "diverge in significant ways." If they do, this "lends further support to the conclusion that Congress did not intend [the statute] to preclude § 1983 constitutional suits."

... The Plaintiffs emphasize the divergence between the rights protected by the SDWA and those protected by their constitutional claims. The Defendants maintain that the § 1983 claims are, at their heart, based on misconduct addressed by the SDWA, arguing that they have the same factual basis as potential SDWA claims and that the allegations made in the Plaintiffs' complaint stem from responsibilities and duties imposed by the SDWA.

The SDWA's citizen-suit provision authorizes action against "any person," which therefore reaches both nonpublic actors as well as the state actors covered by § 1983. *See* 42 U.S.C. § 300j-8(a). But even with some overlap in coverage, the substantive standards within the statute diverge significantly from the protections afforded by the Constitution. The *Boler* Plaintiffs allege violations of several constitutional provisions, including the Contract Clause, Due Process Clause, and Equal Protection Clause. The *Mays* Plaintiffs also allege due process and equal protection violations. All Plaintiffs argue that each of these constitutional rights diverge significantly from the rights and protections provided by the SDWA. We agree.

The distinct coverage of the Equal Protection Clause provides a clear example. The citizen-suit provision allows a plaintiff to file a SDWA action to "enforce ... any requirement prescribed by or under" the statute. The SDWA establishes maximum contaminant levels through its national primary drinking water regulations, which most public water systems may not exceed. *Id.* § 300g-1. These regulations reach only certain harmful contaminants in drinking water, and do not redress harms caused by many other contaminants that are unregulated by the SDWA. Establishing a violation of the statute does not require proof of intent or meeting any specific standard beyond showing contaminant levels in excess of the maximum established by the regulations. The statute would thus cover both intentional and negligent conduct, as long as it violated the regulation.

In a wide variety of circumstances, conduct that violates the SDWA might not violate the Equal Protection Clause, and vice versa. For example, a government entity could provide water through a public system with contaminant levels in excess of national drinking water standards without infringing on any equal protection principles. Likewise, a government entity could provide some customers with water that meets the requirements of SDWA standards, but that is nonetheless dirtier, smellier, or of demonstrably poorer quality than water provided to other customers. The water also could be polluted by a contaminant not regulated by the SDWA. Even though not violating the SDWA, these situations could create an equal protection issue, particularly if such distinction were based on intentional discrimination or lacked a rational basis.

A Due Process Clause example further highlights this divergence in coverage. The *Mays* and *Boler* Plaintiffs both allege that the Defendants denied them due process of law through the state-created danger doctrine, by exposing them to the contaminated water sourced from the Flint River. Establishing a due process violation through the state-created danger doctrine requires showing:

> (1) an affirmative act by the state which either created or increased the risk that the plaintiff would be exposed to an act of violence by a third party; (2) a special danger to the plaintiff wherein the state's actions placed the plaintiff specifically at risk, as distinguished from a risk that affects the public at large; and (3) the state knew or should have known that its actions specifically endangered the plaintiff.

*Jones v. Reynolds*, 438 F.3d 685, 690 (6th Cir. 2006) (citations omitted). The plaintiff "must demonstrate that the state acted with the requisite culpability to establish a substantive due process violation under the Fourteenth Amendment," which varies depending on the circumstances. A deliberate indifference standard is used to establish culpability "in settings [that] provide the opportunity for reflection and unhurried judgments, but … a higher bar may be necessary when opportunities for reasoned deliberation are not present."

A violation of the SDWA that does not meet a deliberate indifference standard, such as a state actor's negligent action resulting in contaminant levels above the established maximum, plainly would not meet the requirements of a due process violation. Likewise, a state actor's deliberately indifferent action concerning contaminants in public water systems, which created a special danger to a plaintiff that the state knew or should have known about, could violate the Due Process Clause without also violating the SDWA, if the hypothetical contaminants did not exceed the statutory maximums or were not regulated by it.

Under some circumstances, actions that violate the SDWA may also violate the Equal Protection Clause or Due Process Clause. The Defendants argue that this is necessarily the case, and that the Plaintiffs' claims could not be pursued without showing a violation of the SDWA. But as noted, that is often not the case, particularly where the SDWA does not even regulate a contaminant harmful to public drinking water users. The contours of the rights and protections of the SDWA and those arising under the Constitution, and a plaintiff's ability to show violations of each, are "not … wholly congruent." This further supports the conclusion that Congress did not intend to foreclose § 1983 suits by enacting the SDWA.…

Having resolved that there is no textual indication in the SDWA that Congress expressly chose to preempt § 1983 claims and that the provisions of the remedial scheme do not demonstrate such an intention, we also find that the contours of the rights and protections found in the constitutional claims diverge from those provided by the SDWA such that we infer lack of congressional intention to foreclose § 1983 claims. The Defendants have not demonstrated that "Congress intended to abandon the rights and remedies set forth in Fourteenth Amendment equal protection jurisprudence" when it enacted the SDWA. Under the governing precedent, primarily that of the Supreme Court, the Defendants have not carried their burden and the Plaintiffs may thus move forward with their cases. We find that the SDWA does not preclude § 1983 claims as pled by the *Boler* and *Mays* Plaintiffs, and reverse the district court's dismissal of their Complaints on that basis.…

[The court then proceeded to consider and reject dismissal of claims under other grounds, including absolute and qualified immunity of government officials. Eds.]

## Notes and Questions

1. **§ 1983 vs. the Safe Drinking Water Act.** As noted by the Sixth Circuit, the Safe Drinking Water Act (SDWA), like most of the federal environmental statutes, has citizen suit provisions allowing private individuals to bring civil actions to "enforce … any requirement" established under the SDWA. As with many other environmental statutes, violations of the SDWA are generally subject to strict liability. § 1983 claims, on the other hand, may present plaintiffs with much more challenging proof standards, such as the Substantive Due Process standard that a state actor acted with

"deliberative indifference." Why then would a private individual like Melissa Mays bring an action under § 1983 instead of under the SDWA citizen suit provision? In fact, Ms. Mays (along with many others) did file a citizen suit under the SDWA. *See Concerned Pastors for Social Action v. Khouri*, 271 F.Supp.3d 960 (E.D. Mich. 2016) (granting plaintiffs' motion for preliminary injunction). What are the relative advantages of each approach for both a private individual and the affected community?

2. **Preclusion?** As noted in the Sixth Circuit's opinion, the district court originally dismissed the § 1983 action relying on the U.S. Supreme Court's decision in *Middlesex County Sewerage Authority v. National Sea Clammers Association*, 453 U.S. 1 (1981). As described by the Sixth Circuit, *Sea Clammers* "determined that the statutory remedies at issue" in that case, including under the Clean Water Act, "were sufficiently comprehensive to evince congressional intent to preclude § 1983 claims for *violations of the statute*" (emphasis in original). In dismissing the § 1983 claims by the Flint plaintiffs, the district court seemed to assume that the entire case depended on *violations of the statute*—specifically, in this case, violations of the Safe Drinking Water Act. The district court asserted, "Indeed, here the crux of each of Plaintiffs' constitutional claims is that they have been deprived of 'safe and potable water.' Plaintiffs' allegations are addressed by regulations that have been promulgated by the EPA under the SDWA." *Beatrice Boler v. Darnell Earley*, 2016 WL 1573272 (E.D. Mich. 2016). How accurate do you find that characterization of plaintiffs' constitutional claims? Is there a difference between being "deprived of safe and potable water" and being sold contaminated water the government warrants to be safe and potable? Moreover, after infants and children have been exposed to high doses of lead from their drinking water and suffered neurological impairment, is it realistic to believe that a potential lifetime of adverse health and social consequences will be "addressed by regulations that have been promulgated by the EPA under the SDWA," as the district court suggests?

3. *Sea Clammers* **reconsidered.** *Sea Clammers* involved allegations that the discharge of sewage, sludge, and other waste materials into the Hudson River and New York Harbor resulted in pollution causing the "collapse of the fishing, clamming, and lobster industries which operate in the waters of the Atlantic Ocean." Much of this pollution was permitted or subject to regulation by the EPA and Corps of Engineers under laws including the Clean Water Act. The U.S. Supreme Court decided the Clean Water Act preempted the § 1983 claims by plaintiff Sea Clammers, notwithstanding that the remedy the plaintiffs sought included compensatory damages to the fishing and clamming industry, which the Clean Water Act would not support. Did the Supreme Court in *Sea Clammers* misconstrue the Clean Water Act? For one view, *see* Jeffrey G. Miller, *The Supreme Court's Water Pollution Jurisprudence: Is the Court All Wet?*, 24 Va. Envtl. L.J. 125, 159 (2005) (noting the Court in *Sea Clammers* "made serious errors"). Even so, as the case remains precedent, how exactly does the Sixth Circuit distinguish *Sea Clammers*, involving Clean Water Act violations, from *Boler*, involving Safe Drinking Water Act violations? Drawing on the distinctions noted by the Sixth Circuit, is it possible that future cases involving Clean Water Act violations could support claims under § 1983?

**4. Hypothetical: The Treble Mine.** Five years from now, a massive gold mining operation known as the Treble Mine opens in Alaska, over objections from commercial fishermen and Alaska Natives who fear impacts to local salmon populations. Treble Mine operations depend on construction and maintenance of a three-mile dam to prevent mine tailings with toxic metals from entering the sensitive watershed below. Eight years into mine operations, after a torrential rain in the middle of winter, the dam fails, sending hundreds of millions of tons of mine tailings into headwater streams and completely choking off a dozen formerly vibrant salmon runs. The unpermitted discharge of these tailings into the streams clearly violates the Clean Water Act. The Native Villages who depend on these streams for subsistence fishing ask you for advice on bringing claims for damages under § 1983. Consistent with *Sea Clammers* and *Boler*, how would you structure your arguments in order to prevail on these claims?

**5. Final analysis.** Imagine that you lived in a small town with a large percentage of minority and low-income residents. Your local water authority provides semi-annual reports identifying chronic violations of standards under the Safe Drinking Water Act. According to the water authority, the violations may affect the taste and smell of your water, but are not predicted to affect human health. The water authority, like the rest of your local government, is struggling financially, but it is slowly making upgrades to water infrastructure. The upgrades are expected to fix the SDWA violations, but at the current pace of funding and construction, completion of the upgrades may take twenty years or more. Meanwhile, you learn that the next town over, with a predominantly white and middle-class population, is making similar upgrades but expecting to complete its construction within three years, given proportionally greater funding by the state government. In this scenario, if you wanted to ensure the protection of drinking water in your community, would you prefer to file civil litigation under the Equal Protection Clause, an administrative complaint under Title VI, or a claim for damages under § 1983? What are the pros and cons of each legal strategy?

# Chapter 5

# Standard Setting

## A. Introduction

Environmental agencies are generally charged with preventing, reducing, or cleaning up environmental contamination. Agencies enlist an array of regulatory tools in their effort to protect human and environmental health. The choice of tool is often specified by Congress in one of the various environmental statutes (e.g., the Clean Air Act, the Clean Water Act) that direct agencies' efforts, but sometimes this choice is left to the agencies. In either event, environmental agencies are responsible for shaping the contours of the relevant regulatory measure—for example, determining what concentration of sulfur dioxide ($SO_2$) in the ambient air is adequately protective of human health; deciding what level of mercury emissions reductions is technologically feasible; or devising an emissions trading regime for the contaminants that contribute to smog. When agencies undertake these varied tasks—discussed in this chapter under the umbrella of "standard setting"—their orientation is general. That is, they typically set standards that apply broadly, to an entire geographic region (e.g., national air quality standards) or an entire category of industrial sources (e.g., coal-fired utilities). These standards are also typically fashioned with an eye toward protecting the "average American," although there are important instances in which agencies are directed to ensure that more sensitive or vulnerable individuals are also protected. Agencies then translate these generic standards into more local, source-specific requirements when they issue permits to individual polluting facilities, a topic that is taken up in Chapter 6: ("Environmental Permits").

While the permitting process has long been recognized as raising issues of environmental justice, agencies' prior efforts to set the standards that will be incorporated into these permits also have implications for environmental justice. What happens when a standard ensures that the ambient air in a given region is healthy, but permits localized "hot spots"—areas of concentrated pollution—that coincide with environmental justice communities? What happens when a national standard governing mercury emissions is designed to protect those who consume an average quantity of fish that harbor mercury, but those in particular groups (e.g., Asian Americans, Native Americans) consume much greater quantities of such fish? This chapter takes up these questions of environmental justice in standard setting. The first section provides an overview of some of the most commonly employed regulatory tools and the statutory authorities for these tools. The next two sections consider examples from agencies' efforts to set standards to address, respectively, air and water pollution. The final section focuses on the environmental justice implications of market-based approaches and emissions trading.

## 1. An Introductory Note on the Taxonomy of Standards

Environmental standards are the foundation upon which all regulatory requirements rest. Broadly speaking, there are three approaches that comprise the mainstay of agencies' standard-setting efforts. Some standards are made by reference to what is a safe level for humans and the environment. These are called **"health-based"** or **"risk-based" standards** and are often expressed by the ambient amount of a pollutant that is deemed safe. For example, EPA may announce that if the air contains over X amount of sulfur dioxide per cubic meter over an eight-hour period, the air will be deemed unhealthy. If there are too many exceedances of this standard, then the airshed will be deemed to be in "nonattainment" with the national ambient air quality standard (NAAQS).

**"Technology-based" standards**, on the other hand, are set by reference to what is currently technologically feasible to achieve, regardless of whether this standard results in a healthy environment. For example, EPA may announce that new facilities emitting sulfur dioxide in nonattainment areas must control their air emissions to the level of the "lowest achievable emissions reductions" possible, and "LAER" becomes the standard. It may be that achieving LAER will still result in troubling ambient conditions; conversely, it may be that achieving LAER will require emissions reductions beyond those necessary to reach healthful conditions.

A third type of standard is termed **"technology-forcing"** because it is made by reference to technology not yet available, but is intended to force the development of such cleaner technologies. For example, in 1990 Congress mandated that manufacturers of automobiles must find a way to reduce tail pipe emissions by 10% below 1990 emissions by 2004. The auto industry was then in a position of having to develop the technology to achieve these reductions (also called "rollbacks") in order to have vehicles certified for sale by that date. When promulgated, this was a technology-forcing standard because in 1990 the technology to achieve this level of reduction had yet to be developed.

The standards that appear to most concern environmental justice advocates are health-based standards. Some claim that these standards are often insufficiently protective because they are made by reference to their effect upon healthy adult males. In addition, many such standards are developed in isolation, a "chemical by chemical approach" that does not factor in the possibility that the exposed individual may use the resource more than the average citizen, may be subject to a range of other pollutants, may be vulnerable because of certain genetic predispositions or health conditions, or may have fewer preventive and health care resources available.

But technology-based standards also may raise environmental justice issues. While these standards may require fairly significant reductions in emissions or discharges from each source—for example, a 90% reduction in mercury emissions at each coal-fired power plant—they say nothing about how many such sources may be permitted to operate in a given area. It is entirely possible that the effect of multiple sources, each having reduced its emissions by the required 90%, will cumulatively pose a level of mercury that is unhealthful for those exposed. Given that, as discussed in Chapter 1, polluting sources are often concentrated in minority or low-income communities, even the most stringent technology-based standards may leave unaddressed the question of community members' health.

Regardless of which type of standard they employ, current federal environmental laws do not directly address environmental justice issues. As advocates and scholars have argued, however, there nonetheless are opportunities within these statutes for integrating environmental justice concerns into agencies' substantive standard-setting efforts. The next section canvasses several of the major environmental statutes and highlights the sources of legal authority that might be tapped to enable agencies to consider and address environmental justice concerns.

## 2. Legal Sources of Authority

### Richard J. Lazarus & Stephanie Tai, *Integrating Environmental Justice into EPA Permitting Authority*

26 ECOLOGY LAW QUARTERLY 617, 631–649 (1999)

*Clean Air Act*

The Clean Air Act (CAA) presents EPA with more opportunities to integrate environmental justice concerns into the Act's substantive standards than the Agency has utilized. The national ambient air quality standards (NAAQS) that serve as the Act's cornerstone are illustrative. Pursuant to the CAA, EPA administrators must promulgate NAAQS to protect "public health" with an adequate margin of safety. It is well settled that Congress intended for EPA to consider especially sensitive subpopulations in determining what pollutant levels would meet the "public health" standard. Pollutant levels that pose no health hazard to average healthy individuals may nonetheless present significant hazards to some individuals who, because of preexisting physical conditions, have heightened vulnerabilities. The Act, accordingly, instructs EPA in developing the "air quality criteria" upon which the NAAQS are based to include information on "those variable factors ... which of themselves or in combination with other factors may alter the effects on public health or welfare." ...

EPA's statutory authority in this respect is also of a continuing nature. It does not end once a NAAQS is first promulgated. Pursuant to CAA Section 109(d), EPA is required to revise air quality criteria and standards at a minimum of every five years or as needed to ensure their adequacy in light of new information and changing circumstances....

Section 112 [dealing with controls for hazardous air pollutants] also includes two other subsections relevant to environmental justice priorities. Section 112(c)(3) and

Section 112(k) both authorize EPA to consider the aggregate effects of multiple sources of hazardous air pollutants, especially those emitted in urban areas....

*Clean Water Act*

... The water quality standard provisions of the [Clean Water Act (CWA)] offer another opportunity for EPA to exercise its authority to consider and address environmental justice concerns. Under the CWA, states must establish water quality standards applicable to waters within the states' borders. Unlike the CAA's NAAQS, which are nationally uniform, these state water quality standards may not only vary between states, but need not be uniformly applied to all water bodies within any one state. A state may legitimately apply different levels of water quality protection to different water bodies depending on the specific uses (for example, recreation, transportation, or industry) the state designates for each body of water. EPA oversees a state's promulgation of water quality standards primarily to ensure that the standards are consistent with the state's "designated uses" but also to ensure compliance with EPA's nondegradation policy, which guards against unwarranted degradation of existing uses of water and associated water quality. CWA permits must ensure compliance not only with the Act's various technology-based effluent limitations, but also with the state water quality standards....

The water quality program is especially relevant to environmental justice because it involves EPA and the states making a series of judgments with clearly distributional consequences. For instance, EPA's nondegradation policy, which protects "existing uses" of water, should provide protection to such existing uses by environmental justice communities, including those that are economically or culturally dependent on the subsistence use of water....

*Federal Insecticide, Fungicide, and Rodenticide Act*

The Federal Insecticide, Fungicide, and Rodenticide Act (FIFRA) confers substantial authority on the EPA Administrator to address environmental justice concerns. EPA's principal responsibility in administering FIFRA is its registration of pesticides to guard against "unreasonable adverse effects on the environment." Environmental justice advocates are interested in FIFRA's administration for many reasons, one of which is the substantial threat to the health of farmworkers posed by the unreasonably dangerous use of pesticides. FIFRA provides EPA with significant authority to eliminate these unreasonable risks through tactics as varied as use restrictions, disposal restrictions, labeling requirements, registration denials, and conditional registrations....

\* \* \*

## Notes and Questions

1. **Cumulative impacts and synergistic risks?** If EPA's authority under the federal environmental statutes is as broad and discretionary as Professors Lazarus and Tai suggest, why has the agency arguably failed to promulgate standards that are protective enough to address cumulative impacts and synergistic risks? As you read the materials in this chapter, consider whether these failures stem from a lack of legal authority,

from an incomplete scientific understanding or insufficient engineering capability, or from a lack of political will.

**2. Judicial deference and public health.** A quick review of environmental cases can lead one to the conclusion that EPA will frequently get sued regardless of the standard promulgated, i.e., either the industrial stakeholders or environmental stakeholders will be dissatisfied, or possibly both. Those wishing to uphold EPA's decision will point to case law affording the agency great deference in technical matters. Those wishing to defeat the agency's decision will use a variety of arguments generally premised upon the failure of the agency to follow its legislative mandate, thus acting outside of the relevant statute's scope. It is likely that the ultimate success of these arguments will depend upon the inclination of the courts to be deferential to EPA. In reviewing the materials in the next section, in addition to judicial deference, also consider the importance of the NAAQS from the standpoint of public health as well as what is at stake with the establishment or revision of these standards.

# B. The Case of National Ambient Air Quality Standards

As noted by Professors Lazarus and Tai, two important standard-setting provisions allowing for integration of environmental justice concerns are sections 108 and 109 of the Clean Air Act, under which EPA is authorized to establish and periodically revise NAAQS for certain air pollutants, called "criteria" pollutants. As stated above, ambient standards refer to the amount of pollutant in an environmental medium (like an airshed or water body) over a period of time. Presently, only a handful of pollutants are regulated under this section, as opposed to the extensive list of hazardous air pollutants regulated under another section of the Clean Air Act (Section 112). Despite the relatively fewer number of NAAQS, regulation of these pollutants is the heart and soul of the Clean Air Act because these pollutants are both serious in their health implications and are difficult to regulate because they come from numerous and diverse sources. **NAAQS presently cover six pollutants** — particulate matter, sulfur dioxide ($SO_2$), ozone, nitrogen oxides, carbon monoxide, and lead. Emissions from industrial facilities, refineries, chemical plants and electric utilities, motor vehicle exhaust, gasoline vapors, and chemical solvents are some of the major sources of oxides of nitrogen ($NOx$) and volatile organic compounds (VOC), which form ground-level ozone. Ozone at ground level is a harmful air pollutant and the main ingredient in "smog."

One of the most controversial features of setting the NAAQS is that the endeavor is supposed to be entirely "cost blind," meaning that the EPA cannot consider how costly it will be to achieve the national standards. Theoretically, NAAQS are supposed to reflect allowable concentrations of these pollutants in the outdoor air that are protective of public health "allowing an adequate margin of safety," even if achieving such levels will shut down entire industries and cause significant economic harm. 42 U.S.C. § 7409(b)(1). These standards are not as draconian as they appear, however, because economic considerations can play a significant role in how the standards are implemented. States and tribes have several opportunities to consider economics and costs in developing their **state implementation plans** (SIPs) or **tribal implementation plans** (TIPs), which are plans submitted to EPA demonstrating how the state or tribe proposes to come into attainment with NAAQS within a given time frame.

Many regions in the U.S. do not meet the NAAQS. This failure has significant health and environmental justice implications. Environmental attorney Curtis Moore explains some of the harmful health impacts of particulate matter and ozone:

> A large body of compelling evidence demonstrates that particulate matter is associated with early and unnecessary deaths, aggravation of heart and lung diseases, reduction in the ability to breathe normally, and increases in respiratory illnesses, leading to school and work absences. As particulate levels rise, so do runny or stuffy noses, sinusitis, sore throat, wet cough, head colds, hay fever, burning or red eyes, wheezing, dry cough, phlegm, shortness of breath, and chest discomfort or pain, as well as hospital admissions for asthma and bronchitis. Studies have shown that chronic cough, asthma, and emphysema rise among nonsmok[ers] ...; bronchitis and chronic cough increase in school children as do emergency room and hospital admissions.... In plain terms, at levels commonly encountered, particulate pollution kills and disables Americans, especially children, the elderly, and those who are ill....

> [I]t is clear that the impacts of ozone exposure are grave. The body of evidence that ozone causes chronic, pathologic lung damage is overwhelming. At levels routinely encountered in most American cities, ozone burns through cell walls in lungs and airways, tissues redden and swell, cellular fluid seeps into the lungs, and over time their elasticity drops. Macrophage cells rush to the lung's defense, but they too are stunned by the ozone. Susceptibility to bacterial infections increases, possibly because ciliated cells that normally expel foreign particles and organisms have been killed and replaced by thicker, stiffer, nonciliated cells. Scars and lesions form in the airways....

> As ozone levels rise, hospital admissions and emergency department visits do the same. In some laboratory animals, cancers appear. Children at summer camp lose the ability to breathe normally as ozone levels rise, even when the air is clean by reference to the former federal standard, and these losses continue for up to a week....

Curtis Moore, *The Impracticality and Immorality of Cost-Benefit Analysis in Setting Health-Related Standards*, 11 TULANE ENVTL. L.J. 187, 195–198 (1998).

SO₂ also can present significant health effects. Short-term exposures to $SO_2$ can harm the human respiratory system, making children and people with asthma particularly susceptible. High concentrations of $SO_2$ lead to the formation of other sulfur oxides, which can react with other compounds in the atmosphere to contribute to particulate matter.

According to the most recent CDC estimates,

**current asthma prevalence increased from 2001 to 2010.** There were no significant changes in rates for hospital outpatient department visits, [emergency department] visits, or hospitalizations, whereas risk-based rates for private physician office visits declined. Asthma death rates decreased from 2001 to 2009. Over the long term, asthma prevalence rose more slowly after 2001 than during 1980–1996, asthma hospitalizations declined since 1984 and deaths declined since 1999.

**The health effects, in turn, appear disproportionately to affect people of color and the poor.** Among white persons, current asthma prevalence increased at a rate of 1.4% per year to a prevalence of 7.8% in 2010. Among black persons, current asthma prevalence increased at a rate of 3.2% per year to 11.9% in 2010. By ethnicity, current asthma prevalence rose among Hispanic persons at a rate of 3.2% per year to 7.2% in 2010. Among non-Hispanic persons, prevalence rose at a rate of 1.9% per year to 8.7% in 2010. Current asthma was more prevalent among persons with family income below 100% of the federal poverty threshold (11.2%) than among persons with family income at or above the federal poverty threshold (8.5% for 100% to less than 250% of the poverty threshold, 7.8% for 250% to less than 450% of the poverty threshold, and 6.7% for at or above 450% of the poverty threshold). Asthma prevalence was significantly lower for each successively higher poverty level group. Ctrs. for Disease Control and Prevention, NATIONAL SURVEILLANCE OF ASTHMA: UNITED STATES, 2001–2010 (2012).

For more detail about the disparate impacts of air pollution on African Americans, Hispanics, and Latinos in the United States, *see* Black Leadership Forum et al., AIR OF INJUSTICE: AFRICAN AMERICANS & POWER PLANT POLLUTION 3 (2002) and League of United Latin American Citizens, AIR OF INJUSTICE: HOW AIR POLLUTION AFFECTS THE HEALTH OF HISPANICS AND LATINOS 3–4 (2004).

Once EPA determines that a pollutant may endanger public health, it is required to promulgate **air quality criteria** and a NAAQS for the pollutant. However, because of the scientific uncertainty involved in determining the precise magnitude and duration of exposure that may trigger harmful health effects, EPA has substantial discretion in deciding whether or not to adopt standards for new pollutants. In fact, lead is the only criteria pollutant EPA has added to the initial statutory list, and it did so only because of a successful citizen suit under a previous iteration of Section 108.

The EPA Administrator also exercises substantial discretion in decisions involving revisions to the NAAQS, although not without judicial scrutiny. The Clean Air Act directs EPA to **review the air quality criteria every five years** and to revise the NAAQS "as may be appropriate." 42 U.S.C. § 7409(d). EPA at various times has declined to revise the existing NAAQS for $SO_2$, carbon monoxide, nitrogen oxides, and particulate matter, despite new evidence indicating that levels of exposure below the then-current standards might be harmful. For example, EPA declined to issue a new short-term exposure NAAQS for $SO_2$ (even though the longer averaging times under the existing standard allowed harmful $SO_2$ spikes to occur), a decision the D.C. Circuit Court of

Appeals remanded because of the agency's failure to explain "[w]hy is the fact that thousands of asthmatics can be expected to suffer atypical physical effects from repeated five-minute bursts of high-level sulfur dioxide not a public health problem?" *American Lung Association v. EPA*, 134 F.3d 388, 392 (D.C. Cir. 1998).

When EPA does seek to revise a NAAQS, its decision often generates controversy and, frequently, opportunities for judicial review. EPA's recent revisions to the ozone and particulate standards illustrate the interplay of science, economics, law, and politics that attend EPA's work in this context. In 1997, EPA lowered the ozone standard from 0.12 parts per million (ppm) over a one-hour average to 0.08 ppm over an eight-hour average and added a new standard for particulate matter of 2.5 microns or less. These more stringent standards (in addition to saving thousands of lives) were anticipated to shift many regions into nonattainment status, necessitate the revision of numerous state implementation plans, and consequently have a significant effect on the activities of the regulated community. The following excerpt from a book by Professor Rena Steinzor provides useful background for understanding the controversy surrounding the revisions to the ozone NAAQS and the courts' role in overseeing these revisions.

### Rena I. Steinzor, *Mother Earth and Uncle Sam:*<br>*How Pollution and Hollow Government Hurt Our Kids*
#### 154–156 (2008)

Congress had the foresight to provide a built-in framework for scientific peer review of NAAQS revisions, creating the Clean Air Science Advisory Committee (CASAC) in 1977 amendments to the [Clean Air Act]. CASAC is organized and funded by EPA, but prides itself on its scientific candor and independence. The statute mandates that the NAAQS process depends upon close collaboration between CASAC scientists and EPA staff. The EPA administrator initiates a five-step process when a NAAQS revision is necessary:

1. EPA staff prepares a "criteria document" summarizing the scientific research available on the pollutant and submits it to a CASAC panel for review. Staff and CASAC members then debate the contents of the draft until they develop a revised document that reflects their consensus interpretation of the research.

2. On the basis of the revised criteria document, EPA prepares a "staff paper" summarizing both the science and the policy options for the administrator and submits it to CASAC for review, triggering a new round of collaboration and negotiation.

3. CASAC sends a "letter of closure" advising the administrator on the scientific soundness of the staff documents and offering any advice it chooses to on the policy options.

4. The administrator proposes a new NAAQS and puts the proposal out for [public] comment.

5. The administrator considers all of the above information, including public comments received by the Agency, and determines the final standard.

The statutory language states clearly that the final NAAQS shall be the number that *"in the judgment* of the Administrator" protects public health, making it clear that the person appointed by the president and confirmed by the Senate has full authority to make a final decision....

As it embarked on its consideration of a new ozone standard, CASAC was unanimous on one point: EPA needed to switch from the existing "one-hour standard" designed to address short-term ozone spikes and immediate health effects to an "eight-hour standard" designed to protect against long-term adverse health effects....

While CASAC endorsed the eight-hour metric, the panel differed on what number of parts per million (ppm) of ozone in ambient (outdoor) air should be tolerated; members of the group argued in favor of numbers from 0.08 to 0.12 ppm. After some heated debates, the panel issued the required letter of closure certifying the quality of the staff paper's analysis and allowing EPA Administrator Carol Browner to make a final decision on a new and more stringent NAAQS. She chose 0.08 ppm of ozone measured over eight hours and averaged over three years.

\* \* \*

In reviewing the standards, the D.C. Circuit admonished the EPA by invoking the long-dormant "non-delegation" doctrine (a doctrine that prohibits unduly broad grants of authority from Congress to the executive branch), a legal rationale that provoked vigorous critique by academics. According to the D.C. Circuit, the EPA's interpretation (rather than the statute itself) violated the nondelegation doctrine by not articulating an intelligible principle upon which the standards were based. Ultimately, the U.S. Supreme Court rejected the view of the D.C. Circuit, reversing the latter's call for a reinterpretation that would avoid the supposed delegation of legislative power. The Supreme Court did, however, remand to the EPA for another reason, that is, a better interpretation of the implementation provisions at issue for the ozone NAAQS. *Whitman v. American Trucking Ass'ns*, 531 U.S. 457 (2001).

In March 2008, after considering the results of more than 1,700 new scientific studies of ozone's adverse health effects, EPA again tightened the NAAQS for ozone, to 0.075 ppm. U.S. Envtl. Prot. Agency, National Ambient Air Quality Standards for Ozone, 73 Fed. Reg. 16,436 (March 27, 2008). According to EPA, among the benefits of this revision is an estimated annual prevention (in 2020) of between 420 and 2,300 premature deaths. U.S. Envtl. Prot. Agency, FACT SHEET: FINAL REVISIONS TO THE NATIONAL AMBIENT AIR QUALITY STANDARDS FOR OZONE 3 (2008). Also among the benefits is an estimated annual reduction (in 2020) of 320 cases of chronic bronchitis, 890 nonfatal heart attacks, 1,900 hospital and emergency room visits, 1,000 cases of acute bronchitis, 11,600 cases of upper and lower respiratory symptoms, 6,100 cases of aggravated asthma, 243,000 days when people miss work or school, and 750,000 days when people must restrict their activities because of ozone-related illnesses. *Id.* EPA estimated that the total monetized ozone-related benefits of the new standard would be between $4 and $17 billion per year, while the costs of implementing the new standard would be between $7.6 and $8.8 billion. *Id.*

These revisions also generated controversy, with EPA again being criticized by both industry and environmentalists. Among the criticisms were those leveled by the American Lung Association, which charged that EPA—then in the hands of the George W. Bush administration—improperly selected the relatively more lenient 0.075 ppm standard despite the fact that the CASAC had recommended a more stringent standard, specifically, a standard between 0.060 ppm and 0.070 ppm. They argued that "[t]wo to three times as many people could have been protected from an early death from their exposure to ozone if EPA had followed the scientists' recommendations, according to the EPA's own estimates." American Lung Association, New Ozone Standards Don't Provide Adequate Protection (2008).

In January 2010, EPA—then in the hands of the Barack Obama administration—proposed to strengthen the NAAQS for ozone, stating that "a standard level of 0.075 ppm is not sufficient to provide ... protection with an adequate margin of safety." U.S. Envtl. Prot. Agency, National Ambient Air Quality Standards for Ozone, 5 Fed. Reg. 2938, 2996 (Jan. 19, 2010). EPA then again missed its deadline to revise the ozone standard in 2013. The American Lung Association, Sierra Club, and others again successfully sued EPA to require a review by October 1, 2015. *Sierra Club v. EPA*, No. 13-CV-2809 (N.D. Cal. Apr. 30, 2014). In 2015, EPA revised its ozone standard to the higher end of the range recommended by CASAC, 0.070 ppm. The EPA stated that the standard is especially important for children and people with asthma, will prevent hundreds of thousands of asthma attacks, and creates significant public health benefits, estimated at $2.9 to $5.9 billion annually and outweighing estimated costs of $1.4 billion. U.S. Envtl. Prot. Agency, Fact Sheet: Overview of EPA's Updates to the Air Quality Standards for Ground Level Ozone (2015). In 2019, responding to challenges by both industry and environmentalists, the D.C. Circuit Court of Appeals largely upheld the 2015 ozone standards set by the EPA. *Murray Energy v. U.S. EPA*, 2019 WL 3977557 (2019).

## Notes and Questions

1. **A range of health protection.** For each NAAQS, there is typically a range of potential standards that are plausibly protective given the scientific information available at the time the standard is being considered. EPA chose a 0.070 ppm level for ozone, but not a level of 0.060 ppm that would have been more protective. Comments to the proposed revisions highlighted an extensive body of scientific literature documenting the need for a 0.060 ppm standard and the need to set levels to protect vulnerable subpopulations:

> Importantly, the NAAQS must be set at levels that are not only adequate to protect the average member of the population, but also guard against adverse effects in vulnerable subpopulations, such as children, the elderly, and people with heart and lung disease. In fact, the D.C. Circuit has repeatedly found that if a certain level of a pollutant "adversely affects the health of these sen-

sitive individuals, EPA must strengthen the entire national standard." *American Lung Ass'n*, 134 F.3d at 390 (citations omitted); *see also Coal. of Battery Recyclers Ass'n v. EPA*, 604 F.3d 613, 618 (D.C. Cir. 2010); *Am. Farm Bureau Fed'n v. EPA*, 559 F.3d 512, 524 (D.C. Cir. 2009). EPA must also build into the NAAQS an adequate margin of safety for these sensitive subpopulations. *See Am. Farm Bureau Fed'n*, 559 F.3d at 526.

*Comments of the American Lung Association, Appalachian Mountain Club, Center for Biological Diversity, Clean Air Council, Earthjustice, Environmental Defense Fund, National Parks Conservation Association, Natural Resources Defense Council, Sierra Club on EPA's Proposed Revisions to the National Ambient Air Quality Standards for Ozone*, 79 Fed. Reg. 75234, Docket # EPA-HQ-OAR-2008-0699 at 17 (March 17, 2015).

How is EPA supposed to choose which standard is best? The same commenters reminded EPA that the agency cannot consider the economic cost of meeting the NAAQS:

> In setting or revising a NAAQS, EPA cannot consider the economic impact of the standard—only the impact on public health. Lower courts had long held that costs could not be considered in setting NAAQS, and in 2001, the Supreme Court affirmed this position. Justice Scalia, writing for a unanimous Court, found that the plain language of the statute makes clear that economic costs cannot be considered: "Were it not for the hundreds of pages of briefing respondents have submitted on the issue, one would have thought it fairly clear that this text does not permit the EPA to consider costs in setting the standards." *Whitman*, 531 U.S. at 465.

*Id.* at 18. Should the distributional aspects of adverse health effects play a role in choosing among several plausible options? It seems that asthma sufferers are a particularly sensitive subpopulation and the EPA likely considered this group in arriving at various NAAQS in the past. Should EPA also consider that asthma is increasingly common among the poor and non-white?

**2. Environmental justice analysis?** What are the advantages and disadvantages to letting an environmental justice analysis help guide the agency to a more precise national standard? According to Professors Lazarus and Tai, "[t]he D.C. Circuit's ruling [in *American Lung Association*] suggests more than that EPA possesses statutory authority to consider the special sensitivities of environmental justice communities when establishing air quality standards under the CAA. The CAA may, in this respect, provide an instance in which the federal law mandates such consideration." Lazarus & Tai, *supra*, at 632.

**3. Industry's arguments.** Professor Steinzor relays an argument that has tended to be raised by industry and others who are generally opposed to more stringent regulation, but that nonetheless raises a concern relevant to those seeking social justice:

> [A] discussion of the costs and benefits of clean air would not be complete without a visit to the far right end of the spectrum, where some argue that implementation of the [CAA] actually kills people. The theory behind this

remarkable claim is that the costs of regulation are passed directly on to the consumer in the form of higher electricity prices and more expensive consumer goods. These costs must be absorbed by families and will have an especially devastating impact on people with low incomes because the money lost will not be able to pay for essentials that make people healthier.... The researchers say these "economically transmitted impacts" of the [1997] ozone and particulate matter NAAQS could kill between 2,201 people (for $10 billion in annual regulatory costs) and 22,589 people (for $100 billion in annual costs). Families with incomes below $15,000 in 1994 dollars will pay by far the highest price, accounting for some 40 percent of lives lost at all levels of cost. In a particularly harsh twist, the researchers estimate that 25 percent of the fatalities will occur in African-American households.

Steinzor, *supra*, at 168.

Professor Steinzor goes on to identify the "string of questionable assumptions" that underlies these claims. Can you think of what some of these might be? Even if you agree with Professor Steinzor that these claims rest on faulty premises, it is surely the case that the benefits of more protective standards come at some cost. Bearing in mind the Supreme Court's holding in *Whitman*, how would you structure agencies' decision-making processes to ensure that they consider the appropriate questions, and costs, in this regard?

**4. Risk avoidance.** The debate over the ozone NAAQS provides another illustration of agencies' quiet turn to "risk avoidance" strategies in lieu of "risk reduction." Here the risk avoidance measure employed is a warning, commonly called an "ozone alert" or "Code Red day," that people, especially asthmatics and others with respiratory issues, remain indoors or restrict their level of exertion if they must go outside. As Professor Steinzor observes:

The Clean Air Act does not allow EPA to even consider the alternative of telling people to stay inside when air quality is bad. Instead, the solution of putting the burden on the victim to avoid the risk has become the default reality as a direct result of the powerful combination of a dysfunctional legal framework and hollow government. For the many parents who live in cities afflicted by Code Red days and who bring their children's asthma inhaler every time they venture from home, all of these elaborate, convoluted calculations, research projections and public policy quarrels seem bizarre. To be sure, we drive cars, we depend on a stable supply of electricity, and we value the vast array of products that are available to American consumers. But would we really choose to impose smog on our and other people's children so that some of us have the option of buying the largest SUV on the market? Is it fair to expect the youngest among us to shoulder so much of the burden of allowing pollution to rise to levels that cause clear health problems, even if the economists tell us that such incidents are only worth a few dollars?

Steinzor, *supra*, at 168–69.

How would you propose to resolve the problems Professor Steinzor identifies, i.e., can you imagine a system for asking and answering the value-laden questions that she highlights?

**5. NAAQS and the Executive Order.** Pursuant to the Executive Order on Environment Justice, No. 12898, EPA considered the implications for environmental justice of its most recent revision to the ozone NAAQS in 2015:

> This final rule increases the level of environmental protection for all affected populations without having any disproportionately high and adverse human health or environmental effects on any population, including any minority populations, low-income populations or indigenous peoples. This rule establishes uniform national standards for O3 in ambient air that, in the Administrator's judgment, protect public health, including the health of sensitive groups, with an adequate margin of safety.

> Although it is part of a separate docket (EPA-HQ-OAR-2013-0169) and is not part of the rulemaking record for this action, EPA has prepared a regulatory impact analysis (RIA) of this decision. As part of the RIA, a demographic analysis was conducted. While, as noted in the RIA, the demographic analysis is not a full quantitative, site-specific exposure and risk assessment, that analysis examined demographic characteristics of persons living in areas with poor air quality relative to the proposed standard.... This analysis found that in areas with poor air quality relative to the revised standard, the representation of minority populations was slightly greater than in the U.S. as a whole. Because the air quality in these areas does not currently meet the revised standard, populations in these areas would be expected to benefit from implementation of the strengthened standard, and, thus, would be more affected by strategies to attain the revised standard.

U.S. Envtl. Prot. Agency, National Ambient Air Quality Standards for Ozone, 80 Fed. Reg. 65,291, 65,446 (October 26, 2015).

Does EPA's analysis appear to consider cumulative impacts? Are there alternative ways in which EPA might frame an inquiry into whether its "programs, policies, and activities" "address[] ... disproportionately high and adverse human health or environmental effects ... on minority and low-income populations" pursuant to the Executive Order on Environmental Justice? Chapter 6 investigates the sufficiency and treatment of the NAAQS (whether as a floor or a ceiling for pollution control) to address environmental injustice in the permitting context.

# C. Standards under the
# Clean Water Act

## 1. An Introductory Note on the Statute's
## Different Standards

This section will look at the environmental justice implications of standards through the lens of the Clean Water Act where, like many of the environmental statutes, there is an interplay between health-based and technology-based standards. In this statute, the standards that have been most vigorously implemented are the technology-based standards, generally under the **National Pollutant Discharge Elimination System (NPDES)** program. In this permitting program, a "point source" must acquire a permit before it discharges effluent that contains certain contaminants into a water body. State or tribal governments may obtain authority from the EPA to carry out the NPDES permit program, but the EPA retains oversight authority, including the ability to veto state- or tribally issued permits. NPDES permits typically require the installation of technology-based standards, such as "best available technology" (BAT). BAT is promulgated by reference to industrial sectors under the assumption that all facilities that produce certain products have similar production processes.

It may occur to you that if there are too many point sources discharging pollutants into a small water body, the water resource could be severely degraded despite the installation of BAT. This has in fact been the case in many instances. But the Clean Water Act has provisions designed to prevent this from occurring. The Act envisions a safety net of health-based standards, called **water quality standards**.

Ideally, a water quality standard should be designed so that if the water body meets the standard, it should be safe for certain designated uses. The baseline use is determined by the EPA to be "fishable/swimmable" waters. This means that, for the majority of water bodies, water quality standards should be sufficient to protect persons who swim in and consume fish caught from the water body. Beyond this default standard, states and tribes are free to establish other designated uses for each water segment within their respective jurisdictions. If a water body does not meet the applicable water quality standards it may be categorized as "water quality limited" and point source dischargers (typically industrial and publicly owned treatment facilities) might have to undertake limitations to their processes above the normally required technology-based standards.

Implementation of the safety net of health-based standards involves a difficult procedure. State and tribal agencies must determine how much of a pollutant loading a given water body can take before it exceeds the applicable water quality standards. Once this **"total maximum daily load"** (TMDL) is established, the agency essentially rations the amount each contributor can discharge, resulting in the possibility that some point source dischargers will have their NPDES permits limited further with "waste load allocations."

Thus far, we have been discussing only **point source dischargers**, but runoff from streets, agricultural activities, logging, and other **"non-point" activities** are, in fact, now the primary contributors to degraded water quality. The CWA does not mandate technology-based standards or other direct mechanisms of controlling pollution from these sources, instead relying on states and tribes to enlist land-use planning and other measures to address non-point sources.

**Many water bodies still fail to support their designated uses.** According to the EPA's most recent data, 52% of assessed river and stream miles; 71% of assessed lake, reservoir, and pond acres; and 80% of assessed bays and estuaries are impaired. The picture for the Great Lakes is especially bleak: 98% of assessed shoreline miles and practically 100% of assessed open waters are impaired. U.S. Envtl. Prot. Agency, Water Quality Assessment and TMDL Information: National Summary of State Information (2019). The proliferation of fish consumption advisories provides another measure of our failure to attain healthful waters. According to 2010 data, fish consumption advisories—warning mainly of contamination from mercury, PCBs, chlordane, dioxins, and DDT—covered 42% of the nation's total lake acreage, and 36% of the nation's total river miles. U.S. Envtl. Prot. Agency, Fact Sheet: 2010/2011 National Listing of Fish Advisories (November, 2007).

From an environmental justice perspective, the present state of implementation of the Clean Water Act raises several important issues. First, the promulgation of the default "fishable/swimmable" water quality standards requires an estimate of how much fish people typically eat. As Professor O'Neill illustrates below, individuals' **fish consumption practices** vary considerably, with members of certain communities consuming fish at much higher rates than the "average American." Agencies' assumptions about the fish consumption rates of those affected by its water quality standards can mean the difference between a standard that is adequately protective and one that is likely to result in significant disparities in protection, as discussed in the first excerpt below. Second, tribes may obtain authority to administer various programs under the Clean Water Act. Tribes that run their own water quality programs have been able to address these and other environmental justice concerns, at least to some degree. When tribes exercise their regulatory authority—presenting the unique situation of an "environmental justice community" as regulator—they face a new set of challenges, some of which are illustrated by *City of Albuquerque v. Browner*, the case that comprises the second excerpt below.

## 2. Water Quality Standards

### Catherine A. O'Neill, *Variable Justice: Environmental Standards, Contaminated Fish, and "Acceptable" Risk to Native Peoples*

19 STANFORD ENVIRONMENTAL LAW JOURNAL 3, 43–56 (2000)

... EPA currently assumes a fish consumption rate (FCR) of 6.5 grams/day [when setting water quality standards]. This amounts to approximately one fish meal per month. The 6.5 grams/day value is derived from a diet recall study conducted in the mid-1970s of the general population of the United States, fish consumers and non-consumers alike....

Various studies of fish consumption rates in Puget Sound and the Columbia River Basin ... indicate marked differences among Native American subpopulations and the general population.... According to a 1994 diet recall study conducted by and of the Nez Perce, Umatilla, Yakama, and Warm Springs tribes fishing along the Columbia River, the 50th percentile or median fish consumption rate for tribal members is between 29 and 32 grams per day; the arithmetic mean is 58.7 grams per day; the 90th percentile is between 97.2 and 130 grams per day; the 95th percentile is 170 grams per day; and the 99th percentile is 389 grams per day. The maximum consumption rate is 972 grams per day.

In *Dioxin/Organochlorine Center* [57 F.3d 1517 (9th Cir. 1995)], the EPA employed its default assumption for the FCR, 6.5 g/day. Relying on this standard assumption about exposure, EPA derived a water quality standard, the TMDL for dioxin, by solving the risk equation for concentration with cancer risk held at $1(10^{-6})$. If a particular environmental standard is set, assuming the exposure of the "average American," to result in risk of no more than 1 in 1,000,000, that same standard will result in greater risk to a more highly exposed subpopulation. In *Dioxin/Organochlorine Center*, this greater risk was estimated to be 23 in 1,000,000 or 2.3 in 100,000.

The Ninth Circuit accepted the EPA's choice of an FCR of 6.5 g/day by asserting that the resulting standards would provide "lower yet adequate protection" to higher-consuming Native American subpopulations.... [T]he court held that even if these subpopulations consume 150 g/day of fish and would therefore be subject to excess risk of $2.3(10^{-5})$, "this level of risk protection is within levels historically approved by the EPA and upheld by courts." The court endorsed EPA's argument that "the one-in-a-million risk level mandated by the state water quality standards for the general population does not necessarily reflect state legislative intent to provide the highest level of protection for all subpopulations but could reasonably be construed to allow for lower yet adequate protection for specific subpopulations." ...

\* \* \*

## *Notes and Questions*

**1. Ninth Circuit rationale?** As noted in Chapter 8 ("Environmental Justice and Contaminated Sites"), the EPA generally adopts a risk range of one-in-ten-thousand ($10^{-4}$) to one-in-a-million ($10^{-6}$). If the risks to Native American subpopulations in *Dioxin/Organochlorine Center* were estimated to fall squarely within this range ($10^{-5}$), is there still cause for concern? What is your view of the merits of the "lower but adequate protection" rationale relied upon by the Ninth Circuit?

**2. Addressing heightened risk.** At what point (if any) should agencies be permitted to set standards that are protective of the majority of the population but not similarly protective of "outliers"—members of the population whose susceptibilities and circumstances of exposure place them at the extreme in a population distribution? What if it could be shown that it would be enormously costly to protect these highly susceptible or highly exposed individuals, and that they comprise only a small fraction of the population? How is your response affected if these individuals were revealed to be members of various groups (e.g., various indigenous peoples, Asian-American communities, African-American communities), each of which might have quite different group-based environmental justice claims? Once the identity of the populations at greater risk is clearly known, is it unethical to ignore the heightened risks they face? What difficulties in accommodating the varied and complex histories of different groups might you imagine from the perspective of an environmental agency engaged in standard setting? Professor O'Neill argues:

> The mere fact that highly exposed subgroups exist in a context where the stakes are high necessitates differential treatment by health and environmental agencies.... The more significant the differences in the circumstances of exposure or susceptibility between the subpopulation and the general population, the more suspect an agency decision that fails to disaggregate these groups for differential treatment....

> [O]f the identifiable subgroups that are candidates for differential treatment, some may require agency attention because of their particular *identity*. Here, various moral and legal commitments may come into play. Agencies must address the intersection of variability and the fact that a particular identifiable subpopulation—Native Americans—occupies the high end of a variable exposure distribution.... [But, to date,] agencies have inadequately considered the relevant normative commitments respecting cultural integrity, equality [in the sense of freedom from both exclusionary and cultural discrimination], and process, and have not registered the applicable legal obligations arising from [inter alia] treaties [and] the federal trust responsibility.

O'Neill, *supra* at 75–76, 81. Do you agree?

**3. EPA's current FCR.** EPA now recommends a four-part hierarchy for determining the fish consumption rate on which water quality standards will be based, by which EPA encourages states and tribes, in order of preference, to "(1) use local data; (2) use data reflecting similar geography/population groups; (3) use data from national surveys; and (4) use EPA's default fish consumption rates." U.S. Envtl. Prot. Agency, METHODOLOGY FOR DERIVING AMBIENT WATER QUALITY CRITERIA FOR THE PROTECTION OF HUMAN HEALTH 4–25 (Oct, 2000). In 2014, EPA released a revised, peer-reviewed analysis of fish consumption rates that includes estimates of consumption rates for more types of fish and subpopulations (including estimates by gender, race, ethnicity, and income). U.S. Envtl. Prot. Agency, ESTIMATED FISH CONSUMPTION RATES OF THE U.S. POPULATION AND SELECTED SUBPOPULATIONS (NHANES 2003–2010) FINAL REPORT (April 2014).

**4. The long road to Oregon's water quality standards.** The states, especially, have been exceedingly slow to update their water quality standards, despite the CWA's requirement that states and tribes review and revise their water quality standards every three years (known as a "triennial review"). The fact that a state undertakes revisions to its water quality standards, of course, is no guarantee that the new standards will be adequately protective of affected tribes and other environmental justice communities. First, because agencies typically rely on quantitative risk assessment to set these health-based standards, they require quantitative evidence of the consumption practices of highly exposed groups, and such studies are few and far between (and, as noted in Chapter 3, may not accurately capture even contemporary consumption practices, especially for tribal members). Second, given the considerable costs that may attend a more protective standard, regulated industries generally oppose more protective revisions. Federal and state agencies, moreover, have often been sympathetic to this concern about costs. Oregon's efforts to revise its water quality standards provide a case in point.

> The Oregon Environmental Quality Commission recently adopted revisions to its water quality standards. Oregon, of course, had local data, including the [Columbia River Inter-Tribal Fish Commission (CRITFC)] survey and the Harris and Harper data [documenting consumption practices of tribal elders, traditional members, and subsistence fishing families in the Umatilla tribe and finding the average rate for this population to be 540 grams/day], and so was in the position to adhere to EPA's first preference. In fact, the Oregon Department of Environmental Quality (ODEQ) had constituted a Technical Advisory Committee, which endorsed the use of the values from the CRITFC survey. Specifically, the Technical Advisory Committee formally recommended that ODEQ assign values to the various regulated waters in Oregon depending on the intensity of fishing activity in those waters: it recommended an FCR for low-intensity use at 17.5 grams/day—the EPA's default for the general population; an FCR for intermediate-intensity use at 142.4 grams/day—the EPA's default for subsistence fishers; and an FCR for high-intensity use at 389 grams/day—the 99th percentile value from the CRITFC survey.

> The ODEQ, however, rejected the recommendations of its own Technical Advisory Committee. Instead, it opted for the least protective—and least preferred—option, a statewide FCR at the EPA's national default of 17.5 grams/day.... Oregon finalized its revised standards in May of 2004.

Catherine A. O'Neill, *Protecting the Tribal Harvest: The Right to Catch and Consume Fish*, 22 J. ENVTL. L. & LITIGATION 131, 141–42 (2007).

Can you think of why a state might opt for less stringent standards? Although EPA is required under the CWA to approve or disapprove a state's water quality standards within 90 days, as of August 2006, EPA had still declined to take action on Oregon's controversial standards. Both Oregon's decision and EPA's inaction were sharply criticized by the affected tribes. Oregon and EPA subsequently joined with the Confederated Tribes of the Umatilla Indian Reservation in an effort to revisit the standards that would be led by the three governments. After numerous public workshops, the Oregon Environmental Quality Commission in October, 2008, adopted a new fish consumption rate of 175 grams/day and directed the ODEQ to revise its water quality standards accordingly. *See* Or. Dep't of Envtl. Quality, OREGON FISH CONSUMPTION RATE PROJECT (2008). In December 2010, ODEQ provided a formal public comment period on the proposed revisions and held nine public hearings. The public comment period extended from December 21, 2010, through March 21, 2011, and solicited one thousand and seventy-five written comments. The Commission adopted the revisions to Oregon's water quality standards, which were then submitted to EPA for review and approval in July 2011. Eventually, in October 2011, EPA approved Oregon's new and revised water quality standards that included human health criteria calculated using an FCR of 175 grams/day. EPA APPROVAL OF NEW AND REVISED HUMAN HEALTH WATER QUALITY CRITERIA FOR TOXICS AND IMPLEMENTATION PROVISIONS IN OREGON'S WATER QUALITY STANDARDS SUBMITTED JOINTLY ON JULY 12 AND 21, 2011 (October 17, 2011). In your view, did EPA fully exercise the authority available to it under the CWA to address environmental justice issues?

**5. Delegated standard setting.** Recall that EPA can delegate authority to tribes as well as states to administer programs under the CWA and other statutes. Given tribal members' higher fish consumption rates and ceremonial uses of water bodies, tribes might be more inclined to set more stringent water quality standards. The following case illustrates the political and legal difficulties involved when Isleta Pueblo, a federally recognized American Indian tribe situated in New Mexico, took up the challenge to promulgate strict water quality standards.

## City of Albuquerque v. Browner
### 97 F. 3d 415 (10th Cir. 1996)

*McKay, Circuit Judge:*

… This case involves the first challenge to water quality standards adopted by an Indian tribe under the Clean Water Act amendment.

The Rio Grande River flows south through New Mexico before turning southeast to form the border between Texas and Mexico. Plaintiff City of Albuquerque operates a waste treatment facility which dumps into the river approximately five miles north of the Isleta Pueblo Indian Reservation. The EPA recognized Isleta Pueblo as a state

**Figure 5-1:** The Rio Grande between Albuquerque, NM, and the Isleta Pueblo. Photo: Cliff Villa.

for purposes of the Clean Water Act on October 12, 1992. The Isleta Pueblo adopted water quality standards for Rio Grande water flowing through the tribal reservation, which were approved by the EPA on December 24, 1992. The Isleta Pueblo's water quality standards are more stringent than the State of New Mexico's standards.

The Albuquerque waste treatment facility discharges into the Rio Grande under a National Pollution Discharge Elimination System [NPDES] permit issued by the EPA. The EPA sets permit discharge limits for waste treatment facilities so they meet state water quality standards. Albuquerque filed this action as the EPA was in the process of revising Albuquerque's NPDES permit to meet the Isleta Pueblo's water quality standards....

Albuquerque argues that § 1377 does not expressly permit Indian tribes to enforce effluent limitations or standards under § 1311 to upstream point source dischargers outside of tribal boundaries.... Under the statutory and regulatory scheme, tribes are not applying or enforcing their water quality standards beyond reservation boundaries. Instead, it is the EPA which is exercising its own authority in issuing NPDES permits in compliance with downstream state and tribal water quality standards. In regard to this question, therefore, the 1987 amendment to the Clean Water Act clearly and unambiguously provides tribes the authority to establish NPDES programs in conjunction with the EPA.... [T]he EPA has the authority to require upstream NPDES dischargers, such as Albuquerque, to comply with downstream tribal standards.

... Under the water quality standards provisions of the Clean Water Act, it is the states and tribes which conduct rulemaking proceedings. This is in accord with Congress's intent to preserve a primary role for the states and tribes in eliminating water pollution. The results of state and tribal rulemaking proceedings are then presented to the EPA for approval. The Fourth Circuit has explained the EPA's limited role in reviewing water quality standards proposed by states, stating:

> EPA sits in a reviewing capacity of the state-implemented standards, with approval and rejection powers only....

> [S]tates have the primary role, under § 303 of the CWA (33 U.S.C. § 1313), in establishing water quality standards. EPA's sole function, in this respect, is to review those standards for approval....

Albuquerque also claims that the EPA's approval of the Isleta Pueblo standards was unsupported by a rational basis on the record and was therefore arbitrary and capricious. Albuquerque argues that the EPA was required to reject the Isleta Pueblo's water quality standards unless the EPA had established its own record based on a sound scientific rationale for each particular provision.

The EPA, however, reviews proposed water quality standards only to determine whether they are stringent enough to comply with the EPA's recommended standards and criteria. If the proposed standards are more stringent than necessary to comply with the Clean Water Act's requirements, the EPA may approve the standards without reviewing the scientific support for the standards. Whether the more stringent standard is attainable is a matter for the EPA to consider in its discretion; sections 1341 and 1342 of the Clean Water Act permit the EPA and states to force technological advancement to attain higher water quality. The EPA's letter approving the Isleta Pueblo standards explains that it is approving the standards, despite their departure from the EPA's guidelines, based on the Tribe's authority to adopt standards more stringent than the minimum requirements of the Clean Water Act.

The EPA considered Isleta Pueblo's rationale for each of the standards challenged by Albuquerque, and the tribe's record contains detailed responses to all of the criticisms expressed by the EPA and Albuquerque. The record contains a detailed explanation of the Isleta Pueblo's scientific, technical, and policy reasons for choosing to establish more stringent standards. For example, the Isleta Pueblo stated that stringent standards are justified because of prevailing drought conditions and the need to protect sensitive subpopulations. The EPA concluded that the standards were consistent with the Clean Water Act's requirements and should therefore be approved. The arbitrary and capricious review standard is very deferential; "an agency ruling is 'arbitrary and capricious if the agency has ... entirely failed to consider an important aspect of the problem.'" Albuquerque has not shown that the EPA failed to consider an important aspect of the Isleta Pueblo's water quality standards....

In its next claim, Albuquerque argues that the Isleta Pueblo criteria approved by the EPA are not stringent enough to protect the Tribe's designated use standard described as primary contact ceremonial use. The Tribe describes primary contact ceremonial use as involving the "immersion and intentional or incidental ingestion of water." Albuquerque argues that this requires the river water quality to meet the standards of the Safe Drinking Water Act, 42 U.S.C. § 300f, and the Isleta Pueblo's water quality criteria approved by the EPA fail to protect water used under the ceremonial use standard.

As the district court stated:

> This argument seems far-fetched. The primary contact ceremonial use appears to resemble a fishable/swimmable standard, which assumes the ingestion of some water, more than it resembles a safe drinking water standard, which assumes the ingestion of a volume of water daily.

*Albuquerque* [*v. Browner*, 865 F.Supp. 733, 740 (D.N.M. 1993)]. The federal drinking water standards apply only to a "public water system," which is defined as a system supplying piped water for human consumption serving at least twenty-five persons or having at least fifteen service connections. 42 U.S.C. § 300f(4). The Isleta Pueblo's ceremonial use standard does not convert the Rio Grande River into a public water system. The EPA considered and approved this aspect of the Isleta Pueblo water quality standards. We decline to second-guess the EPA's technical determination, which is entitled to substantial deference, that the Isleta Pueblo's water quality criteria adequately protect its ceremonial designated use standard....

Albuquerque next claims that the EPA's approval of the Pueblo's ceremonial use designation offends the Establishment Clause of the First Amendment. The First Amendment provides in relevant part: "Congress shall make no law respecting an establishment of religion...." U.S. Const. amend. I. Government action does not violate the Establishment Clause if "[t]he challenged governmental action has a secular purpose, does not have the principal or primary effect of advancing or inhibiting religion, and does not foster an excessive entanglement with religion."

The EPA approved Isleta Pueblo's promulgation of "Primary Contact Ceremonial Use" as a designated use of the Rio Grande River within the boundaries of the Indian reservation. The tribe defines "Primary Contact Ceremonial Use" as "the use of a stream, reach, lake, or impoundment for religious or traditional purposes by members of the PUEBLO OF ISLETA; such use involves immersion and intentional or incidental ingestion of water." Albuquerque argues that the EPA's approval of this standard violates all three aspects of the Establishment Clause under *Lemon* [*v. Kurtzman*, 403 U.S. 602 (1971)].

First, Albuquerque argues that the reason for the designated use is explicitly sectarian. The secular purpose requirement does not mean that a law's purpose must be unrelated to religion because that would require "'that the government show a callous indifference to religious groups,'... and the Establishment Clause has never been so interpreted." The EPA's approval of the primary contact ceremonial use designation serves a clear secular purpose: promotion of the goals of the Clean Water Act. The EPA's purpose in approving the designated use is unrelated to the Isleta Pueblo's religious reason for establishing it. The Isleta Pueblo's designation of a ceremonial use does not invalidate the EPA's overall secular goal.

Second, Albuquerque claims that the EPA's action has a primary effect of advancing religion. We disagree. The EPA is not advancing religion through its own actions, and it is not promoting the Isleta Pueblo's religion. The primary effect of the EPA's action is to advance the goals of the Clean Water Act.

Third, Albuquerque asserts the designated use results in excessive governmental entanglement with religion because the Pueblo and the EPA must inquire on an on-going basis whether the standards adequately protect religious uses of the river water. This argument is meritless. "There is no genuine nexus between" the EPA's approval of the ceremonial use standard "and establishment of religion," and the EPA's approval of the standard provides only an incidental benefit to religion. The EPA's approval of the ceremonial use standard does not require any governmental involvement in the Isleta Pueblo's religious practices. Excessive governmental entanglement will not result when the EPA incorporates the Isleta Pueblo's water quality standards in issuing future NPDES permits....

* * *

## Notes and Questions

**1. Framing the issue.** Professor Denise Fort published an article on the dispute shortly before the above opinion was issued. In the article, she discusses a variety of important factual questions that this controversy raised:

> ... [I]n any dispute over water quality standards, the underlying factual questions are likely to be persuasive in how one views the merits of the dispute. For example, are tribal standards unreasonably strict, or are the state's unreasonably lax? How expensive will it be for upstream dischargers to comply with the standards? Should a tribe be allowed to continue its historic use of a river for ceremonial purposes, involving drinking from the river, when alternative water supplies are available, and if the answer is affirmative, should upstream taxpayers bear the cost of making a river safe for those practices? Should upstream polluters be allowed to endanger those who depend on a river, and, is it relevant that those uses predate the upstream discharge? One's views of the legal merits may vary with the answers to these questions. It is noteworthy that a state's standards provide the lens through which these questions are viewed; if tribes were to adopt standards identical to those of the surrounding states, dischargers would have no grounds to object. The Pueblo of Isleta's standards were at issue in the *Browner* case, not the standards set by the State of New Mexico.

Denise D. Fort, *State and Tribal Water Quality Standards Under the Clean Water Act: A Case Study*, 35 NAT. RESOURCES J. 771, 775–76 (1995).

As with the issues concerning water quality standards and fish consumption discussed above, the legal issues in this dispute were framed with reference to the dominant population. Does framing environmental justice issues as deviations from an existing norm affect the analysis? If so, why did the tribe prevail in this case? In what ways is the case helpful in resolving environmental justice disputes outside the context of tribal sovereignty?

# D. Market-Based Approaches

## 1. An Introduction to Market-Based Approaches to Regulation

The previous sections of this chapter focused on health-based standards in the context of air and water quality regulation. To a lesser extent, these sections considered technology-based and technology-forcing standards and recognized the role that these standards play in agencies' efforts to meet ambient, health-based standards.

Critics have argued that technology-based standards and other similar regulatory tools are suboptimal in a number of respects. Most prominently, these critics point out that such traditional "command and control" approaches — which, they argue, require every regulated source to apply identical pollution control equipment and measures — are inefficient. This is so because the costs of compliance may vary considerably among different industrial sectors (for example, it might be less costly for the printing sector to comply with a mandate to curb certain air pollutants than it would be for computer chip manufacturers) and among different sources within a particular industrial sector (for example, it might be less costly for a pulp and paper facility that uses one bleaching process to control its dioxin emissions than it would be for a pulp and paper facility that uses a different process). As a result, economists and other critics have called for greater reliance on economic incentives, or market-based tools, to achieve environmental objectives.

Economic incentives comprise a range of tools that rely on business' economic self-interest, rather than on direct regulation, to reduce pollution and that therefore allow businesses to reduce their pollution in the most cost-effective manner. Market-based tools can take numerous forms: pollution charges or "taxes," which impose a fixed dollar amount for each unit of pollution emitted or disposed; deposit-refund systems (such as bottle bills) in which purchasers receive a refund when an article is properly returned or disposed of; government subsidies or tax breaks for certain environmental behavior; or "cap-and-trade" regimes, which impose a ceiling or cap on total emissions for a given geographic area (which can be local, regional, national, or even global), allocate these total emissions among contributing sources in the form of allowances that entitle the holder to emit a certain quantity of emissions, and then permit these sources to buy and sell the allowances to each other. Within this market, the firms that can control emissions more cheaply will have the incentive to reduce their emissions to a greater degree because they can sell the excess allowances thereby generated to firms that have higher costs of control. As a result, overall emissions are reduced at a lower aggregate cost to industry. As explained in this section, however, market-based approaches, and in particular cap-and-trade regimes, can exacerbate environmental inequities.

*Pathfinder on Economic Incentives*

For general background about market-based approaches, *see* Robert Stavins, *Harnessing the Marketplace*, 18 EPA J. 21 (May/June 1992); Daniel Dudek & John Palmisano, *Emissions Trading: Why Is This Thoroughbred Hobbled?*, 13 COLUM. J. ENVTL L. 217 (1988); and Bruce Ackerman & Richard Stewart, *Reforming Environmental Law*, 37 STANFORD L. REV. 1333 (1985). For one powerful critique of market-based approaches, *see* Frank Ackerman & Lisa Heinzerling, PRICELESS: ON KNOWING THE PRICE OF EVERYTHING AND THE VALUE OF NOTHING (2004). For similar critiques, *see* David Driesen, *Is Emissions Trading an Economic Incentive Program?: Replacing the Command and Control/Economic Incentive Dichotomy*, 55 WASH. & LEE L. REV. 289 (1998), and David M. Driesen, *Trading and Its Limits*, 14 PENN. ST. ENVTL. L. REV. 169 (2006). In addition to the articles discussed in this chapter, other articles exploring the environmental justice implications of market approaches include Thomas Lambert & Christopher Boerner, *Environmental Inequity: Economic Causes, Economic Solutions*, 14 YALE J. ON REGULATION 195 (1997); Lorna Jaynes, Comment, *Emissions Trading: Pollution Panacea or Environmental Injustice?*, 39 SANTA CLARA L. REV. 207 (1998); and Lily N. Chinn, Comment, *Can the Market Be Fair and Efficient? An Environmental Justice Critique of Emissions Trading*, 26 ECOLOGY L.Q. 80 (1999). For critiques of emissions trading in connection with climate change initiatives, *see* Chapter 14 ("Climate Justice").

In an early article, Professor Stephen Johnson discussed the theory and history behind some of the most widely used market-based tools and their environmental justice implications.

## Stephen M. Johnson, *Economics v. Equity: Do Market-Based Environmental Reforms Exacerbate Environmental Injustice?*

56 WASHINGTON AND LEE LAW REVIEW 111, 117–139 (1999)

*Inevitable Inequities in Market-Based Reforms*

... Although the traditional [regulatory] approach clearly has not adequately addressed distributional inequities, market-based approaches will inevitably exacerbate those inequities. While the traditional command and control environmental laws and regulations do not explicitly require the government to avoid actions that disparately impact low-income or minority communities, those laws also do not affirmatively encourage unequal distribution of pollution. By contrast, as explained below, many market-based approaches to environmental protection affirmatively encourage polluters to shift pollution to lower-income communities....

Classical economic theory institutionalizes and exacerbates existing social disparities that are based on unequal distributions of income. As Judge Richard Posner suggested, in a free market economy, in which voluntary exchange is permitted, "resources are shifted to those uses in which the value to consumers, as measured by their willingness to pay, is highest. When resources are being used where their value is highest, we may say that they are being employed efficiently." Although Judge Posner defined "value" in terms of "willingness to pay," on closer reflection it is clear that Judge Posner and other economists incorporated "ability to pay" into the concept of "willingness to pay." Thus, under traditional economic theory, a pollutant trading program, tax program, or similar market-based reform that shifts pollution to low-income communities is operating efficiently and, therefore, desirably because resources, such as clean air and clean water, are shifted to the uses in which the value to consumers, as measured by their willingness (and ability) to pay, is highest. Because wealthy communities are "willing to pay" more for clean air and water than low-income communities, the market operates efficiently when it funnels those resources to those communities rather than to low-income communities. In a free market, low-income communities will never have sufficient financial resources to buy clean air, clean water, and similar environmental and public health resources from wealthy communities or polluters....

[E]conomists admit that economic theory does not make value judgments regarding the distribution of resources or regarding the moral or social implications of "efficient" allocations of resources. Economists admit that economic theory does not address the important underlying question regarding whether an efficient allocation of resources is socially or ethically desirable....

However, environmental law developed and flourished precisely because economic theory, and the free market, did not address those social concerns.... While environmental laws should weigh economic issues, the laws should not substitute economic considerations for the important social considerations that motivated legislators to enact the laws in the first place....

*Pollutant Trading Systems and Potential Disparate Impacts*

Most of the pollutant trading programs that have been implemented in the United States have focused on reducing air pollution.... [T]he EPA began experimenting with pollutant trading under the Clean Air Act in the 1970s. Those early experiments matured into EPA's 1986 Clean Air Act emissions trading policy for "criteria" pollutants, including sulfur dioxide, nitrogen dioxide, particulates, carbon monoxide, lead, and ozone. Under the policy, companies are allowed to build new major air pollution sources or make major modifications to major air pollution sources in areas of the country where national air pollution standards are not being met if the companies build the source to meet certain technology-based standards and enter into an agreement with an existing air pollution source in the area whereby the existing source reduces its pollution output by at least as much pollution as the new or modified source plans to discharge. The policy refers to the reductions as "emission reduction credits," which can be used to "offset" proposed pollution increases. Companies can obtain offsets by entering into agreements with other companies or by reducing the output of pollution from another source that they own in the polluted area where the new or modified source will be sited....

While EPA's emission trading policy was the agency's first major foray into pollutant trading, the sulfur dioxide emission trading program created by the 1990 Clean Air Act Amendments often is cited as a model for future pollutant trading programs at the federal and state levels. The trading program is designed to reduce by half sulfur dioxide emissions from coal-fired electric power plants by early in the next century. During Phase I of the program, which began in 1995 and ends in 2000, 111 of the dirtiest power plants were given annual "allowances" to emit 2.5 pounds of sulfur dioxide for every million Btu consumed by the plant. During Phase II, which begins in 2000, all power plants that produce more than 25 megawatts will be given "allowances" to emit 1.2 pounds of sulfur dioxide for every million Btu consumed by the plant. Total emissions from all of the plants are capped at 8.90 million tons of sulfur dioxide at the end of the program....

While the state and federal pollutant trading programs promise to reduce pollution in a "cost-effective" manner, these programs could disparately impact low-income communities....

First, while some trading programs limit trading to a specific air quality control region, many trading programs do not include any geographic limits on trades. As a result, while trading programs may decrease overall pollution levels, they may increase pollution in certain areas and create "toxic hot spots." Older, heavily polluting industries may find that it is more cost-effective to continue polluting and to buy pollution rights than to install new technologies to reduce pollution. Thus, communities surrounding those industries will be exposed to higher levels of pollution than other communities. Geographic limits on trades will not eliminate the "toxic hot spot" problem, especially if the geographic area in which trades are authorized is fairly large, but the limits could, at least, reduce the potential volume of pollution that will be imparted into a toxic hot spot....

If the trading programs will create toxic hot spots, economic theory suggests that the hot spots will most likely occur in low-income communities.... First, heavily polluting industrial facilities (the facilities that may purchase pollution credits) will more likely be sited in low-income, urban areas than in middle-to-upper-income, suburban areas. Second, low-income communities may be less likely than affluent communities to urge an outdated, heavily polluting industry to implement new pollution controls instead of buying pollution rights. Low-income communities may fear that if they urge the industry to adopt new pollution controls, then the industry will close, depriving the community of essential jobs and tax revenue. Finally, low-income communities often lack the political power to influence industries to adopt new pollution controls instead of buying pollution rights....

*Pollution Taxes, Fees, and Charges and Their Potential Disparate Impacts*

Pollution taxes, fees, and charges promise to reduce pollution in cost-effective ways similar to pollutant trading programs.... Several states impose variable fees on polluters for water pollution permits or air pollution permits based on the volume or toxicity of the pollution authorized by the permit.... [M]any municipalities are implementing variable waste disposal fees … [where] residents pay variable waste disposal fees, which depend on the amount of waste that they dispose, instead of paying uniform fees.…

[P]ollution taxes, fees, and charges … can also perpetuate environmental injustices. First, if governments impose uniform tax rates on pollution discharges based on the volume or toxicity of the discharge without regard to the location of the discharge, pollution taxes could create toxic hot spots in the same manner as pollutant trading systems. It may be more cost-effective for old, heavily polluting industries to pay pollution taxes than to reduce their pollution discharges, especially when the taxes are not set at rates that force polluters to reduce pollution. Unless governments tax pollution in heavily polluted areas at a higher rate than pollution in other areas, only newer, cleaner industries will have any incentive to reduce their pollution.

More significantly, though, pollution taxes could have regressive effects on low-income communities. For instance, low-income households would feel the impacts of an energy tax much more keenly than high-income households because low-income households spend a greater proportion of their income on heat, electricity, and gasoline than high-income households. Similarly, variable-rate waste disposal fees impose more significant financial burdens on low-income residents than high-income residents.…

* * *

## Notes and Questions

**1. The market and information disclosure.** Professor Johnson also argues that providing environmental justice communities with more information about the environmental and public health impacts of pollution trades, and providing them with technical assistance grants to review market-based actions, will help them more effectively participate in market-based environmental programs. Do you agree that this is an effective approach? What limits are there to relying on information disclosure as a strategy for communities to safeguard their interests? Consider that information about environmental risks may be confusing, technical, and difficult to process for most individuals. Are these insurmountable obstacles?

**2. True market preferences?** Professor Johnson uses an illuminating example to identify what may be a fundamental theoretical problem with an efficiency-oriented approach. In a footnote, he explains that:

> Judge Posner relates the following story to explain the economist's definition of "value": Suppose that pituitary extract is in very scarce supply relative to the demand and is therefore very expensive. A poor family has a child who will be a dwarf if he does not get some of the extract, but the family cannot afford the price.… A rich family has a child who will grow to normal height, but the extract will add a few inches more, and his parents decide to buy it for him. In the sense of value used in this book, the pituitary extract is more valuable to the rich than to the poor family, because value is measured by willingness to pay.… [citing Richard A. Posner, ECONOMIC ANALYSIS OF LAW § 1.1, (4th ed. 1992), at 13]. While Posner suggests that the rich family is

more "willing to pay" for the extract than the poor family, it seems that the
rich family is more "able to pay" than the poor family, rather than more
"willing to pay." Posner's definition of willingness to pay, therefore, seems
to incorporate ability to pay.

Johnson, *supra*, at 118 n.43. If willingness to pay is dependent upon our ability to pay,
at least at the lower end of the economic scale, then this standard economic metric
does not accurately reflect true preferences. It would be hard to imagine that heavily
impacted communities near refineries and other large facilities "value" clean air less
than the rest of society. Is such a metric tantamount to a position that the preferences
and values of the poor simply do not count? If so, are market-based environmental
protection mechanisms inconsistent with democratic values, including pluralistic ideals?

**3. The Acid Rain Trading Program** described by Professor Johnson is considered to
be a major success in many respects. In fifteen years, the program reduced $SO_2$ emissions
by 67 percent compared with 1980 levels and 64 percent compared with 1990 levels,
with sources emitting well below the current annual emission cap. U.S. Envtl. Prot.
Agency, ACID RAIN AND RELATED PROGRAMS: 15 YEARS OF RESULTS 1995–2009 (2009).
As economist Robert Stavins explains, however, the assumptions that underlie the acid
rain trading program are different from trading for conventional air pollutants:

> [T]rades [in sulfur dioxide permits] switch the source of the pollution
> from one company to another, which is not important when any emissions
> equally affect the whole trading area. This "uniform mixing" assumption is
> certainly valid for global problems such as greenhouse gases or the effect of
> chlorofluorocarbons on the stratospheric ozone layer. It may also work rea-
> sonably well for a regional problem such as acid rain, because acid deposition
> in downwind states of New England is about equally affected by sulfur dioxide
> emissions traded among upwind sources in Ohio, Indiana, and Illinois. But
> it does not work perfectly, since acid rain in New England may increase if a
> plant there sells permits to a plant in the Midwest, for example.
>
> At the other extreme, some environmental problems might not be ad-
> dressed appropriately by a simple, unconstrained tradeable emission permit
> system. A hazardous air pollutant such as benzene that does not mix in the
> airshed can cause localized hot spots. Because a company can buy permits
> and increase local emissions, permit trading does not ensure that each location
> will meet a specific standard. Moreover, the damages caused by local con-
> centrations may increase nonlinearly. If so, then even a permit system that
> reduces total emissions might allow trades that move those emissions to a
> high-impact location and thus increase total damages.

Robert N. Stavins, *The Myth of Simple Market Solutions*, ENVTL. FORUM. 21 (2004).
Keep these concerns in mind as you consider the next subsection discussing VOC
trading under Rule 1610, the RECLAIM program.

## 2. Emissions Trading

During the 1990s, the South Coast Air Quality Management District in Los Angeles adopted the world's first urban smog trading program and California's first cap-and-trade system. In 2017, the Air District voted to sunset the program. The following excerpt critiques a central component of this program, which allowed stationary sources to satisfy their pollution control obligations by purchasing credits from mobile sources.

### Richard Toshiyuki Drury, Michael E. Belliveau, J. Scott Kuhn & Shipra Bansal, *Pollution Trading and Environmental Injustice: Los Angeles' Failed Experiment in Air Quality Policy*

9 Duke Environmental Law and Policy Forum 231, 242–279
(Spring 1999)

The Los Angeles, California, region provides an ideal testing ground for environmental policies. Los Angeles' environmental problems are severe, its regulatory agencies are sophisticated, its resources are relatively ample, and the region's population is multi-racial and economically diverse.... The South Coast Air Basin, which includes the metropolitan Los Angeles area, suffers the worst air quality in the nation....

... In 1993, SCAQMD [the South Coast Air Quality Management District] approved the first old vehicle pollution trading program in the country, known as Rule 1610 or the "car scrapping program." Rule 1610 allows stationary source polluters (such as factories and refineries) to avoid installing expensive pollution control equipment if they purchase pollution credits generated by destroying old, high-polluting cars. Ideally, an equal or greater amount of pollution can be reduced at a much lower cost by purchasing and destroying old cars than by forcing stationary sources to install expensive pollution control equipment.

Under Rule 1610, "licensed car scrappers" can purchase and destroy old cars. SCAQMD then grants the scrapper emissions credits based on the projected emissions of the car had it not been destroyed, which may then be sold to stationary source polluters (e.g., factories). The stationary sources use the pollution credits to avoid on-site emission reductions that would be required under the technology-based regulatory regime. Rule 1610 requires polluters to purchase credits representing twenty percent more emission reductions than would be achieved through compliance with technology-based regulations for their plant. Although industrial plants avoid emission reductions, the scrapping of older, high polluting cars should result in greater air quality improvements at a lower cost than regulatory mandates.

SCAQMD then adopted the centerpiece of its pollution trading strategy, the Regional Clean Air Incentives Market (RECLAIM), the world's first urban smog trading program.... RECLAIM, a "declining cap and trade" program, mandates annual emission reductions for industry but provides them the flexibility to achieve that goal by either purchasing emission reduction credits or by reducing their own pollution.

SCAQMD's pollution trading programs have resulted in the creation of toxic hot-spots by concentrating pollution in communities surrounding major sources of pollution.... SCAQMD studies indicate that cars destroyed through the Rule 1610 program were registered throughout the air quality management district, a four-county region. Air pollution from these automobiles would have also been distributed throughout this region. By contrast, stationary sources in Los Angeles are densely clustered in only a few communities in this four-county region. As a result of these distribution patterns, Rule 1610 effectively takes pollution formerly distributed throughout the region by automobiles, and concentrates that pollution in the communities surrounding stationary sources.

Most of the emissions credits purchased to avoid stationary source controls have been purchased by four oil companies: Unocal, Chevron, Ultramar, and GATX. Of these four companies, three are located close together in the communities of Wilmington and San Pedro; the fourth facility, Chevron, is located nearby in El Segundo. These companies have used pollution credits to avoid installing pollution control equipment that captures toxic gases released during oil tanker loading at their marine terminals. When loading oil tankers, toxic gases are forced out of the tanker and into the air, exposing workers and nearby residents to toxic vapors, including benzene, a known human carcinogen. Thus, by using pollution credits, these companies are allowed to avoid reducing local emissions of hazardous chemicals in exchange for reducing regional auto emissions. As a result of Rule 1610, the four oil companies created a toxic chemical hot-spot around their marine terminals, exposing workers and nearby residents to elevated health risks....

... The demographics of this hot-spot area starkly contrast with that of the metropolitan Los Angeles region. The residents living in San Pedro and Wilmington, which host a majority of the oil companies emitting hazardous toxic chemicals, are overwhelmingly Latino. Furthermore, the racial composition of communities living near three of the marine terminals ranges from 75 to 90 percent people of color, while the entire South Coast Air Basin has a population of only 36 percent people of color....

The hazards of trading extend beyond the shifting of pollution from a dispersed region to more concentrated localized areas; inter-pollutant trading can also create toxic hot-spots. Many trading programs allow facilities to trade pollution credits generated through reductions in a large variety of chemicals. For example, the Rule 1610 program allows pollution credits to be generated through reductions in [volatile organic compounds] VOCs. VOCs are a family of over 600 chemical compounds, some of which have high toxicity and some of which have low toxicity. VOC trading raises concerns about the difference in toxicity of VOC emissions from marine terminals compared to VOCs from automobiles. For example, benzene levels may be higher in VOC emissions from marine terminals than from cars, which leads to greater exposure and risks concentrated in the communities around the marine terminals.... Therefore, the Rule 1610 program may allow continued release of highly toxic chemicals into certain communities in exchange for small area-wide reductions in much less toxic chemicals....

In addition to concerns about variable toxicity, VOCs also exhibit different degrees of reactivity related to their ability to form photochemical smog. These differences in photochemical reactivity have long been recognized in air pollution regulation and have guided priority setting in the control of VOC sources for smog control. In pollution trading programs, however, if highly reactive VOCs are emitted by purchasing credits earned for reducing low reactivity VOCs, then downwind ozone (smog) formation may be increased rather than reduced....

The complex chemistry of air pollution leads to further problems with pollution trading. Emissions are composed of complex mixtures of chemicals, not the single pollutants often targeted for regulation or trading. We use the term "co-pollutants" to describe the secondary pollutants that inextricably accompany the emission of primary targeted pollutants.... Since pollution trading enables polluters to avoid emission reductions, or even increase emissions, at one location by purchasing credits earned elsewhere, the co-pollutants associated with that emission source may also persist and concentrate around that polluter....

Most states have permitting procedures through which affected community members can advocate for pollution control requirements on facilities. However, pollution trading allows facilities to avoid those permit requirements—usually without the knowledge or involvement of the affected community. Pollution trades made pursuant to Rule 1610 and RECLAIM are not subject to public review or comment. In fact, the public faces numerous difficulties finding out what companies are trading to avoid compliance with pollution control standards. For instance, RECLAIM credits can be purchased from independent brokers, without any environmental agency or public oversight.... In this way, the democratic will, as represented in permit and regulatory requirements imposed after full public review and comment, can be reversed by a simple economic transaction....

* * *

## Notes and Questions

1. **Self-reporting in pollution trading programs.** In addition to the points raised in the excerpt above, environmental attorney Richard Drury and his colleagues also pointed out that the car scrapping program had a substantial number of design flaws that potentially worsened the situation:

> Pollution trading programs primarily rely on industry self-reporting of emission reductions and increases. Based on these self-reports, regulatory agencies must allocate air pollution credits. In Los Angeles, widespread under-reporting, inaccurate modeling, and potential financial windfalls for polluters plague the pollution trading program....
>
> ... The program creates an incentive to under-report actual emissions. By under-reporting their air pollution, the companies can reduce their purchase of emission reduction credits.

Rather than measure actual emissions released, companies estimate emissions using emission factors developed by the Western States Petroleum Association. Emissions factors are surrogate estimates of emissions based on activity level.... Emissions factors are poor surrogates for actual measurements. With margins of error ranging from fifty percent to one hundred percent, emissions factors are highly uncertain, making claimed emission reduction difficult to verify....

Information recently obtained through the Freedom of Information Act reveals that the oil companies did, in fact, measure their emissions. When the actual measurements were compared to reported emissions based on industry emissions factors, striking differences were revealed. Oil companies under-reported their oil tanker emissions by factors between 10 and 1,000. As a result, the oil companies purchased between 10 and 1,000 times too few credits from scrapping old, high-polluting cars to offset their tanker pollution. This persistent problem was completely overlooked by SCAQMD and was only detected through a time-consuming investigation by Communities for a Better Environment....

Several assumptions underlying the Rule 1610 program are also dubious. In order to quantify the credits generated by scrapping a vehicle, SCAQMD assumes that the old cars would have been driven approximately 4,000 to 5,000 miles annually for an additional three years and that the owner of the car would replace it with a "fleet average" automobile. Although these assumptions were based on studies of old car driving patterns, they have not been borne out in reality.

According to [SCAQMD's Chief] Inspector [Bruce] Lohmann and an audit conducted by SCAQMD, many of the cars scrapped through the Rule 1610 program were at the end of their useful life, and would have been destroyed through natural attrition.... Since less than 23,000 cars have been destroyed through the Rule 1610 program in its five-year life, most of these cars are probably among those that would have been destroyed even without the program.

Drury et al., *supra*, at 259–262.

Can these design flaws be overcome or are flaws of this nature endemic to a market program? For example, in designing market programs, should reductions that would have occurred anyway, such as those that occur when a facility shuts down for economic reasons, count as offsets? Should emission reductions that occurred in years past be used for offsets years later? Why or why not? In switching from a traditional system to a market-based system, how should emission credits be allocated among facilities initially?

2. **Reforms to trading programs.** Mr. Drury and his colleagues call for broad reforms in trading programs, including prohibitions on the trading of any toxic sub-

stances, trading between mobile and stationary sources, and "cross-pollutant" trading (trading for credits generated by reduced emissions of less hazardous pollutants). They also argue that a demographic analysis of affected communities should be required before any trading program is approved, and that affected communities should be given the right to review and comment on any proposed trade that would increase or continue the release of toxic emissions in a given community. Agencies should retain the discretion to reject or amend the proposed trade based on community comments. Drury, *supra*, at 283–286.

**3. RECLAIM's sunset.** In 2015, SCAQMD considered revisions to its NOx RECLAIM program. Commenters noted the program's poor track record, and in particular:

> ... representatives for NOx emitters suggested that environmental interests were naïve in solely looking at the prices of short term credits in asserting that NOx RECLAIM credits are priced too low. They claimed that environmental interests failed to look at the price of Infinite Year Block ("IYB") credits. Rather than rebut the claims environmentalists have made that the NOx RECLAIM system is broken because credits prices are too low, the IYB credits only help boost the environmentalists claim. Even with the recent doubling of IYB NOx credits in 2014, the value of IYB credits has been excessively low for over a decade....
>
> The claims of industry lobbyists that the IYB credits are appropriately priced are not true. In fact, like the short term credits, these credits are exceptionally low. Even with a more than doubling of the IYB prices in 2014 compared to 2013, these credits are only 18% of the $609,187 cost established by the District pursuant to section 39616(f) of the California Health & Safety Code, which is set to ensure credit prices do not go too high. That the failure of these IYB credits to even approach 1/5 of the District's ceiling for credit costs just bolsters the excessive number of credits in the NOx RECLAIM system. Overall, the evidence conclusively suggests that the credits are not priced correctly to push for pollution reductions at a level commensurate with what command and control would achieve ...
>
> The evidence presented by the District in this rulemaking indicates that refineries have used the NOx RECLAIM system as a shield from actually installing pollution control equipment ...
>
> ... As it stands now, the NOx RECLAIM program has failed to spur adoption of available pollution technologies for many large facilities, and has accordingly failed to adequately reduce NOx emissions. In addition, it has continued to allow high NOx emissions in the disproportionately impacted neighborhoods near refineries and powerplants, raising substantial environmental justice issues. Thus it has dramatically displayed one of the major flaws of a trading system.

Communities for a Better Environment, Center for Biological Diversity, Earthjustice, Natural Resources Defense Council and Sierra Club, *Letter to South Coast Air Quality*

*Management District Re: Amendments to Regulation XX—NOx RECLAIM* (July 8, 2015) "seeking strengthening of SCAQMD staff's proposal and investigation of alternatives."

To the surprise of many, the SCAQMD Governing Board adopted even weaker regulations than proposed by its staff, as the following excerpt from a complaint, by the same commenters, challenging that decision illustrates:

4. [In] December 2015, the Air District held a public hearing to review a proposed amendment to the admittedly inadequate NOx RECLAIM program. The Air District staff spent three years developing this proposal, and the Governing Board had before it significant technical analysis in the form of a staff report, a California Environmental Quality Act ("CEQA") analysis, and a staff presentation. The supporting documentation for this proposal exceeded two thousand pages.

5. Instead of adopting the staff proposal which was supported by significant evidence before it, the Governing Board that morning introduced a new alternative developed by industry interests. The evidence presented to the Governing Board failed to support the industry proposal. The industry alternative ensured that it would remain cheaper for certain large companies to buy pollution credits rather than install life-saving pollution controls over the next seven years.

6. Over the objections of its own staff, the Governing Board approved this industry-proposed plan. In doing so, the Board left in place a NOx RECLAIM program that is indefensible under State law.

7. Because of the urgent need to clean up pollution in the South Coast air basin and the harsh consequences associated with this pollution, including causing more deaths than all traffic accidents and crime-related deaths in the region, … [Petitioners] challenge the unlawful NOx RECLAIM program that the Air District currently implements. Importantly, as codified in the Health and Safety Code, the California Legislature requires that if air districts implement market-based programs, like NOx RECLAIM, these programs must achieve emissions reductions equivalent to direct pollution reduction programs (sometimes referred to as "command and control" programs). The NOx RECLAIM program does not live up to this mandated standard, and instead perpetuates a program where some of the largest polluting sources like refineries simply pay to pollute, instead of installing life-saving pollution controls. California's Health and Safety Code demands more. While the Governing Board of the Air District has discretion to make quasi-legislative decisions, this discretion is not boundless. The Governing Board's discretion, just like any other government agency, is bounded by law and fact. Here, the Governing Board deviated far outside the bounds of what is allowed under California law—specifically, California's Health and Safety Code. As such, judicial intervention is needed to correct this injustice.

*Communities for a Better Environment et al. v. South Coast Air Quality Management District*, Cal. Super. Ct. No. BS161399 Verified Petition for Writ of Mandate and Complaint for Declaratory and Injunctive Relief (March 9, 2016).

The complaint included two causes of action: the first challenged the program itself for allowing total emissions greater than what would be emitted under a command and control technology-based standard; and the second challenged the Air District's procedure for approving the revisions. The Superior Court agreed in part with Petitioners and held that the Governing Board abused its discretion in rejecting the Staff Proposal without conducting a further hearing and receiving additional public comment, remanding to the Governing Board for further proceedings consistent with its order. *Communities for a Better Environment et al. v. South Coast Air Quality Management District*, 2017 WL 8950317 (November 6, 2017).

The State Air Resources Board had also weighed in and expressed significant concern with the Board's December 2015 vote:

> As you know, emissions of NOx contribute to atmospheric fine particulate (PM2.5) matter and ozone. Meeting federal air quality standards for ozone and PM2.5 is critically important for protecting the health of residents in the South Coast Air Basin. U.S. EPA has classified the South Coast Air Basin as an extreme ozone nonattainment area. The Basin also recently missed the 2015 deadline for meeting the 35 ug/m3 PM2.5 standard.... The District is authorized by statute to implement a market-based program in lieu of a traditional facility-by-facility BARCT rule as long as it meets the requirements set out in State law. Specifically, Section 39616 authorized the District to adopt the RECLAIM alternative market based mechanisms only if the program results in aggregate emission reductions that are equivalent to application of command and control programs ...

California Air Resources Board, *Letter to Dr. Barry Wallerstein, Executive Officer, South Coast Air Quality Management District* (January 7, 2016).

In March 2017, with mounting pressure from affected community residents, elected officials, environmental and environmental justice groups, and other regulators, the SCAQMD ordered the sunset of the RECLAIM program and convened a working group of stakeholders and experts to examine the future of the program and to develop options and timing for the transition to a command-and-control regulatory structure. Discuss the potential drawbacks of market-based systems that the history of RECLAIM, and especially events leading to its sunset, highlight. To what degree do you think environmental justice concerns, versus compliance with the Clean Air Act, played into the decision to sunset the program?

**4. Market-based vs. command-and-control.** How would you design a market-based mechanism to best achieve environmental justice? Is this even possible, or are command-and-control and other standard-setting mechanisms always preferable?

# Chapter 6

# Environmental Permits

## A. Introduction

As we saw in Chapter 1 with the case of the PCBs landfill in Warren County, many environmental justice challenges appear in the context of facility permitting. There are good reasons why this occurs. First, consider the immediacy of the adverse impacts on a local level, such as toxic air emissions, chemicals that are discharged into waterways, dust, increased truck traffic through neighborhood streets, noise, odor, and at times increased vermin and rodents. Understandably, residents in overburdened communities often view a new facility or a facility expansion as the proverbial straw that breaks the camel's back. Permit proceedings also raise concerns about whether the facility operator will comply with the permit terms, thus injecting into permit proceedings issues such as subsequent enforcement and potential contamination. In a sense, the permit is the gateway to environmental inequity that may stem from inadequacies that may exist in enforcement, cleanup, and even standard-setting activities.

More often than not, community groups are first made aware of matters only when public notice requirements of permit proceedings have been triggered. At that point, the community may be placed in a reactive position and must attempt either to challenge a plan for siting of a facility that is fairly far along, or to seek concessions in the form of marginally more protective permit terms or mitigation measures beyond those directly required by existing regulations. This mission often pits community groups against the facility sponsor and permitting officials—both of whom may have become committed to issuing the permit—and may unfairly cause community groups to be characterized as anti-development or "NIMBY" (Not In My Back Yard) oriented.

This chapter explores both the legal authority under environmental statutes to impose additional permit conditions (or to deny the permit altogether), as well as the difficulties encountered in attempting to change the permitting status quo to better respond to environmental inequities. For the most part, neither the federal government nor most states have legislation specifically addressing environmental justice in permit proceedings. To find legal authority to address these concerns, affected communities and their lawyers often ask regulatory officials and the courts to look to more broadly worded provisions in environmental statutes and regulations, such as provisions to "protect health and welfare." This chapter will examine how federal and state permitting officials have responded to environmental justice claims based on these pro-

visions. Other sources of legal authority, such as provisions under constitutional provisions or planning statutes, are explored in Chapters 4 and 11, respectively.

# B. Federal Authorities to Ensure Environmental Justice in Facility Permitting

As you read the following short excerpt, isolate the precise statutory language that
you, as a lawyer, would use to argue that the permitting official may legally consider
a community's claims that it is already unfairly overburdened with environmental
pollution, risk, and nuisance impacts, and that the permit should contain additional
requirements or be denied altogether.

### Richard J. Lazarus & Stephanie Tai, *Integrating Environmental Justice into EPA Permitting Authority*

26 ECOLOGY LAW QUARTERLY 617, 620–642 (1999)

*Background: The Meaning of "Environmental Justice" in the EPA Permitting Context*

… In the context of an EPA permitting decision, the core expression of environmental justice is that EPA should take into account the racial and/or socioeconomic
makeup of the community most likely to be affected adversely by the environmental
risks of a proposed activity. This involves two steps: the identification of the environmental justice community and the incorporation of that community's concerns
into the permitting process. Taking into account the makeup of the community does
not mean that EPA must automatically deny a permit solely because the affected area
is a community of color or low-income. The Agency's inquiry into these characteristics
of the community is, however, necessary to allow the Agency to make an informed
permitting decision regarding the actual environmental and health effects of a permit
applicant's proposed activity.…

Some of the environmental justice concerns that can be addressed through permit
conditions are discussed below. They include the enhancement of a community's capacity to participate in environmental enforcement and compliance assurance, assessment of risk aggregation or cumulative risk, and identification of
disproportionality in risk imposition. The relevance of each of these concerns to the
permitting process is fairly clear. What is less clear to those officials responsible for
issuing the permits is whether they have the necessary authority to consider such
concerns and to take actions, including the imposition of permit conditions, based
upon those concerns.…

*Survey of Federal Statutory Provisions Authorizing Permit Conditions or Denials Based on Environmental Justice*

The history of environmental law is replete with instances when broadly worded
statutory language or regulations have been successfully enlisted in support of arguments that the federal government has authority or obligations beyond those initially

contemplated by the regulated entities, environmentalists, affected communities, or even the government itself....

The [Clean Air] Act's nonattainment provisions provide [] potential environmental justice opportunities. [Nonattainment means an airshed that does not meet health-based air quality standards for certain pollutants. Eds.] Section 173 describes the requirements for a nonattainment permit. An explicit permit requirement in the Act mandates that [a permit cannot be granted unless] "an analysis of alternative sites, sizes, production processes, and environmental control techniques for such proposed source demonstrates that benefits of the proposed source significantly outweigh the environmental and social costs imposed as a result of its location, construction, or modification." The references to both "social costs" and "location" serve as strong bases for EPA's assertion of statutory authority to take environmental justice concerns into account in evaluating the "location" of a facility seeking a nonattainment permit....

In the context of permitting, the CAA provisions of greatest interest are those that may allow EPA (or a state permitting authority that has assumed permitting responsibility pursuant to CAA Section 502) greater discretion in using the permitting process to increase community participation and build community enforcement capacity. Section 504 would seem to confer on EPA just such authority. Subsection (a) provides that "[e]ach permit issued under this subchapter shall include ... such other conditions as are necessary to assure compliance with applicable requirements of this chapter...." A major component for achieving compliance assurance under the CAA is the citizen suit provision of that statute. Without that provision acting as a credible enforcement threat, there is no assurance of compliance. Therefore, Section 504(a) may authorize EPA to impose upon those receiving CAA permits the condition that they take certain steps to enhance the affected community's ability to ensure that the permitted facility complies with applicable environmental protection laws. Such conditions could range from simply providing more ready access to the information necessary to overseeing the permitted facility's operation and compliance to working to increase the resources of citizen groups participating in environmental oversight and compliance assurance.

To that same effect, Section 504(b) authorizes EPA to prescribe "procedures and methods for determining compliance," and Section 504(c) requires that each permit "set forth inspection, entry, monitoring, compliance certification, and reporting requirements to assure compliance with the permit terms and conditions." There is nothing on the face of the statute to preclude either Section 504(b)'s "procedures and methods" or Section 504(c)'s "requirements to assure compliance" from extending to permit conditions that enhance the community's own capacity to oversee the permitted facility's compliance....

Section 402 of the [Clean Water Act] ... is likely the most significant potential source of permit conditioning authority [under that statute]. Section 402 provides that the Administrator may issue a permit for the discharge of any pollutant: "upon condition that such discharge will meet either (A) all applicable requirements under [various sections of the CWA], or (B) prior to the taking of necessary implementing actions relating to all such requirements, such conditions as the Administrator determines are necessary to carry out the provisions of this chapter." A broad construction of clause (B) could confer on the Administrator wide ranging authority to impose permit conditions promoting environmental justice....

＊ ＊ ＊

## Notes and Questions

1. EPA *EJ Legal Tools.* As early as 2000, EPA's Office of General Counsel (OGC) prepared a lengthy memo that similarly found significant authority under numerous statutory provisions for addressing environmental justice issues in the permitting process, including Clean Air Act Section 504, discussed by Professors Lazarus and Tai. During the Obama administration, EPA OGC finally published the legal memo and made it available to the public. EPA OGC, PLAN EJ 2014, LEGAL TOOLS (Dec. 2011), available online at https://www.epa.gov/sites/production/files/2016-07/documents/ej-legal-tools.pdf.

At more than 100 pages, *EJ Legal Tools* provides a broad review of many existing legal authorities that could contribute to pursuits for environmental justice, sweeping across such topics as pesticide registration, research grants, and tribal consultation. In the particular context of Clean Air Act permitting, *EJ Legal Tools* provides this observation:

> EPA's opportunities to advance environmental justice in [Clean Air Act] permitting differ depending on whether EPA or the state is the permitting authority. When EPA is the permitting authority, the Agency controls both the content of the permit and the permit review process. Control over the review process gives EPA opportunities to enhance environmental justice by facilitating increased public participation in the formal permit consideration process (e.g., by granting requests to extend public comment periods or hold multiple public meetings, or by providing translation services at hearings in areas with limited English proficiency). EPA can also take informal steps to enhance participation even earlier in the process, such as inviting community groups to meet with EPA and express their concerns before a draft permit is issued. And when EPA makes permit decisions, the Agency has sufficient legal authority to consider potential disproportionate environmental burdens on a case-by-case basis, with no need to amend existing regulations or guidance documents. In fact, EPA is already following this case-by-case approach in issuing PSD permits consistent with its legal authority.

> When a state is the permitting authority, EPA's role includes commenting on individual permits during the comment period. This presents an opportunity for EPA to advance environmental justice by focusing the state's consideration on potential disproportionate environmental burdens in determining that the permits comply with applicable requirements. EPA can offer comments to states regarding disproportionate burdens arising from permits (although states would not necessarily need to accept and act on

such comments). EPA routinely comments on proposed permits, but has not previously emphasized such issues in comments.

*EJ Legal Tools* at 11–12.

Note EPA's emphasis here on existing authorities to address environmental justice (EJ) concerns, "with no need to amend existing regulations or guidance documents." Why is that important? Does a mere statement of existing authorities seem controversial? Why then did the EPA hold *EJ Legal Tools* from public release for more than ten years?

Consider this observation from the EPA General Counsel: "*EJ Legal Tools* should be viewed as a starting point, rather than as an end point, in the examination of legal authorities. It does not purport to consider every possible contributive authority; rather it focuses on those authorities that appear to be most relevant to the environmental justice challenge as we currently understand it.... Accordingly, *EJ Legal Tools* should be regarded as a living document, subject to future addition and adjustment." *Id.* (foreword by EPA General Counsel Scott C. Fulton). Does this help explain why the release of *EJ Legal Tools* might have been delayed? Are there other explanations you can imagine? Whatever the cause of the delay, *EJ Legal Tools* should be considered, as it says, a fine "starting point" for legal authorities to pursue environmental justice in different contexts.

**2. EPA policies for EJ in permitting.** In addition to *EJ Legal Tools*, recognizing broad legal authorities to address EJ in permitting, EPA guidance documents also encourage consideration of EJ issues in permitting as a matter of agency policy. *See, e.g., EPA Activities to Promote Environmental Justice in the Permit Application Process*, 78 Fed. Reg. 27220 (May 9, 2013). The EPA's most recent policy statement on EJ in permitting appears in EPA's EJ 2020 ACTION AGENDA (2016). For EJ in permitting, the *EJ 2020 Action Agenda* establishes two basic objectives:

> The first is that environmental justice is routinely considered in EPA permitting in all appropriate circumstances. This means that in initiating a permitting action, EPA permit writers will consider whether there are environmental justice concerns present in the community affected by the permit. [Further,] EPA will establish appropriate permit terms and conditions to address environmental justice concerns to the extent supported by the relevant information and law.

> ... The second objective is to build, through engagement in "mutual learning" with state and local co-regulators and other stakeholders, a shared set of tools, best practices and approaches for considering environmental justice concerns in permitting. These tools, practices and approaches will help overburdened communities know how to advocate their concerns and help permitting agencies consider and address them in an appropriate manner.

*Id.* at 16–17.

Consistent with this call for "mutual learning," in 2019, the EPA announced a series of national webinars to assist state and other regulators with addressing environmental justice concerns through the regulatory process. For information on these webinars, check the website for the EPA Office of Environmental Justice at https://www.epa.gov. environmentaljustice.

**3. The Environmental Appeals Board.** Professors Lazarus and Tai also note the willingness of the Environmental Appeals Board (EAB) to endorse conditioning permits on environmental justice grounds:

> The evolving perspective of the Environmental Appeals Board on EPA's authority to base permits on environmental justice grounds can be seen in a series of decisions beginning in September 1993 and continuing to [1999]. Although the Executive Order on Environmental Justice expressly did not enlarge any agency's permitting power, the Order has had a marked effect on the Board's interpretation of the scope of authority available to permitting agencies. Prior to the Order, the Board rejected an environmental justice community's claim that environmental justice concerns should be considered in an air quality permitting process. The Board held instead that permitting agencies lacked environmental justice authority because they were limited to considering whether a facility would meet federal air quality requirements.

> After the Order was issued, the Board seemed to accord increasingly more acceptance to the contention that permitting agencies were able to condition permits on environmental justice grounds.... The net effect of the Order may have been to draw attention to existing areas of authority that the Board had previously overlooked so that agencies had the means to actually comply with the Order.

Richard J. Lazarus & Stephanie Tai, *Integrating Environmental Justice into EPA Permitting Authority*, 26 ECOLOGY L. Q. 617, 655–56 (1999).

**4. The Executive Order.** Although it appears that broadly worded clauses in federal environmental statutes grant authority to condition or deny permits on environmental justice grounds, the willingness of permitting authorities to use their legal authority is critically important. In order to prompt federal agencies to take more aggressive action to address environmental inequities, in 1994 President Clinton issued Executive Order No. 12898, requiring federal agencies to "make achieving environmental justice part of [the agency's] mission by identifying and addressing, as appropriate, disproportionately high and adverse human health or environmental effects of its programs, policies and activities...." [*See* Chapter 10 ("Governmental Initiatives")]. With the Executive Order remaining in place, this message from the highest level of the federal executive branch should prompt permitting authorities to further test the potential of existing sources of authority. However, if permitting officials decline to do so, the role of reviewing bodies becomes essential to the longer-range goal of a protective permitting system. Administrative judges and courts will be increasingly called upon to support these efforts in two respects. The first is to recognize the authorities in omnibus clauses (statutory clauses that provide general authority for agencies to take environmentally protective measures). Beyond that, however, reviewing bodies may prompt the development of substantive environmental justice criteria to be applied to permitting. As you read the following section, consider how the cases decided by the Environmental Appeals Board either support the permitting status quo or encourage the development of more protective permitting approaches.

# In re Chemical Waste Management of Indiana, Inc.
## U.S. EPA Environmental Appeals Board
### 6 E.A.D. 66 (EAB 1995)

On March 1, 1995, U.S. EPA Region V issued a final permit decision approving the application of Chemical Waste Management of Indiana, Inc. ("CWMII") for the renewal of the federal portion of a Resource Conservation and Recovery Act ("RCRA") permit and a Class 3 modification of the same permit for its Adams Center Landfill Facility in Fort Wayne, Indiana. The Environmental Appeals Board has received three petitions challenging the Region's permit decision....

During the comment period on the draft permit and draft modification (collectively the "draft modified permit"), Petitioners and other commenters raised what the parties refer to as "environmental justice" concerns. More specifically, issues were raised as to whether the operation of CWMII's facility will have a disproportionately adverse impact on the health, environment, or economic well-being of minority or low-income populations in the area surrounding the facility. The gist of Petitioners' challenge is that the measures taken by the Region to address the environmental justice concerns failed to conform to the rules governing the permitting process, violated an Executive Order relating to environmental justice, resulted in factual and legal errors and an abuse of discretion, and raised an important policy issue warranting review. For the reasons set forth in this opinion, we conclude that Petitioners have failed to demonstrate that either the Region's permit decision or the procedures it used to reach that decision involved factual or legal errors, exercises of discretion, or policy issues that warrant review. Accordingly, we are denying review of the petitions.

*Background*

The Region issued the HSWA [Hazardous Solid Waste Amendments] portion of the draft modified permit on May 23, 1994. The public comment period began on that date and extended through July 13, 1994. On June 29, 1994, the Region held a public hearing in accordance with the procedures set out in [the applicable regulations]. On March 1, 1995, the Region issued a response to comments and its final permit decision....

During the pendency of CWMII's permit application, Executive Order 12898, relating to environmental justice, was issued. The Order mandates that:

> To the greatest extent practicable and permitted by law.... each Federal agency shall make achieving environmental justice part of its mission by identifying and addressing, as appropriate, disproportionately high and adverse human

health or environmental effects of its programs, policies, or activities on minority populations and low-income populations in the United States....

Section 1-101. *59 Fed. Reg. 7629* (Feb. 16, 1994). The Order also requires that:

Each Federal agency shall conduct its programs, policies, and activities that substantially affect human health and the environment, in a manner that ensures that such programs, policies, and activities do not have the effect of ... subjecting persons (including populations) to discrimination under, such programs, policies, and activities, because of their race, color, or national origin....

Section 2.2 *Id.* At 7630–31.

In response to the environmental justice concerns raised during the comment period on the draft modified permit, the Region held what was billed as an "informational" meeting in Fort Wayne, Indiana, on August 11, 1994. The meeting was attended by concerned citizens, and representatives of CWMII, the Indiana Department of Environmental Management, and the Region. The purpose of the meeting was to "allow representatives of all parties involved to freely discuss Environmental Justice and other key issues, answer questions and gain understanding of each party's concerns." The Region also performed a demographic analysis of census data on populations within a one-mile radius of the facility. The Region ultimately concluded that the operation of the facility would not have a disproportionately adverse health or environmental impact on minority or low-income populations living near the facility....

Under the rules governing this proceeding, the Regional Administrator's permit decision ordinarily will not be reviewed unless it is based on a clearly erroneous finding of fact or conclusion of law, or involves an important matter of policy or exercise of discretion that warrants review. The preamble to [the regulation] states that "this power of review should only be sparingly exercised," and that "most permit conditions should be finally determined at the Regional level...." The burden of demonstrating that review is warranted is on the petitioner. For the reasons set forth below, we conclude that Petitioners have not carried their burden in this case.

We believe it is useful to begin by considering the precise nature of Petitioners' environmental justice claim in the context of this RCRA proceeding and the effect, if any, the issuance of Executive Order 12898 should have on the way in which the Agency addresses such a claim.

"Environmental justice," at least as that term is used in the Executive Order, involves "identifying and addressing, as appropriate, disproportionately high and adverse human health or environmental effects of [Agency] programs, policies, and activities on minority populations and low-income populations...." Some of the commenters also believe that environmental justice is concerned with adverse effects on the *economic* well-being of such populations. Thus, when Petitioners couch their arguments in terms of environmental justice, they assert that the issuance of the permit and the concomitant operation of the facility will have a disproportionately adverse impact not only on the health and environment of minority or low-income people living near the facility but also on economic growth and property values. The main support in the record for this assertion is an environmental impacts study submitted by the City of New Haven. That study purports to "evaluate the potential for human exposure to toxic chemicals derived from the treatment and disposal of chemicals at the Adams Center." It identifies "exposure pathways" by which citizens living near the facility may be exposed to pollutants from the facility, but its central conclusion is that more risk assessment needs to be done before the extent and probability of such exposure can be determined accurately.

Although it is not made explicit in the petitions, it is nevertheless clear that Petitioners do not believe that the threats posed by the facility can be addressed through revision of the permit. Rather, it is apparent that Petitioners believe that their concerns can be addressed only by permanently halting operation of the facility at its present location or, at a minimum, preventing the Phase IV Expansion of the facility. Thus, Petitioners challenge the permit decision, including the modification, in its entirety, rather than any specific permit conditions.

At the outset, it is important to determine how (if at all) the Executive Order changes the way a Region processes a permit application under RCRA. For the reasons set forth below, we conclude that the Executive Order does not purport to, and does not have the effect of, changing the substantive requirements for issuance of a permit under RCRA and its implementing regulations. We conclude, nevertheless, that there are areas where the Region has discretion to act within the constraints of the RCRA regulations and, in such areas, as a matter of policy, the Region should exercise that discretion to implement the Executive Order to the greatest extent practicable....

While, as is discussed later, there are some important opportunities to implement the Executive Order in the RCRA permitting context, there are substantial limitations as well. As the Region notes in its brief, the Executive Order by its express terms is to be implemented in a manner that is consistent with existing law. The Region correctly points out that under the existing RCRA scheme, the Agency is *required* to issue a permit to any applicant who meets all the requirements of RCRA and its implementing regulations. The statute expressly provides that:

> Upon a determination by the Administrator (or a State, if applicable), of compliance by a facility for which a permit is applied for under this section with the requirements of this section and section 3004, the Administrator (or the State) *shall issue* a permit for such facilities.

RCRA § 3005(c)(1), 42 U.S.C. § 6925 (emphasis added). Thus, as the Region observes:

> Under federal law, public support or opposition to the permitting of a facility can affect a permitting decision if such support or opposition is based on issues relating to compliance with the requirements of RCRA or RCRA regulations or such support or opposition otherwise relate to protection of human health or the environment. RCRA does not authorize permitting decisions

to be based on public comment that is unrelated to RCRA's statutory or regulatory requirements or the protection of human health or the environment.

The Region correctly observes that under RCRA and its implementing regulations, "there is no legal basis for rejecting a RCRA permit application based solely upon alleged social or economic impacts upon the community." Accordingly, if a permit applicant meets the requirements of RCRA and its implementing regulations, the Agency *must* issue the permit, regardless of the racial or socio-economic composition of the surrounding community and regardless of the economic effect of the facility on the surrounding community....

Nevertheless, there are two areas in the RCRA permitting scheme in which the Region has significant discretion, within the constraints of RCRA, to implement the mandates of the Executive Order. The first of these areas is public participation. Part 124 already provides procedures for ensuring that the public is afforded an opportunity to participate in the processing of a permit application. The procedures required under part 124, however, do not preclude a Region from providing other opportunities for public involvement beyond those required under part 124. We hold, therefore, that when the Region has a basis to believe that operation of the facility may have a disproportionate impact on a minority or low-income segment of the affected community, the Region should, as a matter of policy, exercise its discretion to assure early and ongoing opportunities for public involvement in the permitting process.

A second area in which the Region has discretion to implement the Executive Order within the constraints of RCRA relates to the omnibus clause under section 3005(c)(3) of RCRA. The omnibus clause provides that:

> Each permit issued under this section shall contain such terms and conditions as the Administrator (or the State) determines necessary to protect human health and the environment.

Under the omnibus clause, if the operation of a facility would have an adverse impact on the health or environment of the surrounding community, the Agency would be required to include permit terms or conditions that would ensure that such impacts do not occur. Moreover, if the nature of the facility and its proximity to neighboring populations would make it impossible to craft a set of permit terms that would protect the health and environment of such populations, the Agency would have the authority to deny the permit. *See In re Marine Shale Processors, Inc.,* 5 E.A.D. 751, 796 n.64 (EAB 1995) ("The Agency has traditionally read [section 3005(c)(3)] as authorizing denials of permits where the Agency can craft no set of permit conditions or terms that will ensure protection of human health and the environment."). In that event, the facility would have to shut down entirely. Thus, under the omnibus clause, if the operation of a facility truly poses a threat to the health or environment of a low-income or minority community, the omnibus clause would require the Region to include in the permit whatever terms and conditions are necessary to prevent such impacts. This would be true even without a finding of disparate impact.

There is nothing in section 3005(c)(3) to prevent the Region from taking a more refined look at its health and environmental impacts assessment, in light of allegations that operation of the facility would have a disproportionately adverse effect on the health or environment of low-income or minority populations. Even under the omnibus clause some judgment is required as to what constitutes a threat to human health and the environment. It is certainly conceivable that, although analysis of a broad cross-section of the community may not suggest a threat to human health and the environment from the operation of a facility, such a broad analysis might mask the effects of the facility on a disparately affected minority or low-income segment of the community. (Moreover, such an analysis might have been based on assumptions that, though true for a broad cross-section of the community, are not true for the smaller minority or low-income segment of the community.) A Region should take this under consideration in defining the scope of its analysis for compliance with § 3005(c)(3).

Of course, an exercise of discretion under section 3005(c)(3) would be limited by the constraints that are inherent in the language of the omnibus clause. In other words, in response to an environmental justice claim, the Region would be limited to ensuring the protection of the health or environment of the minority or low-income populations. The Region would not have discretion to redress impacts that are unrelated or only tenuously related to human health and the environment, such as disproportionate impacts on the economic well-being of a minority or low-income community. With that qualification in mind, we hold that when a commenter submits at least a superficially plausible claim that operation of the facility will have a disproportionate impact on a minority or low-income segment of the affected community, the Region should, as a matter of policy, exercise its discretion under section 3005(c)(3) to include within its health and environmental impacts assessment an analysis focusing particularly on the minority or low-income community whose health or environment is alleged to be threatened by the facility. In this fashion, the Region may implement the Executive Order within the constraints of RCRA and its implementing regulations....

Petitioners also question the Region's efforts to determine whether operation of the facility will have a disproportionate impact on a minority or low-income community. To assess whether there would indeed be a disproportionate impact on low-income or minority populations, the Region performed a demographic study, based on census figures, of the racial and socio-economic composition of the community surrounding the facility. The Region concluded that no minority or low-income communities will face a disproportionate impact from the facility. Petitioners argue that, in arriving at this conclusion, the Region erred by ignoring available census and other information submitted during the comment period that allegedly demonstrate a disproportionate impact of the facility on minority or low-income populations, particularly those at distances greater than one mile. Petitioners particularly criticize the Region's decision to restrict the focus of its study to the community living within a one-mile radius of the facility. Petitioners contend that the facility adversely affects citizens who live further than one mile away from the facility. In its response to the petitions, the Region defends its decision to focus on a one-mile radius for its demographic study, as follows:

> The Region 5 office of RCRA has chosen a one-mile radius for demographic evaluation of disproportionately high and adverse human health or environmental impacts of RCRA facilities upon minority populations and low-income populations, based upon a Comprehensive Environmental Response, Compensation and Liability Act, ... guidance (Hazard Ranking System Guidance Manual, November 1992, EPA 9345.1-07) developed for CERCLA sites without groundwater contamination; however, the demographic evaluation did not exclude the population located outside of the one-mile radius.

As explained above, the Region can and should consider a claim of disproportionate impact in the context of its health and environmental impacts assessment under the omnibus clause at section 3005(c)(3) of RCRA. The proper scope of a demographic study to consider such impacts is an issue calling for a highly technical judgment as to the probable dispersion of pollutants through various media into the surrounding community. This is precisely the kind of issue that the Region, with its technical expertise and experience, is best suited to decide.... In recognition of this reality, the procedural rules governing appeals of permitting decisions place a heavy burden on petitioners who seek Board review of such technical decisions. To carry that burden in this case, Petitioners would need to show either that the Region erred in concluding that the permit would be protective of populations within one mile of the facility, or that, even if it were protective of such close-in populations, it for some reason would not protect the health or environment of citizens who live at a greater distance from the facility. We believe that Petitioners have failed to demonstrate that the Region erred in either of these respects....

* * *

## Notes and Questions

**1. Trigger for EJ analysis?** Notice the EAB's curious holdings in this case. On the one hand, the EAB agrees with the EPA that EPA has no discretion "to redress impacts that are unrelated or only tenuously related to human health and the environment, such as disproportionate impacts on the economic well-being of a minority or low-income community." On the other hand, the EAB holds that "when a commenter submits at least a superficially plausible claim that operation of the facility will have a disproportionate impact on a minority or low-income segment of the affected community, the [EPA] Region should ... include within its health and environmental impacts assessment an analysis focusing particularly on the minority or low-income community whose health or environment is alleged to be threatened by the facility." What exactly would you understand to be a "superficially plausible claim" for this purpose? Does it require presentation of data on pollution levels or community demographics? Would it be satisfied with declarations from community members or simple averments of counsel? Once this "superficially plausible claim" is established, how far does the burden shift to the permitting agency? May a superficially plausible claim by community petitioners be defeated by a superficially plausible denial of disproportionate impacts by a permitting agency?

**2. The bounds of regulatory discretion.** When broadly worded omnibus clauses, such as RCRA section 3005(c)(3), 42 U.S.C. §6925(c)(3), are used to support an environmental justice claim, federal permitting authorities have tended to be fairly conservative in abiding by constraints plausibly inherent in the language of the clause. What are the outer bounds of regulatory discretion to condition or deny a permit based upon environmental justice considerations? Consider the following two cases.

**Figure 6-1:** Chukchi Sea and Beaufort Sea, proposed for Shell oil exploration. Graphic: Tony Anderson, University of New Mexico.

## In re Shell Gulf of Mexico, Inc. & In re Shell Offshore, Inc. (Frontier Discoverer Drilling Unit)

U.S. EPA Environmental Appeals Board
*15 E.A.D. 103 (EAB 2010)*

[This case arose out of plans by Shell Oil to engage in oil exploration in the Arctic Ocean, specifically in the Chukchi Sea on the west and the Beaufort Sea to the east, within the Outer Continental Shelf of the United States. *See* Figure 6-1. Operation of Shell's massive drill rigs would require permits under the Clean Air Act program for Prevention of Significant Deterioration (PSD). While the drill rigs would operate offshore, residents of Alaska's North Slope, including Alaska Native villages, expressed concern about potential impacts of the drill operation in their communities. Represented by Earthjustice and other legal counsel, concerned community members filed challenges to the Clean Air Act permits written by the EPA, resulting in the following decision on appeal to the EPA Environmental Appeals Board (EAB).]

... The Board has held that environmental justice issues must be considered in connection with the issuance of PSD permits. *In re Prairie State Generating Co.*, 13 E.A.D. 1, 123 (EAB 2006), *aff'd sub nom. Sierra Club v. U.S. EPA*, 499 F.3d 653 (7th Cir. 2007); *In re AES Puerto Rico, L.P.*, 8 E.A.D. 324, 351 (EAB 1999), *aff'd sub nom. Sur Contra La Contaminacion v. EPA*, 202 F.3d 443 (1st Cir. 2000); *In re Knauf Fiber Glass GmbH*, 8 E.A.D. 121, 174–75 (EAB 1999) ("*Knauf I*"); *In re EcoElectrica, L.P.*, 7 E.A.D. 56, 67–69 (EAB 1997).

In the present case, AEWC [Alaska Eskimo Whaling Commission and Inupiat Community of the Arctic Slope] and the Region agree that the North Slope communities potentially impacted by Shell's proposed operations include a "significantly high percentage of Alaskan Natives, who are considered a minority under [Executive Order No.] 12898." ... AEWC contends that the Region clearly erred when it concluded that compliance with the existing annual $NO_2$ NAAQS demonstrates compliance with the Executive Order.

### AEWC's Assertions and Region's Response

... Specifically, AEWC argues that the Region neglected to conduct an environmental justice analysis notwithstanding evidence of existing health disparities between Inupiat Eskimos and other U.S. populations, and despite AEWC's requests for such an analysis in its comments on both permits.... AEWC argues that relying on compliance with the applicable NAAQS as evidence of fulfilling the Executive Order means that no PSD permit will ever trigger the requirements of the Executive Order because no permit can be issued if there is a predicted violation, and further, that because EPA recently updated the $NO_2$ NAAQS, there is evidence that the $NO_2$ NAAQS applicable at the time the Region issued the Permits is not sufficient to protect public health....

The Region responds that its environmental justice analysis was adequate, arguing that it "engaged in extensive outreach" with affected communities to evaluate possible effects on minority or low-income communities, aided by the recently developed North Slope Communication Protocol ("NSCP").... In summarizing the analyses of the potential effects the Permits will have on air quality, the Region states that because operation of the Frontier Discoverer and the Associated Fleet will not cause or contribute to a NAAQS violation, it "means that it will not have a significant adverse impact, much less a disproportionately high and adverse human health or environmental effect, on minority or low-income populations." ... and further argues that because the Region has "determined that no such adverse effects will result from the issuance of the permits in this case, the EAB need not address the AEWC Petitioners' argument regarding the sufficiency of Region 10's environmental justice analysis." ...

### Analysis

... The Region's adherence to prior Board precedent stating that compliance with the NAAQS is sufficient to demonstrate compliance with the Executive Order is misplaced. In the context of PSD permit challenges, the Region correctly states that the Board has accepted compliance with the NAAQS as sufficient to demonstrate that emissions from a proposed facility will not have disproportionately high and adverse human health or environmental effects on a minority or low-income population. See, e.g., *Knauf II*, 9 E.A.D. at 15–17; *In re Sutter Power Plant*, 8 E.A.D. 680, 692 (EAB 1999) (describing the NAAQS as the "bellwether of health protection"). However, the Region ignores the unusual context of this case, as well as the reasons that underlie the Board's precedent of looking in part to NAAQS compliance to satisfy the Executive Order.

The cases the Region cites as support for its decisions in the Chukchi and Beaufort Permits, in which the Board upheld a permit issuer's environmental justice analysis based on demonstrated compliance with the NAAQS, do not support the Region's position in this case. See *Shell*, 13 E.A.D. at 405; *Knauf II*, 9 E.A.D. at 16–17; *Ash Grove Cement*, 7 E.A.D. at 414; see also Region's Resp. at 99. First and foremost, in each of the cases the Region cites, no party argued that a later-in-time standard had been proposed or finalized prior to the permit issuer's decision, and thus application of the then-effective standard was not an issue raised in any of the petitions. In addition, in each of the cases cited, the permit issuer provided some analysis or record evidence to demonstrate compliance with the Executive Order that the Board could look to in evaluating Petitioners' claims regarding environmental justice. See *Shell*, 13 E.A.D. at 404–05 (citing statement in the response to comments document that compliance with the NAAQS and additional permit requirements were expected to provide verifiable means of ensuring Shell's drilling project would comply with the CAA and operate in a manner to protect the health and welfare of Native Villages); *Knauf II*, 9 E.A.D. at 16–17 (upholding Region's environmental justice analysis based on inclusion in the record of two memoranda, made available for public comment when the revised permit was issued pursuant to a remand, analyzing demographics of the areas surrounding the proposed facility and assessing whether emissions from the proposed facility would have a disproportionately high and adverse impact on human health or the environment); *Ash Grove Cement*, 7 E.A.D. at 413–14 (upholding Region's finding of no disproportionately high and adverse human health or environmental effects based on the Region's documented analysis of demographic data for the areas surrounding the proposed facility, as well as the Region's decision not to conduct a quantitative risk assessment based on its conclusions that minority and/or low-income populations identified were outside the area principally impacted by Ash Grove emissions). Thus, the cases the Region cites to support its argument that compliance with the then-applicable NAAQS also indicates de facto compliance with the Executive Order are all distinguishable from the Petitions at issue here. Further, the Region's arguments belie the basis upon which the Board relies on the Agency's NAAQS decisions....

The Board's concerns in this case lie with the Region's stated reliance on its demonstration of compliance with the NAAQS in effect at the time of the Permits' issuance despite the fact that the Administrator had finalized the new 1-hour $NO_2$ NAAQS prior to the issuance of the Permits, and thus the Administrator had already concluded, prior to the issuance of the Permits, that the annual $NO_2$ NAAQS alone did not provide requisite protection of the public health.... Despite the Administrator's un-equivocal determination, made prior to the issuance of either final Permit, that the annual $NO_2$ NAAQS alone was not requisite to protect the public health with an adequate margin of safety, the Region nonetheless solely relies on compliance with the then-applicable annual $NO_2$ NAAQS to demonstrate that Alaska Natives living in North Slope communities will not experience disproportionately high and adverse human health or environmental effects.

For the reasons set forth below, the Board remands the Chukchi and Beaufort Permits for the Region to reconsider the adequacy of its environmental justice analysis....

* * *

## Notes and Questions

1. **Compliance with the NAAQS?** Compare this decision of the EAB with the EPA's decision in the *Select Steel* case (discussed in Chapter 4). Both cases query whether the proposed operations will result in violations of the Clean Air Act's National Ambient Air Quality Standards (NAAQS). In neither case is there any showing of likely NAAQS violations. And yet, the two cases result in markedly different outcomes. What can explain these differences? Is the EAB in *Shell Oil* (12 years after *Select Steel*) still convinced that compliance with the NAAQS confirms the absence of disproportionate impacts on minority or low-income communities?

2. **Environmental justice precedent.** In 2011, EPA completed its environmental justice analysis for the Shell permits. On remand, in part because of EPA's air impacts analysis that correctly applied the revised $NO_2$ NAAQS standard, and rejecting other objections to the environmental justice analysis, the EAB "decline[ed] to review the Region's compliance with the Executive Order and applicable Board precedent." *In Re Shell Gulf of Mexico, Inc. & Shell Offshore, Inc.*, 15 E.A.D. 470, 504 (EAB 2012). Nevertheless, the 2010 EAB decision establishes precedent for the Board to consider environmental justice in permitting. Consider how the next case further illustrates the outer bounds of regulatory discretion to condition or deny a permit based upon environmental justice considerations.

## In re Avenal Power Center, LLC

U.S. EPA Environmental Appeals Board
*15 E.A.D. 384 (EAB 2011)*

[In this case, the Avenal Power Center, LLC, sought approval to construct and operate a new 600-megawatt natural gas-fired power plant in the Central Valley of California, near the communities of Avenal, Huron, and Kettleman City. In support of the project, the EPA issued a permit under the Clean Air Act PSD program. The permit was challenged by concerned members of organizations including El Pueblo Para El Aire y Agua Limpio ("El Pueblo"), Greenaction for Health and Environmental

Justice ("Greenaction"), and the Center for Biological Diversity. On review of the permit, the EAB issued the following decision.]

... El Pueblo, Sierra Club, and Greenaction challenge the Agency's environmental justice analysis and argue instead that the proposed facility will have disproportionately high and adverse human health or environmental effects on residents of Avenal, Huron, and Kettleman City, the three communities in closest proximity to the proposed facility. The Agency argues that the environmental justice analysis itself and the conclusions the Agency made based on that analysis comply with Executive Order 12898 ... Thus, the central question the Board must resolve is: did the Agency meet its obligation to comply with the Executive Order? ...

*Agency's Environmental Justice Analysis*

The Agency included in the Supplemental Statement of Basis a thirty-one page environmental justice analysis that collected and analyzed demographic, health-related, and air quality data.... The demographic analysis indicates that the communities of Avenal, Huron, and Kettleman City contain minority and low-income populations that may be impacted by emissions from the proposed facility....

After the demographic analysis, the Agency described the status of air quality in the area, explaining that it is designated as extreme nonattainment for ozone and as nonattainment for $PM_{2.5}$, and that it is designated in attainment or unclassifiable for $PM_{10}$, annual average $NO_2$, carbon monoxide, $SO_2$, and lead.... The Agency next addressed the limited availability of hourly $NO_2$ monitoring data from Agency-approved monitoring sites, and explained that it decided to use hourly $NO_2$ monitoring information from Hanford and Visalia, the two closest EPA-approved monitors located twenty-eight and forty-six miles from the proposed facility, respectively, to analyze background levels of hourly $NO_2$ at the project site....

In the first part of its environmental justice analysis, the Agency determined that the proposed facility's projected emissions for $NO_2$ (annual average), carbon monoxide (1-hour and 8-hour average), and $PM_{10}$ (24-hour average) will not cause or contribute to a violation of the applicable NAAQS. The Agency concluded that compliance with these NAAQS is sufficient to demonstrate that the proposed emissions for these pollutants over these averaging times will not result in disproportionately high and adverse human health or environmental effects on minority and low-income populations residing near the proposed facility.

In the second part of its environmental justice analysis, the Agency considered the hourly impacts of $NO_2$ concentrations.... The Agency briefly reiterated its previous conclusion that the limited data available from the Hanford and Visalia monitors located closest to the proposed facility indicate that background levels of hourly $NO_2$ "are on par with measured levels of $NO_2$ statewide," and thus background levels of hourly $NO_2$ in the general area of the facility are not disproportionately high as compared to communities throughout the state....

... Contrary to the lack of an environmental justice analysis and the failure to consider short-term impacts of $NO_2$ emissions in *Shell II*, the Agency in this instance provided a thirty-one page environmental justice analysis coupled with a reasoned explanation for why it concluded that the limited information available prevented it from making a determination regarding potential disproportionate impacts caused by short-term NO$_2$ emissions. The Board did not address in *Shell II* whether a permit issuer must make a determinative conclusion after analyzing available, valid data in response to an environmental justice concern. Here, however, the Board finds the Agency's inability to conclude whether short-term NO$_2$ emissions have a disproportionate impact on the populations surrounding the proposed facility is permissible, particularly in light of the facts of this case and the discretion afforded to federal agencies under the Executive Order. The Executive Order does not mandate that the Agency reach a determinative outcome when it conducts an environmental justice analysis, especially when the available valid data is not sufficient to support a determinative outcome. Thus, El Pueblo's and Sierra Club's attempt to selectively interpret the Executive Order and Board precedent to require more must fail. Where, as here, the Agency conducts a substantive environmental justice analysis that endeavors to include and analyze data that is germane to the environmental justice issue raised during the comment period, *see Shell II*, 15 E.A.D. at 160 n.87, and the permit issuer demonstrates that it exercised its considered judgment when determining that it could not reach a determinative conclusion due to the insufficiency of available valid data, the Board will decline to grant review of the environmental justice analysis. *See, e.g.,* *In re Ash Grove Cement Co.*, 7 E.A.D. 387, 417–18 (EAB 1997)....

\* \* \*

## Notes and Questions

1. **Postscript.** After the EAB's decision above, the plaintiffs sought judicial review in the Ninth Circuit Court of Appeals, arguing among other things that the EPA failed to include in Avenal's Clean Air Act permit applicable conditions including recently updated NAAQS for NO$_2$ and SO$_2$. The Ninth Circuit agreed with plaintiffs, vacating the Avenal permit and remanding it back to the EPA in order to fix the permit conditions. *Sierra Club v. U.S. EPA*, 762 F.3 971 (9th Cir. 2014).

2. **Right to appeal.** What provisions confer rights of appeal to the EAB? *See generally*, 40 C.F.R. Parts 71 (Clean Air Act Title V operating permits) and 124 (most other EPA permits). For a useful overview of EAB functions and authorities, *see* EPA, A CITIZEN'S GUIDE TO EPA's ENVIRONMENTAL APPEALS BOARD (July 2018). What if the EPA removed the ability of individuals or community advocates to appeal EPA-issued permits before the EAB? Would the ability to challenge EPA permits in federal court provide the same level of protection and access to justice for minority or low-income communities? Does this hypothetical affect your analysis of the above cases?

3. **Outer bounds?** At a minimum, the *Avenal* case affirmed the precedent for requiring an environmental justice analysis as part of the permitting process. Together, these EAB permitting cases illustrate the tension, on appeal, between the principle of deference to agencies embodied in an abuse of discretion review standard and the counter-balancing policy, embodied in the federal executive order and recognized by

the EAB, that discretion should be exercised in a more protective manner where impacts affect vulnerable communities. The EAB's approach has been to resolve this tension by a more probing review of procedural matters, requiring a detailed environmental justice analysis and good evidentiary support for a claim of disparate impact. As methodologies advance and more specific criteria are developed, by statute or rule, reviewing bodies may have a better basis to evaluate the adequacy of a permitting authority's response to environmental justice concerns. Given the need to substantially improve conditions in overburdened communities, while at the same time affording permit applicants fairness and certainty in the permitting process, how would you devise a more protective permitting scheme that accomplishes these goals?

**4. NEPA's EJ analysis in the permitting context.** Information disclosure laws are more fully discussed in Chapter 12. These same laws also offer a source of leverage for environmental justice advocates. A notable D.C. Circuit opinion concerning the controversial Dakota Access Pipeline (DAPL) addresses such issues. *Standing Rock Sioux Tribe, et al. v. U.S. Army Corps of Engineers, et al.*, 255 F. Supp. 3d 101 (D.D.C. 2017).

> … the D.C. Circuit has permitted challenges to environmental justice analyses under NEPA and the APA, citing *Communities Against Runway Expansion, Inc. v. F.A.A.*, 355 F. 3d 678, 689 (D.C. Cir. 2004) ("The [agency] exercised its discretion to include the environmental justice analysis in its NEPA evaluation, and that analysis therefore is properly subject to arbitrary and capricious review under the APA.").

*Standing Rock Sioux Tribe, supra* 136.

The opinion subsequently rejected the Corps of Engineers' Environmental Assessment (EA) under NEPA for failing to provide an adequate environmental justice analysis which only analyzed impacts of construction, and not spills.

> "The purpose of an environmental justice analysis is to determine whether a project will have a disproportionately adverse effect on minority and low income populations." *Allen v. Nat'l Institutes of Health*, 974 F. Supp. 2d 18, 47 (D. Mass. 2013) (quoting *Mid States Coal. for Progress v. Surface Transp. Bd.*, 345 F.3d 520, 541 (8th Cir. 2003)). The EA takes some steps toward satisfying this purpose. It acknowledges that Standing Rock, a community with a high percentage of minorities and low-income individuals, is based downstream of the Oahe crossing and could be affected by an oil spill, and it observes — without providing any specifics — that a non-tribal community's drinking-water intake is closer to the Oahe crossing than is Standing Rock's. But these statements are not enough to reasonably support the conclusion that the Tribe will not be disproportionately affected by an oil spill in terms of adverse human health or environmental effects. *See* CEQ Guidance at 9.

> The EA is silent, for instance, on the distinct cultural practices of the Tribe and the social and economic factors that might amplify its experience of the environmental effects of an oil spill. *Id.* at 9, 14. Standing Rock provides one

such example in its briefing: many of its members fish, hunt, and gather for subsistence. *See* SRST MSJ at 41. Losing the ability to do so could seriously and disproportionately harm those individuals relative to those in nearby non-tribal communities.

The Corps need not necessarily have addressed that particular issue, but it needed to offer more than a bare-bones conclusion that Standing Rock would not be disproportionately harmed by a spill. Given the cursory nature of this aspect of the EA's analysis, the Court agrees with the Tribe that the Corps did not properly consider the environmental-justice implications of the project and thus failed to take a hard look at its environmental consequences....

*Id.* at 140. Compare the court's review of environmental justice analyses with the EAB's review in the above decisions.

**5. The states.** Some state courts have also turned to state constitutions, plus environmental and information disclosure statutes to find authority to address environmental justice concerns. The following cases illustrate this approach.

# C. Environmental Justice Claims in State Permit Proceedings

## NAACP — Flint Chapter v. Engler

Genesee (Michigan) County Circuit Court
(Transcript of Ruling, May 29, 1997)

*Hayman, Circuit Judge:*

[The case arose out of the Michigan Department of Environmental Quality's (DEQ's) decision to approve an application of the Genesee Power Station Unlimited Partnership for a permit to operate a wood waste incinerator in Genesee Township in 1992. The permit allowed the incinerator to emit lead in the amount of 2.2 tons per year, or 65 tons over its lifespan, which had the potential to increase the concentration of lead in the soil by ten to fifteen percent. The incinerator was located immediately adjacent to a predominantly African American (and heavily polluted) neighborhood near Flint. After the permit was unsuccessfully appealed to EPA's Environmental Appeals Board, the incinerator began operation in 1995. Plaintiffs then filed suit in state court alleging violations of federal and state civil rights and environmental statutes.

The trial judge found that the cumulative impact of multiple sources emitting multiple pollutants imposed a significant burden on the area near the facility, that soil in the area contained levels of lead substantially above statewide background levels, and that at least 50 percent of the children in the northern sector of Genesee County exceeded the maximum level of lead exposure as defined by the health community.]

... In analyzing this case the Court would first note that under Article IV, Section 51 of the Michigan Constitution, it provides: "The public health and general welfare of the people of the State are hereby declared to be matters of primary public concern. The Legislature shall pass suitable laws for protection and promotion of the public health."

Here the Constitution of Michigan has given the representatives of the people of Michigan the authority to pass laws for the protection and promotion of the public health and welfare.

Defendants contend that the Clean Air Act requires them to grant permits when zoning has been approved and the permit meets the NAAQ Standards [National Ambient Air Quality Standards, also commonly referred to as NAAQS]. They argue that they have no authority to deny permits which meet the above stated standards.

This Court disagrees with Defendant's position on this issue. The Clean Air Act and its amendments to same recognize the states' ability to regulate emissions. The act encourages the enactment of uniform State and local laws relating to the prevention and control of air pollution on an interstate level. The act gives primary responsibility for implementation of these interstate standards to State governments, not to the Federal Government. The Federal domain in matters covered by the Clean Air Act has been held not to be exclusive or preemptive of State legislation....

Further, a state may impose pollution control requirements which are more strict than those specified by the Federal plan....

Under the facts of this case, the Court holds that the policies and regulations that are enforced by the State do not go far enough to carry out the duty the State has under the Constitution to protect the health, safety and welfare of its citizens, regardless of their race.

There are some facts in this case that need noting at this point. First, the plant that is at issue in this case was sited in Mt. Morris Township, right at the northeast border of Flint. The relevance of this fact to the decision in this case is that the zoning decision for this plant was made by Mt. Morris Township's local governmental authorities. The significant impacts of pollution fallout will be felt in the City of Flint, by approximately 3,000 white residents to the southeast of the plant and by as many as 50,000 or more African-Americans to the south of the plant. The Plaintiffs are all residents of the City of Flint. Therefore, they had little, if any, standing or political influence to prohibit the zoning approval for the plant in Mt. Morris Township. The elected officials in Mt. Morris did not represent, nor were they elected by City of Flint residents.

Second, the communities in Flint that will be hit by the two tons per year of increased pollution during the estimated 35 years span [sic] of this plant already suffer from significant pollution in the environment. Many of the major polluting facilities are located on the north side of Flint and have been there for many years polluting the environment. The soil in this area of Genesee County has an extremely high lead content. The housing stock is old and many have lead based paint, a major source of lead pollution in the environment. The experts have testified that as many as 50 percent of the children in these communities have lead levels that exceed the national maximum exposure to lead. This causes significant problems for developing children.

Third, since the State has taken the position that they are only concerned with meeting the NAAQ[S], there was no Risk Assessment Study required to determine the impact of introducing this additional two tons of pollution into an environment that already is beyond being safe due to pollution sources....

This Court also finds that Defendant violated the Michigan Air Act by failing to perform a Risk Assessment Analysis in this case. The Michigan Clean Air Act states in Section B: "The Michigan Department of Environmental Quality [M.D.E.Q.] may deny or revoke a permit if installation of the source presents or may present an imminent and substantial endangerment to human health, safety, or welfare, or the environment."

Unless the M.D.E.Q. performs a Risk Assessment to determine the impact of the plant in the surrounding area, at least within a five-mile radius, it cannot conclude that the plant does not violate this provision and must therefore refuse to grant a permit....

Another problem that exists in this case is with the Defendant's failure to provide a meaningful avenue for cities and other governmental units, who are in the situation that Flint is in [here], to have a meaningful and knowledgeable opportunity to have it's [sic] concerns and those of its residents considered in the siting process involving plants that are located in another jurisdiction, but which pollute adjoining governmental units.

And I think that's a big problem in this case. The Department of Environmental Quality is saying, look, we have no authority to decide where the plants are going to be sited. That's a local issue. But in this particular case, you have a local governmental authority deciding to site a plant and it's polluting another community that has no authority to stop that local community from zoning that plant. And there has to be a procedure in place to give those communities an opportunity to be heard.

The State's position that zoning is a local issue is harmful to the health, safety and welfare of citizens who are situated like Flint who do not have a voice at zoning board meetings that are held outside of their communities. In these situations the State must have in place a procedure that gives adjoining communities a fair opportunity to be notified and heard concerning the siting of pollution facilities near their borders that pollute their communities.

There is little or no incentive for Mt. Morris Township to deny zoning to a facility that will pollute an adjoining community. Mt. Morris gets an increased tax base and the residents of the City of Flint will get pollution....

Given that this Court has concluded that the State has violated its constitutional duty to protect the health, safety and welfare of its citizens by failing to enact policies that protect cities like Flint and its residents and give them a fair opportunity to be heard in a meaningful way, this Court concludes that there is no remedy at law and therefore it is appropriate to exercise its equitable power and to grant an injunction against the Michigan Department of Environmental Quality preventing it from granting permits to major pollution sources—and I use the term major pollution sources—until a Risk Assessment is performed and those interested parties and governmental units that will be impacted based upon the Risk Assessment Study are notified and given an opportunity to be heard before the Michigan Department of Environmental Quality....

And it has to also give interested parties and governmental units that [such] study shows will be impacted by the pollution an opportunity to be heard and an opportunity, a meaningful opportunity, not just an opportunity to come in front of the Commission and air their voices, but something meaningful, before zoning is granted for major polluting facilities and permits are granted....

\* \* \*

## Notes and Questions

1. **The bounds of state permitting authority.** The trial court was troubled by the fact that the economic benefits of the plant flowed to persons who lived outside the neighborhood, while residents of the impacted area were unable to obtain jobs from the plant. What is the legal relevance of this finding? The court also found problematic the fact that the impacts of the projects would be felt largely by persons outside the permitting agency's jurisdiction, in the next town. If this is an inevitable consequence of the local nature of most permitting decisions, how should the permitting agency account for this complication? Are there mitigation requirements that it should consider, or should it deny the permit altogether if the impacts reach a particular magnitude?

2. **Postscript.** On appeal, the court of appeals reversed in an unpublished decision, ruling that the trial judge had improperly granted relief based on claims that plaintiffs had not pleaded or raised at trial. See *NAACP—Flint Chapter v. Engler*, No. 205264 (Mich. Ct. App. Nov. 24, 1998). Judge Hayman's opinion nevertheless details a recurring theme: whether an agency has the authority to consider environmental justice impacts where an applicant meets all other technical permitting requirements. Consider the next case.

# Colonias Development Council v.
# Rhino Environmental Services Inc.

138 N.M. 133, 117 P.3d 939 (2005)

*Background*

On September 10, 2001, more than 250 people packed the middle school cafeteria in Chaparral, New Mexico, for a public hearing. The purpose of the meeting was to review an application by Rhino Environmental Services, Inc. (Rhino) for a permit to put a landfill in Chaparral pursuant to the [New Mexico] Solid Waste Act.

Even though the September 11 terrorist attack on the World Trade Center in New York City disrupted the public hearing, emptying chairs the day after the attack, more than 300 people eventually came forth between September 10 and 19, with about sixty actively testifying or conducting cross-examination. Some community members attended the sessions during the day. Others came at night, after driving home from jobs across the border in Mexico and El Paso, Texas. People brought their children and crying babies. They held press conferences. They tried to hang banners protesting the landfill. Some spoke in Spanish, through a translator provided by the Department.

Although a few community members supported the landfill during the hearing, the vast majority did not. Many testified that they did not understand why another landfill had to be placed just a couple of miles from Chaparral, an unincorporated community that lacks infrastructure, political representation, and medical facilities. As a border community consisting primarily of low-income, minority residents, Chaparral has been called New Mexico's largest *colonia* [*colonias* are rural settlements, usually along the United States-Mexico border, that lack safe housing, potable water, wastewater treatment, drainage, electricity, and paved roads. Eds.]....

Despite the overwhelming community opposition, the Secretary, acting through the Director of the Water and Waste Management Division, granted the permit for a period of ten years subject to a list of twenty conditions....

CDC [Colonias Development Council, a nonprofit dedicated to improving conditions in New Mexico *colonias*] appealed that decision to the Court of Appeals, which affirmed the Department's approval of the landfill permit. On certiorari to this Court, CDC acknowledges that community members were given an opportunity to speak but claims the hearing officer erred by interpreting the Department's role too narrowly. In CDC's view, the hearing officer perceived her duty as strictly confined to overseeing the technical requirements of the permit application. As a result, the Secretary approved the landfill permit based on an erroneous assumption that the Department was neither required nor allowed to consider the impact of the proliferation of landfills on a community's quality of life. This perception, CDC contends, ultimately undermined any influence the public's nontechnical testimony could have on the decision to grant a landfill permit....

CDC further contends that the hearing officer erred in refusing to consider testimony regarding the adverse cumulative effects caused by the proliferation of landfills and other industrial sites. CDC claims there are four waste disposal facilities and three industrial sites near Chaparral....

*Discussion*

CDC argues that the impact of the landfill on the community's quality of life, and the general concerns of community members opposed to the landfill, were not considered in determining whether to grant the solid waste permit. It contends that such considerations are required by the Environmental Improvement Act, the Solid Waste Act, and the regulations adopted pursuant to the acts. CDC does not challenge the technical issues addressed in the permitting process....

The Solid Waste Act directs "the establishment of a comprehensive solid waste management program." One purpose of the act is to "plan for and regulate, in the most economically feasible, cost-effective and environmentally safe manner, the reduction, storage, collection, transportation, separation, processing, recycling and disposal of solid waste." Another important purpose is to "enhance the beauty and quality of the environment; conserve, recover and recycle resources; and protect the public health, safety and welfare." ...

In issuing [regulations under the Solid Waste Act], the Board is required to "assure that the relative interests of the applicant, other owners of property likely to be affected and the general public will be considered prior to the issuance of a permit for a solid waste facility." In addition, the Board is required to adopt procedural regulations providing for notice and a public hearing on permit actions.

Pursuant to this statutory authority, the Board adopted regulations providing technical siting criteria. The Board also adopted regulations governing permitting procedures, which encourage public participation.

... [T]he regulations regarding permit issuance state: "The Secretary *shall* issue a permit if the applicant demonstrates that the other requirements of this Part are met *and* the solid waste facility application demonstrates that neither a hazard to public health, welfare, or the environment nor undue risk to property will result." ...

Pursuant to the authority delegated by the enabling statutes, and the regulations adopted to implement those statutes, CDC urges this Court to conclude that the Secretary is required to allow testimony regarding the impact of a proposed landfill on a community's quality of life. Such consideration is required, CDC argues, in order to realize the general purposes of the statutes to confer optimum social well-being, to protect public health, safety and welfare, and to assure that "relative interests" of all parties are considered.

In the view of Rhino and the Department, on the other hand, the purposes of the enabling statutes to promote public welfare and social well-being are addressed in the implementing regulations. Concerns such as landfill proliferation are not mentioned in the regulations, they assert, and cannot be an independent factor in considering whether to issue a solid waste facility permit. The Department sees its role as dictated by the technical regulations. If the siting criteria is met, they argue, the Department has no discretion to deny a permit or impose conditions on one. The Court of Appeals agreed, stating, "[The Department] cannot reasonably be expected to weigh sociological concerns, which it has no expertise in doing. Its role is to pass judgment on the technical aspects of a solid waste site, a subject within its expertise and which it was designed to do." Thus, the Court of Appeals determined that the hearing officer could properly limit evidence relating to "social impact" because the term is not mentioned in the statutes or regulations, and therefore is legally irrelevant.

We think the Court of Appeals' view of the Department's role is too narrow and has the potential to chill public participation in the permitting process contrary to legislative intent. The Solid Waste Act is replete with references to public input and education. The process of applying for a landfill permit attempts to facilitate public participation in several ways. First, the applicant submits an application for a permit, which includes all the technical information required to support the permit, and files notice to the public and affected parties. The Department solicits comments, and once the application is complete, conducts a public hearing, which provides the public and interested parties an opportunity to comment and present evidence. By directing the Department to adopt procedural regulations to provide all persons with a reasonable opportunity to be heard, the Legislature has clearly indicated its intent to ensure that the public plays a vital role in the hearing process....

In finding public participation and the hearing requirement central to the Solid Waste Act, our courts have protected and promoted the role of public input in the Department's decision to issue a permit. In our view, the Legislature did not limit the Department's role to reviewing technical regulations. Instead, our courts have acknowledged that the Secretary must use discretion in implementing the Solid Waste Act and its regulations in order to encourage public participation in the permitting process.

Given the Legislature's goal to involve the public in the permitting process to the fullest extent possible, we do not agree with the Court of Appeals that the Secretary was not allowed to consider testimony relating to the community's quality of life. The Legislature clearly believed public participation is vital to the success of the Solid Waste Act. Members of the public generally are not technical experts. The Legislature did not require scientific evidence in opposition to a landfill permit, but instead envisioned that ordinary concerns about a community's quality of life could influence the decision to issue a landfill permit. While testimony relating to something as broad as "social impact" may not require denial of a permit, the hearing officer must listen to concerns about adverse impacts on social well-being and quality of life, as well as report them accurately to the Secretary. In reviewing the hearing officer's report, the Secretary must consider whether lay concerns relate to violations of the Solid Waste Act and its regulations. Therefore, the Secretary should consider issues relating to public health and welfare not addressed by specific technical regulations....

## Proliferation

Although we hold that the Department must allow testimony regarding the impact of a landfill on a community's quality of life, we agree with the Department that its authority to address such concerns requires a nexus to a regulation. Like the Court of Appeals, we are not persuaded that the general purposes of the Environmental Improvement Act and the Solid Waste Act, considered alone, provide authority for requiring the Secretary to deny a landfill permit based on public opposition. The purposes of the enabling acts, which include the goal of protecting the "public health, safety and welfare," are designed to invoke the general police power of the state. This general expression of legislative police power, without more, does not create a standard for protecting "public health, safety and welfare." Thus, the Court of Appeals was correct to reject CDC's reliance on the purposes of the acts as a statutory mandate to respond to issues that fit ever so loosely under the umbrella of "sociological concerns." Such a broad mandate would offer no guidance to the Department, and violate the well-settled principle that a legislative body may not vest unbridled or arbitrary power in an administrative agency.

Unlike the Court of Appeals, however, we do find that quality of life concerns expressed during the hearing bear a relationship to environmental regulations the Secretary is charged with administering. Although both parties refer to the issues on appeal in a wide variety of ways, including "social impact," "sociological concerns," "social well-being," and "environmental justice," we believe there are legitimate concerns at the core of CDC's claim that are within the purview of the Secretary's oversight role. Contrary to the Department's position, the impact on the community from a specific environmental act, the proliferation of landfills, appears highly relevant to the permit process.

As we have discussed, the regulations implementing the Solid Waste Act demand more from the Department than mere technical oversight. The regulations regarding permit issuance direct the Secretary to issue a permit if the applicant fulfills the technical requirements *and* "the solid waste facility application demonstrates that neither a hazard to public health, welfare, or the environment nor undue risk to property will result." The regulations also require all solid waste facilities to be *located* and operated "in a manner that does not cause a public nuisance or create a potential hazard to public health, welfare or the environment." The regulations do not limit the Secretary's review to technical regulations, but clearly extend to the impact on public health or welfare resulting from the environmental effects of a proposed permit.

Landfill opponents presented testimony that Chaparral is a residential, low income border community that is being overrun by industrial sites including numerous pre-existing landfills. If this is true, we think it is reasonable for the Department to consider whether the cumulative effects of pollution, exacerbated by the incidences of poverty, may rise to the level of a public nuisance or hazard to public health, welfare, or the environment. If proliferation has an identified effect on the community's development and social well-being, it is not an amorphous general welfare issue, but an environmental problem. The adverse impact of the proliferation of landfills on a community's quality of life is well within the boundaries of environmental protection. Thus, the testimony regarding the impact of the proliferation of landfills is relevant within the context of environmental protection promised in the Solid Waste Act and its regulations. For that reason, the Secretary must evaluate whether the impact of an additional landfill on a community's quality of life creates a public nuisance or hazard to public health, welfare, or the environment.

The Department concluded as a matter of law that granting the permit would not result in a public nuisance or a hazard to public health, welfare or the environment. These conclusions, however, were made only after the Department incorrectly found that lay testimony relating to living near multiple disposal facilities was beyond the scope of the Secretary's authority for granting or denying a landfill. In our view, the Department's own regulations not only allow, but require consideration of the cumulative effect of large-scale garbage dumps and industrial sites on a single community.

As the regulations indicate, the Department cannot ignore concerns that relate to environmental protection simply because they are not mentioned in a technical regulation. The Department has a duty to interpret its regulations liberally in order to realize the purposes of the Acts. Because the impact of the proliferation of landfills and industrial sites on a community is relevant to environmental protection, we conclude that the Solid Waste Act and its regulations require the Department to consider whether evidence of the harmful effects from the cumulative impact of industrial development rises to the level of a public nuisance or potential hazard to public health, welfare or the environment.

*Remedy*

Because of the potential chilling effect of the hearing officer's error, we direct the Secretary to afford CDC a reasonable opportunity at a limited public hearing to tender additional evidence regarding the impact of proliferation.... Rhino shall have a reasonable opportunity to respond. We further instruct the Secretary to reconsider the public testimony opposing the landfill and explain the rationale for rejecting it, if the Secretary decides to do so. We are not suggesting that the Secretary must reach a different result, but we do require, as the Act itself requires, that the community be given a voice, and the concerns of the community be considered in the final decision making....

* * *

## Notes and Questions

1. **The meaning of *Rhino*.** The *Rhino* decision by the New Mexico Supreme Court represented a landmark for the jurisprudence of environmental justice, the first state decision requiring consideration of "non-technical" factors such as socioeconomic status of the surrounding population and cumulative impacts from existing facilities. Consider for a moment, however, had the decision gone the other way. If you were

the officer presiding over this hearing, could you explain to the hundreds of community members who showed up to attend the public hearing (even during the national trauma of 9/11) that nothing they might say would matter to your decision unless it concerned the technical specifications for the proposed landfill? As technical comments could perhaps more easily be submitted in writing, what then would be the purpose of any public hearing? Fortunately, the hearing officer's disregard for community input was rejected by the highest court in the state, establishing not just a new precedent for the State of New Mexico but also a model for other states to follow.

2. **Codification of *Rhino*.** In the wake of the *Rhino* decision, the New Mexico Environment Department promulgated regulations enumerating factors to be considered if a community impact assessment is applicable to permit proceedings under the State's Solid Waste Act. *See* N.M. CODE R. §20.9.3.8 D(2)(a)–(j). For a discussion of this case, *see* Kristina G. Fisher, *The Rhino in the Colonia: How* Colonias Development Council v. Rhino Environmental Services, Inc. *Set a Substantive Standard for Environmental Justice*, 39 ENVTL. L. 397 (2009).

3. **The benefits and burdens test.** Following *Rhino*, the Pennsylvania Supreme Court reached a similar conclusion and upheld environmental justice criteria for waste siting established by the Pennsylvania Department of Environmental Protection despite the absence of any specific statutory mandate. Pennsylvania took a different approach, however, requiring among other things, that the project proponent of a waste disposal facility demonstrate that the project's benefits, including social and economic benefits, clearly outweigh its burdens, including social and economic harms. In *Eagle Envtl. II, L.P. v. Commonwealth Dept. of Envtl. Protection*, 584 Pa. 494, 884 A.2d 867 (Pa. 2005), a landfill permitting case, the state supreme court endorsed this "benefits and burdens" test and rejected the argument that Pennsylvania's police power was exceeded because police power only protects the public against harm and does not extend to providing public benefits. In that case, the benefits and burdens were described as follows:

> Eagle cited the following potential short term benefits: disposal of debris in the event of a disaster; payments for health and safety training courses for landfill operators; and use of coal excavated from the site. Eagle identified additional real short term economic benefits: jobs for local residents at the landfill; increased employment at businesses associated with or located near the landfill; increased local, state and federal income taxes as a result of increased employment; higher real estate taxes; a $2 dollar per ton host fee to the township (as specifically authorized by [Pennsylvania law]); and provision of a recycling drop-off center. Eagle further noted real long term benefits of the project: replacement of wetland acreage (although the project would disturb .17 acres of wetlands, the disturbed wetland would be replaced with .42 acres of wetlands); improvement of the roads leading to the landfill; benefit to wetlands in the form of landfill runoff and reduced erosion; recla-

mation of a strip mine, and the resulting visual enhancement and increased soil fertility.

In contrast, Eagle identified harms resulting from the landfill and described how those harms could or could not be mitigated. The potential harm of a malfunction of the leachate treatment plant could be mitigated by proper operation of the plant and utilization of a leachate storage tank [Leachate is a liquid that percolates through a landfill, potentially transporting contaminants beyond the containment system. Eds.]. Eagle recognized the potential negative impact on the residents of the area but concluded that any impact would largely be anticipatory and could be alleviated by working with the residents. Eagle acknowledged sediment-laden runoff as a harm but asserted that it could be mitigated by erosion and sedimentation control features, and various measures relating to sediment required by other regulations. Furthermore, the resulting sedimentary ponds would be beneficial to aquatic life and migratory birds. Eagle observed that an increased risk of fires, emergencies, and accidents that could result from the project would burden the local emergency services, but could be mitigated by contingency planning, fire protection measures, and payments to the local fire departments to cover the increased burden. Eagle further noted the short term harms caused by waste hauling trucks which include fumes, visual impact, noise, spills, and odors. Eagle offered to mitigate these harms by insuring that the trucks are well maintained and that other measures would be employed to reduce the dust, noise, and odors resulting from the site.

Eagle acknowledged the long term harms of the project. After closure of the landfill, the land, which is currently woodland, would be converted to grassland. Eagle argued that, although the conversion could be viewed as a harm, it could also be seen as a benefit because it would increase species diversity in the area. Another long term harm is the negative aesthetic aspect of the landfill, however, Eagle planned to mitigate this by planting vegetation around the perimeter of the landfill.

*Id.* at 501–02, 871–72.

Based upon the foregoing, how would you decide whether the permit should be issued? Would an impact assessment approach change your determination?

**4. Comparing the states.** The cases adjudicating environmental justice claims in permit and related proceedings under state laws by no means uniformly provide remedies to affected communities. Some state courts have been reluctant to find environmental justice requirements in statutes that do not expressly include them. *See, e.g., Pine Bluff for Safe Disposal v. Ark. Pollution Control & Ecology Comm'n,* 354 Ark. 563, 127 S.W.3d 509, 521–22 (2003) (in connection with an air and hazardous waste permit, finding no adverse health effects to *any persons* will result from the Facility's emissions); *Hinds County v. Mississippi Com'n on Environmental Quality,* 61 So.3d 77 (Miss. Sup. Ct. April 14, 2011) (finding no obligation to perform an in-depth environmental justice review and deferring consideration to the Permit Board).

On the other hand, where statutes specifically require consideration of environmental justice or environmental equity, state courts will enforce those requirements. *See, e.g., Hartford Park Tenants Ass'n v. R.I. Dep't of Envtl. Mgmt.*, No. C.A. 99-3748, 2005 WL 2436227 (R.I. Super. Ct. Oct. 3, 2005) (provisions under the state's Industrial Property Remediation and Reuse Act, a cleanup statute). However, even in these instances, they will defer to agency interpretations of how extensive the considerations must be and will narrowly interpret statutory mandates. *See, e.g., Harrelson Materials Mgmt. v. La. Dept. of Envtl. Quality*, No. 2006 CA 1822, 2007 WL 1765563 (La. Ct. App. June 20, 2007) (demolition, debris, and landfill permit); *In re Gaeta Recycling Co.*, 2007 WL 609161 (N.J. Super. Ct. Mar. 1, 2007); *Bronx Envtl. Health & Justice, Inc. v. N.Y. City Dept. of Envtl. Protection*, No. 25754/04, 2005 WL 1389360 (N.Y. Sup. Ct. May 11, 2005) (solid waste facility permit); *City of Brockton v. Energy Facilities Siting Bd.*, 469 Mass. 196, 14 N.E.3d 167 (Mass. Sup. Ct. July 31, 2014) (finding it appropriate for judicial review of application of environmental justice policy, but deferring to agency determination to not apply heihtened review under the policy).

**5. Informed decision-making.** Some successful attempts to add additional permit conditions have targeted another key aspect of permitting: information disclosure laws. In *Communities for a Better Environment et al. v. City of Richmond et al.*, 184 Cal. App. 4th 70 (2010), community groups successfully challenged the City of Richmond's approval of a permit to allow the refining of a heavier, and more polluting, crude oil feedstock at the Chevron Richmond Refinery. While Chevron denied this central purpose of their permit, the company had filed Securities and Exchange Commission forms identifying the central purpose of their project to enable this crude switch. Consequently, the California Court of Appeal held that Chevron's informational document was deficient under the California Environmental Quality Act and failed its informational purpose. For a discussion of how this permitting challenge contributed to community organizing that tilted the balance of power in Richmond, California, *see* Steve Early, Refinery Town: Big Oil, Big Money, and the Remaking of an American City (Beacon Press 2017).

**6. Remedies?** How would you assess the overall approach to environmental justice claims in the permitting context? Do claims reflect concerns for both procedural justice and distributive justice? What kinds of remedies are available to address each concern? Does it matter whether the claims are premised upon state law or federal law?

**7. The permit applicant's perspective.** If you were the lawyer for a permit applicant, how would you advise your client regarding the inherent uncertainty and potential delay associated with addressing environmental justice concerns? Former developers' lawyer and now Professor Michael Gerrard stresses involvement of the community at an early (pre-application) stage:

> At this early stage, a little bit of community opposition can go a long way. If the sponsor has several different options for where to site the project, protests in one community and silence in another may point to the path of least resistance. If it is the type of project that a community might accept if it were modified in certain ways, at this preliminary stage modifications are

often rather easy, before heavy investments have been made in design and engineering.

Michael B. Gerrard, *Stopping and Building New Facilities*, in THE LAW OF ENVIRON-MENTAL JUSTICE 511 (Michael B. Gerrard & Sheila R. Foster eds., 2d ed. 2008). For additional suggestions for the permit applicant, *see* EPA, *Promising Practices for Permit Applicants Seeking EPA-Issued Permits: Ways to Engage Neighboring Communities*, 78 Fed. Reg. 27220, 27226–27233 (May 9, 2013).

# D. Case Study: The Atlantic Coast Pipeline

After the unenlightened decision in *Select Steel* (1998), we have seen administrative bodies (e.g., the EPA's Environmental Appeals Board in the *Shell Oil* case) and state courts (e.g., the New Mexico Supreme Court in the *Rhino* case) begin to embrace principles of environmental justice in citizen challenges to environmental permits. Relatively few of these cases have proceeded to appeals in federal court and the kind of published decisions students often see in casebooks. The following decision is one of these rare cases. As you read this case, consider what arguments seemed most persuasive on behalf of the plaintiffs and what law ultimately grounded the decision.

## Friends of Buckingham v. Virginia Air Pollution Control Board
### 947 F.3d 68 (4th Cir. 2020)

Friends of Buckingham and the Chesapeake Bay Foundation, Inc. (collectively, "Petitioners") challenge the Virginia Air Pollution Control Board ("Board")'s award of a permit for construction of a compressor station on behalf of Intervenor Atlantic Coast Pipeline, LLC ("ACP") in the historic community of Union Hill in Buckingham County, Virginia (the "Compressor Station"). The Compressor Station is one of three such stations planned to support the transmission of natural gas through the ACP's 600-mile pipeline (the "Pipeline"), which is projected to stretch from West Virginia to North Carolina....

Petitioners filed this petition for review against the Board and its chairman, and the Virginia Department of Environmental Quality ("DEQ") and its director (collectively, "Respondents"), raising two assignments of error. First, Petitioners contend the Board erred in failing to consider electric turbines as zero-emission alternatives to gas-fired turbines in the Compressor Station. Second, they contend the Board erred in failing to assess the Compressor Station's potential for disproportionate health impacts on the predominantly African-American community of Union Hill, and in failing to independently evaluate the suitability of that site.

As explained below, we agree with Petitioners and vacate and remand to the Board.

This petition for review is governed by a complex intertwining of local, state, and federal laws and regulations. Therefore, we first set forth the law at play before turning to the facts at hand.

Pursuant to the Clean Air Act ("CAA"), 42 U.S.C. §§ 7401–7671q, the Environmental Protection Agency ("EPA") is tasked with establishing national ambient air quality standards ("NAAQS") for certain "criteria" pollutants. 42 U.S.C. § 7409. Criteria pollutants are pollutants which EPA has determined may endanger the public health or welfare, and they include: sulfur dioxide, carbon monoxide, nitrogen dioxide (referred to herein as "NOx"), ozone, particulate matter, and lead....

Once set by the EPA, the NAAQS are then implemented by nationwide limitations on mobile sources like vehicles, and on new or modified stationary sources; and, relevant here, by state implementation plans ("SIP"s), which implement the NAAQS through emission limitations on stationary and mobile source.

There are two types of stationary sources: major emitting sources and minor emitting sources. A major source is one that has the "potential to emit two hundred and fifty tons per year or more of any air pollutant," and a minor source is one that falls below that benchmark. 42 U.S.C. § 7479(1). The Compressor Station is indisputably a minor source, as it has the potential to emit 43 tons per year....

CAA "establishes a program of cooperative federalism that allows the [s]tates, within limits established by federal minimum standards, to enact and administer their own regulatory programs, structured to meet their own particular needs." The federal NAAQS are merely "[pollutant] concentration ceilings," that "allow[] an adequate margin of safety," 42 U.S.C. §7409(b)(1), and "protect not only average healthy individuals, but also 'sensitive citizens'—children, for example, or people with asthma, emphysema, or other conditions rendering them particularly vulnerable to air pollution." However, the CAA makes clear that "air pollution control at its source is the primary responsibility of States and local governments." 42 U.S.C. § 7401(a)(3). Therefore, states are tasked with adopting a SIP "which provides for implementation, maintenance, and enforcement of [primary and secondary NAAQS] in each air quality control region (or portion thereof) within such State."

Virginia's SIP is set forth predominantly in Title 9 of the Virginia Administrative Code. New minor stationary sources with emissions above a certain level must receive an air permit issued pursuant to Article 6 of Chapter 80 of the Virginia Administrative Code ("Permit" or "Article 6 Permit") by DEQ or the Board. See 9 Va. Admin. Code § 5-80-1120(A). ACP applied for an Article 6 Permit on September 17, 2015. DEQ took ACP's application and elevated it to the Board for approval.

Pursuant to Virginia's SIP, all new stationary sources, whether major or minor, are subject to BACT [Best Available Control Technology] review. See 9 Va. Admin. Code § 5-50-260(B) ("A new stationary source shall apply best available control technology for each regulated pollutant for which there would be an uncontrolled emission rate equal to or greater than the levels in 9 Va. Admin. Code § 5-80-1105 [providing charts of exemption levels in tons per year for various pollutants]."). This is so even though *federal* law does not require a BACT analysis of minor sources....

In addition to the SIP, Virginia law also contains a Commonwealth Energy Policy, which "[e]nsure[s] that development of new, or expansion of existing, energy resources or facilities does not have a disproportionate adverse impact on economically disadvantaged or minority communities." Va. Code Ann. § 67-102(A)(11). Likewise, one of the "[e]nergy objectives" of the Commonwealth Energy Policy is to "[d]evelop[] energy resources and facilities in a manner that does not impose a disproportionate adverse impact on economically disadvantaged or minority communities." ....

The Board is a seven-member citizen board selected by the Governor "from the Commonwealth at large on the basis of merit without regard to political affiliation." The Board is empowered to "make, or cause to be made, such investigations and inspections and do such other things as are reasonably necessary" to discharge its duties. For example, the Board may "call upon any state department or agency for technical assistance" in performing its duties.

The Board often calls upon DEQ to provide technical support and help the Board to fulfill its obligations. In general, DEQ can review permit applications, prepare draft permits and related documents, review and respond to comments from the public, and hold public hearings. Either the Board or DEQ can issue minor source Article 6 Permits, but when the Board does so, as in this case, it must consider:

> (i) the verbal and written comments received during the public comment period made part of the record, (ii) any explanation of comments previously received during the public comment period made at the Board meeting, (iii) the comments and recommendation of [DEQ], and (iv) the agency files.

Va. Code Ann. § 10.1-1322.01(P). If the Board adopts the recommendation of DEQ, it "shall provide in writing a clear and concise statement of the legal basis and justification for the decision reached." Likewise, if the Board's decision varies from DEQ's recommendation, the Board must "provide a clear and concise statement explaining the reason for the variation and how the Board's decision is in compliance with applicable laws and regulations." ....

Because natural gas transported through the Pipeline must remain pressurized, ACP sought to construct three compressor stations in different locations along the Pipeline — one in West Virginia, one in Virginia (the Buckingham County location at issue here), and one in North Carolina.

ACP claims the Compressor Station site in Buckingham County is "the only feasible location" because: (1) "it allows the ACP to interconnect with the existing Transco pipeline"; (2) "it was available for [ACP] to purchase commercially"; and (3) "the Federal Energy Regulatory Commission ('FERC') ruled out the only other site that met the previous two criteria...

After the Permit application was complete, DEQ provided several comment periods. On August 16, 2018, at the beginning of the first 30-day comment period, DEQ held an informational session for the residents of Buckingham County. DEQ representatives stated that, before the Board would take final action on the permit application, it would consider all comments. They also assured all public commenters that they could address the Board at a public meeting. After the comment period closed, DEQ conducted a public hearing on September 11, 2018, and heard proposed comments. Almost 200 people attended, and 60 people made oral comments. DEQ extended the comment period by 10 days. Over the 40-day comment period, DEQ received more than 5,300 comments. "Many comments" expressed "concerns about the potential for disproportionate impacts of the proposed facility on the African American population in Union Hill."

On November 8, 2018, the seven-member Board held its first public hearing. DEQ presented its summary of public comments from the 40-day comment period for the Board's consideration. These comments included concerns such as whether the "[f]acility should use electric turbines" instead of natural gas turbines, criticism that EPA's "[a]ir quality standards [are] not adequately protective," and "[e]nvironmental [j]ustice" and "[s]ite suitability issues." More than 80 people spoke at the hearing, and the Board made the following statements to and inquiries of DEQ officials:

- "[W]hat can you tell me about the demographics of Union Hill? I'd like to know about the community. I'd like to know about the race, the age distribution, anything you know about the health status of the community."

- "I thought [DEQ presented] a very narrow construction of what environmental justice means, and the reason I feel it's important for me to point that out is because I do think that site suitability and environmental justice are wrapped up together."

- "[H]ow is it that DEQ interprets [the Commonwealth Energy Plan] with respect to its obligations to consider environmental justice?"

Based on these concerns, the Board deferred consideration of the Permit. One week later, Governor Ralph Northam removed two Board members who had voiced concerns about the disproportionate harm to Union Hill and replaced them with two new members....

On January 8, 2019, the Board held its final meeting. A DEQ official made a brief presentation, [] stating that "[r]egardless of the demographics of the area surrounding the compressor station, [it] will not cause a disproportionate adverse impact to the community" for two reasons: first, the residents surrounding the Compressor Station site "are already breathing air that is cleaner than the air breathed by 90% of the residents of Virginia"; and second, although "air modeling does indicate...a slight increase in air pollution concentration [from the Compressor Station], the increase is slight."

The [Board] voted unanimously on January 8, 2019, to adopt DEQ's recommendation and approve the Permit. In doing so, individual Board members made statements on the record. Specifically, the Board Chairman stated, "For purpose of my review, I have assumed that [the community around the Compressor Station] may be an E[nvironmental] J[ustice] community." Another member said the same. ("I ...have assumed that the community at issue is an environmental justice community."). The Board as a whole issued a one-page Decision Statement the same day, stating simply that the Permit was "prepared in conformance with all applicable statutes, regulations, and agency practices"; the limits and conditions in the permit "have been established to protect public health and the environment"; and "all public comments relevant to the permit [were] considered."...The Permit was issued the following day.

Petitioners filed this timely petition for review of the grant of the Permit. We possess jurisdiction pursuant to the Natural Gas Act, 15 U.S.C. § 717r(d)(1) (providing the "United States Court of Appeals for the circuit in which a [natural gas] facility...is proposed to be constructed...or operated shall have original and exclusive jurisdiction over any civil action for the review of an order or action of a...State administrative agency acting pursuant to Federal law to issue...any permit...required under Federal law")....

Union Hill is a historic community with a high population of African-Americans whose ancestors established the community in the aftermath of the Civil War. Community members founded the Union Hill Baptist Church, as well as the Union Grove Missionary Church, and have buried their dead there for generations. In 2015, ACP bought a neighboring 68.5-acre plot of land and chose that site for the placement of the Compressor Station.

According to the ACP permit application, the Compressor Station's four turbines, with a combined 58,162 horsepower, would burn gas 24 hours a day, 365 days a year. Together, the turbines' combustion of gas accounts for 83% of the facility's projected nitrogen oxide emissions and 95% of its emissions of particulate matter (PM, PM2.5, and PM10), and also generates emissions of toxic materials such as formaldehyde and hexane. FERC determined that the Compressor Station will increase the area's amount of nitrogen oxide pollution and fine particle (PM2.5) pollution, and emit known carcinogens into the community. FERC likewise recognized that pollutants from compressor stations "are known to increase the effects of asthma and may increase the risk of lung cancer."

Friends of Buckingham, Inc., a group of Buckingham County citizens, conducted a demographic survey (the "Friends of Buckingham Survey"). According to Petitioners:

> The study indicated that about 84% of [Union Hill] residents are nonwhite, most of African-American descent — a percentage far higher than the county-wide percentage of African Americans (34.7%). Of the 67 households for which a full set of responses exists, 42 (or 62.6%) are known descendants of formerly enslaved people from area plantations. Eight households reported unmarked slave and Freedmen graves on their property or nearby. An independent analysis found that the area within one mile of the proposed Compressor Station has a population density 51% higher than the county average — and 77% higher than either [ACP] or DEQ identified in community profiles they prepared during the Compressor Station permitting process.

The Friends of Buckingham study also revealed a prevalence of health conditions consistent with national data showing higher rates of respiratory sickness among the African-American population. Thirty-five households reported pre-existing medical diagnoses, chiefly respiratory and heart conditions. Residents of Union Hill, including many elderly residents, reported suffering from chronic ailments including asthma, chronic obstructive pulmonary disease, chronic bronchitis and pneumonia, heart disease, and other conditions that would make them particularly susceptible to air pollution from the Compressor Station.

Petitioners contend that the Board (and to the extent its recommendations were adopted, DEQ), violated Virginia law by "failing to assess the Compressor Station's disproportionate health impacts on the predominantly African-American Union Hill community and the suitability of the site." These arguments are grounded in a Virginia statute, which provides:

> The Board in…approving…permits…, shall consider facts and circumstances relevant to the reasonableness of the activity involved and the regulations proposed to control it, including:
>
> 1. The character and degree of injury to, or interference with, safety, health, or the reasonable use of property which is caused or threatened to be caused;
>
> 2. The social and economic value of the activity involved;
>
> 3. The suitability of the activity to the area in which it is located; and
>
> 4. The scientific and economic practicality of reducing or eliminating the discharge resulting from such activity.

Va. Code Ann. § 10.1–1307(E). Petitioners argue the Board failed to consider the potential for disproportionate health impacts under (E)(1), and made an incomplete and misinformed site suitability determination under (E)(3).

We conclude that the Board thrice erred in performing its statutory duty under sections 10.1–1307(E)(1) and (E)(3): (1) it failed to make any findings regarding the character of the local population at Union Hill, in the face of conflicting evidence; (2) it failed to individually consider the potential degree of injury to the local population independent of NAAQS and state emission standards; and (3) DEQ's final permit analysis, ostensibly adopted by the Board, relied on evidence in the record that was incomplete or discounted by subsequent evidence.

Before delving into these issues, we begin with a discussion of environmental justice ("EJ").

"As Justice Douglas pointed out nearly [fifty] years ago, '[a]s often happens with interstate highways, the route selected was through the poor area of town, not through the area where the politically powerful people live.'" *Jersey Heights Neighborhood Ass'n v. Glendening*, 174 F.3d 180, 195 (4th Cir. 1999) (King, J., concurring) (quoting *Triangle Improvement Council v. Ritchie*, 402 U.S. 497, 502 (1971) (Douglas, J., dissenting)); *see also* Nicky Sheats, *Achieving Emissions Reductions for Environmental Justice Communities Through Climate Change Mitigation Policy*, 41 Wm. & Mary Envtl. L. & Pol'y Rev. 377, 382 (2017) ("There is evidence that a disproportionate number of environmental hazards, polluting facilities, and other unwanted land uses are located in communities of color and low-income communities."). "The purpose of an environmental justice analysis is to determine whether a project will have a disproportionately adverse effect on minority and low income populations." *Mid States Coal. for Progress v. Surface Transp. Bd.*, 345 F.3d 520, 541 (8th Cir. 2003). "Although the term 'environmental justice' is of fairly recent vintage, the concept is not." *Jersey Heights*, 174 F.3d at 195 (King, J., concurring).

Of note, on August 16, 2018, Governor Northam's own Advisory Council on Environmental Justice recommended suspending the permitting decision for the Compressor Station "pending further review of the station's impacts on the health and the lives of those living in close proximity."

Indeed, under Virginia law, the Board is *required* to consider "character and degree of injury to . . . health," and "suitability of the activity to the area." Va. Code Ann. § 10.1–1307(E). Both Respondents and ACP acknowledge that Virginia law — including the Commonwealth Energy Policy and factors outlined in § 10.1-1307(E)(3) — "require[s] the Board to consider the potential for disproportionate impacts to minority and low income communities." In fact, no party argues that the Board was excused from considering EJ in its analysis. Therefore, we accept that the Board was required to consider EJ in the Compressor Station Permit approval process. Underpinning Petitioners' arguments here is the idea that not only did the Board consider EJ separate and apart from site suitability, it did not give this point enough consideration.

As explained below, it is clear to us that the Board's EJ review was insufficient, which undermines the Board's statutory duties and renders the Board's Permit decision arbitrary and capricious, and unsupported by substantial evidence.

To begin, Petitioners contend, "Despite access to a wealth of information, the Board failed to make any findings regarding the demographics of Union Hill that would have allowed for a meaningful assessment of the likelihood of disproportionate harm." We agree. The Board was presented with conflicting evidence about whether and how Union Hill was a "minority" EJ population, and it made no finding as to its resolution of this conflict. This is improper under both federal law, and Virginia administrative law.

Throughout the public comment period and public meetings, one of the main points of dispute was whether the Union Hill community could be deemed a "minority" EJ community. As noted by the Board and ACP, the Board deferred its vote twice in order to obtain more information on this issue. Yet in the end, it did not even bother to make a finding on this issue. Rather, at least two Board members "assumed" that Union Hill was an EJ minority community without performing further analysis on what that means.

The minority EJ community designation is important because, if Union Hill is considered a minority EJ community, then information about "African-American populations hav[ing] a greater prevalence of asthma" and other health issues is an important consideration. For example, FERC's analysis in the EIS—upon which DEQ originally relied—outlined all the risks to African Americans from the Compressor Station, e.g., increased risk of asthma and lung cancer, and even noted that African Americans were an "especially sensitive" community for these conditions. But because the African-American population around the Compressor Station did not "exceed the threshold[] for environmental justice populations," it was of no moment. Id. at 2373; *see also id.* at 2372 ("None of the three census tracts within 1 mile of the [Compressor Station] are designated minority [EJ] populations [based on a methodology involving 2013 census data].").

There are multiple pieces of conflicting evidence about the minority population of Union Hill in this record, presented to DEQ and the Board:

- FERC's analysis, which is based on 2013 census data, states that in Virginia, "minorities comprise 30.8 percent of the total population." However, on December 9, 2018, DEQ told the Board that Virginia has an average 37% minority.

- FERC stated that "[n]one of the three census tracts within 1 mile of the [Compressor Station] are designated minority environmental justice populations." But the Friends of Buckingham Study (also called the Fjord Study or Household Study) demonstrates that "the area surrounding the [Compressor Station] is clearly an environmental justice area for minority population." Indeed, a September 2018 version of this Study found that, in an actual door-to-door household survey, minorities make up 83% of residents, with African Americans comprising around 62%. After more households were reached, in January 2019, the percentage of minorities increased to 83.5%.

- DEQ also presented an "EJSCREEN" study from the EPA that "found the minority population around the compressor station to be in the range of 37 to 39%." Yet at an earlier presentation, a DEQ staff member had told the Board, "I wouldn't really rely on" EJSCREEN.

DEQ's final permit analysis submission to the Board says nothing further about EJ. And of course, the Board's decision is only one page long, says nothing about EJ or which stud(ies) it relied on, and even adds a provision in handwriting, professing that "[T]he Board does not adopt any legal views expressed by DEQ regarding the Board's authority under Va. Code Ann. Section 10.1–1307.E," without further explanation.

The Board acted arbitrarily in failing to provide *any explanation* regarding the EJ issue, which makes its extensions of public comments and additional meetings ring hollow. Moreover, under Virginia law, the Board's factfinding would fail under a substantial evidence standard of review because there is conflicting evidence in the record that the Board did not resolve. Virginia law is clear: "It is not unusual for there to be conflicting evidence in contested cases, and it is the job of the agency, as factfinder, to resolve those conflicts." *Virginia Ret. Sys. v. Blair*, 772 S.E.2d 26, 32 (Va. Ct. App. 2015) (emphasis in original).

…If the area around the Compressor Station is indeed an EJ minority community, the demographic and statistics change regarding whether this is [an] "especially sensitive" community for certain conditions. Rather than take this into account in its assumption, the Board merely falls back on NAAQS and state air quality standards not tailored to this specific EJ community. The record is replete with such reliance, up to and including the very last Board meeting:

- DEQ draft permit approval submitted to the Board (October 2018) and final permit approval (January 9, 2019): As to site suitability, "[a]ir quality modeling results indicate compliance with all applicable ambient air quality standards. Therefore, the site is deemed suitable from an air quality perspective."

- DEQ response to comments (incorporated into the Decision Statement) (Oct. 24, 2018): "In reviewing the application for this draft permit, DEQ performed a comprehensive regulatory review with respect to Virginia and federal air quality regulations. This includes the health-based standards promulgated by the [EPA] as [NAAQS], as well as Virginia's own health-based standards for toxic pollutants. [T]he draft air permit requirements are designed to ensure protection of public health and the environment in accordance with the state and federal ambient air quality standards and regulations."

- DEQ presentation to Board (Nov. 9, 2018): "[W]hat we strive to do and what we've done in this case, is to assure that pollution, air pollution from this source, does not harm public health. And we do that by doing the modeling and making sure it complies with all health-based standards.

  Our view is that if all the health-based standards are being complied with, then there really is no disproportionate impact, because everyone is being subjected to the same air pollution but well below health-based standards." …

The Board's reliance on air quality standards led it to dismiss EJ concerns. Even if all pollutants within the county remain below state and national air quality standards, the Board failed to grapple with the likelihood that those living closest to the Compressor Station — an overwhelmingly minority population according to the Friends of Buckingham Survey — will be affected more than those living in other parts of the same county. The Board rejected the idea of disproportionate impact on the basis that air quality standards were met. But environmental justice is not merely a box to be checked, and the Board's failure to consider the disproportionate impact on those closest to the Compressor Station resulted in a flawed analysis....

For these reasons, we conclude that the Board failed in its statutory duty to determine the character and degree of injury to the health of the Union Hill residents, and the suitability of the activity to the area. We vacate and remand for the Board to make findings with regard to conflicting evidence in the record, the particular stud(ies) it relied on, and the corresponding local character and degree of injury from particulate matter and toxic substances threatened by construction and operation of the Compressor Station....

## Notes and Questions

1. **"Not merely a box to be checked."** From the excerpt, where does it appear that the Fourth Circuit derives the notion that "environmental justice is not merely a box to be checked"? Does it come exclusively from the Virginia permitting statute, or does it reflect the development of broader legal principles? If the latter, what are the sources of these legal principles?

2. **"EJ minority community"?** What is the legal significance of whether or not the "area around the Compressor Station is indeed an EJ minority community"? If the EPA has defined "environmental justice" to apply to "all people," shouldn't it be enough that some people in the area of the Compressor Station would be disproportionately impacted by the facility operations? In the outcome of this case, how much weight would you attribute to the Court's considerations of race?

3. **Litigation strategy.** How did the community advocates in this case position themselves for this legal victory? Do there appear to be strategies here that would work in different states or under different environmental statutes?

4. **Better advice?** Note that the Virginia DEQ in this case made the same major mistake that the EPA made in the *Select Steel* case, conflating compliance with national air quality standards and protection of local communities. If you had been the legal advisor to the DEQ in this case, how might you have counseled your clients to proceed with this permitting process and reach a result that would withstand judicial review?

5. **The Atlantic Coast Pipeline.** The Atlantic Coast Pipeline (ACP), proposed to run 600 miles across three states of the Southeast, has raised many concerns for environmental injustice, including its potential impacts on racial minorities, low-income communities, and tribes and indigenous peoples. For more on the ACP, considering challenges to actions by the Federal Energy Regulatory Commission (FERC), see Chapter 12 ("Information Disclosure and Environmental Review").

# Chapter 7

# Public Enforcement

## A. Introduction

On August 26, 1996, Allen Elias, the owner of a fertilizer company located near Soda Springs, Idaho, ordered four workers to enter a large, 25,000-gallon tank in order to clean out sludge from the bottom of the tank. On this hot summer day, the workers entered the tank through a 22-inch manhole at the top, but had difficulty washing out the sludge through a small hole at the end of tank. The workers also reported experiencing sore throats and other health effects from the air inside the tank. Despite repeated requests from one of the workers, Elias failed to provide the workers with any safety equipment or training for the work inside the tank. The next morning, August 27, 1996, the workers attempted to resume the work inside the tank. Two workers entered the tank and began to empty the sludge through the small hole onto the ground. After about 45 minutes, one of the workers, Scott Dominguez, collapsed inside the tank. The second worker got out. Dominguez's colleagues tried but were unable to remove Dominguez from the tank. The fire department eventually had to cut a hole in the side of the tank to remove Dominguez and rush him to the hospital.

Unknown to the workers, the sludge inside the tank was the byproduct of a cyanide leaching process that Elias had patented. After extricating Dominguez from the tank, the fire chief asked Elias whether cyanide could be in the tank. Elias denied knowledge of anything in the tank other than water and sludge. After Dominguez arrived at the hospital, the treating physician suspected Dominguez was suffering from cyanide poisoning and called Elias to ask him if there was a possibility of cyanide in the tank. Elias again replied no. Nevertheless, the physician ordered and administered a cyanide antidote kit, and Dominguez responded positively. Blood tests in the hospital confirmed that Dominguez had extremely toxic levels of cyanide in his body.

A grand jury later charged Elias with a four-count indictment. Count I charged Elias with storage or disposal of hazardous waste without a permit, thereby placing another person in imminent danger of death or seriously bodily injury, in violation of [Resource Conservation and Recovery Act (RCRA)] Sec. 3008(e), 42 U.S.C. § 6928(e). Counts II and III charged Elias with improper disposal of hazardous waste without a permit, in violation of RCRA Sec. 3008(d), 42 U.S.C. § 6928(d). Count IV charged Elias with making material misstatements to federal officers, in violation of 18 U.S.C. § 1001. On May 7, 1999, the jury convicted Elias on all four counts.

Allen Elias was sentenced to prison for 17 years, with the prison sentence sustained after years of appeals. Joel Mintz, et al., A Practical Introduction to Environmental Law at 925 (2017).

One powerful and direct means of pursuing environmental justice is through public enforcement of environmental laws and regulations through government agencies. Activists and academics often overlook public enforcement because it rarely draws public attention or results in appellate decisions you find in a typical casebook. Compared to citizen suits (discussed in Chapter 13), public agencies (federal, state, local, and tribal) bring far more cases each year to address environmental violations, but almost all of these cases settle at some point, outside of the spotlight. From the outside, this can be frustrating for some environmental justice advocates who feel their voices may be ignored in the enforcement process. From the inside of an agency, however, advocates for environmental justice may find tremendous authority and opportunity for taking action to protect vulnerable communities. In this chapter, we will explore these opportunities and authorities, helping environmental justice (EJ) advocates collaborate with enforcement agencies by identifying violations, supporting investigations, shifting agency priorities, and suggesting more appropriate enforcement resolutions. Through this process, this chapter may also encourage EJ advocates to consider public service themselves to further the pursuit of environmental justice.

# B. Historical Critiques

Early concerns for environmental racism included allegations of discrimination in the way that the U.S. EPA enforced federal environmental laws. In 1992, the *National Law Journal* (NLJ) published a report to determine whether in fact EPA's environmental enforcement was discriminatory. *See* Marianne Lavelle & Marcia Coyle, *Unequal Protection: The Racial Divide in Environmental Law*, Nat. L.J., Sept. 21, 1992, at S1–S12. The report reviewed civil judicial enforcement cases resolved by EPA from 1985 to 1991. It also looked at EPA responses to contaminated sites under the Superfund program established by the federal Comprehensive Environmental Response, Compensation, and Liability Act (CERCLA). The report specifically examined all sites listed on CERCLA's National Priorities List (NPL) from 1980 to 1992. The study classified zip codes around the facilities and waste sites into four quartiles, ranging from those with the highest white population and highest income to those with the lowest white population and lowest income.

The NLJ study found that penalties for violations of federal environmental laws were substantially lower in minority communities than in white communities. The overall average penalty for all environmental statutes was 46% lower in minority communities than white communities ($153,067 vs. $105,028). With respect to the effect of a community's income on penalties, the picture was less clear. The report found that the average penalty for all violations was significantly lower in poor communities than in wealthy areas: $95,664 per case compared to $146,993. But this result varied considerably by individual statute. Penalties under four statutes—the Clean Air Act, the Safe Drinking Water Act (SDWA), Superfund, and RCRA—were higher in poor areas, ranging from 3% (RCRA) to 63% (SDWA) greater than in wealthy areas. On the other hand, in Clean Water Act cases average penalties in low-income communities were 91% lower than in upper income areas, and in multi-media cases, the average fine in high-income areas was $315,000 compared to $18,000 in low-income communities. The study concluded that the pattern of penalties varied so markedly depending upon the particular law involved that income was not a reliable predictor of the size of penalties.

The NLJ study also found racial disparities in EPA's response to Superfund sites. In particular, it found that "abandoned hazardous waste sites in minority areas take 20% longer to be placed on the National Priorities List (NPL) than those in white areas" (5.6 years from the date of discovery until its listing on the NPL vs. 4.7 years). The report found that by the time cleanup commenced, this gap had narrowed and minority sites were only 4% behind white sites (10.4 years vs. 9.9 years), although in half of the EPA regions this difference was 12% to 42%. The NLJ study also found that EPA chose less protective cleanup remedies at minority sites, opting for "containment" (the capping or walling off of a waste site) 7% more frequently than permanent treatment methods that reduce or eliminate the volume or toxicity of hazardous substances. At sites located in white communities, EPA ordered permanent treatment 22% more often than containment.

The NLJ study has been criticized on a number of methodological grounds. Critics have argued that the study's use of quartiles to divide cases into white and minority areas resulted in areas being classified as "minority" even though they were not in fact predominantly minority; that the disparities reported were not statistically significant; and that the NLJ study failed to control for other variables that might affect penalties.

Two later studies of the cases reviewed by the NLJ study questioned its conclusions. Professor Evan Ringquist found that the results varied depending on how one grouped the historical data. Professor Ringquist first confirmed the study's findings that penalties from 1985 to 1991 were higher in white communities. However, when Professor Ringquist further examined civil judicial enforcement actions dating back to 1974, he found that from 1974 to 1985, penalties were actually *higher* in minority and poor communities, and that during the entire period from 1974 to 1991, there was little difference in average fines between white and minority communities (and that penalties were higher in poor communities). After controlling for other factors that could influence penalties, Professor Ringquist concluded that "minorities are not disadvantaged by case outcomes in environmental protection, and the case for class bias in these outcomes is weak." Evan J. Ringquist, *A Question of Justice: Equity in Environmental Litigation, 1974–1991*, 60 J. POL. 1148, 1162 (1998).

Researcher Mark Atlas also reevaluated the cases analyzed by the NLJ study using some different methodologies, such as geographic concentric rings around facility locations as the units of analysis (rather than facility zip codes), and correcting for mistakes in EPA's original enforcement database. Atlas found that the income level of an area had no meaningful effect on penalties, and that while a community's race affected penalties, it was in the opposite direction of what the NLJ study found; in other words, penalties *increased* as the proportion of minorities in a community increased. Atlas also concluded that factors which influenced penalties the most were the specific characteristics of the case, such as the types of violations, whether more than one facility location was involved in the violation, and how recently the case was resolved. Mark Atlas, *Rush to Judgment: An Empirical Analysis of Environmental Equity in U.S. Environmental Protection Agency Enforcement Actions*, 35 Law and Soc'y Rev. 633 (2001).

In his critique of the NLJ report, Mark Atlas also noted a number of other possible explanations for variations in penalty amounts. For example, under agency policy, EPA may lower a penalty to reflect a defendant's limited ability to pay; in a minority community, this may help avoid driving a minority-owned business into bankruptcy. As will be discussed later in this chapter, EPA may also lower penalties if the defendant agrees to undertake a "supplemental environmental project," bringing environmental benefits to a local community instead of sending penalty payments to the U.S. Treasury.

While there remains a need for further research on the relation of government enforcement to underserved communities, more recent studies appear to confirm the criticism of the NLJ study and the conclusions of Ringquist and Atlas. *See, e.g.*, Spencer Banzhaf, Lala Ma, & Christopher Timmins, *Environmental Justice: The Economics of Race, Place, and Pollution*, 33 J. Econ. Perspectives 185, 202 (2019) (concluding that while a community's "potential for collective action [is] an important determinant[] of enforcement activities, [] race does not have an independent effect and [] the effect of income is mixed").

## Notes and Questions

1. **Critiquing the critiques.** After all of the attention that the NLJ report received, were you surprised by the subsequent critiques and the conclusion that "race does not have an independent effect" in government enforcement? Certainly, government staff—like everyone else—have personal prejudices that could affect their work. Moreover, on every level of government, within the multitudinous agencies that are responsible for environmental enforcement, there remains plenty of opportunity for racism and other forms of bias in the selection and prosecution of enforcement cases. For one detailed analysis of this potential for bias, including bias in favor of business interests and bias against political controversies, *see* Robert R. Kuehn, *Bias in Environmental Agency Decision Making*, 45 Envtl. L. 957 (2015).

Against this potential for bias, however, imagine this scenario. You are an enforcement attorney in EPA Region 5, based in Chicago. Your regional office has enforcement jurisdiction in Minnesota, and your supervisor assigns you a case concerning leaking drums discovered in a vacant lot in Richfield, Minnesota. What do you know at this moment about the demographics of Richfield, Minnesota? If you know nothing about these demographics, would you take time to investigate this? If you discovered an elementary school next to the vacant lot or a high population of Latino residents in the neighborhood, would that information affect your legal analysis of the possible violations related to the leaking drums or your strategy for how to resolve this case?

In reality, busy, overworked enforcement staff often have little or no understanding of the demographics of a community affected by environmental violations. This is both good and bad. It may be good in confirming the empirical finding that racial discrimination is not a significant factor in enforcement decisions. However, it also represents a missed opportunity for promoting environmental justice. If you are a busy, overworked enforcement attorney, would you rather invest your time seeking monetary penalties for violations in wealthy, white communities or seeking to fix serious health problems in poor, minority communities? To perhaps a surprising extent, enforcement staff do have these choices and opportunities for pursuing environmental justice within government agencies, consistent with the concept of enforcement discretion, discussed below.

**2. Squeaky wheels?** Note that one "important determinant" for enforcement activities, according to empirical studies, is the "potential for collective action." What does that mean? In simplest terms, it may reflect the old adage, "The squeaky wheel gets the grease." As Professor Richard Lazarus further elaborated: "Those who complain, who have greater access, who know how to tweak their Congresspeople to do something, are more likely to get the attention of very busy people. And the people with greater know-how are generally those with greater political and economic resources, who tend to be white." Richard Lazarus, quoted in *Unequal Protection: The Racial Divide in Environmental Law*, NAT. L.J., Sept. 21, 1992, at S3. Of course, from the civil rights movement of the 1960s, we know that political and economic resources are not the only factors in determining "collective action." From the historic March on Washington with Martin Luther King, Jr. in 1963 to the historic Women's March on Washington in 2017, organized communities and masses have learned and demonstrated the power of "collective action" even without the benefits of wealth and political access.

**3. Citizen complaints.** In the nearly 30 years since the observation above by Professor Lazarus, there have certainly been some improvements in access to government. Citizen complaints of suspected environmental violations may always be made to any authorities in person or via telephone. With the advent and increasing accessibility of the Internet, community activists can also file reports online. *See, e.g.,* https://echo.epa.gov/report-environmental-violations (EPA violations reporting website). Reports submitted through the EPA website are assigned tracking numbers to ensure response by the appropriate federal, state, or local authorities. What do you imagine are the advantages and limitations of filing reports online versus in person or on the phone? Do any of these systems work? In one case responding to a tip from a "reliable confidential informant," EPA discovered and removed more than 100 containers with pesticide residue buried illegally in an agricultural area with a heavy concentration of migrant farmworkers. *See* Double H Pesticide Burial Site, https://response.epa.gov/site/site_profile.aspx?site_id=4851.

# C. Enforcement Purposes

Perhaps the most significant problem with the NLJ report was its limited focus on one narrow category of enforcement action (civil litigation) by one government agency (the U.S. EPA). In reality, there are many forms of environmental enforcement, including administrative actions, civil litigation, and criminal prosecution. By far the most common form of enforcement is administrative action, which may include things such as warning letters or agency orders issued without judicial intervention. Notably, the most common environmental enforcement agency is not the U.S. EPA but agencies of the states, tribes, territories, and local governments. Environmental enforcement can be complex, sometimes the subject of a full three-credit course in law school. Nevertheless, this section will provide a quick, analytical framework to explain *why* enforcement response may be important to address certain situations. Once we understand the three broad purposes of enforcement discussed below, we can then move on to considering specific legal authorities providing how environmental justice may be achieved through environmental enforcement.

Much of the above discussion about penalties for environmental violations assumes that penalties are a measure of environmental protection, such that lower penalties produce lower protection and higher penalties provide greater protection. In reality, penalties are simply one method of many for addressing violations of environmental law. Which method is most appropriate in a given case depends in part on consideration of three major purposes for environmental enforcement, which may be described as follows: (1) fix the problem; (2) deter future violations; and (3) level the playing field. To understand these three purposes, imagine that you are still that enforcement attorney for EPA Region 5 in Chicago, which has enforcement jurisdiction in the State of Michigan. In February 2015, you learn through an elevator conversation that an EPA chemist in your building has identified extremely high levels of lead in the drinking water of your hometown of Flint, Michigan. With this information, if you could advise your agency clients on a course of action, what would that be? Would you recommend preparing a civil complaint to file in federal court to seek an assessment of civil penalties? Or would you advise more immediate action to stop people from drinking contaminated water?

In this scenario, the most urgent need may be to "fix the problem," which suggests not years of civil litigation for penalties but an administrative order requiring immediate compliance with drinking water standards (which was actually issued by EPA on January 21, 2016). In time, once safe drinking water is provided (even temporarily with bottled water), the enforcement purpose of "deter future violations" may suggest the agency should seek penalties to punish the violator and encourage future compliance with drinking water regulations; in the most egregious cases, such as Flint, deterrence may even include criminal prosecution and jail time for offenders who put people in danger. Finally, if the violator benefited from the violation (such as saving money by not providing proper water treatment), the purpose of "level the playing field" suggests additional penalties should be recovered so that no other party that incurs the costs of compliance would be placed at a competitive disadvantage for playing by the rules.

For any violation of environmental requirements, enforcement action may be appropriate to serve one, two, or all three of these purposes. The purpose which must be served, or served *first*, may thus dictate the choice or sequence of enforcement tools, whether administrative, civil, criminal, or other action.

## Notes and Questions

**1. Enforcement discretion.** Enforcement agencies generally have broad discretion to choose which violations will become the subject of a government enforcement action. To some activists and commentators, this enforcement discretion may seem alarming. As Professor Kuehn observed in the early years of concern for environmental justice, "In fact, the conditions that give rise to the discriminatory impact of environmental hazards may be even greater when the government acts as enforcer, since few areas of the law invest more discretion in agency employees or are more hidden from the public's view and oversight than an agency's enforcement actions." Robert R. Kuehn, *Remedying the Unequal Enforcement of Environmental Laws*, 9 St. John's J. Legal Commentary 625 (1994).

Under the concept of enforcement discretion, the potential for discriminatory enforcement is certainly real, as courts consistently decline to review cases where agencies refuse to take enforcement action. As the U.S. Supreme Court explained in *Heckler v. Chaney*, 470 U.S. 821 (1985), agency decisions whether to take enforcement action in response to a certain violation require a "complicated balancing of factors." These factors include whether the agency has sufficient resources to undertake the action, whether the agency would be likely to succeed on the merits, and whether agency resources would be best spent on this particular violation instead of other competing concerns. Consistent with this Supreme Court guidance, environmental organizations have occasionally challenged EPA's failure to take an enforcement action, but they have rarely prevailed. *See, e.g., Sierra Club v. Whitman*, 268 F.3d 898 (9th Cir. 2001) (dismissing citizen suit seeking to compel EPA to respond to 128 documented violations of a Clean Water Act permit for a treatment plant in Arizona). In this Arizona case, does EPA's refusal to enforce the Clean Water Act necessarily mean there could be no enforcement to address these 128 violations of the Clean Water Act? What other enforcement options might the Sierra Club or other concerned citizens have considered in this case?

**2. Enforcement and compensation.** Look again at the three broad purposes of environmental enforcement articulated above. How do these three purposes of enforcement align with the four dimensions of justice (distributive, procedural, corrective, and social) discussed in Chapter 1? Can enforcement by the government serve all four of these justice dimensions? Consider just the dimension of corrective justice, which according to the reading in Chapter 1 includes "retributive justice," "compensatory justice," "restorative justice," and "commutative justice." Within this framework, one may see how criminal environmental enforcement, for example, could serve interests in retributive justice. Similarly, Superfund enforcement — focused on cleaning up contaminated sites — may serve interests in restorative justice. Enforcement concepts of the "level playing field" may serve interests in commutative justice. But can government enforcement serve interests in compensatory justice, directing resources to public and private parties who have suffered financial or other injuries from environmental violations?

While government enforcement can serve many dimensions of justice, government enforcement may not be able to serve *every* dimension of justice. Consider the case study of the Duwamish Waterway explored in the next chapter (Chapter 8). If pollution in your local waterway prevents you from eating crabs, shellfish, or flounder, you may feel that you have suffered a loss for which compensation is due. This may be particularly true if you are a subsistence fisher and depend on fish and shellfish to feed your family. But in general, violations of environmental law do not give rise to private rights for compensation. The fact that the Duwamish River, in this case, may exceed water quality standards under the Clean Water Act does not mean that fishers have rights to compensation under the Clean Water Act for losses due to CWA violations.

Penalties for violations of the Clean Water Act typically go to the U.S. Treasury, not to the communities harmed by violations of the Clean Water Act. So too with violations of the Clean Air Act, RCRA, and most other federal statutes.

One exception to this general rule comes under CERCLA § 107(a), which allows statutory claims for **natural resource damages** (NRD). Under an NRD action, natural resource trustees (designated entities of federal, state, and tribal governments) may sue for restoration of impaired resources and damages for lost uses. 42 U.S.C. § 9607(a)(4)(C) (authorizing damage claims for "injury to, destruction of, or loss of natural resources"). Expanding on CERCLA's NRD concept, the Oil Pollution Act § 1002(b) provides a laundry list of possible damage claims for injuries related to oil spills. 33 U.S.C. § 2702(b)(2) (authorizing damage claims for injuries to natural resources, real and personal property, subsistence uses, tax revenues, profits and earnings, and public services). This OPA authority was the primary legal basis for many of the damage claims associated with the BP Deepwater Horizon oil spill in the Gulf of Mexico in 2010.

Another exception to the general rule against compensation through enforcement actions is the possibility of restitution as part of a criminal sentencing. For many convictions under federal law, the U.S. Sentencing Guidelines provide, "In the case of an identifiable victim, the court shall … enter a restitution order for the full amount of the victim's loss …" U.S. Sentencing Guidelines Manual § 5E1.1(a) (2018). Victims of environmental crimes, including crimes in vulnerable communities, may thus find another pathway through environmental enforcement for seeking compensation for their injuries.

Despite these narrow exceptions, the general rule remains that government enforcement will not result in compensation for public or private losses. If such compensation is not available through government enforcement action, are there other legal avenues for seeking compensation for injuries? We will return to this question in Chapter 13, when we consider the authorities for citizen suits and common law remedies.

# D. Enforcement Authorities to Protect Vulnerable Communities

As suggested so far in this chapter, diligent government enforcement of federal pollution control laws, including the Clean Air Act, Clean Water Act, RCRA, CERCLA, and the Safe Drinking Water Act, could go a long way toward achieving the objectives of environmental justice. Many of these federal statutes, and state and local counterparts, share structural similarities and also subtle differences. As you review the key provisions presented below, consider how you might use these provisions in order to protect the health and environment of underserved communities.

**Clean Air Act § 113 (42 U.S.C. § 7413)**

(a)(1) Whenever, on the basis of any information ... [EPA] finds that any person has violated or is in violation of any requirement or prohibition of an applicable implementation plan or permit, [EPA] shall notify the person and the State in which the plan applies of such finding. At any time after the expiration of 30 days following the date on which such notice of a violation is issued, [EPA] may ... (A) issue an order requiring such person to comply with the requirements or prohibitions of such plan or permit, (B) issue an administrative penalty order ... or (C) bring a civil action....

(b) Civil judicial enforcement. [EPA] shall, as appropriate ... commence a civil action for a permanent or temporary injunction, or to assess and recover a civil penalty of not more than $25,000 per day for each violation, or both....

(c) Criminal penalties. (1) Any person who knowingly violates any [specified] requirement or prohibition ... shall, upon conviction, be punished by a fine ... or by imprisonment for not to exceed 5 years, or both.... (4) Any person who negligently releases into the ambient air any hazardous air pollutant ... and who at the time negligently places another person in imminent danger of death or serious bodily injury shall, upon conviction, be punished by a fine ... or by imprisonment for not more than 1 year, or both.... (5)(A) Any person who knowingly releases into the ambient air any hazardous air pollutant ... and who knows at the time that he thereby places another person in imminent danger of death or serious bodily injury shall, upon conviction, by punished by a fine ... or by imprisonment of not more than 15 years, or both....

(e) Penalty assessment criteria. (1) In determining the amount of any penalty to be assessed under this section ... [EPA] or the court, as appropriate, shall take into consideration (in addition to such other factors as justice may require) the size of the business, the economic impact of the penalty on the business, the violator's full compliance history and good faith efforts to comply, the duration of the violation..., the economic benefit of noncompliance, and the seriousness of the violation....

## Clean Water Act § 309 (33 U.S.C. § 1319)

(a)(1)–(3) Whenever ... [EPA] finds that any person is in violation of any condition or limitation [of specified CWA provisions], [EPA] shall ... notify the person in alleged violation and such State of such finding [or] [EPA] shall issue an order requiring such person to comply with such section or requirement, or [EPA] shall bring a civil action....

(c) Criminal penalties. (1) Any person who — (A) negligently violates [specified CWA sections] shall be punished by a fine of not less than $2,500 nor more than $25,000 per day of violation, or by imprisonment for not more than 1 year, or by both.... (2) Any person who — (A) knowingly violates [specified CWA sections] or any permit condition or limitation ... shall be punished by a fine of not less than $5,000 nor more than $50,000 per day of violation, or by imprisonment for not more than 3 years, or by both.... (3)(A) Any person who knowingly violates [specified CWA sections] and who knows at that time that he thereby places another person in imminent danger of death or serious bodily injury, shall, upon conviction, be subject to a fine of not more than $250,000 or imprisonment of not more than 15 years, or both....

(g) Administrative penalties. (1) Whenever [EPA] finds that any person has violated [specified CWA sections], [EPA] ... may ... assess a class I civil penalty [not to exceed $25,000] or a class II civil penalty [not to exceed $125,000].... (3) In determining the amount of any penalty assessed under this subsection, [EPA] shall take into account the nature, circumstances, extent and gravity of the violation, or violations, and with respect to the violator, ability to pay, any prior history of such violations, the degree of culpability, economic benefits or savings (if any) resulting from the violation, and such other matters as justice may require....

## Resource Conservation and Recovery Act (RCRA)

RCRA § 3008 (42 U.S.C. § 6928). (a)(1) [W]henever on the basis of any information [EPA] determines that any person has violated or is in violation of any requirement [concerning the handling of hazardous waste], [EPA] may issue an order assessing a civil penalty for any past or current violation, requiring compliance immediately or within a specified time period, or both, or [EPA] may commence a civil action in the United States district court ... for appropriate relief, including a temporary or permanent injunction....

(e) Knowing endangerment. Any person who knowingly transports, treats, stores, disposes of, or exports any hazardous waste ... in violation of [paragraph (d)] who knows at that time that he thereby places another person in imminent danger of death or serious bodily injury, shall, upon conviction, be subject to a fine of not more than $250,000 or imprisonment for not more than fifteen years, or both....

RCRA § 7003 (42 U.S.C. § 6973). (a) Notwithstanding any other provision of this chapter, upon receipt of evidence that the past or present handling, storage, transportation or disposal of any solid waste or hazardous waste may present an imminent and substantial endangerment to health or the environment, [EPA] may bring suit on behalf of the United States in the appropriate district court.... [EPA] may also, after notice to the affected State, take other action under this section, including, but not limited to, issuing such orders as may be necessary to protect public health and the environment.

### Comprehensive Environmental Response, Compensation, and Liability Act (CERCLA)

CERCLA § 106 (42 U.S.C. § 9606). (a) In addition to any other action taken by a State or local government, when [EPA] determines that there may be an imminent and substantial endangerment to the public health or welfare or the environment because of an actual or threatened release of a hazardous substance from a facility, [EPA] may require [DOJ] to secure such relief as may be necessary to abate such danger or threat.... [EPA] may also, after notice to the affected State, take other action ... including, but not limited to, issuing such orders as may be necessary to protect public health and welfare and the environment.

CERCLA § 107 (42 U.S.C. § 9607). (c)(3) If any person who is liable for a release or threat of release of a hazardous substance fails without sufficient cause to properly provide removal or remedial action upon order of [EPA]..., such person may be liable to the United States for punitive damages in an amount at least equal to, and not more than three times, the amount of any costs incurred by [EPA] as a result of such failure to take proper action....

### Oil Pollution Act [Clean Water Act § 311] (33 U.S.C § 1321)

(e) In addition to any action taken by a State or local government, when [EPA or the Coast Guard] determines that there may be an imminent and substantial threat to the public health or welfare of the United States, including fish, shellfish, and wildlife, public and private property, ... because of an actual or threatened discharge of oil ... from a vessel or facility, [EPA or the Coast Guard] may—(A) require the Attorney General to secure any relief from any person ...; or (B) after notice to the affected State, take any other action under this section, including issuing administrative orders, that may be necessary to protect the public health and welfare.

### Federal Insecticide, Fungicide, and Rodenticide Act (FIFRA)

§ 13 (7 U.S.C. § 136k). (a) Stop sale orders. Whenever any pesticide or device is found by [EPA] ... in any State and there is reason to believe on the basis of inspection or tests that such pesticide or device is in violation of any of the provisions of this subchapter, ... [EPA] may issue a written or printed "stop sale, use, or removal" order to any person who owns, controls, or has custody of such pesticide or device....

§ 14 (7 U.S.C. § 136l). (a) Civil penalties. (1) Any registrant, commercial applicator, wholesaler, dealer ... or other distributor [of pesticides] who violates any provision of this subchapter may be assessed a civil penalty by [EPA] of not more than $5,000 for each offense. (2) Any private applicator ... who knowingly violates any provision of this subchapter subsequent to receiving a written warning from [EPA] ... may be assessed a civil penalty ... of not more than $1,000 for each offense....

(b) Criminal penalties. (1)(A) Any registrant ... or producer [of pesticides] who knowingly violates any provision of this subchapter shall be fined not more than $50,000 or imprisoned for not more than 1 year, or both ... (B) Any commercial applicator of a restricted use pesticide ... who knowingly violates any provision of this subchapter shall be fined not more than $25,000 or imprisoned for not more than 1 year, or both. (2) Any private applicator ... who knowingly violates any provision of this subchapter shall be fined not more than $1,000 or imprisoned for not more than 30 days, or both.

### Toxic Substances Control Act § 16 (15 U.S.C. § 2615)

(a) Civil. (1) Any person who violates [select provisions of TSCA] shall be liable to the United States for a civil penalty in an amount not to exceed $37,500 for each such violation. Each day such a violation continues shall ... constitute a separate violation....

(b) Criminal. (1) Any person who knowingly or willfully violates any [select provision of TSCA] shall ... be subject, upon conviction, to a fine of not more than $50,000 for each day of violation, or to imprisonment for not more than one year, or both. (2) Any person who knowingly and willfully violates any [select provisions of TSCA] and who knows at the time of the violation that the violation places an individual in imminent danger of death or serious bodily injury, shall be subject on conviction to a fine of not more than $250,000, or imprisonment for not more than 15 years, or both.

### Safe Drinking Water Act § 1414 (42 U.S.C. § 300g-3)

(a)(1)(A) Whenever [EPA] finds ... that any public water system ... does not comply with any national primary drinking water regulation in effect ... [EPA] shall so notify the State and such public water system and provide such advice and technical assistance to such State and public water system as may be appropriate to bring the system into compliance with such regulation or requirement by the earliest feasible time.

(a)(1)(B) If, beyond the thirtieth day after [EPA's] notification..., the State has not commenced appropriate enforcement action, [EPA] shall issue an order ... requiring the public water system to comply with such regulation or requirement or [EPA] shall commence a civil action....

## Notes and Questions

1. **Notice of violation.** The Notice of Violation (NOV)—also known as a Notice of Noncompliance and other terms—is to an environmental violator as a warning from a traffic cop might be to a speeding driver: there is a message delivered, but no penalty to pay. How could this kind of agency action help address concerns for environmental justice? Does this minimal action just let violators continue to violate? As one response to this question, consider that enforcement agencies almost never have sufficient resources to fully investigate and prosecute every environmental violation that comes to their attention. An NOV offers an efficient way of drawing attention to a problem and giving the violator an opportunity to fix it. It also documents

the existence of a violation, which may figure into a future penalty calculation considering a history of noncompliance.

Is the issuance of an NOV always required before further agency enforcement action? Compare Clean Air Act § 113(a)(1) with Clean Water Act § 309(a)(1)–(3). What do you find? Also consider the NOV provisions of FIFRA § 14(a)(2) and Safe Drinking Water Act § 1414(a)(1). What policy choices do you see in these unique provisions?

**2. Administrative orders.** As noted above, most federal environmental statutes authorize EPA or other agencies to issue orders requiring immediate compliance with specific environmental requirements. What are the differences between an administrative order and injunctive relief available through a court? Which one is likely to provide a quicker response to environmental problems? An administrative order is not necessarily "self-enforcing"; that is, if the recipient of an order chose to disobey it, the agency may have to go to court to compel compliance with it. So why wouldn't the recipient of an administrative order simply ignore it and wait to see if the agency does go to court to enforce it? In answering this question, look closely at CERCLA § 107(c)(3). Do you see why now?

In practice, few recipients of administrative orders simply choose to ignore them. For example, in January 2011, when EPA discovered crude oil leaking from the head of the Trans-Alaska Pipeline near Prudhoe Bay, EPA issued an administrative order within 24 hours under the Oil Pollution Act [Clean Water Act § 311], requiring the pipeline company to fix the problem. Rather than spend time and money fighting the order, the pipeline company chose to comply with the order and had the leak repaired within a week. U.S. EPA Region 10, In the Matter Of: Trans-Alaska Pipeline System, Pump Station 1, Prudhoe Bay, Deadhorse, Alaska, Docket No. CWA-10-2011-0035, Unilateral Administrative Order for Removal Activities, Jan. 11, 2011.

In the relatively rare case where the recipient of an administrative order refuses to comply with it, the order may usually be enforced by the issuing agency and also by concerned citizens. See, e.g., CERCLA § 310(a)(1) (authorizing citizen suits "against any person ... who is alleged to be in violation of any ... order which has become effective pursuant to this chapter"). In one epic saga, an EPA order against a Canadian mining company under CERCLA § 106 became the subject of a citizen suit filed by an affected tribe in 2004. For backstory on the case, see Michael Robinson-Dorn, *The Trail Smelter: Is What's Past Prologue? EPA Blazes a New Trail for CERCLA*, 14 NYU ENVTL. L.J. 233 (2006). For the latest development after 15 years of litigation, see *Pakootas v. Teck Cominco Metals, Ltd.*, 905 F.3d 565 (9th Cir. 2018) (among other things, affirming award of attorney fees to tribe for prevailing in their action).

**3. Penalty calculations.** Recall the early concern about lower penalty assessments in minority communities. Is there a necessary connection between the level of penalties and the level of environmental protection in a community? Look again at some of the statutory factors for calculating penalties, including gravity of the harm, ability to pay, and "such other matters as justice may require." How would you balance these factors in a case like the drinking water contamination in Flint, Michigan (see discussions in Chapters 3–4), where actions by a municipality on the brink of bankruptcy contributed to the gravest of harms to human health? For efficiency and consistency, EPA and states often use written penalty policies to determine proposed penalties. *See, e.g.*, EPA, RCRA Civil Penalty Policy, June 2003; EPA, Public Water System Supervision Program Settlement Penalty Policy for Civil Judicial Actions and Administrative Complaints for Penalties, May 25, 1994. Nevertheless, consistent with the concept of enforcement discretion, much agency flexibility may go into any particular penalty calculation—creating opportunities for pursuing "justice," however agency staff may choose to define it.

4. **Penalty adjustments.** While the basic structures of the federal environmental statutes have not changed for decades, the maximum penalty amounts specified in the individual statutes have been adjusted over time to reflect inflation. For example, the maximum penalty of $5,000 per violation specified in FIFRA § 14 became a maximum penalty of $20,288 per violation in 2020. Similarly, the $25,000 maximum penalty per day under Clean Air Act § 113(b) became a maximum penalty per day of $101,439 in 2020. EPA, Civil Monetary Penalty Inflation Adjustments, 85 Fed. Reg. 1751 (Jan. 13, 2020). How do these adjustments reflect the purposes of environmental enforcement and opportunities for pursuing environmental justice?

5. **Criminal prosecution.** Look again at the maximum criminal penalties in the environmental statutes excerpted above. Did you know that people can go to jail for breaking environmental laws? How could the threat (and reality) of imprisonment contribute to achievement of environmental justice in minority or low-income communities? Could the threat of jail time also work *against* the interests of environmental justice in some cases?

The prosecution of Allen Elias, noted in the chapter introduction, obtained the first federal conviction for knowing endangerment under RCRA. *U.S. v. Elias*, 269 F.3d 1003 (9th Cir. 2001). While the victim in this tragic case unfortunately suffered permanent brain injury as a consequence of Mr. Elias's callous action, the conviction did send a strong signal to all other business owners and operators about the potential consequences for disregarding the value of worker lives. For the full story behind the Allen Elias case, and the criminal agents and prosecutors who pursued it, *see* Joseph Hilldorfer and Robert Dugoni, THE CYANIDE CANARY (2004).

Less dramatically, federal, state, and local prosecutors may pursue cases that never draw public attention but may have significant potential to promote environmental justice. In one series of cases, for example, prosecutors in Oregon and Washington charged building contractors under Clean Air Act § 113(c), 42 U.S.C. § 7413(c), for violations of rules governing the safe handling of asbestos-containing materials. *See* 40 C.F.R. § 61.145 (Standards for Demolition and Renovation). By failing to provide proper safety equipment, among other things, the contractors endangered the health of demolition workers, many of whom were low-income day laborers and immigrants. *See, e.g., U.S. v. Pearson*, 274 F.3d 1225 (9th Cir. 2001) (affirming conviction and sentencing for asbestos violations during renovation project on U.S. Navy base).

In addition to charges under specific environmental statutes, criminal prosecutions often include charges under general criminal statutes, such as those prohibiting false statements (18 U.S.C. § 1001) and obstruction of justice (18 U.S.C. § 1505). Depending on the circumstances, state and local prosecutors might consider more extraordinary charges. For example, in response to the Flint drinking water contamination, prosecutors obtained indictments against at least nine state and local officials, including employees or former employees of the Michigan Department of Environmental Quality. Charges in this case included misconduct in office, willful neglect of duty, and involuntary manslaughter, recognizing the suspected link between the drinking water contamination and multiple deaths due to Legionnaire's Disease.

**6. FIFRA enforcement.** While often overshadowed by the attention and resources dedicated to other environmental statutes, the Federal Insecticide, Fungicide, and Rodenticide Act (FIFRA) may offer powerful enforcement authorities for protecting the health of farmworkers or other community members facing disproportionate exposure to pesticides. Major requirements of FIFRA include federal registration of pesticide products and the handling and use of registered pesticide products in a prescribed manner.

Under FIFRA, the distribution of unregistered pesticides may result in "Stop Sale" orders and civil penalties. In one recent case, EPA issued Stop Sale orders and administrative penalties against Amazon.com for the distribution of unregistered pesticides. U.S. EPA, In the Matter of: Amazon Services LLC, Consent Agreement and Final Order, Docket No. FIFRA-10-2018-0202, Feb. 14, 2018. In this administrative case, EPA alleged that Amazon had committed nearly four thousand violations of FIFRA in the previous five years. EPA alleged that many of these violations particularly endangered Asian immigrants, who were more likely to use certain unregistered pesticides and less likely to be able to read warning labels printed in English. In settlement of this case, Amazon agreed to pay penalties of $1,215,700 and conduct a "supplemental environmental project" that would provide free online education about FIFRA requirements in English, Spanish, and Chinese.

Beyond pesticide registration, FIFRA requires the safe use and handling of pesticides as well as protection of workers who may be exposed to pesticides on farms, forests, nurseries, and other agricultural workplaces. The FIFRA Worker Protection Standard, 40 C.F.R. Part 170, aims to protect agricultural workers through such measures as personal protective equipment, posted pesticide information, worker safety training, and restricted entry to fields immediately after pesticides have been applied. Farmworkers represent the population segment most at risk from pesticides, with reported pesticide poisonings among farmworkers 25 times higher than the general population (and unreported poisonings potentially vastly higher).

Unfortunately, for purposes of environmental justice for farmworkers, FIFRA has been recognized as "the weakest federal environmental statute" when it comes to enforcement provisions. Michael J. McClary & Jessica B. Goldstein, *FIFRA at 40: The*

*Need for Felonies for Pesticide Crimes*, 47 ENVTL. L. REP. NEWS & ANALYSIS 10767, 10770 (2017). Compare the criminal provisions of FIFRA with those of the Clean Air Act, Clean Water Act, RCRA, or TSCA excerpted above. What is missing from FIFRA? Notice in particular the maximum criminal penalty for a "private applicator," which may include the owner of a large farm. Based upon the maximum jail sentence and fine provided by FIFRA, "a private applicator who knowingly violates a FIFRA requirement and causes the death or serious injury of another person, has committed [only] a 'petty offense.'" *Id.* at 10769. Are the FIFRA enforcement provisions a comment by Congress on the value of farmworker lives? Or on the power of agricultural or chemical lobbies? What else could explain these differences?

7. **TSCA enforcement.** Like FIFRA, the Toxic Substances Control Act (TSCA) is often overshadowed and under-resourced for enforcement purposes, yet may offer significant authority for pursuing environmental justice in certain cases. In general, TSCA focuses on designated categories of toxic chemicals, which EPA may ban or restrict if they are found to pose an unreasonable risk to human health. Under TSCA, for example, EPA at one time attempted to ban the use of most products containing asbestos, recognizing the thousands of deaths in the United States each year from asbestos-related diseases. EPA's ban on asbestos-containing products under TSCA, however, was challenged by industry on procedural grounds and overturned on appeal. *Corrosion Proof Fittings v. U.S. EPA*, 947 F.2d 1201 (5th Cir. 1991). This remained the status quo in 2020, with little prospect for a federal ban on asbestos products in the future.

For purposes of government enforcement, TSCA today is mostly a grab bag of regulatory programs addressing a handful of toxic substances. One such TSCA program concerns the use, distribution, and disposal of items containing polychlorinated biphenyls (PCBs). 40 C.F.R. Part 761. PCBs are often found in old transformers or other electrical equipment, posing particular risks to workers who may be engaged in building maintenance or equipment salvage activities. Another, far broader program for TSCA enforcement concerns required notices that sellers or landlords must provide to prospective home buyers or renters about the potential for lead-based paint in a given housing unit. 40 C.F.R. Part 745. Regular enforcement of the TSCA lead-paint disclosure rules may help address chronic problems with lead poisoning from older housing stock in urban areas.

As with the other federal statutes, most government enforcement of TSCA is administrative and results in a settlement. *See, e.g.,* U.S. EPA Region IX, In the Matter of: McNamara Realty, Consent Agreement and Final Order, Docket No. TSCA-09-2018-0007, Dec. 26, 2018 (administrative settlement requiring payment of $32,000 penalty for alleged violations of TSCA lead disclosure rules). Unlike FIFRA, TSCA has criminal provisions that include felonies such as "knowing endangerment," added by TSCA amendments in 2016. The 2016 TSCA amendments, known as the Frank R. Lautenberg Chemical Safety Act, Pub. L. 114-182 (June 22, 2016), also set new requirements for EPA to review additional substances for potential restriction under TSCA.

**8. Federalism.** Under most federal environmental statutes, including the Clean Air Act, Clean Water Act, RCRA, and the Safe Drinking Water Act, states and tribes may seek and receive authorization to implement the federal program within their jurisdiction. This includes the authority to issue permits and take enforcement action for violations. All states and a growing number of tribes now have authority to implement Clean Air Act programs. Almost every state is now authorized to carry out the Clean Water Act and the Safe Drinking Water Act. (New Mexico may soon be the only exception to state authorization for the Clean Water Act.) State enforcement is essential to the success of most environmental programs, as states contribute enforcement resources, innovation, industry insights, and community sensitivities beyond the capability of the federal government. Environmental groups, however, worry that states are more susceptible to industry capture and that, absent federal controls, states will engage in a "race to the bottom" to attract industry by lowering environmental standards. States (like the federal government) may also become directly responsible for environmental violations in some cases, as with the drinking water contamination in Flint, Michigan.

What balance of state or federal primacy would best serve the interests of vulnerable communities such as the poor and minority communities of Flint? The State of Michigan is authorized to carry out and enforce requirements of the federal Safe Drinking Water Act. In Flint, the Michigan Department of Environmental Quality (MDEQ) clearly failed to do its job enforcing the Safe Drinking Water Act. So too did EPA Region 5, which has oversight authority in the State of Michigan. Of course, agencies can act only through the people within them. Employees within EPA Region 5 and state agencies sounded alarms when they discovered the drinking water contamination in Flint, but unfortunately, agency management failed to support staff concerns. Eventually, both the EPA Regional Administrator and the Director of MDEQ resigned under political pressure. If you were in their position when the drinking water contamination came to light, would you have had the courage to support your staff and fight for the people of Flint, even if it ruffled feathers with the heads of other agencies? Is it possible that agency heads who fail in their duties to the public could become liable to injured parties?

# E. Enforcement Policies to Protect Vulnerable Communities

In addition to the statutory authorities discussed above, government agencies may be able to make use of various policies and administrative tools in order to pursue environmental justice though enforcement activity. Some of these policies are long-standing. In 1995, for example, as part of its initial Environmental Justice Strategy, EPA indicated that it would use its enforcement discretion to focus on environmental justice issues raised by violations in communities disproportionately harmed by environmental pollution. Soon after, EPA began to encourage use of specific enforcement authorities to achieve environmental justice. *See, e.g.*, U.S. EPA, Guidance on Use of Section 7003 of RCRA (1997) ("When prioritizing actions to be taken under Section 7003 … the Regions should give particular consideration to sites and facilities that pose environmental justice concerns").

Under the Obama administration, EPA refocused attention to EJ concerns through its "Plan EJ 2014" initiative. Among other things, Plan EJ 2014 established a three-year plan "to fully integrate consideration of environmental justice concerns into the planning and implementation of [enforcement] program strategies, case targeting strategies, and development of remedies in enforcement action to benefit these [over-burdened] communities." EPA Office of Environmental Justice, Plan EJ 2014 at 57 (Sept. 2011). Plan EJ 2014 was superseded by EPA's EJ 2020 Action Agenda, which among other things promised to "direct[] more enforcement resources to the most overburdened communities and strengthen the role of environmental justice in EPA's compliance and enforcement work." EPA, EJ 2020 Action Agenda at 19 (Oct. 2016).

Beyond EPA policies, a number of state policies also encourage pursuing environmental justice through enforcement activity. The Massachusetts Environmental Justice Policy, for example, provides that the state environmental agencies "shall develop targeted [environmental] compliance initiatives for neighborhoods where EJ populations reside and where local environmental and public health conditions warrant increased attention." Massachusetts Environmental Justice Policy of the Executive Office of Energy and Environmental Affairs 12 (2017). Of course, while such policies may sound good to EJ advocates, they remain far from legal mandates, and perhaps even further from the kind of environmental improvements that underserved communities may demand and deserve. As researchers have observed in the particular context of state EJ policies:

> An ineffective agency policy would not be a shocking thing. After all, we can all imagine situations where policies are declared simply to take a stance on an issue or recognize the plight of a particular demographic group without actually addressing the problem. In our research, we have found that policies on environmental justice, generally, are more effective at recognizing the plight of minority and low-income communities in regards to adverse environmental conditions than they are at actually addressing the problem. By creating a policy on environmental justice, a state's policymakers not only publicly recognize the plight of traditionally disempowered groups, but affirmatively take a stance on the side of protecting these communities. The provisions of environmental justice policies are most often incapable of actually addressing the problem at hand, essentially making these policies more symbolic than authentic.

Tonya Lewis & Jessica Owley, *Symbolic Politics for Disempowered Communities: State Environmental Justice Policies*, 29 BYU J. Pub. L. 183, 186 (2014).

So, beyond symbolism, do agency policies on EJ and enforcement offer any real potential for environmental improvements in underserved communities? This concluding section of the chapter will examine two authentic and demonstrated opportunities for pursuing environmental justice goals through enforcement policies: (1) "enforcement targeting," and (2) "supplemental environmental projects."

## 1. Enforcement Targeting

Enforcement targeting involves how an agency should direct its limited enforcement resources, including field inspectors, legal counsel, travel budget, and laboratory support. Flowing from the concept of enforcement discretion, enforcement agencies have substantial flexibility to determine where and what kind of enforcement actions to bring in response to environmental violations. To address concerns for environmental justice, should agencies devote more enforcement resources to industries with higher rates of regulatory violation? Or to communities where there is a higher share of polluting facilities? Or to communities with higher proportions of minority or low-income residents? Or to communities with higher proportions of adverse health impacts?

In order to answer any of these questions, agencies need access to ready and reliable data, including the locations of polluting facilities, the presence of minority populations, and the incidence of adverse health impacts. While all of this data may exist, it may be spread across myriad databases controlled by disparate agencies and organizations. A continual challenge has been the integration of such information to allow enforcement personnel—and concerned community members—to identify good targets for enforcement actions. Toward that end, EPA and other regulatory agencies, including California EPA, have worked to develop a series of tools using Geographic Information System (GIS) technology. Over time, these GIS tools have carried different names, added more GIS layers, and become easier for both government personnel and community members to use. EPA's current GIS tool for this purpose is known as **EJSCREEN** (explored further in Chapter 12: "Information Disclosure and Environmental Review"). The current version of EJSCREEN is now publicly available at https://www.epa.gov/ejscreen.

As described by EPA:

> EJSCREEN is an environmental justice mapping and screening tool that provides EPA with a national consistent dataset and approach for combining environmental and demographic indicators. EJSCREEN users choose a geographic area; the tool then provides demographic and environmental information for that area. All of the EJSCREEN indicators are publicly available data. EJSCREEN simply provides a way to display this information and includes a method for combining environmental and demographic indicators into EJ indexes.

https://www.epa.gov/ejscreen/what-ejscreen.

Environmental indicators incorporated in EJSCREEN include data on local traffic; toxic air pollutants; proximity to hazardous waste facilities and designated Superfund sites; and percent of older housing stock (indicating potential for lead-based paint). Demographic indicators include percent minority, percent low-income, linguistic isolation, population age 65 or older, and people 25 or older without completed high school education.

Drawing on these indicators, through EJSCREEN and similar GIS tools, interested users can type in an address, zip code, or place name, drop a pin or draw a circle on a map, and get an instant report using standard or customized variables. Standard reports in EJSCREEN display an "EJ Index" for each environmental indicator, comparing the data for the selected location to data from the surrounding state, EPA Region, or the United States. For example, an EJ Index indicating 90th percentile for "Superfund Proximity" indicates a selected location has unusually high potential for exposure to contaminants from one or more designated Superfund sites in the area. For complete guidance manuals and training videos on the use of EJSCREEN, please see the EPA EJSCREEN website.

Using these GIS tools, inspectors may be able to identify areas for targeted inspections in order to protect vulnerable communities. Where environmental violations are suspected or identified by any means, enforcement personnel can gather information quickly about potentially impacted communities in order to help the agency decide whether to take enforcement action and what kind of action might be most appropriate to protect the community. Within EPA, information from EJSCREEN may also help convince the U.S. Department of Justice or a local prosecutor's office to accept an enforcement case for civil litigation or criminal prosecution. At the same time, concerned citizens can use the GIS tools to identify vulnerable communities, suggest facilities for inspection and enforcement, and potentially focus their own resources for citizen litigation (discussed in Chapter 13).

## *Notes and Questions*

**1. Return to Richfield.** Consider the scenario suggested earlier in this chapter, where a pile of leaking drums is discovered in a vacant lot in Richfield, Minnesota. Using EJSCREEN, what can you learn now about potential impacts to vulnerable populations in Richfield? What additional information would you like to know about the location of the drums before making any recommendation for enforcement action?

**2. Other targeting tools.** Besides EJSCREEN, what other tools may be available to government agencies or the general public for use in identifying violations and prioritizing areas for enforcement action? Government agencies may have access to law enforcement databases not generally available to the public. But many other enforcement resources are publicly available, including the EPA's Enforcement and Compliance History Online (ECHO) database, available at https://echo.epa.gov/. Through ECHO, members of the public may search the compliance and enforcement history of regulated facilities across the country. Of course, government enforcers also use many of the same online tools available today to anyone with Internet access. How might you use a program such as Google Earth (https://www.google.com/earth/) for identifying potential environmental concerns in your community?

## 2. Supplemental Environmental Projects

As noted previously, penalties collected for environmental violations typically go into the U.S. Treasury or a state's general fund, not to individuals impacted by the violation. As an alternative, EPA and state policies for **supplemental environmental projects** allow violators to reduce penalties in exchange for undertaking environmentally beneficial projects such as pollution-prevention or pollution-reduction projects, or projects to remedy harms to health caused by a violation. Such projects can include establishment of community health centers, monitoring of environmental or health conditions, establishment of alternative water supply systems, reduction of emissions beyond required levels, and so forth.

For more than 20 years, EPA policy has specifically encouraged SEPs in communities where environmental injustice may be an issue. *See* Final Supplemental Environmental Projects Policy Notice, 63 Fed. Reg. 24,796 (May 5, 1998). For communities impacted by environmental violations, SEPs can bring substantial resources toward restorative justice. For comparison of resource levels, under the EJ Small Grants program managed by the EPA Office of Environmental Justice, EPA may award funding of $30,000 for up to five competitive grant proposals a year in each EPA Region. The EJ Small Grants program has proven a tremendous success in leveraging resources and ingenuity for community improvement across the country. (*See* https://www.epa. gov/environmentaljustice/environmental-justice-small-grants-program for information on the EJ Small Grants program.) And yet, far greater resources may be available to communities through SEPs, which may provide direct funding for an unlimited number of projects in each EPA Region, on the scale of hundreds of thousands — or even *millions* — of dollars. There are many inspiring stories of success with SEPs across the country. However, to date, SEPs have not been used as broadly and effectively as they might be to achieve EJ goals in underserved communities. Obstacles to greater use of SEPs include legal requirements, technical challenges, public information deficits, and lack of transparency in the enforcement process. Such obstacles and also opportunities for greater use of SEPs are explored in the following article.

Patrice L. Simms, *Leveraging Supplemental*
*Environmental Projects: Toward an Integrated Strategy for*
*Empowering Environmental Justice Communities*
47 Environmental Law Reporter News & Analysis 10511, 10521–10525 (2017)

* * *

### II. The Unrealized Potential of SEPs

State and federal environmental enforcement authorities initiate thousands of actions each year in the United States. Environmental enforcement, as a result, is one of the most influential activities when it comes to polluter behavior. And the vast majority of these cases end in settlement agreements, which not only assess penalties but also specify injunctive relief (such as the installation of emission control technology), and often direct violators to undertake remedial steps to address the impacts of their noncompliance (by, for example, performing environmental cleanups). Under the right conditions, the potential for local benefits from such environmental enforcement actions is considerable. Whether this happens or not can be influenced by the degree to which affected communities themselves are involved in selecting the violators' remedial obligations.

While in most cases local communities will not be in a position to directly participate in settlement proceedings in a meaningful way—except where local groups are actually *parties* to the enforcement action—SEPs may offer a tool for such groups, by proxy, to play a significant role. In order to empower local communities in this manner, two things will be necessary: (1) the proper policy architecture to provide communities with access to the settlement process, and (2) access to legal and technical expertise to develop locally valuable off-the-shelf SEPs. For this to happen, states, NGOs, academic institutions, and federal enforcement authorities, with meaningful support from the funding community, will need to cooperate to build an effective and sustainable model for engagement.

### A. Understanding SEPs: A Basic Primer

SEPs are enforcement-related tools through which defendants in environmental enforcement cases can mitigate monetary penalties by agreeing to undertake environmentally beneficial projects that they would not otherwise be obligated to perform. As EPA explains in its SEP policy guidance document:

> SEPs are projects or activities that go beyond what could legally be required in order for the defendant to return to compliance, and secure environmental and/or public health benefits in addition to those achieved by compliance with applicable laws. In settlements of environmental enforcement cases, the United States Environmental Protection Agency ... requires alleged violators to achieve and maintain compliance with federal environmental laws and regulations, take action to remedy the harm or risk caused by past violations, and/or to pay a civil penalty. In certain instances, SEPs may be included in the settlement.... The primary purpose of [EPA's] SEP Policy is to encourage and obtain environmental and public health protection and benefits that may not otherwise have occurred in the settlement of an enforcement action.

EPA further explains, "[a] primary incentive for a defendant to propose a SEP is the potential mitigation of its civil penalty." That is, a defendant who voluntarily elects to undertake a qualifying SEP may end up paying a lower enforcement-related monetary penalty.

> Settlements that include a SEP must always include a settlement penalty that [in the aggregate] recoups the economic benefit a violator gained from noncompliance with the law, as well as an appropriate gravity-based penalty reflecting the environmental and regulatory harm caused by the violation(s)....
> [A] violator's commitment to perform a SEP is a relevant factor for the EPA

to consider in establishing an appropriate settlement penalty.

Thus, when a defendant elects to undertake a SEP, EPA may rely on that fact as a mitigating circumstance to impose a lower final monetary penalty.

At least in the federal context, there are significant limitations imposed on the availability of SEPs, which constrain the extent to which federal agencies can rely on them. As EPA explains:

To include a proposed project in a settlement as a SEP, Agency enforcement and compliance personnel should—

1. Ensure that the project conforms to the basic definition of a SEP ...;

2. Ensure that all legal guidelines are satisfied ...;

3. Ensure that the project fits within one (or more) of the designated categories of SEPs ...;

4. Determine the appropriate amount of penalty mitigation to reflect the project's environmental and/or public health benefits using the evaluation criteria ...; and

5. Ensure that the project satisfies all of the EPA procedures, settlement requirements and other criteria.

Additionally, SEPs cannot involve activities that defendant entities would otherwise be legally required to perform. And SEPs must involve projects that have some nexus to the violation that gave rise to the enforcement action. In this regard, "[p]rojects must relate to the underlying violation(s) at issue in the enforcement action." That is, they must be designed to reduce:

a) The likelihood that similar violations will occur in the future;

b) The adverse impact to public health and/or the environment to which the violation at issue contributes; or

c) The overall risk to public health and/or the environment potentially affected by the violation at issue.

* * *

SEPs are available not just in federal enforcement proceedings, however, but are recognized tools in the context of most state enforcement regimes as well. And in the context of such state programs, they are considerably more flexible—as most of the federal legal and policy limitations do not apply to states. Moreover, EPA (and many states) also specifically recognizes SEPs as a mechanism for obtaining environmental justice-related benefits. EPA says, in this regard:

Defendants are encouraged to consider SEPs in communities where there are [environmental justice (EJ)] concerns. SEPs can help ensure that residents who spend significant portions of their time in, or depend on food and water sources located near the areas affected by violations will be protected. However, due to the nonpublic nature of settlement negotiations there are legal constraints on the information the EPA can share during settlement negotiations.... [T]he EPA strongly encourages defendants to reach out to the community for SEP ideas and prefers SEP proposals that have been developed with input from the impacted community. During the public comment period required for many judicial settlements and certain administrative settlements, community members are afforded an opportunity to review and comment on any of the settlement's terms, including any SEPs that may be part of the resolution.... [B]ecause promoting environmental justice through a variety of projects is an overarching goal, EJ is one of the six critical factors on which SEP proposals are evaluated.... SEPs that benefit communities with EJ concerns are actively sought and encouraged....

Despite these seemingly positive protestations, however, SEPs remain the exception and not the rule in environmental enforcement cases. EPA has issued guidance addressing the involvement of communities in environmental enforcement actions; advocates complain that EPA still does not reliably engage communities in the process of formulating SEPs to ensure that they maximize community input and incorporate measures that most closely reflect community priorities.

SEPs mostly derive from administrative enforcement cases as opposed to judicial enforcement. State and federal environmental enforcement actions, in turn, mostly derive from three statutes: the Clean Air Act (CAA), the Clean Water Act (CWA), and the Resource Conservation and Recovery Act (RCRA). According to a study of enforcement over a 12-year period from 2001 to 2012, the CAA had the highest number of enforcement cases overall, followed by the CWA and RCRA. For each type of action, states brought significantly more cases than did the federal government.

Indeed, according to one study, states are generally responsible for between 80% and 90% of all environmental enforcement actions. However, when considering total penalties collected from such cases, despite the lower numbers of cases, the federal enforcement actions resulted in substantially higher aggregate penalties. The highest penalties were under the CWA, followed by RCRA and then the CAA. For example, federal enforcement of the CWA resulted in more than $500 million in penalties over the time period studied, while state enforcement of the CAA netted only about $100 million.

In light of the large number of enforcement cases and high aggregate dollar value, it seems clear that the opportunities for restorative benefits are rich. However, SEPs continue to be underutilized as a mechanism to address the array of environmental challenges that marginalized communities face. The reasons for this, ultimately, are identifiable, and steps could be taken to empower communities to take greater advantage of SEP-related opportunities.

### III. Conceptualizing a More Integrated Approach: SEP Community Empowerment Partnerships

* * *

## A. Clarifying the Impediments to Full Community Participation in SEP Development

The necessary first step to empowering communities to participate more fully in the development and utilization of SEPs is understanding the source of their current disenfranchisement. Here, the underutilization, or ineffective deployment, of SEPs in service of community-driven objectives can be conceptualized as a problem with three relatively distinct components: (1) a process failure (the absence of institutionalized prompts in the enforcement process to reliably ensure that SEPs are consistently explored as an option); (2) an informational failure (a lack of knowledge on the part of communities about SEPs in general, and about the existence of particular enforcement actions that might provide opportunities to realize SEP-related benefits); and (3) a resource failure (a deficiency in technical, science, health, and legal expertise, available to communities, to develop meaningful projects that best reflect community priorities).

As an initial obstacle to effective community involvement in the formulation of SEPs, the environmental enforcement process is not designed to be an inclusive affair. There are serious confidentiality-related concerns that restrain enforcement authorities from disclosing ongoing enforcement activities, and violators are often unwilling to invite the direct participation of community groups for fear of complicating the enforcement proceedings. The issue of confidentiality in civil settlements is certainly not without its critics—indeed some have more generally advocated for broader transparency, and EPA itself acknowledges the importance of sharing SEP development information with affected communities. However, there is continued resistance to what is perceived as "attempts to transform the court into an advocate ... or an information clearinghouse."

In the end, because of limited access to the process, and relatively short settlement time lines once information does become available, it is simply too late to begin the process of considering SEPs, informing the affected community, and locating and deploying resources to develop community-driven project proposals, after enforcement officials have already effectively completed settlement negotiations with the defendant. Therefore, in order to make full and most effective use of SEPs for the benefit of communities, the structural mechanisms to allow for meaningful participation must be fully in place in *anticipation of* (not in reaction to) the emergence of enforcement-related SEP opportunities.

More important perhaps, enforcement officials typically do not build in procedures to ensure that outreach to potentially affected communities occurs in advance of initiating enforcement, even in ways that might protect the identity of the alleged violators. Nor do agencies typically routinize proactive outreach to communities in advance of geographically focused, or industry-specific, enforcement initiatives— where it might be possible to predict with some accuracy which communities are likely to be affected based on region or on the type of industry subject to enforcement efforts (which, in turn, would provide insights into the kinds of SEPs that might be most promising). In these and other ways, the enforcement process itself is not structurally optimized to facilitate consideration of community-driven SEPs, or generally to maximize community involvement.

In addition to these process flaws, there are some very basic informational impediments to effective community participation. Among these is the fact that marginalized communities are often unaware that SEPs are even an available mechanism for obtaining restorative environmental benefits. And even when communities do know about SEPs generally, they are likely to have little access to information about how to engage with enforcement officials, how to find out about enforcement cases, or how to effectively offer input regarding enforcement-related options.

As a result, even when a community might be inclined to participate, it may never find out about enforcement cases, or even if it does, it may not know how to appropriately engage in order to advocate for a SEP, to offer up its own views about what the community needs, or to otherwise meaningfully participate in SEP development. In order to participate, communities must have access to information regarding what SEPs are and how they work. They must also have access to accurate and usable information about the enforcement process, about how to work with enforcement officials, and about what kinds of enforcement actions are underway or anticipated, or at least what types of enforcement actions are reasonably likely to arise in the future (and therefore what kinds of SEPs are likely to be viable).

Finally, even in the absence of the process- and information-related barriers discussed above, communities will often lack the resources to access the science, health, technical, and legal expertise necessary to meaningfully advocate for particular SEP approaches that would best reflect community priorities. SEP development can be a technically burdensome, procedurally complicated, and legally nuanced undertaking, and may be out of the reach of many communities without professional assistance. The process often involves multiple layers of scientific, legal, and economic analyses, and sometime delicate dealings with enforcement agencies and implementing defendants.

Thus, in order to meaningfully contribute to SEP development efforts, in the absence of some kind of supportive infrastructure, communities may need to independently access and manage a substantial suite of resources. An inability to do so thus may stand as an effective obstacle to meaningful engagement. Accordingly, empowering communities in the context of SEP participation will require mustering resources to put to work on their behalf.

* * *

## Notes and Questions

1. **SEP policy.** EPA's SEP policy has evolved and expanded over time. Any party interested in a SEP as part of an EPA enforcement action should be sure to study the latest version of the EPA SEP policy. As of 2020, the latest policy update (2015) appeared online at https://www.epa.gov/sites/production/files/2015-04/documents/sep updatedpolicy15.pdf.

**2. Nexus.** As noted in the article, a SEP cannot be something already required. However, every SEP approved for a settlement with EPA and most states must have sufficient *nexus* to the underlying environmental requirement. In other words, a SEP project must be close—but not *too close*—to the underlying violation. How do you determine that? One factor for determining sufficient nexus is whether the proposed project will reduce "[t]he adverse impact to public health or the environment to which the violation at issue contributes." EPA, Supplemental Environmental Projects Policy, 2015 Update at 7. The EPA SEP policy further offers that nexus will be "easier to establish if the primary impact of the project is at the site where the alleged violation occurred ... or within the immediate geographic area." For this purpose, the policy defines "immediate geographic area" as "generally ... the area within a 50-mile radius of the site on which the violations occurred." *Id.* n.9.

While "nexus" for purposes of the EPA SEP policy may remain somewhat amorphous, it is clear that SEPs must in some way benefit the particular community impacted by the violation. Thus, SEPs may not include simple cash donations to an alma mater or national environmental organization. As such, SEPs may offer unique opportunities for local groups and grassroots organizations to help direct resources towards unmet needs in their communities.

**3. Categories.** In addition to the nexus requirement, the EPA SEP policy generally requires that an approved SEP fall within at least one of seven defined project categories:

1. Public Health
2. Pollution Prevention
3. Pollution Reduction
4. Environmental Restoration and Protection
5. Assessments and Audits
6. Environmental Compliance Promotion
7. Emergency Planning and Preparedness

SEPs in any of these categories may certainly help communities overburdened with pollution.

Under the Public Health category, for example, EPA Region 8 settled a civil penalty in 2001 with W.R. Grace related to asbestos contamination in Libby, Montana. In the settlement, the company agreed to establish a public health clinic in Libby and provide the clinic with "$2,750,000 in funding ... to pay for medical care for asbestos-related illnesses...." *United States v. W.R. Grace & Company*, Consent Decree, Civ. No. 00-167-M-DMW, May 3, 2002.

Under the category of Emergency Planning and Preparedness, EPA Region 10 settled an administrative penalty in 2013 for violations of the Emergency Planning and Community Right-to-Know Act (EPCRA) in Pierce County, Washington. In this settlement, an oil storage company agreed to provide a rural fire district with an upgrade

**Figure 7-1:** Bike trail through South Valley of Albuquerque (Sept. 2018). Photo: Cliff Villa.

to a "hazardous materials ID processor" and other emergency response equipment. U.S. EPA Region 10, In the Matter of: Targa Sound Terminal LLC, Consent Agreement and Final Order, Docket No. EPCRA-10-2013-0061, Sept. 18, 2013.

Under the category of Environmental Restoration and Protection, EPA Region 6 settled an administrative penalty in 2016 for violations of the Clean Water Act at the wastewater treatment plant in Albuquerque, New Mexico. In this settlement, the water utility agreed to spend at least $400,000 to construct a waterline from the treatment plant to the nearby Valle de Oro National Wildlife Refuge. The new waterline would provide reclaimed water for wetlands habitat at the urban refuge and also for landscaping along a new bike trail that will allow the nearby Latino neighborhood to reach the refuge safely within a surrounding industrial corridor. (*See* Figure 7-1.) U.S. EPA Region 6, In the Matter of: Albuquerque Bernalillo County Water Utility Authority, Consent Agreement and Final Order, Docket No. CWA-06-2015-1777, Mar. 17, 2016.

If you were a community advocate or enforcement attorney within EPA Region 5, what potential SEPs might you imagine for violations of the Safe Drinking Water Act in Flint, Michigan, within the seven SEP categories and meeting the EPA nexus requirement?

**4. States, tribes, and citizen suits.** As noted in the article, the EPA SEP policy only applies to enforcement actions brought by EPA. Almost all states have some version of their own SEP policy, most with analogous provisions to the EPA SEP policy, plus minor variations. The SEP policy for Rhode Island, for example, defines eight categories of SEPs, including a unique category for "Outreach and Education." Rhode Island Dept. of Environmental Management, Policy on Supplemental Environmental Projects (July 15, 2004). Michigan's SEP policy requires "adequate nexus," but defines it without reference to EPA's "50-mile radius." Michigan Dept. of Environmental Quality, Supplemental Environmental Projects for Penalty Mitigation (April 15, 2005). New Mexico requires "nexus to the violation," but defines a SEP narrowly as a project that "occurs within the fence line of the violator's facility, or at facilities that are functionally related to the violating facility and under common operational control." New Mexico Environment Dept., Hazardous Waste Bureau, Hazardous Waste Act Civil Penalty Policy, Rev. 1 (March 2017). Notwithstanding this narrow definition of "nexus," New Mexico settled a large penalty against the U.S. Department of Energy (DOE) with an expansive SEP for RCRA violations at the Waste Isolation Pilot Plant (WIPP) near Carlsbad, New Mexico. In this settlement, as part of a SEP, DOE agreed to pay $34 million to the New Mexico Department of Transportation for repairs to New Mexico roads used to ship radioactive waste to WIPP. While perhaps stretching the concept of "nexus" beyond "the fence line of the violator's facility," the SEP did provide significant resources for infrastructure improvements in a poor state. It also demonstrated the flexibility with which states may consider SEPs in settlement of environmental violations.

SEPs may also be used to settle citizen suits under environmental statutes. The EPA SEP policy does not specifically apply to SEPs resolving citizen suits, so some greater flexibility may be found for SEPs in this context. However, citizen suits settled in the form of a consent decree under certain federal statutes may be subject to review by the U.S. Department of Justice. See, e.g., Clean Water Act § 505, 33 U.S.C. § 1365(c)(3) ("No consent judgment shall be entered in an action in which the United States is not a party prior to 45 days following the receipt of a copy of the proposed consent judgment by the Attorney General and the [EPA] Administrator"); Clean Air Act § 304, 42 U.S.C. § 7604(c)(3) (same). The U.S. DOJ can and does file objections with the court to some proposed citizen suits, including on the basis that the SEP does not conform to the EPA SEP policy. See, e.g., Luke Delgadillo Garcia v. Miller Castings, Inc., United States' Statement of Concern and Recommendation that Plaintiff File a Motion to Enter the Proposed Consent Decree, Case No. 2:17-cv-07408-AB-AGR at 29 (C.D. Cal. May 18, 2018) (submitting that proposed consent decree under the Clean Water Act "appears to have no nexus to the violations alleged" as it remains unclear how the proposed "environmental" project "has anything to do with water quality, the environment, the CWA, or the allegations in the complaint"). To avoid potential DOJ objections and judicial delay of entry for a proposed settlement, counsel for citizen plaintiffs may seek to ensure that any proposed settlement including a SEP does comport with the EPA SEP policy.

Notwithstanding these potential constraints, SEPs as part of citizen suit settlements have provided substantial benefits for communities with environmental justice concerns. For one example of a SEP benefiting the largely low-income, African-American community of Anacostia in Washington, D.C., see Chapter 13 ("Citizen Enforcement and Common Law Remedies").

**5. Public involvement in public enforcement.** Law enforcement, including environmental enforcement, is not typically a public process. As the Simms article acknowledges, "There are serious confidentiality-related concerns that restrain enforcement authorities from disclosing ongoing enforcement actions...." Confidentiality may be essential to maintain the integrity of enforcement processes, to include protecting the presumption of innocence, preserving grand jury deliberations, and preventing political interference in prosecutorial decisions. Confidentiality may also pose particular challenges for the environmental justice principle of meaningful involvement for affected communities. How might one who is dedicated equally to both law enforcement and environmental justice balance enforcement confidentiality and meaningful public involvement? What does Mr. Simms recommend for ensuring opportunities for public engagement in the particular context of SEPs?

A first step might be to acknowledge the important role that affected communities may have in identifying potential environmental violations in the first place. Another step might be to recognize the frequent need for community members to serve as witnesses or sources of information to support enforcement investigations and prosecution. If at some point the enforcement process must proceed into a "black box," where enforcement personnel engage in investigations, deliberations, and recommendations outside the public eye, further opportunities for meaningful involvement may reemerge with opportunities for public comment on proposed civil settlements or plea agreements.

Most civil settlements entered in federal court will allow for public comment between the time a proposed consent decree is lodged with the court and the time the court signs and enters the decree. In contrast with civil settlements entered in court, administrative settlements under federal environmental laws may or may not require an opportunity for public comment before the agreement becomes final. Administrative settlements under TSCA, for example, require no opportunity for public comments. On the other hand, proposed administrative settlements under the Clean Water Act and Safe Drinking Water Act do require an opportunity for public comment and even allow members of the public to request a hearing where they may present evidence and cross-examine witnesses. 40 C.F.R. § 22.45. As in all legal questions, interested counsel are advised to read the applicable rules carefully.

Where proposed settlements may be subject to public review and comment, the public obviously has some opportunity for engagement in the enforcement process. However, even where a settlement requires no public comment, some public involvement may still be allowed. For example, as noted in the Simms article, enforcement staff or defendants involved in settlement negotiations may invite community suggestions for supplemental environmental projects to include in a settlement. To find such opportunities for public input, savvy EJ advocates will watch for public notices through conventional channels, but also cultivate relationships with agency staff, industry counsel, nonprofit leaders, elected officials, media members, and other information networks.

# Chapter 8

# Environmental Justice and Contaminated Sites

## A. Introduction

So far in this book, we have focused on measures to protect people from the effects of future exposures to pollution—identifying risks and setting standards to ensure the health of all people, including poor people and people of color. But what if their health is not protected now, perhaps due to sites in their communities contaminated with toxins such as arsenic and lead? To begin our inquiry on this question, consider the following case.

As of April 1, 2017, more than 270 families had left the West Calumet Housing Complex, in East Chicago, Indiana, with 50 or so families to follow soon. Evacuation from the apartment complex began the previous summer, after soil testing found yards with lead contamination nearly 70 times above the federal standard of 400 parts per million. *See* U.S. EPA, Record of Decision, U.S. Smelter and Lead Refinery Superfund Site, Operable Unit 1 (Nov. 2012). The apartment complex sat next to a sprawling industrial facility, the U.S. Smelter and Lead Refinery, which among other things recovered lead from scrap metal and automotive batteries until it shut down in 1985. *Id.* After government officials recognized the health threat to community members and decided to respond, the massive evacuation experienced many delays caused by challenges such as limited rental options in the area, landlords rejecting government housing vouchers, and residents hesitant to leave the only home they had ever known. According to one report, lifelong East Chicago resident Tara Adams said she had been packed and seeking a new home for herself, her son, and her daughter for many months. However, the temporary housing offered by the government was about 25 miles away in what she worried was a dangerous neighborhood across the state line on Chicago's South Side. "I for sure don't want to move my 19-year-old son into an area where there's a greater chance for him to get shot," Adams said. Tom Davies, *About 50 Families Remain at Lead-Tainted East Chicago Housing Complex, Despite Target to Move,* Chicago Tribune, Apr. 1, 2017.

The West Calumet Housing Complex, now completely vacated and demolished, is part of the USS Lead Superfund Site in East Chicago, Indiana. The site consists of both the former USS Lead facility plus adjoining residential neighborhoods impacted by the lead contamination. The racial makeup of the adjoining neighborhoods is

**Figure 8-1:** EPA contractors sampling and removing contaminated soils and cleaning floors at the residential area of the USS Lead Superfund Site, East Chicago, Indiana. Photos: U.S. EPA.

91% minority, primarily African Americans (53%), followed by Latinos (35%). While the USS Lead Site is unusual in some respects—including the degree of lead contamination within an overwhelmingly diverse community—it is also typical in that disproportionate impacts of the contaminated site fall upon racial minorities and low-income people. According to data published by the U.S. EPA in 2017, minorities comprised almost half (49.3%) of the population within one mile of a Superfund site, despite comprising closer to a third (38.4%) of the U.S. population. U.S. EPA Office of Land and Emergency Management, POPULATION SURROUNDING 1,836 SUPERFUND REMEDIAL SITES (2017). Within the same mile from any Superfund site, compared to their general populations within the United States, the Latino population is approximately 45 percent higher, the Asian population is approximately 63 percent higher, and linguistically isolated households are approximately 62 percent higher.

Designated Superfund sites and tens of thousands of other contaminated properties across the country clearly pose serious challenges for environmental justice. Part B of this chapter will explore some of the legal authorities for addressing contaminated sites in the United States. Part C will then investigate the opportunities available for environmental justice (EJ) advocates to ensure that cleanup processes provide fair treatment and meaningful involvement for all affected communities. Part D will conclude the chapter by considering a case study from Seattle, Washington, where community members engaged in innovative efforts to address a major Superfund site in their own backyard.

# B. Legal Authorities for Cleaning Up Contaminated Sites

For most lawyers and academics, the first (and perhaps only) legal authority they will associate with the cleanup of contaminated sites is the Comprehensive Environmental Response, Compensation and Liability Act (CERCLA). Known commonly as "Superfund," CERCLA is the primary federal statute governing the remediation of spills or releases of hazardous substances in the United States. CERCLA is not, however, the only federal statute that may address spills and releases of hazardous materials in the United States. Different kinds of contamination may require the application of different statutes, including the Resource Conservation and Recovery Act (RCRA) for "hazardous waste" and "solid waste." Different statutes, in turn, may provide different legal authorities and opportunities for community engagement. We will begin by considering the different triggers for each statute, followed by a review of the various sources of funding for cleanup, and the processes under CERCLA for selecting cleanup actions.

## 1. Jurisdictional Triggers for Cleanup Statutes

**CERCLA § 104 (42 U.S.C. § 9604):** (a)(1) Whenever (A) any hazardous substance is released or there is a substantial threat of such a release into the environment, or (B) there is a release or substantial threat of release into the environment of any pollutant or contaminant which may present an imminent and substantial danger to the public health or welfare, the [EPA] is authorized to act, consistent with the national contingency plan, to remove or arrange for the removal of, and provide for remedial action relating to such hazardous substance, pollutant, or contaminant at any time....

**CERCLA § 101 (42 U.S.C. § 9601):** (14) The term "hazardous substance" means [any "hazardous waste" under RCRA, any "hazardous air pollutant" under the Clean Air Act, any "toxic pollutant" under the Clean Water Act, and any substance designated as a CERCLA "hazardous substance" by the National Contingency Plan.] The term does not include petroleum, including crude oil or any fraction thereof....

(33) The term "pollutant or contaminant" shall include, but not be limited to, any element, substance, compound, or mixture, including disease-causing agents, which after release into the environment and upon exposure, ingestion, inhalation, or assimilation into any organism ... will or may reasonably be anticipated to cause death [or] disease, ... except that the term shall not include petroleum, including crude oil or any fraction thereof....

**RCRA § 3008(h) (42 U.S.C. § 6929(h)):** Whenever on the basis of any information the [EPA] determines that there is or has been a release of hazardous waste into the environment from a facility authorized to operate [under interim status before obtaining a final permit for a treatment, storage, or disposal facility], the [EPA] may issue an order requiring corrective action ... or the [EPA] may commence a civil action in the United States district court ... for appropriate relief, including a temporary or permanent injunction.

RCRA § 7002 (42 U.S.C. § 6972): (a) ... [A]ny person may commence a civil action on his own behalf ... (B) against any person, including the United States, and any other governmental instrumentality or agency, ... and including any past or present generator, ... who has contributed or is contributing to the past or present handing, storage, treatment, transportation, or disposal of any solid or hazardous waste which may present an imminent and substantial endangerment to health or the environment....

RCRA § 1004 (42 U.S.C. § 6903): (27) The term "solid waste" means any garbage, refuse, ... or other discarded material, including solid, liquid, semisolid, or contained gaseous material resulting from industrial, commercial, mining, and agricultural operations, ... but does not include solid or dissolved material in domestic sewage, or solid or dissolved materials in irrigation return flows or industrial discharges which are point sources subject to permits under [the Clean Water Act].

Clean Water Act § 311 (33 U.S.C. § 1321) (as amended by the Oil Pollution Act of 1990):

(b)(3) The discharge of oil ... (i) into or upon the navigable waters of the United States [or] adjoining shorelines ... in such quantities as may be harmful ... is prohibited....

(c)(A) The President shall, in accordance with the National Contingency Plan and any appropriate Area Contingency Plan, ensure effective and immediate removal of a discharge ... of oil ... (i) into or on the navigable waters; [or] (ii) on the adjoining shorelines to the navigable waters....

## Notes and Questions

1. **Test your understanding.** Given the jurisdictional triggers above, which cleanup statute would appear most appropriate in the following circumstances:

- Two 55-gallon drums containing human waste appear one morning along a county road through the Winnebago Indian Reservation in Nebraska.

- Five million gallons of jet fuel are discovered to have leaked over a twenty-year period from storage tanks on an Air Force base in Ohio, creating a plume of contaminated groundwater beneath a largely African-American neighborhood.

- A fishing vessel sinks off the Georgia coast, discharging an estimated 2,200 gallons of diesel fuel and contaminating the shoreline of a Gullah community on a nearby island.

- Residents of a poor, rural county in Texas near the border with Mexico supplement their income by picking through an illegal dumpsite in order to salvage metals including cadmium, copper, nickel, and zinc.

- A newly constructed pipeline transporting crude oil from North Dakota to Illinois develops a leak and spills more than 100,000 gallons of oil on an Iowa cornfield.

In the scenarios above, do you find that the jurisdictional elements would be triggered for at least one of the statutes we have considered so far? Do you find that more than one statute may apply in these cases? If so, how would you determine which statute would best support the interests of the local community? In part, the answer may lie in a deeper understanding of each statute, an objective beyond the scope of this book but addressed in other available resources. See, e.g., Joel A. Mintz, et al.,

A PRACTICAL INTRODUCTION TO ENVIRONMENTAL LAW (2017). However, another part of the answer may depend on the unique needs and interests of the local community, a fundamental consideration for environmental justice. For example, even if the Georgia spill impacts fishery resources, could the Gullah community still reject a major federal cleanup operation in favor of protecting the community's privacy on the island?

2. **RCRA vs. CERCLA.** One common question for cleaning up contaminated lands is whether to apply RCRA or CERCLA authorities. As noted above, a RCRA "hazardous waste" is also by definition a CERCLA "hazardous substance." However, a RCRA "solid waste" may extend jurisdiction to materials beyond CERCLA jurisdiction, such as piles of used tires (a hazard due to flammability as well as breeding grounds for mosquitoes in wet climates). On the other hand, CERCLA jurisdiction may reach categories of contamination that RCRA cannot, such as radioactive materials (included on CERCLA's list of hazardous substances at 40 C.F.R. Table 302.4, App. B) and mining wastes (excluded from RCRA regulation by the RCRA Bevill Amendment, 42 U.S.C. § 6921(b)(3)(A)(ii)).

For an active facility with financially capable owners or operators, a facility may undergo cleanup through the RCRA **corrective action** process. In some cases, RCRA corrective action may be the only cleanup authority available, as for sites contaminated only with petroleum products, which would be subject to the CERCLA **petroleum exclusion** noted above. In other cases, a facility may proceed with cleanup under the RCRA corrective action process because of a history of RCRA regulation at the site.

At the USS Lead Superfund Site discussed above, an adjacent industrial property known as the DuPont East Chicago facility was historically one of the largest chemical manufacturing operations in the United States. After operations ceased in the early 2000s, substantial contamination was left behind. Instead of proceeding through CERCLA cleanup like the neighboring properties, the DuPont East Chicago cleanup is proceeding through RCRA corrective action, in part due to the history of RCRA permitting for this facility. The use of different cleanup authorities for contaminated sites in such close proximity naturally led to questions from the East Chicago community about differences in both process and protection. According to the EPA, cleanup under both RCRA and CERCLA should result in protection of human health and the environment. But important differences remain. For example, while CERCLA may have few specific legal requirements for public participation, as will be discussed in Part C, public participation under RCRA corrective action relies almost entirely on discretionary guidance.

3. **National Contingency Plan.** Note the references to the "National Contingency Plan" in both CERCLA and the Clean Water Act. Does that sound like a—plan? In fact, the National Contingency Plan (NCP) is a set of regulations guiding the cleanup of both oil and hazardous substances in the United States. More formally, it is the National Oil and Hazardous Substances Pollution Contingency Plan, 40 C.F.R. Part 300. In a twist upon the usual sequence of a statute followed by implementing regulations, the NCP actually predated both CERCLA and the modern Clean Water Act, but was embraced by Congress when it passed both statutes. Today, the NCP continues

to provide the applicable rules for the cleanup of oil and hazardous substances in the United States and should be consulted regularly when engaged in related activities.

## 2. Funding for Cleanup

Each of the federal statutes noted above establishes a scheme of strict liability for pollution; that is, liability in general does not depend on any proof of intent to cause a spill or release. Rather, liability may be established simply by a party's act causing a spill or even by a party's status within certain categories, such as the past or present owner or operator of a facility from which a release occurred. *See* CERCLA § 107(a), 42 U.S.C. § 9604(a) (establishing four categories of liable parties under CERCLA). This is known in CERCLA as the **"polluter pays principle"** and it has proven a powerful instrument for achieving cleanup actions since CERCLA was passed in 1980. According to one study of data from the 1990s, some three-quarters of remedial actions at designated Superfund sites were in fact conducted or funded by responsible parties. Katherine N. Probst & David M. Konisky, et al., SUPERFUND'S FUTURE: WHAT WILL IT COST? at 43 (2001).

Most of this remedial work is performed by **"potentially responsible parties"** (PRPs) under agreements with the EPA, without the need for litigation. *See* CERCLA § 122, (d), 42 U.S.C. § 9622(d). Cleanups may also be conducted under unilateral administrative order from an authorized agency. CERCLA § 106(a), 42 U.S.C. § 9606(a). For example, much of the ongoing cleanup at the USS Lead Superfund Site in East Chicago is being funded or performed by PRPs including DuPont and the Atlantic Richfield Company under a consent decree with EPA entered in 2014 and a unilateral administrative order issued in 2019.

In some cases, EJ advocates may question whether a party responsible for polluting a site may be trusted with cleaning it up. In such cases, it is important to note that cleanup agreements must be subject to agency oversight, with penalties available for violations of an agreement. CERCLA § 122(k), 42 U.S.C. § 9622(k). Cleanup agreements and orders may also be subject to direct citizen enforcement. CERCLA § 310, 42 U.S.C. § 9659. *See, e.g., Pakootas v. Teck Cominco Metals, Inc. (Pakootas I),* 452 F.3d 1066 (9th Cir. 2006) (Colville Indian Tribe enforcing EPA CERCLA order against Canadian mining company).

For a contaminated site where a liable party does not exist, as with an abandoned property, or where liable parties are unable to pay for cleanup, as with bankrupt companies, or where liable parties simply refuse to pay, one great advantage of CERCLA over RCRA is access to the **Hazardous Substance Superfund**. CERCLA § 111, 42 U.S.C. § 9611. Originally financed by a tax on certain petroleum and chemical industries, the "Superfund" has been sustained since 1995 by congressional appropriations and recovery of costs from responsible parties. In the case of a liable party who is able but refuses to pay for cleanup, the EPA may pay for cleanup actions from the Superfund, and then seek to recover its cleanup costs through subsequent legal action. CERCLA § 107(a), 42 U.S.C. § 9607(a). States, tribes, and other parties may also seek to recover cleanup costs from responsible parties, *id.*, but they do not have access to the Superfund to pay for cleanup actions up front. For a thorough review of CERCLA liability and cost recovery authorities, *see* MINTZ, *supra*, at Chap. 9.

Under CERCLA, there are two broad categories of cleanup (or "response") actions: (1) **removal actions**; and (2) **remedial actions**. Removal actions are generally discrete, short-term responses for relatively smaller problems. *See* CERCLA § 101(23), 42 U.S.C. § 9601(23) (defining "removal"). A removal action might include, for example, a two-day operation to pick up a dozen drums of waste discovered in a field. Remedial actions, by contrast, are typically long-term responses for larger problems. *See* CER-CLA § 101(24), 42 U.S.C. § 9601(24) (defining "remedial action"). A remedial action might include, for example, excavating a million tons of contaminated soil or pumping and treating contaminated groundwater over a period of years. Funding from the Superfund for removal actions is generally capped at $2 million. CERCLA § 104(c), 42 U.S.C. § 9604(c)(1). Exceptions to this cap may be made for removal actions "immediately required to prevent, limit, or mitigate an emergency. . . ." *Id.* For remedial actions, the CERCLA statute places no limitations on Superfund expenditures, where the site has been included on the **National Priorities List** (NPL). Such designated "Superfund sites" may potentially receive hundreds of millions of dollars from the Superfund trust fund for major cleanups, limited only by the availability of funds in any year and competition from other Superfund sites in need of funding.

Beyond CERCLA removals and remedial actions, a third category of funding for contaminated site investigation and cleanup is through the EPA **brownfields** program, along with many state and local analogues. CERCLA defines the term "brownfield site" to mean "real property, the expansion, redevelopment, or reuse of which may be complicated by the presence or potential presence of a hazardous substance, pollutant, or contaminant." 42 U.S.C. § 9601(39)(A) (2002). The EPA estimates there are at least 450,000 brownfield sites across the United States, to include former gas stations, drycleaners, and industrial facilities abandoned in inner cities. The issues involved in brownfields redevelopment are complicated, to say the least. For one early consideration of challenges for brownfields redevelopment, see the following:

> Although the costs of continued inactivity at brownfield sites are potentially immense, they are not well quantified. The types of costs, however, are well understood. Inner-city neighborhoods fail to benefit from jobs that redevelopment might provide. Cities receive lower property tax revenues from brownfield sites, which weakens their ability to provide basic services such as education. Brownfields are unsightly and threaten to contaminate drinking water and cause neighborhood health problems. Vacant properties contribute to high crime rates and deterioration of urban neighborhoods. They encourage further environmental abuse, such as "midnight dumping." Finally, brownfields are conspicuous symbols of the decline of lower-income and minority neighborhoods in which they are overwhelmingly located. They discourage urban investment and contribute to a pervasive sense of poverty and hopelessness. . . .

[B]rownfield redevelopment can take advantage of existing urban infra-
structures. A brownfield site often features excellent water and sewer systems,
and rail and highway access to the metropolitan area, the region, and outlying
areas. Densely concentrated urban areas offer better accessibility to workers
and other advantages. Other potential benefits include aesthetic qualities
such as waterfront access and views, proximity to downtown business districts,
public tax and financing initiatives to support development, access to major
universities and medical centers, and ancillary benefits of spending by reju-
venated industries and their workers on local goods and services....

Despite these potential advantages, brownfields remain abandoned or underutilized. In the eyes of many, this is due to widespread fears of brownfield
developers ... that the cost of cleaning brownfield sites to meet government
standards is both so uncertain and so high that it might outweigh the sites'
market value.... A developer must also be concerned about the uncertainties
caused by state hazardous waste cleanup programs, because it cannot predict
at the outset whether it will be subjected to state or federal regulation. The
states have primary responsibility for sites that do not rise to the threshold
for federal action and for sites that states have decided to regulate in the absence of federal requirements....

Joel B. Eisen, *Brownfields of Dreams?: Challenges and Limits of Voluntary Cleanup Programs and Incentives*, 1996 U. ILLINOIS L. REV. 883, 894–900 (1996).

In part to address developer concerns for liability at brownfield sites, Congress
amended CERCLA in 2002. As indicated below, the Brownfields Revitalization Act
also established important programs for financial assistance with brownfields redevelopment.

## Josephine M. Balzac, *Public Engagement*
## *"Reach In, Reach Out": Pursuing Environmental Justice by Empowering Communities to Meaningfully Participate in the Decision-Making Processes of Brownfields Redevelopment and Superfund Cleanup*

9 FLORIDA A & M. U. L. REV. 347, 356–367 (2014)

On January 11, 2002, President Bush signed the Small Business Liability Relief
and Brownfields Revitalization Act ('the [Brownfields Revitalization Act]'). The
[Brownfields Revitalization Act] amended CERCLA (or Superfund) in several ways,
one of which was by providing funds to assess and clean up brownfields. The Superfund provides funding for brownfields projects. This new law created a "bona fide
prospective purchaser" (BFPP) exemption for those whose potential liability under
CERCLA derived only from the fact that it owns or operates a property or facility.
The BFPP shall not be liable if the "BFPP does not impede the performance of a response action." This exemption was Congress' response to the hesitancy in redeveloping
brownfields due to the potential liabilities surrounding cleanup....

Brownfields grants support revitalization efforts by funding environmental assessment, cleanup, and job training activities. Brownfields redevelopment, if done properly with community participation, can provide a number of improvements to the surrounding community, such as to "improve public health by adding accessible and affordable grocery stores, recreational or green space, community gardens, healthcare facilities, pharmacies and other important amenities important to meet community needs as part of healthier redevelopment and reuse as well as job opportunities for community residents."

The Brownfields assessment grant provides funding for a grant recipient to "inventory, characterize, assess and conduct planning for cleanup and redevelopment and community involvement (outreach)." The grant specifically provides for community involvement, which suggests EPA's intent for the community to participate in assisting with the assessment of brownfields. This allows grant recipients to allocate funds to disseminate information, conduct community outreach, and hold public meetings and workshops. Grantees can receive up to $400,000 to assess hazardous substances and petroleum products over a three-year period....

The Brownfields Program also provides for job training grants to nonprofits and other organizations to "recruit, train, and place predominantly low-income and minority, unemployed and under-employed people living in areas affected by solid and hazardous waste." The goal is to give residents the opportunity to work in green jobs, which reduce environmental contamination and build more sustainable futures for communities.

There are many resources available for community involvement within the brownfields and Superfund programs.... The issue is, however, that communities usually are unaware of the available resources. Agencies and municipalities need to do better jobs at community outreach in order to get the information across. Outreach efforts should include not only notice in the newspaper, but door-to-door, various forms of media (specialty newspaper, radio broadcasts, local news), emails, mail outs, workshops, and public meetings. The content of the information is very important, remembering the audience is the key to success. Additionally, the information on sites needs to be easily accessible, such as by creating a repository, uploading the information online, and quickly providing it upon request....

* * *

The EPA brownfields program remains a resource for addressing contaminated sites across the country. In addition to direct grants for brownfield assessment and cleanup, the EPA's **revolving loan fund** (RLF) program enables many local governments and development authorities to provide low-interest loans for brownfields cleanup and redevelopment. Through this process, the EPA reports that 694 cleanups have been completed as of June 2019, attracting 42,000 jobs and $8 billion in public and private funding. For fiscal year 2019, cities including Atlanta, Kansas City, and Texarkana each received $400,000 in supplemental funding for their RLF programs, along with development authorities including the South Central Planning and Development Commission of Louisiana, the Maine Department of Economic and Community Development, and Salt Lake County Economic Development. U.S. EPA, EPA Announces Nearly $2 Million in Supplemental Funds to Clean Up and Reuse Brownfields Sites, June 21, 2019.

Unlike CERCLA removals and remedial actions, most brownfield cleanups are guided not by federal law, but by state cleanup statutes. Most states have enacted provisions specifically directed at brownfield sites. Many states encourage cleanup of sites through voluntary cleanup programs. Voluntary cleanup programs are a popular means for achieving relatively quick and uncomplicated site cleanups. However, a lack of agency oversight and enforceable cleanup standards may leave some communities uncertain whether cleanup measures will genuinely protect their health. For a review of one local brownfields program, noting both successes and continuing challenges, *see* Jessica Higgins, *Evaluating the Chicago Brownfields Initiative: The Effects of City-Initiated Brownfield Redevelopment on Surrounding Communities*, 3 North-western J. L. & Social Pol'y 240 (2008).

For cleanup of **oil spills**, the Oil Pollution Act of 1990 (OPA), passed in the wake of the *Exxon Valdez* spill in 1989, created a liability and funding program modeled upon CERCLA. OPA added authorities to Clean Water Act § 311 authorizing the EPA (for inland waters) and the U.S. Coast Guard (for marine waters) to issue orders for cleanup of oil spills. *See* 33 U.S.C. 1321(c)(1). Analogous to CERCLA's Superfund, OPA also created an Oil Spill Liability Trust Fund, to be used by the EPA or the Coast Guard where responsible parties are unable or unwilling to perform cleanup actions themselves. OPA § 1012, 33 U.S.C. § 2712. With lessons from the impacts to fisher families and Native Alaskans after the *Exxon Valdez*, OPA also greatly expanded upon the scope of liability for damages from oil spills, to include possible claims for lost profits, lost subsistence uses, and injuries to private or public property. OPA § 1002(b)(2), 33 U.S.C. § 2702(b)(2). This expanded scope of liability became particularly crucial after the BP Deepwater Horizon oil spill in 2010, allowing injured communities including Vietnamese American fisher folks a means to pursue restorative and compensatory justice from BP. For more on the impacts of the BP spill to this community, *see* Chapter 15 ("Disaster Justice").

## 3. NPL Listing

EPA defines the National Priorities List (NPL) as a "list of sites of national priority among the known releases or threatened release of hazardous substances, pollutants, or contaminants throughout the United States, and its territories." Most sites go on the NPL through use of the Hazard Ranking System (HRS). Through HRS, the EPA generates a numerical score for an individual site based upon factors such as releases of contamination to soil, groundwater, and surface water, the size of the population at risk, the potential for contaminating water supplies, the potential for public contact, and the possibility that damage to natural resources might affect the human food chain. *See* CERCLA § 105(c), 42 U.S.C. § 9605(c). Sites that score above 28.5 generally qualify for NPL listing, although the final decision by the EPA whether to list any particular site often follows a protracted, political process, including seeking concurrence on the listing decision from the governor of the affected state.

Once a site goes on the NPL, it generally proceeds through phases of site investigation, remedial action, and then monitoring to ensure that objectives for soil, groundwater, surface water, or other targets have been met. Sites can go on the NPL when they require cleanup, and then come off the NPL when all remedial actions have been completed — a process known as **deletion**. As of early 2020, there were 1,335 sites on the NPL, 424 sites deleted from the NPL, and 51 new sites proposed for the NPL. Due to the challenges posed by extensive contamination, some sites may remain on the NPL for a long time. Many sites currently on the NPL today were part of the first listing of NPL sites in 1983. These include the Bunker Hill Mining and Metallurgical Complex in the Coeur d'Alene Basin of northern Idaho. Importantly, even though a site may remain on the NPL, when units of a site have had all physical actions completed and only a period of monitoring remains, the site may be designated as **"construction complete."** In fiscal year 2018, ten NPL sites reached construction complete. U.S. EPA, SUPERFUND: TRANSFORMING COMMUNITIES, ACCOMPLISHMENTS REPORT, FY 2018. By early 2020, 1,212 NPL sites had reached "construction complete" status over the life of the Superfund program. Before reaching either NPL deletion or construction complete, individual units within an NPL site may be completed and reach a status of **"ready for reuse."** At the Bunker Hill site, for example, while decades more cleanup may remain in rural areas through the river basin, many developed areas have already been fully remediated, including the base of the Silver Mountain Ski Area in Kellogg, Idaho. *See* Figure 8-2.

**Figure 8-2:** Silver Mountain Ski Area within Bunker Hill Mining and Metallurgical Site. Kellogg, Idaho, June 2019. Photo: Cliff Villa.

## 4. Removal Actions

While designated "Superfund sites" such as USS Lead in East Chicago and Bunker Hill in northern Idaho often garner the most attention from the mass media, academic literature, and the legal community, far more contaminated sites are addressed each year without resort to NPL listing. In fiscal year 2018, compared to the ten NPL sites that reached construction complete, there were 242 removal actions completed across the United States and its territories under the EPA's CERCLA authority.

Removal actions are usually conducted by the EPA through a corps of credentialed officers known as **on-scene coordinators** (OSC). Based in EPA regional and field offices across the country, OSCs have the training, authority, and resources to respond to spills, abandoned drums, and other discoveries of contaminated sites, potentially deploying on a moment's notice. *See* 40 C.F.R. § 300.120 (noting that OSCs "shall be predesignated by the regional or district head of the lead agency"). Beyond the EPA, OSCs may be designated by the U.S. Coast Guard and other federal agencies within the scope of their respective jurisdictions. State and tribal governments may also designate OSCs through state or tribal law.

EPA OSCs must, of course, operate within the limitations established by Congress. As noted above, the EPA generally has authority under CERCLA to spend up to $2 million from the Superfund trust fund for sites not included on the NPL. CERCLA also establishes a presumption that all removal actions will be completed within 12 months or fewer. CERCLA § 104(c)(1), 42 U.S.C. § 9604(c)(1) ("obligations from the Fund ... shall not continue after ... 12 months has elapsed from the date of initial response"). For emergency situations and other extraordinary circumstances, as noted above, removal actions may continue beyond 12 months and in some cases for many years. *See, e.g., United States v. W.R. Grace & Co.*, 429 F.3d 1224 (9th Cir. 2005) (approving EPA removal expenditures of more than $50 million over three years where evidence indicated devastating health impacts from asbestos contamination in Libby, Montana).

Removal actions at extraordinary sites such as Libby, Montana, may involve massive excavation of contaminated soils. At other sites, removal actions may require only a few hours to retrieve and safely discard a pile of abandoned drums. In cases of more significant contamination, where long-term remediation may eventually be required, removal actions may include the provision of bottled water or the **temporary relocation** of residences or businesses. For more on temporary relocation, *see infra* at pp. 286–287 (note on Relocation).

# 5. Remedial Actions

Where a contaminated site appears to require more attention than may be addressed through removal authorities, the EPA may embark on the CERCLA remedial process. Under CERCLA, the remedial process generally includes the following major elements:

- **Remedial Investigation (RI):** a study of the nature and the extent of contamination at a site, along with assessment of attendant risks to human health and the environment. An RI may include soil sampling, air monitoring, and groundwater monitoring; collection of blood samples and fish tissues; quantitative assessment of risks to ecological receptors such as fish, birds, and mammals; and quantitative assessment of health risks to children, pregnant women, subsistence fishers, and other vulnerable human populations.

- **Feasibility Study (FS):** an evaluation of alternatives to address unacceptable risks to human health and the environment identified in the RI. The FS may consider treatment options such as incineration or solidification; engineering controls such as constructed landfills and water filtration systems; and institutional controls such as deed restrictions to prevent certain future land uses.

- **Proposed Plan:** an agency proposal for addressing contamination at a remedial site, drawing upon the conclusions of an RI/FS, identifying a preferred alternative, and submitted for public review and comment.

- **Record of Decision (ROD):** a document identifying the selected remedy for a site, including supporting analysis and a response to comments on the proposed plan.

- **Remedial Design (RD):** a collection of engineering plans, architectural drawings, and other specifications necessary to construct the remedy selected in the ROD.

- **Remedial Action (RA):** actual implementation of a selected remedy, which may include excavation of contaminated soil; dredging of contaminated sediments; treatment of contaminated water; temporary or permanent relocation of residents or businesses; establishment of deed restrictions or other institutional controls; and monitoring for a period of years to ensure a remedy is operating properly and successfully.

The remedial investigation and feasibility study are usually conducted simultaneously, with each process helping to inform the other. Hence, they are routinely referred to collectively as the "**RI/FS.**" An RI/FS may be conducted by the EPA or by potentially responsible parties (PRPs) under agreement with the EPA. *See* CERCLA § 104(a), 42 U.S.C. § 9604(a)(1) (EPA may allow a PRP to conduct an RI/FS "when such action will be done properly and promptly" by such party). Whether by the EPA or PRPs, an RI/FS will be overseen by an EPA **remedial project manager** (RPM). 40 C.F.R. § 300.120(f). The RPM must ensure the RI/FS is conducted according to criteria established by the CERCLA statute plus implementing rules in the NCP. CERCLA § 121, 42 U.S.C. § 9621; NCP at 40 C.F.R. § 300.430.

Under the statute, CERCLA establishes an overall command that remedial actions "shall attain a degree of cleanup of hazardous substances ... which assures protection of human health and the environment...." 42 U.S.C. § 9621(d)(1) ("Degree of cleanup"). A second command is that any remedial action must ordinarily comply with any applicable or relevant standard set by other federal or state environmental laws. *Id.* § 9621(d)(2). Such **applicable or relevant and appropriate requirements** (ARARs) commonly include standards for water quality under the Clean Water Act, standards for drinking water under the Safe Drinking Water Act, and standards for treatment and disposal of hazardous waste under RCRA. A third statutory direction is bias towards a remedy that "permanently and significantly reduces the volume, toxicity or mobility of the hazardous substances" at a site—that is, a preference for treatment of contaminated materials instead of merely moving and disposing of contaminated materials elsewhere.

The NCP expands upon these statutory commands by establishing **nine criteria** for remedy selection: overall protection of human health and the environment; compliance with ARARs; long-term effectiveness and permanence; reduction of toxicity, mobility, or volume through treatment; short-term effectiveness; implementability; cost; state government acceptance; and community acceptance. 40 C.F.R. § 300.430(e)(9)(iii). According to EPA, the first two of these (protection of health human and environment and compliance with ARARs) operate as "threshold" criteria: only those alternatives that satisfy these criteria will be among those considered. The next five serve as "primary balancing" criteria, providing the technical bases for choosing among the alternatives remaining on the table. Finally, the last two (state and community acceptance) serve as "modifying" criteria, suggesting ways in which aspects of the preferred alternative might be modified. U.S. Envtl. Prot. Agency, THE FEASIBILITY STUDY: DETAILED ANALYSIS OF REMEDIATION ALTERNATIVES at 2 (1990).

With all the criteria that must be considered, supported by all the data that often must be collected, an RI/FS is often a major undertaking. For so-called "mega-sites," where total cleanup exceeds $50 million, the average time to complete an RI/FS may be five years. Katherine N. Probst & David M. Konisky, SUPERFUND'S FUTURE: WHAT WILL IT COST? at 52 (2001). For some big sites, an RI/FS may take considerably longer. For example, the RI/FS culminating in the 2001 ROD to address contaminated sediments in 40 miles of the Hudson River took 12 years to complete. About the same length of time was required to complete the 2014 ROD for Seattle's Lower Duwamish Waterway, discussed in the concluding section of this chapter.

Many large Superfund sites are administratively divided into **operable units** (OUs) to facilitate more efficient investigation and cleanup. According to the NCP, "Sites should generally be remediated in operable units ... when phased analysis and response is necessary or appropriate given the size or complexity of the site...." 40 C.F.R. § 300.430(a)(1)(ii)(A). The USS Lead Site in East Chicago, for example, is divided into two OUs: OU-1 for the residential areas of the site and OU-2 for the former lead facility. Each OU may be subject to its own RI/FS, leading to the potential for multiple RODs at a single large site.

Despite the enormous effort that may go into completing an RI/FS and ROD for a site, a need for changes may always arise based upon new site information or other factors. If the changes are relatively minor, they may be documented through an **explanation of significant differences** (ESD). CERCLA § 117(c), 42 U.S.C. § 9617(c). If, on the other hand, the proposed changes will "fundamentally alter the basic features of the selected remedy," then the ROD must be amended, triggering essentially the same process required for developing a ROD. 40 C.F.R. § 300.435(c)(2).

The need for an ESD or ROD amendment may be triggered by the findings of a **five-year review**. CERCLA requires these reviews no less often than every five years for any site where contamination remains at the site. CERCLA § 121(c), 42 U.S.C. § 9621(c). Five-year reviews are intended "to assure that human health and the environment are being protected by the remedial action being implemented." *Id.* Where such protection cannot be assured, then the EPA may find that additional actions are appropriate, and the EPA "shall take or require such action." *Id.* Where investigations find that no further response actions are required at a site to meet the cleanup objectives, the RPM may document that finding through an RA report. The RA report, in turn, may be used to support subsequent determinations of **construction complete** and **deletion** (or partial deletion) of the site from the NPL.

## Notes and Questions

1. **How clean is clean?** Perhaps the most vexing question in the CERCLA cleanup process is *How clean is clean?* In other words, how much cleanup should be required for any particular contaminated site? In some cases, this may not be a hard question, as where a dozen drums of waste have been dumped in a field and not yet leaked into the ground. In this hypothetical case, just pick up the drums safely, dispose of them properly, and you're done. Most contaminated sites, however, are not like this. In an urban environment like East Chicago, for example, lead from an old industrial facility may be mingled in the soil with lead from lead-based paint in older housing stock plus lead from the decades of leaded gasoline. In a rural context like the Coeur d'Alene Basin of northern Idaho, lead from old mills and smelters may be mingled with lead that is naturally occurring in the geology that attracted the mining industry in the first place. In these two scenarios, where human health may be significantly impacted by lead exposure, once you begin remediation, how will you ever know when you are done?

CERCLA itself provides very little guidance. The prime directive of CERCLA § 121 to "assure[] the protection of human health and the environment" does nothing to suggest any particular degree of protection. The NCP fills in this blank with at least some guideposts. In general, no cleanup action is suggested where the contamination presents a risk of less than one "excess" case of cancer in one million people. This is often expressed as a $10^{-6}$ cancer risk. On the other hand, cleanup action is recommended where contamination presents a risk of cancer greater than one in ten thousand ($10^{-4}$). In between these two posts, cleanup actions may be discretionary, depending on factors including technical uncertainty. 40 C.F.R. § 300.430(e)(2)(A).

For noncancer impacts, such as the effects of lead exposure on neurological development in children, the NCP provides that "acceptable exposure levels shall represent concentration levels to which the human population, including sensitive sub-groups, may be exposed without adverse effect during a lifetime or part of a life, in-corporating an adequate margin of safety." *Id.* Quantitatively, noncancer risks are often expressed through calculation of a **hazard quotient** (HQ), with an HQ below 1 considered not likely to result in an adverse health impact and an HQ above 1 in-creasing in the risk of adverse health impacts.

Based upon your understanding of quantitative risk assessment from Chapter 3, how confident would you feel about using these risk calculations to determine "how clean is clean" in your community? What vulnerabilities do you see in this approach to determining the appropriate level of cleanup for site? On the other hand, what al-ternatives to this approach do you see, particularly where a site may be situated in an area with multiple sources of contamination?

**2. Institutional controls.** According to the NCP, while CERCLA establishes a pref-erence for treatment of contaminated materials, the EPA also "expects to use a com-bination of methods ... to achieve protection of human health and the environment," including "institutional controls such as water use and deed restrictions ... to prevent or limit exposure to hazardous substances...." 40 C.F.R. § 300.430(a)(1)(iii). The use of institutional controls has been promoted by the EPA, private industry, and some community representatives as an efficient, relatively low-cost means for protecting human health while at the same time accelerating efforts to return contaminated properties to economic reuse. *See, e.g.,* U.S. EPA, LAND USE IN THE CERCLA REMEDY SELECTION PROCESS (May 1995). Institutional controls may include a range of ad-ministrative devices designed to guide human behavior in order to prevent exposure to contamination that may remain at a site. Institutional controls may include pro-prietary controls, such as easements, equitable servitudes, and restrictive covenants; governmental controls, such as zoning and other municipal regulation of land uses; and informational devices, such as warning signs against eating fish from a contam-inated waterway. *See, e.g.,* Figure 8-3 below.

While some intentions behind the use of institutional controls may be laudable, simultaneously promoting community development and the protection of human health, in practice, institutional controls may also prove challenging to implement and even inappropriate as a matter of law and policy. Through the history of the EPA's experience with contaminated sites, three generations of perspectives on insti-tutional controls may be discerned.

In the first generation, the EPA often invoked institutional controls as if the phrase itself would bring the restriction into being. In 1979, for example, near the town of Klamath Falls in southern Oregon, the EPA caught a developer in the act of demol-ishing old military buildings in violation of rules for asbestos abatement. The EPA ordered the developer to cease the demolition immediately and place restrictions on the contaminated property to prevent use for residential purposes. The developer quickly agreed and then proceeded to do the exact opposite, completing the demolition and then building homes directly on top of the asbestos contamination. Endangering the lives of some two dozen families for more than a decade, the asbestos contami-

**Figure 8-3:** Public warning signs along Houston Ship Channel. February 2017. Photo: Cliff Villa.

nation finally came to light in 2002. When it became apparent that the problem could not be fixed readily, community members were relocated in 2005 and the site resembled a ghost town until remedial construction at the North Ridge Estates Superfund Site was completed in 2018. *See* www.epa.gov/superfund/north-ridge-estates. For further examples and analysis of institutional control failures in the CERCLA program, *see* Catherine A. O'Neill, *No Mud Pies: Risk Avoidance as Risk Regulation*, 31 Vt. L. Rev. 273, 313–14 (2007).

In the second generation, the EPA began to recognize that institutional controls such as deed restrictions were not subject to magic incantations and, in fact, might not be enforceable at all under controlling state law. Students of property law may recall a general reluctance of law to support endless restrictions on the use of property (among other things, giving us the famous Rule Against Perpetuities). But what if you really needed to ensure such restrictions in perpetuity? To make certain, for example, that an asbestos disposal cell in your neighborhood would never be used for residential homes? One answer was development of the Uniform Environmental Covenants Act (UECA) in 2003, which has since been adopted by at least half of the states. For the text of UECA and tracking of states and territories where it has been adopted, *see* https://www.uniformlaws.org/committees/community-home?CommunityKey=ce3a1f 73-4bc5-4de2-82a9-f4f54ce70294. In states and territories where UECA or similar legislation has been adopted, property restrictions may be established and enforceable by third parties including the EPA or relevant state agencies, with careful drafting and attention to applicable requirements. For one thoughtful critique of UECA and other institutional controls in the particular context of environmental justice, *see* Andrea

Ruiz-Esquide, *The Uniform Environmental Covenants Act: An Environmental Justice Perspective*, 31 ECOLOGY L.Q. 1007 (2004) (suggesting that reliance on land-use restrictions "leads minority inner-city communities to accept disproportionately higher health risks in exchange for the possibility of jobs and economic development").

In the third generation of perspectives on the matter, many critics began to question the very concept of institutional controls. For example, even if state law allowed perpetual restrictions on land use, is it still a good idea to leave an asbestos dump near a residential neighborhood, tying up use of the land and creating the risk that someone, someday will disturb it? To take another example, imagine if the government said that instead of cleaning up an industrial waterway, it would simply ban all fishing in the waterway, with restrictions to be enforced in perpetuity by local law enforcement. Do you believe that would stop all people from fishing in the waterway forever? Would it stop children? The homeless? Members of Asian-Pacific Islander communities with cultural connections to fishing? Members of Native American tribes with treaty rights to take fish from the waterway? And if the restrictions did stop all these groups from fishing in the waterway, how would that compare to the objectives of environmental justice? Does fair treatment permit banning every member of a community from fishing? Would meaningful involvement allow elected officials to enact a ban on fishing that would bind future generations who could not have voted for it? Keep these questions in mind as you consider the case study on the Lower Duwamish Waterway cleanup in the concluding section of this chapter.

**3. Relocation.** In addition to the use of institutional controls, CERCLA response actions may include the movement of people away from contaminated sites, an action known as **relocation**. CERCLA removal actions may include **temporary** relocation of residents and businesses while remedial actions may provide for **permanent** relocation.

Permanent relocation is exceedingly rare, often considered a remedy of last resort, with many perils including the disruption and possible destruction of community bonds and cultural roots. Additional challenges with relocation appear in the opening vignette to this chapter. What concerns did East Chicago resident Tara Adams express with the plan to move her family 25 miles away to housing in Chicago's South Side? Another concern with permanent relocation is appraisal of property values that may already be depressed by contamination or other features of urban blight. If the government must pay for the property it takes through relocation, how should it determine a fair value: by the market value for the property as contaminated, or the property value as may appear after cleanup?

Most relocations under CERCLA are voluntary; that is, no resident should be compelled to leave against their will in order to avoid site contamination. For contaminated sites in Indian country, Congress added the provision that no tribal members shall be permanently relocated without the concurrence of the affected tribal government. 42 U.S.C. § 9626(b). In any relocation circumstance, there may be individuals who decline to leave. For example, in the case of North Ridge Estates noted above, although 22 families chose immediate evacuation in 2005, two households chose to remain in a residential development that came to resemble an empty movie set. What reasons can you imagine people would give for refusing relocation away from contamination? Are there any circumstances you can imagine where relocation should ever be mandatory to protect public health?

Now consider the opposite problem: where community members want relocation but the government does not believe the contamination warrants relocation. If risk calculations remain imprecise (as they often are), are the subjective concerns of community members enough to warrant relocation? Should community concerns such as anxiety about contamination or the inability of children to play outside safely ever go into a government decision whether to offer relocation to residents? What if it turns out that the government has underestimated the risks and the community concerns are well-founded? For an account of one deeply disturbing, but ultimately successful community effort to obtain permanent relocation from a highly contaminated site in Portsmouth, Virginia, *see* Armen H. Merjian, Washington Park Lead Committee, Inc. v. United States Environmental Protection Agency: *Helen Person and the Landmark Struggle Against Environmental Injustice*, 30 CHICANA/O-LATINA/O L. REV. 65 (2011).

One of the EPA's early experiences with permanent relocation concerned residents affected by contamination from the Escambia Wood Treating Company (ETC) Superfund Site in Pensacola, Florida. Decades of wood treatment activities at the ETC site threatened the health of the predominantly African-American community with exposure to toxic pollutants including dioxin, creosote, and pentachlorophenol. Through formation of a community organization, Citizens Against Toxic Exposure (CATE), residents advocated for relocation, which the EPA agreed to provide in a pilot project in 1995. In all, a total of 358 households were relocated in the ETC action. Years later, the EPA collected feedback from relocated residents, identifying a number of areas for improvement and suggestions for future relocations under CERCLA. *See* U.S. Envtl. Prot. Agency, ESCAMBIA WOOD TREATING COMPANY (ETC) SUPERFUND SITE PERMANENT RELOCATION: FOCUS GROUPS SUMMARY REPORT 3 (undated document).

Any relocation by the federal government, including temporary and permanent relocation under CERCLA, will trigger rights to assistance under the Uniform Relocation Assistance and Real Property Acquisition Act ("Uniform Relocation Act" or URA), 42 U.S.C. §§ 4601 *et seq*. Relocation assistance may include rent, per diem for meals and personal items, moving expenses, utility costs, insurance premiums, transportation to school, boarding of animals, and other out-of-pocket expenses necessitated by the relocation. For comprehensive information on temporary relocation under CERCLA, including checklists and template relocation agreements, *see* U.S. EPA, SUPERFUND RESPONSE ACTIONS: TEMPORARY RELOCATIONS IMPLEMENTATION GUIDANCE (2002). Advocates for community members facing relocation (temporary or permanent) should also be sure to carefully review provisions of the URA itself and implementing regulations at 40 C.F.R. Part 24.

**4. Debunking "Superfund stigma."** Proposals for listing a site on the National Priorities List often draw opposition arguing "Superfund stigma"—the concern that designation of a Superfund site will lower property values in a surrounding community. These concerns are not, however, generally supported by empirical studies of housing prices in relation to NPL listing and site remediation; many studies, in fact, find the opposite.

One study published in 2014 examined neighborhoods near 29 NPL sites in the Los Angeles area, measuring the effects on housing prices from specific phases of the Superfund remedial process. According to this study, placing a site on the NPL resulted in an *increase* in housing values averaging 1.6%. The same study found that a site designation of "construction complete" raised prices an average of 2.8% while site deletion raised prices an average of 7.3%. Ralph A. Mastromonaco, *Hazardous Waste Hits Hollywood: Superfund and Housing Prices in Los Angeles*, 59 Environ. Resources & Econ. 207 (2014). Consistent with these findings, a more recent study of 103 hazardous waste sites in the Twin Cities of Minneapolis and Saint Paul, Minnesota, flatly found "little evidence of stigma effects once a hazardous waste site is remediated." Laura O. Taylor, et al., *Disentangling Property Value Impacts of Environmental Contamination from Locally Undesirable Land Uses: Implications for Measuring Post-Cleanup Stigma*, 93 J. Urban Econ. 85 (2016).

A third study helps to explain the findings of the two studies noted above. According to this third study, "Proposal of a site to the NPL may reduce neighborhood housing prices *when this action provides new information* to the housing market that contamination is severe enough to warrant the potential listing...." Shanti Gamper-Rabindran & Christopher Timmins, *Does Cleanup of Hazardous Waste Sites Raise Housing Prices? Evidence of Spatially Localized Benefits*, 65 J. Envtl Econ. & Mgmt. 345, 347 (2013) (emphasis added). In most communities concerned with environmental injustice, the presence of serious contamination in their midst will hardly represent "new information" to the local housing market. Accordingly, for communities already concerned about pollution in their neighborhood, listing a contaminated site on the NPL may "increase housing prices by signaling that a site has been placed on the path towards remediation." *Id.* Moreover, the same study also indicated that the strongest increases in property values after cleanup are homes associated with the lowest income brackets. In this study, homes at the 10th percentile appreciated an average of 24.4% post-remediation, compared to homes in the upper 90th percentile, which appreciated 18.7% post-remediation. *Id.* at 346. In short, poor homeowners may have the most to gain from NPL listing, in protection of their health as well as in increases in wealth represented by the value of their homes.

**5. Gentrification.** Of course, increasing housing values in any community may bring a number of downsides. Renters, for example, may feel any hope of purchasing a home slip away, and may even find themselves priced out of their neighborhood by rising rents. Rising rents may also create greater challenges for the homeless to find a stable home. Even for current homeowners themselves, who may enjoy an increase in home equity, rising home values may mean rising property taxes as well, which some people on fixed incomes—particularly the elderly—may not be able to afford.

One early perspective on gentrification described it as the "involuntary residential displacement caused by the return of affluent gentry from suburbia to well-located but deteriorated inner city areas." Donald C. Bryant, Jr. & Henry W. McGee, Jr., *Gentrification and the Law: Combatting Urban Displacement*, 25 Wash. U. J. Urban & Contemp. L. 43, 46 (1983). Subsequent scholarship articulated varying views on gentrification. For one provocative exchange, *see* J. Peter Byrne, *Two Cheers for Gentrification*, 46 How. L.J. 405 (2003) and john a. powell & Marguerite L. Spencer, *Giving Them the Old "One-Two": Gentrification and the K.O. of Impoverished Urban Dwellers*, 46 How. L.J. 433 (2003). A contemporary definition by the EPA Office of Environmental Justice defines "gentrification" in neutral terms as "the process of neighborhood change that occurs as places of lower real estate value are transformed into places of higher real estate value." The contemporary EPA definition draws upon the work of scholars and community leaders including participants on the National Environmental Justice Advisory Council in the 1990s, who produced an influential report, *Environmental Justice, Urban Revitalization, and Brownfields: The Search for Authentic Signs of Hope* (Dec. 1996). In this report, instead of a focus on combatting gentrification, the NEJAC focused on promoting what it called "urban revitalization."

> "Urban revitalization" is very different from "urban redevelopment." ... Urban revitalization is a bottom-up process. It proceeds from a community-based vision of its needs and aspirations and seeks to build capacity, build partnerships, and mobilize resources to make the vision a reality. Revitalization, as we define it, does not lead to displacement of communities through gentrification that often results from redevelopment policies. Governments must not simply view communities as an assortment of problems but also as a collection of assets. Social scientists and practitioners have already compiled methodologies to apply community planning models.

*Authentic Signs of Hope* at 12.

What "methodologies" might social scientists and planners recommend to address concerns for gentrification? Is it possible that some solutions to community problems may be found within the communities themselves? What might those community "assets" look like? For further discussion of the concerns for gentrification and displacement as a potential consequence of community cleanup and redevelopment, *see* Chapter 11 ("Land-Use Planning").

# C. Fair Treatment and Meaningful Involvement in Site Cleanup

Advocates for environmental justice might read a statute like CERCLA from end to end and find nothing that requires fair treatment or promotes the values of meaningful involvement. In fact, throughout the CERCLA remedial process, where a site might take a decade or more to reach a selected remedy in a Record of Decision, the only explicit requirement for public involvement in the statute follows completion of an RI/FS when the lead agency must "[p]rovide a reasonable opportunity for submission of written and oral comments and an opportunity for a public meeting at or near the facility at issue regarding the proposed plan...." CERCLA § 117(a)(2), 42 U.S.C. § 9617(a)(2). The statute also, however, requires the EPA to promulgate regulations "to provide for the participation of interested persons" in the selection of removal and remedial actions. 42 U.S.C. § 9613(k). The regulations appear in the National Contingency Plan (NCP), 40 C.F.R. Part 300, and will be considered in this section. Importantly, this section will also examine other opportunities for public involvement in cleanup that appear nowhere in the statutes or regulations but exist nonetheless for advocates who take initiative to find them. To begin this section, we will consider the meaning of "fair treatment" in the cleanup context, where remedy decisions are intended to respond to the unique conditions of each individual site but may sometimes fail to meet objectives for protecting human health or the environment.

## 1. Fair Treatment in the Cleanup of Contaminated Sites

As noted in the prior section, the overall command for CERCLA response actions is the protection of human health and the environment. This standard, of course, is highly contextual and often dependent on unique factors at a given site. Even a "simple" drum removal can pose unique challenges in certain circumstances, such as removal of drums from a sensitive wetland, removal of drums from frozen ground, or removal of drums from a school playground. As such, the actions to address contamination will often vary from one site to another. With such variability, however, what constitutes "fair treatment" in any individual circumstance may be difficult to define. And yet, in most cases, we may truly "know it when we see it."

Consider this scenario.[1] Two contaminated sites in the same state are discovered in the same year: 1989. The source of contamination for both sites is also the same: old drycleaner facilities. The same contaminants, trichlorethylene (TCE) and perchloroethlyene (PCE), are found in soils and groundwater underlying neighborhoods that surround the old facilities. In 2001, both sites reach Records of Decision selecting final remedies for the drycleaner contamination. The selected remedies, however, are strikingly different.

In one ROD, for the Fruit Avenue Plume Superfund Site in downtown Albuquerque, New Mexico, the selected remedy for groundwater contamination was a conventional "pump and treat" system, through which contaminated groundwater is pumped to the surface, treated with filters, and then reinjected into the aquifer.

---

1. Credit for this unfortunately real-life scenario goes to Mara Yarbrough, University of New Mexico School of Law Class of 2020, who first identified the disparate treatment of these two sites and further investigated the cases through an Independent Study with the author in 2019.

**Figure 8-4:** North Railroad Avenue Plume Superfund Site, Española, NM. July 10, 2019. Photo: Olivia Villa.

The total estimated project cost for this system was $11,425,000. By all accounts, the system worked, with remedial objectives met and a portion of the site redeveloped into "a green, sustainable and affordable apartment complex ... that opened in March 2010." U.S. Envtl. Prot. Agency, RETURN TO USE INITIATIVE 2013 DEMONSTRATION PROJECT: FRUIT AVENUE PLUME: ALBUQUERQUE, NEW MEXICO (Sept. 2013).

By contrast, 90 minutes north of Albuquerque, the ROD for groundwater contamination at the North Railroad Avenue Plume Site in Española, New Mexico, and the Santa Clara Pueblo, selected "enhanced bioremediation." This remedy depends on microorganisms to break down the contaminants, with no active treatment of the contamination beyond the injection of organic materials such as emulsified vegetable oil into the groundwater to encourage microorganism growth. The advantage of this technology is that it is cheap. With an estimated present value of $5,822,000, bioremediation would be much cheaper than pump and treat. However, it was also a remedy expected to fail: not anticipated to meet remedial objectives for the contaminated plume even within 30 years. Today, the selected remedy for the North Railroad Avenue Plume Site is indeed failing, with contamination remaining in the deep aquifer and in private wells in Española. In the *Second Five-Year Review Report* for the site, the EPA observed that the selected remedy for the contaminated aquifer "has not functioned as designed and has not been effective in reducing contaminant concentrations." U.S. Envtl. Prot. Agency, SECOND FIVE-YEAR REVIEW REPORT FOR NORTH RAILROAD AVENUE PLUME SUPERFUND SITE, ESPAÑOLA, RIO ARRIBA COUNTY, NEW MEXICO, at 38 (July 2015). To fix this failure, "a vastly expanded [] treatment system ... will be [] required" or else "a different technology such as pump and treat should be considered." *Id.* at xviii.

What can explain the fate of these two sites, so similarly situated from the start in 1989, yet so widely divergent today? Differences cannot be fully explained by geology or hydrology of the sites because both cities occupy a high desert environment in New Mexico situated within the valley of the Rio Grande. Differences in available treatment technologies cannot explain the difference, as both sites had remedies selected in the same year. Could the divergent treatment be explained then by ... implicit bias based on race or class? Consider the following demographics from the EPA's GIS tool EJSCREEN:

> **Albuquerque:** population 559,227; 62% minority population within one-mile radius of Superfund site.

> **Española:** population 10,224; 93% minority population within one-mile radius of Superfund site (50% higher than Albuquerque).

> **Santa Clara Pueblo:** population 1,018; 98% minority population within one-mile radius of Superfund site (58% higher than Albuquerque).

Cases like the one above appear across the United States. Look around and chances are you will find cases of unfair treatment for a contaminated site near you. You may know discrimination when you see it, or when you *feel* it, but students of constitutional law also know that discrimination is notoriously hard to prove. As examined in Chapter 4, under continuing direction from the U.S. Supreme Court, violations of the Equal Protection Clause of the Fourteenth Amendment can only be established by proof of intent to discriminate against a suspect class. *See Washington v. Davis*, 426 U.S. 229 (1976).

## Notes and Questions

**1. What now?** Rather than leaping first to an Equal Protection case, guaranteeing years of litigation and the challenging proof requirement, how might effective advocates for environmental justice begin to address evident cases of unfair treatment such as the North Railroad Avenue Plume in northern New Mexico? Recall that in this case, the **five-year review**—mandated by CERCLA—already confirmed the failure of the selected bioremediation remedy. As the current situation requires either a "vastly expanded" treatment system or else a "different technology such as pump and treat," this does not appear a case where minor changes to the existing remedy may be made through an **explanation of significant differences** (ESD). Under CERCLA, this is a case requiring either an amended record of decision (ROD) or a new ROD altogether. Advocates for environmental justice thus have a vehicle under CERCLA for seeking a change to the existing remedy and pursuing fair treatment for the northern New Mexico site after 20 years of environmental injustice.

**2. The "blunt withdrawal" of jurisdiction.** What if, even after admitting the failure of the bioremediation system, the EPA simply refuses to engage in selecting a new remedy? In this case, effective advocates will find many avenues for advocacy, including within executive and legislative branches of government. As lawyers (or future lawyers), we know there must be options for judicial action as well. Under CERCLA, however, there are express limitations for challenging a selected remedy. CERCLA § 113(h) presumptively bars federal courts from reviewing "challenges to any removal or re- medial actions" selected under the statute until the cleanup work is actually completed. 42 U.S.C. § 9613(h)(4) (authorizing challenges to removal or remedial actions only once the actions are "taken" — past tense). Courts have recognized that this language effects a "blunt withdrawal of federal jurisdiction," *see, e.g., McClellan Ecological Seepage Situation v. Perry*, 47 F.3d 325, 328 (9th Cir. 1995). This "blunt withdrawal" serves the congressional intent of CERCLA to provide for expeditious cleanup of contaminated sites without the delay of litigation — a policy described colloquially as "shovels first, lawyers later."

In the case of the North Railroad Avenue Plume in northern New Mexico, the bar established by CERCLA § 113(h) may not apply at all, as it is clear that the selected bioremediation remedy has indeed been "taken" — and failed, as observed in the 2015 five-year review. This may also be true for every other NPL site across the country where failed remedies languish in a state of endless five-year reviews.

**3. Constitutional challenges?** For contaminated sites where the § 113 bar may apply, such as any site receiving ongoing active remediation under CERCLA, challenge to the selected remedy may be tougher, though not impossible. As the plaintiffs in the Portsmouth, Virginia, case pointed out, while § 113(h) may bar challenges under the CERCLA statute, it might not bar challenges under the U.S. Constitution itself, including challenges based upon the Equal Protection Clause. Courts appear split on the question of whether § 113(h) may preclude constitutional challenges to CERCLA remedies. *See* Robert G. Ruggieri, *Broward v. Environmental Protection Agency: CERCLA's Bar on Pre-enforcement Review of EPA Cleanup Under Section 113(h)*, 13 VILL. ENVTL. L.J. 375 (2002). In the Portsmouth case, the federal court allowed the constitutional challenge, observing that if the § 113(h) bar applied, plaintiffs "could not raise their constitutional claims until the cleanup was concluded," at which point "the case would be moot." *Washington Park Lead Comm. v. U.S. EPA*, 1998 WL 1053712 at 9 (E.D. Va. Dec. 1, 1998).

Surviving the § 113(h) bar, of course, plaintiffs bringing an Equal Protection chal- lenge to a CERCLA remedy must still prove defendant's intent to discrimination in order to prevail on the merits. While this may be a high burden of proof, the Supreme Court has provided guidance identifying a range of factors from which discriminatory intent may be inferred. *See Village of Arlington Heights v. Metropolitan Housing De- velopment Corp.*, 429 U.S. 252 (1977). Among the factors identified in *Arlington Heights* are "a clear pattern, unexplainable on grounds other than race...." *Id.* at 266. In the Portsmouth case, plaintiffs seeking to challenge the EPA's denial of permanent relocation for the largely African American community introduced evidence that of the 19 permanent relocations that had taken place at NPL sites as of 2000, 16 had been in predominantly white communities, and nine had been in "overwhelmingly" white communities with white populations of 97% of higher. Merjian, *supra*, at 94–

95. Only three relocations had taken place in predominantly African-American communities, one of which was based upon an act of Congress and another (the Portsmouth case) the result of litigation. Whether this evident pattern would be enough to support a judicial finding of intentional discrimination, we do not know. We do know, however, that it was enough to induce the EPA (and the U.S. Department of Justice) to settle the Portsmouth case and provide the permanent relocation that the residents sought through the litigation.

4. **Natural resource damages.** Beyond remedial actions to address contamination directly, CERCLA and the Oil Pollution Act further authorize legal actions to restore natural resources, such as groundwater, surface water, wetlands, and other wildlife habitats that may be injured by contamination. *See* CERCLA § 107(a), 42 U.S.C. § 9607(a)(4)(C); OPA § 1002, 33 U.S.C. § 2702(b)(2)(A). In one settlement for **natural resource damages** resulting from mining contamination in the Clark Fork River Basin of western Montana, the Confederated Salish and Kootenai Tribes (CSKT) of the Flathead Reservation received $18.3 million for restoration projects in the Clark Fork River Basin. Funded CSKT projects include $6.4 million for restoration of up to 800 acres of wetlands and $1.5 million for measures to restore the local population of native bull trout, a threatened species under the Endangered Species Act and a traditional food source for the Tribes. *See* Streamside Tailings Operable Unit and Federal and Tribal Natural Resource Damages Consent Decree, No. CV-89-039-BU-PGH (April 19, 1999).

5. **State authorities.** Of course, where community members remain unsatisfied with remedies for contamination under federal law, additional remedies may be found under applicable state, tribal, or local authorities. Like many states, the State of Washington, for example, has its own version of Superfund, the Model Toxics Control Act (MTCA), 70.105D RCW. Among other distinct features, MTCA rejects the CERCLA petroleum exclusion, providing a possible remedy for soils contaminated by mismanaged gas stations and other potential sources of petroleum pollution. As another example, the Minnesota Environmental Response and Liability Act (MERLA), Minn. Stat. § 115B, establishes a Harmful Substance Compensation Program to compensate persons who suffer certain kinds of injury or property damage from contamination in Minnesota. Claims for personal and economic injuries under MERLA may be combined with common law tort claims such as trespass, negligence, nuisance, and ultra-hazardous activity. *See* Madeline Gallo, *From Wood Treatment to Unequal Treatment: The Story of the St. Regis Superfund Site*, 29 L. & INEQUALITY 175, 184 (2011).

One possible limitation on the use of state or other non-federal authorities is an argument based upon federal preemption by CERCLA. In the 2019–2020 term, this question will be squarely before the U.S. Supreme Court in the case of *Atlantic Richfield Company v. Christian*, 390 Mont. 76 (2017), *cert. granted*, (U.S. June 10, 2019) (No. 17-1498), where the Supreme Court of Montana allowed landowners near the former Anaconda smelter to bring an action for restoration damages under state common law.

Whether this decision withstands review by the U.S. Supreme Court will be known shortly after this book goes to press. In any event, as indicated above, where the CER-

CLA remedial process denies fair treatment to affected community members, many avenues remain for seeking environmental justice. Such alternatives may begin with measures provided by CERCLA itself, such as the ROD amendment process called for by the remedy failure at the North Railroad Avenue Plume in New Mexico.

## 2. Required Opportunities for Meaningful Involvement in Site Cleanup

As noted at the beginning of the section, the CERCLA statute requires little in terms of public participation — and nothing like modern understandings of "meaningful involvement." That said, this section will attempt to identify those requirements established by the statute and regulations in the NCP as a form of bottom-line for what community advocates should expect and may demand from the CERCLA process. For cleanup in the RCRA corrective process, even less is specified (there is no equivalent of the NCP for RCRA corrective action), but nonbinding agency policies may help establish some best practices. *See, e.g.*, U.S. EPA, RESOURCE CONSERVATION AND RECOVERY ACT PUBLIC PARTICIPATION MANUAL (Jan. 11, 2017). Of course, state, tribal, and local cleanup authorities may always establish greater requirements for public participation and should always be consulted as appropriate.

CERCLA § 105(a) (42 U.S.C. § 9605(a)): **National contingency plan.** (a) ... The [EPA] shall, after notice and opportunity for public comments, revise and republish the national contingency plan for the removal of oil and hazardous substances....

CERCLA § 105(d) (42 U.S.C. § 9605(d): **Petition for assessment of release.** Any person who is, or may be, affected by a release or threatened release of a hazardous substance or pollutant or contaminant may petition the [EPA] to conduct a preliminary assessment of the hazards to public health and the environment.... If the [EPA] has not already conducted a preliminary assessment of such release, the [EPA] shall, within 12 months after receipt of any such petition, complete such assessment or provide an explanation of why the assessment is not appropriate. If the preliminary assessment indicates that the release or threatened release concerned may pose a threat to human health or the environment, the [EPA] shall promptly evaluate such release ... to determine [whether the site should be added to the National Priorities List].

CERCLA § 117 (42 U.S.C. § 9617): **Public participation.**

**(a) Proposed plan.** Before adoption of any plan for remedial action ... the [EPA] or State, as appropriate, shall take both of the following actions:

(1) Publish a notice and brief analysis of the proposed plan and make such plan available to the public.

(2) Provide a reasonable opportunity for submission of written and oral comments and an opportunity for a public meeting at or near the facility at issue....

**(b) Final plan.** Notice of the final remedial action plan adopted shall be published and the plan shall be made available to the public before commencement of any remedial action. Such final plan shall be accompanied by a discussion of any significant changes (and the reasons for such changes) in the proposed plan and a response to each of the significant comments....

(d) **Publication.** For the purposes of this section, publication shall include, at a minimum, publication in a major local newspaper of general circulation. In addition, each item developed, received, published, or made available to the public under this section shall be available for public inspection and copying at or near the facility at issue.

(e) **Grants for technical assistance. (1) Authority.** [T]he EPA may make grants available to any group of individuals which may be affected by a release or threatened release at any facility which is listed on the National Priorities List.... Such grants may be used to obtain technical assistance in interpreting information with regard to the nature of the hazard, remedial investigation and feasibility study, record of decision, remedial design, selection and construction of remedial action, operation and maintenance, or removal action at such facility.

(2) **Amount.** The amount of any grant under this subsection may not exceed $50,000 for a single grant recipient. The [EPA] may waive the $50,000 limitation in any case where such waiver is necessary to carry out the purposes of this section.... Not more than one grant may be made under this subsection with respect to a single facility, but the grant may be renewed to facilitate public participation at all stages of remedial action.

CERCLA § 113 (42 U.S.C. § 9613):

(j) **Judicial review. (1) Limitation.** In any judicial action under [CERCLA], judicial review of any issues concerning the adequacy of any response action ... shall be limited to the administrative record....

(k) (1) **Administrative record.** The [EPA] shall establish an administrative record upon which the [EPA] shall base the selection of a response action. The administrative record shall be available to the public at or near the facility at issue. The [EPA] may place duplicates of the administrative record at any other location.

(2) **Participation procedures.**

(A) **Removal action.** The [EPA] shall promulgate regulations ... establishing procedures for the appropriate participation of interested person in the development of the administrative record on which the [EPA] will base the selection of removal actions and on which judicial review will be based.

(B) **Remedial action.** The [EPA] shall provide for the participation of interested persons, including potentially responsible parties, in the development of the administrative record ... on which judicial review of remedial actions will be based.... The [EPA] shall promulgate regulations ... to carry out the requirements of this subparagraph.

CERCLA § 122 (42 U.S.C. § 9622): Settlements.

(d) **Enforcement. (1)(A) Consent decree.** Whenever the [EPA] enters into an agreement ... with any potentially responsible party with respect to remedial action ...

the agreement shall be entered in the appropriate United States district court as a consent decree.

**(2) Public participation. (A) Filing of proposed judgment.** At least 30 days before a final judgment is entered under paragraph (1), the proposed judgment shall be filed with the court.

**(B) Opportunity for comment.** The [U.S. Department of Justice] shall provide an opportunity to ... comment on the proposed judgment before its entry by the court as a final judgment. The [DOJ] shall consider, and file with the court, any written comments, views, or allegations relating to the proposed judgment. The [DOJ] may withdraw or withhold its consent to the proposed judgment if the comments ... disclose facts or considerations which indicate that the proposed judgment is inappropriate, improper, or inadequate.

**(i) Settlement procedures.** (1) At least 30 days before any settlement [for the recovery of response costs] may become final ... [the lead agency] shall publish in the Federal Register notice of the proposed settlement....

(2) For a 30-day period beginning on the date of publication of notice ... the [lead agency] shall provide an opportunity for persons who are not parties to the proposed settlement to file written comments relating to the proposed settlement.

(3) The [lead agency] shall consider any comments filed under paragraph (2) in determining whether or not to consent to the proposed settlement and may withdraw or withhold consent to the proposed settlement if such comments disclose facts or considerations which indicate the proposed settlement is inappropriate, improper, or inadequate.

**CERCLA § 310 (42 U.S.C. § 9659): Citizen suits.** (a) Except as provided [elsewhere in CERCLA], any person may commence a civil action on his own behalf (1) against any person (including the United States ... ) who is alleged to be in violation of any standard, regulation, condition, requirement, or order which has become effective pursuant to [CERCLA] (including any provision of an agreement under [CERCLA § 120] relating to Federal facilities); or (2) against the [EPA] where there is alleged a failure of the [EPA] to perform any act or duty under [CERCLA] which is not discretionary....

**NCP at 40 C.F.R. § 300.5: Definitions.** *Community relations* means EPA's program to inform and encourage public participation in the Superfund process and to respond to community concerns. The term "public" includes citizens directly affected by the site, other interested citizens or parties, organized groups, elected officials, and potentially responsible parties (PRPs).

**NCP at 40 C.F.R. § 300.155: Public information and community relations.** (a) When an incident occurs, it is imperative to give the public prompt, accurate information on the nature of the incident and the actions underway to mitigate the damage. OSCs/RPMs and community relations personnel should ensure that all appropriate public and private interests are kept informed and that their concerns are considered throughout a response. They should coordinate with available public affairs/community relations resources to carry out this responsibility by establishing, as appropriate, a Joint Information Center bringing together resources from federal and state agencies and the responsible party.

**NCP at 40 C.F.R. § 300.185: Nongovernmental participation.** [Area Contingency Plans] shall establish procedures to allow for well organized, worthwhile, and safe use of **volunteers,** including compliance with [regulations] regarding worker health and safety.... ACPs also should identify specific areas in which volunteers can be used, such as beach surveillance, logistical support, and bird and wildlife treatment. Unless specifically requested by the OSC/RPM, volunteers generally should not be used for physical removal or remedial activities.

**NCP at 40 C.F.R. § 300.415(n): Community relations in removal actions.**

(1) In the case of all CERCLA removal actions..., a spokesperson shall be designated by the lead agency. The spokesperson shall inform the community of actions taken, respond to inquiries, and provide information concerning the release.

(2) For CERCLA actions where ... the lead agency determines that a removal is appropriate, and that less than six months exists before on-site removal activity must begin, the lead agency shall:

(i) Publish a notice of availability of the administrative record file ... in a major local newspaper of general circulation or use one or more other mechanisms to give adequate notice to a community within 60 days of initiation of on-site removal activity;

(ii) Provide a public comment period, as appropriate, of not less than 30 days from the time the administrative record file is made available for public inspection ...

(iii) Prepare a written response to significant comments....

(3) For CERCLA removal actions where on-site action is expected to extend beyond 120 days from the initiation of on-site removal activities, the lead agency shall ...

(i) Conduct interviews with local officials, community residents, public interest groups, or other interested or affected parties, as appropriate, to solicit their concerns, information needs, and how or when citizens would like to be involved in the Superfund process.

(ii) Prepare a formal community relations plan (CRP) based on the community interviews and other relevant information, specifying the community relations activities that the lead agency expects to undertake during the response; and

(iii) Establish at least one local information repository....

(4) Where ... the lead agency determines that a CERCLA removal action is appropriate and that a planning period of at least six months exists prior to initiation of the on-site removal activities, the lead agency shall at a minimum:

(i) Comply with the [above] requirements

(ii) Publish a notice of availability and brief description of the [Engineering Evaluation/Cost Analysis (EE/CA)] in a major local newspaper of general circulation or use one or more other mechanisms to give adequate notice to a community....

(iii) Provide a reasonable opportunity, not less than 30 calendar days, for submission of written and oral comments after completion of the EE/CA....; and

(iv) Prepare a written response to significant comments....

**NCP at 40 C.F.R. § 300.430(c): Community relations.** (2) The lead agency shall provide for the conduct of the following community relations activities, to the extent practicable, prior to commencing field work for the remedial investigation:

(i) Conducting interviews with local officials, community residents, public interest groups, or other interested or affected parties, as appropriate, to solicit their concerns and information needs, and to learn how and when citizens would like to be involved in the Superfund process.

(ii) Preparing a formal community relations plans (CRP), based on the community interviews and other relevant information, specifying the community relations activities that the lead agency expects to undertake during the remedial response....

(iii) Establishing at least one local information repository ...

(iv) Informing the community of the availability of technical assistance grants.

**NCP at 40 C.F.R. § 300.430(e): Feasibility study. (9)(iii) Nine criteria for evaluation. (I) Community acceptance.** This assessment includes determining which components of the alternatives interested persons in the community support, have reservations about, or oppose. This assessment may not be completed until comments on the proposed plan are received.

**NCP at 40 C.F.R. § 300.435(c): Community relations in remedial design/remedial action.**

(1) Prior to the initiation of [Remedial Design], the lead agency shall review the [Community Relations Plan] to determine whether it should be revised to describe further public involvement activities during RD/RA that are not already addressed or provided for in the CRP.

(2) After the adoption of the ROD, if the remedial action ... differs significantly from the remedy selected in the ROD with respect to scope, performance, or cost, the lead agency ... shall either:

(i) Publish an explanation of significant differences when the differences ... do not fundamentally alter the remedy selected in the ROD ...; or

(ii) Propose an amendment to the ROD....

(3) After the completion of the final engineering design, the lead agency shall issue a fact sheet and provide, as appropriate, a public briefing prior to the initiation of the remedial action.

**NCP at 40 C.F.R. § 300.825: Record requirements after the decision document is signed.**

(b) The lead agency may hold additional public comment periods or extend the time for the submission of public comment after a decision document has been signed on any issues concerning selection of the response action.... All additional comments submitted during such comment periods that are responsive to the request, and any response to the comments ... and any final decisions with respect to the issue, shall be placed in the administrative record file.

(c) The lead agency is required to consider comments submitted by interested persons after the close of the public comment period only to the extent that the comments contain significant information not contained elsewhere in the administrative record file which could not have been submitted during the public comment period and which substantially support the need to significantly alter the response action....

## Notes and Questions

1. **Public comment opportunities.** As indicated in the statutory provisions above, CERCLA requires opportunities for public comment in three general contexts: proposals for the National Contingency Plan; proposals for settlement; and proposals for response actions. Each context will be considered with more detail below.

a. **Public comment on the National Contingency Plan.** As noted earlier in this chapter, the National Contingency Plan (NCP), in a twist on administrative law, represents a set of regulations implementing statutes that came after the regulations. With the passage of CERCLA in 1980, Congress required the EPA to revise the NCP, and the EPA in fact continues to revise the NCP regularly. The most frequent NCP revisions, approximately twice a year, are updates to the National Priorities List, to which new sites are regularly added and from which old sites are deleted or partially deleted. As a federal regulation, the NCP (including the NPL) must proceed through rulemaking for any substantive changes. This process requires, at a minimum, public notice through the Federal Register, an opportunity for public comments, and a published response to comments. *See, e.g.*, 81 Fed. Reg. 62,397 (Sept. 9, 2016) (published notice of final NPL listing for the new "Bonita Peak Mining District" Superfund site, including the Gold King Mine—site of the infamous mine blowout in August 2015).

Under CERCLA, any legal challenges to the NCP, including challenges to proposed NPL listings or proposed NPL deletions, must proceed through the D.C. Circuit Court of Appeals, within 90 days of the rule promulgation. CERCLA § 113(a), 42 U.S.C. § 9613(a). Any failure to observe this jurisdictional rule may result in dismissal of the challenge. *See, e.g., United States v. Asarco Inc.*, 214 F.3d 1104 (9th Cir. 2000) (dismissing challenge to scope of NPL listing for the "Bunker Hill Mining Site," as all challenges to NPL listing remain within exclusive jurisdiction of the D.C. Circuit Court of Appeals). While environmental justice advocates clearly may challenge NPL listings and NPL deletions, may they also challenge EPA *refusals* to list a site? What does CERCLA § 105(d) plus CERCLA § 310(a)(2) tell you?

**b. Public comment on settlements.** Despite the general understanding that community advocates should have a "seat at the table" for deliberations that may affect their communities, one exceptional circumstance may be settlement negotiations, where lawyers for the government and potentially responsible parties (PRPs) often meet in closed-door sessions to hammer out the terms of a proposed agreement. Due to the nature of many negotiations, the law generally supports limited protections for "settlement confidentiality." *See, e.g.,* Federal Rules of Evidence 508: Compromise Offers and Negotiations. Closed-door sessions, however, may give rise to community concerns that the government may engage in less than "arms-length" negotiations and provide "sweetheart deals" to favored parties, at the expense of public interests.

Against such concerns, CERCLA provides specific opportunities for public review and comments on proposed settlements for both cleanup actions and cost recovery. Public comments on a proposed settlement with a PRP may convince a government agency (e.g., EPA or a state) or a reviewing court to modify or reject the settlement. In addition to the (rather vague) standard of "inappropriate, improper, or inadequate" specified in CERCLA § 122(i), federal courts have established a more articulate standard for reviewing CERCLA settlements. "In order to approve a CERCLA consent decree, a district court must conclude that the agreement is procedurally and substantively 'fair, reasonable, and consistent with CERCLA's objectives.'" *State of Arizona v. City of Tucson,* 761 F.3d 1005, 1011–12 (9th Cir. 2014), *citing United States v. Montrose Chem. Corp. of Cal.,* 50 F.3d 741, 747 (9th Cir. 1995). In the *Arizona* case, the City of Tucson and other intervenors challenged settlements proposed by the State of Arizona where the State asserted that the settling defendants were only responsible for less than 0.2% of $75 million in remediation costs at the Broadway-Patano Landfill (a state Superfund site). Agreeing with the intervenors, the Ninth Circuit vacated the district court's order approving the consent decrees, finding that the court "failed to independently scrutinize the terms of the agreements, ... and in so doing, afforded undue deference to the [Arizona Department of Environmental Quality]." *State of Arizona* at 1010.

Given the prospect that trial courts or appellate courts may reject a proposed CERCLA settlement for insufficient basis to conclude the agreement is "procedurally and substantively 'fair, reasonable, and consistent with CERCLA's objectives,'" how might a community advocate argue that community concerns should be addressed at the outset of settlement negotiations rather than the tail-end when the product of negotiations is presented to the court for approval?

**c. Public comment on response actions.** The most common opportunity for public engagement within the CERCLA program is commenting on proposals for CERCLA removals and remedial action. While CERCLA § 117 provides explicit opportunities to comment on proposed remedial actions, the statute leaves comment opportunities in the removal context entirely up to the NCP to define. Look closely at the sliding scale for public involvement in removal actions defined by 40 C.F.R. § 300.415(n). What do you see? Does a removal action that can be completed within 30 days require any opportunity for public comment? Noting the NCP's frequent use of "as appropriate," when, if ever, would it be "appropriate" to hold a public comment period on an action that has already been completed? Under the NCP, when, if ever, is a public comment period mandatory for a removal action?

Whenever public comments are collected under CERCLA, the NCP requires a written response to all "significant comments." What are "significant" comments? Significance, of course, depends at least in part on the scope of the given comment period. A proposal to address an illegal dumpsite in a city park, for example, may have little relation to whether the state auditor should be fired. Environmental justice advocates may assist community members with understanding the scope of any particular comment period and finding more appropriate venues for other community concerns.

Perhaps the most important question concerning public comment on proposed response actions is this: Do public comments make any difference in the final remedy selected? Anecdotally, at least, there is certainly evidence that public comments *can* make a difference. The question is probably most often one of timing and degree. For example, after years of work on a remedial investigation/feasibility study (RI/FS) result in an agency recommendation to construct a large waste repository outside of town, public comments might help strengthen design standards for the repository, but may be unlikely to convince agency decision-makers to construct an on-site waste incinerator instead. The time to advocate for the waste incinerator may have passed years ago in early scoping of alternatives in the FS. To ask the obvious question now, what does this mean for the wisdom of waiting for the first official public comment period in CERCLA, after completion of the RI/FS?

2. **Other public involvement tools.** For all remedial actions, and for removal actions expected to continue for more than 120 days, the NCP establishes a number of specific requirements to promote public involvement besides public comment periods. These include community interviews, a community relations plan, a local information repository, and—for NPL sites—**technical assistance grants.** For sites included on the NPL, most of these functions may be handled or managed by a **community involvement coordinator** (CIC), who may serve as a liaison beyond community members and the on-scene coordinator (OSC) or remedial project manager (RPM), who may be more focused on field work or technical analyses. Each of these community involvement functions will be considered briefly in the notes below.

a. **Community interviews** may be an essential means for an agency to understand the diverse perspectives and needs of a community. Among other things, community interviews may identify the various languages that must be accommodated in public meetings and written materials. Community meetings may also identify the best means of communicating with community members (email? printed factsheets? radio broadcasts? personal appearances in farmers markets or faith-based organizations?). In a community with a high level of distrust of the government, how might you design these interviews for maximum usefulness?

**b. Community involvement plans.** Information from community interviews and other resources will help the lead agency develop the required community relations plan, known more commonly now as a **community involvement plan.** The community involvement plan documents important information about a community such as languages spoken, educational levels, preferred means of communication, and possible meeting venues. As indicated by the NCP at 40 C.F.R. § 300.435, the community involvement plan should be updated from time to time, particularly following completion of the remedy selection process and before construction activities begin. For an excellent example, *see* the Community Involvement Plan for the USS Lead Superfund Site in East Chicago (EPA 2018), available online.

**c. Information repositories.** While much information on contaminated sites is now available online through the ten EPA regional offices and other sources, the NCP still requires the establishment of local **information repositories.** Usually, these will be situated in a local public library, most often now in electronic formats. Where libraries and computers may not be available, local repositories have been established with printed materials placed in any local venue where people visit (including churches and local bars).

**d. Technical Assistance Grants.** Given the enormous data analysis and technical complexities associated with most Superfund sites, Congress through CERCLA § 117 (e) established the availability of **technical assistance grants** (TAGs) for community organizations (often known as **community advisory groups**) to track and participate in the site investigation and cleanup. In addition to TAGs, further technical assistance for community advisory groups may be available through EPA contracts for Technical Assistance Services for Communities (TASC), under which the EPA may provide scientists, engineers, and other professionals to assist communities with certain projects at no cost to the communities. For a comprehensive collection of policies and regulations on TASC and TAG grants, *see* www.epa.gov/superfund/technical-assistance-grant-tag-program.

**3. Española, otra vez.** For a contaminated site such as the North Railroad Avenue Plume Superfund Site in northern New Mexico, where the remedy was selected and implemented long ago but remains demonstrably failing now, how would you use the specific public involvement requirements identified in this section in order to achieve an effective remedy that will protect the health of people in this community?

## 3. Unwritten Opportunities for Meaningful Involvement in Site Cleanup

In addition to all the specific requirements for public involvement identified in the preceding section, there remain countless unwritten opportunities for community advocates to engage meaningfully in cleanup processes. Taking advantage of some of these opportunities may prove the most effective means for community advocates to achieve positive change. As noted above, waiting years for the first required comment period after an RI/FS is completed may mean you have already missed the best opportunity for shaping the final selected remedy. Wouldn't it be better if you could comment much sooner, perhaps on a work plan for conducting the RI/FS? In fact, you may be able to do that—and much more than you might imagine. This section will suggest some concrete measures that may not appear in any statutes or regulations but may nonetheless allow community advocates to engage most effectively in cleanup processes.

**a. Get a job.** Ironically, this may be the most overlooked suggestion in academia, as many students invest in education specifically to seek employment after graduation. But for aspiring EJ advocates, employment—*where?*

Imagine that you genuinely cared about protecting human health in a community with a new NPL site, and you had an opportunity to shape an RI/FS for that site from the very start. There are people who get paid to do that, including attorneys in the regional offices of the U.S. EPA. If this interests you, consider applying to the various EPA regional offices and headquarters offices, which independently hire entry-level attorneys most years through honors attorney programs. Consider applying to the U.S. DOJ Environment and Natural Resources Division, where you also may find more litigation experience. Consider applying to other federal agencies who may have much more opportunity to promote environmental justice than you suspect: agencies to include the U.S. Department of Agriculture, U.S. Department of the Interior, the U.S. Coast Guard, and the Army Corps of Engineers. Consider applying to state agencies, including environmental departments and state AG offices. Consider tribal agencies, local governments, nongovernmental organizations, and private firms of all sizes. What could you do to effect positive change in each capacity?

**b. Get involved.** Short of going to work for an agency or organization directly involved in the cleanup of a contaminated site, you may find other opportunities to get involved in the cleanup process, such as participation through a community advisory group, a neighborhood association, or a faith-based organization. Engage in a community interview with an EPA community involvement coordinator and put your name on an email list for regular site updates. Attend a public meeting when you can, provide a thoughtful public comment when the opportunity presents, and invite your neighbors to join you. Agency staff should understand that they work for you, but they won't know what you want unless you tell them.

**c. Make friends.** Get to know the on-scene coordinator in charge of a removal action. Get to know the remedial project manager (or her team) in charge of developing and implementing the remedial action for the Superfund site. Feel free to call or email them when you have a question or concern. Your new friends can probably get you a document you want much faster (usually via email) than a request for the same under the Freedom of Information Act. Respect their time and expect them to respect yours.

**d. Make a phone call.** The most powerful phone call you can probably ever make is to this phone number: **1-800-424-8802**. This is the phone number for the National Response Center (NRC) in Washington, D.C., staffed around the clock by the U.S. Coast Guard. Dial it if you witness an oil spill or a chemical release anywhere in the United States. Within minutes, your call will be routed to the proper authorities for response in the local area, likely to include a member of the EPA regional response team and state or tribal counterparts. Do not dial this number to report the existence of a stable, designated Superfund site. But dial it in case of a sudden, unexpected release from a Superfund site.

*Does it work?* Recall that in fiscal year 2018, the EPA completed 242 removal actions. Many if not most of those cleanup actions began with a phone call to the NRC. In addition to EPA removal actions, releases identified through the NRC reporting system may be addressed by other state, tribal, or local authorities. In one case, based on a phone call placed by one of the book authors, a pile of old car batteries dumped one night along a popular bike trail was removed within hours once the report was routed from the NRC to local authorities.

Reporting to the NRC is actually mandatory for "[a]ny person in charge of a ... facility" where there has been a release of a hazardous substance above a "reportable quantity." CERCLA § 9603(a), 42 U.S.C. § 9603(a). *See* NCP at 40 C.F.R. Table 302.4 for list of reportable quantities by hazardous substance. For all other concerned members of a community, NRC reports can be a voluntary and expeditious means of ensuring immediate attention to newly discovered contaminated sites.

In addition to NRC reporting, citizen tips and complaints about pollution and contaminated sites may also be made online through EPA and state agency websites. Reporting may also be made anonymously if preferred.

**e. Visit a library.** Not everything you want to know about a site may be available online. An RI/FS report may easily consume several linear feet of shelf space and take forever to download or print. Instead, since Congress commanded there shall be local information repositories, take them up on it. Ask your community involvement coordinator where the local file is housed and browse through it. You don't need a degree in chemical engineering in order to get the gist of most technical documents. Start with the executive summary, bookmark the list of acronyms (you already know a few of them now), and flip through the appendices. When you do find a need for expert advice, see if an expert is already available to the community through a TAG grant or through local colleges and universities. Of course, get to know your local librarians too.

**f. Write a letter.** Even if the only formal comment period for a site is on the proposed plan, this does not limit you from commenting on any other documents in the administrative record. Put comments in writing and put writing in the form of a printed letter. (Emails are too easy for busy people to lose.) Request that the letter be included in the administrative record, and later check the index to the administrative record to make sure your letter is there. If you ever need to challenge a remedy down the road, the challenge will be based upon documents in the administrative record, CERCLA § 113(j), and you want your letter to be available then to support your position. While you are at it, offer to help a neighbor write a letter as well.

**Figure 8-5:** Duwamish River from Duwamish Waterway Park, Seattle, WA. Mar. 27, 2015. Photo: Cliff Villa.

# D. Case Study: The Lower Duwamish Waterway Superfund Site

For many people, the Duwamish River holds special meaning as Seattle's only river, flowing from the south to the north to empty into Elliott Bay. On modern maps, however, the Duwamish River does not exist—and has not existed for a long time since civil engineers deepened its channels and straightened its meanders into the Duwamish *Waterway*. A century of urban runoff plus heavy industrial activity, including cement production, airplane manufacturing, auto shredding, and metals recycling, fouled the waterway with a variety of toxins, much in the way of urban waterways across the United States. While industrial practices and water quality improved with environmental regulations in the 1970s, the sediments at the bottom of the Duwamish Waterway remain contaminated with pollutants including arsenic and polychlorinated biphenyls (PCBs), a human carcinogen now banned from production due to its toxic effects. Driven by concern for PCBs in the fish, the EPA added the Lower Duwamish Waterway (LDW) to the National Priorities List in 2001, beginning a long process of Superfund investigation and remediation. Meanwhile, the Duwamish Waterway continues in active industrial use, flanked by diverse neighborhoods impacted by the pollution. In this concluding section of the chapter on contaminated sites, we will consider the case of the Lower Duwamish Waterway to understand continuing challenges for environmental justice plus emerging solutions to these challenges.

As the waterway cuts diagonally across former mudflats and farmland, the Georgetown neighborhood sits to the north and east, with the South Park neighborhood to

**Figure 8-6:** Fish advisory along Lower Duwamish Waterway. Mar. 2, 2018. Photo: Cliff Villa.

the south and west. Both neighborhoods are more diverse and low-income than Seattle overall, with South Park one of the most diverse neighborhoods in the county. Of approximately 4,264 people living in South Park, approximately 25% were born outside of the United States, with high populations of Latinos and Asian-Pacific Islanders. At the one public elementary school in the community, 83% of students qualify for free or reduced price lunch. The community also includes populations of Native Americans, with three federally recognized tribes holding treaty rights to the river. The Duwamish Valley is also the homeland of the Duwamish Tribe, which remains unrecognized by the federal government but an important presence in the community through its tribal leaders and events hosted in the tribal longhouse. Stakeholders in the cleanup of the Lower Duwamish Waterway further include members of more than 20 ethnic groups across the Seattle area who fish the river and engage in other activities to include picnicking and boating. Subsistence fishers who eat resident fish are most likely to come from Asian-Pacific Islander communities and multiracial backgrounds. *See* U.S. EPA Region 10, *Fishing in the Duwamish River: What Did We Learn and What Do We Do Next?* (Feb. 2017).

Threats from contamination in the Duwamish Waterway led the state health department to issue advisories against eating clams, crabs, and resident fish such as perch and flounder, while promoting salmon as a healthier choice. *See* Figure 8-6. In a prior era of environmental thought, this might have been considered enough to address concerns for pollution in urban waterways. *See, e.g.,* Exec. Order 12898, Sec. 4-4 (Federal agencies shall study "differential patterns of subsistence consumption of fish and wildlife" and "shall communicate to the public the risk of those consumption patterns"). In time, government agencies began to recognize the need for actual cleanup of such contamination, as urged by the work of scholars and activists in environmental justice. *See, e.g.,* National Environmental Justice Advisory Council, Fish Consumption and Environmental Justice (Nov. 2002); Catherine O'Neill, *Variable Justice: Environmental Standards, Contaminated Fish, and "Acceptable" Risk to Native Peoples,* 19 Stan. Envtl. L.J. 3 (2000). With the NPL listing of the Lower Duwamish Waterway in 2001, the EPA recognized the need for inclusive processes to address community concerns throughout the phases of Superfund cleanup. The EPA met the minimum requirements of CERCLA and the NCP. For example, the EPA established a local information repository at the South Park Branch Public Library, prepared an original community involvement plan in 2002, and held a public comment period for the LDW proposed plan in 2013. But the EPA also went much farther to promote meaningful involvement for this diverse community—in some cases farther than ever before.

In addition to inviting comments on the proposed plan in 2013 (a requirement of CERCLA § 117), the EPA held public meetings and collected public comments on draft documents throughout the RI/FS process. Public comments on the RI report, for example, encouraged the EPA to begin a series of early cleanup actions in five areas of the waterway with the most contamination. The five early action areas were substantially completed in 2015, reducing PCBs concentrations in the waterway by half even before the final remedy would begin. During the comment period on the FS, community members requested that the EPA conduct an **environmental justice analysis** on the proposed cleanup alternatives. While EJ analyses have become increasingly common in other contexts such as NEPA reviews, no EJ analysis had ever been done in the context of CERCLA remedy selection. The EJ analysis for the Lower Duwamish Waterway became the first. Predictably, potentially responsible parties (PRPs) questioned the role of this EJ analysis in the LDW remedy selection. In response, the EPA wrote that it "agrees that an EJ analysis is not a separate criterion for CERCLA remedy selection. EPA does maintain that considering it as part of the NCP **nine criteria** for remedy selection is an appropriate means of implementing Executive Order 12898"—the 1994 executive order on environmental justice. U.S. EPA,

Lower Duwamish Waterway Superfund Site Record of Decision — Part 3: Responsiveness Summary at 125 (Nov. 2014).

Throughout the Superfund process for the Lower Duwamish Waterway, community involvement was enhanced through the engagement of a **community advisory group** known as the Duwamish River Cleanup Coalition (DRCC). Founded in 2001, the DRCC brings together interests from neighborhood, environmental, tribal, and small business organizations in order to advocate for community concerns with respect to the Duwamish River. With support from EPA **technical assistance grants** and other sources, the DRCC contracts their own technical advisor to interpret and explain technical reports, site conditions, and cleanup proposals and decisions, thereby facilitating community input into the Superfund planning process. The DRCC also supports related programs such as river tours, educational forums, habitat restoration activities, an annual river festival, and other neighborhood events.

In 2013, the DRCC took a lead role in facilitating community comments during the official comment period on the **proposed plan** for the Lower Duwamish Waterway. The proposed plan generally recommended a mix of dredging some contaminated sediments from the riverbed and capping other contaminated sediments in place, for an estimated total cost of $305 million. During this comment period, the EPA held five formal comment meetings, including one in the South Park neighborhood conducted entirely in Spanish. Due to significant public interest in the cleanup, the EPA extended the comment period from the 30 days, required by the NCP, to 105 days. By the end of this extended comment period, the EPA had collected 2,327 written and oral submissions, in ten different languages. Comments from the DRCC and tribes generally supported the proposed cleanup and advocated for expanded cleanup measures. Comments from PRPs generally advocated for less cleanup and for waiving applicable or relevant and appropriate requirements (ARARs) for sediment cleanup standards. In the final Record of Decision, released in November 2014, no commenter received everything they wanted. However, the EPA did reject the ARARs waiver requested by the PRPs and did agree to expand the scope of cleanup by 25%, from 84 acres of dredging as proposed to 105 acres of dredging as selected, at a total final estimated cost of $342 million. U.S. EPA, Lower Duwamish Waterway Record of Decision, Fact Sheet on the Final Cleanup Plan (Nov. 2014).

Since the EPA released the final ROD in 2014, community members have remained engaged in the LDW Superfund process. One hundred and eighty-seven community members contributed comments for an update of the community involvement plan for the Lower Duwamish Waterway. Among other creative ideas captured in the updated plan, community members suggested holding information sessions during soccer practices within the Latino community; coordinating through churches, youth organizations, and karaoke nights within the Vietnamese community; and working with community services for recent immigrants from Somalia, Sudan, Kenya, and other East African nations. The EPA must continue to engage in formal and informal con-

**Figure 8-7:** Daniela Cortez and mural at Duwamish Waterway Park. Seattle, WA. March 30, 2019. Photo: Olivia Villa.

sultation with tribal governments. The EPA must also continue collaborations with agency partners on all levels of government in order to ensure efficient and effective cleanup actions and to avoid overloading community members with repeated requests for input. U.S. EPA, Lower Duwamish Waterway Superfund Site: Community Involvement Plan (Oct. 2016). One particularly fruitful collaboration between the EPA and the local health department resulted in the training and engagement of more than 20 "Community Health Advocates," who help explain technical information and promote safe fish consumption within their own communities.

Meanwhile, as cleanup proceeds on the Lower Duwamish Waterway, the people of South Park will live their lives and improve their environment through their usual means and ingenuity. On a brilliant spring day in March 2019, in the heart of the South Park neighborhood, the Duwamish Valley Youth Corps (another program of the DRCC) unveiled an extraordinary mural painted by the young people on an industrial building looming over the Duwamish Waterway Park. *See* Figure 8-7. As youth leader Daniela Cortez (15) explained the significance of the mural, including the origin story of the Duwamish people and the rich mix of cultures in her community today, you knew from the pride in her voice and surety of her words that the future of this "EJ community" was in very good hands.

## Notes and Questions

**1. Community involvement tools.** Of all the tools for promoting community involvement identified in this case study, which ones seemed most meaningful to you? What other tools, not identified here, would help reach underserved people in your community? Consider, for example, how you would best reach children, seniors, or homeless populations. What might you hope to learn from each of these groups that could assist in developing a more protective remedy or a remedy most likely to receive community support?

**2. EJ analysis.** For a contaminated site in a community such as South Park with a large population of low-income people and people of color, how would you evaluate the argument for conducting an EJ analysis under CERCLA, given that "environmental justice" is not one of CERCLA's **nine criteria** for remedy selection?

**3. Opposition?** While most community members of the Duwamish Valley appeared to support the proposed cleanup, or expansion of cleanup, consider the situation where a majority of public comments opposed the cleanup entirely, perhaps concerned that gentrification might consume the last affordable neighborhood in Seattle. Does the government still have an independent responsibility to proceed with cleanup to protect the public health?

**4. Back to East Chicago.** From the opening vignette of this chapter, recall the temporary housing offered to Ms. Adams in Chicago's South Side, 25 miles away from the community where she grew up. Using the tools for community engagement discussed in this chapter, how might you advocate for a remedy that would allow Ms. Adams to return home someday to East Chicago, Indiana, after the cleanup is complete?

# Chapter 9

# Environmental Justice in Indian Country

*There is just no getting around the fact that applying the concept of environmental justice to situations that affect the communities of Indian reservations is tricky. If environmental justice problems are characterized by disproportionate impacts on communities of color or low-income, then almost every environmental issue in Indian country is an environmental justice issue.*

Dean B. Suagee, *Environmental Justice and Indian Country*, 30 HUMAN RIGHTS 16 (2003).

## A. Introduction

Native Americans (to include Alaska Natives and Native Hawaiians) and other indigenous peoples may share many of the environmental challenges and burdens of other communities of color and low-income populations. Historic uranium mining in the American Southwest, for one example, has left a legacy of devastating health impacts to citizens of the Navajo Nation and other nearby tribes. *See* Eric Jantz, *Environmental Racism with a Faint Green Glow*, 58 NAT. RESOURCES J. 247, 251 (2017) ("During the uranium boom of the 1950s to 1980s, 80–90 percent of uranium extraction occurred on or adjacent to indigenous lands"). Recent protests led by the Standing Rock Sioux Tribe against the Dakota Access Pipeline drew national and international attention to the siting of industrial facilities near the lands of indigenous peoples. *See, e.g.*, Rebecca Solnit, *Standing Rock Protests: This Is Only the Beginning*, THE GUARDIAN, Sept. 12, 2016.

And yet, as observed above by the late distinguished lawyer and Indian law scholar Dean Suagee, applying environmental justice concepts in Indian country and among indigenous peoples in the United States can be "tricky" for many reasons. Among other things, "disproportionate impacts" on "low-income communities" could implicate almost every Indian reservation, where poverty rates are almost three times higher than elsewhere in the United States and health disparities across a range of ailments are pronounced. *See, e.g.*, Indian Health Service, *Indian Health Disparities* (April 2018). Moreover, questions of environmental justice in Indian country require unique considerations of history, culture, tribal sovereignty, and political identity. Congress defined "Indian country" to include "all land within the limits of any Indian reservation," together with "all dependent Indian communities" within the United States and "all Indian allotments." 18 U.S.C. § 1151. Other conceptions of "Indian country," however, may sweep across broader landscapes, from the Arctic coastal plain of the Inupiat people on the North Slope of Alaska to the hardwood forests of the Menominee Tribe in Wisconsin to the high desert Pueblo communities of New Mexico. Some tribal lands, such as the Wind River Reservation in Wyoming, stretch across vast open spaces. Other tribal lands, however, lie within urban or suburban environs. In Florida, the Fort Lauderdale metropolitan area includes the Hollywood Reservation of the Seminole Tribe. In Massachusetts, the rich and famous share Martha's Vineyard with the Mashpee Wampanoag Tribe.

As of 2020, in the United States, there were 574 tribes recognized by the federal government across 35 states. In addition to these federally recognized tribes, other tribes may be recognized only by state governments. These include the Elnu Abenaki Tribe in Vermont; the Ramapough Lenape Nation in New Jersey; and the Duwamish Tribe, whose homeland includes present-day Seattle. Of course, enrolled tribal members and other indigenous people may live anywhere they choose, on or off tribal lands, while retaining strong connections to ancestral landscapes. As such, environmental justice for Indian tribes and indigenous peoples must always consider the unique environments and individual concerns that each case may present.

*Pathfinder on Environmental Justice in Indian Country*

Comprehensive background on Indian law is provided in Felix S. Cohen's HANDBOOK OF FEDERAL INDIAN LAW (Nell Jessup Newton et al., eds., 5th ed. 2012). An introduction to many environmental issues in Indian country can be found in the treatise, William H. Rodgers, Jr., ENVIRONMENTAL LAW IN INDIAN COUNTRY (2005). More contemporary cases and analyses may be found in the latest edition of the casebook, Judith V. Royster, Michael C. Blumm, & Elizabeth Kronk Warner, NATIVE AMERICAN NATURAL RESOURCES LAW: CASES AND MATERIALS (4th ed. 2018). A comprehensive discussion of tribal governments' authority to manage environmental matters within their jurisdiction and to secure environmental justice in Indian country can be found in James M. Grijalva, CLOSING THE CIRCLE: ENVIRONMENTAL JUSTICE IN INDIAN COUNTRY (2008). Some key federal documents include Indian Sacred Sites, Exec. Order No. 13007, 61 Fed. Reg. 26,771 (May 29, 1996); Consultation and Coordination with Indian Tribal Governments, Exec. Order No. 13175, 65 Fed. Reg. 67,249 (Nov. 9, 2000); the EPA Policy for the Administration of Environmental Programs on Indian Reservations (Nov. 8, 1984) ("1984 Indian Policy"); the EPA Policy on Consultation and Coordination with Indian Tribes (May 4, 2011); and the EPA's Policy on Environmental Justice for Working with Federally Recognized Tribes and Indigenous Peoples (July 24, 2014).

In addition to the sources excerpted in this chapter, other articles on environmental justice concerning Indian country and indigenous peoples include Dean B. Suagee, *Turtle's War Party: An Indian Allegory on Environmental Justice*, 9 J. ENVTL. L. & LITIG. 461 (1994); John P. LaVelle, *Achieving Environmental Justice by Restoring the Great Grasslands and Returning the Sacred Black Hills to the Great Sioux Nation*, 5 GREAT

PLAINS NAT. RESOURCES J. 40 (2001); Jana L. Walker, et al., *A Closer Look at Environmental Injustice in Indian Country*, 1 SEATTLE J. FOR SOC. JUST. 379 (2002); Michael S. Houdyshell, *Environmental Injustice: The Need for a New Vision of Indian Environmental Justice*, 10 GREAT PLAINS NAT. RESOURCES J. 1 (2006); Catherine A. O'Neill, *Environmental Justice in the Tribal Context: A Madness to EPA's Method*, 38 ENVTL. L. 495 (2008); James M. Grijalva and Daniel E. Gogal, *The Evolving Path Toward Achieving Environmental Justice for Native America*, 40 ENVTL. L. REP. NEWS & ANALYSIS 10905 (2010); Elizabeth Kronk Warner, *Application of Title VI in Indian Country: The Key Is Tribal Sovereignty*, 6 FLA. A&M U. L. REV. 215 (2011); Rebecca Tsosie, *Climate Change and Indigenous Peoples: Comparative Models of Sovereignty*, 26 TULANE ENVTL. L.J. 239 (2013); D. Dapua 'ala Sproat, *An Indigenous People's Right to Environmental Self-Determination: Native Hawaiians and the Struggle Against Climate Change Devastation*, 35 STAN. ENVTL. L.J. 157 (2016); Hillary M. Hoffmann, *Fracking the Sacred: Resolving the Tension Between Unconventional Oil and Gas Development and Tribal Cultural Resources*, 94 DENV. L. REV. 319 (2017). A wealth of information about environmental issues facing Native Americans and indigenous peoples can be found on the website of the Indigenous Environmental Network, a national grassroots network of indigenous groups working on environmental issues, available at http://www.ien earth.org/. Another excellent resource on a broader range of legal issues in Indian country may be found on the blog Turtle Talk, available at https://turtletalk.blog/.

# B. Special Factors for Environmental Justice in Indian Country

While effective advocates must always consider the individual circumstances of any particular matter, many common interests and concerns may be discerned when it comes to environmental justice for Indian tribes and indigenous peoples. In the excerpt that follows, Elizabeth Kronk Warner, a law school dean and legal scholar who writes at the intersection of Indian law and environmental law, sets the stage for this chapter by examining several special factors to consider for the pursuit of environmental justice in Indian country.

### Elizabeth Kronk Warner, *Environmental Justice: A Necessary Lens to Effectively View Environmental Threats to Indigenous Survival*

26 TRANSNAT'L L. & CONTEMP. PROBS. 343–354 (2017)

... [I]ndigenous communities are often environmental justice communities. Although there are many similarities, environmental justice claims arising in Indian country within the United States differ from indigenous communities elsewhere throughout the world. These differences include considerations of tribal sovereignty (where applicable), unique obligations owed by the domestic state to indigenous communities (such as the federal trust responsibility in the United States), and the unique connection between many indigenous communities and their environment, as well as potential international considerations. Each of these considerations are discussed in detail below.

## A. Tribal Sovereignty

Indigenous communities differ from other environmental justice communities due to their status as sovereign governments within some domestic nation states, such as the United States. While other environmental justice communities typically come together as informal groups whose legal rights flow from environmental laws, the legal rights of indigenous communities, with sovereign status, flow from their sovereignty and their related historical management of the land and resources. For example, in the United States, Native nations exist as entities separate from state and federal governments. A myriad of historical legal developments led to this separateness. American Indian tribes are extra-constitutional, meaning that tribes exist apart from the U.S. Constitution. In the early 19th Century, the U.S. Supreme Court affirmed the separateness of Native nations. In *Cherokee Nation v. Georgia*, the U.S. Supreme Court held that American Indian tribes were "domestic dependent nations," highlighting their separateness from both state and federal governments. In *Worcester v. Georgia*, the U.S. Supreme Court further clarified the separateness of American Indian tribes, finding that the laws of the states are "void, and of no effect" within the exterior boundaries of American Indian tribal territory.

Although the federal government's perception of tribal sovereignty has ebbed and flowed significantly since the Court released the *Worcester* decision, "[i]n the modern era, as tribes have increasingly assumed governmental functions formerly performed by the Bureau of Indian Affairs and Indian Health Service, the relationship between the federal government and the tribes is often described as a government-to-government relationship." Moreover, Congress has indicated its recognition of tribal sovereignty by passing the Indian Self-Determination and Education Assistance Act and by subsequently amending various federal statutes to allow for increased tribal governance.

Accordingly, environmental justice claims arising in Indian country within the United States differ from claims arising elsewhere given the inherent sovereignty still possessed by Native nations. Environmental justice claims raised by Native nations "must be consistent with the promotion of tribal self-governance." This is because environmental justice claims arising from within Indian country include not only racial considerations but also political considerations. The additional consideration of tribal sovereignty is crucial to any discussion of environmental justice claims arising in Indian country. Specifically, an environmental injustice occurs if courts fail to consider the sovereignty of Native nations, because Native nations cannot meaningfully participate in the legal process if courts fail to consider something so essential to Native nations as their sovereignty. Moreover, the government-to-government relationship with American Indian tribal nations forces "the federal government [to] be prepared to defend vigorously the environmental self-determination that tribes already have." Therefore, courts consider Native nations' sovereignty when evaluating claims in order to ensure an environmentally just result as well as a trust relationship between Native nations and the federal government.

## B. Federal Trust Relationship with Native Nations

Beyond the consideration of tribal sovereignty, indigenous communities must also incorporate special obligations owed by the domestic nation to them in their environmental justice claims. Thus, indigenous communities within the United States have a unique trust relationship with the federal government. Consequently, "the United States has a trust responsibility to each tribal government that includes the protection of the sovereignty of each tribal government." The trust relationship between the Native nations and the federal government emerged from the many cessions of both land and external sovereignty. The U.S. government owes federally recognized Native nations fiduciary obligations related to the management of tribal trust lands and resources. Today, Native nations may regularly assume governmental functions that were previously held by the federal government.

To better understand the trust responsibility that the federal government owes to Native nations, it is helpful to look to the history between the sovereigns. The federal trust responsibility doctrine has been the subject of many court decisions related to Indian country over the past two centuries. The doctrine originated from Chief Justice Marshall's opinion in *Cherokee Nation v. Georgia*. With the emergence of the federal trust responsibility doctrine, the federal government began to hold lands in trust for tribal governments. Five decades later, the Court reaffirmed its commitment to this doctrine in *United States v. Kagama*. In the 20th Century, the Court used the federal trust responsibility doctrine to define the scope of review of congressional legislation related to Indian country. Thus, Congress must act as a trustee when taking action within Indian country. Furthermore, "because of the trust responsibility, it is well settled that statutes affecting Indians 'are to be construed liberally in favor of the Indians, with ambiguous provisions interpreted to their benefit.'"

Recognition of the federal trust responsibility is not limited to the courts. President Nixon recognized the federal trust responsibility in his 1968 Special Message to Congress on the Problems of the American Indian:

> The special relationship between Indians and the Federal government is the result of solemn obligations which have been entered into by the United States Government. Down through the years, through written treaties and through formal and informal agreements, our government has made specific commitments to the Indian people. For their part, the Indians have often surrendered claims to vast tracts of land and have accepted life on government reservations.

Subsequent administrations have reaffirmed and expanded upon Nixon's recognition of the federal trust responsibility doctrine.

In sum, any Indian environmental justice claim should be considered under the federal trust responsibility doctrine. Failure to include consideration of this responsibility again results in Native nations being deprived of meaningful participation in the consideration of claims.... Under the federal trust responsibility doctrine, the federal government owes to Native nations a duty that ensures natural resources are sustained. This obligation extends to the federal government as a whole and should be upheld by the federal judiciary. In evaluating an environmental justice claim arising in Indian country, federal courts must be mindful of, and uphold, the federal government's trust responsibility to Native nations. Failure to do so results in an environmental injustice.

### C. Unique Tribal Connection to the Land and Environment

Indigenous communities' claims differ from many other environmental claims because many indigenous cultures and traditions are tied to the environment in a manner that traditionally differs from that of the dominant society. As Frank Pommersheim points out, land "is important to Indian people in a multitude of ways: beyond subsistence, land is the source of spiritual origins and sustaining myth which in turn provides a landscape of cultural and emotional meaning. The land often determines the values of [their] human landscape." Analogous connections to the environment and the land among indigenous communities stem from the fact that many indigenous cultures are "land-based," meaning that they are connected to a certain location or area. Many individual indigenous people and communities also possess a spiritual connection with land and the environment. These communities

> continue to have a deep relationship with ancestral homelands for sustenance, religious communion and comfort, and to maintain the strength of personal and interfamiliar identities. Through language, songs, and ceremonies, tribal people continue to honor sacred springs, ancestral burial places, and other places where ancestral communities remain alive.

The spiritual connection between many Native nations and their surrounding environment is crucial to the self-determination of these communities.

Therefore, many communities facing environmental challenges may also encounter devastating impacts to their culture, spirituality, and traditions. Such spiritual, cultural, and historical connections to the affected land play an important role in any environmental justice claim arising in indigenous territory because land, identity, and sovereignty/self-determination are uniquely connected within indigenous communities. Failure to consider these interconnections will negatively impact the quality of the indigenous community's participation in the legal process.

### D. International Considerations

Beyond domestic legal considerations, principles of international law should also be considered when evaluating the environmental justice matters impacting indigenous communities. As a starting point, there are some principles under international law applicable to all people that are helpful when discussing indigenous rights from an environmental justice perspective. For example, domestic states have an obligation to respect the human rights of individuals subject to their authority. Moreover, OAS [Organization of American States] Member States recognize the right to hold property as a human right under both Article 21 of the American Convention on Human Rights and Article 17 of the Universal Declaration of Human Rights. The right of development was also recognized in 1986 by the U.N. General Assembly via the Declaration on the Right to Development ("Declaration"), which is important for indigenous peoples because it refers to both persons and peoples as rights holders.

International law also contains provisions that are specific to indigenous peoples. Adopted in 1989, the International Labour Organization's Convention Concerning Indigenous and Tribal Peoples in Independent Countries ("ILO 169") is a foundational document on the rights of indigenous peoples. Notably, ILO 169 recognizes the right of indigenous peoples to "exercise control ... over their own economic, social and cultural development" and participate in development that "may affect them directly." Furthermore, Article 14 of the Convention guarantees that indigenous peoples' "rights of ownership and possession ... over the lands which they traditionally occupy shall be recognized," and Article 16 states that indigenous peoples "shall not be removed from the lands which they occupy."

Building on ILO 169, the U.N. Declaration on the Rights of Indigenous Peoples ("UNDRIP") was adopted by the U.N. General Assembly in 2007. This international declaration supports and reaffirms the rights of indigenous peoples. On December 16, 2010, former president Barack Obama announced that the United States endorsed the UNDRIP. UNDRIP's articles pertaining to indigenous self-determination, property, and redress are of particular importance. UNDRIP Article 3 states "[i]ndigenous peoples have the right to self-determination." Article 8 states "[i]ndigenous peoples and individuals have the right not to be subjected to forced assimilation or destruction of their culture." Article 10 states "[i]ndigenous peoples shall not be forcibly removed from their lands or territories. No relocation shall take place without the free, prior and informed consent of the indigenous peoples concerned and after agreement on just and fair compensation and, where possible, the option to return." Article 26 states "[i]ndigenous peoples have the right to the lands, territories and resources which they have traditionally owned, occupied or otherwise used or acquired ... States shall give legal recognition and protection to these lands, territories and resources." Finally, Article 28 states that "[i]ndigenous peoples have the right to redress, by means that can include restitution or, when this is not possible, just, fair and equitable compensation, for the lands, territories and resources which they have traditionally owned or otherwise occupied or used, and which have been confiscated, taken, occupied, used or damaged without their free, prior and informed consent."

... In conclusion, environmental justice requires that courts consider the unique aspects of environmental justice communities to ensure adequate access to substantive or procedural justice. Environmental justice issues arising in Indian country encapsulate considerations that differ from claims arising from other environmental justice communities. These considerations include tribal sovereignty, the obligations of domestic states to indigenous communities including the federal trust responsibility owed by the United States toward Native nations, international legal considerations, and the unique cultural and spiritual connection many indigenous communities have with their land.

\* \* \*

## Notes and Questions

1. **Tribal sovereignty.** Perhaps the most defining distinction for environmental justice in the tribal context follows from the notion of tribal sovereignty or "self-government." In its 1984 Indian Policy, the U.S. EPA acknowledged, "In keeping with the principle of Indian self-government, the [EPA] will view Tribal Governments as the appropriate non-Federal parties for making decisions and carrying out program responsibilities affecting Indian reservations, their environments, and the health and welfare of the reservation population." While this acknowledgment may seem unremarkable now after the passage of decades, at one time states broadly assumed jurisdiction for all environmental regulation within their state borders, even on tribal lands. *See Washington Dept. of Ecology v. EPA*, 752 F.2d 1465 (9th Cir. 1985) (rejecting argument by state agency for jurisdiction to implement hazardous waste program on "Indian lands"). In recognizing tribes as "the appropriate non-Federal parties" for making decisions concerning tribal lands, the EPA also recognized the obligation to engage with tribes in **"government-to-government consultation"** on matters affecting tribes. In 2000, President Clinton signed Executive Order No. 13,175 "to strengthen the United States government-to-government relationships with Indian tribes" and "to establish regular and meaningful consultation ... with tribal officials...." Consultation and Coordination with Indian Tribal Governments, Exec. Order No. 13175, 65 Fed. Reg. 67,249 (Nov. 9, 2000). The federal duty to engage in tribal consultation, however, has often led to confusion over two common questions: (1) What "decisions" will require government-to-government consultation? and (2) Who may speak for the tribal government on these decisions?

On the first question of what decisions should trigger tribal consultation, agencies may have published guidance indicating "non-exclusive" categories of actions appropriate for government-to-government consultation. The EPA, for example, has identified a "non-exclusive list of EPA activity categories [] normally appropriate for consultation if they may affect a tribe." Such activities include regulations, policies, permits, budget planning, civil enforcement, and emergency response. *See* EPA Policy on Consultation and Coordination with Indian Tribes 5 (May 4, 2011). Considering these categories of activities, imagine a proposal to construct a gas refinery on tribal lands. Then imagine a deadly explosion at this refinery five years after it begins operations. In these two contexts, what EPA activities might trigger government-to-government consultation and how might such consultation support (or hinder) the aims of environmental justice?

On the second question, concerning who speaks for the tribal government, regular phone calls or email exchanges between staff for tribal and federal agencies may certainly be encouraged to resolve technical questions on a draft document, for example. However, as some decisions may only be made by designated officials of state or federal government, some decisions concerning tribal interests may only be made by designated tribal authorities, such as a tribal council or a tribal governor or chairman. On this point, EPA's guidance observes, "The appropriate level of interaction" may vary according to factors including "past and current practices" and "the continuing dialogue between EPA and tribal government...." *Id.* at 1. How helpful does this guidance seem to you? What are the potential consequences for a failure to consult with the appropriate tribal officials? If you were a federal attorney for the Army Corps of Engineers considering approval of a new oil pipeline crossing a river near tribal lands, what steps might you take to ensure the "appropriate level of interaction" for your particular case?

2. **Federal trust relationship.** In the excerpt above, Kronk Warner asserts that "any Indian environmental justice claim should be considered under the federal trust responsibility doctrine." What do you understand that to mean? If "fair treatment" and "meaningful involvement" comprise the hallmarks of environmental justice as defined by the EPA, do we need another definition of environmental justice for application in Indian country? Paralleling the substantive concern of "fair treatment" and the procedural concern of "meaningful involvement," courts and experts in the field of Indian law have observed that the federal trust responsibility involves both substantive and procedural duties owed by the federal government to Indian tribes. Consider the following.

Procedurally, the federal government owes a duty "to consult with Indian tribes in the decision-making process to avoid adverse effects on treaty resources." *Klamath Tribes v. U.S.* 1996 WL 924509 (D. Or. 1996), *quoting Lac Courte Oreille Band of Indians v. Wisconsin*, 668 F. Supp. 1233, 1240 (W.D. Wis. 1987). As indicated in the preceding Note 1, the federal duty to consult with tribes, or engage in "government-to-government" consultation, also arises from federal recognition of tribal sovereignty. For both purposes, the EPA defines tribal consultation as "a process of meaningful communication between EPA and tribal officials prior to EPA taking actions or implementing decisions that may affect tribes." EPA Policy on Consultation and Coordination with Indian Tribes 1 (May 4, 2011). Compare this EPA definition of "tribal consultation" to the EPA definition of "meaningful involvement" for purposes of the EPA's conception of "environmental justice" as presented in Chapter 1. Does "tribal consultation," for purposes of satisfying the federal trust responsibility, mean anything more than the "meaningful involvement" of tribes in decisions where tribes may be affected? If so, how would you describe this difference?

Substantively, the federal trust responsibility requires federal agencies to affirmatively protect the interests of tribes whenever the federal agency undertakes any action. Courts describe this responsibility as the federal government "charg[ing] itself with moral obligations of the highest responsibility and trust," *Seminole Nation v. United States*, 316 U.S. 286, 297 (1942), to be judged by "the most exacting fiduciary standards." *Cobell v. Norton*, 391 F.3d 251, 257 (D.C. Cir. 2004). At the same time, the federal government "has an 'overriding duty ... to deal fairly with Indians.'" *Id.*, quoting *Morton v. Ruiz*, 415 U.S. 199, 236 (1974). Is this federal duty to "deal fairly with

Indians" the same duty of "fair treatment" required by the EPA standard for environmental justice? Is it something more, or should it be? The Supreme Court has recognized, under the Constitution, that it may be appropriate to treat American Indians differently, because of their membership in tribes—unique political bodies with long-standing relationships to the federal government. *See Morton v. Mancari*, 417 U.S. 535 (1974). As Professor James Grijalva explains:

> The government-to-government and fiduciary relationships between tribes and the United States alters the constitutional concept of equal protection that underlies environmental justice; while American Indian citizens of the United States are entitled to fair treatment like other people of color, their dual citizenship in Indian tribes allows for different legal treatment, a sort of "measured separatism," reflected in an entire title in the United States Code of federal laws devoted specifically and exclusively to Indians and Indian country.

James Grijalva, *Closing the Circle: Environmental Justice in Indian Country* (2008) at 8.

While recognizing the federal trust responsibility owed to tribes, courts have limited the scope of remedies for trust violations. In a string of cases, the U.S. Supreme Court has held that damages for violations of the trust duty may only be obtained where the federal government agreed to accept affirmative management responsibility through a specific "rights-creating statute or regulation." *U.S. v. Navajo Nation*, 537 U.S. 488, 503 (2003); *U.S. v. White Mountain Apache*, 537 U.S. 465, 475 (2003); *U.S. v. Jicarilla Apache Nation*, 564 U.S. 162, 174 (2011).

In addition to denial of damages for violation of the federal trust responsibility, courts have also denied injunctive relief. In the lawsuit by the Standing Rock Sioux Tribe challenging completion and operation of the Dakota Access Pipeline, amici including the Association on American Indian Affairs argued that the federal trust responsibility supported the Tribe's request for injunctive relief "based upon the heightened fiduciary duties of the trust doctrine." Brief of *Amici Curiae* Association on American Indian Affairs, et al., In Support of Plaintiff Standing Rock Sioux Tribe's Motion for Summary Judgment, Case No. 1:16-cv-1534-JEB, Feb. 21, 2017, at 15. Without reaching this argument, the district court did find that the Corps of Engineers in this case violated legal mandates flowing from the standard definition of environmental justice, as will be discussed further in Chapter 12 ("Information Disclosure and Environmental Review"). *Standing Rock Sioux v. U.S. Army Corps of Eng'rs*, 255 F.Supp.3d 101, 140 (D.D.C. 2017). Unfortunately for the plaintiff tribes, in denying the requested injunctive relief, the court allowed Dakota Access to complete construction of the pipeline and put the pipeline into operation.

In denying the requested injunctive relief, did the court apply the wrong standard for an environmental justice claim in Indian country? How might you have ruled on this question, and why?

**3. Tribal connections to land.** Kronk Warner observes that "many indigenous cultures ... are tied to the environment in a manner that traditionally differs from that of the dominant society." She specifically notes unique connections to land for purposes of sustenance, family identities, and cultural and spiritual practices. For one colorful illustration of this "unique tribal connection to the land," law professor Jeanette Wolfley, an enrolled member of the Shoshone-Bannock Tribes and their legal counsel, offered this anecdote:

> In the summer of 2008, the Yellowstone National Park (YNP) cultural anthropologist contacted me to request information about the cultural significance of certain sites in the YNP. She asked if some Shoshone and Bannock elders would be willing to make a trip to YNP and visit certain sites and advise the park officials about the areas. About twenty elders from Fort Hall and I took several trips to meet with the YNP officials.
>
> Several events during the trips remain with me. First, the NPS's recognition that the Shoshone and Bannock were original inhabitants of YNP, and the desire of the park officials to seek tribal ecological knowledge, place names, and wisdom about cultural areas. Second, the recitation of the official YNP policy declaration to the elders advising them that the park's resources were federal property and were not to be removed, disturbed, or impacted in any manner.[2] Third, many elders' telling me that they had never been to the YNP as they were told they were prohibited. Fourth, the beginning of a collaborative and cooperative relationship with park officials that remains today.
>
> [Footnote 2]: This declaration [of federal property] fell on deaf ears who either did not hear the declaration, did not understand the detailed English rules, or preferred an elder's interpretation who told the others in the Shoshone language that the park was Shoshone and Bannock lands, and they were welcome to gather what they wished on the trip. The third version was preferred by all, and when the bus stopped at the first park site and the elders pulled out their gathering bags, the cultural anthropologist was horrified. And so, the YNP and tribal relations began.

Jeanette Wolfley, *Reclaiming a Presence in Ancestral Lands: The Return of Native Peoples to the National Parks*, 56 NAT. RESOURCES J. 55, 56 (2016).

Where indigenous people maintain "unique connections" to certain lands, what does the EJ principle of "fair treatment" require? Would fair treatment in the above anecdote sustain a flat ban on all gathering at Yellowstone National Park? Or would fair treatment recognize the historical ties of the Shoshone-Bannock people to the land now designated as Yellowstone National Park and allow for limited gathering by certain individuals? If limited gathering should be allowed, how might such a system be administered?

Besides matters of sustenance, how might other unique connections to land be served by applications of federal environmental law? As we have seen already in Chapter 5 ("Standard Setting"), the federal Clean Water Act can be used to set standards for surface water to protect uses including cultural or religious practices by an Indian tribe. *See City of Albuquerque v. Browner*, 97 F.3d 415 (10th Cir. 1996) (upholding EPA's approval of water quality standards established by the Isleta Pueblo to protect "religious or traditional" uses of water flowing in the Rio Grande through the Isleta

Pueblo Indian Reservation). Likewise, the federal Comprehensive Environmental Response, Compensation, and Liability Act (CERCLA) may be used to clean up contaminated sites for designated tribal uses. For example, at the Midnite Mine on the Spokane Indian Reservation of eastern Washington, the EPA selected a remedy of more than $150 million to address uranium contamination and protect future uses defined by the Spokane Tribe to include "recreational and cultural activities, such as hunting, fishing, plant gathering, and youth education." EPA, Midnite Mine Superfund Site, Record of Decision (Sept. 2006) at 2–36, 2–95. More recently, the EPA has embraced the use of CERCLA authorities to support tribal treaty rights and other unique considerations for cleanup in the tribal context. *See*, EPA, Consideration of Tribal Treaty Rights and Traditional Ecological Knowledge in the Superfund Remedial Program (Jan. 17, 2017) (recognizing that "the tribal lifestyle may result in different risks, such as higher fish consumption rates due to subsistence fishing" and that "a portion of a site may be a sacred/ceremonial area or an area of cultural sensitivity that warrants consideration in remedy selection/implementation").

In addition to CERCLA and the Clean Water Act, how might other environmental laws support the "unique connections" between certain tribes and lands? Could the Clean Air Act, for example, be used to compel stronger protections for viewsheds in sacred landscapes? On the flip side, could tribal industries demand special relief from federal land disposal requirements?

**4. International law.** Beyond the consideration of domestic laws such as CERCLA and the Clean Water Act, Kronk Warner suggests that some "principles of international law" may be "helpful when discussing indigenous rights from an environmental justice perspective." Principles of international law may derive from "hard law" such as treaties and customary international law as well as "soft law" such as nonbinding rules and declarations. One source of hard law cited by Kronk Warner is the American Convention on Human Rights, a treaty ratified by most nations in the Western Hemisphere, but not including Canada and the United States. The 2007 UN Declaration on the Rights of Indigenous Peoples (UNDRIP) is an example of "soft law" that is not, of itself, intended to bind nation-states. Over time, soft law may develop into hard law through administrative practice, judicial decisions, and other future developments. For a comprehensive review of related principles of international law, *see* Edith Brown Weiss, et al., INTERNATIONAL LAW FOR THE ENVIRONMENT 146 (2016).

Principles of international law, as Kronk Warner suggests, may be helpful to identify certain norms and expectations for conduct between sovereign entities, such as between the United States and the United Kingdom, or between the Navajo Nation and the United States. Violations of these norms may be discussed and addressed through formal and informal mechanisms where parties are committed to acting in good faith. Where such commitment is lacking, however, principles of international law may be difficult to enforce. In 2011, for example, Navajo tribal members ("Diné") filed a petition with the Inter-American Commission on Human Rights (IACHR), a body charged with investigating alleged violations of human rights by parties of the Organization of American States (OAS). In the petition, the Diné petitioners alleged that the United States had violated their rights under the 1948 American Declaration of the Rights and Duties of Man by subjecting the Diné to continued exposure to radioactive contamination from uranium mining and processing. *See* Petition, Eastern Navajo Diné Against Uranium Mining, et al. v. United States of America, Inter-American Commission on Human Rights, Organization of American States (2011). In response to this petition, the IACHR issued no findings, rulings, or recommendations for eight years (and counting), and in 2019 proposed to close out the case due to its own inactivity.

Nevertheless, since the adoption of UNDRIP in 2007, advocates for indigenous rights have increasingly sought to address their concerns through international mechanisms. In the protests against the Dakota Access Pipeline, for example, the Chairman of the Standing Rock Sioux Tribe traveled to Geneva, Switzerland, to testify before the UN Human Rights Council on September 20, 2016. Nine days later, the Human Rights Council directed the Special Rapporteur on the rights of indigenous peoples to extend her charge "To examine ways and means of overcoming existing obstacles to the full and effective protection of the rights of indigenous peoples...." UN Human Rights Council, Resolution 33/12: *Human rights and indigenous peoples; mandate of the Special Rapporteur on the rights of indigenous peoples* (Sept. 29, 2016).

Responding to this charge, in early 2017, the UN Special Rapporteur engaged in a fact-finding mission to the United States, with the purpose "to assess the impacts of energy development projects ... on Indian tribes living both within and outside of reservations." In this mission, which included visits with Indian tribes in Arizona and New Mexico, "Special attention was paid to the Dakota Access Pipeline and its impact on indigenous peoples, including the Standing Rock Sioux tribe and other tribes indirectly affected by the pipeline." In her final report, the Special Rapporteur identified many concerns regarding the federal government's approval of energy development projects in the West, the Dakota Access Pipeline in particular. She also made a number of related recommendations. Among these, the Special Rapporteur emphasized that "Consent, not consultation, should be the policy to allow for the government-to-government relationship necessary to fulfill the principles set forth in [UNDRIP]." Even so, the Special Rapporteur recognized that the Dakota Access Pipeline had already become operational by the time of her report, leaving her office little option but to "continue to monitor the situation...." UN Human Rights Council, *Report of the Special Rapporteur on the rights of indigenous peoples on her mission to the United States of America* (Aug. 9, 2017).

## C. Tribes as Resource Managers

Indian tribes own approximately 56.6 million acres of land in the lower forty-eight states. Some of these lands are rich in hard rock minerals, timber, oil, natural gas, wildlife, and other natural resources. For instance, according to one report, underlying Indian reservations is approximately half of all uranium deposits, one-third of all western low-sulfur coal, and twenty percent of all known oil and natural gas reserves in the United States. Mary Christina Wood, *Indian Land and the Promise of Native Sovereignty: The Trust Doctrine Revisited*, 1994 UTAH L. REV. 1471, 1481 (1994). The following excerpt considers the issues raised by tribes' status as governments with management authority over tribal lands and resources recognized by the federal policy of tribal "self-determination" that emerged in the 1970s.

### Rebecca Tsosie, *Tribal Environmental Policy in an Era of Self-Determination: The Role of Ethics, Economics and Traditional Ecological Knowledge*

21 VERMONT LAW REVIEW 225 (1996)

As Indian nations assume greater responsibility for managing tribal lands under the rubrics of tribal sovereignty and the federal self-determination policy, they are able to exercise more autonomy over environmental decision-making. That decision-making process, however, raises significant legal issues, ethical conflicts, and economic considerations.... [T]ribal environmental policy must be responsive to the interacting forces of traditional ecological knowledge, western science, economics, and tribal systems of ethics....

*Tribal Environmental Authority in the Era of Self-Determination*

... In 1970, President Richard Nixon called for a new federal policy of self-determination for American Indians. The self-determination policy represented a welcome change from the previous federal policy of "termination," which sought to abolish the federal trusteeship over Indian tribes, dismantle the reservations, and end the Indian tribes' unique status as "domestic, dependent nations." The self-determination policy, intended to "strengthen the Indian's sense of autonomy without threatening his sense of community," encouraged tribes to assume control over many of the federal programs being administered on the reservation....

The federal policy of self-determination has also encouraged tribes to consolidate their land bases and exercise control over their natural resources, thereby reversing earlier federal policies that placed control over land and resources with the Bureau of Indian Affairs, often to the clear detriment of the tribes. These newer policies are significant because natural resource development has long been a predominant means of economic development on many reservations. In particular, the extractive industries, such as coal, uranium, oil, and gas, have played a major role in reservation economic development. Along with their fiscal contributions, however, the extractive industries have brought mining, milling, and smelting operations to Indian lands, causing pollution of reservation lands, waters, and air passages....

Environmental conditions on the reservation are therefore subject to a dual legal structure of federal and tribal law, providing added complexity to the notion of "environmental self-determination." Although tribal values and norms regarding environmental use should serve as the basis for tribal environmental policy under the principle of "self-determination," tribal policy is in fact heavily impacted by the values and norms of Anglo-American society, embodied in federal environmental law and policy....

*The Role of Indigenous Land Ethics in Guiding Tribal Environmental Law and Policy*

The diversity among American Indian people makes defining an "indigenous land ethic" somewhat difficult. Nevertheless, the similarities among indigenous world views regarding the environment cannot be discounted....

*Traditional Indigenous Environmental Ethics: Finding the Common Ground*

"[I]ndigenous" people ... generally refers to the "original inhabitants of traditional lands" who maintain their traditional values, culture, and way of life. Those collective values and ways of life are encompassed within the notion of "traditional ecological knowledge," which is "the culturally and spiritually based way in which indigenous peoples relate to their ecosystems." Thus, the concept of traditional ecological knowledge comprises both indigenous systems of environmental ethics and the group's scientific knowledge about environmental use that has resulted from generations of interaction.... Many of these principles, such as the concept of caring for the land for the benefit of future generations, have parallels among other Native American peoples throughout Canada and the United States. The similarities among American Indian environmental perspectives may stem from the fact that virtually all traditional Indian cultures had "land-based" rather than "industrial" or "market" economies.... A central feature of many indigenous world views is found in the spiritual relationship that Native American peoples appear to have with the environment....

Professor Ronald Trosper has drawn on several tribal traditions to construct a model of "traditional Indian world views" premised on four basic principles: "community," "connectedness," "the seventh generation," and "humility." ... Trosper's model of traditional world views, as affirmed by other scholarship, has several important aspects: a perception of the earth as an animate being; a belief that humans are in a kinship system with other living things; a perception of the land as essential to the identity of the people; and a concept of reciprocity and balance that extends to relationships among humans, including future generations, and between humans and the natural world.

*The Role of Indigenous Ethics in Guiding Tribal Environmental Policy*

The influence of traditional ethics and environmental knowledge on contemporary tribal policy cannot be underestimated. Indeed, there are many examples of successful implementation of traditional ethics in contemporary tribal environmental management. However, there are also many examples of tribal policy built on what appear to be Anglo-American norms, particularly in the case of industries such as mining and waste disposal, which also serve non-Indian interests....

*Incorporation of Traditional Values into Environmental Policy*

Notably, there are several examples of indigenous communities successfully applying traditional norms and values to community development projects. For example, the Zuni Pueblo instituted a comprehensive agricultural project that restores community control over food production and implements traditional methods consistent with the Zuni's unique environment such as "field rooting" and "dry farming." Jim Enote, the director of the Zuni Conservation Project, describes the goals of the project as being based on traditional Zuni knowledge: "Reaching a modern vision of Zuni sustainability requires developing full partnerships with the Zuni people and promoting the status of Zuni values, traditional knowledge, and resource management practices." ...

The Confederated Salish and Kootenai Tribes of the Flathead Reservation in Montana have developed a comprehensive environmental regulatory and land use management scheme that rests heavily on traditional values. For example, the Salish and Kootenai Natural Resources Department developed the "Mission Mountains Tribal Wilderness Management Plan" ("Wilderness Plan") to prescribe how the Tribe will manage natural resources and human uses within the Wilderness. In the Plan's statement of policy, the Tribal Council acknowledges that:

> Wilderness has played a paramount role in shaping the character of the people and the culture of the Salish and Kootenai Tribes; it is the essence of traditional Indian religion and has served the Indian people of these Tribes as a place to hunt, as a place to gather medicinal herbs and roots, as a vision-seeking ground, as a sanctuary, and in countless other ways for thousands of years.

An important part of the Wilderness Plan is the preservation of cultural and historical resources. The Flathead Culture Committee was given a critical role in determining specific policies and actions to govern specific sites. In some cases this has resulted in barring public access to certain ceremonial and religious sites. The Flathead Culture Committee explains the importance of the Mission Mountains:

> Our elders have many stories to tell about experiences in the mountains in hunting, berry picking and about Indian people seeking their powers in the mountains. They have become for us, the descendants of Indians, sacred grounds. Grounds that should not be disturbed or marred. We realize the importance of these mountains to our elders, to ourselves, and for the perpetuation of our Indian culture because of these stories. They are lands where our people walked and lived. Lands and landmarks carved through the minds of our ancestors through Coyote stories and actual experiences. Lands, landmarks, trees, mountain tops, crevices that we should look up to with respect.

A central purpose of the Wilderness Plan is to preserve the wilderness for future generations. As one tribal Committee noted: "These mountains belong to our children, and when our children grow old they will belong to their children. In this way and for this reason these mountains are sacred." The mountains are thus preserved for future generations out of a "reverence for the land, its community of life, and what it means to the Indian culture more than out of a need to enjoy the benefits of direct use." Other documents developed by the Confederated Tribes to regulate environmental and land use on the reservation similarly speak to preservation of the tribal homeland and to ensure that natural resources on the reservation "survive and inure to the benefit of future generations."

The Northern Cheyenne Tribe is [an] example of an Indian nation that has applied traditional norms both to overcome the detrimental impacts of previous federal policies and to set a more positive direction for future policies. The Northern Cheyenne Reservation sits over the Fort Union coal formation, which stretches from northern Colorado to Canada, and houses an estimated 5 billion tons of coal worth approximately $400 billion. A significant number of the Northern Cheyenne Tribe are committed to maintaining traditional values and have resisted efforts to strip-mine the vast coal reserves, even though tribal unemployment rates continue to hover at 50%. During the 1970s, the Bureau of Indian Affairs leased more than half of the Cheyenne Reservation in Montana for coal mining. The leases provided for minimal lease royalties (17 cents per ton) and had no environmental safeguards. The Northern Cheyenne Tribe formed a committee to study ways to void the leases. After the Tribe brought its first lawsuit, federal legislation canceling the leases was enacted in 1980. The Northern Cheyenne Tribe's resistance to coal mining provides a sharp contrast to the neighboring Crow Tribe, which is heavily engaged in coal mining and has opposed the Northern Cheyenne Tribe's attempts to secure enhanced protection for air quality.

The Northern Cheyenne Tribe was the first Indian nation to petition the EPA under regulations to the Clean Air Act to redesignate the reservation air quality as "Class I," a class reserved for near-pristine air quality. This was an important step in mitigating the air quality impacts of the two power plants directly north of the Reservation at Colstrip, Montana. The need for pristine air quality was a means of perpetuating the Northern Cheyenne commitment to the holistic preservation of the Cheyenne "environment, culture, and religion." ...

*Tribal Environmental Policy That Departs from Traditional Norms*

There are several categories of land use that appear to be inconsistent with the traditional environmental norms that we have explored, including coal strip-mining, uranium mining, and siting solid, hazardous, or nuclear waste repositories on tribal land. Both the mining industry and the waste industry carry the potential of severe environmental degradation and, as a result, would appear to be diametrically opposed to traditional indigenous land ethics. Yet both industries have found homes on some Indian reservations. Why?

[T]o a large extent, all Indian nations have been subjected to successive federal policies which encouraged the exploitation of mineral resources on Indian lands. In the late nineteenth century and early twentieth century, Indian treaty lands were often removed from Indian ownership and trust status to facilitate mineral exploitation. For example, the Crow Reservation once encompassed 39 million acres, including vast stores of coal, oil, and natural gas. After several land cessions, the Crow Reservation now encompasses only 2.2 million acres, although the Tribe has reserved mineral rights in certain of the ceded lands. Other lands remained in tribal ownership but were leased out for mineral development by BIA officials convinced, as was Commissioner of Indian Affairs Cato Sells, that it is "an economic and social crime ... to permit thousands of acres of fertile land belonging to the Indians and capable of great industrial development to lie in unproductive idleness." ...

[M]any tribal members continue to protest mining operations on reservation lands, contending that such industry dries up precious water supplies, pollutes water, and endangers the health of people and livestock. The mining companies, however, point to the economic benefits they have offered to tribal communities, including increased funding for education. Given these competing claims, tribal decisions on mining policy are not clearly "right" or "wrong." Nor can tribal governments be faulted for trying to maximize the gain from on-going resource development by renegotiating lease agreements. In many cases, after nearly a century of mineral exploitation, there was no realistic opportunity to go back to a pristine natural world that would enable a traditional land based economy to flourish. The traditional land bases had been badly eroded, open mines and mineral tailings were located throughout many reservations, and many tribal members were dependent upon jobs with the local mines....

The "Not in My Backyard" movement among urban environmentalists and concerned citizens and increasingly stringent state environmental regulations have promoted the recent trend of waste disposal companies to approach tribal governments. The quasi-sovereign trust status of Indian lands has long exempted them from many types of state regulation, and the remote locations of many reservations appeal to the waste industry....

[N]ot all tribes agree that the waste business imperils Indian lands and communities. The Salt River Pima-Maricopa Community in Arizona has opened a second phase of its solid-waste landfill, established in the early 1980s. The Campo Band in California is proceeding with its landfill project after a heated battle with local non-Indians who opposed the project. Interestingly, by 1993, all members of the Campo Band supported the waste project and its only opposition has been from non-Indian residents of the adjacent community. Why was the sentiment at Campo different from Dilkon, Rosebud, or the Los Coyotes Reservation, also located in Southern California, where tribal members finally rescinded the Tribal Council's approval of a waste facility?

Poverty is obviously a factor in Campo's decision, but it is a factor that Campo shares with the tribes that have defeated such proposals. In 1987, when Campo first started considering the landfill proposal, the tribal unemployment rate was 79%, and more than half of those who were employed earned less than $7,000 per year. Another factor in Campo's decision was that the Tribe's relatively small, remote, and arid reservation offered no other realistic opportunities for economic development. In the late 1800s, the Tribe was removed from its arable traditional lands to an area that one BIA official at the time described as "so nearly worthless that a living by farming is out of the question." ...

[Another factor,] tribal sovereignty, raises different issues: that is, whether opposition by non-Indians is seen as an attack on the tribe's ability to engage in self-determination as a sovereign government. In the Campo case, non-Indian activists pressured state legislators to introduce legislation that would extend state regulation to waste facilities on Indian land, constituting a blatant attempt to intrude on tribal sovereignty. [Daniel] McGovern, [a former EPA official who has written about the Campo project], suggests that if tribal members perceive a threat to their sovereignty, they tend to unite against the off-reservation forces, even if that means supporting a decision that may be contrary to certain traditional norms about appropriate land use. Thus, the value of maintaining tribal sovereignty may prevail over the value of protecting the integrity of the land. In fact, the Campo landfill represents some risk of permanent groundwater contamination, and thus, potential loss of the ability to even live on the reservation. However, the risk to sovereignty appears to have been perceived as the more immediate threat....

### Concluding Thoughts

... Tribal governments who depart from traditional norms to engage in nontraditional economic development are responding to a complex history and set of realities. As the above cases demonstrate, these departures may be caused by a lengthy history of competing values imposed by federal policy, by values formulated as a protective response to ensure the continuation of tribal sovereignty, by values stemming from economic dependency on earlier development decisions, and by the cultural loss that has become endemic to many reservations as a result of loss of traditional lands, resources, and a certain measure of sovereignty....

\* \* \*

## Notes and Questions

1. **Indigenous land ethic.** Professor Rebecca Tsosie recognizes that the diversity among American Indian peoples makes any definition of an "indigenous land ethic" difficult. Even so, she cites the work of Professor Trosper and others to identify a number of common indigenous values toward land and natural resources. After reviewing these common values, consider how each may apply to the cases noted below concerning tribal management of natural resources.

2. *Nance v. U.S. EPA.* In some instances, tribes may appear on the opposite sides of environmental issues and litigation. In a case referenced by Professor Tsosie, federal courts upheld EPA's approval of the Northern Cheyenne Tribe's redesignation of its reservation from Class II to Class I (pristine) air quality standards, over the objections from the neighboring Crow Tribe, whose "primary concern ... was clearly the potential impact of such a redesignation on their ability to mine coal...." *Nance v. U.S. EPA*, 645 F.2d 701, 711 (9th Cir. 1981), *cert. denied sub nom Crow Tribe of Indians v. U.S. Environmental Protection Agency*, 454 U.S. 1081 (1981). How should the EJ dimensions of distributive justice and procedural justice apply in the case of an environmental dispute between tribes? Are there more appropriate procedural mechanisms than federal court? Years after the *Nance* case concluded, the Northern Cheyenne's Class I redesignation resulted in substantial impacts to off-reservation industry. As Professor Grijalva reported:

EPA forced the Montana Power Company to redesign its proposed coal-fired energy facility in Colstrip, Montana, in order to protect air quality on the

Northern Cheyenne reservation thirteen miles away. And the Crow Tribe, whose own reservation was immediately upwind of the Northern Cheyenne reservation, abandoned plans for a similar facility when feasibility studies predicted a nearly $300 million pollution control cost increase attributable to the Northern Cheyenne redesignation.

Grijalva, *supra*, at 22. Is this the right result for purposes of environmental protection? For indigenous rights? What common elements of "indigenous land ethics" would be supported (or aggrieved) by the outcome of this case?

**3. Campo landfill proposal.** In another case referenced in the excerpt by Professor Tsosie, the Campo Kumeyaay Nation (formerly Campo Band of Mission Indians) sought to authorize construction of a commercial solid waste landfill on its reservation lands near San Diego, California, just north of the border with Mexico. As Professor Tsosie notes, Campo tribal members broadly supported the landfill proposal as one potential avenue for economic development. Other commenters, however, viewed the landfill proposal as an example of environmental injustice, with commercial developers attempting to take advantage of a tribe's economic desperation. Local, non-Indian activists succeeded in legal challenges to the landfill proposal, attacking EPA's authority to treat the Campo tribe as a state for purposes of solid waste regulation. *See Backcountry Against Dumps v. U.S. EPA*, 100 F.3d 147 (D.C. Cir. 1996).

After the D.C. Circuit decision in 1996, the Campo tribe continued pursuing the landfill proposal for the next two decades, with the cooperation of federal agencies including the EPA and the Bureau of Indian Affairs (BIA). In February 2010, the BIA issued a Draft Supplementary Environmental Impact Statement for the landfill proposal. 75 Fed. Reg. 8986 (Feb. 26, 2010). However, later that same year, the Campo tribe finally voted to abandon the landfill proposal, and the Campo landfill was never built. In the meantime, the Campo Kumeyaay Nation opened a new casino in 2001 and a 50-megawatt wind farm in 2005. Planned expansions of the wind farm could triple the existing wind power generation, increasing revenues to the tribe and contributing to greenhouse gas reductions in San Diego County. Is this a "win" for environmental justice, which found its start in opposing waste disposal sites in poor, rural, and minority communities? Is it a win for tribal sovereignty? On a practical level, what is the likely consequence for the lack of an approved site for waste disposal on the reservation? The pervasive problem of open dumping on Indian reservations will be touched upon in the next section of this chapter.

**4. National Bison Range Management.** For generations, tribes have acted as managers of natural resources, including fish and wildlife, in accordance with their particular systems of law and custom. *See, e.g.*, William Rodgers, et al., THE SI'LAILO WAY: INDIANS, SALMON, AND LAW ON THE COLUMBIA RIVER (2006) (detailing the extensive history of Indian management respecting salmon in the Columbia River Basin). Recent efforts have included extensive habitat restoration and wildlife management on the Flathead Indian Reservation in western Montana by the Confederated Salish and Kootenai Tribes (CSKT), mentioned by Professor Tsosie in the excerpt above. Under auspices of the Tribal Self-Governance Act, 25 U.S.C. §§ 458aa, the CSKT have managed their own conservation areas and also petitioned to assume management of the National Basin Range, a 19,000-acre national wildlife refuge in the heart of the Flathead Reservation. Bison on the Range today descended from wild bison saved from extinction by tribal members at the turn of the century. For background on the CSKT quest to manage the National Bison Range, *see* Brian Upton, *Returning to a Tribal Self-Governance Partnership at the National Bison Range Complex: Historical, Legal, and Global Perspectives*, 35 PUB. LAND & RESOURCES L. REV. 51 (2014). The CSKT proposal was supported by the Obama administration in 2016 but rejected by the Trump administration in 2017. With your understanding of indigenous land ethics and traditional ecological knowledge, as suggested by Professor Tsosie, what arguments could you make for or against future management of the National Bison Range by the CSKT?

**5. The Culverts Case.** Many tribes maintain rights to natural resources by treaties with the U.S. Government. These include the treaties negotiated in 1854–1855 by Territorial Governor Isaac Stevens with tribes of the Pacific Northwest. Under the **Stevens Treaties**, many Northwest tribes retained rights to gathering (e.g., of food, fuel, and medicine) on "open and unclaimed lands" and rights to fishing "at all usual and accustomed grounds...." *See Washington v. Washington State Comm'l Passenger Fishing Vessel Ass'n*, 443 U.S. 658 (1979). In the famous *Boldt* decision, U.S. District Court Judge George Boldt determined that the Stevens treaty language reserving the tribal rights to take fish "in common with" white settlers meant that treaty tribes could "shar[e] equally the opportunity to take fish." *United States v. Washington*, 384 F. Supp. 312, 338 (1974), *aff'd*, 520 F.2d 676 (9th Cir. 1975).

The litigation ultimately confirmed a tribal right to 50 percent of the fish harvest, both on and off-reservations. At the same time, the tribes also pursued a right to protection of fish habitats. In 1980, the district court agreed, finding that "[t]he fundamental prerequisite to exercising the right to take fish is the existence of fish to be taken." *United States v. Washington*, 506 F. Supp. 187 (W.D. Wash. 1980), *vacated*, 759 F.2d 1353 (9th Cir. 1985). In 2001, litigation was filed against the State of Washington for the protection of fish habitat in what has come to be known as the Culverts Case. In 2007, the U.S. district court in the Culverts Case found that highway culverts constructed and maintained by the State of Washington obstructed fish migration in violation of the tribal treaty rights to fish. *United States v. Washington*, 2007 WL 2437166 (W.D. Wash. 2007). In 2017, the Ninth Circuit Court of Appeals affirmed, 827 F.3d 836 (9th Cir. 2016), and in 2018, the U.S. Supreme Court affirmed 4–4 by a divided court. *Washington v. United States*, 138 S.Ct. 1832 (2018). For a thorough review of the history, holdings, and theoretical underpinnings in the Culverts Case, *see* Royster, et al., NATIVE AMERICAN NATURAL RESOURCES 649–662 (4th ed. 2018).

Following the Culverts Case, the U.S. Supreme Court has continued to demonstrate strong support for enforcing tribal treaty rights. *See, e.g., Wyoming v. Herrera*, 139 S.Ct. 1686 (2019) (Crow Tribe's 1868 federal treaty right to hunt on "unoccupied

**Figure 9-1:** Road sign along NM 550, Navajo Nation. Photo: Cliff Villa.

lands of the United States" continued beyond Wyoming statehood in 1890); and *Washington State Dept. of Licensing v. Cougar Den, Inc.*, 139 S.Ct. 1000 (2019) (Washington State fuel tax preempted by right-to-travel provision of 1855 treaty with Yakama Nation). Particularly encouraging, for advocates of tribal treaty rights and the federal trust responsibility, is the separate concurrence in *Cougar Den* by Justice Gorsuch (joined by Justice Ginsburg), concluding with the extraordinary summation, "[T]oday and to its credit, the Court holds the parties to the terms of their deal. It is the least we can do." *Id.* at 1016.

As demonstrated by the 2019 decisions of the U.S. Supreme Court, reinforcing principles from cases such as the *Boldt* decision and the Culverts Case, assertion of treaty rights can provide advocates with powerful authority for protecting natural resources in Indian country. Can the same powerful authority for protecting fish, for example, also help to protect *people*—the traditional focus of environmental justice? How might you frame such arguments? Is the traditional EJ focus on people still appropriate when considering the values associated with *indigenous* people? What does the road sign depicted in Figure 9-1 suggest?

## D. Tribes as Environmental Regulators

Beyond management of land, wildlife, and other natural resources in Indian country, there is the question of who will regulate concerns such as air emissions, water pollution, and contaminated sites in Indian country. As we have seen, the major federal pollution control laws in the United States, such as the Clean Air Act and the Clean Water Act, primarily adopt the model of **cooperative federalism**, under which the federal government (largely, the U.S. EPA) sets national standards for other governments (largely, states) to implement. When Congress passed the original versions of the pollution control laws (e.g., the Clean Air Act in 1970 and the Clean Water Act in 1972), Congress supported state roles in environmental regulation, but for the most part failed to consider the proper role of tribes in the same.

Initially, states may have simply assumed that they had jurisdiction to regulate all environmental matters within their state lines, to include tribal lands within their borders. After this assumption was rejected by courts, *see Washington Dept. of Ecology v. EPA*, 752 F.2d 1465 (9th Cir. 1985), many states and tribes entered cooperative arrangements to ensure environmental protection across respective lands and resources. However, it also became clear that some major pollution concerns fell within regulatory gaps, to be filled either by the tribes themselves or by the U.S. EPA. In the Pacific Northwest, for example, the absence of air quality regulations established by individual tribes compelled the EPA in 2005 to promulgate the Federal Air Rules for Indian Reservations ("the FARR"). The FARR established air quality rules applicable to 39 Indian reservations across Oregon, Washington, and Idaho, setting some of the first reservation standards for public health and welfare concerns such as agricultural burning, particulate matter, and visibility. For general background on the FARR and links to specific regulations, *see* www.epa.gov/farr. The FARR is directly enforceable by the EPA; however, tribal employees may receive (and have received) credentials to carry out FARR inspections on their reservations. *See generally*, U.S. EPA, *Guidance for Issuing Federal EPA Inspector Credentials to Authorize Employees of State/Tribal Governments to Conduct Inspections on Behalf of EPA*, Sept. 30, 2004. For a thorough and timely examination of the challenges for regulating air pollution on Indian reservations, *see* Arnold Reitze, Jr., *The Control of Air Pollution on Indian Reservations*, 46 ENVTL. L. 893 (2017).

As for environmental regulation by tribes themselves, tribal authority in Indian country generally stems from two sources. "First, Indian tribes possess inherent powers to govern their territories. Although those powers may be limited by federal law in certain respects, tribes nonetheless retain substantial authority over matters affecting tribal health and welfare." Cohen, *supra*, at 784. Within this realm, tribes may enact tribal environmental codes and provide for enforcement through tribal agency proceedings and in tribal court. "Second, Indian tribes may exercise powers authorized by Congress. In the environmental context, Congress has authorized tribes to assume primary regulatory authority, or primacy, for administering most federal environmental programs in Indian country." *Id.* at 784–785. Congress established this authority through a series of statutory amendments by which tribes, upon application to EPA, may seek and obtain status for "treatment in the same manner as a state" (TAS).

Typical TAS provisions are illustrated in the following example from Section 301(d) of the Clean Air Act:

(1) [T]he [EPA] — (1) is authorized to treat Indian tribes as States under this chapter....

(2) ... Such treatment shall be authorized only if—

(A) the Indian tribe has a governing body carrying out substantial governmental duties and powers;

(B) the functions to be exercised by the Indian tribe pertain to the management and protection of air resources within the exterior boundaries of the reservation or other areas within the tribe's jurisdiction; and

(C) the Indian tribe is reasonably expected to be capable, in the judgment of the Administrator, of carrying out the functions to be exercised in a manner consistent with the terms and purposes of this chapter....

42 U.S.C. § 7601(d). Boiling down the requirements above, tribes generally must establish in their TAS application that they (1) are federally recognized; (2) have legal authority for implementing the desired program (e.g., with appropriate regulatory codes); and (3) are logistically capable of carrying out the desired program (e.g., with inspection resources).

Beyond the Clean Air Act, for TAS provisions in other statutes, see the following—

- Clean Water Act: Sec. 518(e), 33 U.S.C. § 1377(e)

- Safe Drinking Water Act: Sec. 1451, 42 U.S.C. § 300j-11

- Comprehensive Environmental Response, Compensation, and Liability Act (CERCLA): Sec. 126(a), 42 U.S.C. § 9626(a)

- Federal Insecticide, Fungicide, and Rodenticide Act (FIFRA): Sec. 23, 7 U.S.C. § 136u

Curiously, Congress never included TAS amendments in either the Resource Conservation and Recovery Act (RCRA), regulating the treatment, storage, and disposal of hazardous wastes; nor the Toxic Substances Control Act (TSCA), addressing the safe management of toxic substances. For those concerns, tribes may need to rely upon either direct enforcement by the EPA or exercise of their "inherent powers to govern their territories." Cohen, *supra*, at 784.

As tribes have built capacity for implementing environmental programs over time, the question has arisen how tribes will ensure environmental justice for tribal members and others subject to the tribe's environmental authority. As we have already seen in this chapter, tribes may bring different perspectives to the EJ principles of "fair treatment" and "meaningful involvement," for example. To the extent that a tribe's perspective differs from EPA definitions and expectations, could that difference endanger a tribe's TAS application or program implementation? On the other hand, could there be consequences if a tribe deliberately conforms its views to established criteria? Professor Darren Ranco points to a crucial paradox facing tribes as they contemplate seeking TAS status: "the more closely a tribal program resembles a federal or state program, the more likely it is to survive litigation; but the more a tribe tries to build a program that reflects its own cultural values, the greater the risk to its own tribal sovereignty...." Darren Ranco, *Models of Tribal Environmental Regulation: In Pursuit of a Culturally Relevant Form of Tribal Sovereignty*, 56 FED. LAWYER 46 (2009).

Confronting this paradox, Professor Jeanette Wolfley searches for and suggests resolutions in the excerpt that follows.

## Jeanette Wolfley, *Tribal Environmental Programs: Providing Meaningful Involvement and Fair Treatment*
### 29 J. ENVTL. L. & LITIGATION 389 (2014)

Over the past two decades, Indian tribes throughout the United States have begun to develop and implement tribal environmental programs based on their inherent sovereignty and amendments in federal environmental laws. Tribal governments are directly responsible and accountable for the health and welfare of their people and reservation residents and are in the best position to meet their people's needs and community interests. Accordingly, tribes are in the process of defining their tribal authority by planning and developing the basic frameworks and institutions for protecting air quality, preserving water quality, and managing contamination and hazardous and solid waste pollution caused by industrial society. Regulating polluting activities and other threats to lands, waters, and vital cultural resources is imperative for tribes to continue their way of life and maintain a homeland in which present and future generations of the tribe may flourish.

As tribes begin administering their environmental programs, including establishing boards, commissions, and drafting codes and regulations, they must weigh carefully the concepts of public participation, meaningful involvement, and due process in decision-making affecting Indian and non-Indian reservation citizens, industry, and state interests. As discussed in this article, many tribal programs have assumed these obligations and have promulgated rules, regulations, and policies; established standards; issued or denied permits for proposed activities with full public participation and due process; and taken compliance and enforcement actions against violators of environmental laws.

This Article proposes that there must be an understanding of, or reference to, the tribal values of due process within the tribal culture and context. And a tribal institution—through rulemaking or review by a tribal administrative agency, dispute resolution board, or tribal court—must be given the opportunity to articulate the cultural and social norms of due process. It is through the tribal process that tribes can best preserve, strengthen, and incorporate native concepts of equity and justice, and build communication, cooperation, and support within the tribal community. This represents tribal sovereignty in action. Indeed, due process, if premised on the native way of life, may well introduce the "genius of tribally held values" to a majority society....

### Policies Supporting Meaningful Involvement and Fair Treatment

At the time a tribe assumes authorization to develop and implement a federal environmental program, the tribal environmental program should simultaneously seek ways to provide for due process and public participation. In addition to federal requirements for public participation and due process, there are sound policy reasons that support these principles. This Section presents three policy reasons supporting the establishment of participation and due process procedures including: (1) promoting good governance, (2) respecting the interests of community members, and (3) protecting and promoting tribal sovereignty. These are presented to articulate to tribal governments the importance of, and legal requirements for, providing meaningful involvement and fair treatment when developing and implementing federal environmental programs.

## A. Providing Good Governance

... Governments have a broad set of responsibilities including protecting the health and safety of its citizens or members, improving the community's quality of life through education, planning, property protection, and securing a viable economic future. With this wide range of responsibilities, governments are frequently tasked with balancing competing interests, particularly in the environmental area. Governments often mediate conflicts between those concerned with protecting the environment and those seeking to ensure long-term economic stability through development and use of natural resources, or between individual landowner interests and the interests of the greater community.

To be credible, government officials must demonstrate transparency and accountability in their decision-making. This "[t]ransparency minimizes the opportunity for preferential treatment and the advancement of private interests over public good." Transparency means that information should be provided in easily understandable forms and media. It should be freely available and directly accessible to those who will be affected by governance laws, regulations, and policies and procedures, as well as the outcomes resulting therefrom. "Consolidating and then openly sharing processes and procedures assures citizens that decisions are made fairly." This includes any decisions made and any enforcement taken in compliance with established rules and regulations. A government is accountable to those who will be affected by its decisions or actions as well as the laws and regulations created.

The fundamental exercise of sovereignty by a government includes not only power but also the responsibility to establish a governmental infrastructure and institutions that provide for sound decision-making. These institutions create avenues for the public and local community to participate in policymaking and establish mechanisms for consultation with the community. It also requires the implementation of the laws and regulations in a manner that recognizes the interest of its citizenry and in the case of tribal governments, tribal members and nonmembers residing on the reservation. Good governance requires the set of laws governing the actions of individuals be maintained through an impartial and effective legal system. Good governance also informs the community, educates its citizens, builds public trust, and seeks to improve both the citizens' and community's quality of life. Responsive government also includes the capacity to comprehend and respond to the individual community member's needs and priorities and to mediate conflicts with the community through an established process.

Providing opportunities for public participation can strengthen tribal government and sovereignty, improving the tribes' relations with the rest of the community and with off-reservation communities. Participation by the local community and the public is a key cornerstone of good governance. Participation needs to be informed and organized. Support from the community, by recognizing the legitimacy of tribal institutions, increases a tribe's ability to exercise its sovereignty and authority and will likely result in less interference from external parties. In turn, a tribe is better able to protect and preserve its resources, land base and homeland.

Of course, it should be clear that good governance is an ideal that is difficult to achieve in its totality. But still, these ideals are viewed as legitimate and if governments seek to attain such goals their actions will be perceived as fair and just. Fairness, in turn, is equated with procedural regularity, adequate opportunity to be heard, and nondiscriminatory treatment.

## B. Respecting the Interests of Community Members

Tribal environmental program decisions affect the entire social, cultural, and spiritual beliefs as well as the political fabric of a community because such decisions impact communal rights to live on, use, harvest, conserve, and transfer lands within the reservation, and the land, itself, as community. Accordingly, tribal members have a legitimate stake in the decisions affecting the environment and land base in which they hold a communal interest. Indeed, on many reservations individual tribal members own a majority of the land base as a result of the allotment era. Moreover, communal ownership and kinship places certain duties and responsibilities on some tribal members with respect to the land resources, and all the living beings of the environment.

Tribal leaders, in addressing the myriad of important issues pertaining to running a government, must also be cognizant of the traditional values of respect, reciprocity, humility, and connectedness as they relate to land and tribal members. Often, certain individuals, traditional and religious tribal leaders, advocate the critical importance of cultural integrities to preserve the beauty and stability of the community, to protect the health and welfare of the residents, and to plan for future generations. These voices, comments, and opinions serve an important role in the tribal institutional setting.

Tribal leadership often calls upon federal agencies to recognize tribal interests and to consult with them on federal decisions based upon the trust obligations owed to the tribes. Similarly, tribal members expect and request their tribal leadership to recognize, as many tribal leaders do, the responsibilities they have to the membership, such as informing the membership of proposed tribal government actions and enabling the membership to voice an opinion in support or in opposition to governmental decision-making impacting their rights, natural resources, welfare, and daily lives. Moreover, promotion of local tribal participation is crucial to the credibility and sustainability of reforms in policy, laws and regulations, and the establishment of environmental programs. Community members do not always expect to get everything they want, but they do expect to be heard, taken seriously, and informed of tribal council decisions and processes. Indeed, the impetus for establishing tribal environmental programs is to clean up contamination, confront ecological degradation, improve the overall quality of life for tribal community members, and preserve the treaty-reserved homelands.

Moreover, tribal decision-making seeks to reflect the history, experience, culture, and wishes of the unique people and community it serves. Tribal members share culture, customs, traditions, kinships, and history with the tribal leaders that are elected or appointed as part of the established tribal government. Governance structures and issues differ from reservation to reservation; therefore, the solutions to governance matters must be tailored individually. Traditionally, tribal decisions were not taken lightly in Indian societies but were carefully deliberated, sometimes for days or weeks, by kinship-clan groups, elders, spiritual leaders, and tribal leaders. The groups varied from tribe to tribe. Building consensus and gaining community support were priorities before tribal leadership took action. Today, as part of this deliberative process, tribal environmental institutions should seek out comments and opinions of elders, culture committees, individuals impacted, and the community as a whole.

The federal policies of assimilation and allotment have been abandoned, but their legacy remains. One feature of this legacy on many reservations is a large population of nonmember landowners, who are members of other tribes or are non-Indian. Also, non-tribally-owned businesses and industry have existed on some reservations for many years prior to tribes establishing environmental programs. Tribal governments face the challenge of how to accommodate the interests and rights of nonmembers, while still exercising tribal self-government. It is however vitally important to involve the private sector and the general public in governance initiatives....

## C. Protecting and Promoting Tribal Sovereignty

Tribal sovereign autonomy and self-government, a principled foundation for Indian law, has weathered over 150 years of U.S. jurisprudence, and indeed, insulating tribes against the passage of time is a consistent theme in the law. Additionally, tribal separatism remains both a focal point for modern Indian policy and for tribes themselves. A priority implicit in tribal separatism is maintaining a homeland in which both present and future generations of the tribe may live. A viable tribal land base is the linchpin to other attributes of sovereignty. The tribal territory forms the geographical limits of the tribe's jurisdiction, supports a residing population, is the basis of the tribal economy, and provides an irreplaceable place for cultural traditions often premised on the sacredness of land. Through control over Indian lands and resources, Indian nations maintain a degree of economic self-sufficiency necessary to Indian self-determination. Justice Black once observed the attachment that tribal people have to their established homelands as follows:

> It may be hard for us to understand why these Indians cling so tenaciously to their lands and traditional tribal way of life. The record does not leave the impression that the lands of their reservation are the most fertile, the landscape the most beautiful or their homes the most splendid specimens of architecture. But this is their home — their ancestral home. There, they, their

children, and their forebears were born. They, too, have their memories and
their loves. Some things are worth more than money and the costs of a new
enterprise.

Land and natural-cultural resources will always occupy an important place in Indian
cultures. Accordingly, tribes have a vital stake in resource and environmental management to preserve their homelands and their sovereignty.

Similarly, tribes should be aware of public perceptions about the role of tribal government in providing fundamental fairness to all residents of the reservation. To
many non-Indians, the reservation remains a foreign place and the governmental
structure is a mystery. While territorial jurisdiction is a vital aspect of self-government,
policy makers have noted, "[i]n most cases, non-Indians vigorously reject any type
of regulation by the tribe." Some states voice concerns about law and order and the
efficiency of government, and view tribal regulation as unduly lax in comparison to
their own programs. There are also questions about the ability of tribal governments
to guarantee due process and fairness. Many of these criticisms are based upon a lack
of knowledge and understanding of the structures of tribal governments, anecdotal
evidence, unwillingness to recognize tribal institutions, and outright prejudice.
Whether they are unfounded or not, the public and community perception of tribal
institutions and their environmental programs should be recognized by tribal governments. Tribes should work to address these misconceptions.

Some of these same concerns were leveled at tribal courts in a 1978 report, developed by the National American Indian Court Judges Association that assessed the
strengths and weaknesses of tribal courts. The Judges Association describes serious
problems with political interference, inadequate tribal laws, and a tendency toward
summary judgment when defense counsel was absent. However, the Association also
found many strengths in the tribal court system including quick access to a fair forum,
the ability to bridge the gap between law and Indian culture, and a dedicated judiciary
with increased respect from federal courts, agencies, and tribal governments. The
recommendations included professional training for judges, enhanced funding for
facilities and equipment, and insulation of tribal courts from political pressures.
Since 1978, Congress has provided substantial appropriations directly to tribal courts
to address their infrastructure building needs, training for staff with federal courts,
and law and order code drafting. This assistance has greatly improved the administration of justice throughout Indian country. Moreover, some commentators have
found that tribal courts are "no less protective—and much more accessible—than
federal courts have been in protecting civil rights on Indian reservations."

... Institutional support needs to come from both the Indian and non-Indian
communities as well as the regulated industry. Non-Indian companies that pursue
mineral or other natural resource development affecting the tribal environment are
accustomed to deriving some regulatory certainty from written laws and regulations.
The establishment of advisory committees or boards can also lend support to a fair
and meaningful system. Dialogue among the tribes and industry can foster mutual
understanding of the need to define and make known specific environmental concerns.

Importantly, these forms of public involvement enable the tribes to obtain sound input and receive information that can assist the tribe in its thoughtful deliberations and decision-making. A structured, open process can instill a careful weighing of concerns and issues by tribal program officers, council members, and community members. This approach is similar to existing traditional tribal processes.

Some tribes have already instituted these types of measures to defray the disapproval of, and challenges to, tribal authority, and should allay the concerns of EPA and state interests. Tribes define for their community what due process means based upon their traditions and how due process should be implemented to meet the needs of their community, protect their lands and people, and ultimately protect their sovereignty....

[A] critical point to remember is that environmental justice issues affecting Tribes must always be viewed against the backdrop of tribal sovereignty, the federal trust responsibility owed by the United States to Tribes, and the government-to-government relationship treaty rights. Unlike other environmental justice communities, tribes are self-governing regulators and tribes define and ensure environmental justice within their own communities.

\* \* \*

## Notes and Questions

1. **The "paradox."** In the excerpt above, how does Professor Wolfley respond to the paradox identified by Professor Ranco? Can tribal governments implement environmental programs on their lands while harmonizing the interests of both tribal sovereignty and environmental justice? What steps does Professor Wolfley suggest to resolve potential conflicts?

2. **Defining EJ principles for tribes.** Professor Wolfley continues in the article to suggest a number of available authorities—beyond EPA criteria—which tribes may consult for articulating their own understanding of principles such as fair treatment and meaningful involvement. These available sources include oral traditions, tribal constitutions and codes, the Indian Civil Rights Act, federal environmental statutes, federal common law, and principles of administrative law. What advantages might each of these authorities offer as tribes seek to define environmental justice terms for themselves?

3. **TAS today.** Despite the concerns noted above, tribal governments have invested substantial time and effort to obtain TAS approvals. The process for obtaining TAS approval can be onerous. For one tribal perspective on this process, *see* Jill Elise Grant, *The Navajo Nation EPA's Experience with "Treatment as a State" and Primacy*, 21 NAT. RES. & ENVT. 9 (2007). Recent reforms by the EPA may bring some relief from TAS application requirements. *See, e.g.*, 81 Fed. Reg. 30,183 (May 16, 2016) (eliminating certain application requirements for obtaining TAS for water quality standards). Additional reforms may certainly be anticipated.

Surmounting the onerous process, many tribes have celebrated success in obtaining and defending TAS approvals. For the Isleta Pueblo, to take one early example, the decision in *Albuquerque v. Browner*, 97 F.2d 415 (10th Cir. 1996) [excerpted in Chapter 5 ("Standard Setting")] did not just uphold a water quality standard approved by the EPA; it affirmed the Pueblo's right to determine the uses of its own water resources as the Rio Grande flowed through the reservation. For Professor Grijalva, the bottom-line on TAS appears to be this:

> We might hope the time comes when the preservation of American indigenous culture needs no federal agency, court or legislative body. Until that day, tribal primacy for federal environmental programs may well be the most effective means for addressing environmental injustice in Indian country because it can be conducted in a culturally relevant manner, as defined by the culture itself.

Grijalva, *supra*, at 200.

In agreement with Professor Grijalva's pragmatic conclusion, tribes today remain actively seeking TAS approvals from the EPA. As of October 2019, 62 tribes had obtained TAS approval for setting their own water quality standards. These included the Quinault Tribe in the State of Washington, which obtained TAS approval on September 20, 2018. As of May 2019, more than a dozen tribes had obtained TAS to implement at least some part of the Clean Air Act. These included the Pueblo of Santa Ana in New Mexico, which obtained TAS approval on May 14, 2019.

**4. Open dumps.** As noted above, Congress never managed to amend the Resource Conservation and Recovery Act (RCRA) to add TAS provisions authorizing tribes to assume primacy for programs in hazardous waste treatment, storage, and disposal. Partly as a result of this congressional failure, partly a consequence of poverty on many Indian reservations, and partly due to the opportunities presented by large, rural landscapes, illegal dumping has been a pervasive problem in Indian country. In 1994, Congress acknowledged the problem with the Indian Lands Open Dump Cleanup Act, 25 U.S.C. §§ 3901–3908, which noted the existence of "at least 600 open dumps on Indian and Alaska Native lands...." To address this problem, Congress directed the Indian Health Service (IHS) to conduct studies and inventories of open dumps on reservations lands and to provide tribal governments with "financial and technical assistance ... to close such dumps ..." 25 U.S.C. § 3904. For early background on the problem of illegal dumping on tribal lands and the Indian Lands Open Dump Cleanup Act, *see* Dean Suagee, *Turtle's War Party: An Indian Allegory on Environmental Justice*, 9 J. ENVTL. L. & LITIGATION 461, 473–479 (1994).

In the inventory completed under the Act in 1998, the IHS identified substantially more open dumps on Indian lands than the congressional estimate in 1994. As of 2016, the inventory contained more than 4,600 open dumps on Indian lands, with "actions ... reported at 1,300 of these sites to either close, clean-up, or upgrade the site to bring it into compliance with EPA's municipal solid waste disposal standards." EPA and IHS, *Proposed Approach to Improve Open Dumps Data and Solid Waste Projects and Programs in Indian Country* (May 2016) at 2–3. According to this latest estimate, at least 3,300 open dumps thus remain in need of attention on Indian lands.

In 2017, the IHS and the EPA entered into an agreement to coordinate agency efforts in this area. *See* Memorandum of Understanding Between the Dept. of Health and Human Services and U.S. EPA to Improve Open Dump Data, Solid Waste Projects and Programs in Indian Country (Jan. 16, 2017). Under the MOU, the agencies agreed to provide training, technical assistance, and financial assistance to tribal governments in order to continue efforts to assess and close illegal dumps on tribal lands.

In addition to these collaborative agency efforts under the Indian Lands Open Dump Cleanup Act, could open dumps on Indian lands be addressed more directly through other environmental laws such as RCRA and CERCLA? Look closely at the jurisdictional triggers of RCRA Sec. 7003(a), 42 U.S.C. § 6973(a), and of CERCLA Section 104(a), 42 U.S.C. § 9604(a). Do you see authority here for dealing with junk cars, used motor oil, old paint cans, household trash, or even human waste? Hint: consider the RCRA definition of "solid waste" and CERCLA definitions of "hazardous substances" and "pollutant or contaminant." If RCRA and CERCLA may apply to these wastes, what authorities and resources may each statute bring to bear to address the problem of open dumps on Indian lands?

5. **EJ and indigenous peoples.** As a final question for this chapter, consider all the suggestions provided in the excerpt from Professor Wolfley for how tribal governments may satisfy the aims of environmental justice, as the tribes themselves may define. Then consider what may happen when a tribe is unable to achieve such aims. A principle of cooperative federalism provides that where a state fails to protect its people by, say, failing to enforce drinking water standards in Flint, Michigan, then the federal government retains the authority and obligation to step in and assure such protection. Does the same principle authorize and obligate the federal government to protect tribal members or other residents of an Indian reservation?

For many advocates of indigenous rights, this question may prove difficult to resolve, potentially creating tensions between tribal sovereignty and the federal trust responsibility. It also raises concerns about the EPA's commitment to environmental justice and the overarching agency mission to protect the public health and environment. To address this difficult question, in October 2011, the EPA Office of International and Tribal Affairs asked the National Environmental Justice Advisory Council (NEJAC) "to provide advice and recommendations about how the Agency can most effectively address the environmental justice issues in Indian country ... and those facing indigenous peoples both on and off reservations." NEJAC, *Recommendations for Fostering Environmental Justice for Tribes and Indigenous Peoples* (Jan. 15, 2013). In response to this charge, the NEJAC formed an Indigenous Peoples Work Group with diverse backgrounds and expertise to conduct research and analysis. In a final report back to the EPA in January 2013, the NEJAC provided 24 specific recommendations. NEJAC, *supra*, at 10–16. Among these recommendations, the NEJAC advised the EPA to "seek input and the meaningful involvement and engagement of tribal and indigenous communities, state-recognized tribes, and other indigenous stakeholders in the Agency's decision-making processes...." *Id*. at 11. In implementing this recommendation, the EPA should seek input from tribal elders, youth, college students, and tribal members who work off the reservation "in addition to tribal government representatives." In other words, the EPA's role in ensuring environmental justice on tribal lands should not be limited to government-to-government consultation with tribal officials. In simplest terms, the NEJAC advised, "EPA needs to consult with tribal governments and [also] meaningfully engage the tribal members and tribal community." *Id.*

Embracing many of the NEJAC's recommendations, the EPA Administrator in the following year issued a new policy, *EPA Policy on Environmental Justice for Working with Federally Recognized Tribes and Indigenous Peoples* (July 24, 2014). The new policy "affirm[ed] EPA's commitment to provide to federally recognized tribes and indigenous peoples in all areas of the United States and its territories and possessions ... fair treatment and meaningful involvement in EPA decisions that may affect their health or environment." *Id.* at 1. The new policy established 17 principles for carrying out this EPA commitment in Indian country. Under the broad theme of "Promoting Environmental Justice Principles in EPA Direct Implementation of Programs, Policies, and Activities," the policy established principles to include the following:

The EPA consults with federally recognized tribes and provides meaningful involvement opportunities for indigenous peoples throughout the United States, and others living in Indian country....

- The EPA seeks to be responsive to the environmental justice concerns of federally recognized tribes, indigenous peoples throughout the United States, and others living in Indian country....

- The EPA uses legal authorities, as appropriate, to advance environmental justice goals in its work throughout the United States, including in Indian country....

**6. Hypothetical: The Kickapee Dump Site.** Given the principles above, consider this scenario. On Monday morning, the EPA receives notice of a 13-year-old boy hospitalized for acute mercury poisoning. State health officials believe the boy was exposed to mercury he found in a glass jar in an illegal dump near his home on the Kickapee Nation in eastern Oklahoma. The Kickapee Nation is a federally recognized tribe and the open dump where the mercury was found has been on an inventory maintained by the Indian Health Service (IHS) since 1998. Although the open dump has been on the IHS inventory for more than two decades, nothing has been done in any way to close the dump site or restrict access to it. The property containing the open dump is within the Kickapee reservation but owned in fee by the family of one of the members of the tribal council. When the mercury poisoning is brought to the attention of the tribal council on Tuesday morning, the tribal council puts the matter on the agenda for their next meeting in four weeks. Meanwhile, news of the mercury incident spreads through the community and attracts the attention of other youth on the reservation. On Thursday afternoon, two young people from the reservation are treated for acid burns from an old car battery they found in the same dump site.

You are an attorney for the EPA Region 6 office in Dallas, Texas, which has jurisdiction over matters in Oklahoma. You are aware that the EPA emergency response program has the funding, technical capacity, and legal authority under CERCLA for addressing the dump. Depending on the size of the dump, it is possible that EPA contractors could excavate and remove the entire dump over the weekend, thus preventing any further incidents from this particular site. How do you advise your EPA management to proceed?

# Chapter 10

# Governmental Initiatives to Promote Environmental Justice

## A. Introduction

In addition to considering environmental justice when environmental agencies perform core governmental functions such as standard setting, enforcement, and cleanup, governmental agencies at all levels have attempted to address environmental inequities through a wide range of broader initiatives. This chapter examines how environmental justice issues have been addressed at different levels of governance, including international, federal, state, and tribal. A few states, notably California and New York, have enacted more robust and specific environmental justice legislation. This chapter also examines those efforts and other state initiatives. Moreover, because environmental justice is a crosscutting issue, some agencies have elected to address disparities through broad-based collaboration among public and private actors in many fields and at different levels of governance. This chapter concludes by discussing the progress of this strategy and some of the interagency and collaborative initiatives that have been undertaken to date.

## B. Environmental Justice at the International Level

The United Nations has increasingly recognized the connection between environmental protection and human rights. In 2011, the UN Guiding Principles for Business and Human Rights (commonly called the Ruggie Principles) recognized that some of the worst human rights abuses occur amid conflict over the control of territory (often involving extractive industries) and called on states to protect and businesses to respect human rights in all their activities. These principles built on, and expanded, the UN Declaration on the Rights of Indigenous Peoples, which emphasized the rights of indigenous peoples to their lands and territories (Art. 26), and required that states obtain free prior and informed consent before making development plans in indigenous territories (Art. 19) or storing hazardous materials on indigenous lands (Art. 29).

In 2015, the United Nations Human Rights Council appointed Professor John Knox as the first Special Rapporteur for Human Rights and the Environment. Due to his work, there is now a significant body of information about the contours of a human right to a healthy environment. Much of this work underscored the connection between environmental justice and the human right to a healthy environment. Indeed, the Framework Principle 3 on Human Rights and the Environment emphasized that "[s]tates should prohibit discrimination and ensure equal and effective protection against discrimination in relation to the enjoyment of a safe, clean, healthy and sustainable environment." In Spring 2019, the second Special Rapporteur for Human Rights and the Environment, Prof. David Boyd, released a report on the right to breathe clean air as a human right. This report emphasized that air pollution disproportionately harmed poor people and poor communities and focused on intersectionality between poverty and discrimination. In 2019, UN the Human Rights Council adopted a resolution expressing alarm at the violence directed against environmental defenders, and, stressing the intersectional nature of violations and abuses against them, recognized the need to pay particular attention to women human rights defenders, as well as "indigenous peoples, children, persons belonging to minorities and rural and marginalized communities."

The UN Environment Programme similarly adopted an Environmental Defenders policy that defined environmental defenders as "anyone (including groups of people and women human rights defenders) who is defending environmental rights, including constitutional rights to a clean and healthy environment, when the exercise of those rights is being threatened." The Defenders policy establishes a Rapid Response Mechanism, which allows vulnerable environmental defenders to contact UN Environment confidentially in order to request legal and political assistance.

# C. Federal Initiatives

In the United States, as early as 1971, the White House Council on Environmental Quality issued an annual report acknowledging that racial discrimination adversely affects the urban poor and the quality of their environment. However, it was not until the early 1990s that a concerted effort was undertaken to address this and other disparities in environmental protection. In 1992, the U.S. EPA released the first governmental report comprehensively examining environmental justice. Shortly thereafter, the EPA established what later became the Office of Environmental Justice and convened a 25-member National Environmental Justice Advisory Council (NEJAC) to the EPA. In 1994, the first formal policy directive was issued by the White House subjecting all agencies to the following executive order.

# 1. The Executive Order on Environmental Justice

## Executive Order 12898:
## Federal Actions to Address Environmental Justice in Minority Populations and Low-Income Populations
### February 11, 1994

*Section 1-1. Implementation.*

1-101. Agency Responsibilities. To the greatest extent practicable and permitted by law..., each Federal agency shall make achieving environmental justice part of its mission by identifying and addressing, as appropriate, disproportionately high and adverse human health or environmental effects of its programs, policies, and activities on minority populations and low-income populations in the United States and its territories and possessions, the District of Columbia, the Commonwealth of Puerto Rico, and the Commonwealth of the Mariana Islands.

1-102. Creation of an Interagency Working Group on Environmental Justice.

(a) Within 3 months of the date of this order, the Administrator of the Environmental Protection Agency ("Administrator") or the Administrator's designee shall convene an interagency Federal Working Group on Environmental Justice ("Working Group"). The Working Group shall comprise the heads of the following executive agencies and offices, or their designees: (a) Department of Defense; (b) Department of Health and Human Services; (c) Department of Housing and Urban Development; (d) Department of Labor; (e) Department of Agriculture; (f) Department of Transportation; (g) Department of Justice; (h) Department of the Interior; (i) Department of Commerce; (j) Department of Energy; (k) Environmental Protection Agency; (l) Office of Management and Budget; (m) Office of Science and Technology Policy; (n) Office of the Deputy Assistant to the President for Environmental Policy; (o) Office of the Assistant to the President for Domestic Policy; (p) National Economic Council; (q) Council of Economic Advisers; and (r) such other Government officials as the President may designate. The Working Group shall report to the President through the Deputy Assistant to the President for Environmental Policy and the Assistant to the President for Domestic Policy....

1-103. Development of Agency Strategies.

(a) Except as provided in section 6-605 of this order, each Federal agency shall develop an agency-wide environmental justice strategy ... that identifies and addresses disproportionately high and adverse human health or environmental effects of its programs, policies, and activities on minority populations and low-income populations. The environmental justice strategy shall list programs, policies, planning and public participation processes, enforcement, and/or rulemakings related to human health or the environment that should be revised to, at a minimum:

(1) promote enforcement of all health and environmental statutes in areas with minority populations and low-income populations;

(2) ensure greater public participation;

(3) improve research and data collection relating to the health of and environment of minority populations and low-income populations; and

(4) identify differential patterns of consumption of natural resources among minority populations and low-income populations.... Federal agencies shall provide additional periodic reports to the Working Group as requested by the Working Group....

*Sec. 2-2. Federal Agency Responsibilities for Federal Programs.*

Each Federal agency shall conduct its programs, policies, and activities that substantially affect human health or the environment, in a manner that ensures that such programs, policies, and activities do not have the effect of excluding persons (including populations) from participation in, denying persons (including populations) the benefits of, or subjecting persons (including populations) to discrimination under, such programs, policies, and activities, because of their race, color, or national origin.

*Sec. 3-3. Research, Data Collection, and Analysis.*

... 3-302. Human Health and Environmental Data Collection and Analysis.... [E]ach Federal agency, whenever practicable and appropriate, shall collect, maintain, and analyze information assessing and comparing environmental and human health risks borne by populations identified by race, national origin, or income. To the extent practical and appropriate, Federal agencies shall use this information to determine whether their programs, policies, and activities have disproportionately high and adverse human health or environmental effects on minority populations and low-income populations; ...

*Sec. 4-4. Subsistence Consumption of Fish and Wildlife.*

4-401. Consumption Patterns. In order to assist in identifying the need for ensuring protection of populations with differential patterns of subsistence consumption of fish and wildlife, Federal agencies, whenever practicable and appropriate, shall collect, maintain, and analyze information on the consumption patterns of populations who principally rely on fish and/or wildlife for subsistence. Federal agencies shall communicate to the public the risks of those consumption patterns.

4-402. Guidance. Federal agencies, whenever practicable and appropriate, shall work in a coordinated manner to publish guidance reflecting the latest scientific information available concerning methods for evaluating the human health risks associated with the consumption of pollutant-bearing fish or wildlife. Agencies shall consider such guidance in developing their policies and rules.

*Sec. 5-5. Public Participation and Access to Information.*

... (b) Each Federal agency may, whenever practicable and appropriate, translate crucial public documents, notices, and hearings relating to human health or the environment for limited English speaking populations.

(c) Each Federal agency shall work to ensure that public documents, notices, and hearings relating to human health or the environment are concise, understandable, and readily accessible to the public....

*Sec. 6-6. General Provisions.*

6-601. Responsibility for Agency Implementation. The head of each Federal agency shall be responsible for ensuring compliance with this order. Each Federal agency shall conduct internal reviews and take such other steps as may be necessary to monitor compliance with this order....

6-606. Native American Programs. Each Federal agency responsibility set forth under this order shall apply equally to Native American programs. In addition, the Department of the Interior, in coordination with the Working Group, and, after consultation with tribal leaders, shall coordinate steps to be taken pursuant to this order that address Federally recognized Indian Tribes....

6-608. General. Federal agencies shall implement this order consistent with, and to the extent permitted by, existing law.

6-609. Judicial Review. This order is intended only to improve the internal management of the executive branch and is not intended to, nor does it create any right, benefit, or trust responsibility, substantive or procedural, enforceable at law or equity by a party against the United States, its agencies, its officers, or any person. This order shall not be construed to create any right to judicial review involving the compliance or noncompliance of the United States, its agencies, its officers, or any other person with this order.

* * *

## Notes and Questions

1. **Enforceability?** An important limitation of the Executive Order on Environmental Justice ("Executive Order") is section 6-609, an express provision stating that the executive order does not create any new rights enforceable at law or equity, a provision common to such executive orders. Of what practical value is the executive order given this limitation? In fact, the executive order has been cited by courts and administrative boards as authority for requiring agency action. *See, e.g., Standing Rock Sioux Tribe v. U.S. Army Corps of Engineers*, 255 F.Supp.3d 101, 136 (D.D.C. 2017); *In re* Shell Gulf of Mexico, Inc., 15 E.A.D. 103 (EAB 2010). How have courts found related agency duties despite the express provision that the Order does not create any new enforceable rights?

2. **President Clinton's memorandum.** A companion memorandum with the executive order noted that "[t]he purpose of this separate memorandum is to underscore certain provisions of existing law that can help ensure that all communities and persons across this Nation live in a safe and healthful environment." Memorandum on Environmental Justice, 30 WEEKLY COMP. PRES. DOC. 279 (Feb. 11, 1994). The memorandum explicitly referred to Title VI of the Civil Rights Act of 1964, and directed agencies to ensure that programs or activities receiving federal financial assistance "do not directly, or through contractual or other arrangements, use criteria, methods, or practices that discriminate on the basis of race, color or national origin." *Id.* As discussed in detail in Chapter 4, the Title VI initiative has had a torturous and,

some would argue, unfortunate history, but it may still be a viable tool to pursue environmental justice in limited circumstances. The memorandum also directed agencies to "analyze the environmental effects, including human health, economic and social effects, of Federal actions, including effects on minority communities and low-income communities, when such analysis is required by [the National Environmental Policy Act]." *Id.*

**3. How did the Clinton administration do?** A group of law professors surveyed the actions of federal agencies in responding to the Executive Order through 2000. The survey provided interesting insights into the ways agencies sought to accomplish the goals of the Order. Ultimately, the authors concluded:

> All of the federal agencies surveyed pay homage to EJ [environmental justice] to some extent. A few have made major institutional investments in promoting and achieving EJ. Clearly, substantial federal environmental resources are now directed at minority and low-income communities, especially in brownfield development and lead-based paint remediation efforts…. [On the other hand] [m]eaningful community participation in decisionmaking is still lacking in some agencies….
>
> … The agencies vary in how far they have progressed. Repackaging and identifying existing programs was the norm, with a trend towards undertaking discrete new projects. Integrating EJ into program design has been relatively rare, and comprehensive assessment and analysis exceedingly uncommon. Based upon the agency responses, there appears to be only a few instances in which agencies have incorporated EJ principles and protections into programmatic design…. While all agency actions that reduce disparities are admirable and constitute an advance, clearly full integration is the strategy most likely to result in significant, long-term progress….

Denis Binder, et al., *A Survey of Federal Agency Responses to President Clinton's Executive Order 12898 on Environmental Justice*, 31 ENVTL. L. REP. 11,133, 11,149–11,150 (2001). Other reports since have criticized, in particular, the adequacy of EPA's implementation of the executive order. *See* Nat'l Acad. of Pub. Admin., ENVIRONMENTAL JUSTICE IN EPA PERMITTING: REDUCING POLLUTION IN HIGH RISK COMMUNITIES IS INTEGRAL TO THE AGENCY'S MISSION (2001); U.S. Comm'n on Civil Rights, NOT IN MY BACKYARD: EXECUTIVE ORDER 12898 AND TITLE VI AS TOOLS FOR ACHIEVING ENVIRONMENTAL JUSTICE (2003) (reviewing programs of EPA, Department of Housing and Urban Development, Department of Transportation, and Department of Interior); U.S. Comm'n on Civil Rights, ENVIRONMENTAL JUSTICE: EXAMINING THE ENVIRONMENTAL PROTECTION AGENCY'S COMPLIANCE AND ENFORCEMENT OF TITLE VI AND EXECUTIVE ORDER 12898 (2016) (although the EPA took steps to incorporate procedural environmental justice obligations into its core missions, it had not incorporated environmental justice as a substantive right into its decision-making). For an in-depth discussion of the executive order compliance initiatives by several federal agencies, *see* Bradford C. Mank, *Executive Order 12898, in* THE LAW OF ENVIRONMENTAL

JUSTICE: THEORIES AND PROCEDURES TO ADDRESS DISPROPORTIONATE RISKS 101, 103 (Michael B. Gerrard & Sheila R. Foster eds., 2d ed. 2008).

**4. The George W. Bush administration** appeared to take a different approach to environmental justice. Most striking was the shift in focus by EPA. In 2001, EPA redefined its interpretation of environmental justice to mean environmental protection for everyone, and de-emphasized the need to focus special attention on minority and low-income populations, including these populations along with all others. *See* Memorandum on EPA's Commitment to Environmental Justice from Administrator Christine Todd Whitman to Assistant Administrators (Aug. 9, 2001). EPA's shift was sharply criticized in a 2004 report by the agency's Inspector General. The report noted that:

> [The EPA] indicated it is attempting to provide environmental justice for everyone. While providing adequate environmental justice to the entire population is commendable, doing so had already been EPA's mission prior to implementation of the Executive Order; we do not believe the intent of the Executive Order was simply to reiterate that mission. We believe the Executive Order was specifically issued to provide environmental justice to minority and/or low-income populations due to concerns that those populations had been disproportionately impacted by environmental risk.

Office of Inspector Gen., U.S. EPA, EVALUATION REPORT: EPA NEEDS TO CONSISTENTLY IMPLEMENT THE INTENT OF THE EXECUTIVE ORDER ON ENVIRONMENTAL JUSTICE, REP. NO. 2004-P-00007 at ii (2004).

## 2. Government Use of Race Classifications

The Bush administration's change in approach was likely influenced by a different philosophy of governance coupled with the evolving constitutional jurisprudence in the area of equal protection law, including the 2003 Supreme Court decision in *Grutter v. Bollinger*. This case involved an Equal Protection challenge to the use of race for admissions to the University of Michigan Law School for the purpose of promoting a diverse student body. Although the case was decided in a context different from environmental protection, in reading the following excerpt of the decision, consider how the case bears upon the actions of the EPA in devising a strategy to alleviate racial environmental disparities.

### Grutter v. Bollinger
### 539 U.S. 306 (2003)

… Enrolling a "critical mass" of minority students simply to assure some specified percentage of a particular group merely because of its race or ethnic origin would be patently unconstitutional.…

To be narrowly tailored, a race-conscious admissions program cannot "insulat[e] each category of applicants with certain desired qualifications from competition with all other applicants." Instead, it may consider race or ethnicity only as a " 'plus' in a particular applicant's file"; *i.e.*, it must be "flexible enough to consider all pertinent elements of diversity in light of the particular qualifications of each applicant ... and to place them on the same footing for consideration, although not necessarily according them the same weight." ... It follows that universities cannot establish quotas for members of certain racial or ethnic groups or put them on separate admissions tracks. The Law School's admissions program, like the Harvard plan approved by Justice Powell [in *Regents of the University of California v. Bakke*, 438 U.S. 265 (1978), Eds.], satisfies these requirements. Moreover, the program is flexible enough to ensure that each applicant is evaluated as an individual and not in a way that makes race or ethnicity the defining feature of the application. The Law School engages in a highly individualized, holistic review of each applicant's file, giving serious consideration to all the ways an applicant might contribute to a diverse educational environment. There is no policy, either *de jure* or *de facto*, of automatic acceptance or rejection based on any single "soft" variable....

... [T]estimony indicated that when a critical mass of underrepresented minority students is present, racial stereotypes lose their force because nonminority students learn there is no "minority viewpoint" but rather a variety of viewpoints among minority students....

[Justice Powell's] holding for the Court in *Bakke* was that a "State has a substantial interest that legitimately may be served by a properly devised admissions program involving the competitive consideration of race and ethnic origin." ... In [his] view, when governmental decisions "touch upon an individual's race or ethnic background, [such individual] is entitled to a judicial determination that the burden he is asked to bear on that basis is precisely tailored to serve a compelling governmental interest." Under this exacting standard, only one of the interests asserted by the university survived Justice Powell's scrutiny....

First, Justice Powell rejected an interest in " 'reducing the historic deficit of traditionally disfavored minorities in medical schools and in the medical profession' " as an unlawful interest in racial balancing. Second, Justice Powell rejected an interest in remedying societal discrimination because such measures would risk placing unnecessary burdens on innocent third parties "who bear no responsibility for whatever harm the beneficiaries of the special admissions program are thought to have suffered." Third, Justice Powell rejected an interest in "increasing the number of physicians who will practice in communities currently underserved," concluding that even if such an interest could be compelling in some circumstances the program under review was not "geared to promote that goal." Justice Powell approved the university's use of race to further only one interest: "the attainment of a diverse student body." ...

[N]othing less than the " 'nation's future depends upon leaders trained through wide exposure' to the ideas and mores of students as diverse as this Nation of many peoples." ...

Justice Powell was, however, careful to emphasize that in his view race "is only one element in a range of factors a university properly may consider in attaining the goal of a heterogeneous student body." ...

Context matters when reviewing race-based governmental action under the Equal Protection Clause.... In *Adarand Constructors, Inc. v. Peña*, we made clear that strict scrutiny must take "relevant differences into account." Indeed, as we explained, that is its "fundamental purpose." Not every decision influenced by race is equally objectionable, and strict scrutiny is designed to provide a framework for carefully examining the importance and the sincerity of the reasons advanced by the governmental decisionmaker for the use of race in that particular context....

[The] benefits [of a diverse student body] are substantial. As the District Court emphasized, the Law School's admissions policy promotes "cross-racial understanding," helps to break down racial stereotypes, and "enables [students] to better understand persons of different races." These benefits are "important and laudable," because "classroom discussion is livelier, more spirited, and simply more enlightening and interesting" when the students have "the greatest possible variety of backgrounds." ...

[S]tudies show that student body diversity promotes learning outcomes, and "better prepares students for an increasingly diverse workforce and society, and better prepares them as professionals." These benefits are not theoretical but real, as major American businesses have made clear that the skills needed in today's increasingly global marketplace can only be developed through exposure to widely diverse people, cultures, ideas, and viewpoints....

For this reason, the diffusion of knowledge and opportunity through public institutions of higher education must be accessible to all individuals regardless of race or ethnicity. The United States, as *amicus curiae*, affirms that "[e]nsuring that public institutions are open and available to all segments of American society, including people of all races and ethnicities, represents a paramount government objective." And, "[n]owhere is the importance of such openness more acute than in the context of higher education." ...

Properly understood, a "quota" is a program in which a certain fixed number or proportion of opportunities are "reserved exclusively for certain minority groups." ...

In contrast, "a permissible goal ... require[s] only a good-faith effort ... to come within a range demarcated by the goal itself," and permits consideration of race as a "plus" factor in any given case while still ensuring that each candidate "compete[s] with all other qualified applicants ..."

... The Law School does not, however, limit in any way the broad range of qualities and experiences that may be considered valuable contributions to student body diversity. To the contrary, the 1992 policy makes clear "[t]here are many possible bases for diversity admissions," and provides examples of admittees who have lived or traveled widely abroad, are fluent in several languages, have overcome personal adversity and family hardship, have exceptional records of extensive community service, and have had successful careers in other fields....

Narrow tailoring does not require exhaustion of every conceivable race-neutral alternative. Nor does it require a university to choose between maintaining a reputation for excellence or fulfilling a commitment to provide educational opportunities to members of all racial groups....

Narrow tailoring does, however, require serious, good faith consideration of workable race-neutral alternatives that will achieve the diversity the university seeks....

Accordingly, race-conscious admissions policies must be limited in time.... In the context of higher education, the durational requirement can be met by sunset provisions in race-conscious admissions policies and periodic reviews to determine whether racial preferences are still necessary to achieve student body diversity.

\* \* \*

## Notes and Questions

1. **The EPA's response.** In 2005, partially in response to the unfavorable Inspector General report noted above, the EPA released a new draft environmental justice framework and strategy for public comment. The framework listed twelve potential priorities: reducing asthma attacks; making fish/shellfish safe to eat; making drinking water safe; reducing exposure to waterborne pathogens; revitalizing brownfields and contaminated sites; reducing the incidence of childhood lead poisoning; reducing exposure to mercury; reducing exposure to pesticides; reducing exposure to air toxics; assuring compliance; increasing environmental health along the U.S. borders; and promoting healthy schools. The agency then requested that commenters rank these goals. *See* U.S. EPA, Working Draft of Environmental Justice Strategic Plan 3–4 (2005). EPA also reiterated its view that environmental justice means environmental protection for all, stating "[e]nvironmental justice is achieved when everyone, regardless of race, culture, or income, enjoys the same degree of protection from environmental and health hazards *and* equal access to the decision-making process to have a healthy environment in which to live, learn, and work." *Id.* at 2 (emphasis in original).

2. **Missing the mark?** The draft framework and strategy provoked a storm of criticism from environmental justice organizations, members of Congress, and others. Illustrative of some of the criticism are the following comments submitted to the EPA by community groups in the San Francisco area, who noted that:

> ... [T]he Plan ignores the mandate of [the] Executive Order, which, by its title, specifically requires "Federal Actions to Address Environmental Justice in Minority Populations and Low-Income Populations." ... [Moreover,] EPA is asking commenters to rank a list of twelve potential national environmental justice priorities on a scale of greatest to least importance. This ranking scheme creates an artificial and meaningless ordering of important priorities that are not comparable and fails to take into account the cumulative health and environmental effects experienced by minority and low-income populations that are frequently exposed to disproportionately high levels of mul-

tiple environmental hazards at the same time.... [N]either the Strategic Targets nor any of the twelve proposed national environmental justice priorities address the interests of minority and low-income populations as is required by Section 1-103 [of the Executive Order], and likewise, they do not address areas where EPA's policies and programming are lacking with respect to those populations. Instead, by definition, EPA's Environmental Justice Strategic Plan applies to "all people regardless of race, color, national origin, or income." The Plan by omission fails to identify and then target low-income or minority communities facing multiple hazards and thereby defeats any focus upon these communities.

Letter to U.S. EPA commenting on the 2005 Draft Environmental Justice Strategic Plan submitted by the Golden Gate University Environmental Law and Justice Clinic on behalf of Bayview Hunters Point Community Advocates, the Chinese Progressive Association, People Organizing to Demand Environmental and Economic Rights, and Our Children's Earth Foundation (July 15, 2005).

**3. EPA's rationale.** EPA explained in its response to comments on the draft strategy:

EPA's use of racial classifications as a basis for making decisions would raise significant legal issues. Several Supreme Court decisions, such as *Adarand Constructors, Inc. v. Pena,* 515 U.S. 200, 227 (1995), and *Grutter v. Bollinger,* 539 U.S. 306, 326 (2003), provide that, whenever a racial classification is used as a basis for any federal, state, or local government decision, courts must apply a strict scrutiny standard of review. To survive strict scrutiny, the government must demonstrate that it uses the racial classification to achieve a compelling governmental interest and that the use of the racial classification is narrowly tailored to serve that interest.

The compelling governmental interests for most EPA decisions are protecting human health and the environment and achieving the fair treatment and meaningful involvement of all people regardless of race, color, national origin, or income with respect to the development, implementation, and enforcement of environmental laws, regulations, and policies. To pass the narrow-tailoring test, the Agency would have to show that no race-neutral alternative is available to achieve those compelling interests. However, in general, EPA has race-neutral alternatives for achieving its compelling governmental interests.

U.S. EPA, DRAFT ENVIRONMENTAL JUSTICE STRATEGIC PLAN THEMATIC RESPONSE TO COMMENTS (2005). The 2005 Draft Environmental Justice Strategy was not finalized. Instead, the EPA in its more general EPA strategic plan (a 184-page document governing overall agency priorities), made several references to "environmental justice," albeit, as noted earlier, environmental justice was re-defined to include protection of all people. The agency noted that:

EPA is establishing measurable environmental justice commitments for eight national priorities: reducing asthma attacks, reducing exposure to air toxics, increasing compliance with regulations, reducing incidence of elevated blood lead levels, ensuring that fish and shellfish are safe to eat, ensuring that water is safe to drink, revitalizing brownfields and contaminated sites, and using collaborative problem-solving to address environmental and public health concerns. We will promote environmental justice in all aspects of our work by training staff; providing guidance, online tools, and other resources; sharing information about successful strategies; and enhancing staff skills in working with community-based organizations. We will continue to use dispute resolution, facilitation, listening sessions, and other consensus-building techniques and to convene stakeholders to address environmental and public health issues....

U.S. EPA, 2006–2011 EPA STRATEGIC PLAN: CHARTING OUR COURSE 94, 114 (2006). The plan also directed the EPA to identify strategies to ensure that resources reach "disproportionately exposed" communities. *Id.* at 83.

**4. Should race matter?** The issues raised in *Grutter v. Bollinger,* and the conflicting views of the EPA and the EPA's own Inspector General, mirror broader and continuing debates on the place of race in determining public policy in the United States. In a later case concerning race-conscious school placement, Chief Justice John Roberts declared, "The way to stop discrimination on the basis of race is to stop discriminating on the basis of race." *Parents Involved in Community Schools v. Seattle School District,* 51 U.S. 701, 748 (2007). Is this an example of pragmatic advice for a presumably post-racial society—or denial of the profound role that race and racism still play in American life? Consider the following rebuttal to Chief Justice Roberts from Associate Justice Sotomayor:

> My colleagues are of the view that we should leave race out of the picture entirely and let the voters sort it out. We have seen this reasoning before....
>
> Race matters. Race matters in part because of the long history of racial minorities' being denied access to the political process. And although we have made great strides, "voting discrimination still exists; no one doubts that."
>
> Race also matters because of persistent racial inequality in society—inequality that cannot be ignored and that has produced stark socioeconomic disparities....
>
> And race matters for reasons that really are only skin deep, that cannot be discussed any other way, and that cannot be wished away. Race matters to a young man's view of society when he spends his teenage years watching others tense up as he passes, no matter the neighborhood where he grew up. Race matters to a young woman's sense of self when she states her hometown, and then is pressed, "No, where are you *really* from?", regardless of how many generations her family has been in the country.... Race matters because of the slights, the snickers, the silent judgments that reinforce that most crippling of thoughts: "I do not belong here."

*Schuette v. Coalition to Defend Affirmative Action,* 572 U.S. 291, 380 (2014), Sotomayor, J., dissenting.

Assuming that racial disparities do in fact continue today, is it possible for a strategy that does not explicitly consider race to alleviate these disparities? Will attempts to improve measures related to environmental justice concerns for "all people regardless of race, color, national origin, or income" achieve parity? How is this different from the EPA's general mission to protect the environment? Alternatively, can the EPA use racial criteria to evaluate whether its general strategy is, in fact, alleviating racial disparities (even if not explicitly considered in the strategy itself)? Why might the use of race in the former context be problematic to the agency, but not in the latter? Would it be better to adopt a more conservative approach (and avoid litigation) or adopt a more aggressive approach and take the position that we need race-conscious strategies in order to alleviate racial disparities?

Since income is not a suspect classification, can (and should) the agency take targeted initiatives in low-income communities? Will that likely alleviate racial disparities as well?

## 3. Recent Federal Strategies for Environmental Justice

Professor Rachael Salcido suggests "this de-emphasis on racial minorities and low-income populations would defeat the entire premise of the need for environmental justice." Rachael E. Salcido, *Reviving the Environmental Justice Agenda*, 91 CHI.-KENT L. REV. 115, 138 (2016). "It would seem that President Barack Obama, as the first African-American president, would be uniquely able to focus the national government's attention on this lack of equal access to the fundamental necessities of a healthy life." *Id.* at 121.

**Rachael E. Salcido,**
*Reviving the Environmental Justice Agenda*
91 CHICAGO-KENT LAW REVIEW 115, 122–125 (2016)

... When candidate Barack Obama was on the campaign trail in 2008, he pledged to make environmental justice a priority. Existing laws have not successfully led to rights protections and minorities still endured the unequal burden of pollution.... While E.O. 12898 provided a sufficient framework for using existing laws to minimize environmental injustice, the executive took too little action to ensure that its requirements were being met....

*EJ Plan 2014 and EJ Plan 2020*

... Appointed as EPA administrator by President Obama, Lisa P. Jackson made environmental justice a priority. EPA developed a plan, finalized in 2011, entitled Plan EJ 2014, to serve as a "roadmap for integrating environmental justice (EJ) [concerns] into its programs, policies and activities." Here, it should be emphasized that President Obama beyond his own leadership and visibility on the issue ensured continued priority and leadership by his appointment of Administrator Jackson. The success of any initiative can be thwarted by lack of leadership; it should not be overlooked that among various choices the particular identification of Administrator Jackson ensured that the issue would receive adequate attention during her tenure.

Administrator Jackson stated that she was "committed to making environmental justice an essential part of our decision making." She noted that from the outset of her service she had been meeting with communities to listen to their concerns. EJ 2014 was a manifestation of the EPA's identification in its strategic plan for 2011–2015 to make expanding the conversation on environmentalism and working for environmental justice agency priorities.

Therefore, EJ 2014 was broad and inclusive, an approach that reflects the various ways EPA can further environmental justice objectives. The roadmap approach of EJ 2014 consisted of the development of nine implementation plans. The implementation plans contained "goals, strategies, activities, deliverables, and milestones." The three parts of EJ 2014 divided actions into 1) cross-agency focus areas, 2) tools development areas, and 3) program initiatives.

The cross-agency focus areas include actions EPA would take to incorporate EJ into rulemaking, consider EJ in permitting, and to use compliance and enforcement to advance EJ. Next, EPA would work to support community-based programs. The final area of cross-agency focus of the plan was to engage other federal agencies in implementing E.O. 12898 into their programs.

The tools development focus areas were equally important to the mission of advancing EJ. EPA committed to developing tools related to science, law and information to support EJ objectives. In terms of resources, the EJ plan identified the need for an improved system of delivering financial and technical assistance for communities engaged in EJ work....

Thus, with the production and implementation of EJ 2014, Administrator Jackson made clear that the agency would indeed be embarking on a "new era of outreach and protection for communities historically underrepresented in EPA decision-making." In February 2014, the EJ 2014 progress report identified areas where goals have been met and where further progress is required.... Moreover, as the 2004 [Inspector General's] report critically identified, EPA had not adequately defined the role of the Office of Environmental Justice (OEJ). But according to the progress report on EJ 2014, the OEJ was now situated to continue the work to implement EJ 2014 plan elements. The EPA expects OEJ to play a leading role in the long-term implementation of EJ tools, and work as the coordinator among various regions and national programs.

There is reason to be hopeful that current momentum will continue. EPA recently released its draft of a further roadmap toward achieving environmental justice through its programming EJ 2020. Seeking to build on the work it has done with EJ 2014 as a foundation, the new strategy has identified making a "visible difference" in communities a key priority.

EJ 2020: over the next five years, EPA will focus on

- Deepening environmental justice progress in EPA's programs to improve the health and environment of overburdened communities

- Collaborating with partners to expand our impact in overburdened communities

- Demonstrating progress on outcomes that matter to overburdened communities

\* \* \*

## Notes and Questions

**1. Success?** Professor Salcido highlights other actions to further environmental justice during the Obama administration. *Id.* at 122–129 (including data collection, grant programming and regulatory and enforcement actions). *See* Chapter 7 for a more detailed discussion of government enforcement actions. Professor Zokovitch Paben adds, "[m]ost of the Obama administration's environmental justice successes resulted from the implementation of Plan EJ 2014." Jeanne Zokovitch Paben, *Plan EJ 2014: Fact or Fiction: A Critique of the Obama Administration's Efforts on Environmental Justice*, 41 WM. & MARY ENVTL. L. & POL'Y REV. 1, 18 (2016). According to Professor Paben, the EPA's claimed accomplishments under the Plan include incorporating EJ into rulemaking; considering EJ in permitting; advancing EJ through compliance and enforcement; supporting community-based programs; fostering administration-wide action; developing science, legal, and information and resources tools; issuing EPA policy on EJ for working with federally recognized tribes and indigenous peoples; and providing mandatory trainings for all employees. She remarks:

> It is clear that EPA sees Plan EJ 2014 as a great success and, in fact, it has had significant success in integrating environmental justice considerations in the day-to-day work at EPA. It is also clear that some cross-agency progress on environmental justice was made. If the measurement of success is based on what the Clinton Executive Order set forth, then EPA largely accomplished that goal. Specifically, EPA identified both its major actions in which environmental justice issues are implicated as well as its major substantive programs where environmental justice considerations should be made.

*Id.* at 19. Consider how success might be measured for implementation of agency plans such as EPA's Plan EJ 2014 and the EJ 2020 Action Agenda. Does "success" look differently for agencies and community activists?

**2. What about Title VI?** Plan EJ 2014 specifically recognized Title VI of the Civil Rights Act and EPA's civil rights program as critical components in advancing environmental justice. Nevertheless, as Professor Paben observes:

> There is no mention of Title VI in the EPA Accomplishments Table....

> In 2015, EPA issued a third progress report under Plan EJ 2014 ... The Progress Report ... details three [settlements of important Title VI issues] ... Little of it actually documents the completion of significant tasks, and certainly not those on the level of the accomplishments documented for the other implementation plans in the EPA Accomplishments Table.

Zokovitch Paben, *supra* at 29. In public comments to the draft implementation framework for EJ 2020, a number of environmental and community groups highlighted the relationship between the EPA's environmental justice work and Title VI, and that the connection should be referenced and incorporated into the EJ 2020 action plan. The EPA declined to do so. U.S. EPA, Draft EJ 2020 Action Agenda Framework, EPA's Response to Public Comments, 16–17 (2015).

**3. Federal legislation?** Do we need new federal legislation to address concerns for environmental justice? Environmental justice attorney and scholar Jeremy Orr observes the importance of the codification of environmental justice protections by federal statute. Orr notes:

> There have certainly been various environmental justice bills introduced in both chambers of Congress over the past three decades, but none of them have ever made it out of committee and to the floor for a vote. The most notable of past environmental justice bills was the Environmental Justice Act of 1992, sponsored by civil rights activist and U.S. Representative John Lewis. It was the first federal bill directly aimed at eradicating racial inequalities in the application of environmental laws and policies.

Jeremy Orr, *Environmental Justice Act of 2017: A Fighting Chance for Frontline Communities*, 24 Hastings Envt'l L.J. 303 (2018).

U.S. Senator Cory Booker and Representative Raul Ruiz introduced the Environmental Justice Act of 2017. The latest iteration introduced by Congressional Democrats in 2020 would mandate consideration of the cumulative impacts of the Clean Air Act and the Clean Water Act with respect to permitting decision. In addition, the 2020 bill would establish a fund for fossil fuel companies to transition from greenhouse gas-dependent economies. Also, the bill would broaden rights for environmental justice communities and develop new federal grants and program authority to address environmental and public health concerns.

**4. Actions to limit federal initiatives.** Other administrations could mirror the Bush administration's efforts to weaken actions at the federal level. Nevertheless, significant "police power" remains at the state and local levels of government, which the following section examines.

# D. State Initiatives

States have responded in a variety of ways to the challenges raised by the environmental justice movement. While a handful of states have not taken any action and others have taken only modest steps, some have been fairly aggressive. California and New York, in particular, have taken steps warranting discussion.

# 1. California Initiatives

California has (with considerable sustained effort) enacted several environmental justice bills. California's primary statute, SB 115, requires the California Environmental Protection Agency (Cal/EPA) to follow principles that closely parallel the provisions of President Clinton's executive order. SB 115 was passed in 1999 after five other environmental justice bills were vetoed by former Governor Pete Wilson in the prior seven years. Under the bill, Cal/EPA is required to promote enforcement of health and environmental statutes and conduct its programs and policies "in a manner that ensures the fair treatment of people of all races, cultures, and income levels." It is also required to develop a model environmental justice mission statement for its constituent departments. *See* CAL. GOV'T CODE § 65040.12 (1999); CAL. PUB. RES. CODE §§ 72000–01 (1999). Subsequent legislation also requires Cal/EPA to ensure that environmental justice considerations are addressed in carrying out reviews by the agency under the California Environmental Quality Act (the state's version of NEPA), and to make recommendations for ensuring that public documents, notices, and hearings are understandable and accessible to the public, including translation for limited-English-speaking populations. *See* Ellen M. Peter, *Implementing Environmental Justice: The New Agenda for California State Agencies*, 31 GOLDEN GATE U. L. REV. 529 (2001). California's climate change legislation, AB 32 and subsequent policies, incorporate environmental justice considerations into regulations adopted to reduce greenhouse gas emissions, *see* Chapter 14 ("Climate Justice").

AB 32, also known as the Global Warming Solutions Act, spurred significant debate over its established cap-and-trade program, and arguably revealed a split in the environmental and environmental justice movements. The following article by policy expert and strategist on building an equitable green economy, Vien Truong, illustrates the investments in environmental justice, or "disadvantaged" communities, as a result of SB 535, a statute designed to further implement the Act.

## Vien Truong, *Addressing Poverty and Pollution: California's SB 535 Greenhouse Gas Reduction Fund*

49 HARVARD CIVIL RIGHTS-CIVIL LIBERTIES L. REV. 493, 515–526 (2014)

... Immediately after the passage of SB 535, the Greenlining Institute and others began organizing to ensure that the goals of SB 535 and AB 1532 would be realized and translated into jobs and investments in priority disadvantaged communities. Advocates formed the appropriately named "SB 535 Coalition," led by the Greenlining Institute, the Asian Pacific Environmental Network, the Coalition for Clean Air, and Public Advocates. The SB 535 Coalition created webinars to inform leaders across the country about the new laws and their potential impact, as well as the new investments they would bring to disadvantaged communities. The Coalition also created online surveys for community leaders about what investments would have the greatest effect in their communities. Respondents listed programs that they believed would reduce GHG emissions, as well as those that would create jobs, improve the quality of life in the community, and support local economies. The Coalition continued to inform the broad public about the new laws, the cap-and-trade program, and how they could participate....

*Allocating Funds to Disadvantaged Communities*

SB 535 requires that the cap-and-trade revenues be allocated so that 25% of funds benefit disadvantaged communities and 10% are invested inside the geographic boundaries of disadvantaged communities. The law directs CalEPA to identify the State's most disadvantaged communities for investment opportunities by looking at their geographic, socioeconomic, public health, and environmental-hazard problems. The statute gives CalEPA some criteria for identifying disadvantaged communities— such communities may be (1) areas disproportionately affected by pollution and other hazards that can lead to negative public health effects, exposure, or environmental degradation; or (2) areas with a concentration of people who are of low income and suffer from high unemployment rates, low levels of homeownership, high rent burden, or low levels of educational attainment.

CalEPA's Office of Environmental Health Hazards Assessment ("OEHHA") created a screening methodology to help identify the areas disproportionately harmed by environmental and socioeconomic burdens. This unprecedented tool allows the State to scientifically identify the disproportionate environmental harms, which contributes to a better understanding of the relationship between race/ethnicity and the pollution burdens facing communities in California. Under the direction of CalEPA, OEHHA conducted a series of regional public workshops to get input on a draft cumulative impacts screening tool. The screening tool, named "CalEnviroScreen," was released in 2012. The tool maps the environmental, health, demographic, and socio-economic data of various areas (currently by zip code, but future versions will use census tracts) to create a screening score for communities across the state. These maps show which areas of the state have the highest pollution burdens and vulnerabilities. CalEnviroScreen guides investments under SB 535 but also helps the State and other stakeholders identify areas that have the most need for assistance....

*Benefits of SB 535*

Cap-and-trade auction revenues offer California the opportunity to further the State's climate, air-quality, public-health, and economic goals. If used as intended, strategic investments may not only accelerate the State's transformation in GHG-emissions-reducing sectors, but also revitalize areas that have been historically underserved....

... Thanks to cap-and-trade revenues, California, for the first time, has significant funding to directly aid disadvantaged communities. The Governor's proposed budget for 2014–2015 estimates that cap-and-trade revenues will be $850 million: $225 million of which would be directed to programs that benefit disadvantaged communities. And this is only the first year of allocations. While future revenue is unpredictable, cap-and-trade revenues are likely to be high. In fact, some have deemed these revenues "California's new gold."

SB 535, through its goals of investing in programs that provide co-benefits, helps California move toward an equitable green future. Creating a green economy is beyond a political or legislative challenge; it is a moral challenge. The challenge is whether the State will create greener, more sustainable communities for the wealthy few, or make such improvements a reality for those who need them most. There are areas in California that have suffered disproportionate levels of pollution, poverty, and unemployment; in allocating the funds captured by cap-and-trade, we can and should make sure that those areas are prioritized.

*Limits of SB 535*

… First, SB 535 provides only a floor for investments in disadvantaged communities. The State must invest much more than this minimum—10% of revenue generated by cap-and-trade auctions—to counter the decades of pollution in low-income communities and communities of color.…

… Second, policymakers must better define the requirement that 25% of investments "benefit" disadvantaged communities. Under the current law, "benefit" can be interpreted broadly.…

… Third, policymakers must use a consistent metric to allocate the cap-and-trade funds via the budget process every year. Reallocation each year creates uncertainty about which programs will be funded and for how many years. Funds are then also subject to some additional unpredictability because they are distributed through agencies before going to the community.…

… Fourth, SB 535 implementation should include an explicit role for community members and other stakeholders to guide and shape the allocation of revenue. Those who work or live in the community know best what the community needs.…

… In 2013, the Public Policy Institute of California found that 52% of Californians agreed that it was very important to spend cap-and-trade revenues in low-income or disadvantaged communities (31% agreed that it was somewhat important to spend this money in low-income communities). SB 535 is a popular policy, but it must be implemented to fulfill its intent and requirements if it is to continue garnering support from disadvantaged communities. If there is not evidence of a growing green economy in disadvantaged communities, these communities will see the hope of a green economy as mere hype.

* * *

## Notes and Questions

1. **Real benefits?** In 2016, California passed AB 1550, which now requires 25 percent of proceeds from cap-and-trade revenues be spent on projects *located in* disadvantaged communities. Does this new legislation cure the first limit of SB 535 described above?

2. **Investments in disadvantaged communities.** Several California programs, outside of SB 535, have since also targeted "green" investments in disadvantaged communities.

AB 523 directs at least 25 percent of California Energy Commission Technology Demonstration and Deployment funding to projects located in and benefitting disadvantaged communities. AB 2672 required the California Public Utilities Commission to analyze solutions to provide San Joaquin Valley disadvantaged communities access to affordable energy. Implementation of the bill resulted in the Commission's approval of a $56 million investment for pilot projects in 11 San Joaquin Valley communities, providing energy-efficiency upgrades, solar benefits, and job training, while reducing energy costs and pollution. *See* Commissioner Martha Guzman Aceves, *CPUC Provides San Joaquin Valley Residents with Cleaner and Safer Energy Options*, WORKING FOR CALIFORNIA, A MONTHLY NEWSLETTER FROM THE CPUC (Jan. 2019). California's targeted investment focus has even reached the local level: California enacted SB 1000 (2016), which required all cities and counties to include climate adaptation and resiliency strategies in the safety elements of their general plans. SB 1000 has four core requirements: identify disadvantaged communities; identify objectives and policies to reduce the unique or compounded health risks in disadvantaged communities; identify objectives and policies to promote civil engagement in the public decision-making process, and identify objectives and policies that prioritize improvements and programs that address the needs of disadvantaged communities.

3. **Revisiting race.** What theories of justice does California's definition of "disadvantaged community" and subsequent distribution of greenhouse gas cap-and-trade revenues raise? Are there other benefits or drawbacks to such designation for "environmental justice" communities? What are the limitations imposed by the U.S. Supreme Court decision in *Grutter*? Similarly, CalEnviroScreen currently does not factor in race/ethnicity due to California's Proposition 209, which banned affirmative action by amending the California Constitution to prohibit state institutions from discriminating on the basis of race, sex, or ethnicity. Cal. Const. art. I, sec. 31. CalEnviroScreen also does not currently identify tribal government land. *See* Michelle Roos, E4 Strategic Solutions, CLIMATE JUSTICE SUMMARY REPORT. CALIFORNIA'S FOURTH CLIMATE CHANGE ASSESSMENT at 27 (2018). California state agencies have since developed and continue to develop additional and more inclusive mapping tools.

4. **Process vs. substance.** In considering SB 115 and subsequent California environmental justice initiatives, does each initiative focus on process or on substantive guarantees? *See* Caroline Farrell, *SB 115: California's Response to Environmental Justice—Process over Substance*, 1 GOLDEN GATE U. ENVTL. L.J. 113, 126 (2007). SB 115 explicitly recognizes the fact that disproportionate impacts occur and should be addressed. This can be a valuable tool for communities fighting for environmental justice. *Id.* at 123. When should considerations of process end and substantive efforts begin? Or are the two considerations parallel, and if so, to what degree?

Compare federal initiatives with California initiatives. More recently, California agencies have begun adopting environmental justice policies and implementation plans. In 2018, the California State Lands Commission convened an Environmental Justice Working Group to develop recommendations for the California State Lands Commission update of its environmental justice policy. The resulting policy incorporates the following goals: promote equity; increase awareness of the commission's work; increase and support equitable public access; identify and engage with impacted communities; analyze proposed projects to reduce impacts to and increase benefits for environmental justice communities; honor the importance of tribes' ancestral homelands; build trust and form relationships with local communities, tribal communities, and environmental justice groups; support cleaner industry; advance climate equity; increase public participation; and promote greater agency accountability. CA State Lands Commission Environmental Justice Policy (2018). In 2019, the California Public Utilities adopted, subject to review and update every two years, an "Environmental and Social Justice Action Plan" with the goal of expanding public inclusion in commission decision-making and improving services to targeted communities across California. California state agencies have also established environmental justice advisory panels, for instance the Air Resources Board's Environmental Justice Advisory Committee (AB 32) and the Energy Commission and Public Utilities Commission's Disadvantaged Communities Advisory Group (SB 350). The California Attorney General's office has also established a Bureau of Environmental Justice within the Environment Section at the California Department of Justice to oversee, investigate, and enforce the law to protect people and communities that endure a disproportionate share of environmental pollution and public health hazards.

**5. Federal preemption and state action.** To what degree can states regulate environmental justice issues in areas subject to federal preemption? In 2016, California Attorney General Kamala Harris provided comment on the environmental impact report for the Valero Benicia Refinery Crude-By-Rail Project. The project proposed to allow the refinery to receive and process up to 100 tank cars of flammable and explosive fracked oil feedstock by railway. Valero argued that the Interstate Commerce Commission Termination Act prohibited the City of Benicia from taking rail-related impacts, including significant environmental and public health impacts, into account while deciding on the project. The Attorney General responded:

> … [w]here a local agency is vested with discretionary authority to determine whether to approve a project within its jurisdiction, California law requires the agency to analyze and disclose the full scope of the project's foreseeable impacts [under CEQA]. This requirement ensures that the agency is fully informed of the consequences of its action, and thus that any discretionary action is ultimately in the public interest. This legal duty is not circumscribed by ICCTA for this Project. In fact, for Benicia to turn a blind eye to the most serious of the Project's environmental impacts, merely because they flow from federally regulated rail operations, would be contrary to both state and federal law.

Letter from California Attorney General, Kamala Harris, to City of Benicia on the Draft Environmental Impact Report for the Valero Benicia Crude-By-Rail Project (April, 2016). *See also Friends of Eel River v. N. Coast R.R. Auth.*, 3 Cal. 5th 677, 690 (2017).

## 2. New York Initiatives

In December 2019, Governor Andrew Cuomo of New York signed into law a new statute establishing a permanent environmental justice advisory board to operate under the New York Department of Environmental Conservation. The advisory board will provide guidance to state agencies in order to advance environmental justice across the state. Similarly, New York City has taken a series of steps designed to promote environmental justice within the city.

### Rebecca Bratspies, *Protecting the Environment in an Era of Federal Retreat: The View from New York City*
#### 13 Florida International University L. Rev. 5, 26–30 (2018)

In April 2017, New York City passed two new Local Laws on Environmental Justice. As he signed the bills, Mayor de Blasio characterized them as "recogniz[ing] the historic injustices that have disproportionately fallen on low-income residents and communities of color—with the burden of pollution and climate change—and offer[ing] a different path forward. Environmental justice advocates were quick to emphasize that "as Trump moves backwards" New York City is moving forward on environmental justice. The City agreed. Daniel Zarrilli, New York City's Chief Resilience Officer, characterized these laws as a direct response to the lack of federal leadership on the issue. Costa Constantinides, chair of City Council's Environmental Protection Committee, echoed the sentiment that these laws are part of New York City's response to federal disengagement with environmental law in general, and environmental justice in particular.

The first Environmental Justice Law, Local Law 60, requires the City to delimit boundaries of environmental justice communities around New York City, and to issue recommendations for legislation, policy and budget initiatives that could address environmental justice concerns within those communities. To facilitate community empowerment, this Local Law also directs the creation of an Environmental Justice Portal on the City's website. This portal will contain relevant maps, data, studies and other information.

The second Environmental Justice Law, Local Law 64, requires city agencies to develop plans to incorporate environmental justice into their decision-making processes. The Act also requires the Mayor to establish an Interagency Working Group on environmental justice and tasks the Working Group with developing a comprehensive environmental justice plan. The goal of this Law is to incorporate environmental justice concerns into all City decision-making and to identify opportunities for promoting environmental justice.

Together these two new laws should put New York City on a path to finally address its long-standing and thorny issues of environmental injustice. These laws build on New York City's recognition that environmental justice and environmental protection are "inexorably linked." In addition, City Council continues to move forward with other environmental justice bills. For example, a bill introduced in 2017 would require that 100,000 trees be planted in environmental justice communities within five years. This measure, which has the full support of environmental justice advocates, would go a long way toward reducing the heat island effect in those communities over the medium and long-term. In the meantime, the Mayor's office is moving forward with a parallel plan called Cool Neighborhoods, which also involves tree plantings as well as a cool roofs initiative. In announcing this program, Mayor de Blasio acknowledged that the urban heat islands in NYC pose a "threat that falls disproportionately on communities of color and the elderly." In addition, planting trees improves local air quality, beautifies neighborhoods, and provide a host of intangible benefits associated with wellness. Perhaps most importantly from an environmental justice perspective, children living on tree lined streets are less likely to develop asthma.

Asthma is a significant environmental justice issue, with African American and Latino children experiencing much higher rates of asthma than white children. In New York City, asthma rates have tripled in the past three decades and are now the leading cause of emergency room visits, hospitalizations and school absenteeism. Children living in minority neighborhoods are at much higher risk. Outdoor air quality varies widely, with environmental justice communities more likely to have poor air quality. The new Environmental Justice Local Laws will help document these disparities, and will focus the attention of City officials on methods to resolve these disparities. However, indoor air quality can also contribute to asthma. City Council's Committee on Housing and Buildings recently held hearings on a bill that would increase building owner's responsibilities with regard to indoor asthma allergen hazards. This bill has the strong backing of environmental justice advocates. If enacted, this bill will make a significant difference in childhood asthma for the City's most vulnerable residents.

* * *

Other states also continue to innovate in tackling environmental justice issues and the range of approaches is growing, showing that this area of law and policy continues to mature. Pub. Law Research Inst., UC HASTINGS COLLEGE OF THE LAW & AM. BAR ASS'N, ENVIRONMENTAL JUSTICE FOR ALL: A FIFTY STATE SURVEY OF LEGISLATION, POLICIES AND CASES (4th ed. 2010).

State responses have been traditionally diverse. Several states have statutes that seek to limit the geographic concentration of waste facilities or that allow decision-makers to consider "soft" criteria such as the socioeconomic status of the host community in permit decisions about waste facilities. A number of states have sought to increase public participation in their programs, and others have convened environmental justice task forces or advisory groups. The recommendations of these task forces generally include increasing public participation in agency decisions, improving public education and outreach by agencies, heightening awareness among agency staff about environmental justice issues, collecting better data about environmental disparities, facilitating community-industry dialogue, and targeting enforcement efforts in environmental justice communities. A smaller number of states have gone further and adopted formal environmental justice policies or established environmental justice positions within state government. In several states the primary response has been to conduct research into the extent of environmental disparities.

The UC Hastings Fifty State Survey, cited above, identifies trends as states continue to innovate in tackling environmental justice issues:

> … Community participation and education mechanisms, as in years past, represent the most prevalent techniques of addressing environmental justice concerns. Substantively, permitting and facility siting decisions remain a major focus for state rules and programs. However, in a departure from initiatives identified in our prior studies, a growing number of states, Maryland for example, are using land use planning techniques such as buffer zones, to improve environmental conditions, reduce potential health risks, and prevent environmental degradation in at-risk communities.
>
> In addition, several states have begun addressing global climate change, and a few of those states—California, for example—specifically reference environmental justice concerns in their climate change initiatives.…
>
> We have noted an increase in the number of states pursuing positive collaborative, problem-solving approaches or economic incentives to address environmental justice. For example, several states account for environmental justice in brownfields grant programs and public private partnerships.
>
> A final noteworthy thread is that many states have environmental enforcement policies that seek to address environmental justice issues. For example, we found at least seven states that incorporate environmental justice into Supplemental Environmental Projects policies. Moreover, some states focus on enforcement procedures in environmentally burdened communities, while other states rely upon grants and community education.

*Id.* at iv–v.

* * *

## Notes and Questions

**1. New York state of mind.** On December 23, 2019, Governor Andrew Cuomo signed A1564/S2385, creating a new Article 48 of the Environmental Conservation Law. The new statute established a Permanent Environmental Justice Advisory Group to "monitor compliance" with environmental justice policy across the State of New York. The new environmental justice policy of New York begins with this declaration: "It is hereby declared to be the policy of this state that all people, regardless of race, color, religion, national origin or income, have a right to fair treatment and meaningful involvement in the development, implementation and enforcement of laws, regulations and policies that affect the quality of the environment." How does this policy statement from the State of New York compare to the prevailing definition of "environmental justice" established by the U.S. EPA, as discussed in Chapter 1?

**2. Best practices?** The most popular state responses seem to be creating environmental justice advisory committees or environmental justice policies, and enhancing public participation and education mechanisms. Why do you think this is the case? Bearing in mind experiences in California and New York, which approaches would you like to see adopted in your state? Can you think of other approaches that would help to alleviate environmental disparities?

Are tribal governments in a relatively better position to help alleviate environmental disparities? Consider the material in the next section.

# E. Tribal Initiatives

In managing tribal lands and resources, tribes today must contend with a legacy of colonialism and non-tribal management that presents a formidable set of challenges for tribal efforts to address environmental harms. Numerous aspects of United States policy have worked in concert to separate American Indian peoples from their aboriginal lands, to usurp these peoples' inherent authority to govern the use of their lands and resources, and to undermine their ability to make environmental management decisions as a practical matter through a host of actions that ensured conditions of economic poverty and social distress. Moreover, although tribes were legally recognized as sovereign nations within the United States in early decisions by the U.S. Supreme Court—"domestic dependent nations"—the federal government in fact has exercised broad decision-making authority over mineral and timber extraction; fishing, hunting, and wildlife management; and land and water use. As discussed in Chapter 9 ("Environmental Justice in Indian Country"), these federal management decisions continue to have an enormous impact on tribes' resources and rights and, in turn, on the health of tribal people. Professor David Rich Lewis estimates that these decisions have "scarred thousands of acres with minimal protection for inhabitants":

> Beginning as early as 1900 with the discovery of oil on Osage land, nonrenewable resource development has unleashed some of the most environmentally destructive forms of exploitation. Today, mine and drilling sites, roads and machinery, tailing pipes and settling ponds threaten tribal land, water, air, health, and lifestyles. Inequitable leases and federal, state, and tribal government mismanagement have compounded these problems.

David Rich Lewis, *Native Americans and the Environment: A Survey of Twentieth-Century Issues*, 19 Am. INDIAN Q. 423, 431 (1995). The consequences of this mismanagement have been left for tribal governments to address today; in many cases, they present daunting challenges to tribal environmental regulatory efforts.

Tribes' recent efforts to reinvigorate tribal management over tribal lands and resources comprise important steps toward ameliorating environmental injustice in Indian Country. Efforts to this end include tribes' exercise of their inherent authority to manage the lands and resources over which they have jurisdiction (the issue of tribal jurisdiction is itself often contested, with tribes having to defend their claims against surrounding states and others); tribes' efforts to obtain delegation of authority to administer programs under the Clean Water Act, the Clean Air Act, and other federal environmental statutes; and tribes' devotion of personnel and resources to a host of other environmental management endeavors. *See, e.g.,* William H. Rodgers, Jr., *Tribal Government Roles in Environmental Federalism,* Nat. Res. & Env't, Winter 2007, at 3; Timothy C. Seward, *Survival of Indian Tribes Through Repatriation of Homelands,* Nat. Res. & Env't, Winter 2007, at 32; Mary Christina Wood & Zachary Welcker, *Tribes as Trustees Again (Part I): The Emerging Tribal Role in the Conservation Trust Movement,* 32 Harv. Envtl. L. Rev. 373 (2008). An example of one such tribal effort by the Isleta Pueblo is discussed in Chapter 5 ("Standard Setting").

Professor Charles Wilkinson notes that tribes generally devote a substantial proportion of their governmental resources to environmental protection—often far greater amounts, relatively, than their federal and state counterparts. *See* Charles Wilkinson, Messages from Frank's Landing: A Story of Salmon, Treaties, and the Indian Way 94 (2000). In absolute terms, however, tribal expenditures may still be modest. Many tribes are still working to address poverty and other pressing social issues, and many are still laboring to build the administrative infrastructure necessary to address the environmental problems they face. On the one hand, tribes and their members often possess a wealth of expertise as environmental managers—including traditional ecological knowledge born in many instances of generations of residency in place. On the other hand, funding is a perennial issue for many tribal governments. Professor Judith Royster elaborates:

> In environmental matters, Indian tribes acting as governments face both tremendous opportunities and enormous obstacles. Perhaps the most significant obstacle to tribes' assertions of their environmental rights is money. Despite the recent success of some tribal casinos, many Indian reservations remain among the poorest communities in the nation. Tribes have neither the economic base nor the monetary resources to undertake major environmental protection programs, generally from scratch, without substantial federal financial assistance. Although the federal government has offered limited funding for tribes, the lack of money has been identified as the "key problem" in a study of tribal actions to protect reservation water quality. As one scholar has noted, "[w]hatever else environmental justice means[] in Indian country," it must include sufficient funding for tribes to develop effective environmental programs designed to serve tribal needs and protect tribal values.

Judith V. Royster, *Native American Law, in* The Law of Environmental Justice: Theories and Procedures to Address Disproportionate Risks 199, 213–14 (Michael B. Gerrard & Sheila R. Foster eds., 2d ed. 2008) (quoting Dean Suagee). By comparison, scholars note, substantial federal financial assistance has been provided to state environmental programs for decades.

While advocates point to greater tribal control over traditional and culturally important lands and resources as the solution to environmental injustice for American Indian people, some familiar issues may arise as tribal governments contemplate proposed economic development projects and otherwise regulate economic activities within their jurisdiction. Ms. Jana Walker, attorney and former member of the NEJAC Subcommittee on Indigenous Peoples, and her colleagues raise this point: "But what of potentially 'bad' development decisions made by Tribes? As pointed out by some scholars, recognition of tribal self-government 'does not mean that every decision of a Tribe is beyond scrutiny on environmental justice grounds' ...". Jana L. Walker, Jennifer L. Bradley & Timothy J. Humphrey, Sr., *A Closer Look at Environmental Injustice in Indian Country*, 1 SEATTLE J. FOR SOC. JUST. 379, 391 (2002) (quoting Dean Suagee). At times, impacted communities within tribal lands are in open opposition to proposed developments supported by tribal authorities, and the alliances formed by these opposition campaigns sometimes include non-Indian advocacy organizations. Or, in other instances, non-Indian advocacy groups may challenge tribal developments that have spillover effects beyond the boundaries of tribal lands. This raises a host of sensitive issues for the tribes. Suffice it to say that when tribal governments act as regulators there are different issues, such as tribal self-determination, to be considered than when federal, state, or other governments act as regulators. Several of these issues are elaborated on in Chapter 9 ("Environmental Justice in Indian Country").

# F. Collaborative Approaches

Environmental regulation has been steadily moving in the direction of greater "stakeholder" participation by public institutions and private firms and individuals who are affected by environmental regulation. This trend appears as well in governmental initiatives to promote environmental justice. Through these collaborative approaches, a lead agency, like the EPA, typically will convene a group of governmental officials from other federal agencies and from state and local governments, as well as business firms, environmental and environmental justice organizations, and community residents, to attempt to leverage resources and effectively address (usually localized) environmental justice issues. As you read this section, consider how these collaborative approaches might incorporate different perspectives.

The concept of a collaborative process is deceptively simple and appealing. Although it makes eminent good sense, there are a variety of reasons why well-meaning collaborative processes may fail and end up doing more harm than good. Although collaborations can take various forms—from advisory groups to oversight groups—most in the environmental justice context involve public and private actors attempting to identify and address interrelated environmental problems on a local scale. These place-based efforts often require some devolution of authority in order to implement more innovative strategies, but at the same time must maintain accountability to traditional regulatory authorities. As explained by Professor Sheila Foster:

There are at least two recognizable strands of devolved collaboration currently in practice. The first involves mostly ad hoc local groups that are concerned with diverse issues in natural resources planning and management. The second features more formalized, local working groups that focus on land use and pollution control decisions. Both strands expand the influence of, and demand deeper participation by, public and private local actors in environmental and natural resource decisions. Yet, neither strand requires a complete abdication of government authority and responsibility over those decisions. Accountability to central government decision-makers is preserved through a multilateral relationship whereby local actors supplement central regulatory authorities, which in turn support local efforts. In both strands, regulators (and sometimes legislators) expect to, and often do, use the proposals and recommendations of community-based participants to manage natural resources in accordance with local values, reformulate minimum performance standards, or impose additional conditions and monitoring requirements on regulated sources.

Sheila Foster, *Environmental Justice in an Era of Devolved Collaboration*, 26 HARV. ENVTL. L. REV. 459, 473 (2002).

One early collaborative effort was spearheaded at the federal level. In 1999, the Interagency Working Group on Environmental Justice (IWG) established an Integrated Federal Interagency Environmental Justice Action Agenda. The Action Agenda led to a number of interesting demonstration projects involving collaboration among government agencies, communities, and private parties. Some of these projects, and the philosophy underlying the collaborative approach of the Action Agenda, are described by Charles Lee of the EPA's Office of Environmental Justice and author of the landmark *Toxic Wastes and Race* study (*see* Chapter 1).

## Charles Lee, Submission to the National Environmental Policy Commission*

### (May 15, 2001)

*IWG Interagency Action Agenda*

... Because of the enormous complexity and interrelated/multi-faceted nature of the issues that make up the concept of environmental justice, a primary challenge facing the IWG was to develop a mechanism which can leverage the benefits of many important federal initiatives and public-private partnerships....

... [T]he Action Agenda is spearheading the development of a distinctively new collaborative model for achieving environmental justice.... In order for this model to work, it requires not only cooperation and coordination among Federal agencies,

---

* These written comments were submitted in connection with a presentation made on December 15, 2000, at the Newark, New Jersey Listening Session of the National Environmental Policy Commission.

**Figure 10-1:** Charles Lee, EPA Office of Environmental Justice. Washington, D.C. March 12, 2019. Photo: Cliff Villa.

but leadership and direction from place-based partnerships of all relevant stakeholder groups. . . .

To test and develop the collaborative model of the Action Agenda, the IWG has sponsored 15 demonstration projects, almost all of which [are] geographically based and which embrace a plethora of environmental justice issues and stakeholder communities. Presently, the IWG is developing, with input from all stakeholders, criteria for evaluating these current projects and criteria for selecting possible future projects. . . .

*Background: IWG Collaborative Model*

Collaborative processes requires [sic] the building of genuine partnerships among all relevant parties, and the process results in better understanding for all participants of the perspectives and concerns of each party. Constructive processes are geared toward local[ly] solving problems, which require proactive, pragmatic and innovative strategies. The resulting action must be solution-oriented and of benefit to impacted communities (who must be at the center of the decision making process) and relevant stakeholders.

. . . Environmental health and quality of life concerns which often spark environmental justice disputes more often than not include issues of environment, housing, transportation, urban sprawl, community infrastructure, economic development, capacity building and others. In addition, there are special concerns with respect to Tribes and indigenous populations.... No single agency can adequately address the multi-faceted dimensions of any environmental justice situation.... Without focused and concerted efforts on the part of multiple agencies, the singularly directed initiatives of a given agency, no matter how well intentioned, fall short in the face of the overwhelming challenges presented by the combined ills of environmental, social and economic distress on impacted communities.

A cautionary note: The collaborative model is not appropriate for all environmental justice situations. Some of the most intractable and difficult issues affecting impacted communities may in fact only be resolved in litigation....

On May 24, 2000, EPA formally announced the [Action Agenda] on behalf of the eleven participating federal departments and agencies, including the initial round of fifteen National Demonstration Projects [Below are selected examples of some of the projects. Note the diversity of the issues addressed. Eds.]....

*Selected Demonstration Projects Protecting Children's Health & Reducing Lead Exposure through Collaborative Partnerships*

Location: East St. Louis, Illinois

Population: African American

Issue: Lead Screening and Abatement

Partners: 17 different organizations, including St. Mary's Hospital, East St. Louis, St. Clair County, EPA, HUD, USDA, USACE

Activities:

- Screen over 3,000 children for blood lead
- Conduct lead-based paint assessments
- Conduct site assessments in abandoned lots where children play
- Participate in worker training program
- Initiated phytoremediation project
- Develop outreach and education, including video
- Leveraged over $4 million in federal funding
- Designated a National Brownfields Showcase Community ...

*Metlakatla Indian Community Unified Interagency Environmental Management Task Force*

Location: Annette Islands, Alaska

Population: Alaska Native

Issue: Environmental cleanup and restoration

Partners: Tlingit & Haida Indian Tribes, BIA, DOD, EPA, FAA-DOT, USCG-DOT; Metlakatla Indian Community Unified Interagency Environmental Management Task Force

Activities:

- Develop Master Plan for cleanup and restoration of Metlakatla Peninsula
- DOD anticipates commitment of $2.5 million for site assessment
- Protect traditional use of food resources
- Planning to promote economic development through tourism and commercial fishing
- Designated a National Brownfields Showcase Community ...

*Addressing Asthma Coalition in Puerto Rico: A Multi-Faceted Partnership for Results*

Location: Puerto Rico

Population: Children in Puerto Rico

Issue: Protect children's health

Partners: PR Dept of Health, Pediatric Pulmonary Program, PR Lung Association, HRSA, ATSDR, CDC, EPA

Activities:

- Two strategic planning conferences involving over 1,000 people in NYC and Puerto Rico
- Support development of the Asthma Coalition of Puerto Rico
- Increase public awareness and professional training
- Coordinate better between asthma care providers and insurance companies
- Institute asthma research and surveillance programs ...

*Easing Troubled Waters: Farm Worker Safe Drinking Water Project*

Location: State of Colorado

Population: Migrant Farm workers

Issue: Public Health

Partners: Plan de Salud del Valle, High Plains Center for Agricultural Health and Safety, National Center for Farmworker Health, CO DPH, CO DOL, CO DOA HRSA, EPA, DOL, USDA Colorado State Agricultural Extension

Activities:

- Develop GIS maps of migrant farm worker camps and drinking water sources
- Assess water quality data for camps
- Recommend changes to federal policy regarding testing of migrant worker water sources
- Develop interagency and community plan to address communication and education needs

- Build sustainable network to implement policy and communications changes ...

* * *

## Notes and Questions

1. **Effective collaboration?** As the demonstration pilot projects illustrate, there are a variety of agencies that can participate both "horizontally" and "vertically." Sister federal agencies often agree to participate initially because of the mandate of the Executive Order. However, because environmental hot spots implicate local land-use decisions, the participation of municipal, county, regional, and state agencies is indispensable. The participation of the business sector is also a key component to many projects. Yet, how do these various agencies and stakeholders get together in a collaborative effort, and what is the framework that is most likely to result in tangible results to the impacted area?

A May 2001 forum convened by the International City/County Management Association (ICMA), entitled Building Collaborative Models to Achieve Environmental Justice, provided interesting insights into the successes and failures of the IWG demonstration projects. At the conference, long-time environmental justice activists began by explaining why collaborative efforts were necessary, but extraordinarily difficult to implement in light of a skepticism that still exists in impacted communities—a view that stems from their experiences with governmental agencies that previously exhibited hostility to environmental justice claims. Government regulators noted that the task was difficult initially because the federal government operates on big issues and big policies, while communities work on a different scale; the "levers of decision-making" were necessarily different and not easily subject to coordination. The participants appeared to agree that certain components are critical to successful collaborative partnerships. Among them are:

- There must be a high level of community education and empowerment about the issues. Environmental justice advocates, in particular, argued that a well-organized community group was a critical component of the process;
- Early resident and community involvement and visioning is key. All other stakeholder participants should recognize that the community is different from all other stakeholder groups;
- There must be development of a clear action plan;
- The partnership must include the community, businesses and government agencies;
- Collaborating must include "win-win" scenarios for many stakeholders;
- There must be a commitment to facilitate conflict resolution, where appropriate. Sometimes, parties engaged in a conflict cannot work their way through the conflict by themselves and may need to find a third person that has a sensitivity to the issues; and

- There must be sufficient resources to address the problem. One can better leverage available resources by interagency coordination.

INT'L CITY/COUNTY MGMT. ASS'N, REPORT: FORUM ON BUILDING COLLABORATIVE MODELS TO ACHIEVE ENVIRONMENTAL JUSTICE (2001).

Perspectives differed, however, concerning the interplay between collaborative partnerships and collateral, more adversarial proceedings, such as litigation. Environmental justice advocates were clear in their view that there must be recognition that the collaborative process has limitations. Thus, they maintained that there are some issues that require resolution by litigation or other methods. They saw no problem with these proceedings occurring simultaneously and collaterally to the collaborative processes. In fact, one activist noted that her organization had collaterally participated in proceedings that resulted in a $150,000 fine against one of the partners. Business stakeholders, on the other hand, viewed collateral litigation as disruptive of and counterproductive to the collaborative effort. Some questioned whether litigation might preclude potential partners from joining a collaborative project. What is your view about the interplay between these approaches? Should groups forgo litigation where they are involved in collaborative projects such as those described above?

**2. A note of caution.** In an article examining a proposal by the Conservation Alliance (an environmental organization dedicated to preserving grassland ecosystems) to establish the Greater Black Hills Wildlife Protection Area, Professor John LaVelle, an Indian Law scholar and member of the Santee Sioux Nation, sounds a note of caution about the proposal. *See* John P. LaVelle, *Rescuing Paha Sapa: Achieving Environmental Justice by Restoring the Great Grasslands and Returning the Sacred Black Hills to the Great Sioux Nation*, 5 GREAT PLAINS NAT. RESOURCES J. 40 (2001). In its proposal, the Conservation Alliance specifically notes that "[o]ne group which must be consulted throughout the process would be those Native Americans whose traditional and current territory might be involved. Native American participation should be encouraged as a way to open the door to a broader discussion about the past and a common future on the Great Plains." *Id.* at 42–43. However, the sort of consultation envisioned by the Conservation Alliance—presumably a form of collaboration— cannot proceed in a way that does not consider the ongoing claims of the Sioux Nation. Professor LaVelle explained:

> In contemplating the possibility of establishing a "Greater Black Hills Wildlife Protected Area," the "treacherous history" of the dispossession of *Paha Sapa* should give the Conservation Alliance pause to consider carefully the political, moral, and ethical implications of how it chooses to proceed with its proposal. The advocates of the proposal must be willing to clarify and deepen their commitment to achieving justice through the proposal's development beyond the mere avowal that Indian people "must be consulted" and that "Native American participation should be encouraged." As Professor [Frank] Pommersheim reminds us, "[j]ustice emanates from conversation rather than declaration," and with respect to *Paha Sapa* in particular there

remains an urgent "need for enduring and honest dialogue." Hence, any "conversation" or "dialogue" about our "common future on the Great Plains" must begin by acknowledging that the dispossession of the Black Hills from the Great Sioux Nation is a *present and ongoing* injustice, and not simply a doleful moment in a "broader discussion about the past."

What the Conservation Alliance must conscientiously avoid—and what the Sioux tribes must vigilantly guard against—is the prospect of advancing a policy scheme that charts a course toward a "common future" in which the intolerable and continuing injustice of the dispossession of *Paha Sapa* is further "legitimized" under the guise of "protecting" or "restoring" or "renewing" the environment. If that were to happen—the Lakota, Dakota, and Nakota people's aspirations for the return of the sacred Black Hills were to be sacrificed once again under the edict that the invaders "simply need that country ... [as] part of the geography of hope"—then the plan for "[r]enewing the Great Plains" will have failed to help realize "the dream of dwelling on an earth made whole." Instead, the Conservation Alliance will have opened yet another "tragic[] chapter in the history of the Nation's West" by effectively deploying environmental colonialism to exacerbate the ethnocide manifested in the dispossession of *Paha Sapa*.

*Id.* at 69–71. How might a collaborative process to restore this area—unquestionably in the best interest of all—proceed?

**3. Another note of caution.** Professor Sheila Foster also probes the collaborative process—one strongly oriented towards consensus—for potential bias. She too introduces a cautionary note:

Even with broad representation, however, devolved collaborative processes can be highly problematic from a substantive point of view. As critics of consensus aptly observe, the theory of consensus itself contains an inherent ideological bias. Its emphasis on securing unanimous agreement through the identification of common interests ("win-win") can be antithetical to achieving substantive justice. Such emphasis can skew the process in favor of the outcome which reflects the lowest common denominator acceptable to all parties. The problem with outcomes reflecting the lowest common denominator is that, while the process can be deemed "legitimate" in a democratic process sense, its outcome may reflect a type of "domination by means of leveling." In other words, it tends to leave out difficult, unpopular, or minority concerns, and may orient the process away from sorely needed innovative solutions that address these concerns.

The substantive bias also reveals itself in the very mechanisms upon which consensus depends. Consensus simultaneously stresses agreement and compromise while "veiling the increased potential for coercion by leaders" of collaborative groups. The primary mechanism through which this coercion is practiced is the veto power possessed by each participant. This veto power can force agreement by threatening complete failure of the process if it is exercised. Given current disparities in material resources and social capital, "those with greater power possess and [will] frequently use their prerogative to exert substantial influence over other members and, through them, the content of group decisions." In this way, by forcing agreement through coercion, more powerful and knowledgeable participants are able to co-opt dissident viewpoints that may be critical to seeking more creative, and just, decisions.

By ignoring, marginalizing, or co-opting difficult questions of distributional justice, or other pressing policy dilemmas, consensus processes at their most benign replicate the status quo. Communities disproportionately bearing the costs of current environmental policy and natural resources management may not be left any worse off by consensus solutions, but they will not likely be helped by them either. At their most dangerous, consensus solutions may change the status quo for the worse, exacerbating existing distributional disparities. In the final analysis, the outcomes from some consensus-based process will no more reflect the "public interest" than the problematic pluralistic processes they replace.

Foster, *supra*, at 49394.

Do you agree with Professor Foster that collaboration may simply replicate the problematic processes it replaces and may be unlikely to promote substantive justice? In light of these potential biases, is collaboration worth the effort? What are the potential gains? How would you structure collaboration to avoid some of the pitfalls discussed above?

# Chapter 11

# Land-Use Planning

## A. Introduction

Overburdened communities potentially can rely on a range of legal and political tools to remedy disproportionate environmental harms. These include utilizing civil rights remedies (see Chapter 4), challenging permitting decisions (Chapter 6), seeking to enforce the requirements of pollution control statutes (Chapter 7), pressing for Superfund cleanups (Chapter 8), or bringing common law actions (Chapter 13). Many of these approaches are reactive—they are employed by a community to stop a proposal for an unwanted facility, or to mitigate harm at an existing site. The next two chapters examine several approaches that are more proactive. This chapter discusses first, the benefits of, and barriers to, using planning and zoning mechanisms to address disparate siting patterns, and second, the novel approaches that advocates have utilized to ensure environmental justice in local land-use decisions.

*Pathfinder on Environmental Justice and Land-Use Planning*

For a useful treatise on land-use planning generally, see Julian Juergensmeyer, et al., LAND USE PLANNING AND DEVELOPMENT REGULATION LAW (4th ed. 2018). For cases and other related materials, see John R. Nolon, et al., LAND USE AND SUSTAINABLE DEVELOPMENT LAW: CASES AND MATERIALS (9th ed. 2017). In addition to the articles noted elsewhere in this chapter, readers interested in land-use planning as a tool for pursuing environmental justice may also review Benjamin F. Wilson, *It's Not "Just" Zoning: Environmental Justice and Land Use*, 49 URB. LAW. 717 (2017); Heather E. Campbell, et al., *Local Zoning and Environmental Justice: An Agent-Based Model Analysis*, 50 URB. AFF. REV. 521 (2013); Jenny J. Tang, *Public Participation in Brownfield Redevelopment: A Framework for Community Empowerment in Zoning Practices*, 3 SEATTLE J. ENVTL. L. 241 (2013); Patricia E. Salkin, *Environmental Justice and Land Use Planning and Zoning*, 32 REAL EST. L.J. 429 (2004); and Rose A. Kob, *Riding the Momentum of Smart Growth: The Promise of Eco-Development and Environmental Democracy*, 14 TUL. ENVTL. L.J. 139 (2000).

# B. Planning and Zoning Changes

The excerpt below advocates greater reliance on planning and zoning mechanisms to address disparate siting patterns.

## Craig Anthony Arnold, *Planning Milagros:*
## *Environmental Justice and Land Use Regulation*

### 76 Denver University L. Rev. 1, 8–133 (1998)

... Local neighborhoods can use land use planning to articulate visions for what they want their communities to be, and negotiate land use regulations to implement these visions. In other words, they would not be merely late participants in using existing rules to stop (or attempt to stop) current proposals for unwanted land uses, but also pre-siting participants in developing the rules that will determine what will and will not go in their neighborhoods....

*Land Use Planning & Regulation: Another Vision of Environmental Justice*

Land use planning and regulation offer several advantages for achieving environmental justice goals. First, an owner or operator of a prospective [Locally Undesirable Land Use] LULU would have much more difficulty obtaining approval for siting the LULU in a minority or low-income neighborhood, if the comprehensive plan and zoning ordinances prohibited the LULU in that neighborhood than if they allowed the LULU, either by right or conditionally. Assume that a waste company wants to locate a hazardous waste incinerator in a low-income, Hispanic neighborhood. If the city zoning code prohibits hazardous waste incinerators in every zone except I-3, and the zoning map does not designate any land in the target neighborhood as I-3, the waste company will need a zoning amendment, as well as use-specific environmental permits. If the city's comprehensive plan provides for non-industrial uses only in the neighborhood or explicitly states that waste facilities are not appropriate for that neighborhood, the waste company also will need an amendment to the comprehensive plan. The waste company nonetheless might have enough political and economic power to obtain all the needed approvals, but it will face several obstacles.... Furthermore, the neighbors will have more government approvals to challenge in litigation....

*Comprehensive Plan*

The first land use regulatory mechanism is the comprehensive plan. Zoning regulations that implement low-income and minority neighborhoods' goals may be legally ineffective if they are not preceded by amendments to the city's comprehensive plan to reflect those goals....

*Amendments to Zoning*

[T]he crux of land use regulation for environmental justice will be the amendment of existing zoning codes. Most low-income and minority communities that suffer or risk exposure to environmental harms exist in areas with zoning classifications that currently permit intensive uses. Because people of color and the poor live near and among a higher proportion of industrial and commercial uses than do white, high-income people, an appropriate land use regulatory response for cities would be to change the permitted uses in those areas to correspond more closely to the residents' desired neighborhood environment, as well as their health and safety needs....

Zoning map amendments change the zoning district designation for a particular parcel, tract of land, or set of parcels. Although rezoning has been used to allow intensive uses in neighborhoods of color and low-income communities, grassroots environmental justice activists might seek zoning map amendments to change more intensive use designations in their neighborhoods to less intensive use designations, a technique known as "downzoning." For example, a low-income minority neighborhood might contain several parcels zoned for heavy industrial use in close proximity to residences, schools, churches, health care facilities, and the like. Residents might seek to rezone some or all of these parcels for less intensive, yet economically viable, commercial uses....

*Flexible Zoning Techniques*

... Buffer zones ... both help and hurt low-income people and people of color. Buffer zones are use designations that create a buffer or transition between a less intensive use, such as single-family residential, and a nearby more intensive use, such as commercial or industrial. The buffer zone exists between the two areas to minimize the impact of the more intensive use on the less intensive, more sensitive use.

The most frequent type of buffer between single-family residential areas and industrial or commercial areas is medium-or high-density residential uses.... Buffer zones are perhaps one of the major reasons why low-income and minority neighborhoods have so much industrial and commercial zoning: the multi-family housing, where many low-income and minority people live, is purposefully placed near the industrial and commercial uses to create a buffer that protects high-income, white, single-family neighborhoods. Zoning practices place large numbers of poor and minority people near intensive uses because traditional zoning and planning theory values most the single-family residence, instead of the integrity and quality of all residential areas.

[L]ow-income and minority neighborhoods need buffers to protect them from intensive industrial and commercial activity. Buffer zones can also include physical screening, landscaping, significant set backs, open space, and even low-intensity commercial uses like offices, shops, churches, and medical care facilities. Environmental justice advocates can use the concept of buffer zoning but redefine it to protect low-income and minority residences....

*Exactions*

.... Exactions require the developer to provide the public either real property (land, facilities, or both) or monetary fees as a condition for permission to use land in ways subject to government regulation. These dedications and fees provide the public facilities necessitated by new development, including schools, parks, open space, roads, sidewalks, public utilities, fire and police stations, low-income housing, mass transit, day care services, and job training programs.... Already, various federal, state, and local environmental regulatory programs require developers to dedicate land or pay fees to mitigate the environmental impacts of development in ecologically sensitive areas. A comprehensive environmental justice land use program, though, might include environmental impact fees and dedications for inner-city industrial and commercial development. The exactions would be based on the various environmental and social impacts of intensive uses and LULUs on the surrounding neighborhood(s), not just the publicly funded local infrastructure, and would be earmarked for ameliorating amenities in the affected neighborhood(s)....

*Limits to Land Use Regulations as Environmental Justice Tools*

The land use regulatory model of environmental justice, while promising for many low-income communities of color, contains inherent limits. Among these limits are legal constraints on land use regulation that are largely designed to protect the private property rights of landowners. Courts, increasingly protective of private property rights and skeptical of local political processes, have eroded the well-established judicial presumption that zoning decisions are valid by imposing greater scrutiny on decisions about land use regulation.... The final limits to land use regulation as an environmental justice strategy are political and economic. How successful, as a practical matter, will grassroots neighborhood groups be in changing land use patterns in low-income communities and communities of color? There is reason for a mix of sober realism and thoughtful optimism.... Local government is likely to regard changes to existing industrial or commercial zoning as politically or fiscally inconvenient, especially when these uses cannot be relocated to higher-income, lower-minority areas without political conflict. Indeed, many local governments engage in "fiscal zoning," favoring industrial and commercial uses because these uses generate tax revenues without creating expensive demands for local services in the way that single-family residences do, particularly through public school costs....

\* \* \*

## Notes and Questions

**1. Rezone or focus on nonconforming uses?** What is your response to Professor Arnold's question about the political and economic obstacles to changing land-use patterns? How successful are community activists likely to be in getting their neighborhoods rezoned to exclude industrial uses? What kind of organizing strategy might accomplish these goals, and where does the lawyer fit in that strategy? Another approach suggested by Columbia law professor Michael Gerrard is for local governments to focus attention on prior nonconforming uses. He argues that municipalities "may wish to survey their nonconforming uses and determine whether any of them pose such health and environmental problems that they should be targeted for closure, either immediately as public nuisances or later through an amortization process." Michael B. Gerrard, *Environmental Justice and Local Land Use Decisionmaking, in* Trends in Land Use Law From A to Z 148 (Patricia Salkin ed. 2001). How would your strategy to focus on nonconforming uses differ from or parallel your approach to rezoning?

**2. Disparate political power.** Professor Alice Kaswan highlights Professor Arnold's concern regarding disparate political power before local government:

> In sum, minority and poor communities are less likely to have effective voting power and less able to participate effectively in land use planning and zoning decisions than other communities, thus lessening the likelihood that their preferences are equally met. Existing evidence supports this theory. In a study of thirty-one census tracts in seven cities, Professor Craig Anthony Arnold found that "low-income, minority communities have a greater share ... of industrial and commercial zoning, than do high-income white communities." He observed that industrial uses were frequently permitted near residential homes in low-income communities of color, "creating the very sort of incompatibility of uses that zoning is designed to prevent." Commercial uses were "also located in greater concentrations in low-income, high-minority neighborhoods than in high-income, low-minority neighborhoods." Many of these "commercial" uses were industrial in character, including vehicle storage yards, warehousing, machine shops, drilling, and the like. While these differences in zoning could have been caused by differing preferences, Professor Arnold also notes a wide variety of other factors that are not related to community preferences: "intentional discrimination by government decision makers, institutional discrimination embedded in the land use regulatory system, market forces.... lack of political power or resources, or most likely some complex and variable combination of many or all of these.

Alice Kaswan, *Distributive Justice and the Environment*, 81 N.C. L. Rev. 1031, 1110–1111 (2003). Professor Kaswan also discusses the impact of race in diminishing political power, details a variety of state laws that override local zoning, such as for the siting of hazardous waste facilities, power plants, and prisons, and the overall history of zoning in the United States that itself established and furthered these and other barriers to equitable local land-use and planning decisions. *Id.* Documents such as the Cerrell Report, prepared for California Waste Management in 1984 and which developed demographics that represent those "least likely to resist" (including rural communities, those open to promises of economic benefits, low-income communities, and Catholic communities) land-use decisions, further color the history of disproportionate siting of "locally undesirable land uses."

Despite this stark historical backdrop, however, communities continue to organize to leverage political power to drive local land-use policies and decisions. A notable land-use tool that Professor Arnold raises is the "setback" between industrial and residential uses. Imposition of such protective measures has been met with both political and legal resistance.

# Letter from California Attorney General, Xavier Becerra, to the Mayor, City Councilmembers, and Planning Commission Members of the City of Arvin Regarding Proposed Ordinance for Regulation of Petroleum Facilities and Operations

available at https://www.oag.ca.gov/system/files/attachments/press-docs/
comments-arvin-oil-and-gas-ordinance.pdf (June 2018)

## *City of Arvin*

Arvin is home to a predominantly Hispanic, low-income community with a high percentage of young children as compared to other California communities. The City's residents experience serious air quality and related public health problems. Arvin ranks as one of the most overburdened communities in California.... In addition to air quality and related public health issues, Arvin's residents are also exposed to high levels of pesticides ... and drinking water contaminants.... The City's residents are especially vulnerable to pollution exposure given their high rates of poverty ... and unemployment ... and low levels of educational attainment.

The City is located in the southern end of the San Joaquin Valley in Kern County. The majority of oil and gas production in the state occurs in the San Joaquin Valley, and this region suffers from chronic air pollution. Oil and gas production is a source of pollutants such as hydrogen sulfide, benzene, formaldehyde, hexane, and xylene. There are a number of active oil and gas sites located within the City. These sites contribute to the City's air pollution problems. In March 2014, eight Arvin families were evacuated after a toxic gas leak was detected from an underground oilfield production pipeline located near their homes. Following this incident, the Department of Oil, Gas and Geothermal Resources ("DOGGR") imposed a $75,000 fine on the owner and operator of the pipeline.

## *The Ordinance*

The Ordinance was developed at the direction of City Council in order to replace the City's existing regulations of oil and gas production that were adopted in 1965, more than 50 years ago. The Ordinance will institute various requirements related to the siting of oil and gas sites within Arvin's boundaries for the stated purpose of protecting public health, safety and the environment.

In particular, the Ordinance designates the specific zones in the City where oil and gas sites are allowed and prohibited. The prohibited zones include the City's residential zones, the pedestrian-oriented mixed-use overlay zone, the professional office zone, the neighborhood commercial and restricted commercial zones, the automobile parking zone, the architectural design zone, the precise development zone, and the open space zone....

... In addition, the Ordinance specifies setbacks for oil and gas sites. Under the Ordinance, new oil wells must be located more than 300 feet from the property boundaries of any public school, public park, clinic, hospital, long-term health care

**Figure 11-1:** Oil well in agricultural field. Arvin, California. April 17, 2019. Photo: Cliff Villa.

facilities, residences or residential zones (with some exceptions), and commercially designated zones....

*The Adoption of Setbacks and Prohibited Zones to Protect Public Health Is Reasonable*

... In light of Arvin's severe air pollution problems, the overall disproportionate pollution burdens experienced by Arvin's residents, and the community's vulnerability to that pollution, the proposed setbacks and prohibited zones in the Ordinance are reasonable to reduce air pollution and public health impacts from oil and gas operations within the City. Indeed, as the proposed Findings of Fact supporting the Ordinance recognize, the deleterious impacts of oil and gas operations, including odors, air pollution and particulate matter, "are not localized, but can be spread" at distances of more than 1,500 feet....

... Importantly, the proposed restrictions will not prohibit all oil and gas operations in the City but rather the Ordinance will allow such operations to continue in a manner that prevents the future placement of wells near designated sensitive areas. The Ordinance will not prevent the operation of existing oil and gas wells located within the prohibited zones or setbacks if these sites can demonstrate vested rights....

*The City Has Authority to Adopt Zoning and Setback Provisions for Oil and Gas Sites*

The Ordinance's proposed prohibited zones and setbacks are within the City's power to regulate land uses within its jurisdiction. As the California Supreme Court has explained, "[l]and use regulation in California historically has been a function of local government under the grant of police power contained in article XI, section 7 of the California Constitution." (*Big Creek Lumber Co. v. Cty. of Santa Cruz* (2006)

38 Cal. 4th 1139, 1151.) Thus, a "city ha[s] 'the unquestioned right to regulate the business of operating oil wells within its city limits, and to prohibit their operation within delineated areas and districts, if reason appears for so doing.'" (*Beverly Oil Co. v. City of Los Angeles* (1953) 40 Cal.2d 552, 558.) Indeed, a city's authority to regulate zoning within its boundaries is "one of the most essential powers of the government, one that is the least limitable." (*Id.* [citing *Chicago & Alton R. Co. v. Tranbarger* (1915) 238 U.S. 67, 68].) Consistent with these principles, California's appellate courts have found that the "[e]nactment of a city ordinance prohibiting exploration for and production of oil, unless arbitrary, is a valid exercise of the municipal police power." (*Hermosa Beach Stop Oil Coalition v. City of Hermosa* (2001) 86 Cal. App. 4th 534, 555. The City of Hermosa Beach found that the ban "is necessary to preserve the environment, as well as to protect the public health, safety and welfare of people and property" within the city. (*Ibid.*) The court upheld the ban, concluding it is "presumptively a justifiable exercise of the City's police power." (*Ibid.*)

### The Setbacks and Prohibited Zones Provisions Are Not Preempted by State Law

The Attorney General's Office understands that some commenters have asserted that the Ordinance is preempted by state regulation of oil and gas operations. "[W]hen local government regulates in an area over which it traditionally has exercised control, such as the location of particular land uses, California courts will presume, absent a clear indication of preemptive intent from the Legislature, that such regulation is not preempted by state statute." (*Big Creek Lumber Co.*, 38 Cal. 4th at p.1150 [emphasis in original].) As the California Supreme Court has explained, local zoning ordinances prohibiting oil and gas drilling within the local jurisdiction's territory are legal. (*See Pacific P. Assn. v. Huntington Beach* (1925), 196 Cal. 211, 217; *Beverly Oil Co. v. City of Los Angeles* (1953), 40 Cal. 2d 552, 558.)

... Indeed, as the Attorney General has recognized, while state oil and gas regulations likely preempt any local regulations of subsurface oil and gas activities, local regulations of surface activities for purposes such as environmental protection and public safety, among others, are not necessarily preempted by state laws. (59 Ops. Cal. Atty. Gen. 461, 479–480 (1976).) The prohibited zones and setback provisions of the Ordinance are not regulations of subsurface activities. Rather, as discussed above, the provisions are zoning and land use regulations adopted for the purpose of protecting public health and safety from the impacts of oil and gas activities. Consequently, in light of the above analysis, the prohibited zones and setback requirements in the Ordinance are not expressly preempted by state law....

Under the standards for implied preemption, the proposed setbacks and prohibited zones in the Ordinance are not preempted by implication. First, and as discussed above, state law has not completely occupied the field of regulation related to the location of oil and gas activities for purposes of protection of public health, safety and the environment. (*See* Pub. Resources Code, § 3690; 59 Ops. Cal. Atty. Gen. at p. 481 ["[t]he state does not appear to have occupied [the field of well location] to the exclusion of local entities"].) ...

Second, the proposed setbacks and prohibited zones do not duplicate state law....

Third, the setbacks and prohibited zones do not contradict state regulation of oil and gas activities. The proposed local restrictions were developed to protect public health and the environment and do not interfere with the state's goal to develop and utilize oil and gas resources. Specifically, the Ordinance will not prevent the operation of oil and gas wells currently existing within the prohibited zones and/or setbacks if these sites can demonstrate vested rights and will not eliminate future access to sub-surface oil and gas resources located in the restricted areas....

* * *

## Notes and Questions

1. **Industry's aggressive stance.** Evidently, the public review process for this proposed ordinance was fraught with allegations of illegality, and as discussed below, protection of property "vested rights." The reality of a small rural community, like Arvin, entering into protracted litigation against the oil industry was daunting to City officials, even with the support of several community-based organizations, in particular the Committee for a Better Arvin and the Center on Race, Poverty & the Environment, that played significant roles in organizing the residents' awareness and support of the ordinance. The Attorney General's letter also relied on scientific reports and cited a number of other jurisdictions in oil-producing states, such as Texas, and other local jurisdictions in California, such as the City of Carson, that have incorporated setbacks. On July 18, 2018, the Arvin City Council voted unanimously to approve the proposed oil and gas ordinance. Discuss the importance of the Attorney General's letter in addressing the political power dynamic described by Professors Arnold and Kaswan. How and why do you think the Attorney General chose to submit a letter regarding this proposed ordinance? If you were the Deputy Attorney General charged with drafting the letter, what other evidence would you have gathered, or have wanted to be available?

2. **Community members in political office.** At the time of the vote, Arvin's City Council consisted of Mayor Jose Gurrola, elected mayor of Arvin in 2016 at the age of 23 and with the campaign promise of addressing oil and gas operations, and three council members all under the age of 30. Similarly, for an interesting discussion of how the dispute over siting a polychlorinated biphenyl (PCB) disposal site in Warren County, North Carolina, led community members to successfully seek political office, and how their resulting political power prevented additional PCB facilities from being sited in the county and led to detoxification of the landfill, *see* Dollie Burwell and Luke W. Cole, *Environmental Justice Comes Full Circle: Warren County Before and After*, 1 GOLDEN GATE U. ENVTL. L.J. 9 (2007).

3. **Vested right to pollute?** The Arvin City Council and the Attorney General were very clear that the proposed ordinance did not infringe on "vested rights," or, the right to operate under already permitted oil and gas operations. Why? The claim of vested rights is often the first to be used by developers seeking to protect existing and permitted infrastructure. *Avco Community Developers, Inc. v. South Coast Regional*

*Comm'n*, 17 Cal. 3d 785 (1976) is a leading California case on vested rights, and there is a long history of jurisprudence holding generally that there is "no vested right to pollute," and imposing limitations on use of the doctrine. *See also People v. County of Kern*, 39 Cal. App. 3d 830 (1974), *Mobil Oil Corp. v. Superior Court*, 59 Cal. App. 3d 293 (1976), *Standard Oil v. Feldstein*, 105 Cal. App. 3d 590 (1980). Under what circumstances can local government's police power overcome a claim of vested rights?

Exactions often raise Fifth Amendment challenges if there is not a sufficient nexus between the exaction required of the developer and the activity regulated. What kinds of exactions could be imposed upon, for example, a manufacturing facility emitting toxic chemicals? A buffer zone, a park, a community center? How closely must the exaction mitigate the effects of the regulated activity to survive a takings challenge? The leading takings cases in the context of exactions are *Dolan v. City of Tigard*, 512 U.S. 374 (1994) and *Nollan v. California Coastal Comm'n*, 483 U.S. 825 (1987).

**4. Principles for equitable planning.** In another article, Professor Arnold identified eighteen principles for "planning for environmental justice, or equitable planning" that he argues can be incorporated into any local planning process. What are the core principles that you would identify in such a list? Professor Arnold notes that "effective planning for environmental and land use justice requires good information about environmental conditions in communities with a relatively high percentage of low-income people or people of color." He suggests that agencies should gather this information by conducting "environmental justice audits" that provide demographic, historical, cultural, environmental, land use, and economic information about a local community. Tony Arnold, *Planning for Environmental Justice*, PLAN. & ENVTL L. at 7–8 (2007). The following excerpt illustrates environmental justice land-use policies that have been successfully adopted, and some that have not.

### Emily Bergeron, *Local Justice: How Cities Can Protect and Promote Environmental Justice in a Hostile Environment*
32 NATURAL RESOURCES & ENV'T 8, 12 (2018)

… Many cities across the country have already sought to address actions impacting environmental justice through specific laws as well as by employing local land-use planning and zoning ordinances.

In 2009, Cincinnati became the first city to enact an environmental justice ordinance. Title X, Chapter 1041, Envtl. Justice, Ordinance 210-2009. The ordinance requires an environmental justice permit to be issued by the Office of Environmental Quality for any expansion or construction of hazardous waste facilities or hazardous air pollution point sources within city limits. The permit application must be reviewed by an Environmental Justice Board composed of health experts and community members. The ordinance also requires the permit process to follow all accepted procedures of good governance, including the allowance of public input (through public commenting), transparency, and community empowerment. Touted by many as groundbreaking, Cincinnati's environmental justice ordinance has not yet taken effect. By its terms, the law becomes effective only after the city council provides funding for implementation. To date, the council has yet to do that. Despite the lackluster outcome of its environmental justice ordinance, Cincinnati has been successful in utilizing Title X, Chapter 1001 on Air Quality, a provision controlling odors and air pollution that is grounded in nuisance law. The city has not been required to utilize this aspect of the [air quality] ordinance recently; however, it has proved an effective tool in helping to modify the behavior of at least some industrial facilities near residential neighborhoods. Although the city suspended the enforcement of the law when the Office of Environmental Management fell victim to financial limitations, in 2004 the city council enlisted the Hamilton County Department of Environmental Services to enforce the provisions of the [air quality] ordinance after numerous complaints were registered by individuals clustered near industrial facilities and waste sites. Matt Leingang, *This Air Stinks*, THE CINCINNATI ENQUIRER (Mar. 26, 2004); Kevin Aldridge, *City's Clean Air Act Targets Polluters*, THE CINCINNATI ENQUIRER (May 6, 2004).

Los Angeles's city council, in April 2016, unanimously approved special land-use restrictions for some of the city's most polluted neighborhoods to improve air quality and residential quality of life in areas with high concentrations of industrial uses. Los Angeles, CA, Ordinance No. 184246 (2016). The new requirements impose additional, more rigorous citywide codes and create new development standards in what are known as "Clean Up Green Up" (CUGU) Supplemental Use Districts. The CUGU initiative designated three of these special districts in predominantly Latino communities (Boyle Heights, Wilmington, and Pacoima).

Los Angeles's ordinance subjects all industrial businesses in CUGU districts to very specific site-planning requirements, ranging from lighting and enclosures to setback prescriptions. To better mitigate the impacts of proximity to industrial land uses, the CUGU district standards also place site-planning requirements on the publicly habitable spaces adjacent to industrial operations. The ordinance showcases the ability of localized approaches to environmental justice to target areas of concern. Specifically, it includes a citywide conditional use permit requirement for asphalt manufacturing and refinery facilities as well as citywide mandates for higher rated air filters in new developments built near freeways. The ordinance also pushes for greater enforcement for existing regulations.

Los Angeles's city attorneys have also taken up the environmental justice cause by creating the Environmental Justice and Protection Unit of the Los Angeles City Attorney's Office, which has been charged with enforcing state and city environmental statutes through criminal and civil actions. The special unit prosecutes matters from environmental crimes like illegal disposal of hazardous waste and toxic materials to civil actions for matters like lead paint abatement. The city attorney's office also frequently partners with other government agencies tasked with protecting the environment.

In New Jersey, the Camden City Sustainability Ordinance requires that all applicants for new development or modifications of existing developments submit an Environmental Impact and Benefits Assessment (EIBA) to the city's planning department. *See* Ordinance Approving Sustainability Requirements for the City of

Camden (Jan. 13, 2015). The ordinance, developed and advocated for by the Camden Green Team, the New Jersey Department of Environmental Protection's Office of Environmental Justice, the City Planning Department, and community stakeholders, requires that the EIBA attest to the fact that the development will not adversely affect the air and water quality of proximate neighborhoods and, additionally, that quality of life issues are addressed. Applicants are also "encouraged" to adopt best management practices. Although the guidance documents for drafting an EIBA have not been initialized, a preliminary draft indicates that developers must consider, among other things, whether disadvantaged populations are at greater risk of exposure to environmental hazards, whether residents have been involved in the planning process, and whether negative externalities are minimized. City of Camden, Dept. of Planning and Dev., Draft Environmental Impact and Benefit Assessment Guidance Document (Feb. 10, 2015).

North of Camden, Newark, a city suffering from environmental pollution from its dense transit network, industry, and waste and sewer treatment facilities, enacted its own law. The new ordinance mandates that developers request environmental permits to inform the city of environmental impacts. Ordinance of the City of Newark, N.J., 6PSF-e (2016). Pursuant to the ordinance, Newark's Environmental Commission, which is responsible for reviewing the developer's initial site plan application, advises the Central Planning Board, Zoning Board of Adjustment, and the public of potential cumulative pollution impacts. The ordinance also directs the Environmental Commission to establish a baseline for environmental conditions to help establish and address the environmental injustices that have led to unhealthy, concentrated levels of pollution in the city's poorest communities. The law requires industrial and commercial development proposals with environmental permit requirements to submit specific information about cumulative environmental impacts and gives decision-makers and the public critical information to encourage better decisions regarding sustainable development. *See id.*

... Not all cities have been as receptive to enacting environmental justice ordinances. For example, New Bedford, Massachusetts, rejected a proposed ordinance that would have required any building project that triggers certain state and federal environmental reviews to also obtain a city environmental justice permit. Proposed General Ordinance of the City of New Bedford, Art. 1, § 12-11 (2016). The ordinance would have required public notice and mandated that the city employ an environmental justice examiner to ensure that facilities would not pose an excessive risk to public health or a safety risk nor create a public nuisance. Unfortunately, opponents called the law a job killer, and ultimately the town council voted 4–7 against the proposed ordinance. Jeanette Barnes, *Environmental Justice Ordinance Blocked in Council*, SOUTHCOAST TODAY (Dec. 9, 2016).

* * *

## Notes and Questions

1. **Evaluate these measures.** Notably, Cincinatti's environmental justice ordinance was never fully implemented, and was largely repealed in 2010 due to city budget

deficits. As Professor Sheila Foster notes, more commonly found statutes addressing distribution of waste and other unwanted facilities require decision-makers to consider "soft criteria" in permit decisions, such as "the socioeconomic status of the host community, community perceptions, psychic costs, the potential for change in property values, and the cumulative health risks presented from other environmental sources in the host community." Typically, however, there is no statutory guidance for the weight decision-makers must give these factors in the permitting process. Sheila Foster, *Impact Assessment, in* THE LAW OF ENVIRONMENTAL JUSTICE: THEORIES AND PROCEDURES TO ADDRESS DISPROPORTIONATE RISKS 295, 323–24 (Michael Gerrard & Sheila Foster eds., 2d ed. 2008). Do Professor Foster's observations still apply to the above initiatives? Recall Professor Kuehn's taxonomy of the four kinds of justice embodied in environmental justice principles (*see* Chapter 1). Do these environmental justice ordinances achieve distributive, procedural, corrective, or social justice?

**2. CUGU.** Under Los Angeles' new Clean Up Green Up policy, new and expanding businesses must reduce the environmental impact on neighboring residents with buffer areas, landscaping, and other measures. Another measure mandates higher air filtration standards in new developments within 1,000 feet of a freeway. The ordinance also created an ombudsperson to assist local businesses with implementing these new regulations. For further discussion of this ten-year campaign that involved a coalition of community organizations and residents, academic researchers, foundation officials and other allies employing tactics centered on community organizing, such as "ground truthing," toxic tours, and documenting cumulative impacts, see Carla J. Kimbrough, *Los Angeles' "Clean Up, Green Up" Ordinance: A Victory in the Environmental Justice Fight*, NAT'L CIV. REV. (Spring 2017).

**3. The need to address displacement.** Of the 18 factors Professor Arnold proposes for equitable planning, one stands out in particular cases where communities successfully clean up and green up: prevent the displacement or expulsion of local residents by gentrification, redevelopment, new development, or brownfield remediation. Arnold, *supra* 7. As America's affordable housing crisis worsens, the need for measures to prevent displacement becomes even more apparent. Broad coalitions have emerged to tackle this serious issue. For instance, in California, the United Neighbors in Defense Against Displacement (UNIDAD) coalition is the product of a community collaboration formed to prevent the displacement of residents in South Central Los Angeles and to improve the health and economic well-being of low-income communities of color through responsible development.

In 2017, UNIDAD released the "People's Plan," the "culmination of contributions from hundreds of residents of South Central Los Angeles who have brought with them the lived experience and wisdom derived from struggle, survival and thriving in response to the many beauties and atrocities that have made South Central ground zero for movements of Black liberation, Immigrant rights and Indigenous sovereignty." The People's Plan provided recommendations in four broad categories: create a net gain of affordable housing and stop displacement; promote inclusive economic development that supports local workers and businesses; prioritize environmental justice and enhance community health; and strengthen community leadership in the land-use planning process. UNIDAD, *The People's Plan, available at* http://www.unidad-la.org/wp-content/uploads/2017/06/peoples-plan-report-FINAL.pdf (2017). The Los Angeles City Council adopted many of the People's Plan recommendations for its South and Southeast Community Plans. Advocates have expressed the need for inclusion of more specific anti-displacement policies, but at a minimum, this campaign has embedded policies developed by the affected low-income communities as part of their local land-use legal framework.

# Chapter 12

# Information Disclosure and Environmental Review

## A. Introduction

For more than half a century, information generation, analysis, and disclosure to the public has been a cornerstone of environmental law in the United States. In theory, this legal commitment to environmental transparency undergirds legal mechanisms designed to promote informed public participation in environmental decision-making and to provide remedies for noncompliance with environmental laws. As such, environmental policymaking embraces Justice Brandeis's oft-quoted observation that "sunlight is the most powerful disinfectant." Access to accurate and timely environmental information is particularly important for environmental justice. Such information can be a catalyst for social change. Access to environmental information undergirds the organizing and advocacy work central to environmental justice. It also facilitates effective community participation in rulemaking, and lays the groundwork for citizen suits, which are a statutory creation intended to allow affected members of the public to enforce environmental laws on their own, without requiring intervention by government agencies. EPA has previously acknowledged that "a basic tenet of risk communication in a democracy is that people and communities have a right to participate in decisions that affect their lives, their property, and the things they value." EPA, *Seven Cardinal Rules of Risk Communication* (April 1988).

Professor Sarah Lamdan had this to say about the centrality of environmental information:

> In our modern-day world, environmental information is the backbone of environmental law and regulation, playing a critical and necessary role at every level of environmental decision-making. Navigating this arena and dealing with the divergent interests of the different groups that participate in environmental activities and policymaking can often make accessing environmental information a very thorny and complicated venture. A 2014 account of a U.S. Environmental Protection Agency (EPA) battle over environmental information in the agricultural context underscores the complexities of environmental information and its access. As one reporter, frustrated with EPA's attempts to balance environmental information access and personal privacy, cynically described the events:

The Environmental Protection Agency (EPA) walked into court in Minnesota last week and asked a judge to issue an order to stop the federal agency from sharing information about some of the biggest polluters of our nation's waterways with the American public. That's right, the agency that is charged with protecting your environmental health is working hard to make sure ... that you don't have access to information. It would be shocking if it weren't so sadly commonplace....

EPA is often put in a difficult position, information-wise, recognizing both the importance of protecting the privacy of information that polluters report to the agency and also the key role of public participation in the Agency's programs. EPA recognizes that every environmental issue and effort benefits from public participation, and that environmental information access is vital to that participation. Citizen awareness is crucial to all facets of environmental preservation and the progress on environmental safety and welfare.

Sarah Lamdan, Environmental Information: Research, Access & Environmental Decisionmaking 1–3 (2017).

Professor Browne C. Lewis makes the case that "in order to effectively combat environmental discrimination, people must have access to quality information." She argues that a primary driver of disproportionate placement of environmental hazards in minority and low-income communities is the residents' lack of information about potential risk. If she is correct, access to environmental information must be part of the solution to remedy environmental injustice. Access to environmental information can educate community members, empowering them both to successfully oppose new projects in their neighborhoods that present environmental hazards, and to advocate for removing existing hazards from environmental justice communities. Browne C. Lewis, *What You Don't Know Can Hurt You: The Importance of Information in the Battle Against Environmental Class and Racial Discrimination*, 29 Wm. & Mary Envt'l L. & Pol'y Rev. 327, 328 (2005).

Regulators seem to agree. In 2015, EPA issued guidance titled *Guidance on Considering Environmental Justice During the Development of Regulatory Actions*. This guidance emphasized the key role of public participation as a tool for facilitating environmental justice and focused on three central questions:

This Guide empowers decision-makers responsible for developing rules to determine early in the process the level of focus and effort that is necessary and appropriate to achieve the E.O. 12898 goals. This approach can and should balance the need to make sure that strong, environmentally protective rules are promulgated in a timely way while ensuring EJ is considered to the maximum extent practicable where it has potential to impact regulatory decisions. To achieve these goals, the Guide directs rule-writers and decision-makers to respond to three core EJ questions...:

1. How did the public participation process provide transparency and meaningful participation for minority populations, low-income populations, tribes, and indigenous peoples?

2. How did the rule-writers identify and address existing and/or new disproportionate environmental and public health impacts on minority populations, low-income populations, and/or indigenous peoples?

3. How did actions taken under #1 and #2 impact the outcome or final decision?

This chapter will describe the access to information laws that environmental justice advocates rely on to organize for social and political change as well as to bring lawsuits challenging governmental and/or private action. The chapter will also identify how these laws create some gaps where information about environmental justice communities is missing and will describe some strategies for bridging those gaps.

# B. The National Environmental Policy Act

## 1. Introduction to NEPA

The National Environmental Policy Act (NEPA) is the oldest and best-known environmental disclosure statute. Generally characterized as a "look before you leap" statute, NEPA plays a critical role in gathering information about the environmental impacts of proposed agency actions. Section 102(c) of NEPA requires that "all agencies of the Federal Government shall ... include in every recommendation or report on proposals for legislation and other major Federal actions significantly affecting the quality of the human environment, a detailed statement by the responsible official on—

(i)   the environmental impact of the proposed action,

(ii)  any adverse environmental effects which cannot be avoided should the proposal be implemented,

(iii) alternatives to the proposed action,

(iv)  the relationship between local short-term uses of man's environment and the maintenance and enhancement of long-term productivity, and

(v)   any irreversible and irretrievable commitments of resources which would be involved in the proposed action should it be implemented."

42 U.S.C. § 4332(c).

NEPA cuts across the entire federal government, requiring that every federal agency perform an environmental review known as an Environmental Impact Statement (EIS) for "major Federal actions." Actions subject to this requirement include permit decisions, adoption of agency policy, formal planning, agency projects, and a slew of other actions potentially of interest to environmental justice communities.

NEPA implementing regulations are issued by the Council on Environmental Quality (CEQ), a small agency within the Executive Office of the President. These regulations outline how federal agencies must comply with NEPA. The CEQ requires that every agency adopt its own NEPA implementing procedures under the framework regulations provided by the CEQ. These CEQ regulations define "effects" or "impacts" to include "ecological ... aesthetic, historic, cultural, economic, social or health, whether direct, indirect, or cumulative." 40 C.F.R. § 1508.8.

There are clear windows for public participation in NEPA proceedings. CEQ regulations and guidance require agencies to seek public input at various points in the NEPA process, such as when determining the scope of matters to be included in the EIS ("scoping"), 40 C.F.R. § 1501.7, after issuing a draft EIS and after issuing a final EIS but before final decisions have been made about the project. 40 C.F.R. § 1502.8 Agencies also are required to hold public hearings when there is substantial controversy surrounding a project or substantial interest in a hearing. Additionally, agencies must respond to all public comments submitted on the draft EISs. This finalized environmental review is a final agency action subject to judicial review.

### Pathfinder on NEPA

For a thorough overview of the NEPA statute, regulations, and case law, *see* Joel A. Mintz, et al., A Practical Introduction to Environmental Law, Chap. 3 (2017). For general background about NEPA and environmental justice, *see* Uma Outka, *NEPA and Environmental Justice: Integration, Implementation, and Judicial Review*, 33 B.C. Env. Aff. L. Rev. 601 (2006); Browne C. Lewis, *What You Don't Know Can Hurt You: The Importance of Information in the Battle Against Environmental Class and Racial Discrimination*, 29 Wm. & Mary Envtl. L. & Pol'y Rev. 327 (2005). The regulations implementing NEPA, which are binding on all federal agencies, can be found at 40 C.F.R. §§ 1500–1518. For a discussion of the extent to which NEPA requires consideration of environmental justice issues, *see* U.S. EPA, *Final Guidance for Incorporating Environmental Justice Concerns in EPA's NEPA Compliance Analyses* (1998); CEQ, *Environmental Justice Guidance Under the National Environmental Policy Act*; Alan Ramo, *Environmental Justice as an Essential Tool in Environmental Review Statutes: A New Look at Federal Policies and Civil Rights Protections and California's Recent Initiatives*, 19 Hastings W.-N.W. J. Envtl. L. & Pol'y 41, 49–50 (2013).

Some of NEPA's provisions seem particularly well-suited for incorporating environmental justice concerns into the agency decision-making process. For example, unlike most pollution control statutes, NEPA requires that agencies evaluate the cumulative impacts of proposed projects. Read broadly, this requirement could impose a duty on agencies to consider the pre-existing concentration of industrial facilities, health risks, and environmental exposures in a community.

NEPA has a number of important limitations that affect its effectiveness as a tool for environmental justice. First, NEPA applies only to actions carried out by, funded by, or with some regulatory nexus to the federal government. Most pollution control permits are issued not by EPA, but by states (or in some instances tribes) that have been granted authority to implement federal environmental programs in lieu of EPA. Since NEPA only applies to *federal* actions, the actions of a state permitting agency may be outside of NEPA's purview. Sixteen states plus the District of Columbia and Puerto Rico have adopted similar statutes to fill this gap. These statutes, known as state environmental policy acts (SEPAs), govern projects approved by state or local agencies. *See, e.g.,* Washington State Environmental Policy Act, R.C.W. 43.21C; California Environmental Quality Act, Cal. P.R.C. §§ 21000–21004. They impose analogous information and participation requirements on state and local environmental decision-making. Increasingly, states require that the SEPA reviews include an assessment of potential climate impact, including additional greenhouse gas emissions.

Second, NEPA's broad public participation requirements do not apply unless the agency decides that it may be required to prepare an EIS. The EIS is a major document in which an agency examines the environmental impacts of its proposed action—it is through the EIS process that the agency may consider direct or indirect ecological, aesthetic, historical, cultural, and health impacts, as well as cumulative impacts. An EIS must identify alternatives to the proposed project and appropriate mitigation measures. However, NEPA only requires that agencies prepare an EIS under statutorily specified circumstances—courts have repeatedly interpreted Congress's use of the terms "major," "federal action" and "significantly" in the text of Section 102 of NEPA as indicating a legislative intent to narrow the statute's scope. In many cases, instead of an EIS, an agency will prepare a (theoretically) less-detailed Environmental Assessment (EA). One official purpose of an EA is to determine whether an EIS may be required for a proposed federal action. *See* 40 C.F.R. § 1508.9(a). Project proponents often prepare an EA, however, in order to support a Finding of No Significant Impact (FONSI), which is a determination by the federal action agency that no EIS is necessary for the proposed action. Over time, many EAs have grown to rival the volume and complexity of many EISs. For the Dakota Access Pipeline (DAPL), which in 2016 attracted international attention and outcry led by tribes and indigenous rights groups, the Corps of Engineers prepared an EA instead of an EIS. The DAPL EA was 983 pages—and the reviewing court found it was still inadequate. *Standing Rock Sioux Tribe v. U.S. Army Corps of Eng'rs*, 255 F. Supp. 3d 101 (D.D.C. 2017) (remanding to the Corps of Engineers).

The overwhelming majority of projects subject to NEPA do not involve the preparation of an EIS. Most now either result in a FONSI following completion of an EA or are excluded from the NEPA process from the start through use of a "categorical exemption." By regulation, a federal agency can categorically exclude actions expected not to "individually or cumulatively have a significant effect on the human environment." Although intended to target minor maintenance or procurement, categorical exclusions have been used to exclude some major issues of concern like noise from FAA flight paths or the proposed border wall and associated infrastructure on the United States-Mexico border. In one flagrant case of abuse, the former Marine Minerals Service used a categorical exclusion to exempt from NEPA the construction of deepwater wells in the Gulf of Mexico, leading to the worst oil spill in U.S. history

**Figure 12-1:** Earthjustice attorney Stefanie Tsosie, representing Standing Rock Sioux Tribe in litigation against the Dakota Access Pipeline. Seattle, WA. March 28, 2019. Photo: Cliff Villa.

and devastating impacts on communities of the Gulf Coast. *See* Oliver A. Houck, *Worst Case and the* Deepwater Horizon *Blowout: There Ought to Be a Law*, 40 Envtl. L. Rep. News & Analysis 11033 (2010).

Even when an agency prepares an EIS, that does not ensure protection for environmental justice communities. Federal courts have interpreted NEPA as imposing only procedural rather than substantive requirements on federal agencies. Agencies thus fulfill their NEPA obligations when they consider and fully disclose the environmental impacts of proposed projects. NEPA does not require that agencies select the less environmentally harmful alternatives identified in the EIS, nor does it require that agencies adopt mitigation measures to reduce the environmental impacts of a project that are identified in the EIS. As the Supreme Court has explained, NEPA "merely prohibits uninformed—rather than unwise—agency action." *Robertson v. Methow Valley*, 490 U.S. 332, 351 (1989). SEPAs vary in this regard; while many are similarly procedural, several require that state agencies minimize or avoid significant adverse impacts (for example, Minnesota, New York, and California).

Further narrowing NEPA's scope, federal courts have ruled that EPA does not have to comply with NEPA when the environmental assessment and public participation procedures required by an EPA regulatory action are "functionally equivalent" to those mandated by the NEPA process. EPA thus does not comply with NEPA, when, for example, it issues hazardous waste permits under the Resource Conservation and Recovery Act (RCRA). As a result, when EPA issues a permit under RCRA, the agency does not have to consider socioeconomic impacts or project alternatives, as required by NEPA, and the RCRA permitting process provides fewer opportunities for public participation than NEPA. EPA also has been successful in arguing that it does not have to prepare EISs in connection with cleanup orders under Superfund. Congress has created express statutory exemptions from NEPA for a number of EPA programs, such as all actions under the Clean Air Act and many under the Clean Water Act.

* * *

## Notes and Questions

1. **Toothless?** Although NEPA is often criticized as weak because it does not impose any substantive requirements on federal agencies, many scholars contend that it can nonetheless be of considerable value to environmental justice communities because it serves as an information-gathering, educational, and organizational tool. For example, mandated disclosure of alternatives and mitigation measures can leave the agencies more vulnerable to criticism and result in pressure for them to take steps to mitigate adverse project impacts they might have otherwise overlooked. Likewise, the environmental review process can create important opportunities for organizing community opposition and ensuring community comments are included in the administrative record—to be used if and when it becomes necessary to seek judicial review of any final agency action.

2. **The "Mitigated FONSI."** For advocates of environmental justice, another important opportunity to engage in the NEPA process might come before an action agency issues a FONSI. In reaching a finding that a proposed action will not significantly affect the environment, an agency may rely on mitigation measures to avoid an adverse effect. See 40 C.F.R. § 1508.20 (definition of "mitigation"). Thus, many EAs will conclude with a "mitigated FONSI." One example is the mitigated FONSI for the Dakota Access Pipeline, which, according to the Corps of Engineers, was the result of "over 250 interactions" between the Corps, Dakota Access, and "consulting parties" including tribal governments, historic preservation officers, and other "interested parties." The DAPL mitigated FONSI also followed a public comment period on the draft EA and, according to the Corps, "formal government-to-government consultation with tribal representatives." Following all this process, the DAPL FONSI provided the following:

> The majority of potential impacts would be mitigated by [Horizontal Directional Drilling (HDD) beneath river crossings], by which Dakota Access would install the pipeline beneath sensitive resources without surface disturbance, and allow pipeline construction to proceed with the fewest possible

impacts. Additional mitigation measures are set out in the Environmental Construction Plan; the Stormwater Pollution Prevention Plan; the Spill Prevention, Control, and Countermeasure Plan, the HDD Construction Plan; the HDD Contingency Plan; the Unanticipated Cultural Resources Discovery Plan; and the Geographical Response Plan. Unavoidable impacts to land use and vegetation would be temporary and land would return to current land use once construction is complete.

U.S. Army Corps of Engineers, Mitigated Finding of No Significant Impact, Environmental Assessment, Dakota Access Pipeline Project at 3 (July 25, 2016).

Given all this evident process and apparent mitigation of anticipated impacts, why do you imagine the Standing Rock Sioux Tribe and other parties remained so concerned about completion and operation of the Dakota Access Pipeline, to the point where litigation continues today? Is it a question of procedural injustice? Distributional injustice? Both?

**3. The EIS goes global.** The impact assessment approach pioneered by NEPA has been widely emulated around the world. In the vernacular of international environmental law, "Environmental Impact Assessments" (EIAs) have found their way into international treaties like the Convention on Environmental Impact Assessment in a Transboundary Context (Espoo Agreement); the Madrid Protocol to the Antarctic Treaty of 1991; the Convention on Biological Diversity; and the North American Agreement on Environmental Cooperation. Supporters claim that these measures ensure deliberate and transparent analysis of the consequences of environmental decision-making, and promote environmental democracy. By informing and facilitating public involvement in government decisions on actions impacting their communities, these processes can foster the community engagement and support needed to make sure development decisions are politically and environmentally sustainable. Indeed, in its 2010 decision *concerning Pulp Mills on the River Uruguay (Argentina v. Uruguay)*, the International Court of Justice found that the practice of environmental assessments "in recent years has gained so much acceptance among States that it may now be considered a requirement under general international law." [2010] ICJ Rep. 14 ('Pulp Mills'), at paragraph 204. What do you think accounts for the singular attractiveness of this approach? Do you see any limitations?

**4. Pro forma?** One critique of this information-based approach notes that "information disclosure statutes intended to create transparency can instead merely become pro forma filing requirements." Under the Oil Pollution Act of 1990, adopted in the wake of the *Exxon Valdez* environmental disaster, BP had to submit a spill response plan for regulatory approval before drilling could began. However, BP's Gulf of Mexico Oil Spill Response Plan listed walruses, sea otters, sea lions, and seals as the "sensitive biological resources" at risk in the event of an oil spill, even though none of those animals live in the Gulf of Mexico. BP clearly generated these documents by cutting and pasting from prior environmental assessments rather than by conducting the independent analysis required by law. "The fact that the Plan was approved raises questions about whether regulators read the documents before approving them."

Rebecca Bratspies & Sarah Lamdan, *The Human Right to Environmental Information*, *in* Human Rights and the Environment: Indivisibility, Dignity, and Legality (2018).

## 2. Agency Guidance on NEPA and E.O. No. 12898

Many commentators have argued for a broader reading of NEPA to address environmental justice issues. Since President Clinton issued the 1994 Executive Order on Environmental Justice, E.O. No. 12898 (Feb. 11, 1994) (discussed in Chapter 10), federal agencies have sought to adapt the NEPA process to take into account environmental justice concerns. The Executive Order included two key information gathering and disseminating directives. Section 3 of the Executive Order specifically recognized the importance of research, data collection, and analysis, particularly with respect to the multiple and cumulative exposures to environmental hazards that environmental justice communities face, and Section 5 of the Executive Order required that agencies work to ensure effective public participation and access to information about environmental justice issues. Specifically, Section 5-5(b) of the Executive Order suggested that each federal agency may "wherever practicable and appropriate, translate crucial public documents, notices and hearings, relating to human health or the environment for limited English speaking populations," and Section 5-5(c) directed that agencies "work to ensure that public documents, notices, and hearings relating to human health or the environment are concise, understandable, and readily accessible to the public."

In 1997, the CEQ issued *Environmental Justice Guidance Under the National Environmental Policy Act*. This CEQ guidance, which was intended to implement E.O. No. 12898, acknowledged that "[e]nvironmental justice issues may arise at any step of the NEPA process and agencies should consider these issues at each and every step of the process, as appropriate." *Id.* at 8. To that end, the CEQ guidance identified core environmental justice information that should be considered as part of a NEPA analyses. Such core information would include the demographic composition of the affected area; health data addressing multiple or cumulative exposure to environmental hazards; and social, economic, or other factors that might amplify the environmental effects of the proposed agency action. Where NEPA documents had traditionally analyzed impacts on broadly defined affected areas and populations, the CEQ guidance called on agencies to determine whether an area impacted by a proposed project includes low-income populations, minority populations, or Indian tribes, and whether the proposed action is likely to have a disproportionately high and adverse human health or environmental impact on these populations. Agencies were also directed to consider the potential for multiple or cumulative exposure, historical patterns of exposure to environmental hazards, and cultural differences which may lead certain communities to experience impacts more severely than the general population. For example, the guidance notes, "data on different patterns of living, such as subsistence

> ## The following steps may be considered, as appropriate, in developing an innovative strategy for effective public participation:
>
> - Coordination with individuals, institutions, or organizations in the affected community to educate the public about potential health and environmental impacts and enhance public involvement;
>
> - Translation of major documents (or summaries thereof), provision of translators at meetings, or other efforts as appropriate to ensure that limited-English speakers potentially affected by a proposed action have an understanding of the proposed action and its potential impacts;
>
> - Provision of opportunities for limited-English speaking members of the affected public to provide comments throughout the NEPA process;
>
> - Provision of opportunities for public participation through means other than written communication, such as personal interviews or use of audio or video recording devices to capture oral comments;
>
> - Use of periodic newsletters or summaries to provide updates on the NEPA process to keep the public informed;
>
> - Use of different meeting sizes or formats, or variation on the type and number of media used, so that communications are tailored to the particular community or population;
>
> - Circulation or creation of specialized materials that reflect the concerns and sensitivities of particular populations such as information about risks specific to subsistence consumers of fish, vegetation, or wildlife;
>
> - Use of locations and facilities that are local, convenient, and accessible to the disabled, low-income and minority communities, and Indian tribes; and
>
> - Assistance to hearing-impaired or sight-impaired individuals.

**Figure 12-2:** CEQ, *Environmental Justice Guidance Under the National Environmental Policy Act* at 13 (1997).

fish, vegetation, or wildlife consumption and the use of well water in rural communities may be relevant to the analysis." *Id.* at 14.

The CEQ guidance directed agencies to develop strategies for overcoming "barriers to meaningful participation" and to include diverse constituencies from affected communities in the NEPA process. It also suggested some pathways for agency compliance with the public participation mandate.

With respect to NEPA's alternatives analysis, the CEQ guidance instructs that the distribution and magnitude of any disproportionate adverse effects should be a factor in the agency's identification of the "environmentally preferable alternative" for a project (which agencies are required to identify in a Record of Decision following preparation of an EIS). *Id.* at 15. Moreover, in developing mitigation measures, the CEQ guidance directed agencies to solicit views from the affected populations throughout the public participation process and proposed that mitigation measures should reflect the views of affected low-income populations, minority populations, or Indian tribes to the maximum extent practicable. However, the CEQ Guidelines made it clear that identifying disproportionate impacts did not "preclude a proposed agency action from going forward, nor does it necessarily compel a conclusion that a proposed action is environmentally unsatisfactory." The CEQ guidance also makes clear that the Executive Order "does not change the prevailing legal thresholds and statutory interpretations under NEPA and existing case law." *Id.* at 9.

During the Obama administration, EPA issued two key guidance documents for incorporating environmental justice into agency decision-making. Environmental Protection Agency, FINAL GUIDANCE ON CONSIDERING ENVIRONMENTAL JUSTICE DURING THE DEVELOPMENT OF AN ACTION (2015); Environmental Protection Agency, FINAL TECHNICAL GUIDANCE FOR ASSESSING ENVIRONMENTAL JUSTICE IN REGULATORY ANALYSIS (2015). EPA described these guidance documents as an effort "to advance environmental justice and to protect the health and safety of the historically under-represented in the environmental decision-making process—minority, low-income, and indigenous populations, and tribes—who are often most at risk from environmental hazards." The guidance documents provided direction on when environmental justice should be considered during rulemaking, and on how to do so in an analytical fashion.

* * *

### Alan Ramo, *Environmental Justice as an Essential Tool in Environmental Review Statutes: A New Look at Federal Policies and Civil Rights Protections and California's Recent Initiatives*
19 HASTINGS W.-N.W. J. ENVTL. L. & POL'Y 41, 48–50 (2013)

[The EPA] followed CEQ with its own guidelines on environmental justice in which it presented a number of examples of how environmental justice may be brought into the project environmental review process. The guidelines recognize that, due to unique cultural or socioeconomic challenges facing minority or low-income communities, some cumulative impacts or resource utilization may not be apparent during a typical scoping or screening of a project. As the EPA guidance states:

> This includes subsistence living situations (e.g., subsistence fishing, hunting, gathering, farming), diet, and other differential patterns of consumption of natural resources. If a community is reliant on consumption of natural resources, such as subsistence fishing, an additional exposure pathway may be associated with the community that is not relevant to the population at large. Similarly, dietary practices within a community or ethnic group, such as a diet low in certain vitamins and minerals, may increase risk factors for that group.

Due to historical zoning practices and an imbalance of power resulting from poverty and racism, minority and low-income communities may face multiple exposures to toxic hazards with few resources to mitigate these exposures. The guidance recognizes the importance of these factors when addressing cumulative impacts:

> This includes such issues as whether affordable or free quality health care is available and, whether any cultural barriers exist to seeking health care. Many

low-income and/or minority communities lack adequate levels and quality of health care, often due to lack of resources or lack of access to health care facilities....

Other indirect effects which a low-income or minority population, due to economic disadvantage, may not be able to avoid, that will have a synergistic effect with other risk factors (e.g., vehicle pollution, lead-based paint poisoning, existence of abandoned toxic sites, dilapidated housing stock).

Thus, the guidance calls for demographic analysis at the beginning of project review. If vulnerable subpopulations will be exposed, "this should trigger both an enhanced outreach effort to assure that low-income and minority populations are engaged in public participation and analysis designed to identify and assess the impacts. Also, a positive response to this question should increase the team's sensitivity to the potential for cumulative impacts."

In theory, this approach is merely assuring a more thorough environmental analysis. The guidance seems to denote, however, that typical everyday analysis might overlook many of these factors. Thus, demographic analysis is necessary to ensure that a more proper effort with an appropriate level of sensitivity is conducted in order to root out what should be determined, under conventional environmental review analysis, to be significant impacts. The guidance states that their intent is to "heighten awareness of EPA staff in addressing environmental justice issues within NEPA analyses and considering the full potential for disproportionately high and adverse human health or environmental effects on minority populations and low-income populations...."

\* \* \*

## Notes and Questions

1. **Your turn.** Are there other ideas that you think should be included in agency guidance to address environmental justice concerns?

2. **Lost in translation?** Should EPA and other agencies be required to translate NEPA documents whenever a project will impact a community that has a significant percentage of members who do not speak English? How large a percentage should this be? What if there are numerous, monolingual subpopulations within the affected community — should agencies be required to translate documents into multiple languages? Should entire documents be translated, or only summaries and/or important documents? (As noted, EISs and even EAs can sometimes be several hundred pages long.) What other approaches should be explored? Should technical assistance be provided to help communities participate in the NEPA review process?

3. Federal transportation agencies have issued multiple directives for how to address environmental justice concerns in their own NEPA documents. The Department of Transportation (DOT) issued EJ Order 5610.2(a) requiring that all programs and activities be evaluated to determine whether they would have disproportionately high

adverse impacts on minority or low-income populations, considering the "totality" of individual and cumulative effects. It also specifies measures to be taken to mitigate such impacts. In 2012, the Federal Transit Administration (FTA) issued an Environmental Justice Circular which was intended to ensure that FTA funding recipients avoided, minimized, or mitigated disproportionately high and adverse health and environmental effects, including social and economic effects, on minority populations and low-income populations. The Circular also required FTA funding recipients to incorporate environmental justice principles into their wider transportation planning and decision-making processes, as well as into project-specific environmental reviews. The Federal Aviation Administration (FAA) uses Order 1050.1E: *Environmental Impacts: Policies and Procedures*, to comply with E.O. No. 12898 by incorporating environmental justice principles into its NEPA processes. In addition, the FAA Office of Airports has issued guidance for compliance with environmental justice requirements in Chapter 10 of the *Environmental Desk Reference for Airport Actions*.

## C. EJSCREEN

In 2015, EPA released **EJSCREEN**, an environmental justice mapping and screening tool intended to help the agency meet its responsibilities related to the protection of public health and the environment. EJSCREEN created a nationally consistent data set and Geographical Information System (GIS) tool for combining environmental and demographic indicators in maps and reports. EPA intended EJSCREEN to both be a tool that would assist agency decisionmakers in implementing the environmental justice guidance documents, and a resource for the wider public.

EJSCREEN pulled together data from the Clean Air Act, the Resource Conservation and Recovery Act, the Clean Water Act, the Emergency Planning and Community Right-to-Know Act, and other key federal statutes. It draws demographic information obtained from the U.S. Census Bureau's American Community Survey (ACS). EJSCREEN then pairs this demographic information with environmental hazard exposure data oriented around eleven environmental indicators, including:

- Air pollution:
  - $PM_{2.5}$ [particulate matter] level in air
  - Ozone level in air
  - NATA [National Air Toxics Assessment] air toxics:
    - Diesel particulate matter level in air
    - Air toxics cancer risk
    - Air toxics respiratory hazard index;
- Traffic proximity and volume: Amount of vehicular traffic, and distance from roads;
- Lead paint indicator: Percentage of housing units built before 1960, as an indicator of potential exposure to lead;

- Proximity to waste and hazardous chemical facilities or sites: Number of significant industrial facilities and/or hazardous waste sites nearby, and distance from those:
  - National Priorities List (NPL) sites
  - Risk Management Plan (RMP) Facilities
  - Hazardous waste Treatment, Storage, and Disposal Facilities (TSDFs);
- Wastewater discharge indicator: Proximity to toxicity-weighted wastewater discharges.

In doing so, EJSCREEN operationalizes Professor Paul Mohai and Robin Saha's "distance based method" for assessing proximity to environmental hazards. Paul Mohai & Robin Saha, *Reassessing Racial and Socioeconomic Disparities in Environmental Justice Research*, 43 DEMOGRAPHY 383 (2006); *Racial Inequality in the Distribution of Hazardous Waste: A National-Level Reassessment*, 54 Soc. PROBL. 54,343 (2007). This method rejects reliance on census tract data to assess environmental justice impacts because census tracts can vary widely in size, and populations tend to be clustered within those tracts. The distance-based method instead draws a circle around the exact location of the hazardous sites, considers the demographic characteristics of populations within a specified distance of the hazard to communities located farther away. Mohai and Saha demonstrated how comparing the population demographics within that specified distance from the environmental hazard to the wider population of the community uncovers otherwise hidden demographic disparities between host neighborhoods and non-host areas. Paul Mohai & Robin Saha, *Which Came First: People or Pollution? Assessing the Disparate Siting and Post-Siting Demographic Change Hypotheses of Environmental Injustice*, 10 ENV. RES LET. 11508 (2015).

EJSCREEN allows environmental justice advocates, regulators, and others to easily connect environmental and demographic characteristics of any specific location in the United States. This information can be used to screen for areas that may be candidates for additional consideration, analysis, or outreach by making environmental and demographic information readily available in a consistent form. EJSCREEN could thus shape implementation of permitting, enforcement, and compliance practices.

For example, by opening EJSCREEN (https://ejscreen.epa.gov/mapper/) and dropping a pin on the border of Northern Manhattan and the Bronx on an EJSCREEN map, a user can learn about the populations and relative exposure to environmental hazards of the population within a one-mile radius of that pin. EJSCREEN can then provide information about the environmental hazards within a one-mile radius of the pin. Clicking on another tab provides the demographics information for that same one-mile radius.

EJSCREEN comes with a disclaimer that it "does not identify 'EJ communities.'" Nevertheless, EJSCREEN could potentially be used to establish consistent baselines for techniques to be used in defining environmental justice communities. Currently, agencies select their own methodologies for considering the impacts of a project on

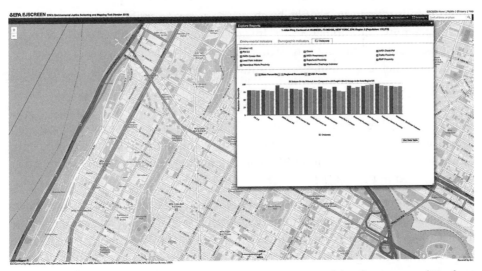

**Figure 12-3:** Screen shot from EPA EJSCREEN depicting environmental data for area around Northern Manhattan and the Bronx (2019).

minority and low-income communities. The only caveat is that the methods selected must be reasonable and adequately explained. *See Standing Rock Sioux Tribe v. U.S. Army Corps of Eng'rs*, 255 F. Supp. 3d 101, 137 (D.D.C. 2017) (parameters of envi-

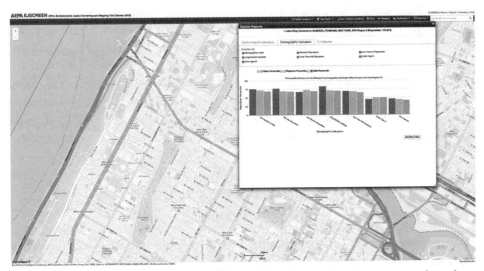

**Figure 12-4:** Screen shot from EPA EJSCREEN depicting demographics for area around Northern Manhattan and the Bronx (2019).

ronmental justice review "should 'be chosen so as not to artificially dilute or inflate the affected minority population.'"). In light of this requirement, EJSCREEN might be a logical tool for building consistency in how various federal agencies answer the question of whether a population constituted an environmental justice community.

### Notes and Questions

1. **Your neighborhood?** Check out EJSCREEN on your computer, drop a pin on your neighborhood, and run a default report. What do these results tell you about concerns in your local community? What do you know about your community that is *not* reflected in the results?

2. **Other GIS tools.** The EPA encourages all federal agencies, states, municipalities, tribal governments, and community advocates to use EJSCREEN as a common platform across jurisdictional boundaries in the United States. However, states and other governments and organizations remain free to develop and use other GIS tools to identify potential areas for environmental justice concerns. One such other tool, released in 2012, is CalEnviroScreen, now in use by state agencies throughout California. For more on CalEnviroScreen, *see* Chapter 10 ("Governmental Initiatives to Promote Environmental Justice").

3. **"EJ communities."** As noted above, EJSCREEN comes with a disclaimer that it "does not identify 'EJ communities.'" However, prior versions of EPA's GIS tool (e.g., "EJSEAT") did exactly that, quickly flagging a given geographic area as either an "EJ community" or not. What are the relative advantages and disadvantages of such a ready designation? From the perspective of a government regulator? From the perspective of a community advocate? Can you imagine why some community activists would desire designation as an "EJ community" while other community members would strongly resist that designation? In the case study below concerning the Atlantic Coast Pipeline, can you see how delineation of an "EJ community" (or "EJ population") may be used by project proponents to the detriment of affected communities?

## D. Community Participation in the NEPA Process

As the materials below show, the initial parameters used to define what constitutes a community for purposes of an environmental justice analysis can be outcome determinative. A recent decision by the Federal Energy Regulatory Commission (FERC) highlights how advocates might use data developed by EJSCREEN to try to reshape agency decisions.

### Atlantic Coast Pipeline
#### 161 FERC 61,042 (Oct. 13, 2017)

[In 2017, FERC issued a "Certificate of Public Convenience" authorizing construction of the Atlantic Coast Pipeline Project over the strenuous objection of environmental justice advocates. Before doing so, the commission prepared an environmental impact statement for the project under NEPA that included an environmental justice analysis.]

### 3. Major Environmental Issues and Comments on the Final EIS

....

#### ii. Environmental Justice

253. Executive Order 12898 requires that specified federal agencies make achieving environmental justice part of their missions by identifying and addressing, as appropriate, disproportionately high and adverse human or environmental health effects of their programs, policies, and activities on minorities and low-income populations. The Commission is not one of the specified agencies and the provisions of Executive Order 12898 are not binding on this Commission. Nonetheless, in accordance with our usual practice, the final EIS addresses this issue.

254. In accordance with EPA guidance, the final EIS followed a three-step approach for environmental justice reviews: (1) determine the existence of minority and low-income populations in the project area; (2) determine if the resource impacts are high and adverse; and (3) determine if any identified high and adverse impacts fall disproportionately on environmental justice populations. If the federal agency finds that any of these conditions are not present, the agency may then conclude its review and determine the action is not sited in a discriminatory manner on low-income or minority communities.

255. The construction and operation of the proposed facilities would affect a mix of racial/ethnic and socioeconomic areas in the ... project area. However, not all impacts identified in the final EIS would affect minority or low-income populations. The primary adverse impacts on the environmental justice communities associated with the construction of projects would be the temporary increases in dust, noise, and traffic from project construction. These impacts would occur along the entire pipeline route and in areas with a variety of socioeconomic backgrounds. We also received numerous comments expressing concern about minority and low-income communities near the proposed Compressor Station 2 in Buckingham County, Virginia. Based on the methodology used in the final EIS, of the three census tracts within one mile of Compressor Station 2, one is a designated low-income community, and none of the tracts were designated as minority environmental justice populations.

256. Atlantic ... would implement a series of measures that would minimize potential impacts on the communities, including environmental justice communities, near project facilities. For example, Atlantic ... proposes to employ proven construction-related practices to control fugitive dust, such as application of water or other commercially available dust control agents on unpaved areas subject to frequent vehicle traffic. Similarly, Atlantic ... will implement noise control measures during construction and operation of the projects.

257. In response to comments regarding specific environmental health concerns of minority communities, including African American populations, the final EIS considered in greater detail the potential risks of impacts falling on these communities, and what those effects would be. Due to construction dust and compressor station

emissions, African American populations near [two of the] projects could experience disproportionate health impacts due to higher rates of asthma within the overall African American community. However, health impacts from construction dust would be temporary, localized, and minor. Health impacts from compressor station emissions would be moderate because, while they would be permanent facilities, air emissions would not exceed regulatory permittable levels. While the final EIS discusses the potential for the risk of impacts to fall disproportionately on minority communities, it further notes that, in relation to comments received regarding Compressor Station 2's effects on African Americans, the census tracts around the station are not designated as minority environmental justice populations. Therefore, by following the methodology outlined above, the final EIS concludes, and we agree, that the projects will not result in disproportionately high and adverse impacts on environmental justice populations as a result of air quality impacts, including impacts associated with the proposed Compressor Station 2. Further, no disproportionately high and adverse impacts on environmental justice populations as a result of other resources impacts will be expected as a result of the projects.

* * *

By contrast, environmental justice advocates argued strenuously that the commission's conclusions were inaccurate. They noted that the commission did not consult with four state-recognized Indian Tribes, even though the pipeline would cross their traditional territories and the overwhelming majority of at least one of the Tribes members live in counties that would be affected by the pipeline.

They objected that the commission acted unreasonably when it used bifurcated analytical standards for its environmental justice analysis. For identifying impacted low-income communities, the commission used the conventional method of population within a one-mile radius of the project. However, for determining whether the minority population within one-mile radius of the project constitutes an environmental justice community, the commission instead compared minority population percentages in census tracts near the pipeline with the percentage of minorities in the county.

## Joint Comments by Public Interest Groups on Draft Environmental Impact Statement
### In the Matter of Atlantic Coast Pipeline
### (Apr. 5, 2017), pp. 66–71

The DEIS analysis of minority populations is remarkable in its contorted logic used to minimize the relative impact on people of color. It notes that "[i]n North Carolina, minorities comprise 30.5 percent of the total population. The percentage of minorities in the North Carolina census tracts within 1 mile of ACP ranges from 12.5 to 95.5 percent. In 13 of the 42 census tracts, the minority population is meaningfully greater than that of the county in which it is located." FERC uses this result to reinforce its conclusion that there are no disproportionate impacts on environmental justice populations.

Remarkably, unlike using poverty data in census tracts within one mile of the pipeline corridor to compare to the state as a whole, FERC's study only compares minority population percentages in census tract near pipeline with the percentage of minorities in the county in which this occurs. As most of the North Carolina counties along the proposed pipeline corridor have minority populations significantly above the state average this greatly minimizes the apparent disproportionality in minorities impacted. Northampton County, for instance, is 58% African American, compared to a state average of 22%. A comparable analysis to disproportionate impacts on low-income residents would use a comparison to state minority populations, and would result in a dramatically different conclusion....

Environmental justice analyses are mandatory in Federal environmental documents, but there is no standard method for computing disproportionate impacts. As such, the research community has long raised concerns about potential misapplication....

[T]he analysis fails to identify major impacts on American Indian populations living along the preferred pipeline route. Data from the DEIS shows that in North Carolina alone, approximately 30,000 American Indians live in census tracts along the route. This number represents one quarter of the state's American Indian population and 1% of the entire American Indian population of the U.S. The environmental justice analysis is silent on this issue, but instead concludes that the preferred route has no disproportionate impacts on minority communities. It draws this conclusion by counting up the number of census tracts with "meaningfully greater" minority populations than the county in which it they are located. Failure of the environmental justice analysis to detect these impacts is based on at least two flaws in the method.

The first flaw is that the environmental justice analysis aggregates results from counties treated as separate comparison groups but fails to account for variations in population size and racial make-up among counties. County-level data can provide valuable comparison statistics for targeted census blocks, but when the baseline data change for each county (as is the case here), county-level results cannot be compared to draw conclusions about impacts along an entire project route. Regulators may be able to adjust the existing analysis for changes to baseline data on a county-by-county basis, but even this analysis lacks the ability to draw statistical conclusions. A more robust method would involve pooling all of the impacted census tracts for each state, and comparing this test population with a suitable reference population comprising appropriate non-affected census tracts from each state. This method would allow regulators to (1) compute disproportionality rates from the demographic profiles of test and reference populations and (2) determine whether these rates are statistically significant....

Second, the definition of "meaningfully greater" is flawed. [The Draft EIS] defines "meaningfully greater" as ten percentage points higher than the comparison group. By defining differences in terms of percentage points, the analysis masks relevant information in areas where minority (or poor) populations are both very small and very large. At the small end of the scale, a reference population that comprises, say, 2% minority individuals would require that the test population be at least 12% minority in order to identify a disproportionate impact. In this example, the minority population would have to be impacted at six times the rate of the reference population before registering as disproportionate. At the other end of the scale, the reference populations themselves become an environmental justice consideration. If a reference population is mostly made up of minority populations that the environmental justice analysis is intended to study, then the choice of reference population becomes suspect, raising the question "meaningfully greater" than what?

The current analysis takes a single, interstate project and breaks it down into a series of county-level projects for evaluating impacts on minorities. In doing so, the analysis masks large disproportionate impacts on minority populations, particularly American Indians and African Americans in eastern North Carolina. According to the executive summary of the DEIS, the public benefits of the project are realized at the regional scale and not necessarily in the counties or census tracts adjoining the pipeline route. For these reasons, FERC should conduct a new environmental justice analysis that considers the nature of this pipeline as a single, inter-state project and considers reference populations more carefully given the stated motivation for the project.

\* \* \*

## Notes and Questions

1. **EJ community designations?** Consider FERC's conclusion above that "of the three census tracts within one mile of Compressor Station 2, one is a designated low-income community, and none of the tracts were designated as minority environmental justice populations." Designated by whom? As noted previously, EJSCREEN will not assign such designations. Does that leave individual agencies like FERC to invent designations of their own? Is this a case where an official designation of "EJ community" by EJSCREEN would aid the interests of concerned community members?

2. **In your own words.** As simply as possible, how would you restate the central critique expressed by the community comments above?

# E. Judicial Review of NEPA Analyses

Very few cases have addressed either the impact of the Executive Order on Environmental Justice, or the role that the CEQ and EPA guidance should play in decisions under NEPA. As an initial matter, since Section 6-609 of the Executive Order provides that it does not create any private right of action to judicial review, some courts have held that they lack jurisdiction to consider challenges to environmental justice analyses carried out under the Order. *See Citizens Concerned About Jet Noise, Inc. v. Dalton,*

48 F. Supp. 2d 582, 604 (E.D. Va. 1999). Other courts treat environmental justice analyses like any other agency decision-making process in the EIS, finding that such an analysis is reviewable under an arbitrary and capricious standard. *See Sierra Club v. Federal Energy Regulatory Commission*, 867 F.3d 1357, 1369 (D.C. Cir. 2017). Under such a review, the agency's analysis

> must be reasonably and adequately explained, but the agency's choice among reasonable analytical methodologies is entitled to deference. As always with NEPA, an agency is not required to select the course of action that best serves environmental justice, only to take a "hard look" at environmental justice issues.

*Id.* at 1369. *See also, Latin Americans for Social and Economic Justice v. Administrator of the Federal Highway Administration*, 765 F.3d. 447, 475–76 (6th Cir. 2014); *Communities Against Runway Expansion, Inc. v. Federal Aviation Administration*, 355 F.3d 678, 688–89 (D.C. Cir. 2004); *Senville v. Peters*, 327 F. Supp. 2d 335 (D. Vt. 2004).

Most of the rulings that reach the question of whether the environmental justice analysis is adequate have, under principles of deference to the agency, upheld the agency decision. However, in one recent case, challenging completion and operation of the Dakota Access Pipeline, the district court rejected the environmental analysis of the U.S. Army Corps of Engineers, partly on the basis that the area of analysis was improperly selected. *Standing Rock Sioux Tribe v. U.S. Army Corps of Engineers*, 255 F. Supp. 3d 101, 136 (D.D.C. 2017).

One relatively early case in which a NEPA environmental justice analysis was fully explored involves the Nuclear Regulatory Commission (NRC), an independent regulatory agency not technically covered by the Executive Order, but that nonetheless voluntarily agreed to be bound by it in 1994. In 1997, the Atomic Safety and Licensing Board (Board) of the NRC heard a challenge to a Final Environmental Impact Statement (FEIS) prepared for a proposal by Louisiana Energy Services (LES) to build an $855 million uranium-enrichment facility in the midst of two historically black communities in Claiborne Parish, Louisiana (the project was known as the Claiborne Enrichment Center, or CEC). The Board issued the following ruling.

### In the Matter of Louisiana Energy Services, L.P.
45 N.R.C. 367 (1997)

This Final Initial Decision addresses the remaining contention — environmental justice contention J.9 — filed by the Intervenor, Citizens Against Nuclear Trash ("CANT"), in this combined construction permit-operating license proceeding.... The Applicant plans to build the CEC on a 442-acre site in Claiborne Parish, Louisiana, that is immediately adjacent to and between the unincorporated African-American communities of Center Springs and Forest Grove, some 5 miles from the town of Homer, Louisiana.... The site, called the LeSage property ... is currently bisected by Parish Road 39 (also known as Forest Grove Road) running north and south through the property.... [Center Springs] lies along State Road 9 and Parish Road 39 and is located approximately [a third of a mile] to the north of the LeSage property.... [Forest Grove] lies approximately [two miles] south of the site along Parish Road 39.... The two community churches, which share a single minister, are approximately 1.1 miles apart, with the LeSage property lying between them.

The community of Forest Grove was founded by freed slaves at the close of the Civil War and has a population of about 150. Center Springs was founded around the turn of the century and has a population of about 100. The populations of Forest Grove and Center Springs are about 97% African American. Many of the residents are descendants of the original settlers and a large portion of the landholdings remain with the same families that founded the communities. Aside from Parish Road 39 and State Road 9, the roads in Center Springs or Forest Grove are either unpaved or poorly maintained. There are no stores, schools, medical clinics, or businesses in Center Springs or Forest Grove.... [F]rom kindergarten through high school the children of Center Springs and Forest Grove attend schools that are largely racially segregated. Many of the residents of the communities are not connected to the public water supply. Some of these residents rely on groundwater wells while others must actually carry their water because they have no potable water supply....

The Intervenor's environmental justice contention is grounded in the requirements of [NEPA].... Subsequent to ... the Staff's issuance of the draft EIS, on February 11, 1994, the President issued Executive Order [on Environmental Justice, No.] 12898.... Although Executive Order 12898 does not create any new rights that the Intervenor may seek to enforce before the agency or upon judicial review of the agency's actions, the President's directive is, in effect, a procedural directive to the head of each executive department and agency that, "to the greatest extent practicable and permitted by law," it should seek to achieve environmental justice in carrying out its mission by using such tools as [NEPA].... Thus, whether the Executive Order is viewed as calling for a more expansive interpretation of NEPA as the Applicant suggests or as merely clarifying NEPA's longstanding requirement for consideration of the impacts of major federal actions on the "human" environment as the Intervenor argues, it is clear the President's order directs all agencies in analyzing the environ-mental effects of a federal action in an EIS required by NEPA to include in the analysis, "to the greatest extent practicable," the human health, economic, and social effects on minority and low-income communities....

*Impacts of Road Closing/Relocation*

The Intervenor [asserts] that the FEIS is deficient because if [sic] fails to address the impacts of closing Parish Road 39, which currently bisects the LeSage site and joins the communities of Forest Grove and Center Springs. Dr. Robert Bullard [a so-ciologist and prominent environmental justice scholar] testified.... that if the road is not relocated it would impose upon the residents of Center Springs and Forest Grove an additional 8- or 9-mile trip by way of Homer to go from one community to the other.

Additionally, Dr. Bullard asserted that even if Parish Road 39 is relocated around the site, the Staff incorrectly concluded in the FEIS that the impacts would be very small and not pose unacceptable risks to the local community. According to Dr. Bullard, it is apparent that the Staff did not even consult with any of the residents of Forest Grove and Center Springs before reaching its conclusion for if it had, the Staff would have found that Forest Grove Road is a vital and frequently used link between the two communities, with regular pedestrian traffic....

[T]he FEIS indicates that the road relocation will add approximately 120 meters (0.075 mile) to the traveling distance between State Roads 2 and 9 and will add an additional 600 meters (0.38 mile) to the 1,800 meter (1.1 mile) distance between the Forest Grove Church and the Center Springs Church, which are the approximate centers of the respective minority communities....

The Staff's FEIS treatment of the impacts of relocating Parish Road 39 does not discuss Forest Grove Road's status as a pedestrian link between Forest Grove and Center Springs and the impacts of relocation on those who must walk the distance between the communities on this road. In the FEIS, the Staff calculates how much additional gasoline it will take to drive between the communities when the road is relocated and the added travel time the road relocation will cause for various trips....

Dr. Bullard testified, however, that Forest Grove Road is a vital and frequently used link between the communities with regular pedestrian traffic. Neither the Staff nor the Applicant presented any evidence disputing Dr. Bullard's testimony in this regard. Further, the Bureau of Census statistics introduced by the Intervenor show that the African American population of Claiborne Parish is one of the poorest in the country and that over 31% of black households in the parish have no motor vehicles. Again this evidence is undisputed. It thus is obvious that a significant number of the residents of these communities have no motor vehicles and often must walk. Adding 0.38 mile to the distance between the Forest Grove and Center Springs communities may be a mere "inconvenience" to those who drive, as the Staff suggests. Yet, permanently adding that distance to the 1- or 2-mile walk between these communities for those who must regularly make the trip on foot may be more than a "very small" impact, especially if they are old, ill or otherwise infirm. The Staff in the FEIS has not considered the impacts the relocation of Forest Grove Road will have upon those residents who must walk. Accordingly, we find that the Staff's treatment in the FEIS of the impacts on the communities of Forest Grove and Center Springs from the relocation of Parish Road 39 is inadequate and must be revised.

*Property Value Impacts*

Intervenor [also] asserts that property values in the neighboring communities will be adversely affected by the facility and that this economic effect will be borne disproportionately by the minority communities that can least afford it....

In support of [this] assertion...., Dr. Bullard testified that the general "benefit streams" to counties with large industrial taxpayers do not have significant positive effects on low income minority communities, which are already receiving a dispro-portionately low share of the services offered by the county....

The Staff's treatment of the economic impacts of the CEC on property values in the FEIS does indeed recognize that the CEC will depress some property values while increasing others, but the Staff fails to identify the location, extent, or significance of impacts. Further, although the FEIS generally indicates the CEC is likely to increase both housing and land prices because of increased demand and the benefits capture effect, the Staff makes no attempt to allocate the costs or benefits. Dr. Bullard directly challenges the Staff's failure to assess the impacts of the CEC on property values in the communities of Forest Grove and Center Springs asserting that when facilities like the CEC are placed in the midst of poor, minority communities, the facility has negative impacts on property values in the immediate area of the plant. For the reasons specified below, we find his testimony on the negative economic impact of the CEC on property values in these minority communities reasonable and persua-sive....

Dr. Bullard explained that unlike white residents of the parish, the black residents of Forest Grove and Center Springs face substantial "housing barriers" that preclude them from leaving when a large industrial facility is sited in the midst of their resi-dential area. As a consequence, these already economically depressed communities must fully absorb the further adverse impact of having a heavy industrial facility nearby making them even more undesirable. He testified that the beneficial effects on housing values from increased demand by new migrating employees and the benefit capture effect relied upon by the Staff in the FEIS will have no effect on these minority communities that currently receive almost no parish services, are virtually 100% African American, and are inhabited by some of the most economically dis-advantaged people in the United States. As Dr. Bullard stated, it is "extremely unlikely" new workers to the area will seek to live in Forest Grove and Center Springs. Dr. Bullard concludes that these factors lead to an overall negative impact on property values in the minority communities that must host the CEC....

The Staff witnesses made no attempt to explain how or why Dr. Bullard might be mistaken.... Indeed, given the Staff's recognition in the FEIS that there will be some negative impacts on property values from the CEC, it is difficult to envision an eco-nomic rationale that would demonstrate those adverse impacts from the CEC are likely to occur to properties well removed from the facility, such as in Homer or Hay-nesville, as opposed to the Forest Grove and Center Springs areas next to the facility.... By the same token, the opinions of [two witnesses for the applicant that] the effect that industrial facilities often increase property values in the vicinity of a facility are far too general to draw any reasonable conclusions about the impacts on property values in the circumstances presented here. Likewise, Mr. LeRoy's [another witness for the applicant] testimony about the positive impact on lakefront vacation home values from the construction of nuclear power plants is neither useful nor reasonable in making a comparison with the economically disadvantaged minority communities of Forest Grove and Center Springs. Certainly, the reality of Forest Grove and Center Springs hardly seems comparable to the description of Lake Wylie in Applicant's Exhibit 19, which states that "the Catawba plant was built on a beautiful lake, dotted with hundreds of expensive homes and homesites." Nor do these communities resemble the description of Lake Keowee in Exhibit 19 as "one of the most prestigious resort/retirement communities in the United States [which] is less than a mile from Oconee Nuclear Station. At Keowee Key more than 1,500 people golf, boat, fish, relax and retire next door to a nuclear plant."

On this basis, we find that the Staff's treatment in the FEIS of the impacts from the CEC on property values in the communities of Forest Grove and Center Springs is inadequate....

* * *

## Notes and Questions

1. What is different about the NEPA analysis demanded by the Board and the type traditionally prepared by federal agencies? Is it the particularized focus on how the project will impact very small subpopulations of larger communities? Is it the Board's careful attention to the project's social and economic impacts? The Board seems to embrace Dr. Bullard's longstanding view that achieving environmental justice requires examination of "who pays and who benefits" from industrial development. Note also that, although the Board requires an environmental justice analysis, it specifically declines to decide whether the executive order calls for a more expansive interpretation of NEPA or merely clarifies NEPA's existing requirement that impacts on the human environment be analyzed. Should it matter?

2. The Board's decision elsewhere quotes Dr. Bullard's testimony that the NRC Staff did not consult with any of the residents of Forest Grove and Center Springs before reaching its conclusion about the negative impacts of relocating the road, and that if it had "the Staff would have found that Forest Grove Road is a vital and frequently used link between the two communities, with regular pedestrian traffic." *See id.* at 403. Does this in effect impose a duty to implement special outreach and public participation efforts in NEPA cases raising environmental justice concerns?

3. Apart from its claims relating to the FEIS' failure to analyze the project's social and economic impacts, the citizens group alleged that the NRC's siting process was racially discriminatory. The group presented testimony from Dr. Bullard showing that at each successive stage of the siting process, the communities under consideration became poorer and more predominantly African American, culminating in the selection of a site that was 97 percent African American and extremely poor. Bullard also testified that the applicant's use of facially race-neutral siting criteria—such as eliminating sites close to sensitive receptors like hospitals, schools, and nursing homes—disadvantaged poor and minority communities by reinforcing the impacts of prior discrimination that had left them without such institutions. The Board found that this evidence raised a "reasonable inference that racial considerations played some part in the site selection process," and remanded for a more complete investi-

gation. Responding to the agency's contention that its decision was based solely on technical and business criteria, and that there was no specific evidence that racial considerations motivated the decision, the Board wrote that racial discrimination "cannot be uncovered with only a cursory review of the description of the [site selection process]. If it were so easily detected, racial discrimination would not be such a persistent and enduring problem in American society. Racial discrimination is rarely, if ever, admitted." *See id.* at 391–92.

On appeal, a panel of the NRC reversed this part of the Board's order, holding that NEPA is not "a tool for addressing problems of racial discrimination." The panel noted that the CEQ's Guidance on Environmental Justice (discussed above) encourages agencies to consider impacts on low-income and minority communities, but "neither states nor implies that if adverse impacts are found, an investigation into possible racial bias is the appropriate next step." *See In re La. Energy Services, L.P.,* 47 N.R.C. 77, 101 (1998). Is the NRC opinion sound? Should there be no recourse under NEPA against a decision that results from a racially biased decision-making process? Recall the emphasis that NEPA places on procedure and meaningful public involvement in agency decisions. Could this be a basis for arguing that further review of the NRC's decision is warranted?

**4.** The NRC panel upheld the part of the Board's NEPA decision that is reproduced above. In April 1998, after this ruling, Louisiana Energy Services dropped its application to construct the CEC. In 2004, the NRC issued guidance indicating that as an independent agency, the NRC is not bound by E.O. No. 12898 or by the CEQ guidance. The NRC specified that it considered NEPA to be the only basis for considering environmental justice contentions in licensing proceedings. The guidance also reiterates that the NRC will not consider issues of racial bias as part of a NEPA claim. 69 Fed. Reg. 52,040, 52044–45 (Aug 24, 2004).

# F. The Emergency Planning and Community Right-to-Know Act

Over the past three decades, right-to-know and information-disclosure statutes have become increasingly popular as an alternative to conventional regulation. These laws serve numerous objectives. One, they improve the efficient functioning of the market by remedying information gaps facing consumers and workers. Such laws also are premised on an entitlement rationale; the underlying notion is that members of the public have a "fundamental right to know" what chemicals are "out there," to which they are being exposed. These laws also promote citizen power and advance democratic decision-making. Armed with more information, citizens can make better-informed decisions and are thus in a better position to bargain with private corporations and government. Finally, such measures provide indirect incentives for industry to undertake self-regulation and thereby reduce risky activities, help avoid accidents and facilitate emergency planning, and add to the database that helps government agencies determine the need for additional regulation.

The most well-known information disclosure law is the Emergency Planning and Community Right-to-Know Act (**EPCRA**), 42 U.S.C. §§ 11001–11050. Section 313 of EPCRA authorizes EPA to establish and maintain a Toxic Release Inventory (TRI) of facilities that manufacture, import, process, or use certain types of chemicals. Section 313(d) outlines the criteria by which chemicals are added to the TRI, including chemical toxicity, potential adverse impacts on human health if exposure were to occur, and certain types of illnesses or health conditions that may be associated with potential exposure to the chemical. Section 313(f) establishes a general reporting threshold of 10,000 pounds for toxic chemicals used at a facility during a calendar year, and 25,000 pounds for toxic chemicals manufactured, imported, or processed at a facility during a calendar year. This data is then shared with the public via an EPA website. For reporting year 2019, the TRI covers 767 individual chemicals and 33 chemical categories.

### Sarah Lamdan & Rebecca Bratspies, *Taking a Page from the FDA's Prescription Medicine Information Rules: Reimagining Environmental Information for Climate Change*
40 U. Ark. Little Rock L. Rev. 573, 581–588 (2018)

...EPCRA emerged in response to two Union Carbide chemical disasters: one in Bhopal, India, and another in Institute, West Virginia. In 1984, faulty operations at a Union Carbide pesticide manufacturing plant in Bhopal, India, led to a massive explosion. Over half a million people were exposed to airborne toxic chemicals; tens of thousands died or suffered severe injuries. Less than a year later, a storage tank exploded at another Union Carbide plant, this one in Institute, West Virginia. The resulting toxic cloud injured scores of nearby residents.

In both Bhopal and Institute, residents were caught unaware and unprepared. First responders faced added dangers because they lacked knowledge about the chemical substances at issue and thus could not take appropriate protective measures. Doctors treating the injured had no idea what symptoms to expect or what treatments would be effective. These chemical disasters became human disasters, and lack of information magnified the harms.

In November 1986, less than two years after the Bhopal disaster, Congress enacted EPCRA to respond to the need for accurate, timely information about chemical risks.... [EPCRA] included sweeping public information access provisions. Through these provisions, EPCRA ... sought to transform industrial chemical practices "from a secretive alchemy to a publicly posted overload of papers, training materials and neighborhood emergency maps." The resulting statutory and regulatory schemes provided for information disclosure to make public the chemical hazard data needed to improve awareness, planning, and preparation for potential disasters....

EPCRA governs local and state emergency planning for potential disasters involving hazardous chemicals, the right of the public to access information on chemical hazards in their community, and the reporting responsibilities for facilities that use, store, and release hazardous chemicals. The law has four major provisions: emergency planning obligations; emergency release notifications; reporting requirements for hazardous chemical storage; and the creation of a toxic chemical release inventory. These provisions are markedly different from more traditional "command and control," "end of pipe" governance that limit hazardous discharge. Instead, EPCRA uses regulation to proactively promote chemical disaster awareness and preparation. The theory behind EPCRA is that public access to data helps communities make informed decisions about the chemical hazards in their midst. The law prioritizes public participation (hence the "right-to-know" language in its title). Indeed, EPCRA is the only U.S. environmental law that arguably creates a stand-alone right of environmental information access. EPCRA mandates the public availability of two major types of information: (1) emergency plans and (2) information about toxic releases....

The most well-known information access provision in EPCRA is the one that requires the EPA to create and maintain an inventory of toxic chemicals, or Toxics Release Inventory (TRI). The TRI has been credited with reducing chemical emissions in the United States by twenty-one percent since 2006. While these reductions are highly significant, the TRI has also produced a less concrete but equally important outcome in the context of information policy, "serv[ing] as a constant example of the vital role information plays in a democracy, and the importance of the public's right to know." Beyond the TRI, which reports on past releases, EPCRA also helps communities plan for future emissions by providing information to the public through Local Emergency Planning Committees (LEPCs). LEPCs are composed of local participants including elected officials; police, fire, civil defense, and public health professionals; environmental, transportation, and hospital officials; facility representatives; members of the media; and community groups who develop and review local emergency response plans and disseminate disaster preparation information to the public ...

Unfortunately, ... [EPCRA is] plagued with implementation issues on local, state, and federal levels. EPCRA ... mandated programs are typically low priorities, thinly staffed with small budgets. Violations often go unchecked, and fines for noncompliance are light and sparsely enforced. Worse, many states actively restrict access to the chemical data that EPCRA was designed to make public, citing fears about unintended uses of the information to promote terrorism or interfere with trade secrets.

\* \* \*

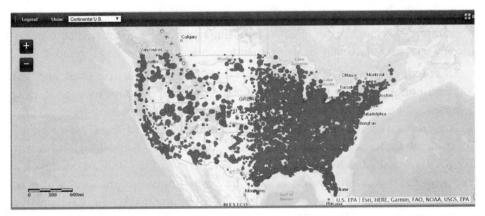

**Figure 12-5:** Geographic distribution of TRI-reporting facilities (2017). Source: https://gispub.epa.gov/trina2017/facilities.html?webmap=3c1480ef7c05470ab4410cb4b6c92298.

## Notes and Questions

1. What are the tensions between disclosure and corporate privacy with regard to toxic releases? How should regulators resolve legitimate disagreements between these public and private interests?

2. Supporters such as Bradley Karkkainen claim that the TRI it is a "watershed, pioneering the systematic use of performance monitoring and benchmarking as regulatory tools." Bradley Karkkainen goes on to assert that:

> the ready availability of TRI data also enhances transparency and account-
> ability to external parties. It subjects the environmental performance of
> facilities and firms to an unprecedented degree of scrutiny by their peers,
> competitors, investors, employees, consumers, community residents, en-
> vironmental organizations, activists, elected officials, regulators, and the
> public in general.... TRI-generated transparency thus unleashes, strength-
> ens, and exploits multiple pressures, all tending to push in the direction
> of continuous improvement as facilities and firms endeavor to leapfrog
> over their peers to receive credit for larger improvements or superior per-
> formance.

Bradley C. Karkkainen, *Information as Environmental Regulation: TRI and Performance Benchmarking, Precursor to a New Paradigm?* 89 GEORGETOWN L.J. 257, 260-
262 (2001).

These claims found support in a study claiming that being ranked in the Top 10 worst polluters did cause facilities to reduce their releases. *See* Wolfram Schlenker and Jason Scorse, *Does Being a "Top 10" Worst Polluter Affect Environmental Releases? Evidence from the U.S. Toxic Release Inventory*, Cornell University Working Paper (2012). Critics acknowledge the program's success but point out that the program currently covers only a small fraction of the more than 75,000 chemicals manufactured in the United States. Clifford Rechtschaffen, *Reforming the Emergency Planning and Community Right to Know Act in* CPR FOR THE ENVIRONMENT 32, 34–35 (Center for

Progressive Reform 2007). Moreover, concentrated animal feeding operations (CAFOs) are statutorily exempted from EPCRA's reporting requirement, as are small businesses and facilities manufacturing or using chemicals below the statutory thresholds.

3. Kathryn E. Durham-Hammer suggests that TRI's success is overstated, and that "the assumption that companies will change their use and release of hazardous waste because they are ashamed of being flagrant polluters in comparison to their competitors ... is not based on convincing empirical evidence ... [and] is pure speculation." She contends that, "Communities cannot safely rely on EPCRA and TRI data because EPCRA allows facilities to report their own data, and requires only an estimate if a true measurement is not feasible. EPCRA establishes no means for communities or the EPA to confirm facilities' self-made reports.... By giving discretion to reporting entities, the EPA also allows entities to change their estimation methods to achieve 'paper reductions.'" Kathryn E. Durham-Hammer, *Left to Wonder: Reevaluating, Reforming, and Implementing the Emergency Planning and Community Right-to-Know Act of 1986*, 29 Colum. J. Envtl L. 323, 337–38, 347–48 (2004).

4. Studies using TRI data have documented that reporting facilities are disproportionately sited in poor communities and communities of color. Ryan Johnson, Kim Ramsey-White, and Christina H. Fuller, *Socio-demographic Differences in Toxic Release Inventory Siting and Emissions in Metro Atlanta*, 13 Int. J. Environ. Res. Public Health 747 (2016); Kerry Ard, *Trends in Exposure to Industrial Air Toxins for Different Racial and Socioeconomic Groups: A Spatial and Temporal Examination of Environmental Inequality in the U.S. from 1995 to 2004*, 53 Social Sci. Res. 375 (2015). Is an information disclosure law like TRI likely to be useful in remedying these disparate environmental burdens? Who is most likely to access and use the information made available through the TRI? Environmental justice activists generally are strong supporters of the TRI program (including expanding and strengthening its provisions).

5. The most well-known state information disclosure law is California's Proposition 65, which requires businesses to warn the public prior to exposing them to listed carcinogens or reproductive toxins. In addition to covering the types of industrial emissions subject to TRI, the statute also extends to exposures from workplace hazards and consumer products, the latter being the area in which it has had its most significant impact. In particular, Proposition 65 has generated reformulations of dozens of consumer products containing toxic chemicals, including brass faucets, ceramic ware, calcium supplements, plastic clothing, wooden playground structures, and portable classrooms. Clifford Rechtschaffen and Patrick Williams, *The Continued Success of Proposition 65 in Reducing Toxic Exposures*, 35 Envtl. L. Rep. 10850 (2005). Given Proposition 65's success in the consumer marketplace, should warning statutes be used more broadly in place of direct regulation of toxic substances? What are the pros and cons of such an approach?

# G. International Law and the Human Right to Environmental Information

Developments in international law have taken up the relationship between environmental justice and transparency and expanded it. Access to environmental information has become central to the emerging international framework of state environmental obligations, both those obligations a state owes to its own citizens and those it owes to other states. For example, Principle 10 of the 1992 Rio Declaration proclaimed state duties to share environmental information with the public, to create opportunities for participation in environmental decision-making, and to ensure effective access to judicial and administrative proceedings, including redress and remedy. The United Nations Framework Convention on Climate Change enshrined some of these duties into law, obliging states to "encourage the widest possible participation" and to "promote and facilitate ... public access to information" concerning climate change. The 2030 Agenda for Sustainable Development mandated a regulatory framework (including laws, policies, and practices) conducive to furthering public participation in environmental decision-making.

There are detailed regional agreements spelling out governmental obligations vis-à-vis environmental information: in Europe, *UNECE Convention on Access to Information, Public Participation in Decision-Making and Access to Justice in Environmental Matters* (adopted 25 June 1998, entered into force 30 October 2001) 2161 UNTS 447 (commonly called the **Aarhus Convention**), and in Latin America, the *UNECLAC Regional Agreement on Access to Information, Participation and Justice in Environmental Matters in Latin America and the Caribbean* (adopted March 4, 2018) LC/CNP 10.9/5.

While the Latin American Agreement has not yet come into force, the Aarhus Convention has a two-decade history of implementation. Article 1 of the Aarhus Convention declares:

> In order to contribute to the protection of the right of every person of present and future generations to live in an environment adequate to his or her health and well-being, each Party shall guarantee the rights of access to information, public participation in decision-making, and access to justice in environmental matters in accordance with the provisions of this Convention.

The Aarhus Convention then defines environmental information broadly (Art. 2), details what constitutes adequate access to information (Art. 4), specifies the steps states must take to collect and disseminate environmental information (Art. 5), and identifies the kinds of public participation in environmental decision-making that the convention intends to facilitate. (Arts. 6–8). The UN Economic Committee for Europe (UNECE) maintains an online database of caselaw related to the Aarhus Convention. https://www.unece.org/env/pp/tfaj/jurisprudenceplatform.html.

Two other European agreements require member states to collect and disseminate environmental information: the *Convention on Environmental Impact Assessment in a Transboundary Context*, (commonly referred to as the **Espoo Convention**), and *the UNECE Protocol on Strategic Environmental Assessment to the Convention on Environ-*

*mental Impact Assessment in a Transboundary Context* (adopted 21 May 2003, entered into force 11 July 2010) 2685 UNTS 140, UN Doc ECE/MP.EIA/2003/2 (commonly referred to as the **Kyiv Protocol**). The European Parliament adopted Council Directive 2003/4, which requires that environmental information be "progressively made available and disseminated to the public in order to achieve the widest possible systematic availability and dissemination to the public."

Access to environmental information and participation in environmental decision-making also features prominently in the emerging human right to a healthy environment. Indeed, five of the sixteen principles that the UN Special Rapporteur on Human Rights and the Environment identified as framework principles for human rights and the environment were about access to information:

**Framework principle 5:** States should respect and protect the rights to freedom of expression, association and peaceful assembly in relation to environmental matters.

**Framework principle 6:** States should provide for education and public awareness on environmental matters.

**Framework principle 7:** States should provide public access to environmental information by collecting and disseminating information and by providing affordable, effective and timely access to information to any person upon request.

**Framework principle 8:** To avoid undertaking or authorizing actions with environmental impacts that interfere with the full enjoyment of human rights, States should require the prior assessment of the possible environmental impacts of proposed projects and policies, including their potential effects on the enjoyment of human rights.

**Framework principle 9:** States should provide for and facilitate public participation in decision-making related to the environment and take the views of the public into account in the decision-making process.

### *Pathfinder on International Right of Access to Environmental Information*

Rio Declaration on Environment and Development (adopted 14 June 1992) A/CONF.151/26 (Vol 1), 1760 UNTS 79; Convention on Environmental Impact Assessment in a Transboundary Context, UNECE Convention on Environmental Impact Assessment in a Transboundary Context (adopted 25 February 1991, entered into force 10 September 1997) 1989 UNTS 309 (Espoo (EIA) Convention); UNECE Protocol on Strategic Environmental Assessment to the Convention on Environmental Impact Assessment in a Transboundary Context (adopted 21 May 2003, entered into force 11 July 2010) 2685 UNTS 140, UN Doc ECE/MP.EIA/2003/2 (Kyiv (SEA) Protocol); Report of the Special Rapporteur on the issue of human rights obligations relating to the enjoyment of a safe, clean, healthy, and sustainable environment, A/HRC/37/59 (Jan. 24, 2018); Framework Principles on Human Rights and the Environment, A/HRC/37/59 (Jan. 24, 2018).

# Chapter 13

# Citizen Enforcement and Common Law Remedies

Earlier chapters of this book examined responses by governmental agencies to promote environmental justice in the regulatory context—setting standards, issuing permits, cleaning up contaminated sites, and so forth. We now turn to efforts by citizens to use the courts to achieve environmental justice goals. An excellent, practical guide to various legal theories that can be used to advance environmental justice is THE LAW OF ENVIRONMENTAL JUSTICE: THEORIES AND PROCEDURES TO ADDRESS DISPROPORTIONATE RISKS (Michael B. Gerrard & Sheila R. Foster eds., 2d ed. 2008).

Before we look at specific enforcement tools, however, we consider an important threshold set of issues that underlies environmental justice lawyering. Recall that as a political movement, environmental justice is premised on the principle that affected communities should speak for themselves and community empowerment is central. In light of this, to what extent should environmental justice activists rely on legal strategies at all? When is litigation appropriate, and what is the proper role of the lawyer in environmental justice disputes? What is the meaning of the phrase, *lawyers should be on tap, not on top*, and how does that apply to environmental justice?

## A. The Role of the Lawyer and Litigation

Environmental justice activists may have an ambivalent relationship with the legal system and with lawyers. On the one hand, legal representatives can play a powerful and essential role in advocating on behalf of communities. In addition, lawyers working with community groups are often activists in their own right and deeply committed to the principles and goals of environmental justice. On the other hand, many activists and community residents distrust lawyers and the legal process. In their view, past reliance on legal processes and procedures has resulted in the historic inequitable distribution of environmental harms. Lawyers may take over disputes from community leaders and frame issues in narrow legal terms that do not seem to address the community's concerns. Moreover, communities will rarely, if ever, be able to match the legal resources of the government or private entities.

## 1. Environmental Justice Lawyering

The following article from 1994 was written by Francis Calpotura, a long-time community organizer in Oakland, California. How much of the perspectives shared here do you believe prevail today?

### Francis Calpotura, *Why the Law?*

THIRD FORCE (May/June 1994)

I was once told by an organizer friend of mine that lawsuits are a tactic to be used during a fight when you want to (a) end the campaign and move on to another issue, (b) inspire your members by showing that you are not afraid to take on these bastards, or (c) force the hand of your opposition to react to your initiative during a stalemate.

In none of these instances, I remember, is a lawsuit a strategy for winning a fight. It is always a tactical move. So where does this penchant for legal strategies come from? Indigenous community organizations normally don't have lawyers (some don't even have paid staff) on their payroll; environmental organizations do. I would argue that the alliance of community organizations with the proliferating Environmental Law Centers around the country has resulted in legal strategies for winning environmental justice fights, to the detriment of direct-action, community-oriented strategies.

The political implications are serious. A legal strategy affects how the issues that confront a community are understood. For example, the fight by [activists in the Georgia Sea Islands against development] was framed as a "preservation" issue in order to employ a variety of zoning and endangered species laws to delay development. This cut on the issue fails to show the racial and class character of the developer's strategy, something organizing for community control and equitable development would do to a much greater extent.

In addition, a legal strategy takes the fight away from arenas in which people can have some direct influence—their politicians, local development company offices, residences of the CEO, bank offices, etc.—to a place where they don't, i.e., in some chamber controlled by a judge where only the lawyers are allowed to speak (and only in English). This strategy does not facilitate the building of a cohesive, imaginative and militant base of people willing to employ various tactics on the opposition. This has great implications on how deep our organizational base is, and how leaders get developed....

\* \* \*

### *Notes and Questions*

**1. The effect(iveness) of litigation.** Do you agree with Mr. Calpotura's misgivings about relying on legal strategies? From the perspective of community groups, is it true that a lawsuit is never a strategy for winning a fight but is always a tactical move? Professors Gregg Macey and Lawrence Susskind explore the impact on the West Dallas

Coalition for Environmental Justice of turning from an approach with community organizing at its center to one focused on litigation in *The Secondary Effects of Environmental Justice Litigation: The Case of West Dallas Coalition for Environmental Justice v. EPA*, 20 Va. Envtl. L.J. 431 (2001). They note that the group's emphasis shifted from cumulative exposure stories that had prompted many residents to join the coalition, to scientific testing and gathering evidence to support the litigation. As a result, "the perceived need for protests, meeting attendance, testimony at hearings, and picketing around industrial land uses (as well as the use of stories of long-term exposure) diminished." *Id.* at 454. The authors also found that the coalition began to rely more heavily on lawyers to communicate with its members and to keep track of its internal operations, causing "[s]ocial networks, which accounted for the Coalition's initial growth in membership … to erode." *Id.* at 456. Overall, their assessment of a litigation strategy is mixed; they conclude that "[w]hile the choice of litigation … has yielded a number of positive outcomes for local residents [including cleanup and closure of some contaminated sites and increased blood lead testing of children], cumulative exposure and the need for resident relocation, two of the driving forces behind the initial building of social networks in 1989–90, remain unaddressed." *Id.* at 472–73.

2. **What role should be played by lawyers** who represent communities in environmental justice controversies? Does the late attorney/activist Luke Cole, whose excerpt follows, differ from Francis Calpotura in his view of the role that a lawyer can take in an environmental justice battle?

## Luke W. Cole, *Empowerment as the Key to Environmental Protection: The Need for Environmental Poverty Law*

### 19 Ecology Law Quarterly 619, 661–679 (1992)

*Client Empowerment*

"Client empowerment" occurs when a lawyer's practice helps clients realize and assert greater control over decisions which affect their lives. Empowerment is also a process which enables individuals to participate effectively in collective efforts to solve common problems.… Client empowerment is about creating in the client community the dynamics of democratic decision making, accountability, and self-determination—ideals which one would like to create in society.

In the environmental poverty law context, empowerment means enabling those who will have to live with the results of environmental decisions to be those who actually make the decisions. "Community-based" and "community-led" are key descriptive and prescriptive phrases for the environmental poverty lawyer, who should seek to decentralize power away from herself and to her clients. The client empowerment model is thus the reverse of the legal-scientific mode of lawyering used by mainstream environmental groups. Rather than solving a problem *for* a community, the empowerment model calls upon attorneys to help community members solve their own problems.

"Empowerment law" is more a *method* than a *product*, a practice through which the lawyer helps the group learn empowering methods of operation. Empowerment of clients is the answer to the political organizers' eternal question: "What happens when we go away?" By helping people take control over the decisions which affect their lives, an attorney leaves the community stronger than when she arrived....

*Law as a Means, Not an End....*

While our first instinct as lawyers might be to use legal tactics, they may not achieve the results our clients desire. Other tactics may be more useful in generating public pressure on an unresponsive bureaucracy or polluting corporation: tactics such as community organizing, administrative advocacy, or media pressure. Because environmental problems are political problems—some government official is allowing one actor to pollute the neighborhood of another—non-legal tactics often offer the best approach. As is so often the case, there may not even *be* a legal solution to the problem faced by the community. Or, the legal approach may radically disempower a client community and thus should be avoided. Translating a community's problems into legal language may render them meaningless.... Finally, lawsuits take fights into the arena most controlled by the adversary and least controlled by the community....

*Three Questions for Effective Advocacy*

Activists for social change have long relied on [the following] three questions in evaluating prospective strategies and tactics. These three questions parallel the three tenets of environmental poverty law:....

*Will the strategy educate people?* This broad question fits the empowerment model of legal services because education is a key to empowerment. Environmental poverty lawyers must broadly construe their concept of "education"—it should encompass education of a client or client group by the lawyer, education of policymakers or decisionmakers, and education of the public. Further, the educational process should be two-way: a lawyer must not only educate her clients, but also be educated by them. By increasing the community's knowledge, and others' knowledge of the community's problems, the community's persuasive power is necessarily strengthened.

*Will it build the movement?* Group representation is a self-conscious strategy to build local movements by developing local community groups. Community groups and their lawyers should look for tactics that draw new members into a group, rather than alienate potential supporters. An environmental poverty law model which is based on community education and empowerment will necessarily "build the movement," while a narrow legal approach will almost certainly fail to build anything.

*Does the strategy address the cause rather than the symptoms of a problem?* Environmental issues—like most legal services issues such as housing, health care access and (un)employment—are systemic. The disproportionate burden borne by poor people is a direct result of the system of economic organization in the United States and the corresponding inequities in the distribution of political power. Legal solutions to the environmental problems faced by poor people most often treat only the symptom, the environmental hazard itself. Embracing non-legal approaches, and legal approaches which treat the law as a means rather than an end, can help environmental poverty lawyers attack the root cause of the environmental problems faced by their clients, political and economic powerlessness....

### What Does It Look Like? Public Participation in Kettleman City

Kettleman City is a small farmworker community located in California's San Joaquin Valley. The community is ninety-five percent Latino, and seventy percent of its 1,100 residents speak Spanish in the home. Most residents work in the agricultural fields that stretch out in three directions from the town. Many of Kettleman City's residents have lived there for years and own their own homes, purchased with low-interest loans from the Farmers Home Administration.

Kettleman City also hosts the largest toxic waste dump west of Louisiana. Established without the community's knowledge or consent in the late 1970s, Chemical Waste Management's (CWM) Kettleman Hills Facility is a Class I toxic waste landfill. Just four miles from town, it may legally accept just about any toxic substance produced.

In 1988, CWM proposed to build a toxic waste incinerator at the dump. A Greenpeace organizer tipped off the Kettleman City community about the proposal and gave residents information on toxic waste incinerators. Feeling that the incinerator would threaten their health, homes, and livelihoods, Kettleman City residents organized a community group, *El Pueblo para el Aire y Agua Limpio* (People for Clean Air and Water), held demonstrations, and pressured their local officials. In 1989, they also secured the legal representation of the California Rural Legal Assistance Foundation (CRLAF).

The young lawyer handling the case—his first—was faced with a dilemma [the lawyer was in fact the author, Luke Cole. Eds.]. The Kings County Planning Department, the local agency responsible for granting permits for the project, had issued a dense, tedious, more than 1,000-page Environmental Impact Report (EIR) on the proposed incinerator. The County had refused to translate the EIR into Spanish, despite repeated requests from Kettleman City residents. Kettleman City residents wanted to take part in the EIR process. The lawyer needed comment on the EIR, so that the administrative record would reflect the deficiencies of the document and the process. The lawyer faced a choice: the traditional mode of environmental lawyering or a new environmental poverty law approach.

*Traditional approach.* In the traditional model of environmental advocacy, the lawyer reads and analyzes the EIR document, shares parts of it with selected experts, and then writes extensive, technical comments on the EIR on behalf of a client group. These comments are submitted to the agency and form the basis of later lawsuits if the agency does not respond adequately.

*Lawyering for social change model.* The lawyer attempts to involve and educate the community while addressing the root of the problem: that the County is ignoring and dismissing the needs of Kettleman City residents without fear of repercussions because the residents are not organized.

**Figure 13-1:** Lupe Martinez of the Center on Race, Poverty, & the Environment (CRPE). Founded in 1989 by attorney Luke Cole, CRPE helped organize the largely Spanish-speaking agricultural community to defeat the proposed hazardous waste incinerator at Kettleman City, California. Delano, CA. April 16, 2019. Photo: Cliff Villa.

*Environmental poverty law in Kettleman City: How it worked.* The lawyer chose the latter strategy. Working with several key leaders in the community, he and a CRLAF community worker held an initial series of three house meetings in Kettleman City. Each meeting was held in a different home, and all were held on the same day.

At a typical meeting, the community leaders would explain the incinerator proposal to eight to ten residents. The lawyer would then describe parts of the EIR and the County's response to the community's requests. The residents would ask questions, which the leaders and the attorney would answer to the best of their abilities. Discussions among the residents would ensue about the incinerator and why it was to be located in Kettleman City. The conversations were not limited simply to the incinerator, however. Residents would tell stories of health symptoms they had experienced (which they blamed on the existing toxic waste dump), of past dealings with County officials, and of other incidents they felt were important. Since the meetings involved almost entirely monolingual Spanish-speakers, the meetings were held in Spanish, with the community worker translating for the lawyer.

At the end of each meeting, the leaders and the attorney would ask each person present to write a letter of comment on the EIR to the Planning Commission. The letters—almost all in Spanish—questioned the Planning Commission about the incinerator, and also asked to have the EIR documents translated so that Kettleman residents could take part in the process. The meetings were as inclusive as possible: if a person was not literate, he or she would dictate a letter to a more educated Kettleman resident; children were encouraged to write as well. Out of the first three meetings, the community group generated twenty-five letters of comment on the EIR.

At the first meetings, people were asked to hold future meetings in their own homes, with five to eight of their neighbors. The community worker followed up with community leaders to ensure that the meetings continued. Over the course of the following three weeks more house meetings were held, and many more letters were written. When the EIR's public comment period closed, the record contained 162 comments from individuals—126 of them from Kettleman City residents. More importantly, 119 of the comments—seventy-five percent of all comments by individuals on the EIR—were in Spanish.

Although the results of such organizing are difficult to quantify—except, of course, for the large volume of letters—the letter-writing campaign served several important purposes. It brought Kettleman City residents together to learn about and discuss the incinerator. It allowed community leaders to bring Kettleman City residents up to date on the project. It informed the community of upcoming opportunities for participation, including a hearing before the Planning Commission. It encouraged individuals to take action—writing a letter—and to express themselves both in the house meetings and on paper. It validated residents' experiences with and concerns about the incinerator and the siting process by creating an opportunity to discuss and affirm them. People could collectively share other individual problems, tell their stories, and, through that process, see the commonality of their experiences. Lastly, the letter-writing campaign allowed residents to tell their stories to the Planning Commission, to act as "experts" in their own case.

Rather than gathering the residents' stories and translating them into narrow legal points (or even into English), the lawyer sought to facilitate the people of Kettleman City speaking for themselves. By asking others to hold meetings in their homes, the attorney and the community leaders fostered a sense of ownership of the campaign among members of the community. And finally, the letters created a stunning administrative record. The County could no longer claim that Kettleman residents and Spanish-speakers were not interested in the project: more than ten percent of the community had written letters to the Planning Commission. The attorney had helped create what he needed—the administrative record—in a way which fostered community action rather than shifting it.

The letter-writing campaign was an instance of empowering the client using group representation and non-litigation avenues. Ironically, by using tactics other than litigation, the campaign facilitated the litigation that ultimately resulted. The Kings County Board of Supervisors ultimately approved the incinerator proposal, and the environmental poverty lawyer was forced to take the County to Court. The Court overturned the County's approval, in part because of the County's exclusion of Spanish-speakers.

The letter-writing campaign also provided solid answers to the three questions environmental poverty lawyers must ask themselves. It educated people both in the community and in the County government. The campaign built the movement by bringing house meetings into new homes and involving residents who had not participated in the group to that point. Finally, it addressed the root of the problem, by using the EIR public comment process as an organizing focus and forcing the County decision makers to listen to the people of Kettleman City.

By contrast, a traditional approach would have educated Kettleman City residents that they were not intelligent or able enough to take part in the process. It would have reinforced, rather than challenged, what Joel Handler calls the "psychological adaptions of the powerless—fatalism, self-deprecation, apathy, and the internalization of dominant values and beliefs." The traditional approach would not have built the movement and would have perpetuated, rather than confronted, the problem of the people of Kettleman City not being heard. A traditional approach would not have highlighted the need for Spanish translation of the EIR, which was so apparent after the campaign. As Señor Auscencio Avila wrote, in Spanish, demanding a Spanish translation of the EIR, "To not do this is to keep the community ignorant of what is going to happen, and to keep the community without any political power, and to suppose that we do not have the mental ability to deal with our own problems."

*  *  *

## Notes and Questions

**1. Community empowerment.** Should empowerment of communities be the primary goal of attorneys? How effective of an advocacy, or even litigation, tool is the principle for environmental justice communities to speak for themselves? In the next excerpt, Professor Helen Kang, depicting the struggle for environmental justice in Bayview-Hunters Point in San Francisco, details the importance of following this core principle of environmental justice.

### Helen H. Kang, *Respect for Community Narratives of Environmental Injustice: The Dignity Right to Be Heard and Believed*
### 25 WIDENER LAW REVIEW 219, 246–260 (2019)

Human beings have an inherent need to tell stories, to tell them their way, and to have them heard. Otherwise, human beings feel disrespected—sometimes to the core of their being. Psychologists explain that storytelling is part of our human need as cognitive beings to order and understand ourselves and the world around us— indeed, one might say, our very existence. With few exceptions, the legal system has traditionally failed to acknowledge the necessity of client stories....

… Communities telling stories of environmental injustice receive varying degrees of respect from their audience in the legal system. To be sure, government actors are not monolithic, and they display different degrees of respect for environmental injustice narratives. As ultimate decision makers, however, agencies are generally not seen as respectful of community narratives of environmental injustice, both in providing a forum to tell the stories and responding to them. Opportunities for public comment in government decision making is one glaring example. Core environmental justice principles, which many government agencies have adopted, include the recognition that communities have a right to participate in environmental decision making, including the right to comment publicly. In practice, however, public comment opportunities are restricted, both in scope and time. In the City of San Francisco, for example, a citizen appealing a land use decision is provided ten minutes of time to make what can be very involved arguments, and the public is provided three minutes of comment time. In some instances, the comment time is halved for translation. Sometimes, police are called in with K-9 units to a public forum where environmental decisions are being made. Thus, rather than make community participants feel part of the process, these public comment procedures amplify the impression that their stories are not worthy of airing and are of little or no consequence in the legal arena. Over time and over repeated experiences of similar small and large incidents involving different polluting facilities, and reinforced by legal procedures that restrict public participation, the message is that their experiences do not matter. At the same time, these community participants perceive that voices of others who have more resources appear to matter more. This experience is corrosive to our clients' view of politicians who are paid to represent them and the system as a whole. A key barrier to accommodating and responding to these stories of environmental injustice is of course race—the issue that the Black Lives Matter movement and, even more recently, the Poor People's Campaign have brought importantly to the fore, even as some powerful people mistakenly believe that we are blissfully in a post-racial period. Another key barrier is how we view low-income people. And, much has been written about how and why stories from environmental justice communities are discounted: race, sex, and class have everything to do with it. Just as much has been written about the challenges lawyers may have in accommodating client narratives because of similar reasons.

For teachers and advocates outside the field of environmental law, such as criminal justice, antipoverty, and civil rights, this idea—that we seek to make central the stories of our clients in the classroom—may not be anything new. In the environmental field, however, we deal with organizational clients whose representatives are often lawyers and not necessarily community advocates or residents in heavily polluted neighborhoods. In addition, many of us environmental advocates may not have background in movement lawyering or racial justice. Some of us may be still learning about environmental justice lawyering and, if we honestly assess our own attitudes, we may even have to say that we share more than we would like to admit with agency representatives who dismiss community residents....

... Environmental justice stories take a long time to tell, listen to, and digest. Consider the Bayview-Hunters Point's environmental justice story.... The long story encompasses the history of blacks in this nation and discrimination that is very much alive—virulent, even, in this day—and corrosive to the soul. The story encompasses the history of blacks in what is assumed by most to be a progressive city, the impact of pollution on blacks in Bayview-Hunters Point, and ultimately their rapid displacement, even as the area is getting cleaned up and beautified for largely newcomers.

The story encompasses the repeated disrespect that various regulatory actors in the system have shown residents of Bayview-Hunters Point through failing to listen and achieve meaningful changes....

... As some prominent thinkers have pointed out over generations in different forms, and most recently, Alicia Garza of the Black Lives Matter movement and Ta-Nehisi Coates, bell hooks and James Baldwin before them, black lives have not mattered. This context, in every way, matters to our clients in the discussion of environmental justice. Without that recognition, as teachers and students, we will fail to connect with our clients and respect their dignity....

... Equally important as the broad context of race and socioeconomics is the local context of environmental justice. As Vernice Miller-Travis, the founder of WE ACT for Environmental Justice, stated,

> "I also learned that if you really want to get to the bottom of environmental injustice, then you have to understand the relationship between race, land use and zoning. In communities of color, local government has set in place a practice of residential segregation. That was the case in the 1940s and 50s, and it is still the case today."

**Figure 13-2:** Vernice Miller-Travis. Duke University, North Carolina. March 9, 2019. Photo: Cliff Villa.

For Bayview-Hunters Point residents, that context includes what happened when the first black residents moved into Bayview—that is, government-created segregation at Hunters Point. The context also includes the history of displacement of black residents from the Fillmore-Western Addition neighborhood in the city, which was once a thriving cultural center for the city's black residents. In the name of "redevelopment," black residents from Fillmore-Western Addition were forced to move. Some of the residents displaced from Fillmore-Western Addition moved to Bayview-Hunters Point. That history of massive displacement is still fresh in the minds of community leaders. Redevelopment is an idea that historical residents of Bayview-Hunters Point distrust.

Also relevant to this local context is the racialization and marginalization of Bayview-Hunters Point and its residents. "Since the 1960s, powerful representations have depicted the Bayview as fundamentally distinct from the rest of the city, binding the area's physical decay, poverty, and other urban problems together with a perceived cultural and racial difference." This type of characterization, "popularized in the mass media, depoliticized the problem of black poverty and related social inequalities by locating their origins in the moral economy of the isolated 'ghetto' household, rather than in the political economy of the greater society." Thus, as Professor Lindsey Dillon argues, even as Bayview-Hunters Point activists contributed greatly to local, national, and international discourse on equity and race and made contributions to economic, social, and political life, they were viewed as different. In other words, they were viewed as "other."

Moreover, and possibly as a result of such marginalization, city politicians and administrators have long excluded Bayview-Hunters Point residents from many decisions that have affected them. Decisions from which they have been excluded include many of the environmental decisions affecting the neighborhood in the redevelopment of the shipyard and nearby Candlestick Park stadium area.... Remarkably, in September 2014—just months after Tetra Tech released its conclusion about the first discovery of sampling fraud and the NBC Investigative Unit reported additional fraud—the city's Office of Community Investment and Infrastructure decided that it would use explosive devices to implode Candlestick Park stadium, without any input from nearby residents. Implosion, which this agency approved as a method of demolition, is a much cheaper method than mechanical demolition, but unsuitable for a windy and densely populated areas, such as the Bayview-Hunters Point neighborhood. Implosion of the stadium likely would have involved a great amount of harmful particulate matter. Although the city did not provide information on the tonnage of concrete that would be reduced to dust, the buildings at Candlestick Point used 200,000 tons of concrete and, thus, implosion would have produced a phenomenal amount of particulate matter. Up to one-third of the total dust that would have been generated from the stadium demolition would have been released within a matter of minutes from implosion, in a neighborhood that already suffers from high rates of asthma and ischemic heart disease, conditions particulate matter could worsen. The air pollution would have spread to a large area, aided by the windy conditions of the neighborhood. At least one health study expresses concerns about even brief exposure to implosion dust:

"[t]he difficulties in protecting public health in the large downwind geographic area affected by implosion dust clouds suggest that implosions in metropolitan areas should be prohibited."

Nevertheless, the city chose to document this implosion decision in an "addendum" to environmental review documents, which by law is not required to be publicly noticed. The addendum itself, labeled simply as "Addendum 3 to Environmental Impact Report," gave no indication that the stadium would be imploded—something nearby residents who lived a football's throw from the stadium would consider highly relevant.

In hiding, at worst, or neglecting to make available the information in a meaningful fashion, the city planning and redevelopment offices kept in the dark local activists that they suspected would oppose the plan. The city succeeded, such that the president of the Bayview Hill Neighborhood Association, which represents residents living near the stadium, did not know of the plan until shortly before the planned implosion. In failing to engage the nearby community, the city offices even rejected the advice of air district staff, who counseled the developer, Lennar Urban, "to concentrate on a robust and transparent community outreach," and "to fully explain the implosion plan to the community." In response, in an unusually frank and tone-deaf written acknowledgement of the disturbing attitude underlying community engagement in the neighborhood, the city and the developer rejected group meetings to explain implosion: apparently, Lennar Urban wanted to "avoid a 'herd mentality.'" Such explicitly coded wording was rightly offensive to nearby residents (and reprehensible to me, their legal counsel)....

\* \* \*

## Notes and Questions

1. **Context and connections to other injustices.** Professor Kang also details the benefit of residents illustrating the prevalence of pollution in their neighborhood as an important factor to provide context to the client's position, in particular regard to cumulative impacts. *Id.* at 260–262. Client narratives also illustrate the subsequent disparity in health outcomes. *Id.* at 262–264. Finally, Professor Kang adds that a community's sustained and persistent fight, and successes against systemic injustice, provides critical context. *Id.* at 264. How do each of these factors benefit a campaign? How does this holistic contextualization benefit litigation? Discuss the importance of providing a forum for listening to the narratives of environmental injustice, as in the stories from the residents of Bayview-Hunters Point and Kettleman City.

2. **Radical lawyering.** As Luke Cole's depiction of efforts in Kettleman City makes clear, lawyers following an empowerment model must adjust to a nontraditional role, since community lawyering often entails a combination of political, organizing, and legal strategies. Three community lawyers who worked on a successful effort to preserve open space in Boston's Chinatown offer the following advice about building relationships between lawyers and the communities they represent:

> Do not assume "trust" exists simply because of shared ethnicity, race, or language ability.... Regardless of the similarities between lawyer and client, the client

sees the lawyer first as a "lawyer." For many, the legal profession represents the hostile, inaccessible, and insensitive legal system that permeates and complicates their lives....

*Build trust by learning about the community....* We mean learning about its history, its geography, and the various players, institutions, and organizations that constitute the community.... Such in-depth knowledge enabled us to identify what sorts of strategies, both legal and non-legal, might be viable and appropriate during the ... struggle.

*Build trust by establishing a permanent presence within the community....* Besides serving on boards of community-based organizations, [community lawyers] need to volunteer their time and skills and use their legal training to further the best interests of the community on myriad issues. Examples include conducting community legal education on relevant topics such as immigration, workers' rights and American government structure; mentoring community youth; and assisting community functions.

Zenobia Lai, Andrew Leong & Chi Chi Wu, *The Lessons of the Parcel C Struggle: Reflections on Community Lawyering*, 6 Asian Pac. Am. L.J. 1, 27–28 (2000). Can lawyers realistically undertake all of these various activities? Or are these tasks better performed by community organizers, activists, and others? What about in situations when a lawyer represents a community group or residents that are geographically far away?

3. **Ethical considerations.** Lawyers engaged in community activism must keep in mind the roles they are playing and be cognizant about issues of legal ethics. For instance, before an attorney has been retained by a community group, does the duty of confidentiality apply? Suppose the lawyer is privy to discussions about a planned illegal protest outside a facility? Likewise, could a lawyer who goes door to door organizing neighbors to oppose a power plant be accused of improperly soliciting clients? In short, how does a lawyer separate her role as an activist from her role as an "officer of the court"? For more discussion of these issues, *see* Irma Russell & Joanne Sum-Ping, *Issues of Legal Ethics in Environmental Justice Matters, in* The Law of Environmental Justice: Theories and Procedures to Address Disproportionate Risks 471 (Michael B. Gerrard & Sheila R. Foster eds., 2d ed. 2008).

4. **Conflict of interest with community-based organization and community residents?** The American Bar Association is clear that an attorney owes ethical duties to the "duly authorized constituents" of the organization represented. Model Rules of Prof'l Conduct R. 1.13. What ethical issues are raised if a grassroots organization's goal begins to deviate from that of its members?

5. **Participatory vs. Power Models.** Virtually all environmental laws provide the opportunity for public participation in the decision-making process. Luke Cole describes two approaches that community groups can follow in utilizing these public participation provisions in the context of a land-use permitting decision. Under the first approach, which he terms the "participatory" model, groups take part in every stage of the administrative process that provides an opportunity for public input—

commenting on draft documents, attending scoping meetings and public hearings, and so forth. The second, or "power," model is premised on the assumption that participation by community groups in the administrative process almost never helps them change undesirable outcomes and that their sole focus should be on the decision point and in actively trying to reach the actual decisionmakers. Luke W. Cole, *Legal Services, Public Participation and Environmental Justice*, 29 CLEARINGHOUSE REV. 449 (Special Issue 1995). If you were representing a community group, which approach would you advise your client to follow? Are the two approaches mutually exclusive? Is participation in the administrative process largely a futile and co-optive exercise? Does it provide an opportunity for educating and organizing community groups? Or is it likely to lead to a slightly improved project that is more resistant to later legal challenge? As illustrated below in regards to standing, a recent example of a successful motion to intervene allowed continued participation by environmental and community groups in a proceeding to defend San Luis Obispo County for its decision to deny a crude-by-rail project that resulted in, at least at the time of writing, the abandonment of the fossil fuel infrastructure expansion project. One distinct disadvantage of not participating in the administrative process is that a party may be denied the right to pursue an issue that was not raised in earlier administrative proceedings, and in some instances, may not be able to file a claim for failure to exhaust administrative remedies. *See, e.g.,* CAL. PUB. RES. CODE § 21177 (California Environmental Quality Act).

## 2. A Note on Environmental Law Clinics

As of 2020, there were approximately four dozen environmental law clinics at law schools throughout the country, and some of them have been at the forefront of representing community groups in environmental justice matters. Law students are often permitted to practice law under attorney supervision prior to their admission to the bar under state student practice rules, established by state bar associations or, in some instances, by state supreme courts.

With aggressive advocacy on behalf of environmental justice clients, however, the clinics themselves also have come under attack. The most prominent example occurred in the late 1990s in Louisiana, where complaints by business organizations and then-Louisiana Governor Mike Foster against the Tulane Environmental Law Clinic led the Louisiana Supreme Court to greatly restrict the state's student practice rules. The business organizations charged, among other things, that "the individual faculty and students' legal views [at Tulane] are in direct conflict with business positions." These complaints arose from the clinic's representation of citizens living in the low-income, eighty-four percent African American industrial corridor town of Convent, in St. James Parish, Louisiana. The residents opposed a plan by Shintech, a multinational petrochemical firm, to build a polyvinyl chloride plant that would result in emissions of over three million pounds of air pollutants per year, including close to 700,000 pounds of toxic air pollutants. (The project is discussed in more detail in Chapter 1.)

As a result of administrative appeals filed by the clinic, EPA vetoed the state's proposed air permit for the facility and accepted the citizens' Title VI civil rights complaint for investigation. As the controversy over the plant grew, Shintech eventually dropped its plans to site the facility in St. James Parish and opted to build a smaller facility elsewhere in the state. *Environmental Law Clinic Raises Environmental Justice ... And a Hostile Reaction from the Governor and the Louisiana Supreme Court*, TULANE ENVTL. L. NEWS, Winter 1999 at 1.

It appears that the revised Louisiana student practice rules adopted in 1999 were designed to preclude representation of virtually all of the community and environmental organizations served by the Tulane clinic in the prior ten years. For example, the rules prohibit student clinicians from representing any group unless an organization certifies that at least fifty-one percent of its members are considered indigent under federal Legal Services Corporation guidelines, and prohibit clinicians from representing individuals or organizations if any supervising attorney or clinician contacted them for the purpose of representation. LA. SUP. CT. R. XX. By contrast, in other states, eligibility for clinic representation is based on whether an organization itself can afford to hire an attorney. The story of the attack on Tulane's clinic is vividly recounted in Robert R. Kuehn, *Denying Access to Legal Representation: The Attack on the Tulane Environmental Law Clinic*, 4 WASH. U. J. L. & POL'Y 33 (2000). Professor Kuehn's account is replete with details of conflicts of interest, corrupt political practices, business intimidation, and unequal justice.

## Notes and Questions

**1. Organization member confidentiality?** What concerns are raised by requiring members of organizations to disclose personal financial information in order to obtain legal representation?

**2. What would you have done?** Business pressure on the Tulane clinic and on the law school was intense—some alumni withdrew their contributions to the law school, and others threatened to refuse to hire students who had participated in the clinic. If you had been a student in the clinic at the time, would you have risked a possible future job in Louisiana in order to represent the clients of the clinic?

**3. Attacks continue.** Law clinics at other schools likewise have come under pressure to drop their representation of community groups in controversial environmental disputes; this has included pressure from other practicing attorneys and lawmakers. For instance, in 2010, lawmakers debated a measure to cut money for the University of Maryland's law clinic if it did not provide details to the legislature about its clients, finances, and cases. *See* Hope M. Babcock, *How Judicial Hostility Toward Environmental Claims and Intimidation Tactics by Lawyers Have Formed the Perfect Storm Against Environmental Law Clinics: What's the Big Deal about Students and Chickens Anyway?*, 25 J. ENVTL. L. & LITIG. 249 (2010). Is it ethical for attorneys to attack law clinics for representing community groups on environmental matters? For discussion of this issue, *see* Robert R. Kuehn, *Shooting the Messenger: The Ethics of Attacks on Environmental Representation*, 26 HARV. ENVTL. L. REV. 417 (2002). For a broader review of attacks on law clinics generally, with suggestions for avoiding undue inter-ference, *see* Robert R. Kuehn & Bridget M. McCormack, *Lessons from Forty Years of Interference in Law School Clinics*, 24 GEO. J. LEGAL ETHICS 59 (2011).

**4. SLAPP suits.** Community groups may encounter similar pressures in the form of a Strategic Lawsuit Against Public Participation (SLAPP). SLAPPs are retaliatory actions filed by private developers or project applicants against organizations or in-dividuals who oppose a project through litigation or other forms of advocacy. At their core, SLAPPs are a reaction to some political action; i.e., some effort to influence a government decision. Because they seek damages that easily can bankrupt a com-munity or public interest group if successful, SLAPPs can chill public participation. As Professor Sheila Foster points out, however, most SLAPPs are successfully defended, particularly on grounds that the underlying activity is protected by the First Amend-ment's right to petition the government. She also notes that "the landscape of SLAPP litigation has become increasingly unfavorable to plaintiffs who bring SLAPPs, due to recent legislation that recognizes the antidemocratic nature of such lawsuits." Sheila Foster, *Public Participation, in* THE LAW OF ENVIRONMENTAL JUSTICE: THEORIES AND PROCEDURES TO ADDRESS DISPROPORTIONATE RISKS 225, 248–49 (Michael B. Gerrard & Sheila R. Foster eds., 2d ed. 2008).

Nevertheless, such aggressive strategies are still employed in response to successful environmental justice campaigns. A recent campaign that resulted in litigation by youth groups from Southeast Los Angeles against the oil industry is a notable example. In November 2015, Youth for Environmental Justice, South Central Youth Leadership Coalition, and the Center for Biological Diversity sued the City of Los Angeles, arguing that the City was not complying with its responsibilities under the California Envi-ronmental Quality Act and instead, "rubber stamping" oil drilling applications without considering environmental, health, and safety impacts, thereby imposing less protective conditions on drilling in majority Latino and African-American communities. An oil industry trade group intervened in the case. Without the participation of the intervenor, the City, the youth groups and the Center for Biological Diversity settled the case and the City adopted more protective policies. The oil industry group challenged the set-tlement, accusing the City and nonprofits of settling the claims pursuant to a "strategy" of "secret[] and collusive negotiations," objecting to the settlement and seeking a de-cision on the merits of the case. The California trial court agreed, but was reversed by the Court of Appeal. The Court of Appeal reasoned that the oil industry could not establish a probability of prevailing on the merits of its claim under California's anti-SLAPP statute, Code of Civil Procedure section 425.16. *Youth for Environmental Justice et al. v. City of Los Angeles et al., California Independent Petroleum Association*, Super Ct. No. BC600373 (2019) (not certified or ordered for publication as of the date of drafting). For a recent review of SLAPP suits in response to environmental citizen suits, *see* James M. Redwine, *Does It Hurt to Get SLAPPed? A Study of the Perils of Citizen Involvement*, 32 NAT. RESOURCES & ENVT. 15 (2017) (noting that while "Courts have had little trouble in dispensing with SLAPP actions," SLAPPs remain a popular industry tactic "to increase the physical, mental, and financial cost" of citizen litigation).

# B. Private Enforcement:
# Citizen Suits

When community groups turn to the courts, one set of enforcement tools available to them is found in the major federal environmental laws. These statutes authorize suits by private parties for violations of federal law, and allow citizens to sue in the absence of any economic injury and without demonstrating that harm to the environment has occurred. Citizen plaintiffs in these cases can obtain penalties or injunctive relief directing a polluter to comply with the law, but not damages for any harm suffered. These laws also often provide for the recovery of attorney fees and costs. Some state environmental statutes also have citizen suit provisions, but they are far less common than under federal law.

In the article excerpted above, Professor Kang identifies that most environmental justice litigation falls into one of the following categories: cases challenging siting of new sources of pollution or expansion of existing sources; cases challenging rulemaking; and cases against existing pollution sources. Before environmental justice attorneys apply litigation as a tool in a campaign, however, they must be wary of a number of barriers to bringing such suits to further the environmental justice movement.

## 1. Legal Requirements for Filing Suit

In order to bring an action alleging a violation of federal environmental law, plaintiffs must satisfy various threshold procedural requirements. For a more detailed discussion *see* Ellen P. Chapnick, *Access to the Courts*, in THE LAW OF ENVIRONMENTAL JUSTICE: THEORIES AND PROCEDURES TO ADDRESS DISPROPORTIONATE RISKS 395 (Michael B. Gerrard & Sheila R. Foster eds., 2d ed. 2008).

Plaintiffs must first demonstrate that they have a right to sue under the statute that they are seeking to enforce. Virtually all of the major federal pollution-control and waste statutes contain a citizen suit provision authorizing suits by "any person" or "any citizen." *See, e.g.*, Clean Air Act § 304, 42 U.S.C. § 7604; Clean Water Act § 505, 33 U.S.C. § 1365; RCRA § 7002, 42 U.S.C. § 6972; CERCLA § 310, 42 U.S.C. § 9659; Safe Drinking Water Act § 1449, 42 U.S.C. § 300j-8; Endangered Species Act § 11(g), 16 U.S.C. § 1540(g). Citizen suits are generally authorized in two circumstances: in suits against a regulated entity for a violation of any standard or requirement of the act's substantive provisions (enforcement actions); and in suits against an agency for failure to perform a nondiscretionary duty, such as meeting a statutory deadline. Virtually all of the citizen suit provisions require that, at least sixty days before filing an enforcement action, plaintiffs must provide notice to government enforcement agencies and the alleged violator of their intent to sue. Suits are generally authorized after sixty days, provided that no government agency has commenced and "is diligently prosecuting" a civil or criminal action for the same violation.

For those environmental laws, such as the National Environmental Policy Act (NEPA), that do not have citizen suit provisions, citizens may bring claims under the general review provision of the Administrative Procedure Act (APA), which authorizes suits for persons "adversely affected" by a final agency action. *See* 5 U.S.C. §§ 702–04.

The Supreme Court also significantly limited the reach of citizen enforcement actions in *Gwaltney of Smithfield Ltd. v. Chesapeake Bay Foundation*, 484 U.S. 49 (1987), in which it held that, because of the way the citizen suit provision of the Clean Water Act is worded, citizens cannot sue defendants for wholly past violations of that law. The *Gwaltney* decision had far-reaching implications because the great majority of environmental citizen suits are filed under the Clean Water Act and because several other federal statutes have similarly worded citizen suit provisions (although not the Clean Air Act, which authorizes citizen suits for repeated past violations). In addition, citizen suits against states for damages under environmental statutes are barred as a result of several Eleventh Amendment decisions. *See Seminole Tribe v. Florida*, 517 U.S. 44 (1996) (Congress lacks authority under Article I of the Constitution to abrogate states' Eleventh Amendment immunity from private suits in federal court); *Alden v. Maine*, 527 U.S. 706 (1999) (Congress lacks authority to abrogate states' immunity from private suits in state courts).

Apart from enforcement actions against violators, citizens can also challenge actions taken by administrative agencies, such as the adoption of regulations and the issuance of permits. Such actions are generally subject to judicial review provided certain preconditions are met, including that the agency actions be "final," that they are "ripe for review," and that plaintiffs have exhausted administrative remedies or otherwise raised their objections in earlier proceedings before the agency. Agencies' decisions about whether or not to initiate an enforcement action are generally not reviewable by the courts. *Heckler v. Chaney*, 470 U.S. 821 (1985).

In addition to establishing a statutory right to sue and meeting other procedural preconditions, plaintiffs suing in federal court must demonstrate constitutional **standing to sue**. Several Supreme Court decisions in the 1990s made it considerably more difficult for environmental plaintiffs to prove standing, although this trend was slowed down with the Court's decision in *Friends of the Earth v. Laidlaw*, 528 U.S. 167 (2000).

Standing derives from Article III, section 2 of the U.S. Constitution, which limits the jurisdiction of federal courts to "cases" and "controversies." To establish constitutional standing, a plaintiff must prove (1) an **injury in fact** that is concrete, affects the plaintiff in a personal and individual way, and is actual or imminent; (2) that the injury complained of is **fairly traceable** to the actions of the defendant (causation); and (3) that an order in the plaintiff's favor will **redress** the injuries complained of (redressability). *Lujan v. Defenders of Wildlife*, 504 U.S. 555, 560–61 (1992). The Court has also imposed a "prudential limitation," one that can be altered by Congress, which requires that the plaintiff's injury arguably falls within the zone of interests that the statute the plaintiff is enforcing is designed to protect. In *Bennett v. Spear*, 520 U.S. 154 (1997), the Supreme Court held that citizen suit provisions authorizing "any person" to sue—the language typically used in federal environmental statutes—establish the broadest possible zone of interests, authorizing any party with constitutional standing to sue. An association has standing to bring suit on behalf of its members when one or more of its members would otherwise have standing to sue in their own right, when the interests at stake are germane to the organization's purpose, and if neither the claim asserted nor the relief requested requires the participation of individual members in the lawsuit. *See Hunt v. Wash. State Apple Adver. Comm'n*, 432 U.S. 333 (1977).

In its seminal decision in *Sierra Club v. Morton*, 405 U.S. 727 (1972), the Supreme Court held that injury to aesthetic and environmental values may be sufficient to establish standing, provided that the plaintiffs are among those personally injured. In the 1990s, the Supreme Court issued three additional decisions on environmental standing. In the first case, *Lujan v. National Wildlife Federation*, 497 U.S. 871 (1990) (sometimes referred to as "Lujan I"), plaintiffs challenged a decision of the Bureau of Land Management to open 180 million acres of federal land to possible mining and oil and gas claims. A plaintiff organization filed affidavits from two of its members alleging that they used and enjoyed federal lands in the vicinity of about two million acres, approximately 4,500 acres of which were impacted by the BLM's action. The Court held that these allegations were insufficient to establish injury and that to prove standing, a plaintiff had to demonstrate that they actually use or visited the specific parcels of land affected by the BLM decision. Two years later, the Court issued its opinion in *Lujan v. Defenders of Wildlife*, 504 U.S. 555 (1992) (sometimes referred to as "Lujan II"). Justice Scalia delivered the opinion of the Court, finding that conservation and environmental plaintiffs

> did not demonstrate that they suffered an injury in fact ... [because] they failed to show that one or more of their members would thereby be directly affected apart from the members' special interest in the subject. Affidavits of members claiming an intent to revisit project sites at some indefinite future time, at which time they will presumably be denied the opportunity to observe endangered animals, do not suffice, for they do not demonstrate an "imminent" injury. Respondents also mistakenly rely on a number of other novel standing theories. Their theory that any person using any part of a contiguous ecosystem adversely affected by a funded activity has standing even if the activity is located far away from the area of their use is inconsistent with this Court's opinion in *Lujan v. National Wildlife Federation*, 497 U.S. 871. And they state purely speculative, nonconcrete injuries when they argue that suit can be brought by anyone with an interest in studying or seeing endangered animals anywhere on the globe and anyone with a professional interest in such animals.

*Id.* at 562–557. A plaintiff claiming only a generally available grievance about government, unconnected with a threatened concrete interest of his own, does not state an Article III case or controversy. *Id.* at 571.

In *Citizens for a Better Environment, et al. v. Union Oil Company (Unocal) and Tosco Oil Company*, and *Communities for a Better Environment, et al. v. Exxon*, a number of Bay Area environmental organizations and private individuals challenged Unocal's and Exxon's discharge of excessive amounts of selenium into the San Francisco Bay in violation of the oil companies' pollutant discharge permit limits. As a result of settlements reached in the two cases, the oil companies agreed to implement water treatment systems to comply with their selenium discharge permit limits and to contribute millions of dollars to local foundations to fund projects dedicated to the health of the San Francisco Bay and its ecosystem. *CBE v. Unocal* also established landmark precedent in the Ninth Circuit Court of Appeals, holding that citizens may sue polluters for violating their permit limits when previous government enforcement against those violations is inadequate. *See Citizens for a Better Environment v. Unocal Oil Co.*, 83 F. 3d 1111 (9th Cir. 1996).

However, in the third major standing case of the 1990s, *Steel Company v. Citizens for a Better Environment*, 523 U.S. 83 (1998), plaintiffs sued a manufacturing company for its failure to file reporting forms required under the federal right-to-know law (the Emergency Planning and Community Right-to-Know Act, or EPCRA) from 1988 to 1995. The defendant had filed the overdue forms after receiving plaintiffs' sixty-day notice of intent to sue and before the litigation was initiated. The Supreme Court ruled that where a defendant has come into compliance at the time the complaint is filed, plaintiffs lack standing to bring a claim for civil penalties, at least where the penalties are awarded to the federal treasury, because such penalties could not redress plaintiffs' injuries. The Court held that in these circumstances plaintiffs (even those directly injured by defendant's noncompliance) share only an "undifferentiated public interest" in seeing the law complied with.

In *Friends of the Earth v. Laidlaw Environmental Services*, 149 F.3d 303 (4th Cir. 1998), the Fourth Circuit decided an issue not addressed by *Steel Company*. If a defendant is in violation at the time a plaintiff files a complaint but comes into compliance at some other point during the litigation, does the plaintiff still have standing to sue for penalties? In *Laidlaw*, environmental groups and individual residents sued the operator of a hazardous waste incinerator for violating its Clean Water Act permit. The trial court found that Laidlaw had committed hundreds of violations through unpermitted discharges of toxic pollutants, including mercury, into the North Tyger River. At least 36 violations occurred after plaintiffs filed their complaint, and the court imposed a penalty of over $400,000. The trial court also found that Laidlaw had been in substantial compliance with its permit for several years by the time of the final order in the case, and denied plaintiffs' request for injunctive relief. The Fourth Circuit, relying on *Steel Company*, held that plaintiffs lacked standing to proceed because their only remaining relief requested was civil penalties paid to the federal treasury, and such penalties could not redress any injuries that plaintiffs had suffered. To the surprise of many, the Supreme Court reversed in *Friends of the Earth v. Laidlaw Environmental Services*, 528 U.S. 167 (2000). Justice Ginsburg delivered the opinion of the Court and, in particular, found "To the extent that [civil penalties] encourage defendants to discontinue current violations and deter them from committing future ones, they afford redress to citizen plaintiffs who are injured or threatened with injury as a consequence of ongoing unlawful conduct.... We recognize that there may be a point at which the deterrent effect of a claim for civil penalties becomes so insubstantial or so remote that it cannot support citizen standing. The fact that this vanishing point is not easy to ascertain does not detract from the deterrent power of such penalties in the ordinary case.... In this case we need not explore the outer limits of the principle that civil penalties provide sufficient deterrence to support redressability."

In an important subsequent portion of its opinion, the *Laidlaw* Court addressed the related question of **mootness**. Defendant argued that plaintiffs' claim for penalties was moot because it had voluntarily come into substantial compliance with its permit after the complaint was filed, and later permanently closed the facility at which the violations had occurred. The Court ruled that a case "might become moot if subsequent events made it absolutely clear that the allegedly wrongful behavior could not reasonably be expected to recur," but that the "heavy burden" of demonstrating this rested with the party asserting mootness. The Court found that the effects of Laidlaw's voluntary compliance and facility closure were disputed facts that had not been litigated at the trial court, and remanded this question to the lower courts. *Id.* at 189, 193–94.

*Laidlaw* did not overrule *Steel Company*, distinguishing it on the grounds that *Steel Company* involved violations that had stopped by the time the complaint was filed, while *Laidlaw* concerned violations that stopped after the lawsuit was filed but before trial. But the logic underlying the *Steel Company* decision—that penalties awarded to the federal treasury as opposed to the plaintiffs themselves cannot redress the injuries of plaintiffs alleging statutory violations—is clearly undermined by *Laidlaw*'s conclusion that plaintiffs' injuries could be redressed by the imposition of civil penalties (which likewise go the federal treasury) and that "all penalties have some deterrent effect."

## Notes and Questions

1. **Scalia's dissent.** Dissenting from the majority's opinion in *Laidlaw*, Justice Scalia would have denied standing to sue for local residents who refused to engage in activities such as fishing and swimming in the river because of concerns for the contamination. Dismissing these community concerns as nothing but "subjective apprehensions," Justice Scalia pointed to the lack of data documenting exceedances of water quality standards in the river. How might you respond to this argument? Can "subjective apprehensions" cause real harm—measurable, for example, in terms of physical stress or lost property values? Moreover, is it possible that one environmental medium such as surface water may meet applicable standards but other media, such as air, groundwater, or river sediments may violate standards? Particularly with the discharge of mercury into the North Tyger River, might residents have reasonable or "objective" concerns with consuming local fish?

2. **Standing as a barrier?** In light of the above cases, to what degree do you believe that the standing doctrine is an impediment for would-be environmental justice plaintiffs? Recall that under the "injury in fact" prong of the analysis, the courts focus

upon injury to the plaintiff, not necessarily injury to the environment. Are worries regarding anonymity of members, for fear of retaliatory immigration action, for instance, set aside by judicial precedent? Because environmental justice claims are often centered upon disproportionate burdens, cumulative impacts, and synergistic effects, how would you assess the ability of such plaintiffs to prove injury in fact sufficient for constitutional standing? In an unpublished California court decision, the County of San Luis Obispo Superior Court granted a motion to intervene to environmental justice and environmental groups to protect the groups' efforts expended at the administrative stage of environmental review of a crude-by-rail project. *Phillips 66 Company v. County of San Luis Obispo*, 16CV-0502 (2017). Phillips 66 sued the county after the Board of Supervisors upheld a Planning Commission decision to deny a permit to build a 1.3-mile rail spur that would allow the company to import 6.6 million gallons of crude oil a week by rail to its Santa Maria Refinery. In evaluating the environmental and environmental justice groups' direct and immediate interest in the litigation, the court reasoned

> The Moving Parties, however, are focused on the environmental review process, and their ability to participate in it — whether generally under the second cause of action or specifically as to this Project under the first cause of action. Here, a favorable ruling for Petitioner on the first cause of action would preclude any further public participation ... in the administrative proceedings. In light of the Moving Parties' missions to protect and conserve the environment, as well as their participation in the administrative proceedings on this Project, the Moving Parties have shown a direct and immediate interest in protecting their ability to continue to participate in and protect the environmental review process as it relates to this specific Project ...

How does this result square with other standing jurisprudence? What implications arise for procedural rights? How viable is this route to claim standing for environmental justice advocates? Does this affect your consideration of the participatory versus power models described by Luke Cole?

## 2. The Practicalities of Private Enforcement

Apart from the legal hurdles discussed above, there are important practical concerns with bringing citizen suits. Professor Eileen Gauna provides an overview of the obstacles for community groups to use federal statutes as part of their campaigns. Eileen Gauna, *Federal Environmental Citizen Provisions: Obstacles and Incentives on the Road to Environmental Justice*, 22 Ecology L.Q. 1 (1995). Professor Gauna particularly observes that "[a] community group with limited resources will find it difficult to obtain information about public risks that may not be readily apparent, and secondly, will find it difficult to mobilize to influence agency response or initiate court proceedings...." *Id.* at 46. On the one hand, she concludes that "[i]t would be relatively easy to train citizens in poor and minority communities to detect and prosecute Clean Water Act violations." On the other hand, Professor Gauna is more skeptical of the

Clean Air Act as a viable tool, due in large part to the "problem of obtaining reliable data to detect and prove the violation." She identifies an additional disincentive: the facility in question might employ community residents. "Compliance monitoring might place some community residents in fear of losing their jobs...." Professor Gauna also illustrates another problem linked to enforcement of CERCLA: "citizens on or near contaminated areas can obtain relief under CERCLA citizen suit provisions only after EPA elects to take action." *See* Chapter 8 ("Environmental Justice and Contaminated Sites") and CERCLA § 113(h), 42 U.S.C. § 9613(h) (the "bar on pre-enforcement review"). In addition, despite the benefits of attorney's fees and recovery of costs under citizen suit provisions, Professor Gauna warns that

> The citizens group must find an environmental lawyer who is willing to take the case without any guarantee that the plaintiffs will prevail. Few private attorneys are willing to undertake expensive lawsuits on behalf of underfinanced citizens groups, especially without the incentive of a contingent fee arrangement or an hourly rate agreement backed by a retainer....
>
> Underfinanced citizens groups face other practical problems. Recovery of legal costs occurs, if at all, at the end of the lawsuit. Meanwhile, the citizens group must be able to finance the lawsuit, which may require significant discovery costs, expert witness fees, and transportation costs (if the suit is not local). The practical difficulty of financing complex environmental citizen suits, combined with substantive and procedural limitations of enforcement suits generally, presents substantial impediments to court access for community-based environmental justice groups in low income and minority communities....

*Id.* at 79. It is also important to remember how and whether litigation will benefit the environmental justice movement. Professor Kang applies litigation to the three questions for effective advocacy posited by Luke Cole, and concludes that piecemeal litigation targeting a discrete source of pollution or a particular regulation is likely to fail that test for community empowerment. As a consequence, systemic environmental problems may only rarely be addressed through litigation alone. *See* Helen H. Kang, *Pursuing Environmental Justice: Obstacles and Opportunities—Lessons from the Field*, 31 WASHINGTON U. J. L. & POL'Y 121, 141–145 (2009).

## Notes and Questions

1. **Litigation as leverage.** Returning to a central question of this chapter, after considering the barriers and practicalities of litigating cases to pursue environmental justice, is there any point? Professor Kang emphasizes that litigation may be the only way for community residents to get a seat at the table with regulators and sources of pollution.

> Litigation is uniquely successful in motivating pollution sources to negotiate with community groups. Lawsuits force corporate decisionmakers to consider the merits and practicalities of their position at every stage of the case — from answering the complaint, to deciding whether to file motions to dismiss or for summary judgment, and eventually to devising positions for mandatory

settlement conferences. The same is true when the lawsuit is filed against a regulator. Lawsuits force regulators to retract decisions that are without basis. In addition, where judicial decisions are necessary for statutory or regulatory interpretations, litigation is the only available recourse. *Id.* at 136–137.

2. **EPA's ECHO.** As Professor Gauna comments, the mere identification of non-compliance may pose a significant barrier to any litigation efforts. One tool that should prove helpful to communities in detecting noncompliance is a website established by the EPA in 2002 that provides enforcement and compliance information to the public on more than 800,000 regulated facilities. The site contains data about a facility's inspection history, penalties assessed, and compliance status under the Clean Air Act, Clean Water Act, and RCRA. The website, Enforcement and Compliance History Online (ECHO), may be visited at https://echo.epa.gov/.

3. **The catalyst theory.** As noted by Professor Gauna, many environmental statutes provide for an award of attorney's fees to "prevailing parties," or in some cases, "substantially prevailing parties." In *Buckhannon Board & Home Care v. West Virginia*, 532 U.S. 598 (2001), the Supreme Court held that a party is only "prevailing" when it obtains judicial relief from the court, either through a judgment on the merits or through a court-ordered consent decree. The Court rejected the view, which had been widely followed by the lower courts, that a plaintiff is entitled to fees where it achieves its desired result because the lawsuit brought about a voluntary change in the defendant's conduct (the so-called "catalyst theory"). The impact of the ruling may be to discourage a significant number of citizen actions from being brought, since defendants will be able to foreclose an award of fees by voluntarily agreeing to the relief requested by the plaintiffs and rendering the case moot.

Other environmental statutes, including the Clean Air Act, the Endangered Species Act, the Safe Drinking Water Act, and the Toxic Substances Control Act, contain different fee-shifting provisions from the "prevailing party" standard at issue in *Buckhannon*. Instead, they authorize fees "whenever the court determines that an award is appropriate" (or similar language). Post-*Buckhannon* cases under these statutes have continued to allow fee recoveries under the catalyst theory. *See Sierra Club v. EPA*, 322 F.3d 718 (D.C. Cir. 2003) (Clean Air Act); *Loggerhead Turtle v. County Council of Volusia*, 307 F.3d 1318 (11th Cir. 2002) (Endangered Species Act). In your view, does the different wording suggest that Congress intended attorney fee recovery to be more difficult under some environmental statutes?

4. **"Diligent prosecution"?** Citizen suits may be precluded when the government is "diligently prosecuting" an action against the violator. Not infrequently, citizens will file suit where the government has taken some enforcement action, but citizens contend it is too weak or ineffectual to constitute "diligent prosecution." Court decisions on the issue of "diligent prosecution" are fairly well divided between those finding "diligent prosecution" and precluding citizen enforcement and those rejecting it and allowing citizen suits to proceed. Attorneys Thomas Mullikin and Nancy Smith argue that the "diligent prosecution" bar should be interpreted broadly to preclude citizen suits where the government has acted:

Diligence is the act of remedying the violations in any manner that the state decides. The mere fact that the state does not take the precise action that plaintiffs would prefer does not constitute lack of diligence.... [C]ollaborative and innovative environmental protection efforts between a state agency and regulated industry may be thwarted by the threat of potential citizen suits. In essence, these suits would second-guess an agency's discretion after the settlement.... If industry is subject to additional enforcement action, namely the prospect of penalties in excess of those already imposed by the agency, then they are less likely to negotiate the resolution of their violations. Clearly, this would result in the unnecessary proliferation of litigation.

Thomas S. Mullikin & Nancy S. Smith, *Community Participation in Environmental Protection*, 21 UCLA J. ENVTL. L. & POL'Y 75, 78, 80–81 (2002–03).

Professor Jeffrey Miller offers a contrary perspective, arguing that the courts frequently accord more deference to government prosecutions than Congress intended, and notes that it is the violators rather than federal and state prosecutors who argue that the prosecutorial choices should be accorded great deference. He contends that "while some degree of deference is due to prosecutorial decisions, blind deference ignores the fact that Congress authorized citizen suits precisely because government enforcers were not always diligent." Jeffrey G. Miller, *Theme and Variations in Statutory Preclusions Against Successive Environmental Enforcement Actions by EPA and Citizens: Part One: Statutory Bars in Citizen Suit Provisions*, 28 HARV. ENVTL. L. REV. 401, 466 (2004). Which approach do you find more reasonable?

**5. Good neighbor agreements.** Community groups have sometimes negotiated "good neighbor agreements" in which industry commits to ongoing environmental improvements such as pollution prevention, emergency preparedness measures, or broader access to information for the public in exchange for the community settling ongoing challenges and ending protests or negative publicity. *See* Sanford Lewis, *Good Neighbor Agreements: A Tool for Environmental and Social Justice*, SOCIAL JUSTICE (Winter 1996). For a more recent and critical review of good neighbor agreements, examined through a case study from Portland, Oregon, *see* Thalia González & Giovanni Saarman, *Regulating Pollutants, Negative Externalities, and Good Neighbor Agreements: Who Bears the Burden of Protecting Communities?*, 41 ECOLOGY L.Q. 37 (2014). A related approach that has become popular in recent years is a Community Benefits Agreement ("CBA"). A CBA is a contract negotiated between a developer and a local community detailing the benefits that the developer will provide in exchange for community support for a proposed project. For a more detailed discussion of CBAs, including approaches used by local groups, ways to obtain legal leverage for community benefits campaigns, and best practices for memorializing community benefits to ensure enforceability, *see* Benjamin S. Beach, *Strategies and Lessons from the Los Angeles Community Benefits Experience*, 17 J. AFFORDABLE HOUSING 77 (Fall 2007/Winter 2008).

**6. Supplemental Environmental Projects.** As discussed in Chapter 7 ("Public Enforcement"), environmental agencies over the past 20 years have been settling many enforcement cases by agreeing to have defendants undertake environmental mitigation

**Figure 13-3:** Dennis Chestnut, founding director of Groundwork Anacostia River DC, Watts Branch of Anacostia River, Washington, D.C. March 12, 2019. Photo: Cliff Villa.

projects known as "Supplemental Environmental Projects" (SEPs). While subject to a number of criteria and limitations (*see* Chapter 7), SEPs are included frequently in the settlement of citizen suits. SEPs as part of citizen suit settlements have provided substantial benefits for communities with environmental justice concerns. In the Anacostia community of Washington, D.C., for example, settlement of a citizen suit for Clean Water Act violations required a defendant to purchase and deploy floating traps to collect litter that falls into the Watts Branch of the Anacostia River. The floating traps proved highly successful in keeping litter out of the creek and regular maintenance of the traps provides jobs for local youth.

7. **Limits of tribal sovereignty.** Tribes can enact their own environmental protection programs on Indian land, although there are considerable challenges in doing so. Professor James Grijalva argues that tribes also can protect their health and environmental interests by bringing citizen enforcement actions under federal environmental laws. He notes that while some tribes have started exercising direct regulatory authority over activities occurring in Indian country, such programs require time and resources

to develop, and in many areas there currently are no effective federal or tribal programs. Additionally, tribal regulatory programs are constrained by limits on the authority of tribes over non-Indian actors in Indian country or over activities occurring or resources located outside Indian country. He points out that non-Indian land can contain sites and resources of ongoing cultural and religious significance to tribes, where the tribes' use often is protected by treaty, but because the sites are outside Indian country, tribes cannot regulate activities of non-Indians adversely affecting these important areas. By contrast, a tribe suing under a citizen suit provision need not show that it has authority to directly regulate the defendant causing environmental harm, since the basis of the citizen suit is the defendant's violation of federal environmental statutes. Professor Grijalva also notes that SEPs resulting from private enforcement cases can have important benefits for tribes, including restoration of damaged areas, pollution reduction, and development of infrastructure and capacity for tribal regulatory programs. James M. Grijalva, *The Tribal Sovereign as Citizen: Protecting Indian Country Health and Welfare Through Federal Environmental Citizen Suits*, 12 MICH. J. RACE & L. 33 (2006).

## 3. Building Community Enforcement Capacity

What approaches can be used to strengthen private enforcement capacity in low-income communities and communities of color? Consider the following suggestions:

### a. Upwardly Adjusting Attorney's Fees

Most environmental statutes allow prevailing parties in enforcement actions to recover attorney's fees. The appropriate amount of fees is traditionally calculated as the product of a reasonable number of hours times a reasonable hourly rate, the so-called "lodestar" amount. Professor Gauna argues that courts should augment fees awarded to attorneys successfully prosecuting environmental justice enforcement cases:

> [J]udges could allow an upward lodestar adjustment, not as a contingency adjustment, but specifically to encourage and reward private attorneys who undertake enforcement actions in low income and minority neighborhoods (i.e., an "equity adjustment").... Fee shifting in the private attorney general context serves several important purposes, not the least of which is the incentive for citizens to bring suits that provide a recognized social benefit. In the case of environmental citizens suits, the recognized social benefit is the enforcement of environmental laws. One can assume that Congress (and the courts) had this general purpose in mind in developing the present fee shifting system based on a market rate lodestar calculation. However, in allowing attorney's fees based on the lodestar for environmental citizen suits across the board, Congress did not specifically address environmental justice concerns: that minority and low income communities suffer disparate environmental hazards due in part to a relative lack of resources as a class. Therefore, an

upward adjustment is necessary to further another important policy objective that is not already subsumed in the lodestar calculation.

Gauna, *supra*, at 81. What do you think of this approach? Would it be consistent with the Supreme Court's decision in *Grutter v. Bollinger*, 539 U.S. 982 (2003), discussed in Chapter 10 ("Governmental Initiatives"), which limits the use of racial considerations in government decisions?

### b. Technical Assistance to Communities

Environmental justice activists often advocate the idea of providing technical assistance to communities. Such assistance could take a variety of forms, and two examples are described below.

### i. Superfund's Technical Assistance Provisions

As elaborated in Chapter 8 ("Environmental Justice and Contaminated Sites"), Superfund mandates that EPA provide opportunities for public participation before it adopts final cleanup plans. As early as 1986, the Superfund amendments authorized EPA to make Technical Assistance Grants (TAGs) of up to $50,000 to citizens affected by sites listed on the National Priorities List. Communities can use the grants to hire independent technical advisors to help them understand and comment on technical aspects of the cleanup process. Additional technical assistance is now available to community organizations through EPA's contracts for Technical Assistance Services for Communities (TASCs). For additional information on TAGs and TASCs, *see* www.epa.gov/superfund/technical-assistance-grant-tag-program.

### ii. Training and Technology for Communities to Detect Noncompliance

Should state and federal agencies provide local community groups with funding, training, and equipment to independently monitor the environment? Or is it inappropriate for government agencies to promote such capacity since it could lead to enforcement actions against regulated entities? Professor Gauna suggests that "EPA [and the states] could greatly enhance [private] enforcement in poor and minority neighborhoods by training community residents in sampling and monitoring techniques," enabling them to determine whether facilities are in compliance. Gauna, *supra*, at 80. As Professors Robert Collin and Robin Morris Collin point out, citizen monitoring of environmental conditions has a well-respected tradition in this country (dating back to 1890 when the National Weather Service began training volunteers to report daily measurements of air temperatures and rainfall), and there are now hundreds of formal, volunteer water quality monitoring programs at the grassroots level. Many training programs for concerned community members are now available free of charge through webinars and other online materials. Public training programs available through the EPA include instruction on the use of EJSCREEN for identifying communities with potential environmental justice (EJ) concerns for targeted assessment and potential enforcement action. *See, e.g.,* www.epa.gov/environmental-justice. Recent advances in technology may also continue to enhance the ability of community activists to monitor local environmental conditions and collect data for potential use in enforcement actions. *See, e.g.,* Emily G. Snyder, et al., *The Changing Paradigm of Air Pollution Monitoring,* 47 ENVTL. SCI. & TECH. 11,369, 11,373 (2013) (noting that "Lower-cost and easy-to-use air pollution sensors provide citizens and communities with opportunities to monitor the local air quality that can directly impact their daily lives").

The following recent example in Southeast Los Angeles illustrates the monitoring and data challenges associated with private enforcement that Professor Gauna identifies. It also shows the response of local community groups, in particular East Yard Communities for Environmental Justice (EYCEJ), to the shutdown of Exide Technologies, Inc., a lead-acid battery recycling factory in Vernon, California.

### mark! Lopez, *The Truth Fairy Project and the Exide Fights to Come*

*available at* http://eycej.org/the-truth-fairy-project-
and-the-exide-fights-to-come/ (May 2019)

The South Coast Air Quality Management District (AQMD) issued Exide a permit under Title V of the Clean Air Act with limits on arsenic and lead emissions into the air, but recent findings show that Exide was emitting unacceptably high levels of lead and arsenic. Arsenic is a carcinogen, and lead is a neurotoxin that is particularly potent in children, potentially having negative lifetime effects on development and behavior. For more than 30 years Exide polluted the surrounding predominantly low-income Latino communities. The Los Angeles County Department of Public Health and [the California] Department of Toxic and Substance Control (DTSC) confirmed that the impact area spreads at least 1.25–1.75 miles from the site, encompassing 10,000+ residential properties and over 110,000+ residents in East LA, Boyle Heights, Commerce, Bell Gardens, Vernon, Cudahy, Maywood, Bell and Huntington Park.

After years of our members and staff engaging with AQMD to implement regulation to clean up Exide Technologies, and push DTSC to shut down Exide, as of February 2015, the Department of Justice announced the permanent shutdown of Exide Technologies. EYCEJ has been working on environmental health and justice issues in the affected locations for more than a decade and has developed an expertise in leadership development, building partnerships and effectively influencing policies for a healthy environment. Although this is a huge victory, we must work to address comprehensive and efficient cleanup of all properties and communities directly impacted by Exide. This April, after immense pressure from community leaders, Governor Jerry Brown signed a $176.6 million appropriation to fund a first wave of massive soil sampling and cleanup in the impacted communities....

*The Truth Fairy Project*

... As the California Department of Toxic Substances Control (DTSC) went on to take credit for the Federal Government shutting down Exide, and as some politicians applauded themselves for securing cleanup funds they never fought for (and even discouraged us from seeking), we moved to lifting up new priorities on top of this. Sustained cleanup funding, which we won through Assemblywoman Cristina Garcia's battery fee bill. Workforce development and local hire for cleanup work, which DTSC piloted and successfully developed. Understanding and addressing the social and health impacts of Exide's poison, which is the hardest of the tasks and accordingly where we found the least support. We began to move the conversation through our Marina Pando Social Justice Research Collaborative, with our members conducting research on Exide lead exposure and the social and health impacts in our communities. Also, Dr. Jill Johnston of USC's Keck School of Medicine responded to our call.

Dr. Johnston came to us with the idea of collecting children's teeth and studying them for lead exposure. She explained that teeth have rings, similar to trees, and there is a partner lab where they can shave the teeth ring by ring and study the level of exposure, as well as the point in life when exposure took place. As a community based movement we do not have the resources or expertise to engage in a project like this on our own, and this highlights the importance of our partnership with USC's Keck School of Medicine. As an academic institution, they often haven't built trust and credibility in the broader community, and sometimes don't have the skillsets to engage our communities the same as community movements or organizations do, and this highlights the importance of their partnership with us.

... [W]e need to do more research and generate more data. The Truth Fairy Project has included a relatively small sample size. 43 participants in an area that has over 100,000 residents. Here, funding has been an issue, so we call on government agencies and philanthropy to step up so we continue to expose the deeper impacts of Exide. Additionally we need government agencies and philanthropy to step up in Exide impacted communities to support with those of us who are more vulnerable now because of lead exposure.

* * *

## Notes and Questions

1. **Participatory action research.** What are the benefits of monitoring by community residents? What potential disadvantages and limitations may you see? Apply Luke Cole's questions of effective advocacy and the role of the lawyer. How could a lawyer assist in participatory action research? Consider how this community engagement may overcome the common law evidence barriers raised below.

# C. Common Law Remedies

Before the start of the modern environmental movement, common law actions were the primary tool for protecting the environment. Such actions would include torts claims for trespass, negligence, public and private nuisance, and ultra-hazardous activities. Although such actions largely receded into the background with the adoption of the major federal environmental laws beginning in the 1970s, they continued to be used at the local level, and have enjoyed periodic moments of resurgence of interest among practitioners in recent years. For an insightful reflection on the continuing value of common law remedies for environmental harms, *see* Michael Axline, *Differential Access to Justice in Environmental Cases Involving Private Property and Public Laws*, 27 J. ENVTL. L. & LITIG. 21 (2012). For a more comprehensive overview of this complex area of legal practice, *see* Robin Craig, et al., TOXIC AND ENVIRONMENTAL TORTS: CASES AND MATERIALS (2010).

Environmental plaintiffs have achieved some important successes in actions seeking damages from catastrophic spills or accidents and damages for injuries from harmful products such as asbestos. However, tort actions alleging harm from routine, ongoing environmental releases are much more difficult to win. Limited access to medical care can result in a lack of baseline health data prior to exposure. Work environments or other lifestyle factors can often be presented as alternative causal factors. A lack of scientific evidence on the causal connection between certain exposures and health problems poses a significant barrier for plaintiffs, and technical assistance with medical and scientific evidence can be costly. *See* Melissa Tofflon-Weiss & J. Timmons Roberts, *Toxic Torts, Public Interest Law, and Environmental Justice: Evidence from Louisiana*, 26 LAW & POL'Y 259 (2004); *see also* Allan Kanner, *Tort Remedies and Litigation Strategies*, *in* THE LAW OF ENVIRONMENTAL JUSTICE: THEORIES AND PROCEDURES TO ADDRESS DISPROPORTIONATE RISKS 667 (Michael B. Gerrard & Sheila R. Foster eds., 2d ed. 2008).

## Notes and Questions

1. **Common law and pesticides.** Common law claims alleging harm from pesticide exposure have been difficult to maintain because until 2005, most appellate courts had found that the federal law governing pesticide registration (the Federal Insecticide, Fungicide and Rodenticide Act or "FIFRA") preempts state tort law claims related to pesticide warning and use labels. In *Bates v. Dow Agrosciences*, 544 U.S. 431 (2005), however, the Supreme Court reversed this jurisprudence, holding that common law claims for strict or negligent product liability, breach of warranty, and others were not preempted by FIFRA. It also ruled that plaintiffs' fraud and negligent failure to warn claims would not be preempted if state requirements were "equivalent to and fully consistent with" FIFRA's labeling requirements. For a discussion of how the desire to avoid tort claims for negligent testing and design could prompt manufacturers to engage in more testing and create better and safer products, *see* Alexandra B. Klass, *Pesticides, Children's Health Policy, and Common Law Tort Claims*, 7 MINN. J.L. SCI. & TECH. 89 (2005).

**2. The root cause problem.** Professor Kang has observed:

> Clients also commonly ask the clinic to file claims against pollution sources that cause a nuisance. These suits typically allege that facilities emit intense and persistent odors or contaminated dust. Our clinic has received requests to investigate or file lawsuits against a yeast manufacturing company, a Kraft pulp mill, a steel foundry, and a large construction project disturbing naturally occurring asbestos-laden rocks. The clients in these cases describe odors or dust that interrupt their lives and prevent them from fully enjoying their homes, schools, and neighborhoods. The odors and dust deter them from leaving windows open, sitting in their backyards, gardening, walking, biking, and relaxing after work. Like residents living near other sources of pollution, residents who live near a nuisance are burdened with persistent worries about their families' and their own health. Unfortunately, nuisances are not well regulated by state or federal pollution control laws....

> ... I argue that litigation is insufficient to address cumulative pollution or nuisance sources because, in addition to being resource intensive and difficult to pursue, it does not have the potential to cure the root cause of the problem of cumulative pollution. In addition, while litigation may be successful in addressing particular nuisance sources, they tend to cause a nuisance wherever they operate, which suggests that broader national regulation, rather than individual litigation, is necessary to address the problems that they create....

> ... tort litigation is difficult at best, and, even in successful cases, abatement of the problem is not a guaranteed remedy. Moreover, litigation under statutory environmental provisions can only produce relief that incidentally addresses the nuisance. For example, community members may privately enforce permit limits on volatile organic compounds and thereby reduce odors, but the limits may not be set low enough to eliminate the nuisance. In addition, there may be sources of odors other than volatile organic compounds, and a lawsuit to enforce limits on specific chemicals will not address those alternative sources. Professor Morag-Levine has also painstakingly documented that nuisance-based odor regulations administered by regional air quality districts rarely work. Such regimes rely on detection and confirmation of the complaints by government inspectors, who often cannot show up in time to make a confirmation.

Helen H. Kang, *Pursuing Environmental Justice: Obstacles and Opportunities—Lessons from the Field*, 31 WASH. U. J. L. & POL'Y 121, 135–144 (2009).

**3. "Nuisance with a twist."** Nevertheless, environmental justice advocates have successfully applied nuisance theories in campaigns. In the excerpt below, attorney Richard Drury chronicles how the residents of Huntington Park, a low-income, largely Latino community in southeastern Los Angeles, successfully used a public nuisance theory against a concrete crushing and recycling facility.

## Richard T. Drury, *Moving a Mountain: The Struggle for Environmental Justice in Southeast Los Angeles*

38 ENVTL. L. REP. NEWS & ANALYSIS 10338, 10339–10346 (2008)

In November 1993, ... [Aggregate Recycling Systems, Inc. (ARS)] approached the city of Huntington Park [California] with a proposal for a concrete recycling facility for a long-vacant lot.... ARS' owner, Sam Chew, proposed to take concrete debris and crush it for reuse as aggregate for roadbeds and for mixing with cement for new roads and structures. The city issued a permit for the facility and it opened for business....

Two months later, the Northridge earthquake [destroyed portions of the Santa Monica Freeway, just west of Huntington Park].... In its haste to [reconstruct the freeway], CalTrans [the California Department of Transportation] had left itself little time to consider how to dispose of the huge amount of debris that used to be the Santa Monica Freeway. As low bidder on the disposal contract, ARS took in much of the debris, and its formerly small recycling operation quickly became the massive La Montaña, an 80-foot-tall mountain containing 600,000 tons of concrete debris.... ARS moved its crushing equipment to the top of the mountain, and began operating the crushers around the clock in a futile attempt to keep up with the incoming loads.

The continuous crushing operations from the top of the mountain created a massive plume of particulate matter (PM) that blanketed streets up to an inch deep, and covered nearby homes, cars, furniture, food, dishes, and lawns, particularly on the downwind Cottage Street side of the facility, with a layer of sticky concrete dust. Residents of the low-income community, many without air conditioning, were forced to keep their doors and windows closed even in the squelching heat of the Los Angeles summer, and many had to abandon outdoor activities entirely. The highly caustic concrete dust caused many residents to suffer from respiratory problems, including bloody noses, sinus headaches and irritated noses, eyes, and throats. Many area children suffered increased asthma episodes, frequent bloody noses, and breathing difficulty. Some nearby businesses also experienced problems....

To remove La Montaña from Huntington Park and shut down the ARS facility, [Communities for a Better Environment (CBE), a local environmental group] undertook to organize the community, to marshal scientific evidence of the deleterious health effects of the pollution from ARS, and ultimately to take legal action....

[First, Carlos Porras, CBE's Southern California Director] hire[d] veteran community organizer Alicia Rivera, ... [who] went door to door through the Cottage Street neighborhood to hear complaints directly from the people who were affected, and to encourage the neighbors to band together. In a short time, the neighbors were holding weekly house meetings.... The residents, now known as the Los Angeles Comunidades Asembleadas y Unidas para un Sostenible Ambiente, or Los Angeles Communities Assembled and United for a Sustainable Environment (LA CAUSA), decided to begin attending meetings of the Huntington Park City Council to raise their concerns [and].... conducted pre-meeting rallies outside of City Hall.... Word of the popular uprising spread quickly, and soon local newspapers, radio, and television were covering the demonstrations outside the formerly sleepy Huntington Park City Council chambers.... [T]he community was now organized, and the issue of La Montaña had been injected into the politics of Huntington Park.

[Second,] [t]he scientists of CBE ... compiled a compelling mountain of evidence.... CBE retained an independent test lab to gather dust samples upwind and downwind of ARS. The company conducted polarized light microscopy on the samples, finding that 70% of the downwind samples were composed of concrete dust, while only 16% of the upwind samples were concrete.

[Huntington Park's] Mayor Loya obtained support from local doctors and the American Lung Association to test Cottage Street residents for respiratory problems. The study revealed that over one-half of the residents suffered from chronic obstructive pulmonary disease.

LA CAUSA members, supported by CBE staff, demonstrated at the South Coast Air Quality Management District (SCAQMD) to demand air testing by the agency. After meeting initial resistance, the SCAQMD agreed to conduct some tests. Despite giving ARS advance notice of the test dates, the results of the downwind test revealed levels of total suspended particulates (TSP) higher than any ever recorded in central Los Angeles during the entire calendar year.

CBE also retained Los Angeles Unified School District atmospheric scientist Bill Piazza, who conducted sophisticated air quality modeling to demonstrate that PM levels generated by ARS were even higher than those measured by the SCAQMD....

[Third,] recognizing that the options for legal action under environmental statutes were limited, CBE's attorneys turned to the common law. The California Civil Code §§ 3479 and 3480 contain an expansive public nuisance provision. Section 3479 defines a nuisance as:

> Anything which is injurious to health ... or is indecent or offensive to the senses, or an obstruction to the free use of property, so as to interfere with the comfortable enjoyment of life or property, or unlawfully obstructs the free passage or use, in the customary manner, of any navigable lake, or river, bay, stream, canal, or basin, or any public park, square, street, or highway, is a nuisance.

Section 3480 defines a "public nuisance" to be one "which affects at the same time an entire community or neighborhood, or any considerable number of persons, although the extent of the annoyance or damage inflicted upon individuals may be unequal."

CBE was aware of a long line of older California cases finding operations very similar to ARS' to be nuisances.... The common law approach was also advantageous because of the breadth and vagueness of the definition of nuisance under California law: if a nuisance action were brought in trial court, the judge would have broad discretion to determine whether the ARS facility was creating a nuisance and, if so, to balance the equities in determining the appropriate remedy....

In assessing ARS' potential defenses, CBE again saw some advantages to a common law approach. The California courts had held that a company may not claim a "permit defense." That is, a company may not create a nuisance even if it is operating its business under valid governmental permits. The courts had reasoned that a permit does not tacitly allow the company to create a nuisance even though the government has granted it a permit to operate....

The CBE legal team then discovered an interesting twist that offered the advantages of the common law of nuisance but eliminated many of the uncertainties of a nuisance lawsuit. Rather than sue ARS in California Superior Court, the residents and CBE could bring an administrative complaint for public nuisance before the city of Huntington Park. If the city could be persuaded to declare ARS to be a public nuisance, then ARS, not the residents, would have the burden of suing the city in the Superior Court to attempt to reverse the decision. But the result had some risks—the court would apply a highly deferential standard of review and likely support the city's determination either way, as long as it was supported by "substantial evidence." ...

Under [Huntington Park's] nuisance ordinance, any resident could petition to have a facility deemed a public nuisance. The matter would be assigned to an administrative law judge assigned by the city manager, and a decision could be appealed to the city council.... LA CAUSA launched a new organizing campaign to convince the city to institute a quasi-judicial administrative proceeding to determine whether ARS was creating a public nuisance pursuant to the city's nuisance ordinance.... [Thereafter] the city's attorney ... recommended that the city invoke its nuisance ordinance and commence a quasi-judicial public nuisance proceeding, as recommended by CBE and LA CAUSA.... [T]he city council agreed and retained the respected environmental lawyer Colin Lennard to preside as its hearing officer.

Lennard conducted five days of administrative hearings.... CBE's strategy was to combine real-life community experiences with scientific evidence and legal authority. CBE began the proceedings with almost a dozen area residents who testified to their personal experiences living near ARS—breathing problems, nosebleeds, asthma attacks, and hospitalizations. This testimony was supported by an atmospheric scientist, a respiratory health expert, an environmental scientist, and others who testified that ARS was the likely source of the residents' health problems and that the health problems were consistent with high-level exposure to concrete PM....

In defense, Chew primarily argued that the dust was created by Saroyan Lumber [a facility located on the other side of ARS]. His legal argument hinged almost entirely on the partial SCAQMD tests results, which found ARS not to be in violation of Air District regulations.... [H]earing officer Lennard found the SCAQMD's test results largely unpersuasive for a variety of reasons and rejected ARS' arguments.... Lennard found ARS to be creating a nuisance per se because it was violating several provisions of the Huntington Park municipal code.... He also found ARS' operations to constitute a public nuisance within the definitions of California Civil Code §§ 3479 and 3480 because its operations were injurious to the health of its neighbors, were offensive to the senses, and interfered with the comfortable enjoyment of property.

[Lennard issued an order abating the nuisance] requir[ing] ARS to render all of its equipment inoperable immediately and to cease all deliveries of new material to the site. ARS was required to hire an independent consultant to develop a plan to remove all debris from the site in an environmentally responsible manner that included controls for dust, noise, and vibrations, and which would eventually decrease the

**Figures 13-4(a) and (b):** Raul R. Perez Memorial Park. Site of the former "La Montaña" in Huntington Park, CA. Jan. 17, 2020. Photo: Roselynn Loaiza.

pile's height to a maximum of eight feet. ARS was to remove the debris within 60 days....

[In subsequent reviews, the city council affirmed Lennard's order and a superior court found that the city had substantial evidence to support its nuisance determination.] ARS still refused to clean up the concrete mountain, even though it had lost all of its legal challenges. The city then brought a criminal enforcement action against ARS, but the company pled poverty. ARS claimed that without any revenues from the receipt of new aggregate debris or from the sale of crushed material, it did not have funding to comply with the cleanup order....

La Montaña, now idle, loomed over the community for the next seven years....

Then in 2004,.... [the city] secure[d] $2 million in state funding to clean up La Montaña.... At the urging of local community members, the city has since purchased the property and will turn it into a park....

The story of Huntington Park's struggle to remove La Montaña suggests that hybrid legal-political strategies are often most effective for achieving environmental justice. It is possible to achieve results by combining sound legal strategies with direct community organizing that might not be possible through either approach alone....

By bringing the legal strategy into the political arena of a quasi-judicial proceeding before the city council, it was possible to bring political pressure on elected officials to declare what had been obvious for so long—that the ARS facility was a public nuisance and had to close immediately. Elected officials can be swayed by media attention, direct pleas from their constituents, pickets, and other forms of organizing. Such pressures rarely come into play in a judicial proceeding....

\* \* \*

## Notes and Questions

1. **Another tool in the toolbox?** Prominent California attorney Richard Drury explains that his clients turned to nuisance law because of the weaknesses of applicable statutory remedies. Their options under the Clean Air Act were limited because the local air district had granted ARS a mobile source air permit, based on the fact that ARS used movable crushing equipment. The district's mobile source permitting rules were far more lenient than stationary source rules (on the assumption, inaccurate in the case of ARS, that a mobile source would not remain in one location for more than a few weeks). Likewise, the city had initially exempted ARS from review under California's environmental review statute, the California Environmental Quality Act, based on the company's representations that the project would have minimal impacts. In addition, the statute's very short (35 day) statute of limitations for challenging that determination had long since passed. See id. at 182–83. What does the experience of this case suggest about the relative usefulness of common law approaches?

2. **Nuisance and climate change.** In a unanimous 2011 decision, the Supreme Court stated that the Clean Air Act displaced the federal common law of nuisance, leaving

enforcement and regulation to the EPA. *American Electric Power v. Connecticut*, 564 U.S. 410 (2011). In 2017, cities including San Francisco and Oakland challenged oil companies, including BP, Chevron, ConocoPhillips, Exxon Mobile, and Royal Dutch Shell, attempting to use the nuisance doctrine at the state level. The cities alleged that the oil companies had long known of the climate risks posed by fossil fuels to the environment and downplayed those risks with public relations campaigns. The cities sought damages under a public nuisance theory to shift costs for adaptation projects, such as protecting coastlines from flooding, to the oil companies. The defendants removed the case to federal district court. Judge Aslup's opinion rejecting the lawsuit and motion to remand to state court held that Plaintiff's nuisance claims are governed by federal common law, and reasoned "[t]he problem deserves a solution on a more vast scale than can be supplied by a district judge or jury in a public nuisance case." *City of Oakland et al. v. BP et al.*, 325 F. Supp. 3d, 1017, 1024–26 (N.D. Cal. 2018). The plaintiffs have appealed the district court's ruling to the Ninth Circuit. Other cities and counties, including King County in Washington State, Rhode Island, the City of Baltimore, and Marin County, San Mateo County, and the City of Imperial Beach in California, have also mounted similar challenges against the fossil fuel industry. For a more detailed discussion, and for more on other cities' application of tort theory to climate change and adaptation, *see* Albert C. Lin & Michael Burger, *State Public Nuisance Claims and Climate Change Adaptation*, 36 PACE ENVTL. L. REV. 49 (Fall, 2018).

**3. When to use tort law?** Do you think environmental groups should rely more on tort cases as opposed to citizen enforcement actions to deter corporate noncompliance? On the one hand, damages in large tort cases (both actual and punitive damages) can sometimes far exceed the penalties imposed (or even theoretically available) in enforcement actions. On the other hand, establishing liability in a citizen enforcement case typically only requires establishing that a defendant violated a permit requirement, and avoids complex and often insurmountable issues of causation. Which approach is preferable, and under what circumstances? For an example of a legally successful toxic tort lawsuit that failed to make the affected community feel whole, *see* Dennis Love, MY CITY WAS GONE: ONE AMERICAN TOWN'S TOXIC SECRET, ITS ANGRY BAND OF LOCALS, AND A $700 MILLION DAY IN COURT (2006) (describing lawsuit against Monsanto for dumping polychlorinated biphenyls (PCBs) into Anniston, Alabama's local environment over a 40-year period, which resulted in a $700 million settlement).

**4. What would you do?** If you were an attorney for community groups, what would you convey to your clients about the strengths and limitations of citizen suits and common law theories compared to regulation, governmental initiatives, and multi-party collaboration as a means of achieving environmental justice?

# Chapter 14

# Climate Justice

**Figure 14-1:** On the Porcupine River above the Arctic Circle, Joe Tetlichi, son Jamie (driving boat), and nephew Shane return from a caribou hunt. Warming temperatures in the Arctic due to global climate change may increase flammability of boreal forests and thus reduce caribou habitat and caribou herds, with disparate impacts on indigenous subsistence hunters such as the Gwich'in people of the Yukon Territory. Photo: Subhankar Banerjee, Sept. 2001, from ARCTIC VOICES: RESISTANCE AT THE TIPPING POINT (Seven Stories Press, pbk, 2013).

## A. Introduction

There is an overwhelming scientific consensus that the earth's temperature is warming, that humans largely are responsible for this increase in temperature, and that if the world continues on its current path of energy use and economic growth, we run the risk of severe and widespread impacts from climate change. Stopping such disruptive climate change is perhaps the most daunting environmental challenge that we have ever faced.

Historical emissions dating back to the Industrial Revolution have already locked in a certain degree of climate change. That means that even if the world were to cease using fossil fuels and emitting carbon entirely, we would still have to grapple with the consequences of sea level rise and global warming for decades if not centuries to come. This is so for two reasons: first, because most greenhouse gas (GHG) emissions

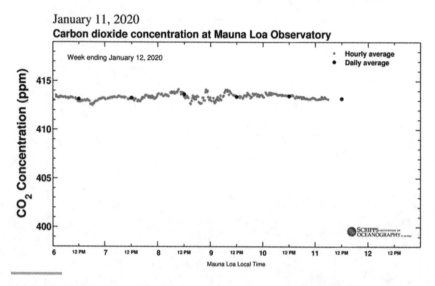

**Figure 14-2:** The Keeling Curve: $CO_2$ Concentration at Mauna Loa Observatory. Source: Scripps Institute of Oceanography SIO.

persist in the atmosphere for decades, and second, because there is a long lag time in the climate's response to the build-up of greenhouse gases (GHG) in the atmosphere. The possibility of limiting global mean temperature warming to 1.5°C—a level that avoids the most catastrophic impacts of climate change—hinges on radically reducing carbon emissions over a very short time period.

In the fall of 2018, the Intergovernmental Panel on Climate Change (IPCC) estimated that there was an eleven-year window to make these changes. To date, we have not stopped emitting greenhouse gases. Instead, carbon emissions are at historic highs and have been increasing rather than decreasing. The environmental justice ramifications of this trajectory are immense. As observed by the IPCC, "People who are socially, economically, culturally, politically, institutionally, or otherwise marginalized are especially vulnerable to climate change.... This heightened vulnerability ... is the product of social processes" that include, for example, "discrimination on the basis of gender, class, ethnicity, age, and (dis)ability." IPCC, 5TH ASSESSMENT REPORT, SUMMARY FOR POLICYMAKERS 6 (2014).

This chapter examines the disparate impacts of climate change and the legal efforts to combat problems at governance scales ranging from the international to the local. Sections B and C provide background about the nature of the problem, including the disparate impacts that will result from climate change. Section D focuses on anticipated impacts of climate change in the United States. Section E explores responses to climate change in the international context, the centerpiece of which is the Paris Agreement. Section F then gives an overview of domestic United States responses to climate change, including initiatives by state governments in the absence of federal leadership. Section G concludes with a quick introduction to the concept of climate adaptation, suggesting some measures that communities may take to minimize or reduce the unavoidable impacts of climate change.

### Pathfinder on Climate Justice

The literature of climate change and climate justice is diverse and mature, with the disparate effects of climate change long recognized by activists, scholars, and policymakers. For the most current and authoritative science on global climate change, see the latest reports of the Intergovernmental Panel on Climate Change, available online at https://www.ipcc.ch/. For climate change science in the United States, one recent and useful resource is U.S. GLOBAL CHANGE RESOURCE PROGRAM, THE CLIMATE REPORT: NATIONAL CLIMATE ASSESSMENT — IMPACTS, RISKS, AND ADAPTATION IN THE UNITED STATES (2019).

Scholarly literature on climate justice is particularly robust. In addition to the works cited elsewhere in this chapter, see Carmen G. Gonzalez, *Climate Justice and Climate Displacement: Evaluating the Emerging Legal and Policy Responses*, 36 WISC. INT'L L. J. 366 (2019); Cinnamon P. Carlarne & JD Colavecchio, *Balancing Equity and Effectiveness: The Paris Agreement & the Future of International Climate Change Law*, 27 N.Y.U. ENVTL. L.J. 107 (2019); Maxine Burkett, *Behind the Veil: Climate Migration, Regime Shift, and a New Theory of Justice*, 53 HARV. C.R.-C.L. L. REV. 445 (2018); Atieno Mboya, *Human Rights and the Global Climate Change Regime*, 58 NAT. RESOURCES J. 51 (2018); Uma Outka, *Fairness in the Low-Carbon Shift: Learning from Environmental Justice*, 82 BROOK. L. REV. 789 (2017); Josephine M. Balzac, *Corporate Responsibility: Promoting Climate Justice through the Divestment of Fossil Fuels and Socially Responsible Investment*, 47 ENVTL. L. REP. NEWS & ANALYSIS 10151 (2017); Nicky Sheats, *Achieving Emissions Reductions for Environmental Justice Communities through Climate Change Mitigation Policy*, 41 WM. & MARY ENVTL. L. & POL'Y REV. 377 (2017); Maxine Burkett, *Climate Disobedience*, DUKE ENVTL. L. & POL'Y F. 1 (2016); Shalanda H. Baker, *Mexican Energy Reform, Climate Change, and Energy Justice in Indigenous Communities*, 56 NAT. RESOURCES J. 369 (2016); Daniel A. Farber, Review, *Climate Justice*, 110 MICH. L. REV. 985 (2012) (reviewing Posner & Weisbach); Eric A. Posner & David Weisbach, CLIMATE CHANGE JUSTICE (Princeton 2010); Alice Kaswan, *Greening the Grid and Climate Justice*, 39 ENVTL. L. 1143 (2009); Maxine Burkett, *Just Solutions to Climate Change: A Climate Justice Proposal for a Domestic Clean Development Mechanism*, 56 BUFF. L. REV. 169 (2008); Paul G. Harris, *Climate Change and the Impotence of International Environmental Law: Seeking a Cosmopolitan Cure*, 16 PENN. ST. ENVTL. L. REV. 323 (2008); Daniel A. Farber, *The Case for Climate Compensation: Justice for Climate Change Victims in a Complex World*, 2008 UTAH L. REV. 377 (2008); Rebecca Tsosie, *Indigenous People and Environmental Justice: The Impact of Climate Change*, 78 U. COLO. L. REV. 1625 (2007).

In addition to scholarly works, many useful materials on climate justice may be found online through various websites. Two of the most useful and reliable websites on climate justice are maintained by the NAACP: https://www.naacp.org/environmental-climate-justice-about/ and the Georgetown Climate Center: https://www.georgetownclimate.org/.

# B. Background on Climate Change

The summary below provides general background about climate change and is drawn largely from the 2018 Special Report: *Global Warming of 1.5°C* from the Intergovernmental Panel on Climate Change (IPCC), the world's most authoritative body on the science of climate change.

The primary cause of global warming is emissions of greenhouse gases stemming from human activities since pre-industrial times. The most widespread greenhouse gas is carbon dioxide, emitted as a result of combustion of fossil fuels such as coal, gasoline, natural gas, and heating oil. Other greenhouse gases include methane, primarily from agriculture and landfills, gases used in refrigerants, nitrous oxide (also stemming largely from agriculture and fuel burning), and black carbon, a form of particulate air pollution produced by biomass burning, diesel exhaust and other sources. Since the beginning of the industrial era, atmospheric concentrations of carbon dioxide have climbed to their highest point in the last half-million years, rising from 275 parts per million (ppm) in the year 1750 to about 411 ppm in 2019 — roughly 40% higher than pre-industrial levels. Nearly half of this anthropogenic carbon was emitted during the last decades of the twentieth century, with the other half accounting for the period between 1750 and 1970. The IPCC projected that to stave off catastrophic climate changes, global emissions would need to fall by 50% by 2030, and reach net zero by 2050. Unfortunately, the trend is going in the other direction, with 2017 and 2018 both being record years for quantities of carbon emitted.

The impacts of climate change already are being felt. In 2017, the globally averaged combined land and ocean surface temperature data show a warming of 0.84 degrees Celsius (1.51 degrees Fahrenheit) above the twentieth-century average. The current global climate is warmer than it has ever been during the past 500 years, and probably warmer than it has been for more than a thousand years. Moreover, the rate of temperature rise is unprecedented. Each of the last three decades has been successively warmer than any preceding decade since 1850, and the four warmest years on record have all occurred since 2014.

The annual mean sea-ice extent in the Northern Hemisphere has decreased over the period 1979 to 2019, with a rate that was very likely in the range of 3.99% per decade. June 2019 marked the second smallest Arctic sea ice extent for June, behind the record low in June 2016. In both of these years, the ice extent shrunk by an area larger than the size California and Texas combined. Sea ice in the Antarctic is disap-

**Figure 14-3:** Flooding in Ocean Park neighborhood of San Juan, Puerto Rico, after Hurricane Maria. Sept. 20, 2017. Photo: Solmari Perez Oliveras.

pearing at an even faster rate. While melting sea ice does not raise sea level, losing bright white sea ice means that more of the sun's heat is absorbed by dark ocean waters, leading to a vicious cycle of warming waters. These changes jeopardize the survival of marine ecosystems, posing a particular threat to charismatic Arctic mammals like the Pacific walrus and the polar bear that depend on the sea ice.

Mountain glaciers throughout the world are disappearing. Changes in winter temperatures are causing more precipitation to fall as rain rather than snow. Since snowpack can be a critical source of water supply, and feeds rivers and streams gradually, the result is less water available in the quantities and during the seasons necessary for human uses. Melting land ice and rising sea temperatures are producing rising sea levels, eroding beaches, and displacing people who live in low-lying areas and on islands.

Moreover, over the past fifty years, cold days and nights have become less frequent, while hot days and nights and heat waves have increased. It is virtually certain that there will be more frequent hot and fewer cold temperature extremes over most land areas on daily and seasonal timescales. Crops and livestock struggle when conditions become too hot, too dry, or too wet. These changes threaten livelihoods and exacerbate food insecurity.

Climate change also impacts human health. While no individual weather event can be conclusively attributed to global warming, warming may already have increased the risk of serious heat waves such as the one that struck Europe in 2003 and caused 35,000 excess deaths. Additionally, high temperatures can put a strain on the electricity grid and related infrastructure, sometimes causing power outages with negative human health effects.

**Figure 14-4:** Climate action sticker in New York City, Dec. 28, 2018. Photo: Rebecca Bratspies.

We also are seeing more extreme weather, including increases in the intensity of tropical cyclones. Increases in the destructive potential of hurricanes are strongly correlated with increases in tropical sea surface temperatures that result from global warming. Most studies have reported increases in the number of Category four and Category five hurricanes in recent decades. This suggests that events like Hurricane Katrina, which devastated the Gulf Coast in 2005, could become the norm and not the exception. Indeed, that has already happened, with Hurricane Sandy (more than double the size of Hurricane Katrina) moving up the Eastern Seaboard in 2012, Hurricanes Harvey, Irma, and Maria wreaking devastation from Houston to Puerto Rico in 2017, and unprecedented wildfires now burning across the West every year.

Scientists predict that if we continue on our current path of greenhouse gas emissions, the impacts of climate change will become increasingly severe, and at some point, may spiral beyond our ability to control or reverse them. In the near term—through the year 2030—our actions may not have much impact on the rate of global warming because our past emissions and inertia in the climate system have already committed us to some degree of warming. Estimated anthropogenic global warming is currently increasing at 0.2 degrees Celsius per decade due to past and ongoing emissions. Human activities are estimated to have already caused approximately 1.0 degree Celsius of global warming above pre-industrial levels, and global warming is likely to reach 1.5 degrees Celsius between 2030 and 2052 if it continues to increase at the current rate. However, while anthropogenic emissions from the pre-industrial period to the present will continue to cause long-term changes in the climate system, these emissions alone are unlikely to cause global warming of 1.5 degrees Celsius. This means that actions we take now (or fail to take) will dramatically affect the rate of warming in the long term.

Impacts from global warming on natural and human systems have already been observed. Climate-related risks depend on magnitude and rate of warming, geographic location, levels of development and vulnerability, and on implementation of adaptation and mitigation options. Experts have identified an increase of 2.0 degrees Celsius (3.6 degrees Fahrenheit) as a threshold beyond which the impacts of climate change are likely to be particularly grave. This benchmark is often cited as constituting "dangerous human interference" with the climate, a term that has legal significance under the United Nations Framework Convention on Climate Change, discussed below. With temperature increases above this level, we risk setting in motion unstoppable "feedback loops" that will exacerbate global warming. For example, the disintegration of large areas of snow and ice will expose darker land surfaces that will in turn absorb more sunlight, raising temperatures and speeding up the further loss of snow and ice. Higher temperatures will thaw the Arctic tundra, causing organic materials in the permafrost to decompose, thereby releasing large amounts of methane. Methane is a powerful greenhouse gas—twenty-one times more potent than $CO_2$.

Climate change will also have profound implications for regional conflicts and global security, as millions of residents are displaced from their homes and conflicts develop over increasingly scarce food, water, and other natural resources. The 2018 Global Compact on Refugees directly addressed the way that climate change and environmental degradation "increasingly interact with the drivers of refugee movements." However, the Global Compact also asserted that climate change and environmental disasters are not "in themselves causes of refugee movements." This assertion is based on the very narrow definition of who is a refugee under international law, and seems out of tune with the UN Institute of Migration projection that 200 million people will be displaced because of climate change by 2050. The World Bank projects that unless urgent measures are taken now, climate change will internally displace more than 140 million people in Sub-Saharan Africa, South Asia, and Latin America alone by 2050. The poorest and most climate vulnerable areas will be hardest hit. Climate-driven 'out-migration' will occur "in areas where livelihood systems are increasingly compromised by climate change impacts. These 'hotspots' are increasingly marginal areas and can include low-lying cities, coastlines vulnerable to sea level rise, and areas of high water and agriculture stress." In other words, millions of people will be forced to migrate from areas affected by rising sea levels and storm surges, as well as from areas that have become too hot or arid to support subsistence agriculture.

Some countries are uniquely vulnerable. For example, 80% of Bangladesh sits in a flood plain, near the rising seas. As Himalayan glaciers melt, they increase water volume in the rivers, leading to riverbank erosion. At the same time, rising sea level means that saltwater intrusions are destroying crop lands and fishing areas. More extreme tropical storms and cyclones continue to hit the country. These manifestations of climate change have already forced hundreds of thousands of Bangladeshis from their homes, and the World Bank projects that number may reach 13 million by 2050.

Similarly, small island states find themselves at the frontline of climate change, with their very existence threatened by rising seas. In late 2018, many of these states came together to issue the Nadi Bay Declaration, expressing deep concern about "the impending grave consequences of climate change," and calling on "the global community to seriously take action to urgently address the warnings of the IPCC Special Report on the dire consequences of lack of urgent actions to address climate change and sea level rise on [small island developing states], and their legal and moral responsibility to account for the loss and damages inflicted on [these states.]" The Nadi Bay Declaration "[a]ffirm[ed] that climate change poses the single greatest threat to the human rights and security of present and future generations of Pacific Island peoples; [and strongly supported] the need for a UN Resolution to establish a Legal Framework to protect the rights of people displaced by climate change that impedes access to basic rights to life, water, food, and housing for many millions of people around the world."

The chart below from the IPCC Special Report vividly conveys the scope and scale of projected impacts from climate change:

## C. The Disproportionate Impacts of Climate Change

Global warming's impacts, while widespread and severe, will not affect everyone equally. As the Chair of the IPCC has stated, "[i]t is the poorest of the poor in the world, and this includes poor people even in prosperous societies, who are going to be the worst hit." Similarly the UN High Commissioner for Human Rights cautioned that "countless lives will be irreparably harmed, starting with those who already face discrimination because of their gender; because of their economic status; because they are members of indigenous peoples or minorities; because they are migrants, or internally displaced; because of their age; or because they are people with disabilities." Indeed, the adverse impacts will fall hardest on people of color and poor people the world over because they are concentrated in areas that will bear the ecological brunt of climate change, and because they often have the least access to the resources

**Share of global cumulative energy-related
carbon dioxide emissions between 1890-2007**

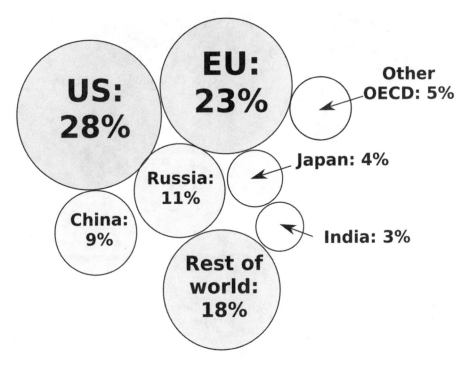

**Figure 14-5:** Percentage share of global cumulative energy-related carbon dioxide emissions between 1890 and 2007 across different regions. Source: Wikimedia Commons, Creative Commons CCO 1.0.

(financial and otherwise) necessary to deal with its impacts. For this reason, responding to climate change is often framed as a justice problem that requires ethical and political responses rather than a problem that calls for purely environmental or physical solutions.

According to the International Energy Agency, the United States alone is responsible for more than a quarter of cumulative global carbon emissions and, together with the European Union, has contributed more than half of total global emissions since the Industrial Revolution. The United States and the European Union together amount to roughly 12% of the world's population, so the per capita contribution disparities are even more stark. And these statistics do not count as American or European emissions those emissions associated with export production in other countries of goods destined for markets in the United States or EU.

Climate change-driven impacts often act as a threat multiplier in that the impacts of climate change compound other drivers of poverty. The countries and communities that have contributed the least to global emissions frequently find themselves on the front lines of climate disruption. These communities tend to be less equipped with the means to cope with the impacts of climate change. This situation gives rise to

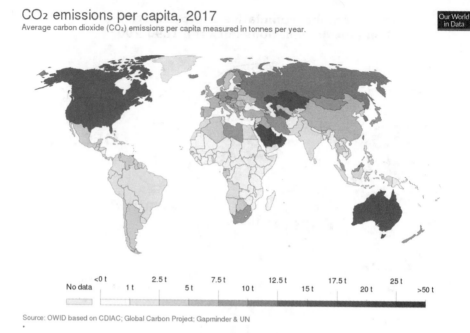

CO₂ emissions per capita, 2017
Average carbon dioxide (CO₂) emissions per capita measured in tonnes per year.

Source: OWID based on CDIAC; Global Carbon Project; Gapminder & UN

**Figure 14-6:** Relative Per Capita CO₂ Emissions for Every Country. Source: OWID based on CDAIC; Global Carbon Project; Gapminder & UN. Retrieved from: https://ourworldindata.org/grapher/co-emissions-per-capita?tab=chart.

calls for climate justice. The story gets more complicated because, in recent years, emissions from some developing countries, particularly India and China, have been growing rapidly. China's national carbon emissions now exceed the combined contributions of the United States and the European Union, even though per capita emissions remain far lower. The climate justice story will only get more complex. The Intergovernmental Panel on Climate Change estimates that, between the years 2000 and 2030, two-thirds to three-quarters of the projected increase in global carbon dioxide emissions will occur in developing countries.

Moreover, whatever steps we take to reduce GHG emissions will by themselves be insufficient to address the challenges of living in a warmer world. We also will have to spend vast sums of money adapting our physical infrastructure and social systems to a world altered by climate change (known as "adaptation" costs). Climate change is likely to exacerbate poverty in most developing countries and create new poverty pockets in countries with increasing inequality, in both developed and developing countries.

The materials below explore in more detail how harm from climate change is likely to be most severe for poorer countries that contributed the least to creating the problem. The first excerpt summarizes some of the major impacts projected for small island states. The second describes the situation for indigenous peoples around the world. The third documents a similar dynamic for environmental justice communities in the United States.

## Maxine Burkett, *Rehabilitation: A Proposal for a Climate Compensation Mechanism for Small Island States*
### 13 Santa Clara J. Intl L. 81, 82–91 (2015)

For more than two decades, vulnerable small island states have sought a means to preserve their lives and livelihoods under threat of the impacts of climate change. Formally organized as the Alliance of Small Island States (AOSIS), small islands have been the source of many novel approaches to climate governance within the United Nations Framework Convention on Climate Change (hereinafter "Framework Convention" or UNFCCC). Perhaps because of their unique vulnerability to its impacts, AOSIS has led a steady drumbeat for urgent and ambitious methods for arresting, and if not, adapting to climate change to survive some of the worst forecast climate phenomena....

A brief introduction to the AOSIS member states quickly reveals their heightened interest in the health and rigor of the Framework Convention. The Alliance is a "coalition of small islands and low-lying coastal countries that share similar development challenges and concerns about the environment, especially their vulnerability to the adverse effects of global climate change." Within the UN system, AOSIS functions as an ad hoc lobbying and negotiating voice for [Small Island Developing States] SIDS, advocating on behalf of roughly 59 million citizens of 44 States and observer countries from across the globe, including the Pacific, Indian, and Atlantic oceans as well as the Mediterranean, Caribbean, and South China Seas. These low-lying coastal states share similar challenges to sustainable economic development, including: geographic isolation, limited resources, dependence on international trade, and pre-existing vulnerability to natural disasters. Further, although their GDPs vary wildly in some cases, most of these countries are middle- or low-income countries, and five also rank among the least developed in the world.

AOSIS countries also have notable vulnerability to climate extremes. The Pacific islands are situated in one of the most natural disaster prone regions and are highly susceptible to—among other disasters—floods, droughts, and tropical cyclones. All SIDS are especially vulnerable to sea-level rise. In the Caribbean, for example, about 70 percent of the population lives on the coast, and regional experts expect that many will have to relocate away from the coasts. In addition, predicted sea-level rise of roughly 3.3 feet by 2100 would "wreak havoc on the region's tourist areas," flood airports, destroy resorts, and—as is already happening—deepen the damage of saltwater intrusion on vital crops. Atoll nations, such as the Marshall Islands, are already experiencing high tides, or "king tides," that surge over sea walls, repeatedly flooding its capital. In the summer of 2013, in an unfortunate coincidence, the tides exacerbated the crisis situation in the northern atolls resulting from devastating drought, which damaged or destroyed local food crops, depleted water tanks, and rendered groundwater unsuitable for human consumption because of high salinity.

SIDS' climate vulnerability is not only the result of the unique exposure to climate extremes but also of the severe impacts that these natural hazards mete on local and national economies. Like many countries, a great proportion of SIDS' economic activity occurs at the coastline, which is particularly true for tourist-dependent island nations. For example, 90 percent of Jamaica's gross domestic product is generated within the coastal zone. Accordingly, any risks to coastal activity will have significant consequence. Not surprisingly, extensive data and a general consensus demonstrate that "developing countries are more economically vulnerable to climate extremes." There are several reasons for this increased vulnerability, including: "less resilient economies" that depend more on natural capital and "climate sensitive activities" such as cropping and fishing; poor preparation for physical hazards; and an "adaptation deficit resulting from the low level of economic development and a lack of ability to transfer costs through insurance and fiscal mechanisms." Accordingly, industrialized countries possess the highest income and account for most of the total economic and insured disaster losses, while fatality rates as well as losses as a proportion of GDP are greater in the developing world. For SIDS, a single disaster has immense ripple effects, severely stressing public financial resources, if not dwarfing annual GDP.

The climate forecast for SIDS is equally troubling. Changes in the "frequency, intensity, spatial extent, duration, and timing of climate extremes" can result in "unprecedented" events. Further, "the crossing of poorly understood climate thresholds cannot be excluded, given the transient and complex nature of the climate system." In other words, scientists anticipate that the known climate-related impacts are set to shift in extreme and novel ways. And, the biggest surprises, though not fully understood, may well come to pass. The IPCC's Special Report on *Managing the Risks of Extreme Events and Disasters to Advance Climate Change Adaptation* (SREX) links anthropogenic activities to known climate extremes, including sea-level rise. Further, it has identified effects like sea-level rise as inevitable. Whereas some climate impacts are avoidable, either through mitigation or adaptation, many are no longer. These unavoidable impacts are ones that cause significant damage regardless of future measures taken to adapt. In addition to land lost to sea-level rise, for example, agricultural land lost to persistent drought, human health impacts of increasing heat events, and the entire collapse of the fishing industry due to increased ocean heat and ocean acidification all constitute unavoidable damage with which SIDS will have to contend. Not only are their territories and economic engines predicted to face significant challenges, SIDS are home to some of the most vulnerable populations—indigenous peoples, internally displaced peoples, and climate-induced migrants. In sum, there are unprecedented climate impacts that efforts to mitigate have failed to address and measures to adapt will fail to prevent or alleviate. And, there are countries and regions in the crosshairs of these impacts.

* * *

## Notes and Questions

1. **Resettlement.** Island nations like Kiribati and Tuvalu may find their lands uninhabitable within the coming decades. If forced by rising seas to abandon their island territory, will Kiribati and Tuvalu still be states? Where would the people go and what would their nationality be?

2. **Compensation?** Professor Burkett advocates for the establishment of a Small Islands Compensation and Rehabilitation Commission to process and pay compensation for loss, damage, and injuries to or displacement of individuals and governments as a result of climate change. She models this proposal in part on the United Nations Compensation Commission created in the wake of Iraq's invasion and occupation of Kuwait. Do you think such a scheme could succeed?

## Randall S. Abate & Elizabeth Ann Kronk, *Commonality among Unique Indigenous Communities: An Introduction to Climate Change and Its Impact on Indigenous Peoples*
### 26 Tulane Envtl. L.J. 179, 181–188 (2013)

Before one can begin to consider the problem of climate change from a legal perspective as it impacts indigenous peoples, one must understand common attributes of many of the world's indigenous communities. By understanding commonalities among various indigenous populations, one can understand more readily the types of legal claims that these communities may bring....

Unlike other populations, indigenous peoples have a tendency to be located in vulnerable locations throughout the world. Indigenous communities are already dealing with impacts of climate change in their daily lives. For instance, the Amazon Rainforest, home to the Yanomami indigenous group, has experienced less rain, severe drought, and higher temperatures. In Canada, indigenous groups such as the Tl'azt'en and the Gitga'at are experiencing unpredictable weather; increased temperatures have contributed to the largest insect infestation in North America [mountain pine beetles], destroying millions of acres of pine trees that [indigenous peoples] rely on, affecting their food supply. In southern Africa, rising temperatures and increased wind speeds have resulted in vegetation loss. As a result, land customarily used for cattle and goat farming is no longer viable for traditional uses. Traditional farming practices in Asia and South America are also threatened by warming surfaces.

In the Arctic, climate change is causing indigenous peoples to lose land and natural resources that are crucial to their subsistence lifestyle. Increasing temperatures related to climate change have caused melting of sea ice and permafrost, resulting in both global and local climate change impacts. For example, greenhouse gases that are trapped in the marshlands of the northeastern Siberian permafrost are being released because of permafrost ice melting, thereby exacerbating global climate change impacts. Climate change is also causing Arctic indigenous groups such as the Sami, Inuit, and Chukchi to suffer severe local impacts to their daily activities such as whaling, sealing, fishing, and reindeer herding. The Inuit's land is experiencing ice melting. Climate change has caused hunting, fishing, and travel in the Arctic to become more difficult, forcing some members to relocate after flooding. Reindeer herders report declining populations because the animals find it increasingly difficult to access food and are more likely to fall through melting ice. Some Arctic species, such as caribou, upon which indigenous peoples rely heavily for their survival, have migrated away from their traditional habitats and ranges due to shifts in weather patterns.

These impacts limit Arctic indigenous peoples' ability to rely on these species because the indigenous peoples, for legal reasons, may be tied to specific areas of land.... As a result of the indigenous peoples' legal connection to the land, it may be impossible for communities to leave land that has been set aside for them in order to follow the changes in species' range land. This in turn decreases many indigenous communities' ability to adapt. In addition, some Arctic species are perishing as a result of climate change....

Perhaps the greatest paradox is that some climate change mitigation efforts are actually compounding the plight of indigenous peoples. Many initiatives, such as biofuels, hydroelectric power, forest conservation, and carbon offsets, which are generally positive measures to address climate change, are often implemented at the expense of indigenous peoples' rights. In this way, many indigenous communities are threatened by initiatives designed to benefit foreign communities.

Biofuels are an alternative source of energy promoted as a climate change mitigation initiative, but it is estimated that 60 million indigenous peoples will be displaced because of biofuel expansion. Indigenous populations in Indonesia and Malaysia have lost forest land because of palm oil plantation expansion. The Guarani tribe of Brazil is losing its ancestral land as Brazil expands sugar cane cultivation to convert into ethanol to meet energy security objectives.

Hydroelectric power is another source of alternative energy and is being used as part of climate change mitigation efforts. Yet hydroelectric dams sometimes occupy indigenous land, destroying their communities. In Borneo, Malaysia, for example, 10,000 indigenous peoples were displaced by the Bakun dam project, flooding 700 square kilometers of surrounding land.

Forest conservation measures and carbon offsets are other initiatives to prevent deforestation and mitigate climate change impacts, but also involve displacing indigenous peoples or otherwise restricting their rights or traditional use of land or natural resources. In Kenya, thousands of Ogiek community members were forced to abandon their homes in the Mau Forest because of the country's conservation efforts, despite the tribe's sustainable existence there for hundreds of years. Moreover, carbon-offsetting initiatives, including reducing emissions from deforestation and degradation (REDD), violate indigenous rights. Apart from concerns regarding the impacts to indigenous peoples, REDD faced many implementation challenges, which led to the creation of "REDD+" as a more effective and flexible form of REDD for the future. REDD's evolution into REDD+ in the years preceding the Fifteenth Conference of the Parties to the United Nations Framework Convention on Climate Change in Copenhagen in 2009 "involved a transition to an enhanced, broad-based approach that includes conservation, sustainable forest management, and forest carbon stock enhancement."

A large portion of the world's forests contemplated in REDD+ schemes belong to indigenous peoples, who fear that such initiatives will cause forced evictions, prevent access, threaten traditional agriculture activity, destroy biodiversity, and violate their rights to their land and natural resources. Under REDD+, developing countries are encouraged to protect their forests, because they can sell stored carbon from the forests as credits to developing countries to offset their carbon emissions. However, until recently, indigenous peoples in developing countries have had limited or no participation in decision-making processes such as REDD+....

In addition to the commonality of the threat from climate change and mitigation efforts, many indigenous communities also share a unique connection to the land that is often not present in the dominant society. This connection is evident through indigenous communities' legal protections and their spiritual and cultural ties to the land. Following colonization from outside societies, many indigenous communities found themselves relegated to certain territories within the dominant nation. For example, in the United States, many tribal nations were removed from their traditional homelands and placed within reservation boundaries that may or may not have been located within the tribe's traditional homeland. As American federal Indian law developed, many of the legal rights possessed by these tribal nations were tied to the reservations where the tribes were relocated. As a result, American tribal nations now have a strong legal interest in the land on which they reside. Additionally, the reservation boundaries often place limitations on the legal rights enjoyed by such tribal nations, as their legal rights may be limited to the territory within the reservation boundaries.

### *Notes and Questions*

1. **Right to redress.** Article 28 of the United Nations Declaration on the Rights of Indigenous Peoples states that:

> Indigenous peoples have the right to redress, by means that can include restitution or, when this is not possible, just, fair and equitable compensation for the lands, territories and resources which they have traditionally owned or otherwise occupied or used, and which have been confiscated, taken, occupied, used, or damaged without their free, prior and informed consent.

Do the impacts of climate change trigger this provision? What about choices made to try to mitigate the impacts of climate change? Is there a way to compensate for the loss of identity and culture?

2. **Risk of violence.** In 2018, more than 160 environmental defenders were murdered. Many of those killed were indigenous peoples. On March 21, 2019, the United Nations Human Rights Council unanimously adopted a resolution recognizing the important and legitimate role of environmental human rights defenders in protecting the environment and in helping States fulfill their obligations under the Paris Agreement. Acknowledging the high levels of risk these advocates face, the resolution called

on States to create a safe and enabling environment for these advocates, to ensure effective remedies for human rights violations, and to combat impunity. The resolution also recognized the need to develop protection mechanisms that take into account the intersecting violations suffered by women, indigenous peoples, and rural and marginalized communities.

# D. Impacts in the United States

On Earth Day 2019, three United States senators announced the formation of the Environmental Justice Caucus. Premised on the notion that all Americans have "the right to breathe safe air, drink clean water and live on uncontaminated land regardless of their zip code, the size of their wallet and the color of their skin," this Senate caucus joins the pre-existing House Bipartisan Climate Solutions Caucus to raise the profile of environmental and climate justice and to seek common ground on climate policy. These legislative developments are particularly important in light of the Trump administration's avowed intention of withdrawing from the Paris Agreement.

In its 2015 *Report on National Security Implications of Climate-Related to Risks and a Changing Climate*, the United States Department of Defense (DOD) characterized the effects of climate change as "an urgent and growing threat to our national security, contributing to increased natural disasters, refugee flows, and conflicts over basic resources such as food and water. These impacts are already occurring and the scope, scale, and intensity of these impacts are projected to increase over time." The DOD has identified a variety of climate risks for military operations, missions, and installations. Of the 3,500 United States military sites around the world, roughly half are already experiencing climate-related impacts like heat, flooding, wildfire, wind, and drought. Indeed, the DOD's 2019 *Report on Effects of a Changing Climate* found that "recurrent flooding, drought, and wildfires" associated with climate change jeopardize all 79 of the military installations included in the analysis. The report also identified climate change as "a source of conflict around the world." Extreme heat events are already putting U.S. soldiers at risk, with over 11,000 heat-related injuries reported between 2014 and 2018.

Aside from the national security risks, the United States has and will continue to experience many of the same devastating impacts from climate change as other regions of the world, although these impacts will be less severe than in some parts of the world due to geographic advantages and greater resources available for adaptation. As discussed below, however, these impacts will hit the poor and communities of color in the U.S. the hardest.

## Congressional Black Caucus Foundation,
## African Americans and Climate Change:
## An Unequal Burden
### 2–3 (2004)

[T]here is a stark disparity in the United States between those who benefit from the causes of climate change and those who bear the costs of climate change....

### Health Effects

It is clear that African Americans will disproportionately bear the substantial public health burden caused by climate change. Health effects will include the degradation of air quality, deaths from heat waves and extreme weather events, and the spread of infectious diseases....

Air pollution is already divided down racial lines in this country, with over seventy percent of African Americans living in counties in violation of federal air pollution standards. The number of people affected will increase as the higher temperatures of global warming are expected to further degrade air quality through increased ozone formation. In every single one of the 44 major metropolitan areas in the U.S., Blacks are more likely than Whites to be exposed to higher air toxics concentrations....

Similarly, at present, African Americans are at a greater risk of [dying] during extreme heat events. The most direct health effect of climate change will be intensifying heat waves that selectively impact poor and urban populations. Future heat waves will be most lethal in the inner cities of the northern half of the country, such as New York City, Detroit, Chicago, and Philadelphia, where many African American communities are located.

African Americans may also be disproportionately impacted by the increased prevalence of extreme weather events and the spread of infectious diseases, such as malaria and dengue fever, primarily in Southern states.... All of these problems are compounded by the fact that Blacks are 50% more likely than non-Blacks to be uninsured.

### Economic Effects

African American workers are likely to be laid off disproportionately due to the economic instability caused by climate change. In general, economic transitions strike hardest at those without resources or savings to adapt. In the United States, drought, sea level rise, and the higher temperatures associated with global warming may have sizeable impacts on several economic sectors including agriculture, insurance, and buildings and infrastructure....

In contrast to the burden of climate change, responsibility for the problem does not lie primarily with African Americans. African American households emit twenty percent less carbon dioxide than white households. Historically, this difference was even higher....

* * *

## Notes and Questions

**1.** As the climate continues to warm, more frequent and severe extreme heat events will disproportionately impact low-income communities, communities of color, socially isolated populations, and the elderly. Deaths caused by extremely hot weather are already a major public health concern in the United States, resulting in more deaths than any other weather-related event. There are large racial disparities in these heat-related deaths. A 2018 Grist report found that roughly half of all New Yorkers who die from heat are African-American—double their share of the population. New York City is not alone in this. Professor Maxine Burkett notes that "[h]eat stress has already been a public health nightmare for the poor and for people of color. As an example, older black males living alone with poor health status suffered a disproportionate share of excess fatalities after the 1996 heat wave in Chicago." Maxine Burkett, *Just Solutions to Climate Change: A Climate Justice Proposal for a Domestic Clean Development Mechanism*, 56 Buff. L. Rev. 169, 177 (2008). Heat-related deaths are more likely to be concentrated in urban areas because concrete and asphalt surfaces there help create the urban "heat island effect," and also because these areas often have worse air quality, and elevated pollution is often associated with heat waves. In addition, urban tree canopy is an important local mitigating factor for extreme heat. Studies in the United States have documented significant disparities in the urban tree canopy, with poor and minority neighborhoods having lower levels of tree coverage.

**2.** As explored further in Chapter 15 ("Disaster Justice"), vulnerability to disasters is a function of both proximity to natural hazards and the social and economic characteristics of a community. As the readings above illustrate, the impacts of global warming experienced by minority and poor communities will be exacerbated because these groups are often the least able to adapt. Their increased vulnerability is not only a function of marginalization or poverty, but also of adaptation planning processes that perpetuate or expand their marginalization. As one social science review of vulnerability to climate change explained:

> Social processes of marginalization and disenfranchisement play important roles in creating patterns of unequal access to resources. Simultaneously, climate change will increase the exposure of populations to environmental hazards, exacerbating the existing unevenness in vulnerability across axes of social difference such as race, class, ethnicity, and gender.... Designing and implementing effective disaster risk reduction and adaptation interventions require attention to these inequalities in the context of ongoing social changes.

Kimberly Thomas, et al., *Explaining Differential Vulnerability to Climate Change: A Social Science Review*, 10 Wiley Interdiscip. Rev. Clim. Change (2019).

Structural racism, which created racial disparities in educational attainment, income, and wealth by perpetuating uneven access to resources, often means that it is more difficult for poor and minority community members to prepare for climate threats. Poor people typically have less access to health insurance, or to homeowner's and renter's insurance. The locations in which they reside are often more vulnerable to the impacts of weather and climate change. Moreover, the buildings they occupy may be poorly constructed and less able to withstand climate hazards. Poor and minority communities thus face heightened climate risks, while enjoying access to fewer preparedness resources. Color blind adaptation policies can further exacerbate inequalities in access to the resources needed to adapt to a changing climate.

3. To what extent are the disproportionate impacts likely to result from climate change part of the larger pattern of disparate environmental harms seen in Chapter 2? What do the similarities/differences suggest about how domestic climate policies should be crafted?

4. The Congressional Black Caucus report notes that poor Americans, regardless of race, also are far less responsible for carbon dioxide emissions than wealthier Americans, "with the average household in the wealthiest decile emitting roughly seven times as much carbon dioxide as the average household in the bottom expenditure decile." UNEQUAL BURDEN, *supra*, at 70. What implications does this have for efforts to control carbon emissions, including the likely political support for such programs?

# E. Climate Justice in International Law and Policy

The international community first addressed climate change with the 1992 United Nations Framework Convention on Climate Change (UNFCCC). The parties to the treaty (which now has been ratified by 192 countries, including the United States), agreed to stabilize greenhouse gas concentrations in the atmosphere with the goal of "preventing dangerous anthropogenic interference with Earth's climate system," although no numerical targets for GHG emissions reductions were set. The Framework recognizes that nations have "common but differentiated responsibilities," reflecting the view that developed countries bear a greater historical responsibility for the problem of climate change and have a greater capacity to take action. In particular, Article 3(1) of the UNFCCC provides that

> The Parties should protect the climate for the benefit of present and future generations of humankind, on the basis of equity and in accordance with their common but differentiated responsibilities and respective capabilities. Accordingly, the developed country Parties should take the lead in combating climate change and the adverse effects thereof.

In late 2015, at the 21st Conference of the Parties (COP 21) to the United Nations Framework Convention on Climate Change, the international community negotiated the Paris Agreement. The Agreement's central aim is to strengthen the global response to the threat of climate change by keeping a global temperature rise this century well below 2 degrees Celsius above pre-industrial levels and to pursue efforts to limit the temperature increase even further to 1.5 degrees Celsius. The Agreement's main mechanism for achieving this goal is through nationally determined contributions (NDCs), which are specific measures to reduce greenhouse gas emissions as determined by the individual nations themselves. After publicly submitting their NDCs, all Parties to the Paris Agreement must report regularly on their emissions and on their implementation efforts. Article 14 of the Paris Agreement provides for a periodic global stocktaking "of the implementation of this Agreement to assess the collective progress towards achieving the purpose of this Agreement and its long-term goals." The Agreement specifies that this stocktaking should be done in a "comprehensive and facilitative manner, considering mitigation, adaptation and the means of implementation and support, and in the light of equity and the best available science." Additionally, the Agreement aims to strengthen the ability of countries to deal with the impacts of climate change. To reach these ambitious goals, appropriate financial flows, a new technology framework, and an enhanced capacity building framework will be put in place, thus supporting action by developing countries and the most vulnerable countries, in line with their own national objectives. The Agreement also provides for enhanced transparency of action and support through a more robust transparency framework.

## The Paris Agreement
### (2015)

*The Parties to this Agreement* ...

*Recognizing* the need for an effective and progressive response to the urgent threat of climate change on the basis of the best available scientific knowledge,

*Also recognizing* the specific needs and special circumstances of developing country Parties, especially those that are particularly vulnerable to the adverse effects of climate change...

*Acknowledging* that climate change is a common concern of humankind, Parties should, when taking action to address climate change, respect, promote and consider their respective obligations on human rights, the right to health, the rights of indigenous peoples, local communities, migrants, children, persons with disabilities and people in vulnerable situations and the right to development, as well as gender equality, empowerment of women and intergenerational equity...

### Article 2

1. This Agreement, in enhancing the implementation of the Convention, including its objective, aims to strengthen the global response to the threat of climate change, in the context of sustainable development and efforts to eradicate poverty, including by:

(a) Holding the increase in the global average temperature to well below 2°C above pre-industrial levels and pursuing efforts to limit the temperature increase to 1.5°C above pre-industrial levels, recognizing that this would significantly reduce the risks and impacts of climate change;

(b) Increasing the ability to adapt to the adverse impacts of climate change and foster climate resilience and low greenhouse gas emissions development, in a manner that does not threaten food production; and

(c) Making finance flows consistent with a pathway towards low greenhouse gas emissions and climate-resilient development.

2. This Agreement will be implemented to reflect equity and the principle of common but differentiated responsibilities and respective capabilities, in the light of different national circumstances....

### Article 4

1. In order to achieve the long-term temperature goal set out in Article 2, Parties aim to reach global peaking of greenhouse gas emissions as soon as possible, recognizing that peaking will take longer for developing country Parties, and to undertake rapid reductions thereafter in accordance with best available science, so as to achieve a balance between anthropogenic emissions by sources and removals by sinks of greenhouse gases in the second half of this century, on the basis of equity, and in the context of sustainable development and efforts to eradicate poverty.

2. Each Party shall prepare, communicate and maintain successive nationally determined contributions that it intends to achieve. Parties shall pursue domestic mitigation measures, with the aim of achieving the objectives of such contributions.

3. Each Party's successive nationally determined contribution will represent a progression beyond the Party's then current nationally determined contribution and reflect its highest possible ambition, reflecting its common but differentiated responsibilities and respective capabilities, in the light of different national circumstances.

4. Developed country Parties should continue taking the lead by undertaking economy-wide absolute emission reduction targets. Developing country Parties should continue enhancing their mitigation efforts, and are encouraged to move over time towards economy-wide emission reduction or limitation targets in the light of different national circumstance.

* * *

## Notes and Questions

1. **Differentiated responsibilities?** What do you think the principle of "common but differentiated responsibilities" articulated in the U.N. Framework Convention on Climate Change means in practice? As a general matter, do you think differentiated responsibility is a workable and desirable rule for addressing international environmental problems? Implementing this approach in the context of climate change is explored in the section below.

2. **Nationally Determined Contributions.** The centerpiece of the Paris Agreement is Nationally Determined Contributions (NDCs). This stands in sharp contrast to the approach of the Kyoto Protocol, where the major industrialized countries (so

called "annex I" countries) had collectively committed to reducing their average annual greenhouse gas emissions between the years 2008 and 2012 to 5.2% below their 1990 levels. Developing countries (so-called "non-annex I" countries) were not required to limit their emissions (and nearly all refused to consider such limits during the negotiations). Why do you think the international community abandoned the Kyoto Protocol approach in favor of the NDCs? Which approach do you think is more likely to succeed?

**3. U.S. NDCs.** The NDCs submitted by the United States included carbon reductions anticipated through the following measures: (1) reduction of emissions from domestic power plants through implementation of the Clean Power Plan under the Clean Air Act; (2) reduction of vehicle emissions through improvements in fuel efficiency; and (3) reduction of methane emissions from landfills and the oil and gas sector. Each of these measures is currently subject to efforts toward repeal under the Trump administration. What are the consequences of a country failing to meet its NDCs? If there is not some international "climate police" with the authority to put a country in jail or otherwise punish violators, why would any country bother to comply with their own NDCs at all?

**4. *1.5°C* Special Report.** The Parties to the Paris Agreement invited the IPCC to provide by 2018 a special report on the impacts of global warming of 1.5°C above pre-industrial levels and related global greenhouse gas emission pathways. The IPCC accepted this invitation. The resulting *1.5°C* Special Report concluded that, if greenhouse gas emissions continue at the current rate, the atmosphere will warm up by as much as 2.7 degrees Fahrenheit (1.5 degrees Celsius) above preindustrial levels by 2040, inundating coastlines and intensifying droughts and poverty. The *1.5°C* Special Report also concluded that the greenhouse gas reduction pledges put forth under the Paris Agreement will not be enough to avoid 3.6 degrees of warming. The UN High Commissioner for Human Rights described the consequences of this degree of climate change as "unthinkable," noting that "entire nations, ecosystems, peoples and ways of life could simply cease to exist."

* * *

## M. R. Allen, et al., 2018: Framing and Context.
### In: *Global Warming of 1.5°C.*

*An IPCC Special Report on the impacts of global warming of 1.5°C above pre-industrial levels and related global greenhouse gas emission pathways, in the context of strengthening the global response to the threat of climate change, sustainable development, and efforts to eradicate poverty*

Human-induced warming reached approximately 1°C (likely between 0.8°C and 1.2°C) above pre-industrial levels in 2017, increasing at 0.2°C (likely between 0.1°C and 0.3°C) per decade (high confidence)....

Warming greater than the global average has already been experienced in many regions and seasons, with higher average warming over land than over the ocean (high confidence). Most land regions are experiencing greater warming than the global average, while most ocean regions are warming at a slower rate. Depending on the temperature dataset considered, 20–40% of the global human population live in regions that, by the decade 2006–2015, had already experienced warming of more than 1.5°C above pre-industrial in at least one season (medium confidence).

Past emissions alone are unlikely to raise global-mean temperature to 1.5°C above pre-industrial levels (medium confidence), but past emissions do commit to other changes, such as further sea level rise (high confidence). If all anthropogenic emissions (including aerosol-related) were reduced to zero immediately, any further warming beyond the 1°C already experienced would likely be less than 0.5°C over the next two to three decades (high confidence), and likely less than 0.5°C on a century time scale (medium confidence), due to the opposing effects of different climate processes and drivers. A warming greater than 1.5°C is therefore not geophysically unavoidable: whether it will occur depends on future rates of emission reductions.... All 1.5°C pathways involve limiting cumulative emissions of long-lived greenhouse gases, including carbon dioxide and nitrous oxide, and substantial reductions in other climate forcers (high confidence). Limiting cumulative emissions requires either reducing net global emissions of long-lived greenhouse gases to zero before the cumulative limit is reached, or net negative global emissions (anthropogenic removals) after the limit is exceeded.

Ethical considerations, and the principle of equity in particular, are central to this report, recognizing that many of the impacts of warming up to and beyond 1.5°C, and some potential impacts of mitigation actions required to limit warming to 1.5°C, fall disproportionately on the poor and vulnerable (high confidence). Equity has procedural and distributive dimensions and requires fairness in burden sharing both between generations and between and within nations. In framing the objective of holding the increase in the global average temperature rise to well below 2°C above pre-industrial levels, and to pursue efforts to limit warming to 1.5°C, the Paris Agreement associates the principle of equity with the broader goals of poverty eradication and sustainable development, recognising that effective responses to climate change require a global collective effort that may be guided by the 2015 United Nations Sustainable Development Goals....

Ambitious mitigation actions are indispensable to limit warming to 1.5°C while achieving sustainable development and poverty eradication (high confidence). Ill-designed responses, however, could pose challenges especially—but not exclusively—for countries and regions contending with poverty and those requiring significant transformation of their energy systems.... Significant uncertainty remains as to which pathways are more consistent with the principle of equity....

Climate change is an integral influence on sustainable development, closely related to the economic, social and environmental dimensions of the SDGs. The IPCC has woven the concept of sustainable development into recent assessments, showing how climate change might undermine sustainable development, and the synergies between sustainable development and responses to climate change (Denton et al., 2014). Climate change is also explicit in the SDGs. SDG13 specifically requires 'urgent action

**Figure 14-7:** Climate Action is Sustainable Development Goal 13. Source: UNCTAD.

to address climate change and its impacts'. The targets include strengthening resilience and adaptive capacity to climate-related hazards and natural disasters; integrating climate change measures into national policies, strategies and planning; and improving education, awareness raising and human and institutional capacity....

* * *

In 2002, the International Climate Justice Network, composed of activists and non-governmental organizations from around the world, released the Bali Principles of Climate Justice. This declaration intended to redefine climate change from a human rights and environmental justice perspective. It was explicitly modeled on *Environmental Justice Principles* developed at the 1991 People of Color Environmental Justice Leadership Summit in Washington, D.C.

## Bali Principles of Climate Justice
29 August 2002

### PREAMBLE

Whereas climate change is a scientific reality whose effects are already being felt around the world;

Whereas if consumption of fossil fuels, deforestation and other ecological devastation continues at current rates, it is certain that climate change will result in increased temperatures, sea level rise, changes in agricultural patterns, increased frequency and magnitude of "natural" disasters such as floods, droughts, loss of biodiversity, intense storms and epidemics;

Whereas deforestation contributes to climate change, while having a negative impact on a broad array of local communities;

Whereas communities and the environment feel the impacts of the fossil fuel economy at every stage of its life cycle, from exploration to production to refining to distribution to consumption to disposal of waste;

Whereas climate change and its associated impacts are a global manifestation of this local chain of impacts;

Whereas fossil fuel production and consumption helps drive corporate-led globalization;

Whereas climate change is being caused primarily by industrialized nations and transnational corporations;

Whereas the multilateral development banks, transnational corporations and Northern governments, particularly the United States, have compromised the democratic nature of the United Nations as it attempts to address the problem;

Whereas the perpetration of climate change violates the Universal Declaration of Human Rights, and the United Nations Convention on Genocide;

Whereas the impacts of climate change are disproportionately felt by small island states, women, youth, coastal peoples, local communities, indigenous peoples, fisherfolk, poor people and the elderly;

Whereas local communities, affected people and indigenous peoples have been kept out of the global processes to address climate change;

Whereas market-based mechanisms and technological "fixes" currently being promoted by transnational corporations are false solutions and are exacerbating the problem; Whereas unsustainable production and consumption practices are at the root of this and other global environmental problems;

Whereas this unsustainable consumption exists primarily in the North, but also among elites within the South;

Whereas the impacts will be most devastating to the vast majority of the people in the South, as well as the "South" within the North;

Whereas the impacts of climate change threaten food sovereignty and the security of livelihoods of natural resource-based local economies;

Whereas the impacts of climate change threaten the health of communities around the world—especially those who are vulnerable and marginalized, in particular children and elderly people;

Whereas combating climate change must entail profound shifts from unsustainable production, consumption and lifestyles, with industrialized countries taking the lead;

We, representatives of people's movements together with activist organizations working for social and environmental justice resolve to begin to build an international movement of all peoples for Climate Justice based on the following core principles:

1. Affirming the sacredness of Mother Earth, ecological unity and the interdependence of all species, Climate Justice insists that communities have the right to be free from climate change, its related impacts and other forms of ecological destruction.

2. Climate Justice affirms the need to reduce with an aim to eliminate the production of greenhouse gases and associated local pollutants.

3. Climate Justice affirms the rights of indigenous peoples and affected communities to represent and speak for themselves.

4. Climate Justice affirms that governments are responsible for addressing climate change in a manner that is both democratically accountable to their people and in accordance with the principle of common but differentiated responsibilities.

5. Climate Justice demands that communities, particularly affected communities, play a leading role in national and international processes to address climate change.

6. Climate Justice opposes the role of transnational corporations in shaping unsustainable production and consumption patterns and lifestyles, as well as their role in unduly influencing national and international decision-making.

7. Climate Justice calls for the recognition of a principle of ecological debt that industrialized governments and transnational corporations owe the rest of the world as a result of their appropriation of the planet's capacity to absorb greenhouse gases.

8. Affirming the principle of ecological debt, Climate Justice demands that fossil fuel and extractive industries be held strictly liable for all past and current lifecycle impacts relating to the production of greenhouse gases and associated local pollutants.

9. Affirming the principle of ecological debt, Climate Justice protects the rights of victims of climate change and associated injustices to receive full compensation, restoration, and reparation for loss of land, livelihood and other damages.

10. Climate Justice calls for a moratorium on all new fossil fuel exploration and exploitation; a moratorium on the construction of new nuclear power plants; the phase out of the use of nuclear power worldwide; and a moratorium on the construction of large hydro schemes.

11. Climate Justice calls for clean, renewable, locally controlled and low-impact energy resources in the interest of a sustainable planet for all living things.

12. Climate Justice affirms the right of all people, including the poor, women, [and] rural and indigenous peoples, to have access to affordable and sustainable energy.

13. Climate Justice affirms that any market-based or technological solution to climate change, such as carbon-trading and carbon sequestration, should be

subject to principles of democratic accountability, ecological sustainability and social justice.

14. Climate Justice affirms the right of all workers employed in extractive, fossil fuel and other greenhouse-gas producing industries to a safe and healthy work environment without being forced to choose between an unsafe livelihood based on unsustainable production and unemployment.

15. Climate Justice affirms the need for solutions to climate change that do not externalize costs to the environment and communities, and are in line with the principles of a just transition.

16. Climate Justice is committed to preventing the extinction of cultures and biodiversity due to climate change and its associated impacts.

17. Climate Justice affirms the need for socio-economic models that safeguard the fundamental rights to clean air, land, water, food and healthy ecosystems.

18. Climate Justice affirms the rights of communities dependent on natural resources for their livelihood and cultures to own and manage the same in a sustainable manner, and is opposed to the commodification of nature and its resources.

19. Climate Justice demands that public policy be based on mutual respect and justice for all peoples, free from any form of discrimination or bias.

20. Climate Justice recognizes the right to self-determination of Indigenous Peoples, and their right to control their lands, including sub-surface land, territories and resources and the right to the protection against any action or conduct that may result in the destruction or degradation of their territories and cultural way of life.

21. Climate Justice affirms the right of indigenous peoples and local communities to participate effectively at every level of decision-making, including needs assessment, planning, implementation, enforcement and evaluation, the strict enforcement of principles of prior informed consent, and the right to say "No."

22. Climate Justice affirms the need for solutions that address women's rights.

23. Climate Justice affirms the right of youth as equal partners in the movement to address climate change and its associated impacts.

24. Climate Justice opposes military action, occupation, repression and exploitation of lands, water, oceans, peoples and cultures, and other life forms, especially as it relates to the fossil fuel industry's role in this respect.

25. Climate Justice calls for the education of present and future generations, emphasizes climate, energy, social and environmental issues, while basing itself on real-life experiences and an appreciation of diverse cultural perspectives.

26. Climate Justice requires that we, as individuals and communities, make personal and consumer choices to consume as little of Mother Earth's resources, conserve our need for energy; and make the conscious decision to challenge and repri-

oritize our lifestyles, re-thinking our ethics with relation to the environment and the Mother Earth; while utilizing clean, renewable, low-impact energy; and ensuring the health of the natural world for present and future generations.

27. Climate Justice affirms the rights of unborn generations to natural resources, a stable climate and a healthy planet.

* * *

## Notes and Questions

1. **Unjust burdens.** The disproportionate burdens that developing countries face seem particularly unjust because these countries are least responsible for climate change. What does this historical distribution suggest about how the responsibility for addressing climate change should be allocated? Should past contributions be more important than current capability (or weighted at all)?

2. **Wrongdoer identity.** Developing countries are adamant that the countries responsible for the historical stock of $CO_2$ that is causing climate change should take the lead in emissions reductions. Developed countries, by contrast, argue that since the harmful climate change implications of carbon emissions were not widely known during the Industrial Revolution, it would be unfair to hold the present generations responsible for the "sins" of their forebearers. They instead argue that responsibility should be allocated based on current emissions, a stance that would require China and India to shoulder a large portion of the burden associated with reducing carbon emissions. Which position do you find more persuasive? Even if they had not been alive during these periods, did individuals in industrialized countries personally gain from the past activities of their countries?

3. As the readings indicate, developing countries face a double, if not triple, whammy from climate change, stemming from geography, limits in adaptive capacity, and potential impacts on the stability of their political regimes. While the costs of adaptation are uncertain and vary dramatically based on emissions scenarios, under any circumstance they are likely to be very large. The UN Environment Programme pegs these costs as between $280 and $500 billion per year by 2050. UNEP, *The Adaptation Gap Report: Status and Trends: The Adaptation Finance Gap* (2018). Does this suggest that massive aid from the developed to the developing world to pay for adaptation programs is needed? The anticipated severity of impacts from climate change are closely linked to the wealth and adaptive capabilities of nations. Does this mean that climate change efforts should only proceed in tandem with development efforts?

4. One often-repeated justification for not acting now on climate change rests on cost-benefit analysis that assumes that future generations are likely to be much richer than current ones. Do you agree with this assumption? If it is incorrect, how does it affect the underlying argument?

5. **Faith-based solutions?** In his 2015 encyclical on the environment, *Laudato Si, On the Care of Our Common Home*, Pope Francis emphasized the connection between

climate change, environmental degradation, and social justice. He wrote "Today, however, we have to realize that a true ecological approach always becomes a social approach; it must integrate questions of justice in debates on the environment, so as to hear both the cry of the earth and the cry of the poor." Do you think that religious traditions and practices contribute to environmental degradation? Do you think that religious teachings can offer a path out of our current environmental conundrum?

# F. Climate Law and Policy in the Domestic Context

From the beginning of the modern era of environmental legislation in the United States, federal law has supported actions to investigate and address climate impacts from air pollution. The Clean Air Act of 1970, for example, authorized the nascent EPA to set air quality standards in order to protect "welfare," which was defined to include the effects of air pollution on "wildlife, weather, visibility, and *climate....*" Clean Air Act § 302, 42 U.S.C. § 7602(h) (emphasis added). Subsequent federal legislation, including the National Climate Program Act of 1978, the Global Climate Protection Act of 1987, and the Global Climate Change Prevention Act of 1990, emphasized the intent of Congress that the EPA and federal government broadly work to identify and avoid or mitigate the dangerous impacts of manmade climate change predicted by scientists.

The legal authority of the EPA to regulate the emission of greenhouse gases (GHG) as an air pollutant under the Clean Air Act was confirmed by the U.S. Supreme Court in *Massachusetts v. EPA*, 549 U.S. 497 (2007). Drawing upon that confirmation of authority, the EPA during the Obama administration established new regulations to reduce carbon emissions from motor vehicles and dramatically improve fuel efficiencies. *See Coalition for Responsible Regulation v. U.S. EPA*, 684 F.3d 102 (D.C. Cir. 2012) (upholding EPA's "Tailpipe Rule" against industry challenge). The Obama administration also used Clean Air Act authorities to promulgate new emissions standards for fossil-fuel burning power plants, through a package of regulations known as the Clean Power Plan. While industry challenges to the Clean Power Plan were pending before the D.C. Circuit, the Trump administration announced the repeal of the Clean Power Plan, substituting for it the "Affordable Clean Energy" (ACE) rule— a program that may actually lead to localized increases in carbon emissions and greater costs to industry, according to some observers. *See* Dan Farber, *ACE or Joker? Trump's Self-Defeating Climate Rule*, LEGAL PLANET, July 25, 2019. Whether the ACE rule will survive legal challenges or the next presidential administration shall be seen. What remains clear for now is that the U.S. EPA retains legal authority under the Clean Air Act to regulate the emission of GHG whenever political will to do so returns. In the meantime, domestic GHG regulation may depend on other levels of governance, including municipal, tribal, and state governments.

California has been one of the states at the forefront of GHG regulation. California's establishment and reauthorization of its GHG cap-and-trade program has been met with significant debate and has arguably drawn distinctions between the traditional environmental and environmental justice movements. Consider the following critique of the first iteration of the GHG cap-and-trade program, the California Global Warming Solutions Act of 2006 (Assembly Bill 32):

> *While GHG emissions do not generally have direct health impacts, co-pollutants such as particulate matter (PM$_{10}$) do. Such emissions are correlated with large GHG emitters reporting that they emit more particulate matter. The largest emitters of both GHGs and PM$_{10}$ also tend to be located near neighborhoods with higher proportions of disadvantaged residents.*

> The neighborhoods within 2.5 miles of the 66 largest GHG and PM$_{10}$ emitters (defined as the top third in emissions of both PM$_{10}$ and GHGs … ) have a 16 percent higher proportion of residents of color and 11 percent higher proportion of residents living in poverty than neighborhoods that are not within 2.5 miles of such a facility…. Compared to other parts of the state, nearly twice as many neighborhoods within 2.5 miles of these highest-emitting facilities are also among the worst statewide in terms of their CalEnviroScreen score. We also found that 40 (61 percent) of these high-emitting facilities reported increases in their localized GHG emissions in 2013–14 relative to 2011–12, versus 51 percent of facilities overall. Neighborhoods near the top-emitting facilities that increased emissions had higher proportions of people of color than neighborhoods near top-emitting facilities that decreased their emissions …

> *While overall, GHG emissions in California have continued to drop from a peak in 2001, we find that, on average, many industry sectors covered under cap-and-trade report increases in localized in-state GHG emissions since the program came into effect in 2013.*

> Only a portion of the state's total GHG emissions are regulated under the cap-and-trade system. For example, the industrial and electrical sectors accounted for about 41 percent of the state's estimated total GHGs emissions in 2014. (The remainder originated from sectors such as transportation, commercial and residential buildings, and agriculture.) As a result, overall emissions and emissions regulated under cap-and-trade can exhibit slightly different patterns. Moreover, not all emissions regulated under the cap-and-trade program occur in state. For example, according to CARB's 2016 Edition of the California GHG Emission Inventory, emissions from electrical power decreased by 1.6 percent between 2013 and 2014. However, when these emissions are disaggregated, we see that it is the emissions associated with imported electricity that decreased, while emissions from in-state electrical power generation actually increased….

> *Between 2013 and 2014, more emissions "offset" credits were used than the total reduction in allowable GHG emissions (the "cap"). These offsets were primarily*

*linked to projects outside of California, and large emitters of GHGs were more likely to use offset credits to meet their obligations under cap-and-trade.*

The cap-and-trade program requires regulated companies to surrender one compliance instrument—in the form of an allowance or offset credit—for every ton of qualifying GHGs they emit during each compliance period. These instruments are bought and sold on the carbon market. The total number of allowances is set by the "cap," which decreases by roughly 3 percent per year in order to meet GHG reduction targets. In 2013 and 2014, most allowances were given to companies for free for leakage prevention, for transition assistance, and on behalf of ratepayers.... Additional offset credits were generated from projects that ostensibly reduce GHGs in ways that may cost less than making changes at a regulated facility.

Regulated companies are allowed to "pay" for up to 8 percent of their GHG emissions using such offset credits. The majority of the offset credits (76 percent) used to date were generated by out-of-state projects ... most offset credits were generated from projects related to forestry (46 percent) and the destruction of ozone-depleting substances (46 percent). Furthermore, over 15 percent of offset credits used during the first compliance period were generated by projects undertaken before final regulations for the cap-and-trade program were issued in 2011, calling into question whether these GHG reductions can be attributed to California's program, or whether they might have happened anyway....

We found that the majority of companies did not use offset credits to meet their compliance obligation; however, those companies that did use offsets tended to have larger quantities of GHG emissions. The top 10 users of offsets account for 36 percent of the total covered emissions and 65 percent of the offsets used. These top offset users included Chevron (1.66 million offsets), Calpine Energy Services (1.55 million offsets), Tesoro (1.39 million offsets), SoCal Edison (1.04 million offsets), Shell (0.62 million offsets), PG&E (0.44 million offsets), Valero (0.43 million offsets), La Paloma Generating Company (0.40 million offsets), San Diego Gas & Electric (0.39 million offsets), and NRG Power (0.33 million offsets).

Lara J. Cushing, Dan Blaustein-Rejito, Madeline Wander, Manuel Pastor, James Sadd, Allen Zhu & Rachel Morello-Frosch, *Carbon Trading, Co-pollutants, and Environmental Equity: Evidence from California's Cap-and-Trade Program (2011–2015)*, PLoS MED. 15(7) (2018).

The reauthorization of California's GHG cap-and-trade regime, through Assembly Bill 398 in 2017, was also met with widespread resistance from the environmental justice community.

... However impressive California's efforts have been to date, the State is nowhere near the 2050 reduction trajectory, which will require even deeper transformative action. Given the scale of the challenge, equivocation and in-crementalism are no longer options on California's path to decarbonization.

Against this backdrop, our legislature recently took the controversial step of passing AB 398, which extended California's greenhouse gas cap-and-trade program — the state's primary strategy for reducing carbon emissions from oil refineries and power plants, both of which are also primary culprits in the fight for environmental justice. Over the years, environmental justice advocates have voiced philosophical objections to pollution trading for com-modifying a social ill that should be eradicated. Yet, the environmental justice community's strongest objections point to California's multiple, fatally flawed attempts to faithfully implement a functioning program. Unfortunately, Cal-ifornia's experiment in the greenhouse gas trade has fared no better.

In striking similarity to Los Angeles's early missteps in its regional RE-CLAIM trading program for other pollutants, AB 32's over allocated and underpriced greenhouse credits quickly flooded the market, disincentivizing some of our state's largest polluters from making actual pollution reduc-tions....

In short, California's cap-and-trade program is not only responsible for allowing some of the state's largest polluters to use dubious offsets, but is motivating some of the worst environmental justice offenders to increase pollution in already-overburdened communities. In a nod to early concerns about equity, a portion of revenue generated from the program was ear-marked to support environmental justice work. Yet, even that feeble attempt to redistribute the program's economic benefits proved illusory when cap-and-trade ceased generating revenue to the State some years ago.

Apparently unsatisfied with the original cap-and-trade giveaways, the oil industry extracted even deeper concessions from the legislature and main-stream environmental groups in the latest round of negotiations to extend the program. In particular, AB 398 included a preemption clause preventing local jurisdictions from imposing separate greenhouse gas reductions on the oil industry — a direct attack on the growing grassroots efforts to secure local caps on refinery emissions in the San Francisco Bay Area. The bill fur-ther carried a price ceiling on the cost of a carbon credit to protect the eco-nomic interests of California's biggest polluters, but lacked any commensurate mechanism to stem the continued flood of unduly cheap credits that allow industry to freely increase pollution and thwart California's path to achieving its 2030 pollution reduction target. Though a companion bill, SB 617, creates new pollution monitoring requirements and localized pollution reduction goals, the environmental justice community has criti-cized the latter bill as lacking the requisite specificity and stringency to guar-antee meaningful local benefits.

Suma Peesapati, *California's Next Environmental Frontier: Climate Justice Leadership*,
24 HASTINGS ENVT'L L.J. 121, 125–127 (2018).

* * *

## Notes and Questions

1. **Cap-and-trade, cap-and-tax, or carbon tax?** At the time of publication, it remains
to be seen whether California can overcome the environmental justice problems inherent in a market-based GHG trading regime. For further discussion of market-
based versus command-and-control-regulation regimes, *see* Chapter 5 ("Standard
Setting"). As Professors Cushing, Wander, Morello-Frosch, Pastor, Zhu, and Sadd
note, the problem of "co-pollutants" cannot be ignored, particularly through a climate
justice lens. This is especially the case, as alluded to by Suma Peesapati, given the
lack of regulation over large stationary sources of GHGs, such as refineries. How
would you re-design California's cap-and-trade program to adequately address the
serious issue of co-pollutants? Alternatively, would either a cap-and-tax or carbon
tax approach to regulating in-state GHG emissions be preferable?

2. **The golden inhaler.** Another component of the California's GHG cap-and-trade
program is the reinvestment of proceeds to "disadvantaged communities," the Greenhouse Gas Reduction Fund (GGRF). For a more detailed discussion of the benefits
of such investment, which to date has totaled more than $9 billion dollars in appro-
priations by the California legislature to state agencies implementing GHG emission
reduction programs and projects, *see* Chapter 10 ("Governmental Initiatives"). As
this investment comes at the cost of co-pollutant "hot spots" around large stationary
sources of GHGs, however, some environmental justice advocates have also referred
to the GGRF as a "golden inhaler." What theories of justice are raised by California's
approach to regulating GHGs?

Nevertheless, in response to actions (or inaction) at the federal level, state action
on climate change is particularly important, and has become increasingly aggressive,
as illustrated in the next article.

## Rebecca Bratspies, *Our Climate Moment Is Now!* *(Or How to Change the Story to Save Our World)*

NEWS AND ANALYSIS, ENVIRONMENTAL LAW. DISRUPTED.
(ELI 2020)

… The current U.S. administration seems set on blocking any such transition.
Most recently, the Trump administration blocked any declaration from the Arctic
Council mentioning climate change or the IPCC's *Global Warming of 1.5°C* report.
Against otherwise universal alarm at the rapid melting of Arctic sea ice, United States
Secretary of State Mike Pompeo suggested that an ice-free Arctic created new global
trade opportunities. Rather than permit the Trump administration to water down

**Figure 14-8:** Vineyards in the San Pasqual Valley, California. Nov. 10, 2019. Grapevines are particularly vulnerable to climate change because they take years to establish—three to four seasons to bear fruit, and at least six years (and sometimes a decade) to produce high-quality berries. Photo: Nadia Ahmad.

the Arctic Council's consensus statements about climate change, the rest of the Arctic Council opted—opted for the first time ever—to end the Council's biennial meeting without a collective declaration. This intransigence is of a piece with Trump's administration's earlier announcement that the United States would withdraw from the Paris Agreement. Indeed, immediately after being confirmed as EPA Administrator, former coal lobbyist Andrew Wheeler explicitly rejected the notion that climate change "is an existential threat," because "most of the threats from climate change are 50 to 75 years out." Wheeler is no aberration. Before his immediate predecessor, Scott Pruitt, resigned amid scandals, he shut down EPA's climate adaptation office, took down EPA's climate change website, and directed agency personnel to downplay the science surrounding climate change. The Trump administration's budget director's characterization of these moves was "we're not spending money on that anymore."

The Trump administration's climate denial is on the wrong side of history. Indeed, the United States' own reporting underscores just how dangerous the administration's climate denial has become. The *Fourth National Climate Assessment*, quietly released in 2018 the day after Thanksgiving, painted a clear picture of the climate change impacts "already being felt in communities across the country." The Report called on state, federal, and local governments to "take aggressive action" to reduce emissions, while also promoting adaptation to locked-in levels of climate changes. Nevertheless, with climate deniers occupying key executive branch positions, the administration alternates between bolstering the coal industry, undoing laws preventing methane and hydrofluorocarbon emissions, and reducing fuel efficiency standards....

Noting that their proposed rollback in emissions limits was "projected to result in only very minor increases in global $CO_2$ concentrations and associated impacts," the administration rationalized that any such increases were too small to matter because climate change was a global issue. This was, of course, precisely the argument the Supreme Court rejected in *Massachusetts v. Environmental Protection Agency*. In that case, President Bush's Environmental Protection Agency (EPA) had argued that because greenhouse gas emissions caused widespread harm, there was no "realistic possibility ... that the relief petitioners seek would mitigate global climate change and remedy their injuries." The U.S. Supreme Court flatly rejected this contention, noting that "the United States transportation sector emits an enormous quantity of carbon dioxide" and that restricting these emissions would be an incremental step that might reduce the risk to some extent. It is nothing short of astonishing to see the federal government recycling these discredited arguments to justify ignoring the IPCC's call for urgent, immediate action.

## I. Moving Forward without the Federal Government

Even as the federal government backslides, large portions of the country are forging ahead. All eyes are on the cities, states, businesses, and other organs of civil society that have pledged to take climate action on their own. The 3,600-member strong *We Are Still In* coalition, for example, has taken up the task of achieving with the United States' nationally determined contribution to the Paris Agreement without federal leadership. Hundreds of subnational and private actors have submitted pledges to reduce their carbon emissions. These commitments put the United States on track to come close to achieving its Paris obligations, even without federal backing.

Key states have recently committed themselves to drastic carbon reductions. Hawaii was first to establish a goal of 100% renewable electricity by 2045. In 2018, California enacted a law requiring that renewables provide 60% of the energy sold in the state by 2030. The law also calls for a path toward 100% zero-carbon electricity by 2045. New York has responded in kind—enacting the Climate Leadership and Community Protection Act which mandates net-zero greenhouse gas emissions by 2050. New Jersey, New Mexico, Puerto Rico, and Washington State have also committed to a path to 100% clean energy in the coming decades. Vermont law requires that the state be 75% renewable by 2032. And Colorado just passed a slew of climate bills committing the state to 90% carbon reductions by 2050, to funding promoting electric

**Figure 14-9:** Wind farm in Whitman County, Washington. Sept. 13, 2019. Photo: Cliff Villa.

vehicle infrastructure, and to promoting a just transition.... Collectively these commitments cover roughly 32% of the nation's population and 21% of its energy generation-related carbon emissions.

... Although the zero carbon goal sounds lofty, several cities and even countries have already achieved it in practice, offering proof of concept for the wider transformation that is occurring. The United States Department of Energy estimates commercially available renewable energy technologies could adequately supply 80% of total U.S. electricity generation in 2050 while balancing supply and demand at the hourly level. The analysis also found that there were multiple pathways to achieve this high renewable energy future, that will result in deep reductions in electric sector greenhouse gas emissions and water use. The United States Energy Information Administration (EIA) forecasts that renewables will be the fastest growing source of electricity generation in the United States. Small-scale solar is growing by leaps and bounds. Despite the Trump administration's best efforts, the EIA projects that coal will continue to shrink, and that US carbon emissions will fall, even without any national leadership. There is still a long way to go, but the trend is in the right direction.

Major cities are also taking steps to drastically reduce their carbon footprints. New York City, in particular, has been forging ahead with climate innovation. A series of concrete climate mitigation steps now bolster New York City's Mayor Bill Di Blasio's assertion that "we're still in" in response to the Trump administration plan to leave the Paris Agreement. Most recently, just in time for Earth Day 2019, New York City

Council passed the *2019 Climate Mobilization Act*. Made up of 6 related bills, the Climate Mobilization Act has been hailed as New York City's "Green New Deal." This legislation will significantly reduce the city's carbon footprint by setting enforceable carbon emissions caps for all buildings of more than 25,000 square feet.... This bill will cut New York City's overall emissions by 4 million tons—roughly equivalent to taking 800,000 cars off the road. While the Climate Mobilization Act will not single-handedly reverse the effects of climate change, it "will be the largest emissions reduction policy in the history of New York City or any city anywhere." Since New York City residential consumers use 1.4% of the electricity in the United States, these changes will make a noticeable dent in the country's overall carbon footprint.

### Notes and Questions

1. **"We're still in?"** International law generally considers the state to be a unitary entity—with the national government as the actor capable of representing the state in international decision-making. If the Trump administration withdraws from the Paris Agreement but state and local decision-makers take actions that achieve the United States' Nationally Determined Contributions (NDCs) anyway, is the United States still part of the Agreement?

# G. Climate Adaptation

Whatever we might do to reduce carbon emissions in the future, whatever regulatory tools, diplomatic frameworks, or technology developments we might embrace, the fact is that the Earth's climate has changed already due to man-made carbon emissions and will continue to change in succeeding generations. An important question then is how people should adapt to these changes in order to meet basic needs and to achieve thriving communities in the future. A corollary question for purposes of this book is how to ensure that climate adaptation happens fairly and inclusively for all affected people and communities. One can easily imagine a scenario, for example, where rising sea levels around South Florida inspire wealthy homeowners to relocate to higher ground, leaving lower-income people locked into mortgages near sea level to face recurrent threats of flooding. What, if anything, may be done to help all people with the adaptations that our rapidly changing climate will require? The answer to this question is varied and continually expanding with developments in law, policy, and technology. In the next chapter, we will explore concepts of climate adaptation through the concept of **resilience** to the impacts of climate-related disasters. For the concluding section of this chapter, we will endeavor primarily to introduce the concept of climate adaptation and suggest valuable resources for continuing study in this dynamic area of law and public policy.

For a comprehensive examination of climate adaptation from multiple perspectives within the legal academy, *see* Michael B. Gerrard & Katrina Fischer Kuh, The Law of Adaptation to Climate Change: United States and International Aspects

(2012). For a quick introduction to climate adaptation generally, see the following excerpt.

## Daniel A. Farber, *Climate Adaptation and Federalism: Mapping the Issues*
### 1 SAN DIEGO J. CLIMATE & ENERGY 259, 261–265 (2009)

Adaptation to climate change is unavoidable. The fact is that some degree of climate change has already begun, and further change is inevitable. This section will survey some of the most likely impacts of climate change and the sorts of adaptation that may be required.

Climate change will raise sea levels, a simple effect with potentially far-reaching consequences. Sea level rise will have substantial impacts on the United States such as causing dramatic losses in wetlands. Because the slope of coastal areas on the Atlantic and Gulf Coasts is low, a forty-centimeter rise in sea level could result in as much as sixty meters of beach erosion and may cost billions of dollars. A half-meter sea level rise would place $185 billion of property in jeopardy by 2100, and the cost of protecting developed areas from a half-meter rise would be $115 to $274 billion. In Dade County [Florida] alone, approximately $10 billion in property is within 65 centimeters of sea level. Thus, sea level rise translates into significant increases in flood risks.

Water supply is another key climate impact. Flood risk and water supply issues can be intertwined, as in the California Delta, where potential levee collapses due to flooding would drastically impair water supplies for much of the state. Meanwhile, in the Southwest, the future of the water supply is uncertain, with potentially major impacts on agriculture. Recent evidence regarding the Southwest is particularly worrisome:

> Scientists also looked at the prospect of prolonged drought over the next 100 years. They said it is impossible to determine yet whether human activity is responsible for the drought the Southwestern United States has experienced over the past decade, but every indication suggests the region will become consistently drier in the next several decades. Richard Seager, a senior research scientist at Columbia University's Lamont-Doherty Earth Observatory, said that nearly all of the 24 computer models the group surveyed project the same climatic conditions for the North American Southwest, which includes Mexico. "If the models are correct, it will transition in the coming years and decades to a more arid climate, and that transition is already underway," Seager said, adding that such conditions would probably include prolonged droughts lasting more than a decade.

Adaptation of water systems to increased flood and drought risks includes a variety of responses. Some involve management of water systems through use of longer-range predictions to guide water reservoir use. Managing water demand is another option, including increased use of market transfer among users or conservation and efficiency improvements. It is also important to evaluate the risks to water infrastructure posed by more severe floods, which may require investment in strengthening existing dams and levees. Additional storage capacity (both surface and groundwater) may also be called for.

The challenge of adaptation will be substantial. *The Stern Report* estimates that the cost of adapting infrastructure "to a higher-risk future could be $15–150 billion each year (0.05%–0.5% of GDP), with one-third of the costs borne by the U.S. and one-fifth borne by Japan." The difficulty of adaptation varies directly with the pace of climate change and the potential increase in extreme events. "Extreme events such as floods and drought cause extensive damage to many parts of society, and thus a critical issue for adaptation is the degree to which frequency, intensity, and persistence of extreme events change." Simply because of higher sea levels, higher flood levels would result, with a possibility that by the end of the century what are now 100-year floods would become 50-year or 30-year floods.

Public health impacts of climate change are also a concern. By midcentury, the number of heat wave days in Los Angeles is expected to at least double over the late twentieth century and quadruple by the end of the century. One of the most vulnerable groups (ages over 65) will double in the United States by 2030. Higher ozone levels due to the increased temperature will cause additional deaths. The probability of large wildfires is also expected to increase by 12% to 53% by the end of the century.

Just as climate impacts are multiple, so are adaptation techniques. Adaptation covers a wide spectrum of responses:

> The array of potential adaptive responses available to human societies is very large, ranging from purely technological (e.g., sea defenses), through behavioural (e.g., altered food and recreational choices) to managerial (e.g., altered farm practices), to policy (e.g., planning regulations). While most technologies and strategies are known and developed in some countries, the assessed literature does not indicate how effective various options are to fully reduce risks, particularly at higher levels of warming and related impacts, and for vulnerable groups. In addition, there are formidable environmental, economic, informational, social, attitudinal and behavioural barriers to implementation of adaptation.

Few of these measures are costless, and some may turn out to be quite expensive. It remains to be seen how different levels of government will participate in this effort.

State and local governments are beginning to understand the need for adaptation. For instance, Chicago has issued a detailed guide to adaptation for municipalities. The guide considers a broad range of impacts, including shoreline erosion, invasive species, health threats from heat waves and increased ozone, damage to key infrastructure, and flood damage.

It is important to understand that climate change adaptation and mitigation can overlap. For instance, green building can be a way of mitigating climate change through reduced energy use, but it can also help adapt to climate change through more efficient water use or internal temperature control. The trend toward green building may push some regulatory decision making from the local level to the state level, and it is easy to imagine that the federal government might step in to promote the move to green building. Similarly, water systems are a significant source of energy use, so water conservation efforts can both respond to climate change and help mitigate future change.

Some adaptation will happen seamlessly through the private sector or via low-visibility actions by various levels of government. Other adaptation efforts will require significant government expenditures or regulatory initiatives. In the American government system, which divides authority between the federal government and state governments and their municipalities, we can confidently predict disputes about who should take the lead.

* * *

Shortly after publication of the article excerpted above, the federal government appeared to take the lead on climate adaptation through a series of initiatives. In 2009, President Obama signed Executive Order No. 13,514, Federal Leadership in Environmental, Energy and Economic Performance (Oct. 5, 2009), which, in addition to setting targets for reduction of greenhouse gas emissions by federal agencies, directed federal agencies to "participate actively" in adaptation planning. Under Executive Order No. 13,514 (2009), later replaced by Executive Order No. 13,653 (2013), each federal agency was directed to "develop or continue to develop, implement, and update" an agency adaptation plan describing "actions the agency will take to manage climate risks in the near term and build resilience in the short and long term...." Executive Order No. 13,653, § 5. While President Trump subsequently revoked Executive Order No. 13,653, see Executive Order No. 13,693, § 8 (May 17, 2018), the federal agency adaptation plans identified a number of adaptation opportunities available to federal agencies, many of which have been or continue to be implemented. *See, e.g.*, THE WHITE HOUSE, PROGRESS REPORT: HIGHLIGHTING FEDERAL ACTIONS ADDRESSING THE RECOMMENDATION OF THE STATE, LOCAL, AND TRIBAL LEADERS TASK FORCE ON CLIMATE PREPAREDNESS AND RESILIENCE (2015) (identifying a range of federal climate adaptation measures such as EPA's "Green Infrastructure Collaborative" to provide funding for local communities to develop advanced stormwater infrastructure).

For climate adaptation planning by states and local communities, a wealth of resources is available through the Georgetown Climate Center's Adaptation Clearinghouse, available online at www.georgetownclimate.org/adaptation. Among the resources available on the Adaptation Clearinghouse is the report excerpted below addressing adaptation strategies particularly to support minority and low-income communities.

## Georgetown Climate Center, Opportunities for Equitable Adaptation in Cities
### 1–2 (2017)

Two of the biggest challenges facing the United States—and the world—are the income inequalities that put the health and well-being of our poorest populations at risk, and climate change, which affects our most vulnerable populations even more than the public as a whole. The effects of climate change—including rising temperatures in urban areas, more polluted air, and increased extreme storms and stormwater—will disproportionally affect overburdened and low-income people and communities who are already facing significant economic and social challenges. Our success or failure in preparing for the impacts of climate change will be measured by how well we protect the most vulnerable and affected members of our communities, already suffering from a range of challenges including lack of economic opportunity, racism, and pollution.

In April 2016, the Georgetown Climate Center (GCC) and the Urban Sustainability Directors Network (USDN) convened a workshop bringing together nearly 50 thought leaders on equity and climate adaptation. The workshop focused on city-level actions that would support social justice goals and better prepare communities for the effects of climate change. Participants included city officials, representatives of environmental justice and social justice organizations, state and federal partners, and funders who support this work. Workshop participants were challenged to reflect on their own planning processes and identify ways that communities can address unequal risks; increase diversity, community participation, and leadership in adaptation planning; and ensure that climate change preparation efforts are benefiting and not negatively affecting those most at risk of impacts. Workshop participants discussed adaptation strategies, policies, and projects that could help cities achieve social justice, economic development, and climate adaptation goals.

… Participants identified the following key lessons over the course of the workshop:

- Achieving equitable adaptation outcomes will require an inclusive process that gives community members, especially low-income residents and people of color, the opportunity to envision and set adaptation priorities and influence investments, policies, and programs pursued in their communities.

- In many cities, a long history of mistrust between public agencies and community members will need to be addressed before and throughout the process for collaborative planning to be successful. This will require a long-term commitment to relationship building that is institutionalized and not project-specific.

- Cities can address inequity within their own agencies by hiring more inclusively and identifying ways that city agencies currently reinforce inequities (e.g., holding meetings at inconvenient times for working people or failing to include interpreters or notices in representative languages).

- Public agencies will benefit from partnering with others, including community-based organizations, community institutions, and foundations, to address climate and equity goals.

- Recognizing that climate change will affect some people and groups disproportionately, cities can address equity concerns by directing resources to those areas and groups facing the greatest risks.

- Equitable adaptation asks city leaders and staff to think not only about how and where they direct resources, but also how certain policies might have negative consequences for particular groups or communities. For example, low-income homeowners in floodplains will face increasing economic strain from rising flood insurance rates; this may force some homeowners to drop insurance coverage, which is the last line of defense in the event that flood impacts occur.

- Climate policies can address larger issues such as poverty, housing security, and racial equity. Likewise, policies and activities that are not traditionally seen as "climate adaptation," such as workforce development and arts festivals, can be linked with adaptation initiatives to improve the economic and social resilience of residents.

- Addressing climate change and equity will involve a long process of experimentation and creativity. Some cities and community-based organizations are already pushing boundaries and trying to identify best practices. Participants in the workshop shared ways that they are integrating equity considerations into their adaptation work; these examples are featured throughout this workshop summary.

* * *

## Notes and Questions

1. **"Adaptation" defined.** The Intergovernmental Panel on Climate Change (IPCC) has defined climate "adaptation" to mean "the process of adjustment to actual or expected climate and its effects. In human systems, adaptation seeks to moderate or avoid harm or exploit beneficial opportunities. In some natural systems, human intervention may facilitate adjustment to expected climate and its effects." IPCC 5TH ASSESSMENT REPORT, SUMMARY FOR POLICYMAKERS (2014). The definition recognizes that adaptation may take place *before* climate impacts are experienced ("anticipatory adaptation") or may follow as a *consequence* of climate impacts ("autonomous adaptation"). What examples of each type of adaptation can you imagine for communities on low-lying Pacific islands affected by rising sea levels?

2. **Adaptation is the solution?** If all efforts toward climate mitigation fail to achieve substantial reduction of greenhouse gases, can climate adaptation save us? May the population of the American Gulf Coast avoid repeated hurricane damage by migrating to the American Midwest? May the American Southwest escape prolonged drought by migrating to the Pacific Northwest?

Addressing the proper role for climate adaptation, the IPCC says this: "Without additional mitigation efforts beyond those in place today, and even with adaptation, warming by the end of the 21st century will lead to high to very high risk of severe, widespread and irreversible impacts globally. . . ." Even more bluntly, "Adaptation can reduce the risks of climate change impacts, but there are limits to its effectiveness. . . ." IPCC, *supra*, at 17–19. What "limits" might you see to the effectiveness of northward migration as a remedy for climate change, particularly for low-income communities and people of color? What alternative adaptation measures does Professor Farber suggest in the brief excerpt above?

**3. Adaptation resources.** As noted by Professor Farber, adaptation requires resources. And as noted by the Georgetown Climate Center, "equitable adaptation" may require the reallocation of resources toward vulnerable communities. Through such investments, "Climate policies can address larger issues such as poverty, housing security, and racial equity." How might that work? To use two examples from the Georgetown Climate Center, how exactly might investments in "workforce development" and "arts festivals" contribute to climate adaptation as well as social equity?

Resources, of course, do not always equate to money and may include such things as training and reference materials, which may be obtained free of charge through such sources as the Georgetown Climate Center's Adaptation Clearinghouse. Among the trove of materials linked through the Adaptation Equity Portal, see the training modules produced by the NAACP: *Our Communities, Our Power: Advancing Resistance and Resilience in Climate Change Adaptation—Action Toolkit.* Here you will find information addressing such diverse topics as community banking, emergency management, and LGBTQ engagement in climate adaptation efforts. Peruse the training modules and see if some ideas here would help your community adapt to anticipated impacts of climate change in your area. In return, what ideas for adapting to climate change might you have to share with others?

# Chapter 15

# Disaster Justice

## A. Introduction

### Mattathias Schwartz, *Maria's Bodies*

NY MAGAZINE (Dec. 22, 2017)

On Wednesday, September 20, the eye of Hurricane Maria cut a slash directly across the island of Puerto Rico, from the southeast to the northwest. It arrived shortly after six in the morning, near the harbor at Yabucoa. Wind gusts peaked at 155 miles an hour, bending palm trees like straws and snapping others off near the roots. The storm's center was 50 to 60 miles across—more than half the length of the island. It rolled at the leisurely pace of about ten miles an hour and hovered above the island's mountainous center well into the morning. The wind tore hundreds of electrical-transmission towers from the ground and carried some of them through the air. Sheets of earth fell from the hillsides, smashing houses and erasing roads. The death toll began immediately: In the town of Utuado, a landslide came through the wall of a house where three elderly sisters had taken refuge, burying them alive.... Bodies began to pile up beyond the capacity of the dark and fetid morgues....

That morning, Carmen Chévere Ortiz, a 41-year-old pharmacy manager, looked out the window of her two-story home in a neighborhood of Toa Baja called Villa Calma and saw her neighbor's patio under inches of water. Chévere Ortiz, who goes by Milly, lived with her mother, one daughter, and five sons. She remembered when Hurricane David had struck the neighborhood in 1979 and her father had carried her under his right arm as they fled. On that day, the water had been high enough that it splashed against the bottoms of her feet. This is a place that floods, Milly thought. She grabbed the car keys and gathered her family. Outside, the water was already approaching the top of the rear wheels of her family's RAV-4. It reeked of sewage. On her way up the street, she shouted out the windows, "The river is coming! Get out! Get out!"

On reaching the highway, Milly saw that seawater from the ocean, whipped up by the winds, was coming in from the Caribbean to the north and meeting the canal waters rising from the south. The rows of houses behind her looked like islands in a muddy lake. Villa Calma, she decided, would need to take refuge inside the neighborhood school, a two-story building surrounded by fences that were sealed with heavy gates....

She took a hook from the back of a red tow truck parked nearby and began to smash it against the locks. The gates opened, and dozens of people from Villa Calma, many soaked by floodwaters and shaking from the wind, took refuge inside. They brought their animals, as well. By nightfall, there were 16 dogs, two cats, a pig, and a half-dozen horses milling around in the courtyard. Inside, the refugees decided to call the school *el Arca*, the Ark.

On that first day, when Hurricane Maria still raged with apocalyptic force, the destruction wrought by the storm was gruesome—and also familiar to anyone who had seen a tornado shuck the roofs off an Oklahoma town or watched Houston flood only a few weeks earlier. When Hurricane Katrina hit New Orleans in 2005, more than 1,800 died, many by drowning, as levees and flood walls failed and the city's poorest neighborhoods were submerged. Puerto Rico has fewer low-lying areas, so the immediate death toll from Maria was substantially smaller.

But Puerto Rico's population of 3.4 million is more vulnerable, and its infrastructure weaker, than anywhere on the mainland. The island's per capita income is $11,688, roughly half as much as the poorest of the 50 states. Its government has let its roads, emergency services, and electrical grid decay as it struggles under massive debt obligations and federally imposed austerity measures. These two factors— poverty and rotting infrastructure—combined with the storm to trigger a second disaster, this one entirely man-made and far more deadly than the storm itself.

\* \* \*

Like exposure to hazardous waste and toxic air pollutants, and the many other threats to human health and the environment already explored in this book, disasters such as Hurricane Maria in 2017 often have disproportionate effects on certain segments of our population, including racial and ethnic minorities, women and children, the elderly, and low-income peoples. While disasters have commonly been viewed as "social equalizers," affecting everyone in a community regardless of status or station, other experts such as Professor Rob Verchick have observed, "In nearly every disaster, it is the poor and other vulnerable groups who suffer most."

After Hurricane Katrina in August 2005, many observers examined the disparate impacts on the largely poor and African American communities in New Orleans through the lens of environmental justice. *See, e.g.,* Eileen Gauna, *Katrina and Environmental Injustice,* JURIST (Oct. 10, 2005) ("Katrina ... was an exceptionally large echo of a socioeconomic political condition known popularly as environmental injustice"); Center for Progressive Reform, *An Unnatural Disaster: The Aftermath of Hurricane Katrina* 6 (Sept. 2005) ("Race, class, and injustice were key dimensions" of government's failure to protect Katrina victims); National Environmental Justice Advisory Council, *The 2005 Gulf Coast Hurricanes and Vulnerable Populations—Recommendations for Future Disaster Preparedness/Response* 3 (Aug. 2006) ("Emerging literature on the issues of environmental justice and vulnerable populations, in the wake of Hurricanes Katrina and Rita, speaks to the need for disaster research, policy, planning, and program implementation to be more historically, socially, and geographically informed"). Environmental justice, or *injustice*, can indeed help explain many of the impacts from disasters on certain populations; the disproportionate impacts of climate change on the people of Puerto Rico through stronger and more frequent hurricanes is certainly one example. However, the emerging study of "disaster justice" may add some unique and valuable dimensions to environmental justice as described in earlier chapters of this book. For one thing, the impacts of disasters on certain populations may not always trace to some human action, such as the siting of a new industrial facility or the burning of fossil fuels; the impacts may result from human *inaction*, such as government's failure to provide for evacuation before a storm. For another thing, the impacts from disasters may be much more immediate. While the risks of toxic exposures, for example, are often measured by increased chances of cancer over a lifetime, the fatalities from a disaster such as Hurricane Maria may begin instantly and tallied over days and weeks. Finally, the potential remedies for disaster injustice may be different in kind from environmental remedies, requiring planning and mitigation measures by expert agencies on down to individual households.

Returning to Hurricane Maria, on September 20, 2017, when the storm made landfall in Puerto Rico with Category 4 winds, the island was devastated. With an electrical grid already weakened by years of decay plus Hurricane Irma two weeks before, the entire population of the island sank into darkness. Two months later, power had been restored to only 26% of the island. By May 2018, power remained spotty across the island and still out in certain locales, leading to declarations of "the largest blackout in American history." Trevor Houser and Peter Marsters, *The World's Second Largest Blackout* (April 12, 2018), https://rhg.com/research/puerto-rico-hurricane-maria-worlds-second-largest-blackout/. With electricity went communications, the storm knocking out almost 90% of cell phone service across the island. FEMA, *2017 Hurricane Season After-Action Report* 2 (July 12, 2018).

The official death toll from Maria stood initially at 64 lives. Closer analysis by the Harvard School of Public Health, however, estimated 4,645 "excess deaths" attributable to Maria, one-third due to "delayed or interrupted health care" after the storm. Nishant Kishore, et al., *Mortality in Puerto Rico after Hurricane Maria*, 379 N. ENGL. J. MED. 162 (July 12, 2018). For the survivors of Maria, the losses of life coupled with damages to private property and public infrastructure seemed almost incalculable. The Federal Emergency Management Agency (FEMA) estimated damages from Hurricane Maria at approximately $90 billion. And Maria was just one of ten named hurricanes in the 2017 hurricane season, which also included Hurricane Harvey (dumping a record 60 inches of rain on Houston, Texas) and Hurricane Irma (requiring a massive evacuation from South Florida). Altogether, the 2017 hurricane season surpassed all others, with total damages estimated on the order of $265 billion. FEMA, *2017 Hurricane Season After-Action Report* at 1.

At the same time as record hurricanes and floods were devastating the Central and Eastern parts of the United States, record wildfires were burning in the West. Massive

**Figure 15-1:** Remains of Journey's End Mobile Home Park after Tubbs Fire in Santa Rosa, CA. Jan. 26, 2018. Photo: Cliff Villa.

fires from Washington State to Southern California consumed not just timberlands but entire communities at the wildland-urban interface. Among a multitude of massive fires in California in the 2017 fire season, the Tubbs Fire in October 2017 charred swaths of Napa and Sonoma Counties, almost leveling the Santa Rosa community of Coffey Park. According to state fire investigators, the Tubbs Fire destroyed 5,636 structures, including more than 4,650 residential buildings, and resulted in 22 fatalities. Cal-Fire, *Tubbs Investigation Report*, Case No. 17CALNU010045 3 (Jan. 20, 2019). At the time, the Tubbs Fire was the most destructive fire in California history. However, the Tubbs Fire was quickly and by far surpassed by the Camp Fire the next year. In November 2018, the Camp Fire incinerated the mountain town of Paradise, California, and surrounding communities, destroying 18,804 structures. Cal-Fire, *Top 20 Most Destructive California Wildfires* (Feb. 19, 2019). The Camp Fire was also the deadliest wildfire in California history, claiming an official count of 86 lives, with the death of an injured 72-year-old man in August 2019.

Besides the staggering losses of life and property, the 2017 hurricanes and the California wildfires demonstrated some of the long-expected consequences of climate change. In the first assessment report by the Intergovernmental Panel on Climate Change, the IPCC predicted in 1990 that rising ocean temperatures may affect "the frequency and intensity of coastal storms and hurricanes." *See* IPCC, *Climate Change: The 1990 and 1992 IPCC Assessments* 106 (July 1992). With anticipated increases in heat, drought, and pests, the IPCC also predicted matter-of-factly, "Losses from wildfire will be increasingly extensive." *Id.* at 88. With further prescience, the IPCC warned, "The most vulnerable human settlements are those especially exposed to natural hazards; e.g., coastal or river flooding, severe drought, landslides, severe wind storms and tropical cyclones." *Id.* at 89. We are now living in the future that the best scientists predicted 30 years ago. How we may endeavor to keep all people safe in this future is the subject of this chapter.

This chapter is not, however, limited to consideration of "natural" disasters. In fact, many disaster scholars and managers now question whether indeed there is such a thing as a "natural disaster." *See, e.g.*, Greg Bankoff, *No Such Thing as Natural Disasters*, HARVARD INT'L REV. (Aug. 23, 2010); *There Is No Such Thing as a Natural Disaster: Race, Class, and Hurricane Katrina* (Chester Hartman & Gregory D. Squires, eds., 2006). Hurricanes and wildfires occur in nature, of course, but in the age of climate change, the fury and frequency of such events may be quite unnatural. Moreover, there is no "disaster" from hurricanes or wildfire until someone is injured in some way. Conversely, some events that we may consider "disasters" may have no basis in nature at all, such as the September 11 terrorist attacks in 2001 and the BP Deepwater Horizon oil spill into the Gulf of Mexico in 2010. As Professor Dan Farber has observed, what marks some incidents as "disasters" is not so much a basis in natural phenomena as the kinds of human impacts and risk management choices a disaster may elicit. Daniel Farber, *Symposium Introduction: Navigating the Intersection of Environmental Law and Disaster Law*, 2011 BYU L. REV. 1783, 1788 (2011). Modern definitions of "disaster" reflect this broader conception. For example, the definition of "major disaster" in the federal Stafford Act includes not just "any natural catastrophe," but also "*regardless of any cause*, any fire, flood, or explosion ... which ... causes damage of sufficient severity and magnitude to warrant major disaster assistance...." Stafford Act § 102(2), 42 U.S.C. § 5122 (emphasis added).

This chapter may therefore consider the justice implications of oil spills and industrial accidents, as well as earthquakes, hurricanes, wildfires, and other "natural" catastrophes. Most importantly, this chapter will also consider measures that both public authorities and private actors may take to help keep people safe from disasters. Recall that on the day Hurricane Maria made landfall in Puerto Rico, Milly had access to a car, her RAV-4, allowing her family to escape from the oncoming floodwaters. Milly's neighborhood of Villa Calma may also have benefited from a common language (Spanish), a safe refuge (the neighborhood school), prior experience with hurricanes (Hurricane David in 1979), and a community spirit that emphasized mutual care and protection. In the vernacular we shall explore in this chapter, Milly's community demonstrated both **vulnerability** to disasters but also **resilience** to the impacts. Following a closer examination of these related concepts, this chapter will survey the emerging field of Disaster Law, focusing on the federal **Stafford Act** and the **Disaster Cycle** of readiness, response, and recovery, to prepare advocates for the pursuit of disaster justice in affected communities. Finally, we will conclude the chapter with two illuminating perspectives following Hurricane Katrina — one a catalogue of disaster *injustice*, the other a vision of how lawyers (and even law students) might help achieve disaster justice for vulnerable communities.

# B. Vulnerability and Resilience

Many disasters may strike suddenly and with little warning. In ancient times and continuing today in some circles, disasters were often accorded supernatural origins, giving rise to potential exemptions from liability for "Acts of God." *See, e.g.,* Clifford J. Villa, *Is the 'Act of God' Dead?,* 7 WASH. J. ENVTL. L. & POL. 320 (2017) (discussing "Act of God" exemptions to liability in federal environmental statutes). In modern times, we may be less inclined to blame the heavens for fates that befall us. Indeed, people who study disasters, from perspectives of law, geography, sociology, or other disciplines, often attempt to predict the impacts from disasters in terms of **vulnerability** and **resilience**. Vulnerability, in general, describes the susceptibility of certain communities or individuals to some form of adverse impact from an incident, including damages to private property or public infrastructure, losses in economic activity or ecosystem services, as well as bodily injury or death. Resilience, in general, describes the capacity of that community or individual to withstand harmful impacts and recover from the incident. This section will explore these related concepts, beginning with an excerpt from one formative article introducing the concept of Disaster Justice.

## 1. Vulnerability

### Robert R.M. Verchick, *Disaster Justice: The Geography of Human Capability*
#### 23 DUKE ENVIRONMENTAL LAW & POLICY FORUM
#### 23, 38–46 (2012)

We can think of "community hazard" as a combination of a community's "physical vulnerability" and its "social vulnerability." Here, "community" means, as a geographer might put it, "the totality of social system interactions" contained within a "defined geographic space." Depending on one's interest, that could be anything from a neighborhood or a census tract, to a city or a county. Physical vulnerability refers to a community's physical exposure to a place-based risk—for example, a flood, an earthquake, or a wildfire. Physical vulnerability should be read to include "geophysical characteristics" (geology, hydrology, climate, and so on), as well as important aspects of the built infrastructure that, if they failed, would present their own difficulties (such as a dam or a nuclear facility). Social vulnerability refers to the susceptibility of a community's population groups to the impacts of a hazard. This susceptibility, as Susan Cutter defines it, "is not only a function of the demographic characteristics of the population (age, gender, wealth, etc.), but also more complex constructs such as health care provision, social capital, and access to lifelines (e.g., emergency response personnel, goods, services)." ... The community-hazard framework expands the scope of disaster policy in significant ways. In this view, the factors are not just geophysical; they are also economic, social, and political. They involve a community's natural infrastructure as well as its built infrastructure. The protection of soil-stabilizing forests and storm-slowing coastal marshes becomes an important consideration in disaster policy. So too do bridge maintenance and regular improvements to data and cellphone networks. This leads us to see the relationship between risk-reduction and the broader concept of "sustainability." The framework's emphasis on the ability to rebound as well as withstand reveals the relationship between risk reduction and the broader concept of "resilience" in all its physical, social, and economic aspects. Within this broader framework—encompassing environmental protection, public works, and more—disaster research has gradually honed in on one social factor of critical concern: inequality.... Studies consistently show that in a disaster, poor people and people of color are more likely to suffer property damage, injury, and death.... The most significant factor, the literature suggests, is that low-income and minority populations are simply more likely to live in older, denser, disaster-prone neighborhoods, with shoddy housing and inadequate services....

Government assistance programs—often crucial in the wake of a large catastrophe—tend to favor middle-class homeowners over less affluent renters or the homeless. Studies following the 1989 Loma Prieta Earthquake in the San Francisco Bay area have documented the many ways that federal assistance programs failed to meet the needs of the homeless, Latino farm workers, and low-income African-Americans. Louisiana's post-Katrina assistance programs raised similar concerns. Using federal funds, the state developed programs to promote the construction of rental housing and to compensate homeowners for the costs of rebuilding. Because of funding limitations, the rental-repair programs were only able to support the repair of less than one-third of the 82,000 rental units lost to Hurricanes Katrina and Rita. As for homeowners, nearly three-quarters of Road Home applicants had gaps between the received rebuilding resources and the actual costs of repair. The average shortfall for African-Americans was roughly $8,000 more than it was for whites. This discrepancy was caused by the grant formula, which was based on a home's pre-storm value, and African-Americans often lived in housing markets with depressed values.

Poor people and people of color also tend to suffer more psychological effects from disaster than victims who are wealthier or white. According to the literature, "poor, minorities, and single mothers may already feel a lack of control over their lives, and the dislocation and increased uncertainty about the future add to underlying and persistent stress." Elderly African-Americans, in particular, have been found to recover more slowly from "psychosocial" trauma than whites, an effect partially attributable to financial insecurity.

While social scientists emphasize the vulnerabilities of race and class, we should not forget that other demographic characteristics are also important. Age is often a big factor. Because the elderly tend to have more health problems, reduced mobility, and fixed incomes, they are often at higher risk of death or injury during disasters. Following the 2003 European heat wave, which killed an estimated 70,000 people, the World Health Organization reported that "in European cities, the elderly suffered the greatest effects of heat-waves," adding that elderly women bore a higher risk of dying than elderly men. In New Orleans, the elderly made up 60 percent of Katrina's death toll. In its investigation of fatalities from the 2011 Japan tsunami, the Japanese newspaper, YOMIURI SHIMBUN, estimated that more than 65 percent of those who died were over sixty years old. Children also tend to be more vulnerable in times of disaster and recovery. Physically, their smaller bodies put them at higher risk for allergies, infections, malnutrition, and other health problems. Children recovering from disasters often require emotional support and counseling to help them process confusing or frightening experiences.

Gender can also play a key role. Women, for instance, were hit particularly hard by Hurricane Katrina. Of the 180,000 Louisianans who lost their jobs after the storm, 103,000—or 57 percent—were female. Of the thousands of households that lost public housing services in New Orleans when they were summarily closed after the storm, 88 percent were headed by women. Men's median annual income rose after the storm, in part due to the rise in heavy-labor jobs like demolition and construction. Women, who were more likely to work in the healthcare, education, and hospitality sectors, saw their median income decline. Such widespread destruction, of course, dramatically increased stress within families, predictably leading to soaring reports of domestic violence. Indeed, research shows that evacuations and disasters are often accompanied by increases in violence against women and girls.

\* \* \*

## Notes and Questions

**1. Physical vulnerability.** After the scenes of devastation in New Orleans following Hurricane Katrina, some people around the country questioned the wisdom of rebuilding a city subject to all the physical hazards of existence between the Mississippi River and the Gulf of Mexico. But how "safe" is your community? Is your community also subject to hurricanes? Floods? Tornadoes? Wildfires? Winter storms? Earthquakes? Between Hurricane Katrina in 2005, Hurricane Sandy in 2012, and the one-two-three assault of Hurricane Harvey, Hurricane Irma, and Hurricane Maria in 2017, we know that the entire Gulf Coast and Atlantic Seaboard are subject to the ravages of hurricanes. We know that the entire West Coast is subject to wildfires. We know that the entire watershed of the Mississippi River is subject to flooding, from Minot, North Dakota, to the Mississippi Delta. The Midwest has twisters. The Southwest faces drought. For a more comprehensive review of physical hazards by geographical regions of the United States, *see* Denis Binder, *The Nature of Extreme Natural Risks in the Natural Environment*, 7 WASH. J. ENVTL. L. & POL. 340 (2017).

Every state is also subject to earthquakes, but some regions are more susceptible than others. The San Andreas Fault most infamously threatens Northern California, triggering the Great San Francisco earthquake of 1906 and the Loma Prieta earthquake of 1989. Even graver danger may be posed by the Cascadia Fault in the Pacific Northwest, recently revealed as capable of producing "the worst natural disaster in the history of North America," with odds of one in three for a massive "Cascadia subduction zone" earthquake in the next 50 years. Kathryn Schultz, *The Really Big One*, THE NEW YORKER, July 20, 2015, at 52, 54. Given this physical hazard in the Pacific Northwest, should Seattle be relocated? Where would it go? If we do not relocate Seattle, may we question the wisdom of any other places where people choose to live?

**2. Social vulnerability.** In the excerpt above, Professor Verchick conceptualizes "community hazard" as a combination of both physical vulnerability and social vulnerability. While the risk of earthquakes and other "natural" phenomena might be estimated by application of geology and other physical sciences, can we also attempt to estimate risks based upon factors of social vulnerability? In fact, as Professor Verchick has noted, geographers including Susan Cutter have developed a "social vulnerability index" (SVI) to estimate and compare risks in communities across the country. As further explained by Professor Verchick:

> Cutter's team began by collecting socioeconomic data for 1990 for all 3,141 counties in the United States. Starting with more than 250 variables, they winnowed the field (through various statistical means) to ... a subset of the eleven most important variables, which "explained 76.4 percent of the total variance among all counties." They were: (1) personal wealth, (2) age, (3) density of the built environment, (4) single-sector economic dependence, (5) housing stock and tenancy, (6) race—African American, (7) ethnicity—Hispanic, (8) ethnicity—Native American, (9) race—Asian, (10) occupation, and (11) "infrastructure dependence" (as in being employed by a transportation service or public utility)....
>
> On this basis, Cutter's team found that "[a]s expected, the vast majority of U.S. counties exhibit moderate levels of social vulnerability." But some regions carried higher risk. With a few notable exceptions, the most vulnerable communities were located in the southern half of the country, stretching from southern California to Florida. These regions not only had greater racial and ethnic variation but were also growing quickly, resulting in crowded, flimsy housing stock. The least vulnerable counties were located mainly in New England, along the eastern slopes of the Appalachian Mountains, and in the Great Lakes Region. In all, 12.5 percent of U.S. counties were deemed "most vulnerable." New York County (otherwise known as Manhattan) ranked first in vulnerability due to density as well as its racial, ethnic, and socioeconomic profiles. Other high-risk counties included San Francisco County, Bronx County, and Benton County—home of the Hanford Nuclear Reservation—the economy of which was dominated by a single public utility. The safest bets, like Poquoson, Virginia, or Tolland, Connecticut, were more homogenous and often presented a face that was more "suburban, wealthy, white, and highly educated."

Verchick, *Disaster Justice*, at 47–48.

**3. Your community?** Building on the work of Susan Cutter and other researchers, the federal Centers for Disease Control and Prevention (CDC) now maintains an online database and GIS tool for identifying the SVI score in any city, county, or region of the United States. Look for it at https://svi.cdc.gov/ or simply type "cdc svi" in any Internet browser. Applying this tool, what is the SVI score for your community?

Which of the eleven variables identified above do you believe may most influence the SVI score for your community?

**4. Age.** In the article from Professor Verchick, how does a person's age relate to their potential vulnerability in a disaster? In a disaster like Hurricane Katrina, who is more at risk: a six-year-old or sixty-year-old? A six-year-old obviously cannot drive a car, wade through flood waters, or comprehend evacuation orders the way we might expect of an adult. Children may also be more vulnerable to toxic exposures in contaminated air, water, food, and land, as explored in previous chapters. In addition, children may be more susceptible to psychological trauma, resulting in a range of behaviors and mental health symptoms including anxiety, depression, bullying, fighting at school, and substance abuse. Tara Powell & Lori K. Holleran-Steiker, *Supporting Children After a Disaster: A Case Study of Psychosocial School-Based Intervention*, 45 CLINICAL SOC. WORK J. 176 (2015) (observing that "Children are one of the most vulnerable groups during and after a natural disaster").

On the other hand, what disproportionate impacts may older people face from a disaster? Consider the following:

> The greatest mortality during and immediately after the 2005 hurricane and subsequent flooding of the Greater New Orleans (GN) area was among the elderly. Those over age 60 — some 15% of the New Orleans population before the storm — accounted for approximately 75% of bodies found immediately after; 40% were over 70. These high mortality rates can be attributed to several factors, including lack of evacuation facilities, infirmities that made evacuation difficult if not impossible, and high levels of poverty and isolation....

Vincanne Adams, et al., *Aging Disaster: Mortality, Vulnerability, and Long-Term Recovery Among Katrina Survivors*, 30 MED. ANTHROPOL. 247, May 30, 2011. Since Hurricane Katrina, every new disaster sadly appears to reconfirm these exceptional risks to the elderly. For one recent, horrific example, following the deadly Camp Fire in November 2018, 77% of the bodies recovered and identified were reported over the age of 65. Laura Newberry, *Poor, Elderly and Too Frail to Escape: Paradise Fire Killed the Most Vulnerable Residents*, L.A. TIMES, Feb. 10, 2019. As Americans continue to age and disasters continue to multiply and expand, how can the law help address this vulnerability? As a matter of Equal Protection jurisprudence under the Fourteenth Amendment, the Supreme Court has afforded no special protection or recognition for age as a suspect class. *See Massachusetts Bd. of Retirement v. Murgia*, 427 U.S. 307 (1976). However, legal protections may be found under federal statutory law, including the federal Age Discrimination Act of 1975, 29 U.S.C. § 6101 (2018) (Subject to certain exceptions, "no person in the United States shall, on the basis of age, ... be denied the benefits of, or be subjected to discrimination under any program or activity receiving Federal financial assistance"). Remedies may also be found under state laws to protect children and the elderly. *See, e.g.,* Cal. Welf. & Inst. Code § 15610.07 (California law defining abuse of an elder or a dependent adult to include physical abuse, neglect, abandonment, isolation, or deprivation of care); NMSA 1973, § 30-6-1D (prohibiting "knowingly, intentionally, or negligently and without justifiable cause, causing or permitting a child" to be abused). How would you want public and private authorities to assure the protection of your own children or parents or grandparents from the risk of disasters?

**5. Disability.** Closely associated with the disproportionate risk of disasters to elderly persons are the risks to people with physical or mental disabilities. Of all the people age 65 and older whose homes were flooded or otherwise damaged by Hurricane Katrina, almost half (48%) reported at least one disability, and more than one-quarter (26%) reported two or more disabilities. Disabilities included visual and hearing impairments, learning and memory difficulties, as well as mobility limitations. Thomas Gabe, Gene Falk & Maggie McCarty, Congressional Research Service, *Hurricane Katrina: Social-Demographic Characteristics of Impacted Areas* at 17 (Nov. 4, 2005). Of course, disabilities are not limited to the elderly, and neither are the associated vulnerabilities to disasters. In the Tubbs Fire of October 2017, for example, one of the deaths in Santa Rosa, California, was a 27-year-old woman in a wheelchair who could not escape the flames that consumed the Journey's End Mobile Home Park. Eloísa Ruano González & Mary Callahan, *Victims Identified in Deadly Sonoma, Napa and Mendocino County Fires*, PRESS DEMOCRAT, Oct. 12, 2017.

What can the law do to protect people with disabilities from the risks of disasters? Among other statutory protections, the Americans with Disabilities Act (ADA), 42 U.S.C. § 12131 *et seq.*, and state analogues might prove of value in the disaster context. Title II of the ADA provides in relevant part that "[n]o qualified individual with a disability shall, by reason of such disability, be excluded from participation in or be denied the benefits of the services, programs, or activities of a public entity, or be subjected to discrimination by any such entity." 42 U.S.C. § 12132. Courts have found the ADA to require public authorities to include the needs of people with disabilities in their planning for disaster response. *See, e.g., Brooklyn Center for Independence v. Bloomberg*, 980 F.Supp. 2d 588 (S.D.N.Y. 2013) (New York City violated ADA by failure to plan for needs of disabled in emergency evacuation, transportation, and sheltering); *Communities Actively Living Independent & Free v. City of Los Angeles*, 2011 WL 4595993 (C.D. Cal) (Los Angeles violated ADA and California Disabled Persons Act by, among other things, failing to include provisions in the State's emergency preparedness program "to notify people with auditory impairments or cognitive disabilities of an emergency").

**6. Gender.** A narrow but significant body of literature has examined the differentiated impacts of disasters on men and women. As indicated in the brief excerpt from Professor Verchick above, gender-based marginalization is a contributing factor in populations' overall social vulnerability. This means that women, girls, and trans or nonbinary people are generally more susceptible to the harmful impacts of disasters than their cisgender male counterparts. Elaine Enarson, a scholar in the field of gender and disaster research, describes how the "human experience" is often universalized in disaster, which overlooks issues specifically affecting women and girls:

The striking disregard for gender in disaster studies is derived in part from generalizations about "human" behavior arising from decades of gender-blind research studies on preparedness, risk communication, emergency response, economic recovery, emergent organizations, public administration, and vulnerability. The result is a body of knowledge that both fails to specifically investigate gender in men's lives, and generalizes the knowledge gained "through men's eyes" to all persons. This covert grounding of disaster theory in men's lives benefits neither women nor men. Perhaps when critical gender studies are integrated into the canon and gender analysis comes to life in practice, we can speak of human experience in disasters.

Elaine Enarson, Women Confronting Natural Disaster: From Vulnerability to Resilience 2 (2012).

What sort of issues are overlooked in a male-centric approach to disaster studies, and at what cost? As compared to men, women are overall more likely to, among other things, live below the poverty line; experience partner abuse and sexual assault; live with disabilities or mental illness; or need access to medical services including for reproductive health. Enarson at 3. These disparities are further exacerbated for women of color as compared to their white counterparts. *Id.* Additionally, literature regarding disaster impacts on trans or nonbinary populations is fairly scarce, but importantly indicates another gender-based area of social vulnerability that is often overlooked in dominant disaster paradigms. *See, e.g.,* J.C. Gaillard, et al., *Beyond Men and Women: A Critical Perspective on Gender and Disaster*, Disasters 429, 433 (2017).

**7. Immigrants.** One vulnerable group not addressed in the Verchick excerpt is immigrant communities. What are the sources of vulnerability in disasters that you might imagine among people coming to the United States from different countries and cultures? Consider the case below, concerning the disproportionate impacts of a winter storm in December 2006 that triggered an epidemic of carbon-monoxide poisonings across the Seattle area:

> The carbon-monoxide cases came quickly that week, with 1.5 million utility customers in the dark.

> Immigrant populations were the hardest hit: Of the 70 people treated in Virginia Mason's hyperbaric chamber, only five spoke English as their first language.

> Early arrivals at Virginia Mason and Harborview Medical Center included three dozen Kent residents, nearly all Somali immigrants who had been cooking and warming themselves over charcoal grills indoors.

> For the Vulnerable Populations Action Team of Public Health—Seattle & King County, formed in 2005 after Hurricane Katrina, "This was our first opportunity to take our planning work and turn it into a response effort," said Carina Elsenboss, a program manager with the health district.

**Figure 15-2:** Front-page headline warning non-English speaking communities about dangers of carbon monoxide poisoning from indoor burning for heat during winter storm. SEATTLE TIMES, Dec. 20, 2006.

As the cases mounted, calls were made to immigrant community groups. Hundreds of fliers in seven languages were distributed and a news conference was held.

Into the next week, churches, grocery stores, restaurants and gathering places of every kind were helping spread the carbon-monoxide warnings, which were eventually produced in 14 languages.

For some, the warnings came too late: On the next Monday, four members of a Vietnamese family were found dead in their Burien home. A generator had been running in their garage.

Jack Booth, *Carbon Monoxide: Last Year's Surprise Killer Still Claims Lives*, SEATTLE TIMES, Dec. 13, 2007. More than just reporting on this case after the fact, the SEATTLE TIMES actually became a part of the story at one point, agreeing with local health authorities to run a front-page, above-the-fold warning to immigrant communities about the dangers of carbon monoxide poisoning from indoor heat sources during this winter storm. *See* Figure 15-2. In this case, what made the immigrant communities so vulnerable to this extreme health hazard? Was it a difference in language, education, or culture? All of the above, perhaps?

After Hurricane Katrina, Congress amended the federal Stafford Act specifically to address vulnerabilities based upon limited English proficiency. *See* Post-Katrina

Emergency Management Reform Act of 2006, Pub. L. No. 109-295, 120 Stat. 1355 (2006), amending Stafford Act § 308, codified at 42 U.S.C § 5151(a) (adding "English proficiency" to list of classes to be protected from discrimination in the distribution of disaster relief). With this amendment, states who fail to provide for Limited English Proficiency communities could be subject to enforcement action including loss of federal disaster assistance.

Beyond language barriers, other important differences may make immigrant communities more vulnerable during disasters. In many immigrant communities, there may be engrained distrust of government, financial institutions, charitable organizations, or legal professionals. With distrust of banks, immigrants may be more likely to maintain savings in cash, which could be lost in a fire or flood. In a disaster, immigrants may worry about the loss of critical immigration documents. Immigrants may also experience heightened levels of prejudice based on national origin. In one notorious incident, for example, then New Orleans mayor Ray Nagin, speaking on camera during a town hall meeting in the wake of Hurricane Katrina, elicited great applause from a crowd by asking, "How do I make sure that New Orleans is not overrun by Mexican workers?" For one harrowing story of discrimination against a Syrian-American family following Hurricane Katrina—and the lawyers who help in the end—*see* Dave Eggers, ZEITOUN (2009).

Finally, many individual immigrants and families may have legitimate concerns about seeking emergency aid and disaster assistance based upon their immigration status. Undocumented immigrants are, in fact, entitled to many forms of emergency care, including temporary shelter, food, water, and medical care. FEMA also maintains, "Your information is confidential [and] FEMA shares that information only with the state and designated agencies that provide disaster assistance, with your permission only." FEMA, *Non-Citizens Can Apply for FEMA Assistance*, Nov. 15, 2016 (encouraging "non-citizen" residents of North Carolina to seek emergency aid and disaster assistance following Hurricane Michael). Nevertheless, FEMA remains a part of the U.S. Department of Homeland Security (DHS), which also includes U.S. Immigration and Customs Enforcement (ICE), so the potential concerns of undocumented persons interacting with FEMA are certainly understandable. For a full analysis of the rights and challenges of immigrant communities in receiving disaster assistance in the United States, *see* Ashley Morey, *No Shelter from the Storm: Undocumented Populations and Federal Disaster Aid*, 11 SEATTLE J. SOC. J. 257 (2012).

As a student-lawyer in a law school clinic, or an attorney in a legal aid organization, how might you advise a client who has immigration concerns as well as substantial injuries or losses from a declared disaster?

## 2. Resilience

In contrast to increased vulnerability, increased resilience can help communities and individuals survive the impacts of disasters and recover quickly. There are many ways to define and conceptualize resilience. Here is one description from Professor J.B. Ruhl:

> Although there are numerous variations, a good working definition [of resilience] as used in natural and social sciences is "the capacity of a system to experience shocks while retaining essentially the same function, structure, feedbacks, and therefore identity." One hallmark of system resilience thus is the capacity to maintain a high level of consistency of behavioral structure in the face of a dynamic environment of change.

J.B. Ruhl, *General Design Principles for Resilience and Adaptive Capacity in Legal Systems—With Applications to Climate Change Adaptation*, 89 N.C. L. Rev. 1373, 1374–76 (2011).

From this beginning, Professor Ruhl proceeds to distinguish two approaches to resilience, what he terms "engineering resilience" and "ecological resilience." According to Ruhl, "The engineering resilience strategy is to devote all system resources to staying near the equilibrium, the goal being to snap back." By contrast, "ecological resilience relies on adjustments to system processes as the means of managing overall system integrity." *Id.* at 1377. Thus, disaster justice advocates might pursue resilience to coastal storm surge either through engineering measures (e.g., higher, reinforced seawalls) or through ecological measures (e.g., reshaping of wildlife habitat or relocation of human communities away from flood zones).

Another way of considering resilience is through the dichotomy suggested previously by Professor Verchick's discussion of vulnerability, considering *physical* resilience and *social* resilience. With *physical* resilience, one might imagine building structures designed to withstand maximum wind speeds anticipated in future hurricanes and typhoons. With *social* resilience, one might imagine a community prepared to help each community member find safe shelter from the storm, as seen in Villa Calma on the day Hurricane Maria made landfall in Puerto Rico. For further exploration of the concept of social resilience and its potential value to traditionally vulnerable communities, consider the following excerpt:

## Sidney Shapiro, *Preface: An Ounce of Prevention*

CENTER FOR PROGRESSIVE REFORM, FROM SURVIVING TO THRIVING:
EQUITY IN DISASTER PLANNING AND RECOVERY iv–vi (Sept. 2018)

The story is now familiar. An area of the United States is battered by a superstorm, hurricane, or other climate disaster, resulting in a calamity for the people who live and work there. The Federal Emergency Management Agency (FEMA) offers emergency assistance, but since it is not enough to address the harms that occurred, Congress acts to provide hundreds of millions of dollars of additional assistance.

But imagine a counter-narrative, with a significantly better outcome. In that story, we would have paid attention—before disaster ensued—to how environmental protection and planning can prevent and minimize the harm that disasters cause to people, their housing, and the infrastructure of our cities, states, and territories. Steps to inform the public about risks, to adopt protective measures, and to enforce health, safety, and environmental standards could have minimized the human suffering and loss and minimized the economic costs associated with recovery.

One reason for our oversight is that we tend to think about the varied functions of government as distinct. Agencies that protect us from health, safety and environmental risks are separate and operate under different laws than do agencies that address human needs, education, and other forms of our collective welfare. So we tend to overlook the role that these protections play in minimizing the impact of disaster. But viewed through a wider lens, all of these agencies' work ideally serves the same goal: promoting social resilience. People and their neighbors are socially resilient when they have the capacity to survive, adapt, and grow in the face of misfortune and change.

These two types of government activities are mutually supportive. As this report details, investments in health, safety, and environmental protection on the front end can reduce the need for financial or other assistance for human needs after disaster strikes. Environmental protection measures cannot prevent all of the harms that will occur in the wake of weather disasters. Nor can social support services and disaster relief alleviate all the loss and suffering in the wake of disasters. By partnering to promote social resilience, these agencies can use their resources more effectively and better achieve their shared goals.

Although the term "social resilience" is relatively new—it gained prominence slightly more than a decade ago in the field of disaster studies—the idea that government can and should help people protect themselves against unexpected events outside of their control is not new. This commitment dates back to the founding of the country and has been a consistent commitment of our country ever since. Since 1776, Congress has passed numerous laws that protect us from economic, social, health and safety risks.

When we fail to prevent and minimize preventable harms, we ignore Ben Franklin's sage advice, "An ounce of prevention is worth a pound of cure." A recent study by the National Institute of Building Sciences highlights the accuracy of that maxim in the context of disaster response. The study recommends measures that governments and property owners can take to reduce the impact of disaster events that would prevent 600 deaths, 1 million nonfatal injuries, 4,000 cases of post-traumatic stress disorder (PTSD), and that would save $6 for every $1 spent on these protections funded through select federal agencies.

We also ignore the reality that our most vulnerable citizens are the ones who suffer the most in violent storms and other disasters. Many people share the heartache of losing a house, valuable keepsakes, and other property. But while these harms are shared among many, the most vulnerable residents are often the people least able to manage the temporary and permanent consequences imposed on them by weather disasters.

*Social resilience* is about the capacity of people and their communities to withstand, recover from, and prosper after disruption. In the case of climate and other weather disasters, measures that promote resilience include natural and human systems that reduce the force of storms or the likelihood of other disasters, preparedness plans that protect people when disaster occurs, and health, safety, and environmental protection measures that focus on anticipating and preparing for weather-related events in ways that prevent (or minimize) harm to people and their property. Resilience is also enhanced by strong social networks, access to information to make sound choices, and policies that recognize and account for the varied needs and capacities of different communities and populations. It is about ensuring people have access to health care, education, and training they need to accommodate the dislocation that occurs when disasters wreak havoc on the communities in which they live.

\* \* \*

Outside of academia, efforts to promote community resilience have been supported broadly by public and private initiatives and at every level of government across the country. *See, e.g.*, Georgetown Climate Center, *Lessons in Regional Resilience: Case Studies on Regional Climate Collaboratives*, Jan. 2017 (discussing resilience initiatives by local governments from Seattle, Washington, to Miami, Florida). On a national level, the U.S. Department of Homeland Security (DHS), together with other federal departments and agencies, has recognized and emphasized the need for building community resilience. In 2011, President Obama issued a formal directive "aimed at strengthening the security and resilience of the United States through systematic preparation for the threats that pose the greatest risk to the security of the Nation, including acts of terrorism, cyber attacks, pandemics, and catastrophic natural disasters." Presidential Policy Directive/PPD—8: National Preparedness, Mar. 30, 2011. For the purpose of this national goal, the directive defined "resilience" to mean "the ability to adapt to changing conditions and withstand and rapidly recover from disruption due to emergencies."

In implementing this directive, DHS under the Obama administration compiled a list of "Community Resilience Indicators," a step toward developing quantitative measurements of community resilience, such as how the Social Vulnerability Index now assists with measuring community vulnerability. While work on the Community Resilience Indicators remains ongoing, a sampling of these indicators appears below to suggest areas where disaster justice advocates may focus efforts to improve community resilience:

## U.S. Dept. of Homeland Security, *Draft Interagency Concept for Community Resilience and National-Level Measures*
### June 2016, at 8–15

**Housing Condition:** Families living in housing units that are well maintained and consistent with current building standards are typically more resilient to hazards than families living in poor housing conditions. Substandard housing may be more susceptible to the impacts of hazards, resulting in property damage, injury, or death during an event and extensive repair costs in both time and money after an event. These costs are especially challenging for the typically lower-income families that occupy housing units with severe problems....

**Healthy Behaviors:** In general, communities with good baseline mental and physical health are more resilient to disasters than communities with high concentrations of health-related needs.... Promoting wellness and encouraging healthy behaviors alongside disaster preparedness can help communities face everyday challenges as well as major disruptions or disasters.

**Environmental Health:** A number of environmental factors, such as air and water quality, can directly affect individual and community health status. Areas with concentrated environmental health risks can increase disaster impacts by increasing underlying vulnerabilities and amplifying the impact on individuals with access and functional needs. Poor air quality contributes to health conditions including cancers, cardiovascular disease, asthma, and other illnesses that can compound disaster vulnerabilities.

**Roadway Condition:** A community's transportation infrastructure is the core of its economy and its disaster response and recovery system. In the response phase of a disaster, sufficient transportation infrastructure ensures that residents can evacuate and emergency responders can reach areas in need. After a disaster, functioning transportation infrastructure is critical for economic and physical recovery. Roads and bridges are a critical part of the transportation infrastructure.

**Energy Assurance:** Without a stable energy supply, health and welfare are threatened, and the U.S. economy cannot function. The Energy Sector is uniquely critical because it provides an "enabling function" across all other critical infrastructure. During emergencies, power service disruptions can have cascading impacts on other systems that pose additional health and safety risks (e.g., inability to heat or cool homes, provide potable water, treat sewage or stormwater runoff, or communicate with emergency responders)....

**Telecommunications Accessibility:** Telecommunications services are integral to the U.S. economy, underlying the operations of all businesses, public safety organizations, and government. Over the last 25 years, communications infrastructure evolved from predominantly a provider of voice services into a diverse, interconnected industry using terrestrial, satellite, and wireless transmission system.

**Cultural Resources Protection:** In the same way that biological diversity increases the resilience of natural systems, cultural diversity can increase resilience of social systems. The maintenance of cultural diversity into the future, and the knowledge, innovations, and outlooks it contains, increase the capacity of human systems to adapt to, and cope with, change.... Promoting the protection of cultural heritage is necessary because of its intrinsic historic or artistic value and because it provides the fundamental spiritual and psychosocial support and sense of belonging communities need during the disaster recovery phase....

**Community Preparedness:** Community preparedness generally focuses on the pre-event actions that residents, businesses, governments, and emergency responders can take to respond to a disaster effectively. For residents and businesses, this includes basic steps, such as developing household or business emergency plans and securing backup energy, communications, food, and water supplies....

**Civic Capacity:** Social connectedness is a critically important element of community resilience capacity. Socially isolated individuals are less resilient than socially connected individuals are because they have less access to shared resources and are vulnerable to mental health challenges. At the community level, concentrations of isolation are a major factor of community vulnerability....

\* \* \*

Government agencies are certainly not alone in their promotion of community resilience and recognition of the indicators noted above. For one final perspective on resilience in this section, consider this observation from the NAACP Environmental & Climate Justice Program, focusing on the resilience indicator identified by DHS as "Civic Capacity":

> A key aspect of community resilience is social cohesion. There are many definitions of social (or community) cohesion; we like this definition from The Organisation for Economic Co-operation and Development: "A cohesive society works towards the well-being of all its members, fights exclusion and marginalization, creates a sense of belonging, promotes trust, and offers its members the opportunity of upward social mobility."
>
> Put simply, a spirit of cooperation defines socially cohesive communities. What does this have to do with emergency management? To have a community that works well together in times of crisis, there must be strong relationships, trust, and a spirit of cooperation, unity, and mutuality to mitigate the shocks of a disaster. In fact, a poll conducted by the Associated Press-NORC Center for Public Affairs Research confirmed that communities that lack social cohesion and trust tend to have a more difficult time recovering from disasters. Therefore, an important (and often overlooked) aspect of emergency preparedness and community resilience is building social cohesion.

NAACP Environmental & Climate Justice Program, *In the Eye of the Storm: A People's Guide to Transforming Crisis & Advancing Equity in the Disaster Continuum* (2018) at 37, https://www.naacp.org/climate-justice-resources/in-the-eye-of-the-storm/.

For one unfortunate example of what "social cohesion" does *not* look like, with potential consequences in the disaster context, the NAACP report offers the following anecdote:

In August 2016 record breaking flooding occurred in Baton Rouge, Louisiana, after over two feet of rain fell over a 72-hour period. The devastation that ensued was significant—the floods were considered the worst natural disaster in the United States since Superstorm Sandy. The floods came the month following the police killing of Alton Sterling and the retaliatory killing of police officers in Baton Rouge. The lack of social cohesion and extreme racial tension in the community significantly negatively impacted flood recovery efforts.

## Notes and Questions

1. **"Engineering resilience" vs. "ecological resilience."** Professor Ruhl's distinction between "engineering resilience" and "ecological resilience" may be readily grasped in the context of natural catastrophes: Can we build a structure strong enough to withstand the next hurricane/flood/fire/winter storm/earthquake (engineering resilience) or can we create a system flexible enough to adjust and adapt to changes without losing its essential identity and function (ecological resilience)? In his article, as suggested by the title, Professor Ruhl theorizes that legal systems, as well as physical structures, can exhibit either engineering resilience or ecological resilience. For one example of engineering resilience in a legal system, Professor Ruhl points to the U.S. Constitution, which "was designed to be hard to alter in design and has proven so...." Ruhl continues, "By contrast, the American common law system offers an example of ecological resilience: it is a highly dispersed structure of courts throughout the nation, all working to craft doctrine under a loose set of process rules.... The result is a high capacity for swings in behavior in response to changing conditions without altering the system's basic structure and process design." Ruhl at 1380–81.

What are the relative advantages you see of each approach to designing a legal system capable of functioning in a disaster context? Do you want hard and fast rules to provide clarity and structure to potentially chaotic conditions? Or do you want the flexibility to adapt to changing conditions and circumstances that cannot possibly be anticipated in advance? Can you have some of both?

To put these questions in a concrete context, consider the BP Deepwater Horizon oil spill in the Gulf of Mexico in 2010. When the *Deepwater Horizon* (DWH) drill rig caught fire on April 20, 2010, killing eleven crewmembers, and sank two days later, crude oil from the well a mile below the surface spewed uncontrolled for at least 87 days. By some official estimates, more than 200 million gallons of oil discharged to waters of the Gulf over this time, making it one of the biggest oil spills in world history and, as President Obama described it, "the worst environmental disaster America has ever faced." As an example of "engineering resilience" in the legal system, the federal Oil Pollution Act, 33 U.S.C. §2702 (2018), clearly made responsible parties, including BP, liable for the costs of cleanup and damages. But what kind of damages? The federal law explicitly provides for recovery of losses in "subsistence use" and "profits and earnings capacity." *Id.* §2702(b)(2)(C), (E). Consider these liability provisions in the unique circumstances of the community described below:

Louisiana is home to roughly 25,000 Vietnamese-Americans, most of them living near the Gulf Coast. Their communities, which grew out of the wave of refugees in the 1970s, are almost all economically dependent on fishing and crabbing. Indeed, it is estimated that thirty to fifty percent of all commercial fishers in the Gulf are of Vietnamese descent. In addition to supporting the local economy, fishing also nourished an array of reciprocal bonds among family, friends, and business associates. Vietnamese-American fishers fed their families with their catch. They bartered it for fruits, vegetables, and other goods. A fisher may donate a recent haul to a spring festival or "pound" (that is, reward) the minister with tuna after a stirring sermon. At a wedding, the bride's family might be showered with a hundred pounds of blue crab.

Verchick, *supra*, at 58–59. Can legal systems ever "engineer" for every circumstance that might be encountered after a disaster? How might the concept of "ecological resilience" apply to protect the interests and values of the Vietnamese-American fisher community in this example?

2. **Social resilience.** Consider the factors contributing to "social resilience" as described by Sidney Shapiro. Which of these factors appear relevant to the epidemic of carbon monoxide poisoning among non-English-speaking communities following the 2006 winter storm in the Seattle area? Do you see this as a case where community education failed to warn people in time to avoid the preventable deaths, or a case where education succeeded in that people could read and understand the warnings once they appeared in appropriate languages during the emergency? Beyond translation of messages, what more did the local health authorities do in this case to save lives within the immigrant communities?

3. **Resilience indicators.** Review the Community Resilience Indicators sampled in the excerpts from the U.S. Department of Homeland Security. Which of these indicators were most prominent, or lacking, in Puerto Rico before Hurricane Maria? To improve resilience before the next major storm strikes the island, how would you prioritize the investment of limited public resources? Obviously, much of the misery on the island after Hurricane Maria followed from the lack of electricity. Imagine going a week without the ability to connect with friends or family via phone, text, social media, or email. Imagine navigating unfamiliar roads without a GIS app. Imagine not knowing where you will find food or drinking water today— and for whatever you do find, not being able to pay with a credit or debit card. If you can imagine such a scenario, as many faced in Puerto Rico after Hurricane Maria, what could you do now to improve your personal resilience or the resilience of your community? Taking the resilience indicators into account, how might a legal system improve resiliency to ensure the rule of law survives during and following a disaster?

4. **Social cohesion.** Note that Shapiro, DHS, and the NAACP report, in various terms, all appear to endorse what the NAACP describes as "social cohesion" as a means for achieving community resilience. How did the Villa Calma community

demonstrate social cohesion when Hurricane Maria made landfall in Puerto Rico? How might the lack of social cohesion have led to adverse impacts from the 2016 flooding in Baton Rouge?

# C. Disaster Law Fundamentals

In the immediate aftermath of Hurricane Katrina in 2005, scholars from diverse fields including emergency management and environmental law began to recognize and develop a new branch of integrated study and practice that soon came to be known as Disaster Law. The first book dedicated to disaster law appeared in 2006 and is now in its third edition. Daniel A. Farber, Robert R.M. Verchick, James Ming Chen, Lisa Grow Sun, DISASTER LAW AND POLICY (3rd ed. 2015). According to lead author Dan Farber, one thing that identifies disaster law as a distinct field is the existence of "a number of distinctive statutes, such as the Stafford Act...." Moreover, and perhaps most importantly, "disaster law as a whole is unified by the concept of risk management," which is the central concern of what Farber calls the "circle of disaster." Daniel Farber, *Symposium Introduction: Navigating the Intersection of Environmental Law and Disaster Law*, 2011 BYU L. REV. 1783, 1790–91 (2011). For the benefit of students, lawyers, and other advocates who may be called upon at some point to assist diverse individuals or communities impacted by disasters, this section provides a very brief introduction to both the Stafford Act and other relevant statutes plus the major elements of the "Disaster Cycle."

## 1. Disaster Law

The Robert T. Stafford Disaster Relief and Emergency Assistance Act, Pub. L. No. 100-707, 102 Stat. 4689 (1988) ("Stafford Act"), amended the Disaster Relief Act of 1974, Pub. L. No. 93-288, 88 Stat. 243 (1974). As amended, the Stafford Act provides the major authority for federal assistance following a declaration by the president of a national "emergency" or a "major disaster." The Stafford Act also provides federal funding for "predisaster hazard mitigation." While no substitute for complete review of the statute itself, we share from the Stafford Act some key provisions:

**Sec. 102. Definitions (42 U.S.C. § 5122)**

(1) "Emergency" means any occasion or instance for which, in the determination of the President, Federal assistance is needed to supplement State and local efforts and capabilities to save lives and to protect property and public health and safety, or to lessen or avert the threat of a catastrophe in any part of the United States.

(2) "Major disaster" means any natural catastrophe (including any hurricane, tornado, storm, high water, winddriven water, tidal wave, tsunami, earthquake, volcanic eruption, landslide, mudslide, snowstorm, or drought), or, regardless of cause, any fire, flood, or explosion, in any part of the United States, which in the determination of the President causes damage of sufficient severity and magnitude to warrant major

disaster assistance under this Act to supplement the efforts and available resources of States, local governments, and disaster relief organizations....

### Sec. 201. Federal and State Disaster Preparedness Programs (42 U.S.C. § 5131)

(a) The President is authorized to establish a program of disaster preparedness that utilizes services of all appropriate agencies and includes — (1) preparation of disaster preparedness plans for mitigation, warning, emergency operations, rehabilitation, and recovery; (2) training and exercises; [and] (3) postdisaster critiques and evaluations....

### Sec. 203. Predisaster Hazard Mitigation (42 U.S.C. § 5133)

(b) The President may establish a program to provide technical and financial assistance to State and local governments to assist in the implementation of predisaster hazard mitigation measures that are cost-effective and are designed to reduce injuries, loss of life, and damage and destruction of property....

### Sec. 308. Nondiscrimination in Disaster Assistance (42 U.S.C. § 5151)

(a) [Regulations issued by the President] shall include provisions for insuring that the distribution of supplies, the processing of applications, and other relief and assistance activities shall be accomplished in an equitable and impartial manner, without discrimination on the grounds of race, color, religion, nationality, sex, age, disability, English proficiency, or economic status.

### Sec. 316. Protection of Environment (42 U.S.C. § 5159)

An action which is taken [pursuant to provisions of this statute], which has the effect of restoring a facility substantially to its condition prior to the disaster or emergency, shall not be deemed a major Federal action significantly affecting the quality of the human environment within the meaning of the National Environmental Policy Act....

### Sec. 401. Procedure for Declaration (42 U.S.C. § 5170)

(a) All requests for declaration by the President that a major disaster exists shall be made by the Governor of the affected State. Such a request shall be based on a finding that the disaster is of such severity and magnitude that effective response is beyond the capabilities of the State and the affected local government and that Federal assistance is necessary.... Based on the request of a Governor under this section, the President may declare under this Act that a major disaster or emergency exists.

(b) The Chief Executive of an affected Indian tribal government may submit a request for a declaration by the President that a major disaster exists....

(c) In providing assistance to an Indian tribal government under this subchapter, the President may waive or adjust any payment of a non-Federal contribution....

### Sec. 402. General Financial Assistance (42 U.S.C. § 5170a)

In any major disaster, the President may —

(1) direct any Federal agency ... to utilize its authorities and the resources granted to it under Federal law ... in support of State and local assistance response and recovery efforts ...

(2) coordinate all disaster relief assistance (including voluntary assistance) provided by Federal agencies, private organizations, and State and local governments ...

(4) assist State and local governments in the distribution of medicine, food, and other consumable supplies, and emergency assistance; and

(5) provide accelerated Federal assistance and Federal support where necessary to save lives, prevent human suffering, or mitigate severe damage, which may be provided in the absence of a specific request....

### Sec. 403. Essential Assistance (42 U.S.C. § 5170b)

(a) Federal agencies may on the direction of the President, provide assistance essential to meeting immediate threats to life and property resulting from a major disaster, as follows:

(1) Utilizing, lending, or donating to State and local governments Federal equipment, supplies, personnel, and other resources ...

(3) Performing on public or private lands or waters any work or services essential to saving lives and protecting and preserving property or public health and safety, including—

    (A) debris removal;

    (B) search and rescue, emergency medical care, emergency mass care, emergency shelter, and provision of food, water, medicine, durable medical equipment, and other essential needs ...

    (C) clearance of roads and construction of temporary bridges ...

    (D) demolition of unsafe structures which endanger the public....

(b) The Federal share of assistance under this section shall be not less than 75 percent of the eligible cost of such assistance.

### Sec. 406. Repair, Restoration, and Replacement of Damaged Facilities (42 U.S.C. § 5172)

(a)(1)(A) The President may make contributions—(A) to a State or local government for the repair, restoration, reconstruction, or replacement of a public facility damaged or destroyed by a major disaster....

### Sec. 408. Federal Assistance to Individuals and Households (42 U.S.C. § 5174)

(a)(1) [T]he President, in consultation with the Governor of a State, may provide financial assistance and, if necessary, direct services, to individuals and households in the State who, as a direct result of a major disaster, have necessary expenses and serious needs....

(h)(1) No individual or household shall receive financial assistance greater than $25,000 under this section with respect to a single major disaster.

(h)(2) The limit established under [the preceding] paragraph shall be adjusted annually to reflect changes in the Consumer Price Index....

### Sec. 415. Legal Services (42 U.S.C. § 5182)

Whenever the President determines that low-income individuals are unable to secure legal services adequate to meet their needs as a consequence of a major disaster ... the President shall assure that such programs are conducted with the advice and assistance of appropriate Federal agencies and State and local bar associations.

### Sec. 416. Crisis Counseling Assistance and Training (42 U.S.C. § 5183)

The President is authorized to provide professional counseling services ... to victims of major disasters in order to relieve mental health problems caused or aggravated by such major disaster or its aftermath.

### Sec. 502. Federal Emergency Assistance (42 U.S.C. § 5192)

(a) In any emergency, the President may — (8) provide accelerated Federal assistance and Federal support where necessary to save lives, prevent human suffering, or mitigate severe damage, which may be provided in the absence of a specific request....

### Sec. 503. Amount of Assistance (42 U.S.C. § 5193)

(a) The Federal share for assistance provided under this title shall be equal to not less than 75 percent of the eligible costs.

(b)(1) Except as provided in paragraph (2), total assistance provided under this title for a single emergency shall not exceed $5,000,000.

(b)(2) The limitation described in paragraph (1) may be exceeded when the President determines that — (A) continued emergency assistance is immediately required; (b) there is a continuing and immediate risk to lives, property, public health or safety; and (c) necessary assistance will not otherwise be provided on a timely basis.

## Notes and Questions

1. **Punctuated equilibrium.** In contrast to federal environmental legislation, which has remained largely stagnant since 1990, federal disaster legislation has been the subject of continual activity by Congress through numerous amendments to the Stafford Act since 1988. Most of these amendments have followed major catastrophes including Hurricane Katrina in 2005, Hurricane Sandy in 2012, and the devastating hurricane plus wildfire season of 2017. *See, e.g.*, the Post-Katrina Emergency Management Reform Act of 2006, Pub. L. No. 109-295, 120 Stat. 1355 (2006); the Sandy Recovery Improvement Act of 2013, Pub. L. No. 113-2, 127 Stat. 4 (2013); and the Disaster Recovery Reform Act of 2018, Pub. L. No. 115-254, 132 Stat. 3438 (2018).

Legal scholars, adopting theory from evolutionary biologists, have described this pattern as "punctuated equilibrium," characterized by periods of relative stasis followed by moments of disjunction that create opportunities for law to advance. *See, e.g.*, Mark Niles, *Punctuated Equilibrium: A Model of Administrative Evolution*, 44 J. MARSHALL L. REV. 253 (2011). Consistent with this pattern, for example, Congress seized upon the post-Sandy legislation to address an original defect in the Stafford Act that allowed the "Governor of an affected State" — but not the head of an affected Indian tribe—to request the declaration of a major disaster or emergency. The amended text in Stafford Act § 401 (major disaster declaration) and § 501 (emergency declaration) fixed this defect, supporting federal principles of tribal sovereignty. *See* Heidi Adams, *Sovereignty, Safety, and Sandy: Tribal Governments Gain (Some) Equal Standing Under the Hurricane Sandy Relief Act*, 2 Am. Indian L.J. 376 (2013).

When the next major catastrophe strikes the United States, what amendments to the Stafford Act or other disaster legislation might you seek at that time on behalf of one of the vulnerable groups considered in this chapter?

**2. "Emergency" vs. "major disaster."** Consider the Stafford Act definitions of "emergency" and "major disaster." Which category of incident is broader? Could either designation encompass contaminated drinking water, or the financial collapse of a local government, both as seen in Flint, Michigan?

In the case of Flint, Michigan, discussed in Chapters 3 and 4, there were actually multiple "emergencies" declared. The first was an emergency declaration under state law that allowed the state to appoint an emergency manager to take over decision-making authority from locally elected officials of a municipality facing financial catastrophe. Sydney L. Hawthorne, *Do Desperate Times Call for Desperate Measures in the Context of Democracy? Michigan's Emergency Manager Law & the Voting Rights Act*, 41 N.Y.U. Rev. L. & Soc. Change 181 (2017). The emergency manager appointed to take over authority from elected officials in Flint, Michigan, allegedly made the decision to switch the city's drinking water source to the Flint River, resulting in the predictable epidemic of lead poisonings and other acute and continuing health impacts in Flint residents. A second "emergency" declaration came under the Stafford Act, through a request by the Michigan Governor on January 14, 2016, and approved by President Obama on January 16, 2016. The Stafford Act emergency declaration authorized "emergency assistance [] to provide water, water filters, water filter cartridges, water test kits, and other necessary related items for a period of no more than 90 days for Genesee County." FEMA, Emergency Declaration Summary, No. FEMA-3375-EM, Jan. 16, 2016.

After all of the emergency declarations for Flint, Michigan, could the president also declare a "major disaster" under the Stafford Act? Review the Stafford Act definition to see if you can find an answer. If the president could declare a "major disaster" in this case, what would be the advantage of doing so? Would there be any disadvantages?

**3. Other "emergency" authorities.** Within a week of the emergency declaration for Flint under the Stafford Act, a third "emergency" was soon declared by the U.S. EPA under authority of the federal Safe Drinking Water Act § 1431, 42 U.S.C. § 300i. The order directed the State of Michigan and City of Flint to take immediate actions to repair the drinking water system. U.S. EPA Office of Enforcement and Compliance Assurance, In the matter of: City of Flint, Michigan, Michigan Dept. of Environmental Quality, and the State of Michigan, Emergency Administrative Order, Jan. 21, 2016.

In addition to authorities under the Stafford Act and Safe Drinking Water Act, many other federal, state, and local authorities allow emergency declarations and response actions. On the federal level, these include the Oil Pollution Act (OPA) to address spills of oil to water and the Comprehensive Environmental Response, Compensation, and Liability Act (CERCLA) to address releases of hazardous substances in the environment. OPA authorities, found in Clean Water Act § 311, authorize designated officials for the U.S. EPA (inland waters) and U.S. Coast Guard (marine waters) to "direct or monitor all Federal, State, and private actions to remove a discharge." 33 U.S.C. § 1321(c)(1)(B)(ii). Similarly, CERCLA provides designated officials with authority to respond immediately to releases of hazardous substances into the environment [§ 104(a)], to issue orders where conditions may present an "imminent and substantial endangerment to the public health or welfare or the environment" [§ 106(a)], and to exceed a presumptive funding cap of $2 million in the event of an "emergency" [§ 104(c)(1)(A)(ii)]. 42 U.S.C. §§ 9604(a), 9604(c), 9606(a).

EPA invoked the emergency authority under CERCLA to exceed the presumptive cap of $2 million in order to respond to the spill of some three million gallons of contaminated water from the Gold King Mine in southwestern Colorado caused by EPA contractors on August 25, 2015. By the end of the emergency action, EPA had spent over $30 million on the response, and may spend hundreds of millions more for long-term cleanup. *See* Clifford J. Villa, *Gold King Mine Spill: Environmental Law and Legal Protections for Environmental Responders*, 2019 Utah L. Rev. 263 (2019). As in the case of Flint, communities affected by the Gold King Mine spill, including the Navajo Nation, requested a "major disaster" declaration under the Stafford Act. The federal government denied these requests. Do you see why?

Given the limited reach of disaster declarations under the Stafford Act, emergency declarations under the Stafford Act and other statutory frameworks may remain important authorities for advocates of environmental justice and disaster justice to consider and seek whenever needed to protect the communities they serve.

**4. Invitation only?** Can the president, through FEMA and other federal agencies, respond to emergencies and disaster situations if no affected state or tribe requests a declaration? Review the excerpted provisions from Stafford Act § 402 (General Federal Assistance) and § 403 (Essential Assistance). What do you see as differences between these two sections in assistance authorities and triggering mechanisms? Why would an affected state or tribe decline to make such a request in a serious emergency or disaster situation?

After Hurricane Katrina, President Bush and his FEMA Administrator Michael Brown were criticized for delaying the federal response to this catastrophe while awaiting specific requests from state officials. Did the Stafford Act require the president to wait for such requests? For one perspective on this question, *see* Stephen M. Griffin, *Stop Federalism Before It Kills Again: Reflections on Hurricane Katrina*, 21 St. John's J. Legal Comment 527 (2007). One important lesson learned from Hurricane Katrina is that the federal government may sometimes need to act to protect affected communities, even without a specific request from the proper government officials. This notion is now embedded in the response doctrine of "leaning forward," which encourages federal agencies to err on the side of acting if they are uncertain whether or not to act in an emergency situation. FEMA, NATIONAL RESPONSE FRAMEWORK (4th ed. 2019) at 7 ("A forward-leaning posture is imperative for incidents that may expand rapidly in size, scope, or complexity, as well as incidents that occur without warning").

**5. Public Assistance.** Often the single largest benefit of a major disaster declaration is the availability of Public Assistance under Stafford Act § 406 to assist state and local government in the "repair, restoration, reconstruction, or replacement" of damaged public facilities or nonprofit facilities. Under this authority, state and local governments regularly receive billions of dollars for repairing or replacing government buildings, public schools, public housing, hospitals, roads, bridges, electrical grids, drinking water and sanitation systems, and other public infrastructure, with a state cost-share of 25 percent.

In the year following Hurricane Maria, for example, FEMA obligated $3.3 billion in Public Assistance to Puerto Rico, reportedly restoring to the island 100 percent of hospitals, 99 percent of drinking water, 99 percent of electrical service, and 99 percent of cell service. FEMA funding for public infrastructure was also supplemented and exceeded by funding from the U.S. Department of Housing and Urban Development (HUD), with $20 billion awarded to the Government of Puerto Rico through Community Development Block Grants. https://www.fema.gov/hurricane-maria.

**6. Individuals and Households Program.** Beyond assistance to public entities and nonprofit institutions, the Stafford Act under § 408 authorizes direct assistance to disaster victims under the Individuals and Households Program (IHP). The IHP authorizes funding for a variety of housing needs, including rent for temporary housing and repairs to owner-occupied housing. Note, however, that IHP benefits are subject to a severe cap under the statute, 42 U.S.C. § 5174(h) (no greater than $25,000 per individual or household with respect to a single major disaster). FEMA has adjusted this cap over time, so that as of October 2019, it stood at $35,500 with respect to any single major disaster. FEMA, Notice of Maximum Amount of Assistance Under the Individuals and Households Program, 84 Fed. Reg. 55,323 (Oct. 16, 2019). If your home was destroyed in an earthquake, fire, or flood, how far would that go toward rebuilding your home?

Many disaster victims obviously rely on homeowners insurance to rebuild, but that does not always work due to common policy exclusions, particularly for damages from floods and earthquakes. Moreover, many older homeowners who have paid off their house may not have homeowners insurance. Many others simply cannot afford insurance. As such, additional assistance is often needed, and sometimes available through programs such as low-interest loans available to individual homeowners through the U.S. Small Business Administration (SBA). After Hurricane Maria, SBA provided $1.8 billion in low-interest to 52,228 homeowners. At the same time, FEMA

provided $1.4 billion to 462,000 households through the IHP program. https://www.
fema.gov/hurricane-maria.

7. **Legal services.** Stafford Act § 415 authorizes the president to provide low-income
individuals with legal services "to meet their needs as a consequence of a major disaster."
What kind of services might this include? Could it include representation of disaster
victims in claims against the federal government for disaster assistance? Would this
present a conflict of interest? In practice, FEMA provides funding to independent organizations such as the American Bar Association Young Lawyers Division (YLD) to
provide "Disaster Legal Services" for declared major disasters. https://www.americ-
anbar.org/groups/young_lawyers/disaster_legal_services/. If you are or will be a "young
lawyer" in the near future, you could be practicing in this area before you know it.

8. **Forward progress?** Consider the opportunities that resources from a major disaster declaration could bring to an underserved community. Could you replace or
redesign some damaged highways to allow for non-motorized transportation? Could
you replace large, old coal-fired power plants and decayed electrical grids with smaller,
community-based solar, wind, or tidal energy sources? Could you replace old buildings
with energy-efficient and climate resilient constructions?

One common complaint about FEMA assistance has been that it is designed simply
to return communities to conditions before a disaster, regardless of whether those
pre-disaster conditions ensured any level of safety. If so, then FEMA in Puerto Rico
might spend billions of dollars to replace a decrepit electrical grid with another
decrepit electrical grid that will fail just as completely as the last one did in Hurricane
Maria. FEMA appears, however, to have recognized this illogic and taken steps to
address it. Among other things, in 2018, FEMA obtained new authority from Congress
to "replace or restore the function of a facility or system to industry standards without
regard to the pre-disaster condition of the facility or system" impacted by Hurricane
Maria. Bipartisan Budget Act of 2018, Sec. 20601, Pub. L. No. 115-123, 132 Stat.
64 (2018). FEMA has also authorized funding for repair of homes to create a "stronger,
more resilient structure ... to withstand future natural events." https://www.fema.gov/
hurricane-maria (discussing replacement of wooden house structure with stronger
concrete house structure).

How far can such improvements go with FEMA funding under Public Assistance
and the Individuals and Households Program? In conjunction with this question,
consider the effect of Stafford Act § 316, waiving requirements for environmental assessments under the National Environmental Policy Act (NEPA) where FEMA funding
will be used for purposes of "restoring a facility substantially to its condition prior
to the disaster or emergency." 42 U.S.C. § 5159. While most environmentalists and
environmental justice (EJ) advocates routinely argue for expanded NEPA analysis to
consider potential impacts of a federal action on diverse communities, are there also
cases where diverse communities may oppose such analysis?

9. **Predisaster mitigation.** Consistent with principles of resilience and the Benjamin
Franklin adage that "an ounce of prevention is worth a pound of cure," the Predisaster

Mitigation (PDM) program established by Stafford Act § 203 provides annual funding to states, U.S. territories, federally recognized tribes, and local communities with the goal "to reduce overall risk to the population and structures from future hazard events." *See* FEMA, *Predisaster Mitigation Grant Program*, https://www.fema.gov/pre-disaster-mitigation-grant-program. As a condition for PDM funding, FEMA requires state, territorial, tribal, and local governments to develop and adopt "hazard mitigation plans." As of January 2020, according to FEMA, all 50 states, 5 territories, 233 tribal governments, and 20,935 local governments have approved hazard mitigation plans in place, covering 87 percent of the U.S. population. https://www.fema.gov/hazard-mitigation-plan-status. For a compilation of ideas for mitigation projects to address the risks of drought, earthquake, flood, wind storms, winter storms, storm surge, tornados, wildfire, and other common hazards, *see* FEMA, *Mitigation Ideas* (Jan. 2013), https://www.fema.gov/media-library/assets/documents/30627.

Based on the prior discussion of vulnerability and resilience indicators, how do you see that mitigation efforts might help promote energy assurance, telecommunications accessibility, healthy behaviors, and social cohesion?

## 2. The Disaster Cycle

Beyond unique statutory authorities such as the Stafford Act, the field of disaster law is also distinguished by its focus on risk management through what some observers describe as a "circle of disaster." Professor Dan Farber suggests it includes stages of "mitigation, emergency response, insurance/liability compensation, government assistance, [and] rebuilding...." Daniel Farber, *Symposium Introduction: Navigating the Intersection of Environmental Law and Disaster Law*, 2011 BYU L. Rev. 1783, 1791 (2011). For purposes of this brief section, we will refer to the "Disaster Cycle" and simplify it to three stages, all conveniently beginning with the letter R, as depicted in Figure 15-3:

**Figure 15-3:** Disaster Cycle. Graphic: Cliff Villa.

Before further consideration of these three R's, we should make a few broad observations from this figure. In general, greater investments in readiness may contribute to a more immediate and effective response when a disaster strikes and faster recovery for the affected communities. Also, as a cycle, there is no beginning nor end. As Lee County, Alabama, for example, recovers from the EF-4 tornado that left 23 dead on March 3, 2019, it must also maintain readiness and respond to the next tornado that touches down in the county. While the stages may thus overlap and blend at times, the Disaster Cycle nevertheless provides a useful framework for comprehending disaster law and policy, as this brief section may demonstrate.

**a. Readiness** (or "preparedness") refers generally to "actions taken to plan, organize, equip, train, and exercise to build and sustain the capabilities necessary to prevent, protect against, mitigate the effects of, respond to, and recover from those threats that pose the greatest risks...." U.S. Dept. of Homeland Security, National Preparedness Goal (2nd ed. Sept. 2015), at A-2 (defining "National Preparedness"). Importantly, readiness in this sense is not merely a static condition of being "ready" to respond to an incident, but also a state of active and continuous preparation for significant and foreseeable threats.

Elements of readiness such as planning, organizing, equipping, and training engage all levels of government, and many businesses, nonprofit organizations, and private individuals. Of course, the capacity to engage in readiness activities is not equally distributed across all communities and individuals. One obvious limitation is available resources. A single parent working two jobs in order to make ends meet each month cannot be expected to have the same capacity to participate in readiness training or to maintain a recommended level of personal savings in case of emergencies. As one review of related studies concluded:

> The literature suggests that socially vulnerable or disadvantaged households have lower levels of disaster preparedness. For example, [multiple studies] all find that earthquake preparedness (that is, possession of first-aid kits, emergency food supplies, evacuation plans, and fire extinguishers) is less common in low income and minority populations. [One 2003 study] finds that both low income and Black households are less likely to have adequate shuttering to protect homes from hurricane damage. Similarly, [a 1999 study] note[s] that Black households have constrained access to hurricane preparedness supplies. Scholars also observe that minority and lower income homeowners are less likely to hold earthquake [] and flood insurance instruments [].

Sammy Zahran, et al., *Social Vulnerability and the Natural and Built Environment: A Model of Flood Casualties in Texas*, Disasters, Oct. 24, 2008, at 539–40.

What can advocates do to address this inequality? First, it is certainly an appropriate role of government to plan for the protection of all people in the event of an emergency or disaster situation. Indeed, much of the planning improvements since Hurricane Katrina have focused on this continuing challenge. On a national level, planning for most emergencies and disasters that require a federal response is led by FEMA through the *National Response Framework*. Recent revisions of the NRF have emphasized protection of the "whole community," which the NRF defines specifically to include "children; older adults, individuals with disabilities and others with access and functional needs; those from religious, racial, and ethnically diverse backgrounds; people with limited English proficiency; and owners of animals, including household pets and service and assistance animals." FEMA, NATIONAL RESPONSE FRAMEWORK (4th ed. 2019) at 5. Accordingly, the unique needs of each of these groups and all other members of a community must be taken into account when governments engage in readiness planning activities.

Consistent with federal law and policy as well as state, local, and tribal policy and legislation, all states and many tribal and local governments have emergency plans in place addressing "all hazards," regardless of whether they represent a "natural" disaster. *See, e.g.*, State of Florida Comprehensive Emergency Management Plan (2018); State of California Emergency Plan (Oct. 2017); State of New Mexico All-Hazard Emergency Operations Plan (Dec. 2016). Planning in each of these documents should address the needs of vulnerable communities and individuals — or be updated to ensure such needs are fully addressed.

In addition to government planning, resources are available to help vulnerable communities and individuals improve their own readiness for emergencies. One good online source of information maintained by FEMA is www.ready.gov, which provides helpful suggestions to family members, including young people, on how to prepare for specific threats such as earthquakes, floods, and winter weather. Recognizing the limited access to and use of online materials by some community members, many planning agencies also offer training in person at convenient locations. In New York City, for example, the *Ready New York* program will send emergency management experts upon request to "your workplace, school, community center, or house of worship" in order to help community members "learn about the hazards you may face in New York City and prepare for all types of emergencies...." https://www1.nyc.gov/site/em/ready/ready-new-york.page.

**b. Response.** Ready or not, when disaster strikes, some response may be required. FEMA defines "response" in this context to include "actions to save lives, protect property and the environment, stabilize communities, and meet basic human needs following an incident." FEMA, NATIONAL RESPONSE FRAMEWORK (4th ed. 2019), at 1. For most emergencies, such as a car crash or house fire, response may be provided entirely by "first-responders," including local law enforcement and fire authorities. Larger, more complex incidents such as a train derailment may require involvement from state or federal authorities. For a major catastrophe such as an earthquake or hurricane in the United States, the public mind may think immediately of FEMA, but the actual assignment of response duties may be different and important for advocates of disaster justice to understand.

One old analogy for FEMA was that it simply "held the checkbook," taking in deposits from Congress and writing checks to reimburse other agencies for services rendered in declared disasters. Since Hurricane Katrina, FEMA has taken a more direct and visible role in managing disasters, but the analogy still holds much truth. The question of "Who does what?" is one with potentially life-or-death consequences, as interagency turf battles at the time of a disaster could be a disaster in itself. To avoid that kind of delay, most response plans designate lead agencies that may be required to meet particular needs during an emergency or disaster, with or without reimbursement from FEMA. For example, under the *National Response Framework*, Emergency Support Function #1 (ESF #1: Transportation), if an earthquake destroyed part of the federal highway system or required closure of national airspace, the designated lead agency would be the U.S. Department of Transportation for purposes of managing those aspects of the disaster response. If the same earthquake breached a levee or impaired a sewage treatment system, the lead agency for response to those concerns would be the U.S. Army Corps of Engineers (ESF #3: Public Works). Likewise, if the earthquake caused an oil spill from a ruptured pipeline, the designated lead agency for responding to the oil spill would be the U.S. EPA (ESF #10: Oil and Hazardous Materials Response). NATIONAL RESPONSE FRAMEWORK (4th ed. 2019), Table 4: Emergency Support Functions and ESF Coordinators.

Similar designations are often made in advance by state, local, and tribal governments, requiring multiple agencies from various levels of governments to coordinate efficiently and effectively in order to achieve a common mission. To establish and maintain such coordination quickly and throughout a disaster response, federal policy (and federal funding) requires all agencies, on every level, to adopt the **Incident Command System (ICS)**. Under ICS, agencies maintain their individual authorities and jurisdiction, but must operate under certain response doctrines, for example, operating within certain organizational structures such as Unified Command. ICS may appear bewildering to most members of the public, but effective community advocates will decipher the bureaucracy, request copies of organization charts and operating plans, and identify particular moments in time and place where community input may be most influential. For a head-start on comprehending the Incident Command System, *see* Clifford J. Villa, *Law and Lawyers in the Incident Command System*, 36 SEATTLE U. L. REV. 1855 (2013).

c. **Recovery.** As defined by FEMA, recovery includes "the restoration and strengthening of key systems and resource assets that are critical to the economic stability, vitality, and long-term sustainability of the communities themselves. These include health (including behavioral health) and human services capabilities and networks, public and private disability support and service systems, educational systems, community social networks, natural and cultural resources, affordable and accessible housing, infrastructure systems, and local and regional economic drivers." FEMA, NATIONAL DISASTER RECOVERY FRAMEWORK (2nd ed. 2016) at 1–2. Among the guiding principles most relevant to vulnerable communities, FEMA emphasizes that the recovery stage (as with readiness) focus on service to the "whole community." By this, FEMA explains—

> Understanding legal obligations and sharing best practices when planning and implementing recovery strategies to avoid excluding groups is critical. Actions, both intentional and unintentional, that exclude groups of people based on race, color, ethnicity, national origin (including limited English

proficiency), religion, sex, sexual orientation, gender identity, age, or disability can have long-term negative consequences on entire communities and
may violate law.

*National Disaster Recovery Framework* at 10. By potential violations of law, FEMA
cites federal statutes specifically including the Americans with Disabilities Act (ADA),
Title VI of the Civil Rights Act of 1964, the Fair Housing Act of 1968, and the Age
Discrimination Act of 1975.

If all of this sounds good (or somewhat abstract), when most people think of
lawyers and the Disaster Cycle, they think immediately of the recovery stage and
questions of compensation. What are the limits of my client's homeowners insurance
policy? Can the federal government be liable for the failures of a levee constructed
by the Army Corps of Engineers? Should BP have to compensate the Vietnamese-
American fishers along the Gulf Coast for injuries to their cultural resources? Should
a local government be liable for constructing public housing in a floodplain? Could
a local government be liable if it refuses to replace public housing in a floodplain?
Could a public utility be liable for power lines that ignite a wildfire during a windstorm? Could a public utility be liable if it preemptively shuts down power lines before
a windstorm and interrupts the flow of oxygen to an elderly person on a Continuous
Positive Airway Pressure (CPAP) machine? Obviously, questions of compensation
after a disaster may keep lawyers employed for a long time and keep justice advocates
searching for better solutions.

# D. Disaster Justice in Practice

Putting all of this together—vulnerabilities and resilience, disaster law and policy—what does Disaster Justice look like in the "real" world? This final section of
the chapter presents two perspectives after Hurricane Katrina. The excerpt from
Bullard and Wright, immediately below, ironically offers a "twenty-point plan" for
how to destroy black communities in New Orleans, along the way cataloguing the
myriad ways that response and recovery efforts after a disaster can lead to greater injuries to vulnerable communities. Following that, the excerpt from Professor Davida
Finger to close this chapter demonstrates how legal advocates (even law students)
may engage directly in seeking justice for vulnerable victims of disaster.

### Robert D. Bullard & Beverly Wright,
### The Wrong Complexion for Protection
(NYU Press, 2012) at 74–78

*A Twenty-Point Plan to Destroy Black New Orleans*

Hurricane Katrina exposed the limitation of local, state, and federal government
operations to implement an effective emergency preparedness and response plan.
As reconstruction and rebuilding move forward in New Orleans and the Louisiana,

Mississippi, and Alabama Gulf Coast region, it was clear that the lethargic and inept emergency response after Hurricane Katrina was a disaster that overshadowed the deadly storm itself. Yet, there was a "second disaster" in the making, driven by racism, classism, elitism, paternalism, and old-fashioned greed. The "Twenty-Point Plan to Destroy Black New Orleans" presented here is based on trends and observations Beverly Wright and I made four months after the devastating storm. Other trend data and observations were added that further illustrate how the "plan" was implemented.

1. *Selectively hand out FEMA grants.* The Federal Emergency Management Agency (FEMA) was consistent in its slow response in getting aid to Katrina survivors. FEMA's grant assistance program favors middle-income households, making it difficult for low-income and black Katrina survivors to access government assistance and directing the bulk of the grant assistance to middle-income white storm victims....

2. *Systematically deny the poor and blacks SBA loans.* The [Small Business Administration] screened out poor applicants and denied black households disaster loans. A December 21, 2005, *New York Times* editorial summed up this problem: "The Poor Need Not Apply." As of that date, the SBA had processed only a third of the home loan applications it had received. However, the SBA rejected 82 percent of the applications it received, a higher percentage than in previous disasters. In well-off neighborhoods like Lakeview, 47 percent of the loans were approved, whereas in poverty-stricken neighborhoods, only 7 percent were. Middle-class black neighborhoods in the eastern part of the city had lower than average loan rates....

4. *Redline black insurance policyholders.* Numerous studies show that African Americans are more likely than whites to receive insufficient insurance settlement amounts. Insurance companies target black policyholders in majority-black zip codes and offer them low and inadequate insurance settlements as a way to subsidize fair settlements made to white policyholders. If black homeowners and business owners were to recover from Katrina, then they had to receive full and just insurance settlements. FEMA and the SBA could not be counted on to rebuild black communities.

5. *Use "greenbuilding" and flood-proofing codes to restrict redevelopment.* Requiring that rebuilding plans conform to "green building" materials and new floodproofing codes priced many low- and moderate-income homeowners and small-business owners out of the market. This hit black homeowners and black business owners especially hard, since they generally had lower incomes and less wealth.

6. *Apply discriminatory environmental cleanup standards.* Failure to apply uniform cleanup standards can kill off black neighborhoods. A full-scale cleanup of white neighborhoods was undertaken to meet residential standards, while no or partial cleanup (industrial standards) took place in black residential neighborhoods. Failure to clean up black residential areas can act as a disincentive for redevelopment. It can also make people sick. Some people used the argument that black neighborhoods were already highly polluted with background contamination "hot spots" that exceeded

EPA safe levels pre-Katrina and thus did not need to be cleaned to more rigorous residential standards.

7. *Sacrifice "low-lying" black neighborhoods in the name of saving the wetlands and environmental restoration.* Some people advocated allowing black neighborhoods like the Lower Ninth Ward and New Orleans East to be "yielded back to the swamp," while allowing similar low-lying white areas to be rebuilt and redeveloped. This is a form of "ethnic cleansing" that was not possible before Katrina. Instead of emphasizing equitable rebuilding, uniform cleanup standards, equal protection, and environmental justice for African American communities, public officials sent mixed signals for rebuilding vulnerable "low-lying" black neighborhoods.

8. *Promote a smaller, more upscale, and "whiter" New Orleans.* Concentrating on getting less-damaged neighborhoods up and running could translate into a small, more upscale, and whiter New Orleans and a dramatically down-sized black community. Clearly, shrinking New Orleans neighborhoods disproportionately shrinks black votes, black political power, and black wealth. A February 2011 *Bloomberg News* headlines read "Census Finds Hurricane Katrina Left New Orleans Richer, Whiter, Emptier." The city lost 140,845 residents, a decrease of 29 percent from 2000. Whites were far more likely to make it back to New Orleans than blacks. The percentage of the population that was black fell to 60.2 percent from 67.3 percent. This drop in population will translate in one fewer congressional seat for Louisiana—now six instead of seven.

9. *Revise land-use and zoning ordinances to exclude.* Katrina could be used to change land use and zoning codes to "zone against" undesirable land uses that were not politically possible before the storm. Also, "expulsive" zoning could be used to push out certain land uses and certain people....

12. *Offer no financial assistance for evacuees to return.* Thousands of Katrina evacuees were shipped to more than three dozen states with no provisions for return, the equivalent of being given a "one-way" ticket. Many Katrina evacuees ran short of funds. No money translates into no return to their homes and neighborhoods. Promoting the "right to return" without committing adequate resources to assist evacuees to return doesn't help.

13. *Keep evacuees away from New Orleans jobs.* The nation's unemployment rate was 5 percent in November 2005. That month, the jobless rate for Katrina returnees was 12.5 percent, while 27.8 percent of evacuees living elsewhere were unemployed. The jobless rate among blacks who had not returned was 47 percent in November 2005, whereas the rate was only 13 percent for whites who had not gone back. Katrina evacuees who made it back to their home region thus had much lower levels of joblessness. This is especially important for African Americans, whose joblessness rate was more than 30 percentage points lower for returnees. The problem was that the vast majority of black Katrina evacuees had not returned to their home region. Only 21 percent of black evacuees—but 48 percent of white evacuees—had returned by November.

14. *Fail to enforce fair housing laws.* In the aftermath of the storm, housing discrimination against blacks was allowed to run rampant. Katrina created a housing shortage and opened a floodgate of discriminatory acts against black homeowners

and renters. In December 2005, the National Fair Housing Alliance (NFHA) found high rates of housing discrimination against African Americans displaced by Hurricane Katrina. In 66 percent of the test runs conducted by the NFHA, forty-three of sixty-five instances, whites were favored over African Americans.

15. *Provide no commitment to rebuild and replace low-income public housing.* Shortly after Katrina struck, even the Secretary of the U.S. Department of Housing and Urban Development (HUD) spoke of not rebuilding all of the public housing lost during the storm. The HUD secretary's statement was a powerful signal to New Orleans poor that public housing might not be around for them to return to.

16. *Downplay the black cultural heritage of New Orleans.* Some officials tried to promote rebuilding and the vision of a "new" New Orleans as if the city's rich black culture did not matter or as it if could be replaced or replicated in a "theme park"-type redevelopment scenario. Developers tried to capture and market the "black essence" of New Orleans without including black people.

17. *Treat mixed-income "integrated" housing as superior to all-black neighborhoods.* First, there is nothing inherently inferior about an "all-black" neighborhood or all-black anything, for that matter. Black New Orleanians who chose to live in neighborhoods that happened to be all black (whites have always had the right to move in or move out of these neighborhoods) should not have been forced to have their neighborhoods rebuilt as "integrated" or "multicultural" neighborhoods. Also, for many blacks, "mixed-income" housing conjures up the idea that 10 percent of the fair-market housing units will be set aside for them. Many blacks are battle-weary of being some generic 10 percent. New Orleans was 68 percent black before Katrina, and most black folks were comfortable with that....

19. *Delay rebuilding and construction of New Orleans schools.* The longer New Orleans schools stayed closed, the longer families with children stayed away. Schools are a major predictor of racial polarization. Before Katrina, more than 125,000 New Orleans children were attending schools in the city. Blacks made up 93 percent of the students in the New Orleans schools. Evacuated children were enrolled in school districts from Arizona to Pennsylvania; three months after the storm, only one of the New Orleans 116 schools was open.

20. *Hold elections without appropriate Voting Rights Act safeguards.* Almost 300,000 registered voters left New Orleans after Katrina. The powerful storm damaged or destroyed 300 of the 442 polling places. Holding city elections posed major challenges in terms of registration, absentee ballots, availability of city workers to staff the polls, polling places, and identification for displaced New Orleanians. Identification is required at the polls, and returning residents might well have lost traditional identification papers (e.g., birth certificates, driver's licenses) in the hurricane.... Holding elections while a substantial portion of African American New Orleans voters were displaced outside of their home district and even their home state is unprecedented in the history of the United States, but also raises racial justice and human rights questions.

* * *

# Davida Finger, et al., *Engaging the Legal Academy in Disaster Response*

10 Seattle Journal for Social Justice
211, 214–23 (2011)

Law clinics have a duty to "respond to the legal services needs of the communities in which they operate." In addition, law clinics are likely to have significant experience lawyering for particularly vulnerable individuals and communities, which usually have the greatest difficulty with disaster recovery.

The Katrina Clinic originated in the fall of 2005, when the entire Loyola University New Orleans College of Law was displaced to Houston, Texas; the University of Houston Law Center hosted the law clinic while Loyola was displaced. Law clinic students and faculty, in association with Lone Star Legal Aid and the University of Houston, worked in Disaster Relief Centers to assist those displaced by Hurricane Katrina who had temporarily settled in Houston.... Loyola students and clinical faculty, with support from the administration, provided critical legal and informational resources, especially for low-income individuals served by the law clinic.... While in Houston, law students assisted over a thousand people in face-to-face meetings or phone interviews at one of the Houston hotline centers.

The law school returned to its New Orleans campus in spring of 2006. For the next three years, the Katrina Clinic operated from the Loyola University New Orleans College of Law as a part of the law clinic. The Katrina Clinic's mission was to provide information, communicate on behalf of, and give legal assistance to individuals on hurricane-related legal civil issues. Over the years that the Katrina Clinic operated at Loyola, law students handled hundreds of individual cases with faculty supervision. The law students also worked on various aspects of class action and impact litigation on post-disaster issues for low-income people. Law students were able to engage with displaced residents, hear their stories, document barriers and hardships, and lay the groundwork for advocacy and litigation.

... The Katrina Clinic bolstered its capacity by serving as a volunteer placement site for hundreds of visiting law students from around the country. Some took advantage of the opportunity to satisfy academic requirements at their home law schools. Visiting law students typically participated for single week periods over various school breaks, with some students returning for multiple visits. The Katrina Clinic coordinated closely with the Student Hurricane Network (SHN) to provide opportunities for volunteer placement and hosted orientations for visiting SHN law students....

Following Hurricane Katrina, low-income people received financial housing assistance from [FEMA].... By speaking with hundreds of evacuees, the Katrina Clinic, in partnership with attorneys from around the country, learned that evacuees faced termination of this assistance without the benefit of adequate notice of the termination and without an opportunity for a pre-termination hearing. As a result, evacuees lost their means to pay rent, to prevent utility shutoffs, or to otherwise secure safe shelter. Students assisted in talking with FEMA grant recipients, gathering extensive information regarding problems with FEMA's rental assistance program, and documenting difficulties with FEMA's recoupment practices. Eventually, a class action lawsuit challenged both the termination of rental assistance and FEMA's widespread recoupment practices. The suit resulted in a settlement of $2.65 million on behalf of those who were wrongfully terminated from rental assistance. The influx of law student volunteers bolstered this litigation effort as students were available to assist with client interviews, callbacks, and administrative appeals to FEMA.

During recovery efforts, displaced people also faced a possible blanket deadline for filing insurance claims. The Katrina Clinic, through student volunteer efforts, provided information about claim deadlines at public meetings, in the newspaper, and on local TV news and radio programs in Orleans and Lafourche Parishes, Louisiana, and in Houston, Texas. In cooperation with other legal services providers, the Katrina Clinic compiled insurance packets with information on negotiating with insurance companies, engaging with the state-sponsored mediation program, and filing a pro se form included in the packet. The clinic provided over six hundred packets.... Ultimately, the Louisiana Supreme Court extended the period for filing claims. The Katrina Clinic filed an amicus curiae brief with the court on behalf of the State Attorney General's Office in that matter....

Louisiana's Road Home Program, which was set up to disburse federal rebuilding funds, also provided extensive advocacy opportunities for students participating in the Katrina Clinic. Homeowners encountered barriers at every turn [including] access to program rules and their own files.... The Katrina Clinic handled hundreds of Road Home appeals and advocated on systemic issues related to Road Home's policies and procedures. The Katrina Clinic also drafted and distributed template appeal forms to assist homeowners in completing their own appeals for wrongful grant calculations. All told, the Katrina Clinic recovered more than $1 million in wrongfully withheld Road Home funds for homeowners. Unfortunately, many homeowners were not able to rebuild given the vast problems with the program.

One of the most common post-disaster issues faced by residents was related to contractor fraud, which became a serious problem after the storm. As residents struggled to return home, they faced a confusing marketplace, where both formal and informal networks of communication had been destroyed. Low-income people and the elderly, desperate to move forward with rebuilding, were particularly vulnerable to predatory rebuilding schemes. As insurance funds and federal recovery dollars began to trickle into the hands of the displaced, unscrupulous contractors—and those pretending to be contractors—were able to take advantage of an already difficult situation. Some contractors absconded with funds completely and others were unable to complete work within promised time schedules.... Under faculty supervision, students met with people experiencing a range of problems connected to these issues. They attempted to reach contractors as well as draft demand letters, in an effort to facilitate rebuilding for vulnerable homeowners. Students also participated in advocacy and mediations and assisted with the preparation of contractor-fraud cases for litigation....

The Katrina Clinic utilized new systems in an effort to meet some of the pressing demands of the unprecedented domestic disasters, including on-site and community-wide intake and information distribution, phone intake and consultation through a dedicated hotline, and online case management. All of these efforts were coordinated with law clinic faculty supervision and institutional support.

… The lessons learned from the Katrina Clinic contribute to a greater collective understanding of how to situate a disaster response at law schools across the nation. With the ever-present threat of disasters, particularly pronounced in the southern region in recent years, law clinics are likely to be at the forefront of post-disaster work for vulnerable and low-income communities. Ideas that have emerged from the experience of the Katrina Clinic might assist with disaster preparation at the institutional level of law schools. They may also serve as part of a framework for developing stronger partnerships between and among law schools for purposes of disaster recovery.

… Finally, to achieve meaningful participation by law students in post-disaster work, law school curricula must include a focus on race, gender, and poverty—the prime markers for social vulnerability in the aftermath of disaster. By teaching with a focus on these issues, law students will be better equipped to understand and serve those who will have the most difficult time recovering, and also the most likely to be left behind in post-disaster rebuilding efforts.

While some of the Katrina Clinic's efforts are easily quantifiable, others are simply not easily measured. Students witnessed the failures and hopes of the Gulf Coast post-disaster recovery efforts; such moments were critically important to their professional development and, for many, their growth as social justice advocates.

\* \* \*

## *Notes and Questions*

1. **Lessons learned for COVID-19 recovery.** Considering the excerpt from Bullard & Wright, which of the injustices observed after Hurricane Katrina might you anticipate as the United States and other countries begin to recover from the COVID-19 pandemic of 2020? Consider the particular impacts that Bullard & Wright identified in the areas of education, housing, insurance, small business, and voting rights. With the lessons learned after Hurricane Katrina, how might these same problems be avoided during recovery from COVID-19?

2. **COVID-19 legal services?** Considering the article by Davida Finger, and the tremendous achievements by Loyola's Katrina Clinic, how might law school clinics, legal aid offices, the ABA's Young Lawyers Division, and other organizations provide legal assistance to vulnerable individuals and communities impacted by the COVID-19 pandemic?

3. **Vulnerability and resilience in context.** Given all the materials in this chapter, coupled with your own knowledge and experience, what factors do you see as contributing the most to either vulnerability or resilience during a pandemic? For one early perspective on vulnerability and COVID-19, see Dan Farber, *Inequality and the Coronavirus*, LEGAL PLANET (Mar. 24, 2020), available online at https://legal-planet.org/2020/03/24/inequality-and-the-coronavirus/.

# Chapter 16

# Food Justice

**Figure 16-1:** Street art in Cali, Colombia. Translation: "At harvest time, we will reap the truth for the peace and reconciliation of our disappeared." The saying refers to the plight of millions of peasants (many Afro-descendent and indigenous) who were forced off their land during the civil war in Columbia. In fact, many were killed or disappeared. The resulting food insecurity drove even more people off their lands. Feb. 23, 2019. Photo: Rebecca Bratspies.

## A. Introduction

From the beginning of the environmental justice movement, advocates recognized that environmental justice included a concern for access to safe food. *See* Principles of Environmental Justice (1991), #3 ("Environmental justice calls for universal protection from ... toxic/hazardous wastes and poisons ... that threaten the fundamental right to clean air, land, water and *food*") (emphasis added). Ensuing concerns for "food justice" have inspired multiple lines of investigation in recent years, including the problem of local "food deserts," the global "energy-food-water" nexus, and the worldwide struggle for food security. In this concluding chapter of the book, we will take a quick look at each of these emerging areas of investigation and practice, with a view toward achievement of the original and enduring principles of environmental justice.

### Pathfinder on Food Justice

For a solid foundation in food law generally, *see* Lisa Heinzerling, FOOD LAW: CASES AND MATERIALS (2019); and Mary Jane Angelo, Jason J. Czarnezki, & William S. Eubanks II, FOOD, AGRICULTURE, AND ENVIRONMENTAL LAW (2013). For an introduction and overview of the food justice movement, *see* Joshua Sbicca, FOOD JUSTICE NOW!: DEEPENING THE ROOTS OF SOCIAL STRUGGLE (2018); and Garrett Broad, MORE THAN JUST FOOD: FOOD JUSTICE AND COMMUNITY CHANGE (2016).

For a selection of contemporary academic literature demonstrating the diversity of concerns and perspectives on food justice, in addition to the articles noted later in this chapter, *see* Ernesto Hernández-López, *Sustainable Food and the Constitution*, 50 ARIZ. ST. L.J. 549 (2018); Dan DePasquale, Surbhi Sarang, & Natalie Bump Vena, *Forging Food Justice Through Cooperatives in New York City*, 45 FORDHAM URB. L.J. 909 (2018); Marc-Tizoc González, *Criminalizing Charity: Can First Amendment Free Exercise of Religion, RFRA, and RLUIPA Protect People Who Share Food in Public?*, 7 UC IRVINE L. REV. 291 (2017); Melanie Pugh, *A Recipe for Justice: Support for a Federal Food Justice Interagency Working Group*, 72 FOOD & DRUG L.J. 341 (2017); Stephen Lee, *The Food We Eat and the People Who Feed Us*, 94 WASH. U. L. REV. 1249 (2017); Julia Guarino, *Tribal Food Sovereignty in the American Southwest*, 11 J. FOOD L. & POL'Y 83 (2015); Margot Pollans & Michael Roberts, *Setting the Table for Urban Agriculture*, 46 URB. LAW. 199 (2014); Anastasia Telesetsky, *Community-Based Urban Agriculture as Affirmative Environmental Justice*, 91 U. DET. MERCY L. REV. 259 (2014); Erika George, *Incorporating Rights: Child Labor in African Agriculture and the Challenge of Changing Practices in the Cocoa Industry*, 21 U.C. DAVIS J. INT'L L. & POL'Y 59 (2014); Emily M. Broad Leib, *All (Food) Politics Is Local: Increasing Food Access Through Local Government Action*, 7 HARV. L. & POL'Y REV. 321 (2013); Christopher J. Curran & Marc-Tizoc González, *Food Justice as Interracial Justice: Urban Farmers, Community Organizations and the Role of Government in Oakland, California*, 43 U. MIAMI INTER-AM. L. REV. 207 (2011); Avi Brisman, *Food Justice as Crime Prevention*, 5 J. FOOD L. & POL'Y 1 (2009); Andrea Freeman, *Fast Food: Oppression Through Poor Nutrition*, 95 CAL. L. REV. 2221 (2007); and Carmen Gonzalez, *Markets, Monocultures, and Malnutrition: Agricultural Trade Policy Through an Environmental Justice Lens*, 14 MICH. ST. J. INT'L L. 345 (2006).

In popular media, *see* Eric Schlosser, FAST FOOD NATION (2001) and the Richard Linklater documentary film of the same name (2006). Valuable online resources include Farmworker Justice (www.fwjustice.org); JustFood.org (www.justfood.org); and USDA Urban Agriculture (https://www.nal.usda.gov/afsic/urban-agriculture).

# B. Food Deserts

The problem of "food deserts" can be seen in almost any community in the United States where there are high populations of low-income and minority people. Instead of Whole Foods or Trader Joe's, Safeway or Piggly-Wiggly, or other full-service grocery stores, poor communities will obtain food from corner convenience stores emphasizing beer and chips, or from fast-food restaurants such as McDonald's, Burger King, and KFC. Such sources offer the advantage of cheap calories, at the expense of nutrition and community health. Potential solutions to this problem are many and varied, some with potential drawbacks, as explored in the following excerpt.

## Deborah N. Archer & Tamara C. Belinfanti, *We Built It and They Did Not Come: Using New Governance Theory in the Fight for Food Justice in Low-Income Communities of Color*

15 Seattle Journal for Social Justice 307–316 (2016)

Meet Anthony. Anthony is eighteen years old and lives with his mother, Mary, in Anacostia, a residential neighborhood in Southeast Washington, D.C. There are no supermarkets in his neighborhood—the closest grocery store is 20 minutes away by bus. One or two corner stores in the neighborhood sell milk, cereal, and other packaged foods. Mary shops for groceries twice a month "when she has the money." On rare occasions she also shops for fruits and vegetables at a farmers market, though she has to travel for over 45 minutes on two buses and a train to reach it. Anthony rarely eats breakfast at home, and when he does it usually consists of dry cereal. His typical breakfast comes from either McDonald's or a hot dog stand he passes on his way to school. If he is home for lunch, he usually has "something like a hot pocket." More often, his lunch comes from his neighborhood McDonald's or a Chipotle near his school. For dinner, he usually eats at McDonald's if he is in his neighborhood or Chipotle if he is at school. On the occasions when Anthony and Mary have dinner together, they eat Chinese take-out; their favorite dishes are orange chicken, chicken nuggets, and fries. Anthony gets food from McDonald's more than any other establishment because "it is cheap and there is one every three blocks" in his neighborhood. Anthony "does not like or dislike" his food options because, as he says, "I'm used to it, it's all I know."

Anthony lives in a food desert—a neighborhood that is more than a mile away from a supermarket or other large retailer that sells fresh fruits and vegetables. In essence, food deserts are communities, both urban and rural, with severely limited access to healthy and affordable food. In the United States, approximately 23.5 million people live in food deserts. Most of these people are Black or Brown. Blacks, Latinos, and Native Americans tend to travel farther, have fewer choices, and pay more for food than Whites. Compared to Whites, Blacks are half as likely to have access to a chain supermarket, while Latinos are a third less likely to have access to a chain supermarket.

While residents of food deserts have difficulty accessing healthy food, they often have easy access to fast food and convenience stores. Fast food restaurants offer high-calorie, filling meals at bargain prices. But fast food affordability comes at a severe cost to residents' nutrition and health. The average distance between an individual's home to a grocery store as compared to a fast food restaurant is relevant to his or her food choices. "When fast food restaurants are closer than supermarkets to a neighborhood, the neighborhood is more likely to make unhealthy food choices." While food deserts are characterized by a dearth of full-service supermarkets, they often have an abundance of small corner markets. However, "fresh and nutritious produce is rarely available at these small stores, and the type of food generally tends to be of poorer quality and less healthy, high in sugars and saturated fats."

In examining food deserts, many researchers found a link between poverty, access to fresh nutritious foods, and diet-related health problems. This link leads to a paradox of poor health: "Many Americans, particularly low-income people and people of color, are overweight yet malnourished. They face an overwhelming variety of processed foods, but are unable to procure a well-balanced diet from the liquor stores and mini-marts that dominate their neighborhoods." Life in food deserts leads to a lack of food security—these are environments in which "all persons [cannot obtain] at all times a culturally acceptable, nutritionally adequate diet through local non-emergency sources."

Food deserts and food insecurity have received considerable attention from various stakeholders, such as state and local governments, community organizations, and private sector institutions. These stakeholders have sought to overcome food insecurity by turning food deserts into oases by providing "access" to fresh, healthy food. However, many of their solutions—building supermarkets and sponsoring farmers markets—have missed the mark. Residents of food deserts did not flock to grocery stores to purchase fruits and vegetables. As a result, many stakeholders blame the residents of food deserts for their own predicament, lamenting, to paraphrase *Field of Dreams*, "we built it but they did not come."

… Food deserts have largely been framed as problems of proximity. If the problem is proximity to grocery stores, then the solution should be simple: create incentives and opportunities to develop grocery stores in underserved, low-income communities of color. Community organizations worked to bring farmers markets, policy makers and government officials provided financial and tax incentives for the development of full-service supermarkets, and the private sector responded by building supermarkets in many underserved communities. In recent years, the U.S. government distributed more than $500 million, through the Healthy Food Financing Initiative, to encourage grocery stores to open in underserved communities. Many states have also invested substantial resources to spur the development of healthy food options in poor communities plagued by diet-related health problems. However, these investments have not always resulted in healthier communities—supermarkets came to food deserts, but, in many of the communities, the residents neither came to the supermarkets nor bought the newly available healthy food.

In some communities, the development of full-service supermarkets did not alter residents' buying habits. Although community members shopped at the new supermarket, they often bought the same foods they previously bought. Several recent studies have documented this phenomenon around the country. For a National Bureau of Economic Research study, residents agreed to allow researchers to track all of their bar-coded food purchases. The study confirmed that low-income neighborhoods had less physical access to healthy food. However, the study also concluded that individual food preferences, not proximity to full-service supermarkets, dominated the choices people made. Participants who were low-income and had lower levels of education but who lived in wealthier communities with proximity to healthy foods made food choices that were similar to the choices made by low-income people living in low-income neighborhoods with less physical access to healthy food.

Similar results were reached in studies of food desert interventions in Philadelphia and in the United Kingdom. In the Philadelphia study, researchers studied the impact of opening full-service supermarkets in food deserts. After studying purchasing habits over six months, the researchers found that the presence of supermarkets did not lead to increased fruit or vegetable intake of residents or impact body mass index. Ultimately, researchers concluded that "the effectiveness of interventions to improve physical access to food and reduce obesity by encouraging supermarkets to locate in underserved areas therefore remains unclear."

Rather than seeing the results of these studies as a prompt to further investigate the complex reasons people experience difficulty accessing healthy food, many have been content to declare the problem of food deserts solved, or to claim that food deserts were never really the threat to public health that many believed them to be. Yet poor nutrition and food insecurity remain, despite the geographical proximity of supermarkets or other sources of whole foods. Indeed, in the aforementioned study by the National Bureau of Economic Research, researchers found that no more than a tenth of the variation in food bought could be explained by people's proximity to a grocery store. One danger in this finding is that rather than further engaging to unearth and address all of the challenges and opportunity costs people face in accessing food, private industry may stop investing in full-service grocery stores in low-income communities, government entities may move to end tax incentives or other benefits, and non-profits may turn their attention and resources to "more pressing" concerns.

Others have taken the publication of these studies as an opportunity to blame the victims, declaring that access was improved and the remaining issues are about individuals having the desire to change behavior. Some in the food justice movement call residents' behavior a "lifestyle choice" and point to a perceived cultural preference for unhealthy, processed foods. For example, in a survey of community-supported agriculture initiatives ("CSA"), managers were asked, "what do you think are some of the reasons that it is primarily European-American people who seem to participate in CSAs?" Respondents did not question access and affordability or raise issues about structural inequalities. Instead, the CSA managers made remarks such as "Hispanics aren't into fresh, local, and organic products," "I believe that food is affordable to all;

it's just a matter of different values...," and "low income people shop elsewhere unless they are given freebies like WIC."

These responses stigmatize the choices of affected communities rather than respond to the systemic and structural barriers that impact access and lead those people to make the choices they do. The result is condemning individuals who may not have the wealth, information, or resources to participate in the food market on the terms set by others. The problem of access to healthy, affordable food is not as simple as reducing the distance a resident must travel to healthy food sources. Advocates, government entities, and members of the private sector must take a step back and examine whether they have truly addressed the access problem by focusing on the meaning of access and the specific barriers for each community.

## Notes and Questions

1. **Food desert.** Do *you* live in a food desert? If you do now, or ever have before, what measures would help you or your neighbors better address needs for safe, nutritious food? Can you think of any legal measures that would also help?

2. **Food "mirage."** As Archer and Belinfanti suggest above, the problem of food deserts may not be solved by simply building new supermarkets in underserved communities. Such efforts, in fact, may lead to the problem of the "food mirage," which occurs when "full service grocery stores appear plentiful but, because food prices are high, healthful foods are economically inaccessible for low-income households." Archer & Belinfanti, *supra*, at 317. Whether food stores are inaccessible by physical distance or by economic circumstances, the result for many community members may be the same.

3. **"Hispanics aren't into" fresh food?** While remarks such as this may surprise (and offend) many Hispanics, cultural differences may play some important part in determining whether or not a business, such as a new supermarket, will be embraced by a local community. In the fall, the air around any successful supermarket in New Mexico should be wrapped in the aroma of roasting chiles. In Seattle, any worthy grocery store must deliver the Copper River sockeye salmon in season. In Queens, New York, tamarind, pigeon peas, and (perhaps most important) plantains are essential ingredients for Puerto Rican cuisine introduced from West Africa to the Caribbean. And in Miami, papayas, mangoes, and coconuts are essential for salsas, marinades, and preserves. In Oakland, stylish cafes serve horchata lattes. To what extent should such unique cultural values determine whether or not the specific needs of a community are being met? Should the interests of procedural justice require that community members be allowed some meaningful involvement in determining the food offerings of any new store proposed for siting in a community? If so, how would this community involvement work?

## C. The Energy-Food-Water Nexus

The Energy-Food-Water Nexus involves global public-private partnerships to provide solutions for energy, water, and food security. The United Nations views this nexus as central to sustainable development. "Demand for all three is increasing, driven by a rising global population, rapid urbanization, changing diets and economic growth." *See* https://www.unwater.org/water-facts/water-food-and-energy/. Agriculture is the largest consumer of freshwater resources worldwide. More than one-quarter of energy use globally is spent on food production and supply. Considering these inextricable links provides keys for environmental justice concerns through science-based policy and decision-making. Governments and organizations can play a role in advancing nexus-informed solutions through support.

The relationship between energy, water, and food is at once both obvious and complex. This complexity can be illustrated in the growing global demand for a very small seed. Hydraulic fracturing — or "fracking" — is an increasingly relied upon method for extracting natural gas from shale formations. Fracking is often highly water intensive, requiring millions of gallons of water to frack a single well. To limit impacts on local water supplies, some fracking operations rely on a gel fracking method that uses less water. However, the gel used in these fracking operations requires an emulsifier produced from the tiny guar seed. The increasing global demand for this more water-efficient fracking method has resulted in a rising demand for guar, with the international price of guar seed rising from US$4 per kilogram to US$30 in less than two years. Consequently, thousands of acres of cropland in India and Pakistan that were otherwise devoted to the production of food have been converted to growing guar. This shift from food production to guar not only impacts local food markets and global energy markets, but results in the fracking jurisdiction externalizing the costs of water scarcity to another region of the world. Fracking operations in the United States may conserve water by using the gel-fracking method in its own region, but the shift from more water-efficient food crops to guar aggravates water scarcity in another region. The guar example typifies the global energy-water-food nexus and is the quintessential example of Garrett Hardin's *Tragedy of the Commons* warning that, in natural resource policy, no effort aimed at conservation, sustainability, or environmental protection will come without some unintended consequences. Rhett B. Larson, Cameron Holley, Diana M. Bowman, *The Energy/Water/Food Nexus—An Introduction*, 59 JURIMETRICS J. 1, 2–4 (2018).

## D. Food Security, Biofuels, and Climate Change

One of the most serious threats from global climate change is disruption of food security. "Food security" has been defined by the UN Food and Agriculture Organization (FAO) as a status where "all people, at all times, have physical and economic access to sufficient safe and nutritious food that meets their dietary needs and food preferences for an active and healthy life." According to the FAO, worldwide hunger had been declining for decades. This positive trend, however, has recently reversed, with more than 820 million people currently food insecure. U.N. FAO, THE STATE OF FOOD SECURITY AND NUTRITION IN THE WORLD (2019). The global rise in food insecurity tracks the increasing frequency of droughts, natural disasters, and other anticipated impacts of climate change. Concerns for food security may be expected to continue without concerted efforts toward both climate change mitigation and climate adaptation.

One suggested response to climate change that has received considerable attention is increasing the use of biofuels — fuels made from plant materials — as an alternative to fossil fuels. The argument for biofuels (also called agrofuels) is that they have the potential to reduce greenhouse gas emissions because the carbon dioxide released from burning them can, in theory, be offset by the carbon dioxide absorbed by the crops grown to make the fuel. (This is in contrast to fossil fuels, which release carbon that has been stored for millions of years under the earth's surface.) Both the United States and the European Union had sought to promote biofuels for transportation in recent years, spurred as much if not more by concerns about energy independence and rising fuel prices as a desire to reduce greenhouse gas emissions. Yet, in recent years, both the United States and the European Union have backtracked on their biofuel ambitions due to concerns about lifecycle emissions, land use, and economics. The United Nations report below addresses how climate change and land use impact food security.

## Intergovernmental Panel on Climate Change, Special Report: Climate Change and Land

An IPCC Special Report on climate change, desertification, land degradation, sustainable land management, food security, and greenhouse gas fluxes in terrestrial ecosystems (Aug. 7, 2019)

Climate change creates additional stresses on land, exacerbating existing risks to livelihoods, biodiversity, human and ecosystem health, infrastructure, and food systems (high confidence). Increasing impacts on land are projected under all future GHG emission scenarios (high confidence). Some regions will face higher risks, while some regions will face risks previously not anticipated (high confidence). Cascading risks with impacts on multiple systems and sectors also vary across regions (high confidence)....

Current levels of global warming are associated with moderate risks from increased dryland water scarcity, soil erosion, vegetation loss, wildfire damage, permafrost thawing, coastal degradation and tropical crop yield decline (high confidence). Risks, including cascading risks, are projected to become increasingly severe with increasing temperatures. At around 1.5°C of global warming the risks from dryland water scarcity, wildfire damage, permafrost degradation and food supply instabilities are projected to be high (medium confidence). At around 2°C of global warming the risk from permafrost degradation and food supply instabilities are projected to be very high (medium confidence). Additionally, at around 3°C of global warming risk from vegetation loss, wildfire damage, and dryland water scarcity are also projected to be very high (medium confidence). Risks from droughts, water stress, heat related events such as heatwaves and habitat degradation simultaneously increase between 1.5°C and 3°C warming (low confidence).

The stability of food supply is projected to decrease as the magnitude and frequency of extreme weather events that disrupt food chains increases (high confidence). Increased atmospheric $CO_2$ levels can also lower the nutritional quality of crops (high confidence).... [G]lobal crop and economic models project a median increase of 7.6% (range of 1 to 23%) in cereal prices in 2050 due to climate change, leading to higher food prices and increased risk of food insecurity and hunger (medium confidence). The most vulnerable people will be more severely affected (high confidence).

In drylands, climate change and desertification are projected to cause reductions in crop and livestock productivity (high confidence), modify the plant species mix and reduce biodiversity (medium confidence).... [T]he dryland population vulnerable to water stress, drought intensity and habitat degradation is projected to reach 178 million people by 2050 at 1.5°C warming, increasing to 220 million people at 2°C warming, and 277 million people at 3°C warming (low confidence).

... The supply of food is defined in this report as encompassing availability and access (including price). Food supply instability refers to variability that influences food security through reducing access. Asia and Africa are projected to have the highest number of people vulnerable to increased desertification. North America, South America, Mediterranean, southern Africa and central Asia may be increasingly affected by wildfire. The tropics and subtropics are projected to be most vulnerable to crop yield decline. Land degradation resulting from the combination of sea level rise and more intense cyclones is projected to jeopardise lives and livelihoods in cyclone prone areas (very high confidence). Within populations, women, the very young, elderly and poor are most at risk (high confidence).

Changes in climate can amplify environmentally induced migration both within countries and across borders (medium confidence), reflecting multiple drivers of mobility and available adaptation measures (high confidence). Extreme weather and climate or slow-onset events may lead to increased displacement, disrupted food chains, threatened livelihoods (high confidence), and contribute to exacerbated stresses for conflict (medium confidence)....

The level of risk posed by climate change depends both on the level of warming and on how population, consumption, production, technological development, and land management patterns evolve (high confidence). Pathways with higher demand for food, feed, and water, more resource-intensive consumption and production, and more limited technological improvements in agriculture yields result in higher risks from water scarcity in drylands, land degradation, and food insecurity (high confidence).

Projected increases in population and income, combined with changes in consumption patterns, result in increased demand for food, feed, and water in 2050 in
all Shared Socio-economic Pathways (SSPs) (high confidence). These changes, combined with land management practices, have implications for land-use change, food
insecurity, water scarcity, terrestrial GHG emissions, carbon sequestration potential,
and biodiversity (high confidence). Development pathways in which incomes increase
and the demand for land conversion is reduced, either through reduced agricultural
demand or improved productivity, can lead to reductions in food insecurity (high
confidence). All assessed future socio-economic pathways result in increases in water
demand and water scarcity (high confidence). SSPs with greater cropland expansion
result in larger declines in biodiversity (high confidence)....

Risks related to food security are greater in pathways with lower income, increased
food demand, increased food prices resulting from competition for land, more limited
trade, and other challenges to adaptation (e.g., SSP3) (high confidence). For food
security, the transition from moderate to high risk occurs for global warming between
2.5°C and 3.5°C in SSP1 (medium confidence) and between 1.3°C and 1.7°C in SSP3
(medium confidence). The transition from high to very high risk occurs between
2°C and 2.7°C for SSP3 (medium confidence). Urban expansion is projected to lead
to conversion of cropland leading to losses in food production (high confidence).
This can result in additional risks to the food system. Strategies for reducing these
impacts can include urban and peri-urban food production and management of
urban expansion, as well as urban green infrastructure that can reduce climate risks
in cities (high confidence).

* * *

Law professor Rebecca Bratspies examines legal and ethical concerns for the use
of genetically engineered crops to address food security in the following article.

## Rebecca M. Bratspies, *Hunger and Equity in an Era of Genetic Engineering*

### 7 UC IRVINE LAW REVIEW 195, 221–33 (2017)

The challenge of resolving food insecurity as populations continue to grow is
often framed as a binary choice: either farmers will have to glean higher yield from
existing farmland under new less favorable conditions, or more land will be converted
to agriculture. The latter option has obvious negative environmental ramifications,
so policymakers focus on techniques designed to increase production on existing
croplands. With this framing, genetically engineered crops are touted as the clear
answer. These claims about genetic engineering are built on a series of contested
propositions. First, that undernourishment is a production problem susceptible to
resolution by increased production. Second, that genetically engineered crops are
necessary to increase yield. Third, that only through genetic engineering can we
rapidly produce crop varietals able to thrive in the face of climate change. If these
propositions were true: *if* undernourishment were a production problem, *and* ge-

netically engineered crops increased yields, *and* these crops were the best way to en-sure continued or increased production as growing conditions deteriorate, this would be virtually unanswerable moral claim. However, there is, as yet, no reason to believe that any of these claims are accurate.

### Do Genetically Engineered Crops Actually Increase Food Production?

Monsanto and other promoters of agricultural biotechnology claim that genetically engineered crops must have a major role in attempts to solve undernourishment in the face of an increasing population. Over the past few decades, genetically engineered crops have been touted as the answer to world hunger, to pesticide overuse, and to negative environmental impacts of agriculture more generally. The assumption is that these crops are necessary to meet the food security needs of a burgeoning human population. As former Secretary of Agriculture Dan Glickman wryly described, the United States' unofficial position toward agricultural biotechnology "was good and that it was almost immoral to say it wasn't good because it was going to solve the problems of the human race and feed the hungry and clothe the naked." Opponents of the technology were accused of fearmongering, fraud, and worse.

Yet, as demonstrated above, food insecurity flows from inequitable distribution of food rather than from underproduction. Arguments about increased yield alone are therefore not responsive to the actual contours of the food insecurity problem. Indeed, this framing marginalizes the importance of more equitable distribution of existing food, and of minimizing food waste.

Moreover, it is not at all clear that genetically engineered crops increase yield. Re-viewing the many dueling studies claiming that crop yields have either increased, held steady, or decreased, the National Research Council concluded that genetically engineered crops "do not have greater potential yield than [non-genetically engineered] counterparts." This conforms with USDA's Economic Research Service's assessment which found the yield record for herbicide tolerant crops to be at best a mixed bag, with some researchers finding increased yield, others finding a decrease, while still others finding no effect on yields. Nor is there a clear case for a net economic benefit to farmers for adopting these crops. The National Research Council specifically noted there is virtually no difference in gross margins between conventional and genetically engineered crops across most of the world. In short, the technology's performance is much more tepid than the extravagant claims made on its behalf.

One thing is clear: two decades of genetically engineered crops has done little to solve the problem of food insecurity. The tantalizing prospect that genetic engineering could help feed the world's hungry has so far "been a somewhat empty promise." Indeed, the pattern has been one in which the benefits claimed for these crops re-peatedly fail to materialize. The National Academy of Science cautions that, "given the uncertainty about how much emerging genetic-engineering technologies will increase crop production, viewing such technologies as major contributors to feeding the world must be accompanied by careful caveats." Many experts continue to assert that conventional breeding, rather than genetic engineering, offers the best hope for increasing yield.

Of course, the current array of genetically modified crops was not engineered with reducing food insecurity in mind, so measuring them against that yardstick is not entirely fair. But that is, in many ways, the problem. These crops were developed by a few large multinational corporations as a tool for enhancing the scope, scale, and profitability of industrial agriculture. They embody a vision agriculture built around private ownership of patented seeds that are licensed, not sold, to farmers. Because farmers can only purchase the right to use seeds for a single growing season, farmers can no longer save seed. Moreover, because this business model is built on trade secrets and patent rights, the free exchange of germplasm and agronomic information—the intellectual cornerstone of agricultural research for most of the past century—is inhibited. That structure at best renders the poorest of the poor invisible to seed developers' decision-making, and at worst, compounds the problems of poverty and food insecurity associated with treating food as global commodities....

*What Are the Equity Ramifications of Genetically Engineered Crops?*

If we recognize, as we must, that food insecurity and undernutrition are not just functions of food production, we are left with questions of equity and power—why do people starve or suffer food insecurity amidst plenty? How do we change the patterns of distribution and consumption that produce these dismal results? Those are not questions of science or of production. They hint at a problem that is not amenable to a technical solution. Yet, purported technical solutions abound.

The decade-long Golden Rice saga is a good illustration of what happens when decision-makers insist on pursuing purely technical solutions to problems created by poverty and inequity. Golden Rice is rice that has been genetically engineered to contain beta carotene in an attempt to ward off vitamin A deficiencies that lead to blindness and death. In 2000, *Time Magazine* profiled Golden Rice on its cover, proclaiming *This Rice Could Save a Million Kids a Year*. Golden Rice instantly became the poster child for biotechnology, a life-saving negation of the assertion that agricultural biotechnology only generated benefits for multinational corporations. Monsanto and other agricultural biotech companies mounted a slick ad campaign using Golden Rice to stake out moral high ground in debates over genetic engineering. These ads sought to inextricably link "the dream of a tomorrow without hunger" to biotechnology as "the science that promises hope." Critics found themselves accused of perpetuating a "nutritional holocaust," and of condemning poor children to suffer and die. Recently, an open letter from 104 Nobel Laureates demanded, "How many poor people in the world must die before we consider [opposition to Golden Rice] a 'crime against humanity'"?

To say that Golden Rice has failed to live up to this "world changing" hype would be a significant understatement. When it was featured on *Time*'s cover, an at-risk child would have had to eat fifteen pounds of Golden Rice per day to obtain the benefits described in the article. Responding to that disconnect, Michael Pollen called it "the world's first purely rhetorical technology" designed "to win an argument rather than solve a public-health problem." Greenpeace, a staunch opponent of genetic engineering, called Golden Rice an "overpriced public relations exercise." Even the Rockefeller Foundation, which bankrolled the Golden Rice project, acknowledged that the industry advertisements and public relations campaigns built around Golden Rice had "gone too far," and were promising benefits that the technology could not, and might never be able to deliver....

Unfazed by these major ethical breaches, advocates of Golden Rice continued to tout the results. Their unwillingness to acknowledge the significance of failing to get proper government approvals or parental consent before feeding children an experimental genetically modified product speaks volumes. Research rules governing prior informed consent are not a technicality—they are all that stand between vulnerable populations and serious exploitation.

The importance of these questions should be self-evident. The choice to pursue a technology-based solution to a problem rooted in poverty had consequences. There are alternative, equally valid perspectives about whether vitamin A deficiency, and by implication issues of hunger and diet-related disease more broadly, are problems in need of technical or social solutions. Had the hundreds of millions of dollars spent developing Golden Rice been instead used to support the pre-existing, albeit less glamorous poverty alleviation efforts, or straightforward initiatives to provide vitamin A supplements directly to vulnerable populations, perhaps today's statistics would look very different. As Peter Rosset, director of Food First, emphasized, "People do not have vitamin A deficiency because rice contains too little vitamin A but because their diet has been reduced to rice and almost nothing else." Poverty is the core issue in vitamin A deficiency and in food insecurity more generally. Technology, by itself, cannot solve the problem.

\* \* \*

## Notes and Questions

1. **The climate change-food security connection.** The Special Report of the IPCC notes, "Risks to food security include availability and access to food, including population at risk of hunger, food price increases and increases in disability adjusted life years...." In your words, how is food security exacerbated by climate change and land-use impacts?

2. **Upside?** Meanwhile, the growing biofuels market and higher agricultural prices could generate important economic benefits in poorer nations. "As such, biofuels may offer an opportunity for developing countries—where seventy-five percent of the world's poor depend on agriculture for their livelihoods—to harness agricultural growth for broader rural development and poverty reduction." United Nations Food and Agriculture Organisation, The State of Food and Agriculture 2008—Biofuels: Prospects, Risks and Opportunities 5–6 (2008). In your view, do these potential benefits compensate for the potentially adverse impacts of increased competition for food and land from biofuels production?

**3.** Criticism about biofuels has intensified as research suggests that biofuels may provide far less reduction in GHG emissions than initially believed, once emissions generated through the life cycle of the fuel, including growing, harvesting, and processing it, are factored into the equation. Corn-based ethanol produced in the U.S., for example, may rely on corn grown with energy-intensive methods and may be manufactured using coal (the most GHG-intensive fossil fuel) as an energy source. Biogeochemist William Schlesinger, global change biologist Beverly Law, systems dynamics expert John Sterman, and international environmental policy expert William Moomaw warned of the dangers of this change on the account of basic science: "We must reduce greenhouse gas emissions now, not increase them." William H. Schlesinger, et al., *Pruitt Is Wrong on Burning Forests for Energy*, N.Y. TIMES (May 3, 2018), https://www.nytimes.com/2018/05/03/opinion/pruitt-forests-burning-energy.html. They argue:

> The simple fact is that cutting and burning trees adds carbon dioxide to the atmosphere, trapping radiant heat from the earth and making the planet warmer. The added carbon dioxide is removed from the atmosphere only if the forest that is cut down is replaced by a new generation of trees. (Trees and other green plants remove carbon dioxide from the air and use it to make leaves, wood and roots through photosynthesis.) But regrowth takes time, a century or more for native forests, assuming they don't fall victim to wildfire or disease. And regrowth never occurs if the land is developed or converted to pasture or farmland.
>
> Moreover, throughout the many decades before the replacement forests can grow enough to remove the extra carbon dioxide from the atmosphere, the previously added gas will thaw more permafrost and melt more ice, make ocean acidification worse, accelerate global warming, speed sea-level rise, increase the incidence of extreme weather, worsen drought and water stress, and hurt crop yields — effects that will persist for centuries or longer.

How would mitigation efforts for climate change benefit or burden food security concerns?

**4.** What are legal and ethical issues to address in the use of genetically engineered food in terms of food security and nutrition concerns?

## E. Food Oppression and Poverty

Attorney and geographer Danielle Purifoy explains food justice as an emerging movement that is to be seen as distinct from the sustainable food movement. She provides the example of food that is served in school cafeterias to illustrate this point. She also observes the proliferation of food policy councils to address community concerns to government officials.

**Figure 16-2:** Hoophouse used to overwinter spinach and other vegetables by Greening of Detroit (now "Keep Growing Detroit"). Detroit, Michigan. March 2014. Photo: Jacqueline Hand.

## Danielle M. Purifoy, *Food Policy Councils: Integrating Food Justice and Environmental Justice*

### 24 Duke Environmental Law & Policy Forum
### 375, 379–82 (2014)

Like environmental justice, food justice centers its activities on achieving equality for low-income and low-access communities. Rather than aiming for food practices and policies—like do-it-yourself food cultivation and expensive fresh food markets—which require significant disposable income and presume easy access to other necessary resources, food justice aspires to establish healthy food as a fundamental right and to eliminate barriers to its access. The term "food justice" is defined in several ways, likely as a result of its recent emergence as a social movement. Some have attempted to define it in terms of the injustices it is designed to combat, such as advocating against "the maldistribution of food, poor access to a good diet, inequities in the labour process and unfair returns for key suppliers along the food chain." Others, like attendees of the 2012 Food + Justice = Democracy conference, define it as "the right of communities everywhere to produce, process, distribute, access, and eat good food regardless of race, class, gender, ethnicity, citizenship, ability, religion, or community." The conference attendees also defined "good, healthy food and community wellbeing" as "basic human rights." In the 2000 edition of the journal *Race, Poverty, and the Environment*, which was devoted to the food system, the editors observed that the environmental justice definition of the environment as the place "where we live, work, and play," could be extended to "where, what, and how we eat." In all these interpretations, the food justice movement is a direct critique of the global industrial food system and the negative impacts of its policies, laws, and practices on human health, the environment, culture, and equity.

One important example of a food justice challenge is the source and quality of food served in school cafeterias. Although problems are pervasive in school food programs across the United States, they are particularly dire in under-resourced public schools, which often do not have the means to create alternative school food programs or to secure resources for farm-to-school programs. However, the food justice framework views impacted communities as leaders in defining the problems and helping to craft viable solutions. In a case study examined in Gottleib and Joshi's *Food Justice*, public school students from New Orleans—a city with a rich local food culture— were served cafeteria food that was imported from distant sources, "tasted terrible" and did not support the local economy. The middle school activists in the study, called the Rethinkers, defined the problem in their schools not only as a matter of where their food came from and its quality, but also as a problem of the broader conditions of the cafeterias where they ate, and the amount of time they were given to eat their food. Their advocacy also extended to support the local shrimp industry, which, as they learned, was being displaced because of imports of cheap, chemical-laden shrimp from abroad. Rather than relying on an authoritative, top-down solution to the problem, the students ensured that they had a say in the outcome, appealing to the school district Superintendent for eliminating "junky eating utensils," using healthy, local food sources, and placing local shrimp on the menus. In this way, Gottleib and Joshi suggest, the movement for food justice is about advancing "opportunities for moving toward a more just, healthy, democratic, and community-based system."

Advocacy around food justice in the United States has manifested in many forms, from activism around domestic food law and policy (most notably, around the federal Farm Bill, which has historically created farm subsidies for commodity crops (e.g., corn, soybeans, wheat) and public assistance funds for food to low-income individuals and families) or around developing programs and institutions designed to reconfigure local and regional food systems such that they will provide all communities with greater and more equitable access to safe, healthy, and local food. Urban agriculture, community supported agriculture (CSAs), kitchen gardens, co-ops, and local food artisans joined the menu of other food initiatives, most of which targeted hunger at an individual level. Food policy councils, first established in Knoxville, Tennessee,

**Figure 16-3:** Cornfield. Walton, Nebraska, Nov. 12, 2019. Photo: Shirley Trout.

in 1981, have rapidly proliferated in the past decade as forums through which concerned citizens and government officials can collaborate on resolving critical challenges to the local food system.

This concentration on local food systems, with which local residents are most familiar, creates new opportunities not only for bolstering local economies, but also for gradually altering the global food system as localized policies are replicated across the nation.

\* \* \*

Attorney Rebecca Goldberg considers the lessons and goals of the food justice movement as ways to involve the concerns of impoverished communities in policy debates. She draws parallels between the food justice movement and the early days of the environmental justice movement.

### Rebecca L. Goldberg, *No Such Thing as a Free Lunch: Paternalism, Poverty, and Food Justice*

24 Stanford L. & Pol'y Rev. 35, 92–97 (2013)

[T]he food justice movement relies heavily on equality-based rhetoric, but the movement has generally failed to grapple with the disparate needs of the various groups it encompasses, or to articulate a coherent vision of an equitable food system. While a grand unifying theory of equitable food policy might be an unrealistic goal, the environmental justice movement — on which the food justice movement has largely patterned itself — provides an excellent model for how the food justice movement might move beyond feel-good discussions about the need for across-the-board justice and toward a deeper analysis of complex problems such as the ones raised in this article. The current struggles of the food justice movement are in many ways reminiscent of the early days of the environmental justice movement, which began with a fairly diffuse coalition of grassroots activists coalescing around concerns about the distribution of environmental harms and their impact on racial minorities and the poor. When lawyers made a somewhat tardy appearance on the scene, it was not immediately clear how the concerns of the grassroots movement could or should translate into legal or policy actions. Soon, however, the environmental justice movement became, among other things, an influential voice for policy-level change, and it continues to wield that influence today.

The environmental justice movement's involvement in policy debates has often led it to confront the types of difficult issues discussed in this article. For example, the environmental justice movement has often faced situations where an impoverished community expresses a preference for a policy that will harm the community's environment. Paternalistic government actions are sometimes available that would protect the community's environment, albeit against the community's wishes. The conflict between the community's preference and the government's power is particularly stark in situations involving Indian tribes, whose ability to self-govern can in many situations be overridden by the federal government. Such situations pose a conflict for the environmental justice movement, because they create tension between two of the movement's central values: anti-discrimination and environmental protection....

Legal scholars of the environmental justice movement have been tremendously involved in grappling with this dilemma, and in using these situations to identify and address flaws in the movement's theory of equality. The specific issue of Indian tribes that want to allow storage of spent nuclear fuel and other hazardous waste on their land has generated a particularly large body of scholarship. For example, one scholar uses a case study of one such tribal decision as the basis for an extensive analysis of Rawlsian theories of justice and their applicability to the environmental justice movement, including a lengthy discussion of what the principle of equality means in that context. Other scholars argue that these particular types of situations necessitate a reconceptualization of environmental justice. "The unique characteristics of Native-American environmental struggles illustrate the epistemological inadequacies of a distributive paradigm of environmental injustice," Sheila Foster asserts, ultimately concluding that these struggles demonstrate that environmental injustice manifests itself not only in unequal distribution of environmental harm, but also in the decision-making process around environmental issues. Alice Kaswan responds to Foster's "community preferences model" by arguing that the specific situation of tribal environmental decision making demonstrates a layering of distributive justice issues on top of sovereignty concerns.

The specific issues of paternalism and equality that the environmental justice movement has focused on are somewhat different from the food policy issues raised in this article. This is because much of the environmental justice literature is about siting disputes that rest on an assumption that some community must bear an environmental burden; the question is how to choose a location. This raises somewhat different questions about equality and justice than are faced by the food justice movement. But the environmental justice movement's scholarship on these topics nonetheless offers a model for how the food justice movement—and particularly, legal scholars of the food justice movement—might begin to engage with the issues discussed in this article.

To be sure, one should not overstate the extent to which the environmental justice movement has resolved the similar issues that it has faced (and continues to face). A mere proliferation of scholarship does not necessarily represent a move toward coherence or relevance, and the debates discussed above have not resulted in any kind of official determination about the environmental justice movement's vision. However, these debates have been one part of the movement's journey from the nascent, doctrinally underdeveloped movement that Gerald Torres described in 1996 to the prominent movement that today commands real influence over federal government policymaking and has the ability to win meaningful legislative victories. This type of effective role in policymaking is only possible if a group is able to take a position on difficult, real-world problems. While the environmental justice movement certainly does not always speak with one voice, enough of its members are able to coalesce behind specific measures—for example, the Obama administration's Plan EJ 2014, which includes among other things a focus on community participation—such that the movement can be effective.

The food justice movement should follow the lead of the environmental justice movement and use the types of difficult questions discussed here to analyze, refine, and express its core values. If it does not do so, the movement will significantly reduce its ability to contribute in a meaningful way to current debates around food policy, many of which involve paternalistic proposals that either target or disproportionately affect the poor. These include not only other proposed uses of zoning to address obesity and other proposals to modify [the Supplemental Nutrition Assistance Program] (SNAP), but also ongoing efforts to improve the school lunch program and otherwise influence what children eat at school; various proposals to limit or influence portion sizes (which can affect low-income consumers who might take advantage of inexpensive large sizes to share one serving among several people); and the numerous recent proposals to tax unhealthy food, which would have a regressive effect on low-income consumers. Broader food justice topics, such as labor and wage protections for farm workers, also implicate questions about paternalism toward disadvantaged groups.

Furthermore, the food justice movement's failure to articulate a coherent vision of justice hinders the movement's ability to analyze any policy, paternalistic or otherwise, that poses a conflict between substantive goals relating to food consumption and what we might call personhood goals such as autonomy. Put differently, this failure of vision makes it hard for the movement to address the tension that so often exists between the substantive goal of healthy food for the poor and other things the poor might value—anything from autonomy to low prices. In short, the movement's ability to participate coherently and productively in almost any difficult food policy debate is questionable until it can address the weaknesses this article discusses.

That process will likely need to begin with an intra-movement conversation—whether through scholarship or other media—that addresses head-on the tensions that the food justice movement so far has largely ignored. As the history of the environmental justice movement shows, it takes time and effort for a movement to transition from observing problems to proposing (and successfully fighting for) workable solutions. That leap cannot be made if the movement's own goals are under-developed to the point where it is paralyzed by issues that force it to choose between competing values.

* * *

Communications and media studies professor Garrett Broad provides recommendations for strategic action for the food justice movement.

### Garrett M. Broad, *After the White House Garden:*
### *Food Justice in the Age of Trump*
13 J. FOOD L. & POL'Y 33, 38–41 (2017)

Grassroots people-power remains a hallmark of the community-based food justice approach, but the ability to pay living wages to educators and organizers, to provide incentives for youth participants, and to build community institutions that contribute to local economic development are all central to sustaining that grassroots power for the long-term. Especially in the face of a hostile federal government, those committed to food justice must work hard to develop and expand projects and programs that are fiscally sound in their approach, as well as demonstrably effective with respect to achieving their educational, organizing, and advocacy goals.

Community-based food justice activists compete for a limited pool of fiscal resources, a pool that is not always allocated on the basis of organizational merit or community need. The resources available to support non-profits in this domain generally come from three main areas — 1) public funding, including modest federal support, state and municipal grants, and through partnerships with public universities; 2) private funding, including from foundations, corporations, private universities, and individual donors; and 3) through self-generated revenue, commonly derived via the establishment of food-focused social enterprises under a non-profit structure. Often following the example of Michelle Obama and the impassioned calls of garden advocates like Michael Pollan and Alice Watters, recent years have seen a significant amount of money spent to create food and garden-based programs in schools and community spaces across the nation. After a season or two of harvest, however, many of them go fallow, perhaps due to a lack of long-term administrative and financial support, or due to a lack of integration into the culture of the community in which they were established.

The takeaway is that community-based food justice organizers and their supporters in law and policy must proactively articulate and demonstrate what makes for successful programs, and then communicate that message to funders, donors, and policymakers at multiple levels of society and government. This means embracing a culture of process and goal-oriented evaluation — bolstered by participatory partnerships with allied professionals and researchers — and from there, having a willingness to shift aspects of strategy when research suggests they could be more effective.

There are many opportunities, for instance, for community food practitioners to embrace new technological innovations that could improve their agricultural productivity, including those that are integrated into urban design and architecture. There are also significant opportunities to encourage social innovations that improve economic viability, particularly efforts that lead to community acquisition of land and property in the face of encroaching real estate development and gentrification. Equitable partnerships between community activists and outside collaborators can build community capacity and prevent stagnation across these domains.

On a related note, organizers and their supporters must also have the courage to point out why some food-based programs are more deserving of support than others. Today, many of the best-funded community food projects are not situated in communities that suffer from food injustice at all, as lower-income communities for whom food is more likely to serve a vital nutritional and organizing need struggle to gain recognition. This is part of a problem that extends well beyond food injustice, as a recent report from the National Committee for Responsive Philanthropy points out: "Philanthropic funding for the people who need it most has lagged behind booming assets, and foundations have continued to avoid strategies that have the greatest potential to change the status quo." Across the social justice landscape, more funding is needed that directly benefits underserved communities, addresses root causes, and provides more dollars as general support and multi-year funding. My own research into this topic points to several key principles that make for effective food justice programs: strong food justice initiatives fundamentally reflect and are shaped by the needs and interests of community members, have clear plans for fiscal and organizational sustainability, and are guided by a vision of social change that connects food injustice to a broader analysis of inequality in America.

On this final point, the years ahead necessitate significant coalition-building and collaborative action between food justice advocates and other movement actors fighting for progressive change. Here again, it is vital to reiterate the power of food as an organizing tool—its centrality to our health and ecology, as well as its universal connection to culture and community, gives food activists a unique ability to incorporate their concerns into the work of others. To be specific, community food advocates can help affordable housing advocates integrate gardens into design efforts, rally food service workers around a living wage, and coordinate with those seeking protection for the immigrants who play such vital roles in the food system. Indeed, one could argue that the best healthy food policies are actually progressive housing, labor, and immigration policies, which can open up the time and financial resources for families and communities to pursue healthier relationships with food. Further, state and municipal programs and policies in these areas can serve as a testing ground that could be scaled up if future federal administrations are more responsive to social justice concerns. In the years ahead, only an integrated approach—one that combines grassroots advocacy, policy development, and broader movement building—will be able to turn these aspirations into reality.

\* \* \*

Law professor Andrea Freeman links the notion of food oppression to social invisibility, decreased social status, and other conditions. Freeman shares the example of milk to illustrate harms posed to vulnerable groups.

### Andrea Freeman, *The Unbearable Whiteness of Milk: Food Oppression and the USDA*

3 UC Irvine Law Review 1251, 1253–54 (2013)

Food oppression is institutional, systemic, food-related action or policy that physically debilitates a socially subordinated group. Politically and financially weak communities absorb the external costs of food oppression, rendering these costs largely invisible to the mainstream. The effects of the oppression also increase the harmed groups' vulnerability by constraining their political voices, reducing their work capacity, and draining the energy of household and community members who must care for the sick and take on the responsibilities that ill members cannot fulfill. In the long term, food oppression diminishes already vulnerable populations in numbers and in power. Illness arising from food oppression also leads to social invisibility, decreased social status, depression, and despair.

Food oppression is a difficult concept for many to embrace because of the powerful rhetoric regarding personal choice that is endemic in the United States. This rhetoric attributes ill health to individual weakness, regardless of the very real constraints that shape nutritional intake, particularly in low-income, urban communities. The focus on the individual that dominates medical, scientific, and social views of health carries harmful consequences. By ignoring the structural aspects that shape consumption choices, this myopic perspective forecloses effective prevention and treatment of illnesses that disproportionately harm vulnerable communities.

Social position, which reflects the amount of privilege individuals possess along multiple axes, including race, class, gender, sexual orientation, physical ability, and immigration status, dictates how much disposable income and access to nutritious food people have. These factors, in turn, largely determine what we eat. More than taste, preference, willpower, or a commitment to health and fitness, structural forces shape diets. When fast food dominates a person's diet, the reasons are complex and manifold. They include government-corporate partnerships that place fast food in schools, government assistance checks that stretch further in a fast food restaurant than a produce aisle, public transportation that fails to provide routes between low-income neighborhoods and grocery stores, and government subsidies that artificially lower the price of fast food. Fast food tends to offer more bang for the buck, calories for dollars, making it a sound economic choice for many low-income African American and Latina/o households.

Fast food corporations exploit these harsh realities by devoting millions of dollars to race-targeted marketing annually, including Spanish-language advertising, McDonald's "365 Black" and "Me Encanta" websites, the reconfiguration of restaurants to accommodate large Latina/o families, and the introduction of culture-specific food items. Health problems linked to fast food, including heart disease, strokes, cancer, and diabetes, affect low-income African Americans and Latina/os more frequently and more seriously than whites. In "Fast Food: Oppression Through Poor Nutrition," I introduced the theory of food oppression to explain how government actions and policy that lead to the dominance of fast food in low-income, inner-city African American and Latina/o communities contribute to these health disparities.

* * *

## Notes and Questions

**1.** Rebecca Goldberg writes about the conflict between community preferences and policy decisions. She writes, "Paternalistic government actions are sometimes available that would protect the community's environment, albeit against the community's wishes." Goldberg provides an example of the conflict between the community's preferences and the government's power in situations involving Indian tribes. What central values are at stake in these conflicts?

**2.** Garrett Broad notes, "The takeaway is that community-based food justice organizers and their supporters in law and policy must proactively articulate and demonstrate what makes for successful programs, and then communicate that message to funders, donors, and policymakers at multiple levels of society and government." What obstacles do food justice advocates confront in conducting outreach to stakeholders, government agencies, and corporations?

**3.** To what extent has rhetoric and media limited or enhanced the discussions surrounding food security and food oppression? For example, how do cultural norms of fast food diets and personal decisions broadly impact food oppression?

# Index